Time Out

Milan

timeout.com/milan

Penguin Books

PENGUIN BOOKS

Published by the Penguin Group
Penguin Books Ltd, 80 Strand, London WC2R ORL, England
Penguin Books USA Inc., 375 Hudson Street, New York, New York 10014, USA
Penguin Books Australia Ltd, 250 Camberwell Road, Camberwell, Victoria 3124, Australia
Penguin Books Canada Ltd, 10 Alcorn Avenue, Toronto, Ontario, Canada M4V 3B2
Penguin Books (NZ) Ltd, cnr Rosedale and Airborne Roads, Albany, Auckland, New Zealand

Penguin Books Ltd, Registered Offices: Harmondsworth, Middlesex, England

First published 2002
10 9 8 7 6 5 4 3 2 1

Colour reprographics by Icon, Crown House, 56-58 Southwark Street, London SE1
and Precise Litho, 34-35 Great Sutton Street, London EC1
Printed and bound by Cayfosa-Quebecor, Ctra. de Caldes, Km 3 08 130 Sta, Perpètua de Mogoda, Barcelona, Spain

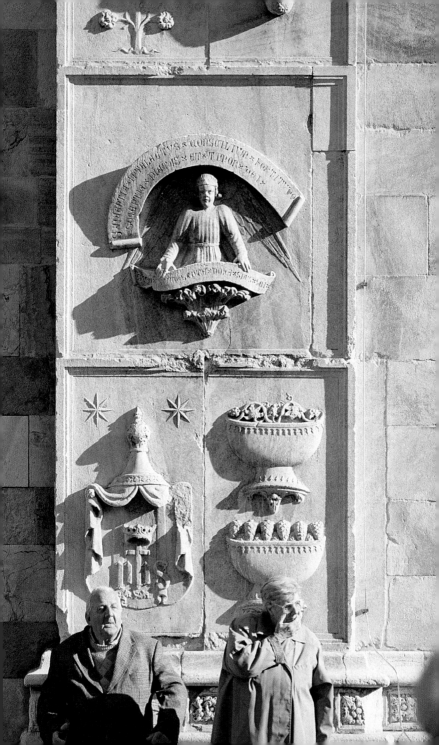

Edited and designed by
Time Out Guides Limited
Universal House
251 Tottenham Court Road
London W1T 7AB
Tel + 44 (0)20 7813 3000
Fax + 44 (0)20 7813 6001
Email guides@timeout.com
www.timeout.com

Editorial
Editor Anne Hanley
Deputy Editor Rosamund Sales
Copy Editor Sophie Blacksell
Listings Researcher Charlotte Sylverstersten
Proofreader Tamsin Shelton
Indexer Marion Moisy

Editorial Director Peter Fiennes
Series Editor Ruth Jarvis
Deputy Series Editor Jonathan Cox

Design
Group Art Director John Oakey
Art Director Mandy Martin
Art Editor Scott Moore
Designers Benjamin de Lotz, Lucy Grant
Scanning/Imaging Dan Conway
Ad Make-up Glen Impey
Picture Editor Kerri Littlefield
Deputy Picture Editor Kit Burnet
Picture Librarian Sarah Roberts

Advertising
Group Commercial Director Lesley Gill
Sales Director/Sponsorship Mark Phillips
International Sales Co-ordinator Ross Canadé
Advertisement Sales (Milan) Margherita Tedone
Advertising Assistant Sabrina Ancilleri

Administration
Chairman Tony Elliott
Managing Director Mike Hardwick
Group Financial Director Kevin Ellis
Marketing Director Christine Cort
Marketing Manager Mandy Martinez
US Publicity & Marketing Associate Rosella Albanese
Group General Manager Nichola Coulthard
Production Manager Mark Lamond
Production Controller Samantha Furniss
Accountant Sarah Bostock

Features in this guide were written and researched by:
Introduction Anne Hanley. **History** Gregory Dowling, Anne Hanley. **Milan & Lombardy Today** Deborah Ball. **The Art of Milan & Lombardy** Clarice Zdanski. **Architecture** Lucy M Maulsby. **The Food of Lombardy** Monica Larner (*Food heaven* Lee Marshall). **Accommodation** Justin Ratcliffe. **Sightseeing** Clarice Zdanski, Anne Hanley (*Alessandro Manzoni* and *I promessi sposi* Gregory Dowling, *Leonardo da Milano* Anne Hanley). **Restaurants** Justin Ratcliffe. **Cafés & Bars** Brian Lagrotteria. **Shops & Services** Karla Bluestone. **Children** Valerie Waterhouse. **Comtemporary Art** Leigh Robb. **Film** Leigh Robb. **Gay & Lesbian** Deborah Ball. **Nightlife & Music** Hilary Walker. **Performing Arts** Leigh Robb. **Sport & Fitness** John Moretti. **Lago d'Orta** Karla Bluestone. **Lago Maggiore** Elisabeta Povoledo. **Lago di Como** Susannah Gold. **Lago di Garda** Gregory Dowling. **Bergamo & Around** Michael Thompson. **Brescia & Around** Susannah Gold. **Mantova & Around** Lee Marshall. **Cremona, Lodi & Around** Piers Grimley Evans. **Pavia & Around** Karla Bluestone. **The Mountains** Valerie Waterhouse. **Directory** Vivian Infantino (*Further Reference, Vocabulary* and *Glossary* Anne Hanley).

The Editor would like to thank:
Carla Chelo, Charlotte Sylvesterstern, Ros, Sophie and special thanks to Lee and Clara Marshall.

Maps by LS International Cartography, via Sanremo 17, 20133 Milan, Italy. The Milan transport map is used by kind permission of ATM.

Photography by Adam Eastland except; page 9, The Art Archive/Monza Cathedral/Dagli Orti, page 16, The Art Archive/Malmaison Musee du Chateau/Dagli Orti, page 63 The Art Archive/Album/Joseph Martin; pages 160, 161 BFI; pages 23, 174 Associated Press/Luca Bruno; pages 7, 14 - 17,19, 27, 94, 209, 224, 228, 243, 249 AKG London; The following photographs were supplied by the featured establishments page 155, page 170

Contents

Introduction

Milan isn't an easy city to like. The mist that turns lakes Como and Maggiore into a wonderland of mountains and slow-moving boats emerging mysteriously from the haze becomes oppressive fog in the city. The torrid summer heat that transforms the rice paddies of the Po Valley lowlands into a vast lake of shimmering emerald green makes the city breathless and stifling. The icy cold that turns Lombardy's relatively undiscovered Alps into a skier's delight cuts through Milan's streets like a knife.

Milan, moreover, won't appeal immediately to your aesthetic senses: it has none of the striking beauty of Venice, Florence or Rome. It is, resoundingly, a modern metropolis, with more than its fair share (by Italian standards) of ugly grey concrete. And the Milanese – and those drawn to the city by its particular ethos – are hard-headed working types, never loosening their designer ties or slipping off their designer heels until the working day is well and truly over and *aperitivo* hour can begin.

But herein lies the city's allure. In Milan, Italian style has been honed to a sharp point. Its denizens might have stepped out of any of the giant designer-label advertising hoardings that peer down archly over every street corner. Its shops – be they fashion, furniture or food – are mouthwateringly chic.

And yet in the midst of so much bustle and style, Milan clings endearingly to those remaining bits of its past that haven't been demolished, bombed, or 'restored' beyond all recognition.

Few cities, for example, can have quite such a lasting fondness for a fourth-century saint (Sant'Ambrogio) who was – in typically Milanese fashion – more of a power-broker than a holy man. But St Ambrose and his feast day determine such fundamental city events as the opening of the season at La Scala and the *Carnevale ambrosiano*, which extends into Lent rather than coming to an abrupt end on Ash Wednesday as happens elsewhere in Italy.

And when a *milanese* offers to meet you by the *colonne*, he or she may be heading for the myriad clubs and bars in southern Milan but still revels in the fact that the point of reference is the 16 second- and third-century AD columns arranged in front of the church of San Lorenzo Maggiore.

Few short-stay visitors to Milan venture further than Leonardo's *Last Supper*. It's a shame. In this guide, we have striven to reveal some of the city's many hidden treasures. Scratch the businesslike surface, and you'll discover that workaday Milan has a cultured, historic heart.

ABOUT THE TIME OUT CITY GUIDES

The *Time Out Milan Guide* is one of an expanding series of Time Out City Guides, now numbering over 35, produced by the people behind London and New York's successful listings magazines. Our guides are all written and updated by resident experts who have striven to provide you with all the most up-to-date information you'll need to explore the city or read up on its background, whether you're a local or a first-time visitor.

THE LOWDOWN ON THE LISTINGS

Above all, we've tried to make this guide as useful as possible. Addresses, telephone numbers, websites, transport information, opening times, admission prices and credit card details are all included in our listings. And, as far, as possible, we've given details of facilities, services and events, all checked and correct as we went to press. However, owners and managers can change their arrangements at any time. Also, in Milan, small shops and bars often

do not keep precise opening hours, and may close earlier or later than stated. Similarly, arts programmes are often finalised very late. Before you go out of your way, we'd advise you whenever possible to phone and check opening times, ticket prices and other particulars.

While every effort has been made to ensure the accuracy of the information contained in this guide, the publishers cannot accept responsibility for any errors it may contain.

PRICES AND PAYMENT

Prices throughout this guide are given in Euros (for more information on the Euro, *see p286*). As this guide was being compiled, not all local businesses had confirmed their Euro rates; there may, therefore, be slight discrepancies in price. Bear in mind that the lire-Euro exchange rate was 1=L1,936.27. If prices vary wildly from those we've quoted, please write and let us know. We aim to give the best and most up-to-date advice, so we always want to know if you've been badly treated or overcharged.

We have noted where shops, restaurants, hotels and so on accept the following credit cards: American Express (AmEx), Diners Club (DC), MasterCard (MC) and Visa (V). Many businesses also accept other cards, including JCB. Some shops, restaurants and attractions take major travellers' cheques.

THE LIE OF THE LAND

We have divided the city into simple areas that do not reflect the neighbourhood names; our relevant area name is given with each venue listed in this guide. The sightseeing chapters and many others are arranged according to these areas. For maps showing the different city areas, *see pp308-311*. Wherever possible, a map reference is provided for every venue listed, indicating the page and grid reference at which it can be found on the street maps.

TELEPHONE NUMBERS

It is necessary to dial provincial area codes with all numbers in Italy, even for local calls. Hence all normal Milan numbers begin 02, whether you're calling from inside or outside the city. From abroad, you must dial 39 (the international dialling code for Italy) followed by the number given in the book – which includes the initial 02. For more information on telephones and codes, *see p289*.

ESSENTIAL INFORMATION

For all the practical information you might need for visiting Milan, including emergency

phone numbers, visa and customs information, advice on facilities for the disabled, useful websites and details of local transport, turn to the **Directory** chapter at the back of the guide. It starts on page 274.

MAPS

The map section at the back of this book includes a map of the Lombardy region, an overview map of the greater Milan area, detailed street maps of the centre, a transport map showing bus, tram and underground lines and a comprehensive street index. Many of the destinations featured in the Lakes & Cities section that begins on page 181 have detailed maps within the appropriate chapters. The maps begin on p303.

LET US KNOW WHAT YOU THINK

We hope you enjoy the *Time Out Milan Guide*, and we'd like to know what you think of it. We welcome tips for places that you consider we should include in future editions and take note of your criticism of our choices. There's a reader's reply card at the back of this book for your feedback, or you can email us at milanguide@timeout.com.

There is an online version of this guide, as well as weekly events listings for 35 international cities, at www.timeout.com.

In Context

History

From powerful duchy to backwater to industrial powerhouse.

Lombardy's prehistoric inhabitants have left us with a fascinating glimpse into their obsessions and skills, hacked into the rocks of the Valcamonica (*see p269*). Through the millennia and right up to the Roman conquest of the zone, the Camun people refined their carving styles, portraying new tools, more realistic animals and more evolved divinities. Down on the marshy plain of the Po river, other Ligurian tribes (the rest of the Italian peninsula was populated by Italic peoples and Etruscans) dwelt in stilt-houses by the side of the region's many lakes.

CELTS, ROMANS AND BARBARIANS

Gallo-Celtic tribes moved across the Alps and into the fertile plains of the Po Valley some time in the fifth and fourth centuries BC, spreading themselves into territory occupied by Ligurians and Etruscans, and pitching camp in the vicinity of what are now Milan, Brescia, Bergamo and Lombardy's other major cities.

These Celts – and particularly the Insubre tribe, whose settlement where Milan now stands had become a large and dominant one – had their hearts set on further expansion

southwards: in 390 BC only the cackling of geese on Rome's Capitol hill tipped sleeping Romans off to the fact that the Celts were about to overrun their city. In the end it was the Romans who pushed their borders northwards into what they termed Cisalpine Gaul (Gaul this side of the Alps); in the 280s they began their drive across the Po Valley from the east, founding colonies as they went and conquering the Insubre town of Mediolanum (Milan) in 222 BC.

It was not all plain sailing for the Roman conquerors: during the Second Punic War (218-201 BC), for example, northern Italy's Celts and Ligurians rallied to the side of Hannibal, helping the great Carthaginian general's exhausted troops to beat the Romans back across the Po.

By 42 BC, however, Rome had exerted its hold over Cisalpine Gaul sufficiently to make it officially part of its Italian territories. In his reorganisation of Italy in 15 BC, Emperor Augustus (30 BC-AD 14) made Milan the capital of the 11th region, Transpadania, which included the towns of Como, Bergamo, Pavia and Lodi, and extended as far west as Turin and Aosta. No longer a mere military garrison, and with municipal and judicial structures in its own right, Mediolanum began to take on the importance to be expected of a city placed so strategically between the Italian peninsula and those areas beyond the Alps where Roman interests were widespread.

In the (relatively) peaceful times that extended from the reign of Augustus the placid agricultural zone of northern Italy flourished: roads were built and rivers made navigable, to the benefit of both communications and trade. And though even the area's elite continued to prefer their country villa-farms over urban residences, towns were endowed with suitably imposing monuments; this was especially true of Mediolanum, the importance of which was growing rapidly.

'Milan became the effective capital of the Western Empire.'

When barbarian tribes began baying at borders in the third century AD, Diocletian (emperor 284-305) reorganised the empire into two halves to streamline its military capacities. From 292 Mediolanum became the effective capital of the western emperor (Byzantium was home to his eastern counterpart, *see p18* **Popes and emperors**), leaving Rome to languish.

As Milan's political and military star was rising, so was its importance as a centre of a new religious sect, Christianity, which according to local legend was brought to the city by St Barnabus (San Barnaba), a friend and companion of St Paul. Under Diocletian and his persecuting successors, Milan chalked up nearly as many top-notch martyrs as Rome (*see p11* **Milan's martyrs**). Constantine the Great (306-37), who reunified the two halves of the empire under his sole control and was only too aware of Mediolanum's strategic importance, diplomatically issued the Edict of Milan (313) putting an end to the persecution of Christians and paving the way for Christianity to become the religion of state. The charismatic St Ambrose (*see p10* **Sant'Ambrogio**) was elected bishop of Milan in 374, remaining in that office until his death in 397. His legendary piety and charity conferred untold prestige on the local Church, giving his successors in the region unrivalled spiritual and temporal clout for centuries to come.

In 402, Emperor Honorius (395-423) transferred the seat of empire to Ravenna, leaving Milan more or less at the mercy of waves of attacking barbarian tribes.

Theodolinda

In the chapel of Theodolinda (*see p102*) in Monza's magnificent Duomo, International Gothic frescos depict Lombard Queen Theodolinda as a blonde bombshell, dressed in the gorgeous clothes of the Visconti age. How much of the queen's story is legend and how much history is difficult to assess. There seems little doubt, however, that Theodolinda – not a Lombard herself – made a big impression on the people she married into.

Her marriage in 589 to Autari, king of the Lombards, was a strategic one for the groom. The bride's father, Duke Garibaldo of Bavaria, would be a useful ally should the Franks try invading Italy. But legend also tells us that Autari visited the duke's court incognito, caught a glimpse of the blonde princess and came away with the conviction that this bit of strategy was not going to be pure self-sacrifice.

When the Franks got wind of the impending nuptials, they invaded Bavaria to put a stop to it. Theodolinda fled south to Verona, however, and the couple were spliced there in great pomp. Their wedded bliss did not last long; Autari died in Pavia in 590. That the young queen had been a hit with the Lombard people was clear, for, contrary to usual practice, they confirmed her as queen, inviting her to choose a new husband. Her choice fell on Duke Agilulf of Turin, whom she summoned to court and regally informed of her decision.

King Agilulf had a reputation as a warrior. He proved equally skilful, however, as a player in the power-balancing game. After an attempt to besiege Rome he allowed himself – to the dismay of some of his more ferocious followers – to be bought off by Pope Gregory the Great. He maintained cautious diplomatic relations with the pope ever afterwards, realising that open

In 452 when Attila the Hun left the city, Milan was a smouldering wreck. It was partially rebuilt, but was then razed again by Goths in 489 and 539. Most of the population had taken refuge in the countryside, and the clergy had fled to Genoa. However, by that time, the fate of the beleaguered city was of little interest to anyone. For after the death of the last western emperor, Romulus Augustulus, in 476, the Latinised Goth who wielded greatest power on the peninsula, Odoacer, had had

hostility would only push the pontiff into the arms of the Byzantines, based in Ravenna. Though an Arian (*see p13* **The Arian heresy**), Agilulf dampened his followers' anti-Roman enthusiasm. The wily Gregory, meanwhile, cultivated a friendship with Agilulf's Roman-style Christian wife.

Never one for doing things by halves, Theodolinda – egged on by Gregory – got down to converting her people. Her husband – for political reasons or from genuine conviction – helped her along by accepting the faith himself. Theodolinda went on to found many churches and monasteries, including a church dedicated to John the Baptist where Monza's Duomo now stands.

It is here that Pope Gregory's most precious gift – a nail from the True Cross – was (and is) kept, incorporated into an Iron Crown.

Agilulf died in 615; Theodolinda reigned alone until 625, then handed the crown to her son. He was deposed the following year by his brother-in-law, who made a last-ditch attempt to restore Arianism. For the next century, Arians and Roman Christians continued to squabble, but by the time of Liutprand (712-44), the Lombards were definitively in the Roman fold. Theodolinda's friendly relations with the pontiff, however, proved more difficult to maintain; in the end, the Lombards were crushed by Franks summoned by a pope.

himself crowned king in what had become northern Italy's most important town: not Milan, but Pavia.

LOMBARDS AND FRANKS

For decades Goths and Byzantines alternately colluded and squabbled for control of the Italian peninsula, heedless of the threat swiftly mounting across the Alps, where various antagonistic tribes of Germanic Lombard peoples were being forged into something

like a unified front by the bloodthirsty King Alboin. In 568 the Lombards began their relatively challenge-free rampage through northern Italy, setting up their capital in Pavia, which fell to the invaders after a siege in 572. The region they overran was a shadow of its former self, its agriculture and infrastructure in tatters. This seemed to matter little to the ruling Lombards, who taxed and oppressed with glee, only becoming slightly less aggressive and hostile after wily Pope

Gregory the Great (590-604) persuaded the Lombard Queen Theodolinda (*see p8* **Theodolinda**) to convert her people from the Arian heresy (*see p13* **The Arian heresy**) to Roman-style Christianity.

Later popes continued to clash with the ever-expanding Lombards, whose territory now extended from the myriad dukedoms of the Po Valley to the far south of mainland Italy. With the Normans of southern Italy also making life difficult for the occupant of the throne of St Peter's, outside help was sought, in the shape of the Franks. At the head of this Germanic tribe in the second half of the eighth century was Charlemagne, a mighty warrior and impressive politician who, although illiterate, had established a glittering court at Aachen from where he had set out to conquer much of western Europe. In 774 Charlemagne turned his attention to Italy, where he crushed the Lombards – at the time under the leadership of King Desiderius, who was Charlemagne's own father-in-law – and added King of the Lombards to a long list of titles.

Pope Leo III (795-816) awarded him yet another – *imperator augustus*, later to be known as Holy Roman Emperor (*see p18* **Popes and emperors**) – in 800. In the short term, it was a sound move, forcing Charlemagne to uphold papal rights against encroaching foes. But after Charlemagne's death, no one could live up to his mighty reputation, and even before his direct family line had died out, his empire had fallen into the hands of bickering lordlings striving to be big fish in very small ponds.

Northern Italy was no exception to this rule. Already, under Lombard and Carolingian rule, religious orders had established control over large swathes of countryside, establishing monasteries in the midst of rich agricultural and pastoral holdings. With Magyar invaders harrying them through the ninth and tenth centuries, locals barricaded themselves into a series of fortified hamlets, each proclaiming its territorial rights over surrounding countryside and laying the foundations of an extensive feudal system that would later come into conflict with the religious oligarchy. Meanwhile, the region's rural poor were being reduced to the level of serfs, obliged to work for a living on lordly estates where ever-larger tracts of woodland – traditionally used for grazing by small-scale stock raisers – were being dug up and cultivated to provide crops to feed a growing population.

With the end of the Carolingian line in 888, northern Italy passed under the control of a series of Frankish *reucci* – kinglets – of little worth, who occasionally found themselves in conflict with the questionable characters named *imperator augustus* by popes kept firmly under the thumbs of Roman nobles.

It was the unwise attempt by kinglet Berengar II to force Adelaide, widow of his predecessor Lothar, to marry him (or possibly his son, Adalbert; sources are divided) that upset this state of affairs. In 961 the eastern Frankish King Otto I responded to a plea for help from the beautiful Adelaide, who had been locked up in a tower on Lake Garda (*see p206*) by her would-be spouse (or maybe father-in-law). Otto invaded Italy, carried Adelaide off (though by that time the feisty lady had escaped to Tuscany under her own steam) and the following year was crowned Holy Roman Emperor in Rome, returning the title to a German.

Sant'Ambrogio

In a near-contemporary mosaic portrait in the church of Sant'Ambrogio, Milan's patron saint, Ambrose (c334-97), looks simple and humble. It's a misleading picture. For this patrician Roman was a man of vast learning, a musician, a writer and an uncompromising weeder-out of heresy; and if his famously charitable works make his saintly status well deserved, his equally famous refusal to knuckle under to temporal authority gives some measure of the man who set the model for centuries of strong Church control in northern Italy.

Ambrose came to Milan as a public official but was proclaimed bishop by the locals in 374, then hastily ordained afterwards. He was an avid studier of the (pagan) ancients, as is obvious from the quotations in and influences on his writings. It was he who imposed his Christian-Neoplatonic ideas on a doubting African convert called Augustine, who would go on to become one of the Church's greatest teachers and a saint.

With a crystal-clear vision of the need for the Church to emerge as a guiding beacon as the Roman Empire declined, he stood up to even the highest powers, refusing to allow Empress Justina to build an Arian (*see p13* **The Arian heresy**) chapel in Milan, and bundling Emperor Theodosius unceremoniously out of his church after news came of a massacre perpetrated on his orders.

Milan's martyrs

Milan is second only to Rome in its collection of early saints and martyrs, many of them given solemn burial by St Ambrose (*see p10* **Sant'Ambrogio**), who had an uncanny knack for sniffing out discarded relics.

Barnabas (**San Barnaba**) is the earliest saint associated with the city. He was a Cypriot Jew and a close friend of St Paul, with whom he travelled on the first-ever missionary journeys of the Church. Near the church of Sant'Eustorgio (*see p91*) are the remains of an ancient font in which Barnabas is supposed to have baptised the Milanese. No other evidence exists of his visit to Lombardy.

St Victor (**San Vittore**) is even more elusive as a historic figure. Legend tells of this soldier's lengthy martyrdom under Emperor Maximianus (286-305), during which he was whipped, stretched on the rack, coated in boiling lead and beheaded. Even the beheading went awry: when they came to bury him he was found dead but intact. In addition to a church and a monastery, he has given his name to Milan's prison (*see p95*).

Other Milanese martyrs – most dug up by Ambrose – tend to go in pairs.

Nabor (**Nabore**) and Felix (**Felice**): soldiers who were beheaded under Maximianus; little more is known of them.

Gervasius (**Gervasio**) and Protasius (**Protasio**): burly twin brothers, also beheaded, perhaps under Nero. Their burial site was revealed to Ambrose in a dream, just when he needed a few fresh relics for a basilica he was about to consecrate.

Vitalis (**Vitale**) and **Valeria**: a later tradition claimed the brothers Gervasius and Protasius to have been the sons of this husband and wife pair. According to legend, they were martyred separately, Vitalis being stretched on the rack and Valeria attacked by pagans outside the city.

Nazarius (**Nazario**) and Celsus (**Celso**): their bodies were found by Ambrose in a garden outside Milan. According to legend, Nazarius was expelled from Milan for comforting Gervasius and Protasius before their martyrdom; on his long wanderings through Gaul and Italy he took charge of the nine-year-old Celsus, who was to be his companion in martyrdom when they finally returned to Milan.

Under Ottos I, II and in particular the devout Otto III, Lombardy's clergy had a field day. Bishops and archbishops still exercised much influence – especially in major cities, which had declined but never died away, ready to bounce back strongly during any brief period of tranquillity and prosperity. They were given precedence over the landed nobility whose uppitiness irked the emperors and whose power was consequently reduced. In Milan, a building boom gave the city a swathe of new landmarks – including the rebuilt basilica of Sant'Ambrogio, *see p95* – in the Romanesque style. Allied with the *cives* – city-dwelling merchants or tradesmen – the clergy were the effective rulers of Lombardy's increasingly wealthy cities from around the start of the new millennium.

AGE OF THE *COMUNI*

By the end of the 11th century, however, the *cives* were demanding a greater degree of control: in Milan, a *consulatus civium*, or town council meeting, was recorded in 1097. Bergamo, Brescia, Como, Cremona and Mantova followed suit in the second decade of the following century. The first of these

meetings was held very much under the clergy's auspices, in the *brolo*, or garden of the bishop's palace. Hence the abundance of later town council offices around Lombardy called palazzo del Broletto.

> ## 'By the end of the 11th century, merchants and tradesmen were demanding more control.'

But increasing civic feistiness also brought the various settlements of the Lombardy region into conflict with each other. Milan, the strongest and wealthiest, imposed its supremacy over Lodi, Cremona, Como and even Pavia, with its imperial connections. This was too much for the Holy Roman Emperor of the time, Frederick Barbarossa (1152-90), who marched across the Alps to bring Milan to heel. At the end of a seven-month siege in 1162, the emperor had the city's fortifications pulled down and the palaces of leading anti-imperial agitators destroyed, and drove the whole populace into the countryside. Hated as Milan was by many of its neighbours, Barbarossa's

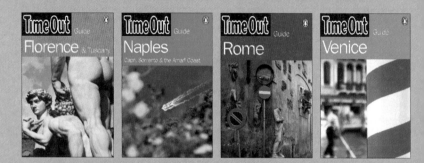

heavy-handed treatment of it failed to endear him particularly to any of the wary cities of Lombardy. In 1167, at a meeting of their representatives at Pontida, the *comuni* (people-run towns) banded together in the Lega Lombarda (Lombard League). Its symbol was an old cart (*il carroccio*) with the Lombard standard flying atop it. And it was – popular lore has it – rallied around this cart that the forces of the Lombard League engaged with and beat back the imperial troops at the Battle of Legnano in 1176 (*pictured p7*). Risorgimento (*see p17*) sentimentalists were later to see this battle – the subject of an opera by Verdi – as the beginning of Italian resistance to foreign tyrants; but if truth be told, it was the emperor as tax-imposer, rather than the emperor as foreign power, that they were fighting against. The moment the Holy Roman Empire ceased to be a threat, the *comuni* returned to their self-interested squabbling.

It is, therefore, eminently suitable that the Northern League of today, *see p24* **Northern League**, should have adopted the *carroccio* as its symbol.

'Trouble arose from conflicts between the aristocracy and pushy parvenus.'

The Battle of Legnano was followed by further skirmishing against the emperor's forces, but in 1183 the Peace of Constance at last awarded Milan the privileges of independence and self-government it had long considered itself more than worthy of. The city could now settle down happily to its own internal bickering. Most of the trouble arose from conflicts between the old aristocracy and the pushy ranks of merchants and tradesmen. They were conflicts that the city's institutions were powerless to solve. Solutions were sought from outside, with the aristos lining up with the pro-empire Ghibelline party, and the parvenus joining the pro-papal Guelphs (*see p18* **Popes and emperors**).

This was yet another indication of Milan's innate inability to free itself from outside interference. Admittedly, geography was against it: Lombardy was inevitably the doorway into Italy for a stream of northern invaders. But the city's habit of wavering between outside powers was the seal to its fate. In 1266, Pope Clement IV summoned Charles d'Anjou from France to deal with Barbarossa's heirs in Sicily. Forced into a decision, Milan's then-dominant Guelph (ie pro-papacy) faction, led by the Torriani family, opted to back the anti-empire movement.

The Arian heresy

Arianism – the version of Christianity espoused by the Lombards – was the first big heresy to get the Church's thumbs down.

Arius (c256-336), a teacher from Alexandria, denied the divinity of Jesus Christ... hardly a minor issue for a faith that had chosen to call itself Christianity. What Jesus was exactly was a matter for heated debate among Arians: for some he was 'unlike' God; for others 'of similar substance'; for others he was 'like' God. The Council of Nicea (325) was summoned to deal with the heresy, and produced the pointedly anti-Arian Nicean Creed. In this decree, the son was categorically labelled 'of one substance with the Father' and therefore divine.

This did not, however, stop a number of later eastern emperors from backing the Arians; finally, though, pro-Nicene support from Emperors Gratian (western 367-83) and Theodosius I (eastern 379-92, and eastern and western 392-5) sealed the heresy's official fate.

Still the heresy spread – perhaps as a reaction against the might of Rome – in Dacia (Romania) among the Goths. It then caught on with Burgundians, Swabians, Vandals and Lombards, who clung to it until Queen Theodolinda (*see p8* **Theodolinda**) took it into her head to convert them. Today shades of Arianism linger among Unitarianists and Jehovah's Witnesses, these latter explicitly citing Arius as a forerunner of their creed.

But if there was one thing you could be sure of in the politics of the time, it was that popes never continued backing winners – those who helped the papacy had a nasty habit of turning on Rome itself. Charles conquered the south and became king of Sicily; true to form, the pope switched allegiance, championed a German candidate for the title of emperor and even backed (traditionally anti-papal) Ghibelline forces in the north.

THE VISCONTI

Among these forces was one Ottone Visconti, an archbishop of Milan who had been ousted by the Torriani family. Ottone seized the initiative, scoring a major victory over the Torriani at Desio in 1277. One year later he was declared *signore* (lord) of the city. The old *comune*

Leonardo da Vinci. *See p15.*

system was over: Milan – like so many other northern Italian cities – was going the way of one-family rule.

In 1294, on payment of 50,000 florins to Holy Roman Emperor Arrigo, Ottone's great nephew and designated successor, Matteo, was given the title of *vicario imperiale* (imperial delegate), a rank that also gave him a claim to authority over Milan's neighbours. He was driven out of Milan in 1302 by the Torriani family, but with support from Emperor Henry VII he made a triumphant return in 1311. From then on, the Viscontis went from strength to strength. In 1330 Azzone Visconti was proclaimed *dominus generalis*. Within the space of a generation the surrounding cities all acknowledged Visconti rule – Bergamo and Novara in 1332, Cremona in 1334, Como and Lodi in 1335, Piacenza in 1336, Brescia in 1337, Asti in 1341 and Parma in 1346.

The family's splendour reached its zenith with the rule of Gian Galeazzo Visconti (1378-1402). He obtained the title of Duke of Milan in 1395 from Emperor Wenceslas. Two years later it was upped to Duke of Lombardy; Gian Galeazza ruled over the second-largest *signoria* in Italy (only the kingdom of Naples was bigger), which included Milan, Pavia, Bergamo, Brescia, Como, Lodi, Cremona, Novara, Vercelli, Alessandria, Valenza, Tortona, Piacenza, Parma, Reggio, Verona, Vicenza, Feltre and Belluno. Gian Galeazzo was a man of culture, whose greatest delight was to curl up with the

classics. But there was nothing wimpish or velvet-glove about his way of exerting command. Local *feudatari* who refused to recognise his authority had their castles razed and were whipped off to prison. A chancellor accused of treachery was wrapped in an ox-skin and walled up alive.

It was under this cultured but ruthless despot that Milan became the largest city in Italy, with a population of around 250,000. Major building projects were embarked upon in the region, including the Certosa (Charterhouse) in Parma – of which Gian Galeazzo personally laid the first stone – and the Duomo (*see p57*) of Milan. When he died of plague in 1402, the great duchy was divided among his heirs, with his wife Caterina left as regent and tutoress.

Elsewhere in the duchy, Gian Galeazzo's death was the signal for other *signori* to raise their heads; Pandolfo III Malatesta declared himself *signore* of Bergamo and Brescia; Facino Cane took over territory in the west. In Milan, meanwhile, Caterina died – perhaps poisoned – just two years after her husband, and their eldest son, Giovanni Maria, was assassinated on his way to church. It fell to the younger son, Filippo Maria, to try and regain control of things. He had inherited his father's ambitious spirit and intelligence, along with his bookish habits and suspicious, closed character. But Milan's further-flung neighbours proved more resilient than in his father's day: despite a number of wars against Florence and Venice, Filippo Maria ruled over a much-reduced duchy, with Bergamo and Brescia going to Venice.

THE SFORZA

When Filippo Maria died in 1447, leaving no male heirs, a group of noblemen attempted to re-establish republican life, setting up the *Aurea repubblica ambrosiana*. Never slow to take advantage of a neighbour's weakness, Venice attacked, grabbing Piacenza and Lodi. The new republican authorities of Milan (rather foolishly) entrusted their defence to Francesco Sforza, husband of Filippo Maria Visconti's illegitimate daughter Bianca Maria (*see p241*) and the closest thing there was to a direct Visconti heir. Francesco won back the lost cities, but then did a secret deal with the Venetians, giving them Brescia and other territories in exchange for their recognition of him as the new duke of Lombardy.

After a brief siege the republican forces in Milan capitulated in 1450. Francesco's rule was even more magnificent than that of Gian Galeazzo Visconti. He transformed the city into a powerful metropolis, building among other things the Castello Sforzesco (*see p70*) and the

Ospedale Maggiore (*see p86*). On his death in 1466 he was succeeded by his pleasure-loving son Galeazzo Maria, whose determination to transform the court into a brothel-cum-circus did not endear him to all his subjects. This was made clear in 1476, when he was stabbed to death in church by three young patricians.

As his son was only seven at the time, Galeazzo Maria's wife gave the regency to a trusty minister and to two of her husband's brothers. The younger, Ludovico Mauro, known as Il Moro (the Moor) due to his dark complexion, was clearly the dominant figure

'Ludovico II Moro's court was one of Italy's great centres of art and culture.'

and very soon he had the reins of power securely in his hands. He proved a good ruler, encouraging agricultural development and the silk industry. Under him, the court became one of Italy's great centres of art and culture, with architects like Donate Bramante (*see p28*) and all-round geniuses like Leonardo da Vinci given free scope.

Only the court of Mantova (*see p232*) could compete for brilliance: there, Ludovico's sister-in-law, the urbane Isabella d'Este, had married into the Gonzaga family and held sway over a centre of high culture. The Gonzagas may not have had Ludovico's military clout, but they could boast a truly great artist in Andrea Mantegna.

Literary icon: **Alessandro Manzoni**. *See p16*.

The life expectancy of these brilliant Renaissance courts as independent entities was, however, short. On a military plane, they hadn't a hope of vying with Europe's great powers. In a fatally flawed attempt to neutralise two birds with one cunningly launched stone (both Naples and France had a claim on the Duchy of Milan through complicated inter-dynastical marriages), Ludovico suggested that King Charles VIII of France might wish to regain the throne of Naples, which had been seized from the French Anjous by the Spaniards. Charles already harboured dreams of becoming a second Charlemagne: Ludovico's invitation was just what he wanted; others came from Florence and the pope; in 1494 he descended through friendly northern and central Italy to an easy victory in the south.

At which point, history repeated itself. Having looted the kingdom of Naples and lost the support of its people, Charles found that Pope Alexander had turned against him, forming a Holy Alliance – including Ludovico – to drive him out. In 1495 Charles was defeated at Fornovo, near Parma, and returned to France. But four years later, France's new king, Louis XII, took his revenge. When he invaded Italy – determined, among other things, to claim his rights over Milan – Ludovico appealed to Emperor Maximilian. The ragged army of Swiss and German mercenaries that the emperor drummed up couldn't match French firepower. With the help of Mantova's Gonzaga family, the French took Il Moro prisoner in 1499; he died in France in 1508.

In the same year French-ruled Milan joined the League of Cambrai, which had been summoned by the great warrior – if not great pope – Julius II to counter the threat posed by Venice's expansion on to the Italian mainland. The League scored a major victory against the Venetians at Agnadello (1509). After which the pope… changed allegiance. In 1513 the French were expelled from Lombardy and Ludovico's son Massimiliano was placed in power.

By this time, however, Lombardy's role as rugby ball in the endless scrimmages between the Great Powers – France, Austria and Spain – was firmly established: for the next three and a half centuries the region was trampled over by foreign armies and swapped about among the great rulers. It was to become a pawn in the Thirty Years War that pitted Catholic leaders against Protestant, and Habsburgs against just about everyone else around Europe.

FOREIGN DOMINATION

The region enjoyed a 14-year semblance of autonomy after France's King Francis I was defeated at Pavia in 1525, his efforts to assert

French hereditary rights over Lombardy stymied by imperial forces. Massimiliano's brother Francesco ruled under the tutelage of Francis's great foe, the Holy Roman Emperor Charles V (a Habsburg, and King Charles I of Spain); but when Francesco died in 1535, Charles assumed power directly. So began 170 years of Spanish domination. The once-proud independent Duchy of Milan became the neglected capital of a province: administered, guarded and taxed by foreigners. This is the wretched, humiliated Milan described in Manzoni's novel *I promessi sposi* (*see p65 I promessi sposi*).

Milan's population fell from 130,000 to around 70,000; industry and agriculture wouldn't recover from the crisis until towards the end of the 17th century. Other Lombard cities, too, were in decline. Mantova was reduced to a mere buffer-state between Milan and Venice. When the last Gonzaga died in 1627, another convoluted war of succession ensued, bringing in its wake invading armies, famine and plague.

In the second half of the 17th century, Milan's religious life was given fresh vigour – albeit of a rather dreary kind – by the imposing Cardinal (later saint) Carlo Borromeo. He was a leading figure of the Counter-Reformation – the movement that had arisen out of the Council of Trent – convened to clean up a hedonistic, corrupt Catholic Church whose authority and clout were being greatly undermined by the spread of militant northern Protestantism. There was certainly no cheery bonhomie about

Napoleon, King of Italy. *See p17.*

the ascetic Carlo; but there can be no denying that he did a good deal to rid the Church of some of the abuses that got the Protestants protesting in the first place.

The 18th century began with the impossibly complicated War of Spanish Succession, following on attempts by French King Louis XIV – a Habsburg – to grab for France all the various European possessions of Spain's last Habsburg monarch, Charles II. In 1706, in the course of this war, Milan was occupied by Eugenio von Savoy (whose Italian/German/French name indicates the complexity of his background) on behalf of Emperor Joseph I of Austria; the Peace of Utrecht (1713), and then the Treaty of Rastadt (1714), confirmed the new occupation.

> ## 'The once-proud independent Duchy of Milan became the neglected capital of an over-taxed province.'

Administratively, the Austrians were a great step up from the Spaniards, who had made it their business to improve as little and tax as much as possible. Various reforms were implemented, one of which was the drawing up of a land register for tax purposes. Suddenly, aristocratic landowners faced the unprecedented need to make their land profitable. This instilled an unusual spirit of enterprise into the land-owning classes, helping to get the economy moving.

The Austrians also did their best to alleviate some of the worst judicial abuses, abolishing ecclesiastic tribunals and the use of torture (to the dismay of some conservative Lombards). The intellectual climate brightened as well, with a number of lively journals being published in Milan and Enlightenment ideas beginning to trickle in among the intellectual classes. Lombardy was undoubtedly the area of Italy most open to new notions from the rest of the Continent. Numerous learned institutions were founded, including the Accademia della Brera (*see p70*), instituted by Empress Maria Teresa in 1776. The Teatro alla Scala (*see p62*) was opened in 1778.

It was thanks to this climate of enlightened thought that Napoleon, whom many earnest optimists at the time saw as embodying the spirit of democratic reform, was received so enthusiastically by the Milanese when he marched into the city in May 1796.

Milan became the capital of his Cisalpine Republic. It was perhaps with rather less enthusiasm, in 1805, that the Milanese watched

Mussolini makes his final appearance, in Milan's piazzale Loreto. *See p19*.

Napoleon assume the crown of Italy in the Duomo – the same iron crown (*see p102*) that had once sat on the heads of the old Lombard kings.

THE RISORGIMENTO

After Napoleon's fall in 1814, Lombardy was restored to Austria. Although the region thrived culturally and economically during the 19th century, the Milanese remained largely hostile to Austrian rule. This hostility found a musical outlet in some of the early operas of Verdi. It finally exploded in the heroic *Cinque Giornate* (Five Days) of 1848: inspired by the spirit of the Risorgimento – the Italy-wide movement to create a united country – the Milanese, in an unprecedented display of united struggle, succeeded in throwing the Austrians out of the city after five days of street fighting. Owing to the military incompetence of Carlo Emanuele of Piedmont, to whom the generally republican leaders of the insurrection had reluctantly turned for aid, the uprising eventually failed. Austrian forces re-entered the city, which, along with the whole Lombardy region, was placed under the iron-fisted control of their commander-in-chief Count Joseph Radetzky. Liberation was postponed until the second war of independence in 1859. This time, under the pressure of combined military intervention by

Popes and emperors

A century and a half before the last Roman emperor in the west – Romulus Augustulus – died during imprisonment by his Germanic conquerors in Naples (476), Constantine the Great had made his eastern capital at Byzantium/Constantinople/Istanbul into the political powerhouse of the Roman Empire.

But so emotionally powerful was the idea of a Europe-wide empire with *caput mundi* Rome at its head, that not even the three ensuing centuries of Barbarian invasions could expunge it from western minds. Through those very dark ages, the pope was – like any bishop of the Christian Church – appointed by the eastern emperor whose hold over the provinces of Italy tightened and slackened as fresh waves of invaders made their presence felt. But with the collapse of the eastern emperor's final stronghold on Italian soil in Ravenna in the 720s – not to mention growing differences between east and west on religious niceties – the pope in Rome felt the need for an iron-fisted, temporal champion of western orthodoxy.

It was the weak and vacillating Pope Leo III (795-816) who, unable to cope with the diplomacy necessary to hold all his potential enemies at bay, plopped a crown on the head of Frankish King Charlemagne (c742-814) when he visited St Peter's in Rome on Christmas Day 800. The pope had no legal right to name anyone *imperator augustus*, never mind this brilliant strategist whose military might had crushed the heretical Lombards in northern Italy. But Charlemagne opted to take his new title seriously, interpreting it as a hereditary one to be passed down to his sons. A long line of Germanic 'Holy Roman Emperors' (though

this name was not used until the 13th century) had begun, to bring successive popes much more grief than aid.

After Charlemagne, the imperial title, like Charlemagne's dominions, became the focus of squabbling and confusion. Under the thumb of powerful Roman families, popes made political imperial appointments of little value through the chaotic ninth century. But when Otto I emerged as eastern Frankish ruler in 936, order began to be restored. Having subdued northern Italy, he made his way to Rome to be crowned emperor by Pope John XII in 962. His 'empire' consisted of no more than present-day Germany and northern Italy. But his successors Otto II (973-83) and Otto III (983-1002) pushed back geographical and moral boundaries. The heir to the imperial throne was known as 'King of the Romans' and the emperor – rather than the pope – came to be seen by some as God's representative on earth.

For the next few centuries popes and emperors were to be engaged in ceaseless and usually fruitless power struggles. Neither, in fact, could do without the other: the emperor needed papal approval, and often enough papal crowning; while the pope frequently needed imperial muscle for defence against threats such as the Normans or, later, the Turks.

In the 12th century the Hohenstaufen family attempted to make the imperial title a family heirloom. They were contested in this by the Wölf family, who had the support of the pope. From this conflict arose the two rival factions of the pope-supporting Guelphs (Wölf) and the emperor-supporting Ghibellines (from the Hohenstaufen family castle of Waiblingen);

the French and the Piedmontese – and with the decisive action of Risorgimento hero Giuseppe Garibaldi and his guerrilla troops – the Austrians were forced to cede Lombardy to Vittorio Emanuele II of Savoy, the first king of a united Italy.

Lombardy was easily the most prosperous and dynamic region of the new united Italy. Though few doubted that the seat of government had to be Rome, Milan clearly considered itself the country's cultural and financial capital. In the years immediately after unification, the city celebrated its new free status by undertaking a number of grandiose

building projects, including the construction of the great Galleria Vittorio Emanuele II (*see p60*) and the remodelling of piazza del Duomo (*see p57*).

On a more practical level, the opening of the San Gottard tunnel through the Alps facilitated trade with northern Europe, and gave another boost, if one was needed, to Lombardy's industry. The flip side of the booming capitalist coin was suffering and unrest among the workers. Support for socialism grew; a general strike in 1898 was repressed with extreme brutality, leaving 81 'subversives' dead and 502 injured. Immediately after World War I there

this rivalry was to tear Italian society apart until at least the days of Romeo and Juliet. In 1160 Emperor Frederick Barbarossa (1155-90), excommunicated by Pope Alexander for his territorial ambitions in Lombardy, set up a rival pope of his own; it was only after he was defeated by the Lombard League at Legnano (*see p106*) and had lost the support of the German bishops that the emperor agreed to a reconciliation with Pope Alexander. Legend has it, however, that as he knelt before the pope in St Mark's in Venice he sulkily muttered, 'Not to you but to Peter.'

An attempt to expand imperial power over the whole of Italy as well as Germany was made by the heirs of Barbarossa, after his son Henry VI (1191-7) married the heiress to the Norman throne of Sicily.

Their son Frederick II – legislator, linguist, philosopher, mathematician and poet – turned southern Italy into a great cultural centre; however, his role as emperor proved more difficult to exercise, with continual papal opposition culminating in excommunication. After Frederick's death, Pope Clement IV (1265-8) saw off his heirs by bringing in Charles d'Anjou from France, who swept down with 30,000 troops and took over the Kingdom of Sicily, publicly decapitating Frederick's 15-year-old son to drive his point home.

For the next two centuries the Holy Roman Empire remained a strictly German affair, and continued to dwindle in international importance. Emperors would occasionally descend into Italy to get a proper papal coronation, but it was not until the 16th century that the office regained any sort of European dignity.

Imperial poise: **Frederick II**.

King Charles I of Spain became Emperor Charles V in 1519 and the title was to remain a Habsburg appanage. Feared by both France and the pope, he was at war on several fronts for most of his reign. Relations between pope and emperor reached an all-time low when Charles's troops sacked Rome in 1527.

Apart from a brief return to prominence during the hideously entangled Thirty Years War, the title became little more than honorific. Few people felt moved to protest when Napoleon did away with it in 1806.

were 445 strikes within the space of a single year; it was in this heady climate that the Fascist party began its thuggish activities, with some of its earliest attacks being launched in Milan against the socialist newspaper *Avanti* (previously edited, curiously enough, by Mussolini himself).

With Fascism firmly established, demonstrations of proletarian discontent magically disappeared. It was not until 1943 that Milanese workers dared to manifest their displeasure once again, bringing several factories in Milan and Turin to a halt; these protests contributed to the downfall of

Mussolini's regime in July the same year. In April 1945 the population of Milan pulled out the old 1848 spirit, rising up against the Nazi-Fascist occupying forces and taking just three days to liberate the city. If there is one thing that characterises the Milanese, it's their determination to improve on past records.

And it was in Milan that the fallen Mussolini made his grisly final public appearance. Having been captured in Dongo (*see p201*) and executed by Partisans in Giulino Mezzegra (*see p200*) on 28 April 1945, Mussolini and his mistress Claretta Petacci were strung up the following day for all to behold in Milan's piazzale Loreto.

Key events

CELTS, ROMANS AND BARBARIANS

5th-4th centuries BC Celtic tribes cross Alps from Gaul to Po Valley occupied by Ligurians.
390 BC Celts almost conquer Rome.
280s BC Romans begin conquest of Po Valley.
222 BC Romans conquer Mediolanum (Milan).
218-201 BC Second Punic War: Celts back Hannibal, beat Romans back across the Po.
42 BC Romans control Cisalpine Gaul.
15 BC Emperor Augustus makes Milan capital of 11th region Transpadania.
1st & 2nd centuries AD Relatively peaceful times. Agricultural northern Italy flourishes.
3rd century Barbarians threaten; Diocletian reorganises the empire into two halves.
292 Mediolanum becomes effective capital of Western Empire.
4th century Empire reunited under control of Constantine the Great (306-37).
313 Edict of Milan legalises Christianity.
374-97 St Ambrose bishop of Milan.
452 Attila the Hun razes Milan.
476 Odoacer, a Goth, crowned king in Pavia.

LOMBARDS AND FRANKS

568 Lombards begin rampage through Italy.
572 Lombards take Pavia, becomes capital.
774 Charlemagne defeats Lombards.
800 Charlemagne made Holy Roman Emperor; after his death (814) empire collapses.
9th-10th centuries Locals live in fortified rural hamlets for protection against barbarians; *reucci* (kinglets) bicker for control.
961 Frankish King Otto I invades; named Holy Roman Emperor in 962; clergy more powerful.

AGE OF THE *COMUNI*

Late 11th century *Consulatus civium* (town council meeting) held in Milan 1097.
Early 12th century Milan takes control over Lodi, Cremona, Como and Pavia.
1162 Holy Roman Emperor Frederick Barbarossa (1152-90) lays siege to Milan, destroys walls and palaces of nobles.
1167 Lombard *comuni* band together in the anti-imperial Lega Lombarda.
1176 Lega beats imperial forces at Legnano.
1183 Peace of Constance grants Milan independence; pro-Empire Ghibellines squabble with pro-pope Guelphs.

THE VISCONTI

1277 Ottone Visconti's Ghibelline forces beat Guelphs; Ottone declared *signore* of Milan.
1294 Matteo Visconti controls all Milan area.

1330s Visconti take control of Bergamo and Novara (1332), Cremona (1334), Como and Lodi (1335), Brescia (1337).
1395 Gian Galeazzo Visconti (1378-1402) made Duke of Milan; 1397 Duke of Lombardy; Milan Italy's largest city, population 250,000.
1402 Gian Galeazzo dies; cities break away.

THE SFORZA

1447 Filippo Maria Visconti dies with no male heir; Milanese republic set up; Filippo Maria's son-in-law Francesco Sforza leads, then betrays, republicans.
1450 Francesco becomes Duke of Lombardy.
1476 Francesco's brother Ludovico Il Moro becomes duke; court is centre of culture.
1499 France's King Louis XII invades Italy, takes Il Moro prisoner.
1513 French expelled from Lombardy; Ludovico's son Massimiliano placed in power.

FOREIGN DOMINATION

1525 Francesco Sforza rules under tutelage of Holy Roman Emperor Charles V.
1535 Francesco dies, Charles V assumes power; 150 years of Spanish rule begins.
1560 Carlo Borromeo made archbishop of Milan; gives religious life new vigour.
1706 Milan occupied by Austria; reforms implemented; Enlightenment ideas arrive.
1796 Napoleon invades, makes Milan capital of Cisalpine Republic; King of Italy (1805).

THE RISORGIMENTO

1814 Lombardy restored to Austria.
1848 Milanese rise up against Austrians in *Cinque Giornate* (Five Days) rebellion inspired by spirit of Risorgimento; revolt quashed.
1859 Second war of independence: Austrians cede Lombardy to Vittorio Emanuele II of Savoy, united Italy's first king.
1898 81 die, 502 injured in general strike protests in industrially modern Milan.
Post-1918 Fascist party emerges; attacks in Milan against Socialist newspaper *Avanti*.
1943 Milanese workers strike, contributing to Mussolini's downfall.
April 1945 Milanese liberate city from German control in three-day uprising.
1960-70s Lombardy is the driving force behind Italy's 'economic miracle'.
1983 *Tangentopoli* scandal erupts in Milan.
1990s Separatist Lega Nord (Northern League) party gains support, representing widespread discontent with Rome.

Milan & Lombardy Today

Pragmatism and creative flair in Italy's economic capital.

Any first-time visitor to Milan just off the train from Venice or Florence will be struck by how un-Italian this northern capital appears. Shrouded in fog during the winter and smothered with smog all year round, Milan has little of the charm and grace for which Italian cities are legendary. The Allies' bombs cleared wide swathes through the city, which were unfortunately filled with monolithic concrete buildings and inelegant *piazze* in the decades that followed, while the no-nonsense, harried Milanese manner could hardly be more different from the relaxed, devil-may-care creed of their southern brethren.

But while the initial impact rarely makes for love at first sight, Milan is a city that manages to meld the pragmatism and affluence of northern Europe with the creative flair and love of the good life that all Italians relish. And while southern Italy appears to in its Latin indolence (much to the irritation of

northerners), the Milanese and their neighbours throughout Lombardy have been the principal engines for economic growth for the entire country for the past three decades.

ITALY'S POWERHOUSE
The inhabitants of Milan and the region of Lombardy are without doubt the worker bees of the nation, having played an integral part in the boom that transformed Italy from a relatively backward, agricultural country at the end of World War II to a world leader in machine tools, design and textiles. The city that is now the financial capital of Italy has its roots as a major commercial trading centre stretching back to Roman times, thanks to its strategic position just south of the key passes through the Alps. Even today, it is unequivocally Italy's most international and cosmopolitan city, as well as one of Europe's richest.

Lombards take great pride in their industriousness, as well they should. The north accounts for three-quarters of Italy's total exports and boasts an unemployment rate of 3.6 per cent, less than half the European average and a fifth of the level registered in the perennially lagging Italian south. Over the years, the region has churned out thousands of sprightly enterprises, some of which are world leaders in their sectors. By 2000 Lombardy easily topped the rest of the country in terms of numbers of businesses, with nearly a fifth of all Italian enterprises located here.

The city of Milan also transformed itself from a provincial northern city at the end of the war into a major financial centre servicing Italy's expanded post-war economy. The emerging wealth of Italy's northern regions in the 1960s and '70s sent money flowing into the coffers of its banks and investment houses. The gradual maturation of international capital markets brought fresh money to Milan's stock market in the 1970s and, in particular, the 1980s. That decade also marked the salad days for Italy's newly born financiers, who launched mini versions of the hostile takeovers and fancy financial operations that were sweeping Wall Street at the time.

The 1970s also saw the explosion of Italian fashion and design in Milan, initially fuelled by the innovative textile groups and clothing manufacturers that dot the Lombard countryside outside Milan. In 1975 Giorgio Armani sold his Volkswagen to finance the founding of his fashion house. Just five years later, he was dressing Richard Gere in the cult classic *American Gigolo*, and gracing the cover of *Time* magazine. Gianni Versace grabbed the world's attention with his ultrasexy party dresses and supermodel-laden catwalk shows. By the 1990s a plethora of names – Max Mara, Gucci and, more recently, Miuccia Prada – had made the catwalks of Milan an indispensable twice-yearly stop for buyers from the US and Asia. Milan's rise was such that some argued that the city had actually overtaken Paris as the most important stop on the fashion circuit by the mid 1990s. While that's debatable, Milan has certainly become one of Europe's most important trendsetting cities.

THE NORTH–SOUTH DIVIDE

The combination of wealth and style has left the Milanese with a distinctly snobby streak. In their clipped accent, most Milanese are happy to complain about the laziness of their compatriots, particularly those in the deep south. In their opinion, most of Italy is living off the sweat of northern brows, while the source of much that ails Italy can be found in

Rome (whose antipathy for Milan is absolutely mutual). The Milan–Rome rivalry is such that cars with Rome licence plates are frequently vandalised if their owners are careless enough to park them on the street.

The federalist/separatist party, the Lega Nord (*see p24* **Northern League**), capitalised on these feelings in the early 1990s, finding fertile ground for its potent mix of anti-Rome diatribes, xenophobia and grandiose secessionist plans; one of its number, Marco Formentini, was elected mayor of the city in 1993.

'Milan's spectacular wealth in the 1980s turned out to have been greased by floods of dirty money.'

Ironically, when the massive bribes scandals that were to hamstring a whole generation of politicians and business figures broke in the early 1990s, it was soon obvious that a considerable part of the corruption that had risen to grotesque proportions during the 1980s had its very roots in Milan. Indeed, Milan's spectacular wealth of that decade turned out to have been greased by floods of dirty money. The symbol of the bribes scandals – dubbed *Tangentopoli*, or Bribesville – became the Milan-based Ferruzzi company and the massive kickbacks it had paid to Roman politicians and executives at state-owned companies in order to create a world-class chemicals conglomerate. The suicide of Ferruzzi's chief executive Raul Gardini in 1993 and a damning investigation into the near-bankrupt group became an indictment of an entire Milanese business class that had ridden the wave of the easy money of the 1980s. And while the level of corruption has surely dropped since the *Mani pulite* (Clean Hands) investigations, funny money still abounds in Milan and Lombardy, encouraged by the reluctance of northerners to pay Italy's sky-high taxes and the close proximity of the Swiss tax haven Lugano.

Although some had feared that the bribes scandals and a new era of austerity in Italy would dampen Milan's spirits, the city was once again the centre of a boom by the late 1990s. This time it was the New Economy that stirred the pot, with a class of young entrepreneurs preaching the gospel of the Internet. The peak of this boom was the 1999 takeover of the former state monopoly of Telecom Italia – one of the largest hostile deals ever done – by a group of Lombardy-based businessmen.

APPEARANCES COUNT

The go-go years of the late 1990s allowed the Milanese to indulge in the material pleasures affluence allows. Even in a country that places inordinate importance on physical appearance, the Milanese – egged on by the presence of world-class fashion houses – are fixated. A Milanese woman would no sooner nip out to the supermarket without full make-up than walk through the streets naked. And Milanese men are arguably the best-dressed in Europe, with a keen eye to their waistline and the cut of their custom-made suit. A recent mania for fitness and beauty farms in Milan has seen the establishment of pricey health clubs where Milanese ladies no longer lunch, but spend their days toning thighs and receiving anti-cellulite massages.

Probably no institution better incarnates Milanese snobbery than La Scala, one of Europe's premier opera houses. La Scala is the ultimate place to see and be seen in Milan, where the city's grey-haired bankers mingle with chief executives and their socialite wives. The event of the season is the debut of the new headline opera on 7 December, the feast day of the city's patron, St Ambrose (Sant'Ambrogio). While occasionally disrupted by paintball-bearing anti-fur activists, opening night – with tickets topping $1,000 a piece – gives the crème of Milanese society the ultimate opportunity to revel in their wealth and status.

Outside of Milan, those industrious Lombards from Brescia or Bergamo are somewhat less showy, but hardly strangers to the good things in life. Many of these entrepreneurs, after years of 15-hour days and admirable thrift, have built up considerable fortunes. But with very few exceptions, they tend to shun the limelight of high society, preferring their routine of family, church and factory. They take refuge in their spectacular villas – behind heavily armed gates – that dot the shores of Lombardy's trio of major lakes, Como, Garda and Maggiore. They're also apt to indulge in boats or fancy cars, with a shiny red Ferrari a perennial favourite for the clan's eldest son.

PROBLEMS AND SHORTCOMINGS

Despite their affluence, the Milanese are remarkably short on civic pride. They are little inclined to devote money or time to beautify their city, one of the ugliest of Italian metropolises. Urban development has been slapdash, with real estate speculators having thrown up eyesores over the years. Milan has just nine square metres of park space per inhabitant, a third of that of Bologna and even less than Venice, a situation

Donatella Versace struts her stuff at the Milan show.

that only contributes to its evident pollution problem. The periphery is a string of factories, hypermarkets and concrete-block monstrosities in which the less-privileged Milanese live. Driven by the smog, those who can escape the city virtually every weekend, fleeing to country homes in the nearby Alps or at the seaside in Liguria. This weekly flight leaves little support for cultural events, which are remarkably thin on the ground for a city the size of Milan.

Furthermore, while in many respects Milan is one of the country's most efficient cities, it nonetheless suffers from the lack of organisation that plagues all of Italy. Its transport system is woefully inadequate, raising constant complaints from industrial groups who say that poor roads and rail networks leave them struggling against nimbler European competitors. Lousy commuter rail services mean that the city is choked with cars. Malpensa, the new airport that was supposed to be Italy's major hub and reinforce its emergence as a major financial centre in Europe, has been a disaster, hobbled by frequent delays in flights and poor services on the ground.

Milan's popular mayor, Gabriele Albertini, has done his best to rectify these shortcomings. The centre-right politician has undertaken a series of urban beautification projects, including a revamping of piazza Cadorna, the restoration of the Castello Sforzesco (*see p70*) and a clean-up of city parks that had fallen prey to drug pushers and the homeless. He has also made a valiant attempt at solving Milan's chronic parking problem and at combatting the graffiti artists that run rampant in the city.

However, the administrative and spending powers of Italian mayors are much more limited than in other parts of Europe and Albertini hasn't been able to make as much headway as originally hoped.

These shortcomings are even more painful at a time when the world economy is slowing sharply. Many Lombard businesses had already been suffering from competition from rivals in eastern Europe and Asia, who can easily undercut the Italians on labour costs and overheads. Furthermore, the single currency in Europe means that Italians can no longer depend on a weak lira to boost orders in slow times. At the same time, foreigners have been arriving in force, looking to offer cheaper and better services in banking, retailing and consulting, and putting many Milanese groups under heavy pressure to get with the times.

Many Milanese are looking to the government of Silvio Berlusconi for relief. A self-made media mogul who hails from Milan, Berlusconi has promised to implement the free-market reforms his northern electorate has long been clamouring for. He has pledged to cut taxes, clean up government waste and fix up Italy's creaky infrastructure. His coalition includes the Northern League, which has been pushing for more local control over the levers of state power.

But reform doesn't come easily to Italy and the economic slowdown has made Berlusconi's task even tougher. In the coming years, Milanese and Lombard businesses are going to have to come up with an extra dose of the ingenuity that has served them so well over the years.

Northern League

The Lega Nord (Northern League) was founded in 1984 by Umberto Bossi, a former electrician with a flair for demagoguery who laboured in anonymity until around 1992. That year marked the eruption of a series of bribes scandals that unearthed deep northern resentment towards the inefficiencies and corruption of Rome's political system. By 1994 Bossi had ridden this wave of popular discontent, and the Northern League had joined the ranks of Italy's major parties, with Bossi becoming a kingmaker for the creation of the first government led by Silvio Berlusconi. (It was also the irascible Bossi who brought the government crashing down from the inside after just seven months in power in December 1994.)

Despite its strong performance in the mid 1990s, the Northern League has gone into

sharp decline since the scandals faded in Italians' minds. Bossi's ranting demands for the independence of what he dubbed 'Padania' – a strip of northern Italy bordering the River Po that stretched, sometimes as far as Tuscany, and shrank with the party leader's ever-changing delusions of grandeur – caused him to lose support among mainstream entrepreneurs. They found his fiery rhetoric overwrought and out of tune with their everyday concerns.

Nevertheless, despite declining support, the League forms a small but important part of Silvio Berlusconi's current government. And despite its decline, there has been no diminution of the feeling among most Lombards that Roman politicians, corruption and the interminable problems of the south remain a millstone around their necks.

Art in Milan & Lombardy

No past Golden Age, but Milan is looking to the future.

Financial and industrial clout is something Milan has long had in abundance. But popes and kings (potential sponsors) and radical bohemians (potential producers) have been sadly lacking, which goes some way towards explaining the city's shortage of 'great' art. But there are other, more complex, reasons too.

Take, for example, the city's long-standing position as underdog and also-ran. Milan was a capital under Diocletian (see p8) during the late Roman Empire, it's true. But Rome had already marked off its territory in terms of artistic and architectural style several centuries before, and Milan simply became a ready receptacle for Roman work, such as the portrait head of Maximinus or the torso of Hercules, both in the Museo Archeologico (see p97).

In the 14th century, under its Visconti overlords (see p11), Milan was a centre of the International Gothic. But art history has never very been comfortable with the idea of the International Gothic as a high point of western art.

In the 15th century, Milanese ruler Ludovico 'Il Moro' Sforza might have created something as splendid as the Florence of Botticelli, Verrocchio and Ghirlandaio had he not been carted off to a French prison, his dream of a great Milan nipped in the bud.

From the early 1500s until it became part of the Kingdom of Italy in the 19th century, Milan was ruled by foreigners. It's understandable, therefore, that indigenous qualities that could be held up as standards for posterity are hard to spot (the 'Lombard realism' recognised as a formative influence on the great baroque painter Caravaggio is one). Like the city itself, Milan's art was under the sway of foreign imports and fashions. Which is not to say that qualified local operators were absent; it just takes a little extra effort to discover them.

Which is another problem in looking at art in Milan: us as viewers. Milan never had an artistic Golden Age like Florence in the 15th century, or Rome in the 16th; it was largely off

Time Out Milan Guide **25**

travel itineraries in the days of the Grand Tour and remains that way in the era of the package tour. What we are 'supposed to see' or 'can't miss' is generally not here. And when it is (for example, **Leonardo da Vinci**'s *Last Supper*, *see p98*, considered the first High Renaissance picture and one of the greatest masterpieces of all time), it has been reproduced so many times that we may find ourselves at a loss when trying to come to terms with the real thing.

The dearth of 'high' art can also be put down to a tendency to turn greatness into something else. This is a truly Lombard characteristic: an exasperating urge not to create *ex novo*, but to add on, remodel, or cover with whitewash. Little remained uninhabited or unused long enough to become 'artistic', 'charming' or 'quaint'. Milan has always been all too glad to bury its past.

So it is not in its 'high' art that the region's uniqueness lies. But forget your Grand Tour preconceptions, and you'll find there is a great deal to see in the city and beyond.

ROMANS AND BISHOPS

Lombardy's earliest artistic expression can be seen in the prehistoric caves and rock art in the provinces of Brescia and Sondrio. The Castello Sforzesco (*see p70*) and the collections in the Musei Civici in the Villa Mirabello (*see p108*) in Varese both contain fine examples.

The advent of the Romans turned Milan – ancient Mediolanum – into the region's most important city. Yet only in the last century – with the construction of the Metropolitana (underground) – did its (very few) ruins emerge. When Mediolanum became the main city of Augustus' XI *regio* in 15 BC, it took the form of a Roman city with walls, *cardo* and *decumanus* and a forum where San Sepolcro (*see p66*) now stands. Great monument building took place at the end of the third century AD, when Diocletian made it the capital of the western half of the empire, and again as Milan emerged as a focal point of early Christianity.

When the charismatic Ambrose became bishop in 374, he embarked on a 'Christian' building campaign that included five basilicas around the city walls and two cathedrals in the centre. Though most were remodelled during the Romanesque period, the fifth-century chapel of Sant'Aquilino in San Lorenzo (*see p90*) has mosaics that reveal the pictorial tastes of the age.

Modern historiography no longer looks upon the early medieval period as the 'Dark Ages'; for Milan, however, it was as black as could be. Humbled and razed by successive waves of barbarian invaders, impoverished Milan was sidelined by flourishing neighbouring towns. Monza and Pavia were favoured by the Germanic Lombards who held sway from the

sixth to the ninth centuries; the crown of Lombard Queen Theodolinda is in the treasury of Monza cathedral (*see p101*).

But in the 12th century, bishops Angilberto II and Ansperto ushered in a new age of monumental splendour for Milan, with a burst of building activity and new city walls. Sant'Ambrogio (*see p94*) is home to the most important artistic works from this period: the ciborium (with recycled Roman porphyry columns and capitals), Angilberto II's gold altarpiece with scenes from the life of Christ and St Ambrose and the mosaics in the apse and sacellum of San Vittore in Ciel d'Oro.

The reconstruction of Sant'Ambrogio in the 11th and 12th centuries inaugurated the great Romanesque period in Milan. The Byzantine, Islamic and Lombard influences on proto-Romanesque sculpture are clearly visible in the decoration on the capitals of the columns and the polychrome-and-gilt stucco of the baldachin. Much of the work of the time was destroyed by later invaders, or subjected to heavy restoration at the end of the 19th century. Luckily, bits and pieces of many no-longer-extant buildings have been preserved in the sculpture museum of the Castello Sforzesco, including an early 'ideological' relief, *St Ambrose Expelling the Arians*, which is signed by **Gerardo** and **Anselmo**, two *maestri campionesi* – master stonecutters from the Campione area, between the lakes of Lugano and Como.

'A 150-year era of Gothic luxury made Milan into a centre of art and culture.'

Another sign of this period's prosperity are the great monastic complexes just outside Milan, such as the Cistercian abbey of Chiaravalle (*see p110*), founded by St Bernard in 1135 and consecrated in 1221. The religious Humiliati (*see p110* **Humiliati**) order – wiped out in the 16th century by the Counter-Reformation zeal of St Charles Borromeo – was also responsible for tremendous building activity, constructing the church of Santa Maria di Brera – now incorporated into the Pinacoteca di Brera (*see p70*) and abbeys at Viboldone (*see p110*) and Mirasole (*see p110*). On the portal of the church at Viboldone (begun in 1176) are sculptures of the Madonna with Child and Saints by another *maestro campionese*, the **Maestro di Viboldone**.

VISCONTIS AND SFORZAS

By the 1330s, the powerful Visconti family had put an end to the free commune of Milan and seized power. Azzone Visconti (*see p13*) ushered

Martyrdom of St Catherine by Lombard Mannerist Gaudenzio Ferrari. *See p29.*

in a 150-year era of Gothic luxury that made Milan into a centre of art and culture – and, briefly, Florence's rival. The wealth of schools represented in the city at the time can be seen in the city's Pinacoteca di Brera (*see p70*). At Viboldone Abbey, the *Last Judgment* attributed to **Giusto de' Menabuoi** is considered one of the finest works of the era.

Azzone was responsible for importing another great Gothic master, **Giovanni di Balduccio**, who brought the imposing sculptural/architectural Pisan style of funerary monument to Milan. His masterpiece – the tomb of Stefano Visconti – is in the church of Sant'Eustorgio (*see p90*); his sculptural decoration on the Porta Ticinese (*see p87*) is still *in situ*. Azzone's successor, Bernabò, favoured sculptor **Bonino da Campione**: his massive equestrian statue of Bernabò in the Castello Sforzesco matched Bernabò's ego.

In painting, the International Gothic flourished in Milan under Bernabò's nephew Gian Galeazzo. 'His' artist was **Giovannino de' Grassi**, one of the many Italian, German and French stonecutters and architects in Milan from 1386 onwards to work on the immense Duomo (*see p57*): his sculpture can be seen on the portals in the south sacristy and on St Catherine's altar in the left nave. Other examples of the refined Milanese culture of the period include **Bonifacio Bembo**'s *Tarocchi* in the Accademia Carrara in Bergamo (*see p218*), and the **Zavattari brothers'** frescos in the chapel of Queen Theodolinda in Monza's Duomo (*see p102*).

Visconti rule gave way to that of the Sforza dynasty, which aimed, at first, to conserve the city's International Gothic tradition. But both the first Sforza duke, Francesco, and his successor, Galeazzo Maria, were aware of the artistic goings-on in central Italy, by that time on to its second generation of Renaissance painters (including **Piero della Francesca**, whose Montefeltro altarpiece is in the Brera). What emerged was a sort of Lombard-Tuscan pastiche, both in architecture and painting. The leading artist of the age was undoubtedly **Vincenzo Foppa**, who blended Mantegnesque and Tuscan influences in his masterpiece in the Cappella Portinari (*see p90*), *Scenes from the Life of St Peter Martyr*.

Galeazzo Maria's half-brother Ludovico 'Il Moro' had very different ideas for Milan: while extending the territory under Milanese control well into present-day Switzerland, he strove to make the city a true centre of Renaissance style. He summoned the most highly acclaimed men of letters, musicians and artists of the time, including **Donato Bramante** and **Leonardo da Vinci**, to his court.

Though Bramante is best known for his Milanese buildings (Santa Maria Delle Grazie and Santa Maria presso San Satiro), he also left his mark in fresco: his *Portraits of Illustrious Men*, now in the Brera, show how extensively the humanistic culture of central Italy had penetrated Lombard territory.

Leonardo – Ludovico's 'engineer' – was commissioned to make a vast equestrian monument to Francesco Sforza, but like so many of the great Tuscan's projects, it failed to get past the planning stage; the model for it was destroyed by French troops after Ludovico was ousted. (A reconstruction by sculptor Nina Akamu can be seen at the Ippodromo, *see p99*).

The most famous ducal commission, however, remains the *Last Supper* (*Il Cenacolo*, *see p98*) in the refectory of Santa Maria delle Grazie, Ludovico's favourite church. A comparison with **Donato da Montorfano**'s fresco of the crucifixion on the opposite wall shows how far ahead of his time Leonardo was.

Milan's museums, however, show that the city has also known how to give credit where it is due. The Brera (whose original study collections were enriched by the holdings of suppressed churches, *see p98*) houses a number of works by **Giovanni** and **Gentile Bellini** including the spectacular *St Mark Preaching in Alexandria*, **Andrea Mantegna**'s *Dead Christ*, and **Raphael**'s *Marriage of the Virgin*. **Piero Pollaiuolo**'s portraits and **Sandro Botticelli**'s *Lamentation over the Dead Christ* are in the Poldi Pezzoli gallery (*see p77*).

THE BORROMEOS AND THE BAROQUE

Leonardo and Bramante had already left the city by the time Ludovico 'il Moro' fell in 1499, but the tradition that had taken root there continued for two decades more. The prolific **Bernadino Bergognone** was the chief representative of Lombard tradition, leaving behind a prodigious amount of work at the Certosa di Pavia (*see p254*) and in Milan (*The Coronation of the Virgin* in the apsidal conch of San Simpliciano, and a series of *Christ and the Apostles* in the sacristy of Santa Maria della Passione). Great convent and monastery churches were built within the city walls, and decorated by **Giovanni Boltraffio** and **Bernardino Luini**.

Holy Roman Emperor Charles V (*see p15*) had works by his Venetian favourite **Titian** (including *The Flagellation*, which was later carried off to Paris by Napoleon) installed in Milanese churches. Towards the middle of the century, another important Venetian work arrived in Milan: **Tintoretto**'s *Christ Disputing with the Elders in the Temple*, now in the Museo del Duomo (*see p60*).

The more austere spirit of the Counter-Reformation – personified in Milan by the all-powerful archbishop-cousins Carlo and Federico Borromeo – brought the first traces of the late Renaissance style, Mannerism. No area of artistic output in the region in the late 16th and early 17th centuries escaped the cousins' influence. Among their favourites was the Cremonese painter **Bernardino Campi**, whose work is cloyingly pious; brothers **Vincenzo** and **Antonio Campi** from Cremona also found fertile terrain in Milan, as did **Simone Peterzano** from Bergamo. But the Lombard Mannerist artist *par excellence* was **Gaudenzio Ferrari** from Valsesia. He appeared on the scene in 1544-5, with frescos in Santa Maria della Pace (now in the Brera) and in Santa Maria delle Grazie.

The baroque hit Milan while Federico occupied the archbishop's throne (1595-1631). A new generation of Milanese painters – **Giovanni Battista Crespi** (aka Il Cerano), **Giulio Cesare Procaccini**, **Il Morazzone**, **Daniele Crespi** – emerged. A series of canvases with *Scenes from the Life of St Charles Borromeo* (1602-10) by Il Cerano and Procaccini are still exhibited in the Duomo from 4 November until 6 January. The church of Sant'Antonio Abate provides a one-stop tour of the period, with works by Procaccini, Il Cerano, Il Morazzone, **Tanzio da Varallo** and **Francesco Del Cairo**. But the single greatest symbol of the cultural spirit of the age remains the Pinacoteca Ambrosiana (*see p65*), founded in 1618 when Federico's own art collection was donated to the Biblioteca Ambrosiana.

FOREIGN RULE, FOREIGN INFLUENCE

During Milan's first stint under Austrian rule in 1706-96, mature baroque and extravagant rococo flourished. The archetypal rococo dabbler **Giambattista Tiepolo** was called on to decorate many Milanese *palazzi* in the 1740s; the Venetian's paintings can be seen on the ceiling of the Sala della Giunta in the Palazzo Isimbardi (*see p81*). Frescos by a precursor of Tiepolo, **Sebastiano Ricci**, adorn the vault of San Bernardino alle Ossa (*see p87*).

The second period of Austrian rul (1815-59) brought Milan closer to the spirit of northern Europe; its open attitude towards liberal ideas made it a capital of the Romantic era, a role epitomised in **Francesco Hayez**'s *Il bacio (The Kiss)* in the Brera.

UNIFICATION TO ABSTRACT EXPRESSIONISM

Milan's annexation into the Kingdom of Italy in 1805 magnified its twofold image: as European city, and as Italian economic success story.

Liberal-leaning private enterprise created great works such as the Cimitero Monumentale (*see p76*), and the the Galleria (*see p60*).

In the arts, an eclectic movement of Lombard historicism sprang up, wandering from the 'Romanesque-Gothic' to the 'Bramantesque' styles of painting. Simultaneously, the avant-garde **Scapigliati school** (Federico Faruffini, Luigi Conconi, and the sculptor Giuseppe Grandi) paved the way for the energetic celebration of modernism, Futurism.

While **Filippo Tommaso Marinetti**, author of the *Futurist Manifesto*, held his famous salon in his home on corso Venezia (a plaque marks the spot where it once stood), **Alessandro Mazzucotelli** and his **Società Umanitaria** were forging a Socialist *arte nuova* in applied arts. Out of this came **Pelizza da Volpedo**'s *Quarto Stato*, now in the Museo d'Arte Moderna, a symbol of artistic commitment to the forces of social change.

The Milan of the interwar years was a contradiction politically and culturally. At the centre of humanitarian Socialism, it was also the birthplace of Fascism. However, the construction of the Palazzo d'Arte in 1932-3 as permanent headquarters for the Triennale exhibition demonstrated the city's connection with contemporary art at an early date. It became a reference point for the first **Novecento group**, whose greatest exponents were the ex-Futurists **Carlo Carrà** and **Mario Sironi**, as well as the neo-impressionist painting of the **Chiaristi** and the expressionism of the young painters of **Corrente** such as **Aligi Sassu** and **Ernesto Treccani**. These last two organised their own gallery, Il Milione, where the first Italian abstract artists met nd where abstract expressionist **Jackson Pollock** was shown for the first time. This period also saw the birth of great collections of contemporary art in Milan.

CONTEMPORARY COMMITMENT

Milan has continued to be a centre for showing and producing art. Among the city's main post-war avant-garde movements are **Fronte Nuovo**; the abstract **MAC**; the 'spatial' and 'nuclear' groups of **Lucio Fontana** (his legacy went to the CIMAC in Palazzo Reale, *see p57*); urban-existential neo-realism gravitating around the Centro dei Gesuiti di San Fedele; **Piero Manzoni**'s conceptual and behavioural art; and the 'pop' art of **Valerio Adami** and **Emilio Tadini**. And examples of urban avant-garde sculpture are scattered around the city, including **Arnaldo Pomodoro**'s piece in piazza Meda.

With a commitment to the contemporary that outstrips other Italian cities, Milan appears to be striving to compensate for its less splendid past.

Architecture

Lombardy is always willing to embrace the new.

In 1646, British traveller and diarist John Evelyn described Milan as 'one of the most princely cities in Europe'. Today Milan has shed its aristocratic veneer and become inescapably modern: skyscrapers puncture the sky, cars race along wide tree-lined streets and subways shake the pavements. This willingness to embrace the new is characteristic of a city that has continued to transform itself in the face of adversity. The heart of Lombardy, Milan sets the tone for the architectural character of the region.

MEDIOLANUM

When they took control of the Celtic settlement where Milan now stands in 222 BC, the Romans applied their usual urban plan to what they called Mediolanum: the central forum was located at the intersection of east–west (*cardum*) and north–south (*decumanus*) axes running between four main gates. The forum was located where the church of **San Sepolcro** (*see p67*) and the **Biblioteca Ambrosiana** (*see p65*) now stand; with some imagination, the rectilinear grid of the Roman city can still be made out in the surrounding streets.

Remains of Mediolanum are few, but hints of its grandeur are visible in the foundations of the imperial palace (*see p97*) and in the graceful Corinthian colonnade that is part of a second-century BC building by the church of San Lorenzo Maggiore (*see p91*).

More extensive vestiges of Roman opulence can be found throughout Lombardy, from the **Tempio Capitolino** built by Vespasian in Brescia in AD 73 (*see p227*) to the magnificent holiday villas constructed by prosperous locals on the shores of Lake Garda at Sirmione and Desenzano (for both, *see p207*).

EARLY CHRISTIANITY AND THE MIDDLE AGES

Fittingly for a city so swift to embrace Christianity, Milan holds one of the most important examples of early Christian architecture: the church of **San Lorenzo Maggiore** (*see p91*). Founded in the fourth century, and constructed with materials scavenged from the nearby Roman circus and amphitheatre, this centrally planned octagonal structure was a point of reference for church design right into the Renaissance.

The quiet Romanesque churches of **San Nazaro Maggiore** (*see p87*) and **Sant'Eustorgio** (*see p90*) and the sturdy brick *campanili* (bell towers) scattered throughout the city are further proof of Milan's importance as a religious centre. But undoubtedly the most evocative of the city's early Christian architectural gems is **Sant'Ambrogio** (*see p95*), founded by the city's much-loved bishop St Ambrose (*see p10* **Sant'Ambrogio**) and constructed between 379 and 386. The interior is built to a basilica plan, a rectangular space adapted from Roman meeting halls to meet the needs of Christian worship. Unlike most of Milan's churches, which give directly on to the street, Sant'Ambrogio is preceded by an arcaded forecourt: the warm red of the brick, coupled with the repetition of the arch in the forecourt and again on the façade, sets this space apart from the chaos of the city and anticipates the ordered stillness of the interior.

As Milan's economic and political power grew, both religious and civic patrons endowed the city and surrounding area with fitting landmarks. In the 12th century the Cistercian abbeys were built outside the city walls; in the 13th new religious orders put up churches, monasteries and convents inside the city. In his *De Magnalibus Urbis Mediolani* (1288), Bonvesin de la Riva described a city with over 200 churches and chapels and a skyline punctuated by 120 *campanili*.

'Religious and civil patrons endowed the city with fitting landmarks.'

The demands of civic authorities were met with grand constructions that in addition aimed to proclaim the city's status as an important commercial centre. The Visconti family that ruled Milan and its dominions from the late 13th century (*see p13*) was responsible for many significant landmarks, including Milan's sculpture-laden **Duomo** (*see p57*). French and German architects were hired by to help with the construction; the flying buttresses, profusion of exterior decoration, and pointed arches on the vaults are characteristic elements of northern Gothic cathedrals.

Amongst Gian Galeazzo's other foundations was the spectacular **Certosa di Pavia** (*see p254*), a monastery intended as a family mausoleum. The façade is rich with sculptural detail and polychrome decoration; however, the more mundane aspects of the monastery complex – such as the great cloister with its monks' cells – are perhaps more impressive.

THE RENAISSANCE

As the Renaissance took hold, the cultured court of Milan's new rulers, the Sforzas, attracted many of the leading architects of the time, including Il Filarete and Donato Bramante.

Trained as a bronze sculptor, the Florentine Il Filarete (Antonio Averulino) worked on St Peter's in Rome before being summoned to Milan by Federico Sforza to create the **Castello Sforzesco** (*see p70*). His most important work in Milan, however, was the **Ospedale Maggiore** (*see p85*): the cruciform plan was an innovation; a typically Lombard mixture of brick and terracotta is masterfully manipulated to create rich patterns of colour and texture.

Bramante's first major work in Milan was the church of **Santa Maria presso San Satiro** (*see p67*). Thwarted by the existing street pattern, which made a regular Latin cross plan impossible, he created the illusion of depth with a *trompe l'oeil* perspective. For Ludovico Il Moro Sforza, Bramante designed a family mausoleum in **Santa Maria delle Grazie** (*see p97*), a new courtyard at Sant'Ambrogio, and a new square in **Vigevano** (*see p257*). All betray a fascination with the architecture of antiquity.

Frustrated by the lack of opportunities open to him in Milan, Bramante left for Rome in 1500, where he went on to design many of the most important monuments of the Renaissance. In 1537 the architect Sebastiano Serlio wrote: 'It may be said that he [Bramante] revived the good architecture that had been buried from the days of the ancients until now.'

Under the rule of the Gonzaga family, the city of Mantova, too, was endowed with splendid Renaissance constructions. Ludovico II Gonzaga had the church of **Sant'Andrea** (*see p237*) built in 1470 to a design by leading architectural theorist Leon Battista Alberti. The **Palazzo Te** (*see p236*), begun in 1525 by Giulio Romano for Federico II Gonzaga, reveals the shift in style from the ordered harmony of the High Renaissance to the playful and sculptural quality of the late Renaissance.

In Bergamo, the lavish Cappella Colleoni at **Santa Maria Maggiore** (*see p216*), commissioned by the famous *condottiere* (mercenary soldier) Bartolomeo Colleoni, was designed by Milanese architect Giovanni Antonio Amadeo.

THE COUNTER-REFORMATION AND BAROQUE

The Council of Trent (1545-63) ushered in an austere age – the Counter-Reformation – a change reflected in Milanese architecture. In the late 16th century, bishops Carlo Borromeo (*see p15*) and his cousin Federico imposed their tastes on the city: critical of the decorative excesses of late

The gracious **Galleria Vittorio Emanuele II**.

medieval architecture, they favoured the simplicity of a restrained classicism. Borromeo was eager to find an architect capable of translating his religious convictions into architecture and turned to the young Pellegrino Tibaldi. Tibaldi's courtyard of the **Palazzo Arcivescovile** (1569-1604) with its double *loggie*, rustication, and inventive use of the orders (*see p294* **Glossary**) – here Doric and Ionic – exemplifies this architect's contribution to the architectural character of the city.

The Counter-Reformation also brought new religious orders with new liturgical requirements: the Jesuit church of **San Fedele** (also by Tibaldi with input from Borromeo) has a wide nave to allow direct visual contact between congregation and priest.

Milan's architects eschewed the florid exuberance that marked the baroque in Rome and Naples; they did, however, show an interest in the baroque's robust and theatrical forms. The façade, interior court and grand staircase of the **Collegio Brera** (the building now houses, among other things, a gallery and library; *see p70*), following a design by Francesco Maria Ricchino from 1627-8, has baroque plasticity and a hint of drama.

Counter-Reformation Lombardy also spawned the phenomenon of *sacri monti*, shrines recreating the Mysteries of the Rosary. The most famous is just outside Varese (*see p108* **Holy Mountains**). This stunning display of devotion comprises 14 chapels, each containing life-size terracotta statues, arranged along a two-kilometre winding incline.

NEO-CLASSICISM

Lombardy passed under Spanish control in 1535; a couple of centuries later the territory passed to Austria. Architect Giuseppe

Piermartini was responsible for the transformation of Milan under Austrian rule. He provided residences for the Habsburg court, restored existing religious buildings to serve the needs of the state, and laid out new public gardens. The **Palazzo Reale** (*see p60*) and the **Teatro alla Scala** (*see p63*) are both by this neo-classical architect.

Napoleon made Milan capital of a new state when he arrived in 1796. To give the city an appropriately French ambience, a grand entrance gates and public buildings were proposed. Though little of this was realised (the Austrians marched back into the city in 1814), the **Porta Ticinese** (*see p89*) by Luigi Cagnola and the **Porta Venezia** (*see p81*) by Ridolfo Vantini are both from this period.

MILAN, ITALY

Italian unification in 1861 brought Milan back to centre stage, as the financial, commercial and industrial heart of Italy. Another bout of town planning reflected the ambitions of city leaders. Milan was to be a gracious urban centre, along the lines of Paris and Vienna, with broad avenues, public parks and the latest in sanitation and public transport systems.

Once again, many of the projects never made it past the drawing board. Among these was a facelift for **piazza del Duomo**: Giuseppe Mengoni won a competition for the job in 1863 but his plan was (perhaps mercifully) only party implemented. His design for the **Galleria Vittorio Emanuele II** (*see p60*) was completed, however. Though common enough in Paris and London, the gracious gallery, with its glass and iron ceiling, was an innovation in Milan. As local builders had no experience with these new materials, a British firm was hired to construct the ceiling.

Though northern European models were imitated, Italian architects of this period were also searching for an appropriate style for their newly united country. Camillo Boito led the debate; his neo-Gothic and polychrome **Casa di Riposo per Musicisti** (retirement home for musicians; *see p100*) is his architectural manifesto. The **Cimitero Monumentale** (*see p75*) is another fine example of late 19th-century eclecticism: many prominent architects of the day were responsible for the elaborate tombs within its walls. The same architects were responsible for 'restorations' of many of Milan's churches, often with greater attention to late 19th-century taste than historical accuracy.

THE TWENTIETH CENTURY

The turn of the century saw an explosion in Europe of experiments in architecture and design. Somewhat late in joining in, Italy made up for lost time after the 1902 decorative arts exhibition in Turin.

The Milanese were among the first to embrace the sumptuous possibilities of the art nouveau offshoot known in Italy as *stile Liberty* (named not very inventively after the Liberty department store in London). Some of the most spectacular examples of this style can be found in and around Milan: among the best is **Palazzo Castiglioni** (*see p81*) by Giuseppe Sommaruga. Slightly later but equally impressive is Giulio Ulisse Arata's surreal **Casa Berri-Meregalli** (*see p81*), where giant figures support drain pipes and animal heads peer out above the windows.

> '**Milan was quick to embrace the sumptuous possibilities of art nouveau.**'

Outside the city, even hydroelectric plants were built with an eye to design. The use of local stone for Gaetano Moretti's power station at Trezzo sull'Adda (*see p104*) was intended to enhance the unity of the building with its surroundings. The power company owners, the Crespi family, also founded the adjacent town of Crespi d'Adda (*see p104*) as a model community for workers in the late 19th century.

After World War I, new attitudes beset architectural design. The first manifestation of the *Novecento* style in architecture is Giovanni Muzio's **Ca' Brutta** (Ugly House) of 1922. The clever pastiche of classical references breaks up the monotony of one of the first large-scale apartment buildings in Milan.

Dissatisfied with the traditional forms and materials of the *Novecentisti*, a young group of architects at the Milan Polytechnic, influenced

The shocking **Novocomum**.

by European modernism, proposed an alternative solution expressing itself through, modern materials such as glass and concrete.

Giuseppe Terragni was a leading figure of this group: most of his work is in his native city of Como. His first building – that shook the Italian architectural community – was Como's **Novocomum** apartment block of 1928-29.

Few Italian architects opposed the inter-war Fascist regime; most scrambled for important government-sponsored projects. Terragni was no exception: his **Casa del Fascio** in Como is an iconic example of Italian Rationalism.

The 1927 competition for a new Milanese master plan set the tone for the architectural transformation of the city. **Piazza San Babila** (*see p80*) and Marcello Piacentini's **Palazzo di Giustizia** (*see p85*) are examples of the monumental excesses of the Fascist era.

After devastating bomb damage to the city during World War II, reconstruction efforts were focused on rehousing the population. The city outskirts became home to experimental residential neighbourhoods such as **Quartiere 8** (1946-66) and **Gallaratese** (1967-74). In the 1950s the centre of the city and its skyline were transformed by Giò Ponti's shimmering **Grattacielo Pirelli** (*see p74*) and BBPR's skeletal **Torre Velasca** (*see p86*). But by no means all of what went up in the city centre and suburbs was innovative or striking: post-war architecture in Milan is, tragically, more memorable for its anonymous blocks in smog-blackened concrete than for its triumphs.

The final decades of the 20th century were marked by internationally renowned building projects such as Marco Zanuso's **Nuovo Piccolo** and the **Teatro Studio** (for both *see p174* **The Strehler legacy**). And still, building activity in Milan shows no sign of abating.

The Food of Lombardy

Cream, cutlets and the ubiquitous *risotto*.

The Milanese are to *cucina italiana* what Leonardo Da Vinci is to Italian art. Like the Renaissance all-rounder, the Lombard capital's culinary repertoire uses varied techniques and borrows flavours from the north, south and abroad to create a school in a class of its own. Like the master whose genius was underpinned by wealthy benefactors, so too the capital of finance and fashion nurtures some talented restaurateurs and sophisticated palates.

> '**The capital of finance and fashion nurtures talented restaurateurs and sophisticated palates.**'

There's a little-known footnote in the history of the La Scala opera house (*see p63*) that says it all about Milan's relationship with what it eats. In the mid 1800s, the costliest boxes housed tiny kitchens. Jewel-clad patrons took their seats and a curtain was drawn in the rear to conceal the cooking. As the curtain went up, Milan's elite settled down to enjoy the evening's Verdi to whispers of *buon appetito*.

A La Scala appearance is a *chef d'orchestre*'s badge of success. Similarly, culinary maestros from Sicily, Tuscany and Puglia use Milan as a stage for their première performances. It comes as no surprise, then, that the world's first commercial cookbook is Lombard. In 1662, Bartolomeo Stefani, court chef to Mantova's Duke of Gonzaga, published *L'Arte di ben cucinare*, divulging the secrets that kept his boss happy and well fed.

GEOGRAPHY

Cooking tips may come from afar, but the ingredients are products of Lombardy's farming traditions and its unique geography. To the north, the Alps block destructive frost; to the east and west, lakes Maggiore and Garda soften extremes of temperature. But two-thirds of Lombard territory is located within the fertile flatlands of the Po river basin.

Lombardy's plains – *la pianura* – are, without a doubt, Italy's farming heartland. Lemon, olive and even palm trees grow where glaciers once scoured the earth. Europe's biggest rice paddies are found here. And the fields of the Po river valley – the Val Padana – are blanketed with clover and barley, which fuel centuries-old dairy and cattle traditions.

CHEESE AND MEAT

From sharp **gorgonzola** cheese, to spreadable **stracchino** (named after tired cows, or *stracchi*, in local dialect), to oozing **taleggio**, Lombardy is a cheese mecca. Towns like Cremona and Crema even have names reminiscent of dairy treats. The olive oil used throughout Italy is replaced in Lombard dishes by butter, and heavy cream is common.

Succulent cuts of meat, in particular veal, are transformed into namesake specialities: *ossobuco alla milanese* (braised veal shanks)

Lombardy produces cured meats.

and *cotoletta alla milanese* (breaded and fried veal chop). Boiled meat dishes are spiced with a chutney called **mostarda** made from mustard oil and plums, figs, or watermelon.

Lombardy also produces cured meats: **bresaola** (paper-thin cuts of dried beef); **culatello** (the centre cut of ham); **salame**

Food heaven

Lombardy has as high a concentration of top-flight restaurants as any Italian region. It is also one of the few areas of Italy where the cult of the celebrity chef reaches almost Gallic proportions. Alongside established names like Gualtiero Marchesi (Gualtiero Marchesi), Nadia Santini (Dal Pescatore), Elio Santin (Antica Osteria del Ponte) and Romano Tamani (L'Ambasciata) are rising stars like Patrick Leveille (Miramonti L'Altro). A small army of gastronomes with money to burn keep these establishments in business and in competition. What follows is a bite-sized selection of the best eating experiences the region has to offer. *See also* **Al Sorriso**, *p190*; **Ristorante Lanterna Verde**, *p262*.

Milan & province

Antica Osteria del Ponte

Piazza G Negri 9, Cassinetta di Lugagnano, nr Abbiategrasso (02 942 0034). **Meals served** *Sept-July* 12.30-2.30pm, 8-11pm Tue-Sat. Closed Aug, 2wks Dec-Jan. **Average** €80. **Credit** AmEx, DC, MC, V.
Classic high-class, French-tending Italian cuisine dished up by old trooper Elio Santin; a little tired for some, but still has many fans.

Il Luogo di Aimo e Nadia

Via Montecuccoli 6, Milan (02 416 886/ www.aimoenadia.com). **Meals served** *Sept-July* 12.30-2pm, 8-10pm Mon-Fri; 8-10.30pm Sat. Closed Aug, 1wk Jan. **Average** €80. **Credit** AmEx, DC, MC, V. **Map** off p310 1A.
Obsessively sourced raw materials, simple but elegant preparations and pleasant, modern-art-decked surroundings are a few of the reasons why Aimo and Nadia has long been a gastronomic temple in a city lacking true genius in the kitchen.

Varese province

Il Sole di Ranco

Piazza Venezia 5, Ranco (0331 976 507/fax 0331 976 620/www.relaischateaux.com/ soleranco). **Meals served** *Mid Feb-Nov* 8-10.30pm Mon; 12.30-2.30pm, 8-10.30pm Wed-Sun. Closed Dec-mid Feb. **Average** €70. **Credit** AmEx, DC, MC, V.
In a quiet village on the shores of Lake Maggiore (*see p187*), this seafood-oriented restaurant has risen to become one of the stars of western Lombardy. Leave room for the spectacular desserts.

milanese (pork salami with garlic and spices); and **carpaccio** (thinly sliced raw beef). These can be admired and acquired at outdoor markets from Sondrio to Cremona. But Milan, Brescia, Bergamo and Mantova are the regional gastronomic capitals. Vendors hawk their goodies on market day with gossip and cooking tips for added value. On a more exalted level are delicatessens – including Peck (see p142) in Milan, a veritable temple to food. It has two floors of earthly delights, from wild boar *prosciutto* to some 3,500 cheeses.

VEGETABLES

Lombardy is not noted for its vegetables, and what it does produce is strictly seasonal. Excellent asparagus fills markets each spring, while autumn is the time for chestnuts, mushrooms and *zucca* (pumpkin).

RICE AND PASTA

Lombardy's *pianura* yields wheat and maize, but no crop is more important than rice. A train trip from Bologna to Milan reveals a landscape of soggy rice paddies as far as the eye can see. In much of Lombardy, consumption of rice outstrips that of pasta. Thick kernels of **carnaroli** or **arborio** rice are slowly simmered to absorb cheese, butter and broth, then vegetables are mixed in.

Rice dishes vary according to area: *risotto alla mantovana* has sausage and onion; *risotto alla valtellinese* is made with cabbage and beans. The resulting mush is divinely decadent; leftovers are fried into crisp cakes (*risotto al salto*). Desserts include rice pudding and *frittelle di riso* (fried rice balls).

Though rice is often preferred, pasta is by no means ignored. *Tortelli di zucca*, or pumpkin-stuffed pasta, is a speciality of Cremona and Mantova provinces. Mantova also produces *agnoli*, or meat-filled pasta. Cooks from Valtellina in the far north adore *pizzoccheri* – buckwheat pasta with cheese, cabbage and potato (see also p264 **Mountain Fare**).

SOUP AND POLENTA

Unlike other Italian soups, Lombard soups can be a main course. *Zuppa pavese* (broth with bread and eggs) and *zuppa di porri e bietole* (with leeks and Swiss chard) is found in rural eateries. *Casoeûla* is a soupy cabbage stew with polenta, pork and sausage.

Brescia province

Il Gambero

Via Roma 11, Calvisano (030 968 009). **Meals served** *Sept-July* noon-2pm, 8.30-10pm Mon, Tue, Thur-Sun. Closed Aug, 1wk Jan. **Average** €48. **Credit** DC, MC, V.
One of the best-value culinary experiences in the region: hurry to try Gavazzi family specials like *sfoglie calde con i salumi* before they double the prices.

Gualtiero Marchesi

Via Vittorio Emanuele 11, località Bellavista Nord, Erbusco (030 776 0562/www. marchesi.it). **Meals served** 12.30-2pm, 7.30-10pm daily. Closed 4wks Jan-Feb. **Average** €110. **Credit** AmEx, DC, MC, V.
Some say the former *enfant terrible* of Italian nouvelle cuisine is losing his touch; others demur. If you like your risotto with gold leaf, this is the place to come.

Miramonti l'Altro

Via Croisette 34, Costorio di Concesio (030 275 1063). **Meals served** 12.30-2.30pm, 8-10pm Tue-Sun. Closed 2wks Aug. **Average** €75. **Credit** DC, MC, V.

Light, creative combinations of locally sourced ingredients from volatile rising star Patrick Leveille: when he's good, he's very very good.

Mantova province

L'Ambasciata

Via Martiri di Belfiori 33, Quistello (0376 619 169/www.ristoranteambasciata.it). **Meals served** *Sept-July* noon-3pm, 8-11pm Tue-Sat; noon-3pm Sun. Closed Aug, 3wks Jan. **Average** €90. **Credit** AmEx, DC, MC, V.
Romano Tamani's complex flavours mirror the ornate decor of this Aladdin's cave. The *tortelli di zucca* are second to none.

Dal Pescatore

Località Runate, Riserva del Parco dell'Oglio. Canneto sull'Oglio (0376 723 001/www. dalpescatore.com). **Meals served** *Sept-July* 8-10.30pm Thur-Sun; noon-2.30pm, 8-10.30pm Mon-Wed. Closed Aug, 3wks Jan. **Average** €100. **Credit** AmEx, DC, MC, V.
Probably Italy's top restaurant; no airs and graces, just spot-on modern Italian cooking from Nadia Santini and impeccable service co-ordinated by hubby Antonio in delightful country house surroundings.

Polenta (boiled cornmeal), served topped with meat or mushrooms, is a common feature of menus in the Valtellina and – in winter – much of the rest of Lombardy. *Pulmentum* was devoured by Roman legions and evolved in peasant cooking because of its hearty consistency and long shelf life.

FISH AND SEAFOOD

Land-locked Lombardy is a surprisingly good place to eat both freshwater fish and seafood. Milan is Italy's biggest sea-fish distribution centre: the morning catch is flown in so quickly that it's often fresher here than on the coast.

Lakes and rivers yield sturgeon and grey caviar in late November. Perch, trout, carp, salmon and eel are also used in lake region cuisine. *Luccio alla gardesana* is pike with capers and vegetables; *coregone in crosta* is freshwater whitefish with fennel seed cooked in a coarse salt crust. **Misoltini** are twaite shad – a kind of freshwater sardine – usually fried.

SWEETS AND DESSERTS

Sweet teeth are catered for with *torta paradiso*, an egg pastry from Pavia, Mantova's *torta sbrisolona* (crumbcake with almonds), or *semifreddo al limone* (lemon ice-cream cake). At Christmas, the region is swamped with *panettone*, a dome-shaped sponge cake, and *torrone* – nougat from Cremona.

FOREIGN INFLUENCES

The vagaries of history have left a culinary aftertaste. Lombardy was part of ancient Rome's Gallia Cisalpina region and a stronghold of the 'barbarian' Lombards. Later centuries brought French, Venetian, Spanish and Austrian invaders.

The region's most famous dish, *risotto alla milanese* (rice with onion, white wine and bone marrow), took its most important ingredient – saffron – from Spanish *paella*. Another well-known speciality, *cotoletta alla milanese*, is a not-so-distant cousin of Austria's *wiener schnitzel*. Even **mascarpone** is said to have been named when an approving Spaniard pronounced the creamy cheese *mas que bueno*.

Today Milan whets the appetites of cosmopolitan gourmets with more ethnic restaurants than any other Italian city. Its culinary curiosity and openness showcase Thai, Mexican and Brazilian food, bagel brunches and excellent sushi. It's just as easy to order an Indian takeaway or grab a falafel as it is to pick up a *tramezzino* – sandwich snacks invented to nourish time-impaired bankers. (Note that the city that's so keen on its quick bite is the birthplace of Italy's, and indeed Europe's, largest fast-food chain, Autogrill. There is one for every 25 kilometres of Italian toll road.)

Market vendors hawk local treats.

LOMBARD WINES

Although premier wine regions surround Lombardy, the region itself is not prominent on the Italian viticulture map. But that doesn't mean its wines should stay corked. Of the 1.7 million hectolitres produced here annually, 26 per cent is DOC (*denominazione di origine controllata*) quality wine.

Lombardy is home to half a dozen wine regions including **Franciacorta** (*see p231* **The wines of Franciacorta**) east of Brescia. Its rolling hills are well suited to vines and the area produces some of Italy's best sparkling wines; **pinot bianco** and **chardonnay** are bottle-fermented in the *champenois* style. Reds from **cabernet franc**, **barbera** and **nebbiolo** (named after the all-pervasive fog, *nebbia*) are aged two years.

> ### 'Land-locked Lombardy is a surprisingly good place to eat seafood.'

Lombardy's most productive wine area is the **Oltrepò Pavese** (*see p258* **Milan's wine cellar**), located, as its name tells us, 'beyond the Po' in the province of Pavia. Much of its **pinot nero** is boxed and sold as cheap plonk, but 15 per cent of Oltrepò's fruit goes into DOC wines. Oltrepò also makes fizzy reds with **barbera** and **bonarda** grapes, though these are not to everyone's taste.

Some of Lombardy's most respected bottles come from Grumello and Valgella appellations in the mountainous Valtellina (*see p263*) area, where **nebbiolo** grapes are harvested from vineyards on steep bluffs with pulleys and cables. Other notable regions are Riviera del Garda Bresciano, Colli Mantovani and Milan's San Colombano DOC.

Accommodation

Accommodation

Milan's hotels are geared to the corporate traveller:
book early and don't expect stunning views from your room.

As northern Italy's richest city and home to the *borsa* (stock exchange), Milan revolves around business and money-making. Consequently, it tends to be expensive. And accommodation is no exception. Unlike other Italian cities that cater mainly to the tourist trade, Milan's hotel prices are definitely geared to the corporate traveller. Don't expect any picturesque views either: the best you can hope for is a room overlooking a quiet courtyard; the worst will be facing a bare brick wall.

That said, there are places offering value for money, such as the charming **Antica Locanda Solferino** or the rustic **Vecchia Milano** (for both, *see p45*). But even places like these tend to be on the high side of the medium-price category. Be prepared to splash out.

During any trade fair at the Fiera di Milano (*see p100*) – and there seems to be something on there most of the time, especially during the

autumn – hotel accommodation in any price category is almost impossible to find and prices are hiked by as much as 30 per cent. Whenever possible, make your room reservation well in advance. You will probably be asked to confirm your booking by fax or to leave a credit card number. If you cancel your reservation less than a day or two before your expected arrival, you may be required to pay for one night.

Milan suffers from a chronic shortage of parking space. Few hotels have their own car park or, if they do, they are pocket-handkerchief sized. To compensate, many have deals with local garages for overnight parking. The price of this service varies considerably, but can be as much as €45. Suffice to say, don't come by car if you can avoid it: you won't need a vehicle anyway, in this compact city with its efficient public transport system.

Utter luxury at the **Four Seasons**. See p43.

STANDARDS AND PRICES

Italian hotels are graded from one star to five star deluxe. *Pensione*, although not an official term, is still used to describe one- and two-star hotels (€93-€130); these are usually family-run affairs where rooms tend to be functional and you may have to share a bathroom. They are often located in rather decrepit buildings, so what you gain in local charm you might end up paying for with musty rooms, paper-thin walls and noisy plumbing. Some lock up early for the night, though staff should provide a key to the main door. A *locanda* was traditionally a cheap place to eat and sleep: nowadays it usually signifies a fancy *pensione* with some olde worlde charm.

Three- and four-star hotels have more facilities and the majority of rooms will have en suite bathrooms. There's a huge disparity in this category between best and worst deals. Higher prices do not guarantee cleanliness or better service. But this disparity can translate into value for money and some of the best hotels in this guide come under this section.

There's not a lot to say about five-star hotels in Milan: as you would expect, they are intimidatingly luxurious and exorbitantly expensive. The emphasis here is on opulence,

but unless you're on your honeymoon or staying on a generous expense account, you're better off staying at the perfectly comfortable accommodation available in central locations for a fraction of the price. When making a reservation be sure prices are quoted including IVA (sales tax): an additional ten per cent on your bill can come as a nasty surprise.

Most hotel rates include breakfast (assume it's included unless otherwise stated in the listings): in the medium to high brackets this is generally a buffet with hot and cold food; further down the scale you'll encounter the kind of dull-tasting coffee that foreign tourists are thought to enjoy with limp-looking *brioche* (croissants) or bread rolls, butter and jam. If you have a choice, pay for the room without breakfast. Go to a local bar instead and enjoy the very Italian custom of knocking back an espresso or cappuccino standing at the bar. It'll cost you less, the pastries will be fresh and the coffee real.

If you arrive at Malpensa or Linate airports with nowhere to stay, avoid the travel agency desks. They will book a hotel for you, but the choice is limited to the places that pay the agency a commission and the cost will be passed on to you. Go into town and head straight for the APT office (via Marconi 1;

The light-filled charm of the **Antica Locanda dei Mercanti**. *See p45.*

02 7252 4301) near piazza Duomo: staff will provide you with a free booklet on hotels that is updated every six months, although you'll have to ring around yourself.

Duomo & Centre

Expensive

De La Ville
Via V Hoepli 6 (02 867 651/fax 02 866 609/ de.la.ville@italyhotel.com). Metro Duomo/bus 61. **Rates** €238.70-€295.90 single; €301.40-€341 double; €511.50 junior suite; €738.10 suite. **Credit** AmEx, DC, MC, V. **Map** p311 A1.
An elegantly refined atmosphere pervades this traditional hotel a short hop from the Duomo and La Scala. The rooms are well appointed and the bathrooms have marble fittings. The adjoining Canova restaurant is open until late for returning theatre-goers; there's a well-equipped fitness centre with sauna and Turkish bath, and conference rooms for business guests. The price reflects the prestigious location, but the quality and services are comparable with the five-star hotels in the area, only a good deal cheaper.
Hotel services *Air-conditioning. Babysitting. Bar. Conference rooms. Disabled: lift, wide doors. Gym. Laundry. Limousine service. No-smoking rooms. Parking (€40 per day). Restaurant. Sauna.* **Room services** *Dataport. Hairdryer. Mini-bar. Room service (7am-midnight). Safe. TV: satellite.*

Four Seasons
Via Gesù 8 (02 77 088/fax 02 7708 5000/ www.fourseasons.com/milan). Metro San Babila or Montenapoleone/bus 73/tram 1. **Rates** €470-€550 single; €540-€630 double; €700-€6,000 suite. **Credit** AmEx, DC, MC, V. **Map** p309 C1.

The most expensive hotel in Milan is housed in a 15th-century convent, with frescos in some of the suites and an idyllic cloistered courtyard. Guests typically include heads of state, wealthy industrialists and film stars. For a hefty price you get a huge bedroom with Fortuny fabrics, pear and sycamore wood furniture, VCR, fax and personal safe, and an opulent marble bathroom big enough to sleep in. The Il Teatro restaurant is ranked among the top five eateries in town. Beyond the means of most, but very, very nice.
Hotel services *Bar. Conference rooms. Disabled: adapted rooms, ramp access. Gym. Laundry service. Limousine service. Parking (€51 per day). Restaurant.* **Room services** *Air-conditioning. Fax. Hairdryer. Mini-bar. Room service (24hrs). Safe. TV: satellite, VCR.*

Grand Hotel et de Milan
Via Manzoni 29 (02 723 141/fax 02 864 0861/ www.grandhoteletdemilan.it). Metro Montenapoleone/tram 1, 20. **Rates** €357.50-€440 single; €440-€511.50 double; €594 junior suite; €825 superior suite; €1,007 deluxe suite. **Credit** AmEx, DC, MC, V. **Map** p309 C1.
A sumptuous five-star hotel dating back to 1863. Housed in an elegant palazzo, the Grand has two highly regarded restaurants, Don Carlos and Caruso, popular with the *après*-theatre crowd. Illustrious guests in the past have included Verdi and Wagner, Stendhal and Hemingway. Extensively renovated in 1993, this is the height of luxury and just a stone's throw from La Scala. Ask about weekend rates: you may be pleasantly surprised.
Hotel services *Air-conditioning. Bars. Conference rooms. Disabled: adapted rooms, ramp access. Gym. Laundry. Limousine service. Parking (€39 per day). Restaurants.* **Room services** *Hairdryer. Mini-bar. Room service (7am-1am). Safe. TV: satellite.*

CAPITOL

MILLENNIUM
W O R L D   C L A S S   H O T E L
MILANO

20144 Milano via Cimarosa 6
tel +39 02 438 591
fax +39 02 469 4724
e-mail booking@capitolmillennium.c

Style:

Suprelative comfort framed in elegance, designed
refined details, for a combination of pleasure, comfor
milanese good taste, for all who love to travel without g
up the creature comforts of home, discovering in
room the elegance and pleasure that Milan offers.

Location:

Near Leonardo's Last Supper in the exclusive residentia
shopping area between the Sforzesco Castle and opposi
Trade Fair, all within a few minutes' walking distance c
Duomo Cathedral and La Scala Theatre.

Accomodation:

Rooms and suites delightfully furnished - comfortable
space - 2 telephone lines with modem connection - Int
by TV - Safe - Trouser press - Linen sheets - Marble
room - Jacuzzi's - Electronic lock - Refrigerator
smoking - Evening turn down - Suites

Facilities and Amenities

2 restaurants, *"La Veranda"* with traditional It
suggestions, *"Atmosphere"* where you can sa
creative dishes - Cocktail Bar - Buffet Break
Garage - on-site fitness centre- Courtesy
Cars - Concierge Service, tickets fo
theatre, sports events and museums.

Spadari

Via Spadari 11 (02 7200 2371/fax 02 861 184/ reservation@spadarihotel.com). Metro Duomo/ bus 73/tram 2, 3, 14, 20, 27. **Rates** €188-€228 single; €208-€268 double; €288 junior suite; €308 suite. **Credit** AmEx, DC, MC, V. **Map** p310 A2.

Small, elegant and in the heart of Milan, the Spadari has been designed as a hotel-cum-exhibition space and a recent renovation project has turned it into a work of art itself. During the restructuring, owner Marida Maitegani and architect Urbano Perini commissioned well-known Italian artists to personalise the rooms. Sculptor Giò Pomodoro made a large wall sculpture and fireplace for the hall. But the most striking feature of the new decor is the soothing blue colour scheme that runs throughout the hotel. Great for art lovers; others might find it naff.

Hotel services *Air-conditioning. Bar. Limousine service. Parking (€20.66 per day). Restaurant. Travel office.* **Room services** *Mini-bar. No-smoking rooms. Room service (7am-11pm). Safe. TV: satellite.*

Moderate

Antica Locanda dei Mercanti

Via San Tommaso 6 (02 805 4080/fax 02 805 4090/www.locanda.it). Metro Cordusio or Duomo/ tram 14, 24, 27. **Rates** €118 single; €130-€210 double. **Credit** AmEx, MC, V. **Map** p310 A2.

The use of 'Locanda' in the name is intended to give an impression of olde worlde charm. Not that this place needs it: just off via Dante, a pedestrian street in the epicentre of town, it's like something out of *A Room With a View*. Fresh flowers, books and magazines are welcome substitutes for the standard TV set. Try and book one of the three top-floor rooms, with private terrace and four-poster beds. Breakfast is served in bed.

Hotel services *Bar. Parking (€23 per day).* **Room services** *Room service (7am-11pm).*

Gritti

Piazza Santa Maria Beltrade 4 (02 801 056/fax 02 8901 0999/www.hotelgritti.com). Metro Duomo/tram 12, 14, 27. **Rates** €90 single; €129 double; €181 triple.* **Credit** AmEx, DC, MC, V. **Map** p308 A2.

Piazza Beltrade is a quiet little square just off via Torino, a busy shopping street just around the corner from piazza Duomo. The rooms are bit tatty and uninspiring, but they are clean and comfortable with modern fittings and all of them have a connection for your laptop. The bathrooms have a choice of shower or bath.

Hotel services *Bar. Parking (€21 per day).* **Room services** *Dataport. Hairdryer. Room service (7am-midnight). TV: satellite.*

Manzoni

Via Santo Spirito 20 (02 7600 5700/ fax 02 784 212/www.hotelmanzoni.com). Metro Montenapoleone/tram 1, 2. **Rates** €131 single; €193 double; €247 suite. **Credit** AmEx, DC, MC, V. **Map** p309 C1.

The Manzoni is quite grand for a three-star, with an impression of space that is usually lacking in this category; the bathrooms are especially roomy. The sombre brown carpet and sky-blue upholstered walls leave something to be desired, but considering the hotel is right slap bang in the middle of the *quadrilatero d'oro*, Milan's chic fashion district, it's still a pretty good deal. Breakfast consists of a buffet brunch with hot and cold food, and there's a garage for parking too.

Hotel services *Air-conditioning. Bar. Conference room. Parking (€13-€30).* **Room services** *Room service (6am-3pm, 6-11pm). TV: satellite.*

Vecchia Milano

Via Borromei 4 (02 875 042/fax 02 8645 4292/ hotelvecchiamilano@tiscalinet.it). Tram 19, 27. **Rates** €55-€85 single; €95-€135 double; €130-€160 triple. **Credit** AmEx, DC, MC, V. **Map** p310 A2.

Friendly staff is just one reason why guests return again and again to this small, wood-panelled hotel. The central location and reasonable pricing are others. The rooms are a bit on the small side and simply furnished, but the building itself is an attractive old palazzo with an inn-like atmosphere. The only problem is parking in the very narrow streets, but there is a garage close by.

Hotel services *Air-conditioning. Bar. Parking (€20 per day).* **Room services** *Room service (7am-midnight). TV: satellite.*

Sforzesco & North

Expensive

Una Hotel Century

Via F Filzi 25B (02 67 504/fax 02 6698 0602/ www.unahotel.com). Metro Centrale FS/bus 60/tram 9, 33. **Rates** €240-€397 single junior suite; €287-€397 double junior suite. **Credit** AmEx, DC, MC, V. **Map** p309 B1.

A modern, nondescript tower-block hotel popular with visiting businessmen. The area around the railway station is not especially inviting and can be downright unpleasant at night, but the hotel itself is set back from the main road. On the Executive Floor all the suites are provided with fax machines, trouser presses and linen bed sheets. The patio/garden is a welcome feature in summer.

Hotel services *Air-conditioning. Bar. Conference rooms. Garden Gym. Laundry. Parking (€21 per day). Restaurant.* **Room services** *Coffee machine. Dataport. Hairdryer. Mini-bar. No-smoking rooms. Room service (6.30am-10.30pm). Safe. TV: satellite.*

Moderate

Antica Locanda Solferino

Via Castelfidardo 2 (02 657 0129/fax 02 657 1361/ info@anticalocandasolferino.it). Metro Moscova. **Rates** €100 single; €150 double; €180 triple. **Credit** AmEx, MC, V. **Map** p309 B1.

The main attraction here is the hotel's location on the corner of via Solferino in the heart of the bohemian Brera district and just five minutes' walk from the Pinacoteca (see p70). But the rooms are also delightful – more typical of a country-style inn than a city hotel – and furnished with Daumier engravings and handcrafted mouldings. Room 10 is the most comfy, decked out with heavy velvet drapes and antique furniture.

Hotel services *Garage (€20 per day). Laundry.*
Room services *Room service (breakfast only). TV.*

Marconi

Via F Filzi 3 (02 6698 5561/fax 02 669 0738/ www.marconihotel.it). Metro Repubblica or Centrale FS/tram 9, 33, 2. **Rates** €88-€140 single; €98-€170 double for single use; €197 double. **Credit** AmEx, DC, MC, V. **Map** p309 B1.

The interior of this family-run hotel is oppressively dark, but some of the rooms look on to a delightful courtyard full of lemon trees and geraniums; breakfast is served out here in the summer. The rooms have standard fittings and tile floors, which keep them cool in hot weather, but can make them a bit chilly in winter, although central heating is fitted throughout the hotel.

Hotel services *Air-conditioning. Bar. Conference room.* **Room services** *Room service (24hrs). TV: satellite.*

Budget

London

Via Rovello 3 (02 7202 0166/fax 02 805 7037/ hotel.london@traveleurope.it). Metro Cordusio/tram 1, 3, 12, 14. **Rates** €88 single; €135 double. Breakfast €8 extra. **Credit** MC, V. **Map** p308 C2.

An excellent budget hotel just around the corner from the Duomo and the Castello Sforzesco. The rooms are simply furnished and a bit pokey, but the lobby and conversation area around the bar are particularly welcoming and the staff are friendly and easygoing. Breakfast can be served in your room. There's a 10% discount if you pay cash. Considering its prime location, the London represents very good value for money.

Hotel service *Air-conditioning. Bar. Parking (€24 per day).* **Room services** *Hairdryer. Room service (7am-10.30pm). TV: satellite.*

Ostello Piero Rotta

Viale Salmoiraghi 1 (02 3926 7095/fax 02 330 0191/www.hotels-aig.org/shop-it/milano.htm). Metro Lotto/bus 68. **Rates** €15.49 per person. **No credit cards. Map** off p308 A1.

The only youth hostel in Milan is out in the suburbs near the San Siro stadium, though the nearby Lotto metro station makes reaching the centre simple. The price of a dormitory bed includes breakfast. The garden provides a welcome escape from city traffic. The staff are not exactly falling over themselves to be helpful and friendly – but that doesn't stop the place being full most of the time.

San Babila & East

Expensive

Sheraton Diana Majestic

Viale Piave 42 (02 20 581/fax 02 2058 2058/ www.sheraton.com/dianamajestic). Metro Porta Venezia/tram 9, 30. **Rates** €160-€416 single; €489-€532 double; €352-€600 junior suite; €672-€1,137 deluxe suite. **Credit** AmEx, DC, MC, V. **Map** p309 C2.

This five-star art nouveau-style hotel is named after the first public swimming pool in Milan, which opened on this site in 1842. The pool has since been replaced with a small garden, dotted with tables that spill out from what is one of the city's most trendy bars. The large rooms are elegantly kitted out with antique furniture while the bathrooms have ubiquitous marble fittings. The hotel restaurant, Il Milanese, is popular with lunching businessmen. The tree-lined viale Piave is conveniently located close to the shops of corso Buenos Aires and the public gardens in corso Venezia.

Hotel services *Air-conditioning. Bars. Business centre. Conference rooms. Disabled: ramp access, adapted rooms. Garden. Gym. Laundry. Restaurants.* **Room services** *Hairdryer. Mini-bar. Room service (7am-midnight). Safe. TV: satellite.*

Moderate

Etrusco

Via AN Porpora 56 (02 236 3852/fax 02 236 0553/ www.hoteletrusco.it). Metro Loreto/bus 62/tram 33. **Rates** €93-€103 single; €134-€155 double. **Credit** AmEx, DC, MC, V. **Map** off p309 B2.

The three-star Etrusco boasts a good price/quality ratio and a convenient location not far from the main railway station. The rooms are exceptionally clean and some have balconies overlooking a charming garden where breakfast is served in the summer. In the winter the heating in the rooms can be individually controlled – a welcome detail in a country where hotel rooms tend to be kept stuffily hot.

Hotel services *Air-conditioning. Bar. Laundry. Parking (free).* **Room services** *Mini-bar. TV: satellite.*

Mazzini

Via Vitruvio 29 (02 2952 6600/fax 02 2951 0253/ www.hotelmazzini.com). Metro Centrale FS or Lima/ tram 5, 20, 33. **Rates** €77-€88 single; €98-€137 double; €134-€178 triple. **Credit** AmEx, DC, MC, V. **Map** p309 B2.

The place to go for if you're looking for something a little more upmarket (shame about the plastic flowers in the lobby, though) that's near the main railway station. Rates vary according to the season and whether there's a trade fair on, but prices are lowest in December, July and August. It's worth asking for the weekend rates too. The rooms are nothing to write home about, but they have double-glazing, air-conditioning and other features not

always guaranteed in a hotel in this price range. Ask for a room overlooking the rear garden.
Hotel services *Air-conditioning. Bar. Parking (€15 per day).* **Room services** *Hairdryer. Room service (7am-midnight). Safe. TV: satellite.*

Budget

Aspromonte

Piazza Aspromonte 12/14 (02 236 1119/fax 02 236 7621/www.venere.it/milano/aspromonte). Metro Loreto/bus 90, 91/tram 33. **Rates** €54-€72 single; €75-€100 double; €102-€124 triple. **Credit** AmEx, DC, MC, V. **Map** off p309 B2.

The piazza from which the hotel takes its name is dotted with two-star hotels and there's not a lot to choose between them. But the Aspromonte has an added attraction in its pretty garden, which has a covered section where guests can take breakfast outside. The rooms look pretty much alike, are decidedly basic and only half of them have air-conditioning (although the owners are planning to install AC in the others).

The playground in the piazza outside makes this a good bet for families travelling with children. Tickets for football matches can be arranged.
Hotel services *Bar.* **Room services** *Hairdryer. Mini-bar. TV: satellite.*

Del Sole

Via G Spontini 6 (02 2951 2971/fax 02 2951 8689/ delsolehotel@tiscali.it). Metro Lima or Loreto. **Rates** €50-€70 double for single use; €70-€85 double; €94.50-€114.75 triple. Breakfast €4 extra. **Credit** AmEx, DC, MC, V. **Map** p309 B2.

This family-owned and family-run hotel just off corso Buenos Aires is almost next door to Pizzeria Spontini, a famous eaterie. A spiral staircase leads from the lobby to a cosy bar/breakfast area. The rooms are clean, with tile floors and standard fittings, and there are two rooms with huge terraces overlooking the courtyard where you can sit outside and sip a glass of plonk during the summer months.
Hotel services *Air-conditioning. Bar. Parking (€7-€15 per day).* **Room services** *TV.*

Ariston: the most stylish eco-hotel in town. *See p49.*

Eden

*Via Vitruvio 20 (02 2048 0343/fax 02 2941 5910).
Metro Centrale FS/bus 60/tram 33.* Rates €80
single; €110 double; €149 triple. Breakfast not
included. **Credit** AmEx, DC, MC, V. **Map** p309 B2.
This cosy two-star is handy for the main railway station. The stairwell could do with a paint job, but all
the rooms have bathrooms (with shower) and air-
conditioning and there's free parking round the back.
The premises are soon to be extended to include a
small garden. Breakfast is not included, but there is
a small bar in the lobby that's open round the clock.
Unusually for a hotel in this category, there is also a
room on the ground floor adapted for the disabled.
On Tuesdays and Saturdays there's a great fruit and
veg market in nearby piazza B Marcello.
Hotel services *Air-conditioning. Bar. Disabled:
adapted room. Parking (free).* **Room services** *TV.*

Nettuno

*Via Tadino 27 (02 2040 4527/02 2940 4481/
fax 02 2952 3819/hotelnettuno.cjb.net). Metro Porta
Venezia or Lima/bus 60/tram 5, 23, 29, 30, 33.*
Rates €33.57-€46.48 single; €51.65-€60.72 double;
€69.72-€87.80 triple; €103.29 quad. Breakfast not
included. **Credit** AmEx, DC, MC, V. **Map** p309 B2.
This cavernous and rather gloomy one-star hotel is
located between the main station and the centre.
Breakfast is not included, but there are hot and cold
drinks dispensers in the lobby and loads of bars and
restaurants nearby. The rooms are spartan, but spacious and clean, and the bathrooms have polished
granite tiles. Reception is staffed around the clock.
Hotel services *Hot & cold drink dispensers.*
Room services *TV.*

San Francisco

*Viale Lombardia 55 (02 236 1009/fax 02 2668
0377/sf@hotel-sanfrancisco.it). Metro Piola/
tram 33.* **Rates** €52-€67 single; €83-€103 double.
Credit AmEx, DC, MC, V. **Map** p310 B/C1.
An attractive, modern two-star hotel with a small
garden and patio close to the Piola metro station. The
rooms are well lit and very clean with simple yet adequate furniture and fittings. If you're visiting in the
summer, be sure to ask for a room with air-conditioning (at the time of writing six rooms were still
without AC). There is also a small meeting room with
fax service available. It's a bit off the beaten track,
but La Matricola pub down the road has a friendly
atmosphere if you fancy an evening drink.
Hotel services *Air-conditioning (some rooms). Bar.
Conference room. Fax.* **Room services** *TV: satellite.*

Porta Romana & South

Expensive

Liberty

*Viale Bligny 56 (02 5831 8562/fax 02 5831 9061).
Tram 9, 30.* **Rates** €106-€129 single; €129-€207
double; €232 suite. Breakfast €10 extra. **Credit**
AmEx, MC, V. **Map** p310-11 B1/2.

A popular though somewhat overrated and over-
priced hotel. Breakfast is not included, but can be
served in your bedroom – far better to get out and
have a cappuccino and *brioche* (croissant) in a bar.
The rooms have standard, modern-ish decor and fittings and four of the bathrooms are equipped with
jacuzzis. What a shame that the effect of the pretty
courtyard garden and gleaming lobby can be spoiled
by some of the moodier members of staff.
Hotel services *Air-conditioning. Bar. Garden.
Parking (€23-€28 per day).* **Room services**
*Hairdryer. Jacuzzi (4 rooms). Mini-bar. Room service
(breakfast only). TV.*

Moderate

Ariston

*Largo Carrobbio 2 (02 7200 0556/fax 02 7200
0914/www.brerahotels.com). Tram 2, 3, 14.*
Rates €123.95 single; €175.60 double; €204 triple.
Credit AmEx, DC, MC, V. **Map** p310 A2.
On the outside the Ariston looks like any other modern, comfortable hotel, but on the inside it is an extraordinary experiment in bio-architectural design: the
lightbulbs consume less electricity; the showers are
designed to save water. Even the water in your tea
is purified, and organic products are served at breakfast. The hotel is conveniently located between the
centre of town and the Naviglio district, with trams
stopping by the front entrance.

Cheap and cheerful **San Francisco**.

Hotel services *Air-conditioning. Bar. Parking (€12.91 per day).* Room services *Room service (7am-11pm). TV: satellite.*

Mercure Relais Milano

Via Conca del Naviglio 20 (02 5810 4141/ fax 02 8940 1012/www.mercuri.com). Metro Sant'Ambrogio/tram 2, 14. Rates €99-€154 single; €106-€175 double for single use; €135-€191 double. Credit AmEx, DC, MC, V. Map p310 B2.

An excellent choice for both business travellers and families, this comfortable three-star hotel is located in a quiet and surprisingly green corner of Milan close to the Naviglio district, with its bars and restaurants. The centre of town is just ten minutes' walk in the opposite direction. The hotel was completely renovated in 1998 and joined the Mercure chain, but the hotel staff have remained helpful and friendly.

Hotel services *Air-conditioning. Bar (breakfast only). Beauty centre. Bicycles (free). Parking (€15.50 per day). Pizza delivery service.* Room services *Hairdryer. Mini-bar. TV.*

Minerva

Corso C Colombo 15 (02 837 5745/fax 02 835 8229). Metro Porta Genova/bus 47/tram 2, 9, 14, 30, 29. Rates €67-€77 single; €96-€113 double; €130-€145 triple. Closed Aug. Credit AmEx, DC, MC, V. Map p310 B1.

Don't be put off by the lacklustre foyer and breakfast area. Or by the rooms, which, although clean, are drearily basic. The real advantage of this no-nonsense three-star hotel is that it's within easy walking distance of the bars and restaurants of the Naviglio district and just across the road from the Porta Genova metro station. The 14 tram, which stops right by the front door, goes all the way to the Duomo. The free car park is another bonus if you're motoring.

Hotel services *Air-conditioning. Bar. Parking (free).* Room services *Room service (breakfast only). TV.*

Sant'Ambrogio & West

Expensive

Antares Hotel Rubens

Via Rubens 21 (02 40 302/fax 02 4819 3114/ www.antareshotels.com). Bus 72, 80/tram 24. Rates €199-€215 single; €265-€295 double; €295-€325 suites. Credit AmEx, DC, MC, V. Map off p308 C1.

A comfortable if rather dull four-star hotel, although the owners have made an effort to brighten things with individual decor in the rooms. It's much used by business travellers visiting the nearby Fiera complex (*see p100*), but it's not really anywhere else of interest, unless you want to take in a football match at San Siro stadium (*see p100*). The buffet breakfast is served on the top floor in the grandiosely named Sala delle Nuvole (Cloud Room): there's a panoramic view across this unexceptional part of the city. Unusually for an Italian hotel there is a whole floor for non-smokers.

Hotel services *Air-conditioning. Bar. Parking (free). Restaurant.* Room services *Dataport. Hairdryer. Mini-bar. Non-smoking floor. Room service (7am-1am). Safe. TV: satellite, pay movies.*

Moderate

Antica Locanda Leonardo

Via Magenta 78 (02 463 317/fax 02 4801 9012/ www.leoloc.com). Rates €95 single; €150-€180 double; €175-€205 triple. Credit AmEx, DC, MC, V. Map p310 B1.

An immaculate little hotel set back from busy corso Magenta in a quiet residential courtyard. The property was renovated in 1997, but already the Italo-Japanese owners are thinking of refurbishing some of the 20 rooms. Heaven knows why, as they are all tastefully and individually decorated with

Location, location, location

Hotels in this guide have been chosen for their charm, historical interest, good value for money and location. You will pay a premium for a hotel in the **centre**, but being within easy walking distance of the city centre's closely packed sights may make it worthwhile.

If it's nightlife you're after, a hotel in or near the buzzing **Naviglio** district (*see p92*) will put you within a stone's throw of innumerable bars, clubs and restaurants. In the summer, the area's streets are closed to traffic: join locals pub-crawling their fume-free way along the canalside hangouts.

Quieter, but still close to the centre, is the **Brera** district (*see p69*), with its bourgeois-cum-bohemian ambience. There are bars and restaurants galore in this area, and there's the Pinacoteca di Brera (*see p70*), too, if you fancy a dose of culture.

Efforts to clean up the area around **Stazione Centrale** (*see p75*) have met with moderate success. It's perfectly safe during the day but can be intimidating at night, although the dangers are more imagined than real. Even a short distance from the station, the atmosphere changes dramatically for the better.

modern or antique wooden furniture and bathrooms with shower and bath tub. There is a cosy breakfast/bar area that is due to be expanded. **Hotel services** *Air-conditioning. Bar. Parking (€23 per day). Safe.* **Room services** *Safe. TV: satellite.*

Ariosto

Via Ariosto 22 (02 4817844/fax 02 498 0516/ www.hotelariosto.com). Metro Conciliazione/tram 29, 30. **Rates** €134.28 single; €191.09 double. **Credit** AmEx, DC, MC, V. **Map** p308 C1.

Via Ariosto is an elegant residential street, handy for both the central sights and the Fiera (*see p100*). The hotel is airy and well lit with a beautiful art nouveau staircase. All the rooms have double-glazing, parquet flooring, and marble tiles in the bathrooms; a couple also have walk-in wardrobes. The TV sets have a VCR incorporated and videos in different languages are available from reception. A small patio garden should be completed by summer 2002. The bar and restaurant area resembles a cafeteria – so eat out. **Hotel services** *Air-conditioning. Bar. Conference rooms. Parking (€22.21 per day). Restaurant. Video hire.* **Room services** *Room service (7am-10.30pm). TV: satellite; VCR.*

King

Corso Magenta 19 (02 874 432/fax 02 8901 0798/ www.hotelkingmilano.com). Metro Cadorna/tram 24. **Rates** €140 single; €204 double; €278 triple. **Credit** AmEx, DC, MC, V. **Map** p308 C1/2.

Centrally located in a picturesque part of town, the King is just down the road from Bar Magenta (*see p130*), a Milanese institution. The hotel was in the process of being renovated as this guide went to press, and the new decor is overly ornate. But the rooms are clean, tidy and quiet, with well-stocked mini-bars, and the buffet breakfast is generous. The atmosphere as you enter the lobby is warm and welcoming. Be aware that there is a surcharge if you cancel a reservation. **Hotel services** *Air-conditioning. Bar. Laundry service.* **Room services** *Hairdryer. Mini-bar. Parking (€20 per day). Room service (7am-midnight). Safe. TV: cable.*

Metro

Corso Vercelli 61 (02 498 7897/fax 02 4801 0295/ hotelmetro@tin.it). Metro Wagner/tram 24. **Rates** €92.96-€134.28 single; €103.29-€185.92 double. **Credit** AmEx, DC, MC, V. **Map** p308 C1.

Following recent renovations, all the Metro's spacious rooms have satellite TV, air conditioning and mini-bar; best of all are the split-level ones with jacuzzis in the bathroom. It's very convenient for the nearby Fiera complex (*see p100*), but expect to pay more when a trade fair is on and make sure you book well ahead. Corsi Vercelli is a bustling shopping street, but the hotel is set back from the road and the rooms are very quiet. You can borrow a bike at reception. **Hotel services** *Air-conditioning. Bar. Bicycles (free). Disabled: adapted room. Parking (€15.49 per day).* **Room services** *Coffee machine. Jacuzzi (3 rooms). Mini-bar. Room service (breakfast only). Safe. TV: satellite.*

Princely decor at the **King**.

Palazzo delle Stelline

Corso Magenta 61 (02 481 8431/fax 02 4851 9097/ congress centre 02 4546 2111/www.hotelpalazzo dellestelline.it). Metro Cadorna/tram 24. **Rates** €102 single; €152 double; €182 junior suite. **Credit** AmEx, DC, MC, V. **Map** p308 C1/2.

This hotel and congress centre is housed in a beautiful 15th-century palazzo with arched cloisters overlooking a grass courtyard and an immense magnolia tree. The tastefully furnished rooms offer total privacy, a world apart from the hubbub of the city. Leonardo da Vinci is said to have grown vines here while painting the *Last Supper* (*see p98*) at the Santa Maria della Grazie monastery across the road. **Hotel services** *Air-conditioning. Bar. Conference rooms. Disabled: adapted suite.* **Room services** *TV (satellite).*

Budget

Piemonte

Via Ruggero Settimo 1 (02 463 173/fax 02 4819 3316). Metro Wagner/bus 61. **Rates** €77 single; €96-€108 double; €128-€145 triple. **Credit** MC, V. **Map** off p308 C1.

This small, family-run hotel is a pleasant surprise: it offers decent-sized rooms with modern fittings at a reasonable price in a peaceful location just off tree-lined via Washington. Well-placed for the Fiera (two metro stops or a brisk walk; *see p100*), the Piemonte is a favourite with business travellers. The bathrooms are in the process of being renovated and there's a pretty garden round the back. **Hotel services** *Air-conditioning. Bar. Garden. Parking (€13 per day). Safe.* **Room services** *TV.*

Sightseeing

Features

Introduction

Plunge into Milan's modern bustle: there's much here that will surprise.

For travellers familiar with Rome, Venice, Florence or the enchanting towns of Tuscany and Umbria, Milan can come as a shock: indeed, you may be hard pushed to reconcile the city with the rest of Italy. Milan is a modern metropolis, with the deafening sounds and hectic rhythms this implies. Many Milanese spend a great deal of energy trying to get away from it. But plunge into its bustle, and Milan has much to offer.

Milan is the commercial and financial hub of Italy, housing the Borsa (stock exchange), Fiera (trade fair) and innumerable bank headquarters. It is also the epicentre of Italian design and the fashion trade, not to mention the communications sector. The only city in Italy where the work ethic is tangible, Milan takes a lot of flack from fellow Italians for its dedication to labour and Mammon.

WORKING MILAN, LIVING MILAN

Most of the city's entrepreneurial activity is concentrated in the city centre and the area known as the **Centro Direzionale** around the **Grattacielo Pirelli** (*see p75*). The ever-expanding **Fiera** (*see p100*) is a trade-driven district in its own right.

Many of Milan's industrial and low-rent quarters – such as the **Navigli** (*see p92*), **Bovisa** (*see p76*) or **Isola** (*see p82*) – are undergoing a rapid transformation into cutesy, trendy zones packed with bars, cafés, art galleries and speciality shops. In other districts – such as the area behind the **Arena** (*see p74*) or around **Porta Venezia** (*see p79*) – growing ethnic enclaves inject a different note into the cityscape.

ANCIENT SITES AND CITY WALLS

The Milanese obsession with revamping and building over has left the city with few ancient remains. **San Lorenzo Maggiore** (*see p91*), with its arcade of Corinthian columns, is perhaps the most satisfying. For more ancient artefacts, head for the **Museo Archeologico** (*see p97*), or the crypt of **Santa Maria della Vittoria** (*see p95*), a recently opened space where finds from ongoing digs are deposited.

The **Duomo** (*see p57*) stands at the historical and geographical centre of an irregularly shaped city; around it are three concentric ring roads: the middle ring, or *bastioni*, corresponds to the 16th-century Spanish walls; the

outermost is more recent and serves to connect the outer suburbs. The ring closest to the centre is known as the Cerchia dei Navigli, and corresponds to the medieval fortifications. The best pieces of gates and city walls – both medieval and Roman – are the **Porta Nuova** (*see p77*) in via Manzoni/piazza Cavour, the **Porta Ticinese** (*see p89*) and the **Pusterla** (*see p95*) at Sant'Ambrogio.

CHURCHES

If the Duomo is a widely known landmark, most of Milan's 100-plus churches will come as a surprise to the visitor. For the most part sandwiched between office buildings and apartment blocks, they bear witness to a more meditative side of Milan where aesthetics triumph over economics.

Most of Milan's churches still function as places of worship. And though not all enforce strict dress codes or visiting hours (the Duomo and **Sant'Ambrogio**, *see p95*, are the strictest), you'll spare yourself outbursts from the sacristan if you cover bare shoulders and legs and refrain from clattering around during mass. Church opening times should be taken as rough guidelines: you will not be allowed to visit during weddings, for example. Some churches have coin-operated lighting systems, audio-visual aids and computerised displays (usually in Italian but sometimes at least partially in English); keep a few coins handy.

MUSEUMS AND GALLERIES

Milan's major galleries have all-day opening times; some remain open until 10pm or later one night a week. Regular winter opening hours are given in this guide; many museums and galleries extend their hours during the summer, so call ahead or visit tourist information offices (*see p290*) for up-to-date information.

Admission to the city's collections is free. Other museums offer discounts for students and over-60s, especially if they hail from EU countries: to benefit, you'll need to show appropriate ID. Many galleries and museums stop issuing tickets half an hour or more before closing time.

TICKETS AND BOOKING

Booking is essential for Leonardo's **Last Supper** (*see p98*), though last-minute cancellations may mean that you get in without a reservation if you're prepared to wait. Many museums and galleries require reservations for groups of seven or more.

You are unlikely to find queues at any of Milan's galleries, though if the temporary exhibits at the **Palazzo Reale** (*see p60*) are blockbusters, advance booking can be a good idea. There is usually a booking charge of €1.04.

During the *Settimana dei beni culturali* (cultural heritage week, *see p291*), which usually takes place in early spring, all publicly owned museums and sites have extended visiting hours and are free of charge.

Note the following cumulative tickets, which can be purchased at the sights themselves:
● Paying areas of the Duomo (*see p57*) and Museo del Duomo (*see p60*), €7.
● Museo del Teatro (*see p61*) and Museo Poldi Pezzoli (*see p77*), €5.16.
● Museo Bagatti Valsecchi (*see p78*) and Museo Poldi Pezzoli (*see p77*), €7.24.
● Museo Diocesano (*see p90*), Cappella Portinari at Sant'Eustorgio (*see p91*) and Cappella di Sant'Aquilino at San Lorenzo (*see p91*), €9.50.

GETTING AROUND

Milan's glorious past is embedded in its prosperous present, with old bits and pieces spread over many square kilometres of modern urban development. Consequently, sightseeing in Milan involves a few preliminary decisions: car, public transport or physical locomotion.

For walkers, Milan's easy because it's flat (with the exception of the Monte Stella park (*see p100*), where debris from World War II was piled up and covered up in the park near the **stadium** (*see p178*). Bear in mind, however, that Milan suffers from a lack of parks and gardens, so most of your strolling will be done in a relentlessly urban landscape.

Milan is served by an extensive public transport system, the ATM, consisting of three subway lines, one light railway, trams and buses (*see also p275*). Ground transport can be extremely slow during the aggravating traffic jams of Milan's rush hours, but the system can take you exactly, or near, where you want to go. A detailed map of ATM services can be obtained at the ATM point at the Duomo metro stop (*see p276*).

Driving is not recommended, especially in the centre, where one-way streets, lack of parking and nightmare rush-hour traffic may put you off driving for life.

If you're aggressive and brave enough to take on the Milanese traffic, cycling is often the fastest way to get around. Bicycles can be rented at selected metro stops during the warmer months. (*See also p279* **Bike hire**.)

Sightseeing

The **Naviglio Grande** in Milan's watery south.

The Duomo &
Central Milan

Milan's religious, literary and financial hub.

Much of what remained of old Milan after 19th-century town planners had had their way with it succumbed to Allied bombing during World War II. **Piazza dei Mercanti** is still more or less intact; almost everything around **piazza del Duomo** is modern. And it buzzes with modern activity: during the day it's peopled with shoppers, tourists and the sharply dressed denizens of the nearby **Borsa** (stock exchange) and banks; in the early evening it's the haunt of *apertivo*-sippers and leisurely window-shoppers; by night, cinema-going crowds pack **corso Vittorio Emanuele**, the pedestrian thoroughfare connecting piazza del Duomo and piazza San Babila (*see p79*).

Around the Duomo

In the fourth century, when the charismatic St Ambrose (*see p10* **Sant'Ambrogio**) held sway in Milan, the area around where the Duomo now stands was the heart of the city. Located hereabouts were two basilicas and a baptistery (all of which were torn down in the 14th century to make room for the Duomo). The political and administrative headquarters were in the nearby **Palazzo Reale** (now a venue for exhibitions and home to the **CIMAC** contemporary art and the **Museo del Duomo** collections). At the time, Milan was not much bigger than that.

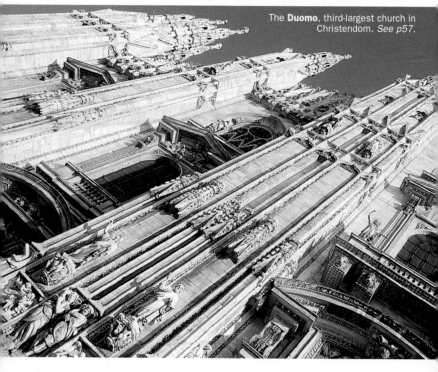

The **Duomo**, third-largest church in Christendom. *See p57.*

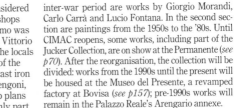

What is now piazza della Scala was considered the outskirts. The cluster of dark little shops and dilapidated houses around the Duomo was demolished in 1865-7 when the Galleria Vittorio Emanuele II – 'Milan's living room' as the locals call it – was built. The structure is one of the earliest examples in Italy of the use of cast iron as architectural ornament. Giuseppe Mengoni, who designed the Galleria, also drew up plans for a major revamp of piazza Duomo, only part of which was carried out.

Note that a cumulative ticket costing €7 allows access to the Duomo roof, and to the Museo del Duomo.

CIMAC (Civico Museo di Arte Contemporanea)

Piazza del Duomo 12 (no phone). Metro Duomo/ bus 50, 60/tram 1, 2, 3, 12, 14, 15, 24, 27. Closed for restoration as this guide went to press; due to reopen May 2002. **Map** p311 A1.

Situated on the second floor of the Palazzo Reale (*see p60*), CIMAC is home to the city's contemporary art collection. Section 1 contains Italian art from the turn of the 20th century until the post-World War II period, including works by Modigliani, the Futurists and the Metaphysical Giorgio De Chirico. From the

inter-war period are works by Giorgio Morandi, Carlo Carrà and Lucio Fontana. In the second section are paintings from the 1950s to the '80s. Until CIMAC reopens, some works, including part of the Jucker Collection, are on show at the Permanente (*see p70*). After the reorganisation, the collection will be divided: works from the 1990s until the present will be housed at the Museo del Presente, a revamped factory at Bovisa (*see p157*); pre-1990s works will remain in the Palazzo Reale's Arengario annexe.

Duomo

Piazza del Duomo (02 864 634 56). Metro Duomo/ tram 1, 2, 3, 12, 14, 15, 24, 27/bus 50, 60. **Open** *Church* 6.45am-6.45pm daily. *Treasury & crypt of San Carlo Borromeo* 9.30am-noon, 2.30-5pm daily. *Baptistery & early Christian excavations* 9.45am-12.45pm, 2-5.45pm daily. *Roof (le terrazze)* Nov-Feb 9am-4.15pm daily. Mar-Oct 9am-5.45pm daily. **Admission** *Church* free. *Treasury & crypt of San Carlo Borromeo* €1. *Baptistery & early Christian excavations* €1.50. *Roof (le terrazze)* by lift €5; on foot €3.30. **Map** p311 A1.

The third-largest church in Christendom (beaten by St Peter's in Rome and the cathedral in Seville), the towering, spiky Duomo dominates the city centre. Construction began in 1386 under the patronage of Bishop Antonio da Saluzzo, who decreed a Jubilee in 1390 to persuade the Milanese to cough up funds or lend a hand on the massive project. The cathedral owes its northern Gothic appearance to the French and German master masons called in to work alongside local Lombard stonecutters and architects. Originally designed in typical Lombard terracotta, the church was clad in cream-coloured marble from Candoglia, on Lago Maggiore (*see p187*), on the orders of the city's ruler, Gian Galeazzo Visconti. Gian Galeazzo envisaged a grandiose structure to equal northern Europe's International Gothic masterpieces. The marble was shipped to Milan on the Ticino river, and then along a network of purpose-built canals (*navigli*). Although consecrated in 1418, the cathedral remained incomplete for five centuries, a fact reflected in the great mixture of styles to be found in the edifice. The façade didn't go on until the early 19th century, when Napoleon did a rush job before crowning himself king of Italy here.

The exterior

Some 3,500 statues adorn the Duomo, around 2,300 of them on the exterior. The oldest are around the apse end, which was built from 1386 to 1447; those along the sides were added as the building of the Duomo progressed, between the late 15th and early 18th centuries. The façade is baroque up to the first order of windows, and neo-Gothic above. The main bronze doors were made between 1840 and 1965. To appreciate the stonework fully, take the lift to the roof from where, on clear days, there are also breathtaking views of the Alps. A roof visit also brings you closer to the *Madonnina* (1774) – the gilded copper figure of Mary on the spire – which is one of the *milanesi*'s best-loved mascots.

Sightseeing

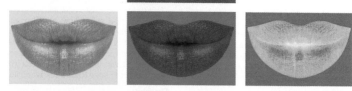

The interior

The 52 pillars of the five-aisled Duomo correspond to the weeks of the year. On their capitals, imposing statues of saints seem to stretch up into the cross vaults of the ceiling. On the floor through the main entrance is a sundial installed in 1768 by the astronomers of the Brera (*see p70*). A ray of light entering the window of the second bay on the right marks noon on the line in the paving.

In the first chapel on the right is the 11th-century sarcophagus of Bishop Ariberto d'Intimiano and a 17th-century plaque commemorating the founding of the Duomo. The stained glass windows in the next three chapels date from the 15th and 16th centuries; the oldest of all, with scenes from the life of Christ, was made in 1470-75 and is in the fifth bay on the right. In the seventh chapel, a window done in 1988 provides a comparison of changing styles.

In the crossing of the transept, the presbytery floor is shiny and worn with signs of the passage of the many millions of pilgrims who, over the centuries, have visited the Duomo, which Cardinal-saint Carlo Borromeo (*see p33*) wanted to serve as his model Counter-Reformation church.

Flanking the 15th-century high altar are two gilded copper pulpits, both 16th-century works. The organ is here, too, its shutters painted with Bible scenes by Giovanni Ambrogio Figino, Camillo Procaccini and Giuseppe Meda.

A nail allegedly from the Cross hangs at the apex of the apse's vaulted roof. Once a year, on the second Sunday of September, the archbishop ascends in the *nivola* (cloud: a curious ornate sort of lift) to bring the nail down and leave it on public display for two days. The bulbous underside of the *nivola* has angels and clouds painted on it; on top, two polychrome angel-candelabras flank a red canopy where the archbishop stands.

In the right transept, the funerary monument to Gian Giacomo Medici was long attributed to Michelangelo, but is now recognised as the work of sculptor and collector Leone Leoni (1560-63) (*see p61* **Casa degli Omenoni**).

On a pedestal in the wall opposite the Medici monument stands an arresting and remarkably lifelike statue of the flayed corpse of St Bartholomew. The statue was done in 1562 by Marco d'Agrate, a follower of Leonardo. Above, the splendid stained glass with St Catherine of Alessandria – who died on the original Catherine wheel – is the work of the Arcimboldo brothers (1556).

The 17th-century sculpture that closes the choir – designed by Pellegrino Tibaldi and carved by the Taurini brothers, Paolo de' Gazzi and Virgilio del Conte – is a masterpiece of its time. The ambulatory windows blaze with fabulous 19th-century stained glass by the Bertini brothers, with scenes from the Old and New Testaments and the Apocalypse. From the ambulatory, stairs lead down to the crypt, where Carlo Borromeo is buried. Entrances to the treasury and the choir, with its 16th-century stucco decoration, are also in the ambulatory.

Galleria Vittorio Emanuele II. *See p60.*

Stylish neo-classical **Palazzo Reale**.

In the left transept, the fantastic monsters on the bronze Trivulzio Candelabra, a masterpiece of medieval goldsmithing, are representations of the arts, professions and virtues. It was made by the great 12th-century goldsmith Nicolas of Verdun.

In the left aisle, the Cappella del Crocifisso (third past the transept) has 16th-century stained glass.

The remains of the earlier churches of Santa Tecla and the Baptistery (where St Ambrose baptised St Augustine in 387) can be reached by descending the stairs just to the left of the entrance.

From 4 November until the Epiphany, the great *Quadroni di San Carlo*, a devotional pictorial cycle with scenes from the life of the saint, are shown in the naves between the pillars. The works are a compendium of 17th-century Lombard painting.

Galleria Vittorio Emanuele II

Piazza del Duomo to piazza della Scala. Metro Duomo/bus 54, 60, 65/tram 15, 23, 27.
Open 24hrs daily. **Map** p311 A1.

Elegant cafés, shops and restaurants and mammoth book and music stores (*see chapter* **Shops & Services** *p131*) line the Galleria, a glass-roofed arcade that was begun in 1865 to a design by architect Giuseppe Mengoni (who plunged to his death from scaffolding a few days before it was opened). The Galleria was inaugurated in 1867 by newly united Italy's King Vittorio Emanuele II. Connecting piazza del Duomo and piazza della Scala, the Galleria is 47m (157ft) high. On the floor are mosaics of the coats of arms of Vittorio Emanuele's Savoia family, plus the symbols of Milan (a red cross on a white field), Turin (a bull), Rome (a she-wolf) and Florence (a lily). In the vault are more mosaics representing Asia, Africa, Europe, America.

Museo del Duomo

Piazza del Duomo 14/via del Arcivescovado 1 (02 860 358/www.internetlandia.com/duomo). Metro Duomo/bus 54, 60, 65/tram 15, 23, 27.
Open 10am-1.15pm, 3-6pm daily. **Admission** €6; concessions €1-13. **No credit cards**. **Map** p311 A1.

The Museo del Duomo houses 14th-19th century sculpture, furniture and stained glass from the cathedral. Among its most precious works is Jacopo Tintoretto's *Christ in the Temple* (1530). A wooden model of the Duomo from 1519 is one of the more fascinating items in a collection documenting the building's interminable construction.

Palazzo Reale

Piazza del Duomo 12 (02 875 672/reservations 02 3932 2737). Metro Duomo/bus 54, 60, 65/tram 15, 23, 27. Open for exhibitions only. **Admission** varies with exhibition. **No credit cards** (except at the telephone booking office, which accepts AmEx, MC, DC, V). **Map** p311 A1.

Milan's original town council office, the Palazzo del Broletto Vecchio, stood on this site from the 11th century. It was replaced with a grander structure around two courtyards in the 14th century under Visconti rule and revamped again in the 16th by the Sforzas. The city's first theatre company was provided with a stage inside in 1598, and Mozart played there as a child; the old theatre was destroyed by fire in 1776, and replaced by the Teatri alla Scala (*see p63*). Giuseppe Piermarini gave the palazzo its present neo-classical look in the 1770s, when he was commissioned to design a residence for Archduke Ferdinand of Austria. Its sumptuous stucco decoration, frescos and inlaid furniture made it one of the most refined and stylistically consistent neo-classical palaces in Europe; only a very small part of the decor survived World War II bombardments. The palazzo is now used for major exhibits – over two million people passed through its door in 2001 – as well as housing the CIMAC contemporary art gallery (*see p57*) and the Museo del Duomo (*see p60*). Check local press for current exhibitions.

Around piazza della Scala: *Milano manzoniano*

The area around piazza della Scala is neo-classical, aristocratic Milan. It is also the zone where Milan – the antithesis of the Italian *città d'arte* (city of art) – redeems itself culturally: besides being home to La Scala, the country's best-known, most prestigious opera house, its streets are indelibly marked with the spirit of Italy's greatest 19th-century novelist, Alessandro Manzoni (*see p64* **Alessandro Manzoni**), who lived, worked and died here.

The northern end of the Galleria Vittorio Emanuele II leads into piazza della Scala, home to the **Teatro alla Scala** and to Milan's city government offices in **Palazzo Marino**. Tucked behind Palazzo Marino, the Jesuit church of **San Fedele** is a fine example of Milanese baroque.

North of the church, beyond the massive façade of the **Casa degli Omenoni**, the **Casa del Manzoni** was the residence of Alessandro Manzoni, curse of Italian school children. Opposite, in piazza Belgioioso, the neo-classical **Palazzo Belgioioso** (No.2; not open to the public) was designed by Giuseppe Piermarini in 1777-81 for Alberico XII di Belgioioso d'Este; the family's heraldic symbols figure large in the decoration of the façade. West of piazza della Scala, **Palazzo Clerici** contains frescos by Giambattista Tiepolo.

Casa del Manzoni

Via Morone 1 (02 8646 0403/www.museidelcentro. mi.it). Metro Montenapoleone/bus 61/tram 1, 2. **Open** 9am-noon, 2-4pm Tue-Fri. **Admission** free. **Map** p311 A1.

Novelist Alessandro Manzoni (*see p64* **Alessandro Manzoni** and *p65* **I promessi sposi**) lived here from 1814 to 1873, when he took a tumble on the steps of nearby San Fedele and died. The ground floor of the house, including Manzoni's study, is perfectly preserved – as befits the home of a literary icon. Also housed in the Casa is the Centro Nazionale di Studi Manzoniani, with a library of Manzoni's works and criticism on the author, and the Società Storica Lombarda.

Casa degli Omenoni

Via Omenoni 3 (no phone). Metro Duomo or Montenapoleone/bus 61/tram 1, 2. Closed to the public. **Map** p311 A1.

Eight muscle-bound Atlases dominate the ornate front of the studio-home that sculptor Leone Leoni built for himself in 1565. Beneath the cornice, a lion savaging Calumny is an example of the creator's famously witty personality. Leoni's magnificent art collection, which included works by Titian and Leonardo's Codex Atlanticus (*see p89* **Leonardo da Milano**) – now in the Biblioteca Ambrosiano (*see p65*) – was broken up long ago.

Palazzo Clerici

Via Clerici 5 (02 878 266). Metro Cordusio/bus 61/ tram 2, 3, 4, 12, 14. Open by appointment only. **Admission** free. **Map** p308 C2.

The result of an 18th-century enlargement of an earlier structure, Palazzo Clerici contains marvellous rococo interiors, including a room frescoed by Giambattista Tiepolo in 1740. A royal residence from 1773 until 1778, the palazzo was sold to the government in 1813 and used by the Appeals Court until 1940. It is now home to the Institute for International Policy Studies (ISPI), which will arrange visits to the Salone del Tiepolo.

Palazzo Marino

Piazza della Scala 2. Metro Duomo/tram 1, 2. Closed to the public. **Map** p311 A1.

Genoese banker Tommaso Marino began building his palazzo to a design by Galeazzo Alessi in 1558. It was not until 1892, however, that architect Luca Beltrami added the façade. The palazzo has been the city government headquarters since 1860. The Cortile d'Onore, with its wealth of sculptural decoration, can be seen from via Marino. Quite inexplicably, local lore cites this palazzo as the birthplace of the fictional nun of Monza, from Alessandro Manzoni's novel *I promessi sposi* (*see p65* *I promessi sposi*).

San Fedele

Piazza San Fedele (02 7200 8027/www.gesuiti.it). Metro Duomo/bus 61/tram 1, 2. **Open** 7.30am-2.30pm, 4-7pm daily. **Map** p310 A2.

San Fedele is the Milanese headquarters of the Jesuit order, and is baroque *per eccellenza*. Pellegrino Tibaldi designed it in 1569 as an exemplary Counter-Reformation church (*see p33*), with its solemn architecture and single nave allowing the priest to keep his eye on the whole congregation. The cupola, crypt and choir were added by Francesco Maria Ricchini (1633-52). The carved wooden choir stalls in the apse came from Santa Maria della Scala, the church demolished to make way for the Teatro alla Scala.

The church is a Who's Who of Milanese baroque and mannerist painting. In the first chapel on the right is Il Cerano's *Vision of St Ignatius* (c1622); in a room leading to the sacristy beyond the second chapel on the right is a *Transfiguration* and *Virgin and Child* by Bernardino Campi (1565). The exuberant carvings on the wooden confessionals and the sacristy (designed by Ricchini and executed by Daniele Ferrari in 1569) liven up so much Counter-Reform sobriety.

Sightseeing

Teatro alla Scala
Piazza della Scala (02 805 3418/Museo del Teatro 02 805 3418/www.teatroallascala.org). Metro Duomo/bus 61/tram 1, 2. **Map** p311 A1.

The Teatro alla Scala closed in 2002, for what theatre luminaries predicted would be a two-year restoration project; meanwhile, performances are being staged at the Teatro degli Arcimboldi. At the time of writing, the future of the Museo del Teatro hung in the balance (though it was expected to move to Palazzo Busca, corso Magenta 71), and regular tours of the opera house had been suspended. For the latest information on visits, call Centro Guide Milano (02 8645 0433).

In 1776, when a fire destroyed the city's main theatre, situated inside the Palazzo Reale (*see p60*), architect Giuseppe Piermarini was called upon to design a new one. His neo-classical masterpiece takes its name from the church of Santa Maria della Scala, commissioned in 1381 by Regina della Scala, wife of Bernabò Visconti, and razed to make way for this temple of culture. It was inaugurated in 1778 with an opera by Antonio Salieri; many of the best-known works of Puccini, Verdi, Bellini and others premiered here. Destroyed by World War II bombings, this great symbol of national pride was rebuilt swiftly. With 1,200sq m (12,900sq ft) of stage and seats for 2,015, La Scala is one of Europe's biggest theatres. Its acoustic is exceptional.

On the evening of 7 December – the feast of Milan's patron saint, St Ambrose – Milan's rich and famous flash jewels and furs galore for the gala opening of the new season. Between acts, they see and be seen in the mirrored Ridotto hall.

The Museo del Teatro, created in 1913, contains a motley collection of sculpture, autographs, paintings and other artefacts related to the theatre. *See also p176* **La Scala moves north.**

Around piazza Affari: Milano finanziario

West of the Duomo, piazza Affari is the site of the **Palazzo della Borsa**, Italy's main stock exchange, and therefore the throbbing heart not only of financial Milan but of the entire country. The square was built between 1928 and 1940.

The regular grid street plan of Roman Mediolanum stretched over the few blocks south-east of piazza Affari: you'll need all your imagination to make it out nowadays.

In what was the Roman forum – and is now a very unspectacular parking lot – stands the Romanesque (and neo-Romanesque) church of **San Sepolcro**; nearby are the 16th-century **San Sebastiano** and **Santa Maria presso San Satiro**, a Renaissance structure concealing a ninth-century one. Situated behind San Sepolcro (the entrance is on the far side, in piazza Pio XI), the **Biblioteca Ambrosiana**

The Pinacoteca Ambrosiana. *See p65.*

contains one of Milan's finest art collections in its **Pinacoteca**. (It was from a balcony on the piazza San Sepolcro side of the Biblioteca Ambrosiana that Mussolini first explained the wonders of Fascism to the multitude).

To the north-east, **piazza Mercanti** was the political and administrative centre of medieval Milan. With its typical market loggia structure, this is the only medieval corner of Milan that survived – more or less unscathed, though with the inevitable Milanese tweaking – the ravages of 19th-century 'improvers' and war-time bombing.

The square was originally closed on all four sides, with the **Palazzo dei Giuresconsulti** making up the whole of the north-east side. This state of affairs came to an end when via dei Mercanti (built 1867-78) was rather cavalierly driven straight through it. The medieval **Palazzo della Ragione** – the old law courts – once stood proud in the middle of the square's buildings: it now gives on to via dei Mercanti on one side and to that part of piazza Mercanti also known as **piazza del Broletto Nuovo** on the other.

The coats of arms of the patrician families who lived around the piazza are much in evidence (see, for example, the **Loggia degli Osii** with Matteo Visconti's shield from 1316), as are portraits of classical scholars and church fathers (see the **Scuole Palatine** of 1645 with its statues of St Augustine and the Latin poet Ausonius), both on the south-west side. The **well** in the centre of piazza del Broletto Nuovo dates from the 16th century.

Alessandro Manzoni

In the Italian literature stakes, Alessandro Manzoni (1785-1873) comes second only to Dante. Outside Italy, he trails way behind. It was not always so: when his great novel, *I promessi sposi*, was first published in the 1820s, it was hailed as a masterpiece by Goethe and Stendhal. But Italy's first – and last – great 19th-century novel was soon overshadowed: composer Giuseppe Verdi became the symbol of that age's cultural heights.

Manzoni and his works remain relevant even today, however, and can still help to understand the particularities of his native country.

Like many Italians past and present, the novelist was a bundle of paradoxes. He was born into an Enlightenment background and was influenced by Romanticism in his early youth, only to undergo a fervent religious conversion at the age of 25. His poetry attempts to reconcile these strongly opposed influences. At its most successful –as in his remarkable poem on the

The **Casa del Manzoni**. *See p61.*

death of Napoleon – it achieves a serenity of detachment that epitomises the Italian skill for compromise. That same skill comes into play in *I promessi sposi*: the vow of virginity so fervently taken by Lucia is shrugged off at the end of the novel when she coolly decides that she doesn't have much choice but to adopt drastic strategies at the time.

Six centuries before, the writings of Dante had made Tuscan the language of the Italian peninsula's educated classes. Manzoni brought this language up to date, 'rinsing his garments in the Arno' as he put it, referring to Florence's river – before revising his original Lombard-ocentric version of *I promessi sposi* for a new edition in 1840.

The result was a vernacular novel, with forms not too far removed from everyday speech, but in a language comprehensible to any educated person in the dialect-divided Italian peninsula: a modern Italian literary language had been created.

However, none of this would count for anything had Manzoni not come up with a ripping yarn: here, his sheer imaginative brilliance came into play. Portrayed with memorable clarity, the characters and episodes of his novels are a part of every Italian's cultural DNA: the pusillanimous parish priest Don Abbondio, the corrupt Nun of Monza and the hysterical persecution of the (allegedly) plague-spreading *Untori* have no less resonance than Pinocchio.

Stranded on the other side of via dei Mercanti, the **Palazzo dei Giuresconsulti** (closed to the public) was built in 1561 as the office of Milan's magistrates, though various reworkings have left little of the original structure; it now houses city council offices and the Chamber of Commerce. The 16th-century structure engulfed the 13th-century **torre** (tower) **di Napo**, which was given a baroque make-over in 1601. The names of the six gates that once allowed access into the square (dei Fabbri, blacksmiths; dei Fustagnari, clothmakers, and so on) give a good idea of the activities that went on around; the names of adjacent *vie* (Armorari, armour makers; Spadari, swordmakers; Cappellari, milliners; Orefici, goldsmiths) are another reminder.

Biblioteca & Pinacoteca Ambrosiana

Piazza Pio XI 2 (02 806 921/www.ambrosiana.it). Metro Duomo or Cordusio/bus 50/tram 2, 3, 4, 12, 14, 24, 27. **Open** *Library* 9.30am-5pm Mon-Fri; *Pinacoteca* 10am-5.30pm Tue-Sun. **Admission** €7.30; €3.65 concessions; *(see also p55)*. **Credit** (accepted weekends only) AmEx, DC, MC, V. **Map** p310 A2.

In 1603 building began on Cardinal Federico Borromeo's *(see p32)* Palazzo Ambrosiano, which was to be the venue for a sweeping cultural project that included a *biblioteca* (library; opened in 1609) and an *accademia del disegno* (art school; 1629) to train artists in the new spirit of the Counter-Reformation. Federico's private art collection was donated to this cultural centre in 1618; it was to form the basis of a collection that would continue to grow over the centuries.

The 172 paintings donated by Federico are still together, housed in rooms 1 and 4-7 of the present-day Pinacoteca. These include Titian's *Adoration of the Magi* and portrait of a man in armour in Room 1; Jacopo Bassano's *Rest on the Flight from Egypt*, Raphael's cartoon for the *School of Athens*, and Caravaggio's *Basket of Fruit* in rooms 5 and 6; and works by Flemish masters including Jan Breughel and Paul Brill in Room 7.

Renaissance masterpieces not from the cardinal's collection are in rooms 2 and 3, including Sandro Botticelli's *Madonna del Padiglione* and Leonardo's *Musician*. The rest of the Pinacoteca contains later works. A lachrymose *Penitent Magdalene* by Guido Reni – darling of the Victorians – is in Room 13 on the upper floor; there are two works by Giandomenico Tiepolo in Room 17. The De Pecis donation of 19th-century works, including a self-portrait by sculptor Antonio Canova, is in rooms 18 and 19. The Galbiati wing houses *objets* such as a lock of Lucrezia Borgia's hair and the gloves Napoleon wore when he met his destiny at Waterloo. The Museo Settala is a replica of a 17th-century 'Wunderkammer' (chamber of wonders): a magnificent jumble of scientific instruments, fossils, semi-precious stones, paintings and books.

I promessi sposi

Not many years ago, when someone rashly proposed removing Alessandro Manzoni's novel *I promessi sposi* (*The Betrothed*) from the school curriculum, the shocked outcry could hardly have been greater if he had suggested turning Milan's Duomo into a hamburger joint.

For despite its stultifying associations with plodding classroom study, this is the Italian novel *per eccellenza*. Moreover, for Italians who manage to shrug off their bad memories – and foreigners approaching the work unscathed – this occasionally preachy historical tome is a gripping page turner.

At the heart of the novel is the classic theme of frustrated love: Renzo and Lucia – the betrothed of the title – are prevented from marrying by the machinations of the wicked Don Rodrigo, who has other, more dastardly, plans for the young lady. Thickening the plot are a wicked nun, a mysteriously nameless brigand leader and a pusillanimous priest; there's a kidnapping and abduction to a mountain fastness, street riots, scenes of famine and a bad bout of plague. Despite the high drama, however, the tone throughout is of convincing historical and psychological realism.

When Manzoni penned his opus (it was published in three volumes between 1825 and 1827), the Italian novel scarcely existed; for this reason he looked northwards for models, and to Walter Scott in particular. Manzoni eschewed Scott's romantically medieval settings. Instead he chose his own Lombardy of 200 years before, undoubtedly because of its analogies with his own day, with the region under oppressive foreign domination.

Indeed, the helplessness of the humble against the arbitrary cruelty of the powerful is a key theme in *I promessi sposi*. Some of the novel's finest moments revolve around string-pulling power play in the higher echelons of both court and Church. In one memorable scene, two minor characters arrange for the transferral of a meddlesome monk who has taken it upon himself to protect Lucia; any follower of contemporary Italian politics will recognise the tried-and-tested techniques.

Shoppers, workers and *aperitivo*-sippers reach the centre by tram.

The Biblioteca (library) is open to bona fide scholars with suitable letters of introduction only. Historical documents – including Leonardo's jottings in what is known as the Codex Atlanticus – are kept firmly under lock and key, with facsimiles only available to library users.

Palazzo della Borsa

Piazza Affari 6/via San Vittore al Teatro 14. Metro Cordusio/bus 50, 58, 60/tram 19, 24, 27. Not open to the public. **Map** p310 A2.

The Milan stock exchange (*borsa*) was founded in 1808 but led an unsettled existence until 1931 when it found a permanent home in the striking Palazzo della Borsa, designed by Paolo Mezzanotte. In pre-computer days, trading went on in a three-floor hall with glass stalls. In the palazzo's cellar are the scant remains of a Roman theatre from the first century AD, destroyed during one of Holy Roman Emperor Frederick Barbarossa's (*see p11*) rampages in 1162. Tours of the theatre ruins, organised by the Chamber of Commerce, had been suspended indefinitely as this guide went to press. For further information, call 02 85 151. The palazzo dominates piazza Affari, the heart of the financial district, constructed like the Borsa, in Rationalist style in 1928-40; the muscle-bound figures dominating façades are pure Fascist mythology.

Palazzo della Ragione

Piazza Mercanti (02 7200 3358). Metro Duomo/tram 1, 2, 3, 12, 14, 15, 24, 27/bus 50, 60. **Open** for exhibitions only. **Admission** varies according to exhibition. **No credit cards. Map** p310 A2.

Now open to the public during exhibitions only, the Palazzo della Ragione was constructed in 1233 for the *podestà* (mayor) Oldrado da Tresseno as the law courts. Oldrado's portrait can be seen in relief on the façade facing piazza del Broletto Nuovo. The palazzo is also known as the 'Broletto Nuovo' – it replaced the Broletto Vecchio, where the medieval Comune of Milan first held its meetings, which stood where the Palazzo Reale (*see p60*) is now located. Markets were held in the ground-floor porticos. Inside, the first-floor Salone dei Giudici (Judges' Room) measures 1,000sq m (10,700 sq ft).

Between the second and third arches on the via Mercanti side of the Palazzo della Ragione is a relief of a 'semi-woolly sow', a reference to the legend that the city of Mediolanum was founded on the site where a wild sow with hairy legs (medio means half, lanum is wool) was seen running about. (Milan's other foundation legends are equally as unlikely: the theory that brothers Medio and Lano founded the city is too suspiciously reminiscent of Rome's Remus and Romulus tale; that the name derives from the German Mai – May, or land where it's always spring – is extremely dubious given Milan's weather).

San Sebastiano

Via Torino 28 (02 874 263). Metro Duomo/tram 2, 3, 12, 14, 12, 15, 24. **Open** 8am-noon, 3-5pm Mon-Sat; 9.30am-noon, 3.30-7pm Sun. Map p310 A2.

When Milan emerged from a bad bout of the plague in 1576, residents heaved a sigh of relief and, to express their thanks, constructed this church on the site where the 14th-century church of San Quilino had once stood. Pellegrino Tibaldi designed the building, though he originally planned a much higher dome; if the heavenly vision of the *Evangelists and Church Fathers* (1832) by Agostino Comerio inside the cupola makes your head spin as it is now, just imagine the effect Tibaldi was originally aiming for. Most of the other unmemorable works are by Federico Bianchi (1635-1719) and Andrea Lanzani (1490-1526).

San Sepolcro

Piazza San Sepolcro (no phone). Metro Duomo or Cordusio/tram 2, 3, 12, 14, 19, 24, 27. **Open** noon-2pm Mon-Fri. **Map** 310 A2.

The forum of Roman Mediolanum occupied the area between piazza San Sepolcro and piazza Pio XI. It was in the heart of the forum that a church dedicated to the Holy Trinity was built in 1030, only to be rebuilt in 1100 and rededicated to the Holy Sepulchre by *milanesi* off to wrest control of that site from the Infidel during the second crusade. The church underwent the usual Counter-Reformatory treatment in the early 17th century; an 18th-century façade was replaced by a neo-Romanesque one in 1894-97. The crypt, which runs the entire length of the church, is all that remains of the original Romanesque structure. A forest of slim columns divides its five aisles; by the apse, a 14th-century sarcophagus has reliefs of the resurrection.

Santa Maria presso San Satiro

Via Torino 9 (02 7202 1804). Metro Duomo/bus 54, 60, 65/tram 2, 3, 12, 14, 15, 24. **Open** 8.30-11.30am, 3.30-5.30pm Mon-Sat; 9.30am-10.30am, 4.30-5.30pm Sun. **Map** p310 A2.

San Satiro (or Satirus) was the brother of St Ambrose (*see p10* **Sant'Ambrogio**). It was to this little-known sibling that a certain Archbishop Ansperto wanted a church dedicated when he left funds for the job in his will in 876.

All that remains of the early structure is the Greek-cross cappella della Pietà and even that was reworked in the 15th century. In 1478, Renaissance genius Donato Bramante was called in to remodel the whole church in order to provide a fitting home for a 13th century image of the Virgin which was said to have bled in 1242 when attacked by a knife-wielding fanatic; the fresco still sits on the high altar. Bramante's gift for creating a sense of power and mass – even in a space as limited as the one occupied by this church – emerges in the powerful, barrel-vaulted central nave that ends in a perspective niche that simulates a deep apse in a space of only 97cm (38 inches).

The cappella della Pietà contains fragments of early medieval fresco decoration and a terracotta sculptural group of the *Pietà* from 1482-3, a typically northern Italian devotional work in which Biblical episodes are treated in diorama fashion.

Castello Sforzesco, Brera & Northern Milan

An imposing fortress, French town planning and a hot nightlife scene.

Sightseeing

Castello Sforzesco. *See p70.*

A rich variety of architecture, urban design and Milanese lifestyles starts with the **Castello Sforzesco**, massive remnant of Milan's Renaissance rulers. The city's French rulers (*see chapter* **History**) imposed a unifying geometrical scheme on this end of town; the elegant *palazzi* along the semicircular **Foro Buonaparte** are still some of Milan's most exclusive real estate.

But the area north of the Duomo also harbours some of Milan's great cultural institutions: the Piccolo group theatres (*see p174* **The Strehler legacy**), the **Pinacoteca di Brera** and the **Triennale**. For colour and flair, look to the very chic **Brera** neighbourhood with its Romanesque churches (often hardly recognisable as such following the attentions of 19th-century 'restorers'), the ethnic enclaves of via Canonica and via Bramante and the up-and-coming **Isola** quarter – once a left-leaning blue-collar stronghold – around Porta Garibaldi station.

Castello Sforzesco & Parco Sempione

When construction of the **Castello Sforzesco** was begun in the 14th century, the area it occupied lay outside the city walls, and was surrounded by woods, much of which were cut down in following centuries to make room for fortifications. Today the castle also houses the eclectic collections of the **Civici Musei**.

During the city's brief period under Napoleonic rule (1796-1814), planners and architects made this out-of-the-way area into a new urban hub consisting of elegant *palazzi* – in largo Cairoli and along Foro Buonaparte – surrounding a green expanse stretching from the Castello to the **Arco della Pace**.

By the end of the 19th century a dense network of medieval shops and dwellings had been razed to make way for via Dante, connecting the Castello with the Duomo

(*see p57*). The **palazzi** along this
pedestrianised thoroughfare were constructed
in the 19th century to match the monumental
feel of the new street. All, that is, except
Palazzo Carmagnola (No.2): despite its
neo-classical façade, this palazzo dates back
to the 14th century, and still retains its original
courtyard. It was here that Ludovico Il Moro
Sforza (*see p15*) lodged his mistress Cecilia
Gallerani, whose illustrious guests included
Bramante and Leonardo da Vinci.

Next door is the original **Piccolo Teatro**
(*see p174* **The Strehler legacy**), founded
in 1947 by Italian contemporary theatre greats
Paolo Grassi and Giorgio Strehler for their
avant-garde company, and now called the
Teatro Grassi.

From largo Cairoli at the Castello end of
via Dante, the semicircular Foro Buonaparte
sweeps left towards the Cadorna commuter
station and right towards the **Teatro Strehler/
Nuovo Piccolo** and **Teatro Studio** (for
both, *see p174* **The Strehler legacy**). The
controversial Nuovo Piccolo – its construction
took 20 years as Strehler and architect Marco
Zanuso dodged accusations of corruption and
mismanagement – stands alongside the equally
divisive Teatro Studio, another Zanuso project
in which the architect gutted the charming
old Teatro Fossati (1858-9) in corso Garibaldi
and turned it into a cylindrical – many call it
uncomfortable – space with traditional Milanese
architectural motifs like the *ringhiera*
(suspended balconies with railings) that
failed to appease bemused locals.

Via Q Sella leads to the **Museo del
Collezionista**, with its fascinating insight
into the lively world of art fakes.

North-west of **Parco Sempione** (*see p74*
All around the garden), beyond the **Arco
della Pace**, corso Sempione – another
Napoleonic legacy – shoots straight as a die
through uninspiring residential suburbs packed
with late 19th- and early 20th-century
apartment blocks towards the municipal
cemetery, the **Certosa di Garegnano** and,
eventually, **Lago Maggiore** (*see p187*).

Certosa di Garegnano
Via Garegnano 28 (02 3800 6301). **Open** 7.30am-
noon, 3-5pm daily. **Map** off p308 A1.
A gem of baroque architecture, this Carthusian
monastery contains stunning fresco decorations by
17th-century artist Daniele Crespi to thank the monks
for granting him sanctuary after he had killed a man.

Museo del Collezionista d'Arte Fondazione Goffredo Matthaes
*Via Quintino Sella 4 (02 7202 2488/www.
museodelcollezionista.com). Metro Cairoli or Lanza/
bus 43, 57, 61, 70, 94/tram 1, 3, 4, 12, 14, 27.*

Open 10am-6pm Mon-Fri; 10am-2pm Sat.
Closed 2wks Aug. **Admission** €6. **No credit
cards. Map** p308 C2.
The fascinating world of art fakes is explored in this
educational museum, which also contains a scientific research lab and art certification office. The
scope of the museum is to help the collector distin-
guish artworks of true value from good imitations.
Twelve rooms house every kind of artwork and
'antique', from copies of the old masters to fabrics.
There are explanations (in English) along the way
of how to test for authenticity.

Brera

In a city where build-'em-big redevelopment
has long been the norm, the narrow, winding
streets of the Brera neighbourhood are a
refreshing change, with their pavements
of porphyry blocks or round river stones.
Traditionally an area of artisans' workshops,
Brera today is full of captivating shops,
boutiques, cafés and nightspots, including
some of the oldest and best jazz clubs in Milan
(*see chapter* **Nightlife**).

From Foro Buonaparte, via Cusani then via
dell'Orso lead east towards Brera. In via Verdi,
to the south, stands the baroque church of **San
Giuseppe**. To the north, via Brera leads into
the heart of the district. Off to the west in the
street of the same name, the **Santa Maria
del Carmine** is one of four (originally)
Romanesque churches hidden in this web
of streets – they sadly fell prey to 19th-century

Santa Maria del Carmine. *See p74.*

Castello Sforzesco

Begun in 1368 by Galeazzo II Visconti as part of the city's fortifications, the Castello kept growing through the 14th century. Filippo Maria Visconti (*see p14*) transformed it into a sumptuous ducal residence. Part of it was demolished in uprisings in 1447, but it was restored to its original splendour by Francesco Sforza in the 1450s.

The court gathered in the Castello by Francesco's son Ludovico II Moro was one of Europe's most refined, with Bramante and Leonardo da Vinci at work there. But when Ludovico was captured by the French in 1499, the castle – like the court – became yesterday's news, and went into decline.

While Milan was under French rule in the early 19th century, the castle's star-shaped bulwarks were knocked down.

By the end of the 19th century, there was talk of demolishing the rest of the red-brick white elephant. Luckily for Milan, architect Luca Beltrami fought tooth and nail to preserve it, coming up with the idea of headquartering the city's various art collections here. From 1893 until 1904, Beltrami oversaw the restoration of the structure, rearranging and rebuilding unashamedly where it didn't quite fit in with contemporary ideas of what a 14th-century castle should look like, but at least saving it from total oblivion.

Coming to a spindly point above the façade is a tower originally by the Florentine architect Antonio Averlino, known as 'Il Filarete' (whose treatise on architecture contains a chapter on the ideal city of Sforzinda, a somewhat toady tribute to his Milanese patrons). The structure here today is, in fact, a 1901-04 re-creation of the 15th-century architect's work, which collapsed in 1521.

Through the gate at the base of the tower, the piazza d'Armi courtyard was being restored as this guide went to press. (The scaffolding hiding the restoration work is disguised by placards illustrating the history of the castle, and is scheduled to come down in 2003-04.) From the piazza d'Armi, gates lead into the Rocchetta (on the left), the oldest part of the castle; and into the Cortile (courtyard) and Palazzo del Corte Ducale (on the right), in Renaissance style. The entrance to the Civici Musei is between the piazza d'Armi and the Cortile del Corte Ducale.

CIVICI MUSEI DEL CASTELLO

The Castello's vast collections cover everything from Renaissance masterpieces to mummies to musical instruments. If you have the time to wander through all the collections – and you'll need most of the day for such an undertaking – it's well worth the effort. Explanations of the works displayed are available (in English) in each room.

restoration. Nearby, one façade of the 17th-century **Palazzo Cusani** (via Brera 15; not open to the public) was remodelled by Giovanni Ruggeri in 1719 in *barocchetta* style, with ornate windows and balconies, while the other was done in neo-classical style by Giuseppe Piermarini. Tradition has it that each of the two Cusani brothers had very different ideas about how they wanted their own private entrance to look. Opposite the Palazzo Cusani is the **Pinacoteca di Brera**, one of Milan's most prestigious art collections.

Another of Brera's 'Romanesque' churches, **San Marco**, stands just beyond the Pinacoteca. **San Simpliciano** is west of here, off via Solferino, while **Sant'Angelo** is east. From piazza Sant'Angelo, largo Donegani leads to via Turati and the **Palazzo della Permanente**, a venue for temporary exhibitions of modern art and a permanent collection of 20th-century Italian art.

Palazzo della Permanente

Via Turati 34 (02 655 1445/www.lapermanente-milano.it). Metro Turati/bus 61, 94/tram 1, 2. **Open** 10am-1pm, 2.30-6.30pm Tue, Wed, Fri; 10am-1pm, 2.30-10.30pm Thur; 10am-6.30pm Sat, Sun. **Admission** €6.20; €4.60 concessions. **No credit cards. Map** p309 B/C1.

Although mainly visited for its temporary exhibitions, the museum houses a permanent collection of Italian paintings, sculpture and graphics from the early 20th century onwards, including Giorgio De Chirico's *Prodigal Son* (1922), Amedeo Modigliani's *Portrait of Paul Guillaume* (1916) and Umberto Boccioni's *Unique Forms of Continuity in Space* (1913). Other artists represented in this single hall on the museum's upper floor include Lucio Fontana, Mario Sironi, Carlo Carrà, Giacomo Balla, Giorgio Morandi and Massimo Campigli.

Pinacoteca di Brera

Via Brera 28 (02 722 631/reservations 02 8942 1146). Metro Montenapoleone or Lanza/bus 61/ tram 1, 2, 3, 12, 14. **Open** 8.30am-7pm Tue-Sun.

Sightseeing

Raccolte d'Arte Antica

The sculpture gallery begins on the ground floor with early Christian and medieval works, including a marble head of the Byzantine Empress Theodora. Dominating Room 2 is an equestrian statue (1363) of Bernabò Visconti by Bonino da Campione. Room 6 contains a bas-relief (1171) from the Porta Romana (*see p86*) showing Milanese scenes after one of Barbarossa's rampages (*see p11*). In Room

8, the Sala delle Asse, are heavily restored frescos attributed to Leonardo da Vinci. There is a series of portraits of the Sforza family attributed to Bernardino Luini in rooms 9 and 10. The Cappella Ducale (duke's chapel, Room 12) was built by Galeazzo Maria Sforza in 1472 and decorated by the leading painters of the day under the direction of Bonifacio Bembo. Room 14 has a 15th-century portal from the Milan branch ▶

Admission *Permanent collection* €5.16.
Collection & exhibitions €7.02. **No credit cards**.
Map p308 C2.

This important collection is often bypassed, even by the Milanese themselves, despite its plethora of works by major Italian artists from the 13th to 20th centuries. The palazzo was begun in 1651 by Francesco Maria Richini for the Jesuits, who wanted it to house their college, astronomical observatory and botanical garden.

In 1776 part of the building was allocated for the Fine Arts Academy. The Pinacoteca (picture gallery) was established as a study collection, with plaster casts and drawings for the students at the Academy. It was enlarged in the Napoleonic era (you can't miss Canova's statue of the diminutive warrior with the body of an ancient Greek athlete in the centre of the courtyard) to house paintings from suppressed religious orders.

The Brera continues to be a great place to learn the basics or improve on your existing knowledge of Italian painting. Thirty-eight rooms are arranged in a circuit that begins and ends with 20th-century

Italian painting. The itinerary starts in Room 1, with works by the major exponents of the leading movements in Italian art from 1910-1950 (Massimo Campigli, Carlo Carrà, Marino Marini, Giorgio Morandi), as well as a few works by European masters who changed the course of art in the early 20th century (Georges Braque, Pablo Picasso). Don't miss Amedeo Modigliani's *Portrait of Moise Kisling* (1915) or Umberto Boccioni's *The City Rises* (1910). The next four rooms cover Italian painting from the 13th to the 15th centuries. Jacopo Bellini's *Virgin and Child* in Room 3 shows how the Venetian painter was influenced by new developments in art in Florence and Padua after 1450. Room 4 hosts works by masters of the International Gothic style, including Gentile da Fabriano's elegant *Valle Romita* polyptych of about 1410.

The next six rooms, numbered 5-9 and then 14, are dedicated to the Venetian Renaissance. In Room 6 are some of the Brera's most outstanding works by artists who marked two centuries of great painting in Venice: the diligent cataloguer of Venetian life Vittore Carpaccio (*Scenes from the Life of the Virgin*,

of the Medici bank and a collection of arms. Although the swords are forged with fierce inscriptions ('I love peace but I bring war'), the small size of the suits of armour makes it difficult to believe such Lilliputian warriors constituted a major threat.

In Room 15, Bambaja's masterpiece, the monument to Gaston de Foix, is a tribute to the Lombard classical style of the early 16th century. De Foix, Louis XII's nephew, was a French military commander who died heroically in Ravenna in 1512. The grand finale is the *Rondanini Pietà*, the statue Michelangelo was supposedly working on up to a few days before his death on 18 February 1564. Although somewhat out of place after the long journey through the Gothic and early Renaissance, it is strangely moving nonetheless.

On the first floor, the Pinacoteca (picture gallery) begins with antique furniture borrowed from the applied arts collections (*see p70*). Highlights include the 15th-century *coretto* from the castle of Torchiara near Parma (Room 16): the box with a pyramid on top was designed to allow the castle's owner, *condottiere* (mercenary leader) Pier Maria Rossi, to hear mass with his lover Bianca Pellegrini da Como without being seen by the indiscreet glances of the congregation. More of Pier Maria's legacy is in Room 17; frescos depict an episode

from Boccaccio's *Decameron* in which the Marquis of Saluzzo inflicts trials on his wife to test her virtue.

The gallery proper begins in Room 20 with a panorama of 15th-century Italian painting. The Veneto is represented by Giovanni Bellini's innocent *Madonna con Bambino* (1470s), Mantegna's majestic masterpiece *Madonna and Child with Saints and Angels in Glory* (1497), and Antonello da Messina's *St Benedict* (1470), with his suspicious gaze. There are also works by the Florentines, including Filippo Lippi with his usual chubby children in the *Madonna dell'Umiltà* (1430s). Room 21 is an extravaganza of Lombard painting from the early to late Renaissance, including Vincenzo Foppa's stoic *St Sebastian* (before 1490) and a *Noli Mi Tangere* (c1508) by Bramantino. The 16th-century schools are represented by the languorous male nudes of Cesare da Sesto's *San Rocco* polyptych (1520s), the melting gaze of Correggio's *Madonna and Child with the Infant St John* (1517) and Moretto da Brescia's *St John the Baptist* (c1520); rooms 23-24, meanwhile, are full of the forced elegance and erudition of the Lombard Mannerists. The Pinacoteca closes with 17th- to 18th-century works: Bernardo Strozzi's fleshy *Berenice* (1630) and the inevitable photographic views of Venice by Canaletto and Guardi.

c1505); the austere geometry of Andrea Mantegna (*Dead Christ* and *St Luke* polyptych, 1455); and two guileless Madonnas and a mournful *Pietà* (1465-70) by Giovanni Bellini. A gallery of 16th-century Venetian portraits follows in Room 7. Although the sitters may be obscure, the authors of these works are certainly in Venice's hall of fame: the giant of Venetian painting, Titian (*Portrait of Count Antonio Porcia*, 1535-40); the introspective Lorenzo Lotto (*Portrait of Laura da Pola*, 1544); Tintoretto's arrogant *Young Man* (1560-65); and the 'pre-Impressionist' style of Palma Giovane in the *Portrait of an Old Man*, with a *Portrait of a Child* on the other side (1590). Room 8 goes back to the 15th century with the pageantry of *St Mark Preaching in Alexandria* (1504-07) by Gentile and Giovanni Bellini. Room 9 houses some of the greatest works of 16th-century Venetian painting: the vibrant colours of Titian's *St Jerome in Penitence* (1555); the dynamic diagonal perspective of Tintoretto's *Finding of the Body of St Mark* (1562-6) and the unrestrained display of sumptuousness that led Paolo Veronese (*Feast in the House of Simon*, 1570)

to be censured by the Inquisition. The fallout from this artistic explosion can be seen in the northern Italian painters on show in Room 14 (il Pordenone, il Romanino, Lorenzo Lotto, Moretto da Brescia, Giovanni Battista Moroni, Gian Girolamo Savoldo, Bonifacio de' Pitati, Paris Bordone, Lambert Sustris, Palma Vecchio). The next three rooms, numbered out of sequence 15, 18 and 19, provide a chance to get a better idea of the styles of Gaudenzio Ferrari, Bramantino, Vincenzo Foppa, Bergognone, Bernardino Luini, the Campi brothers and other personalities that dominated Lombard art during the 15th and 16th centuries.

This regional survey of Renaissance art continues with styles that provide strong contrasts with the classicism of the Florentines or the colour harmonies of the Venetians. There is the expressionism of the Ferrarese (Francesco del Cossa, Cosmè Tura, Lorenzo Costa, Ercole Roberti, Garofalo, Dosso Dossi, rooms 20-22), the overly ornate style of Carlo Crivelli (1430-1494/5) from the Marches region (Room 21), and the warmth of feeling in the work of the Emilian, Correggio (Room 23).

Museo degli Strumenti Musicali

The collection of musical instruments (rooms 36 and 37) is one of the biggest in Europe, with 640 pieces arranged in five sections: strings, plucked instruments, keyboard instruments, winds and exotic instruments. The instruments displayed range from the very rare – such as Giovanni Grancino's 1662 viol, one of the few stringed instruments in the world to conserve its original baroque neck; and violins by the great Stradivarius, *see p244* **Fiddles** – to the very bizarre.

Among the latter are the pochette, a pocket-sized violin used by dancing instructors, and combo guitar-mandolins. Whether or not instruments grab you, take a peek into Room 37, the Sala della Balla, where dames and lords played a sort of tennis. Hanging above this enormous hall are the Trivulzio tapestries, commissioned around 1504. They illustrate the labours of the months.

Civiche Raccolte d'Arte Applicata

This section runs the whole gamut of the so-called minor arts: wrought iron (Room 28); ceramics of the world from the 15th to the 19th centuries (rooms 29-30: don't miss the huge crab by Ferruccio Mengaroni (1920s) in the former, or eccemtric pieces made by architect Giò Ponti (1920s) for Richard Ginori in the latter); Italian and European porcelain (Room 31); liturgical objects, ivories and scientific instruments (Room 32); leather objects (Room 35); and goldsmithing, enamels, small bronzes, textiles and wall coverings.

Civiche Raccolte Archeologiche e Numismatiche

Part of the city's prehistoric and ancient Egyptian collections is housed in the basement beneath the Cortile della Rocchetta (there's more in the Civico Museo Archeologico, *see pxxx*). Archeological artefacts range from the paleolithic to Iron Age, with a fascinating section on the prehistoric lake dwellers who lived in stilt-houses in Lombardy's lakes. The Egyptian collection is less complete, but contains sarcophagi, small pieces of sculpture and the usual mummy. This section of the museum was closed indefinitely for restoration as this guide went to press.

Castello Sforzesco

Piazza Castello (02 8846 3700).
Metro Cairoli, Cadorna or Lanza/bus 43, 57, 61, 70, 94/tram 1, 3, 4, 12, 14, 27.
Open *Castle grounds 8am-8pm daily.*
Museums 9.30am-5.30pm Tue-Sun.
Admission *free.* **Map** *p308 C2.*

Room 24 contains the most famous works in the Brera: Piero della Francesca's eternally immobile *Brera Altarpiece* (1472), Donato Bramante's disturbing *Christ at the Column* (after 1490); and Raphael's *Marriage of the Virgin* (1504). This leads into paintings from central Italy in the 15th and 16th centuries (Room 26). Also in this section are works by the Caracci brothers and other central Italian artists who provided the background against which Caravaggio was working. Caravaggio's own magnificent *Supper at Emmaus* (1605-6) can be seen in Room 29.

Take a break from 17th-century Lombards in rooms 31-33, with vibrant Van Dyck (*Virgin and Child*, 1630-32, room 31) and Rubens (*Last Supper*, 1630-32, room 31), still lifes by Evaristo Baschenis and Jan Fyt (Room 31) and landscapes by Jan Van Goyen and Jan Breughel the Elder (Room 32).

The vast range of 18th-century painting is spread over three rooms, with religious works in Room 34, Venetian painting (views of Venice by Canaletto and Guardi) and Italian portraiture and genre scenes in rooms 35 and 36. The itinerary ends with two rooms of 19th-century Italians: Francesco Hayez's romanticised view of the Renaissance in *The Kiss* (1859) or *The Last Moments of Doge Marin Faliero* (1867), contrasted with his very realistic *Portrait of Alessandro Manzoni* (1841); and Giuseppe Pellizza da Volpedo's *Human Flood*, an early version of his *Fourth Estate*, now in the Civica Galleria d'Arte Moderna (*see p82*).

San Giuseppe

Via Verdi 11 (02 805 2320). Metro Duomo or Cordusio/tram 1, 2. **Open** *7am-6.30pm Mon-Sat; 9am-1pm Sun.* **Map** *p309 C1.*

A baroque façade with statues from the early 19th century hides the octagonal structure of this building, which is considered Francesco Maria Richini's greatest work. The interior is decorated with works by the usual local bunch: the baroque Camillo Procaccini (1620-25) and Andrea Lanzani (1712).

San Marco

Piazza San Marco 2 (02 2900 2598).
Bus 41, 43. **Open** *7.30am-noon, 4-7pm daily.*
Map *p308 C2.*

San Marco was built in 1254 by the Augustinian Lanfranco Settala on the site of a church that the Milanese had dedicated to Venice's patron, St Mark, as thanks to the Venetians for their intervention in the battle against Barbarossa (*see p11*). The façade was redone by Carlo Maciachini in his favourite neo-Gothic style. Inside are nine chapels that provide an overview of Lombard painting during the 16th and 17th centuries.

San Simpliciano

Piazza San Simpliciano 7 (02 862 274).
Metro Lanza/bus 43, 57, 70/tram 3, 4, 12, 14.
Open 7am-noon, 3-7pm Mon-Sat; 7am-noon, 4-7pm Sun. **Map** p308 C2.
One of the oldest churches in the city, San Simpliciano was founded in the fourth century by St Ambrose with the name Basilica Virginum and finished in 401. The original church had a porticoed structure where penitent parishioners and neo-phytes attended mass. The present façade was added in 1870 by Carlo Maciachini, a champion of the neo-Gothic revival; the central entrance dates from the 12th century, however. The apse decoration, the *Coronation of the Virgin*, is by Leonardo da Vinici's follower Bergognone. Note that the early Christian sacellum, with its many relics, is not open to the public.

Santa Maria del Carmine

Piazza del Carmine 2 (02 864 633 65).Tram 1, 3, 4, 12, 14, 27/bus 61. **Open** 7.30-11.30am, 3.30-7pm daily. **Map** p308 C2.
Built in 1250 and rebuilt in 1400, nothing much remains of the original Romanesque church of Santa Maria del Carmine. The present-day façade is the work of Maciachini (1880). The Carmine is full of Milanese history: the tomb (1472) of ducal

All around the garden: Parco Sempione

Extending for 47 hectares (116 acres), the recently spruced-up Parco Sempione is a 19th-century creation. The city's French rulers began carving it out of the remains of the ducal gardens, with orchards, vegetable gardens and a hunting reserve, early in the century.

Only Napoleonic urban planners could have come up with the pompous neo-classical **Arco della Pace** that stands at the head of corso Sempione, Milan's answer to the Champs Elysées. Begun in 1807 to a design by Luigi Cagnola, this triumphal arch was supposed to commemorate Napoleon's victories. Work proceeded too slowly, however, and came to an abrupt halt in 1808 after Napoleon fell from power. It resumed in 1826 – with a few essential changes to the faces in the reliefs – and the arch was eventually inaugurated on 10 September 1838 by Austrian Emperor Ferdinand I. Also from the Napoleonic period is the **Arena Civica**, designed in 1806 by Luigi Canonica. The rulers of the Roman-inspired French Empire used it for open-air entertainment – chariot races and mock naval battles (flooded with water from nearby canals). Today it is used for international athletic events.

The park was landscaped many years later, in 1893, by Emilio Alemagna. He opted for the then-popular 'English garden' fashion, with winding paths, lawns, copses and a lake. Nestling amid the landscape is a host of museums and galleries including the **Civico Acquario** and the **Palazzo dell'Arte (Triennale)**.

Parco Sempione

Metro Cadorna, Cairoli or Lanza/bus 43, 57, 61, 70, 94/tram 1, 3, 4, 12, 14, 27, 30.
Open *Nov-Feb* 6.30am-8pm daily. *Mar-Apr, Oct* 6.30am-9pm daily. *May* 6.30am-10pm daily. *June-Sept* 6.30am-11.30pm daily.
Admission free. **Map** p308 C1/2.

Civico Acquario e Stazione Idrobiologico (Aquarium)

Via Gadio 2 (02 8846 5750/www.acquariocivico.mi.it). Metro Lanza/bus 43, 57, 70/tram 3, 4, 12, 14.
Open 9.30am-5.30pm Tue-Sun.
Admission free. **Map** p308 C2.
Designed by architect Sebastiano Locati in 1906, the aquarium's fantastic art nouveau decorative reliefs in polychrome majolica are some consolation for the lack of hammerhead sharks and killer whales on display. The smattering of the world's marine life here consists of much smaller fry, starting with local fish and swamp life and ending up with uninspiring creatures of the deep from more exotic climes.

Palazzo dell'Arte (Triennale)

Viale Alemagna 9 (02 724 341/www.triennale.it). Metro Cadorna/bus 43,

councillor Angelo Simonetta stands in the right transept; the body of finance minister Giuseppe Prina was brought to the sacristy after he had been massacred by the populace for raising the tax on salt in 1814. The wooden choir (1579-85) houses the plaster models that were used by the artists working in the Duomo in the 19th century.

Sant'Angelo

Piazza Sant'Angelo 2 (02 632 481). Bus 94/tram 41, 43. **Open** 8am-8pm daily. **Map** p309 B/C1.
Built in 1552 to take the place of a Franciscan church the Spanish had destroyed to build defence works, Sant'Angelo is a highly significant work of 16th-century Milanese architecture. The interior is full of paintings by noteworthy Milanese and Lombard artists from the 16th and 17th centuries, including Antonio Campi, Morazzone, Procaccini and a copy of a work by Gaudenzio Ferrari.

Palazzo dell'Arte.

61, 94. **Open** 10am-8pm Tue-Sun.
Admission varies according to exhibition.
No credit cards. **Map** p308 C1/2.
The Palazzo dell'Arte was constructed in 1932-3 by Giovanni Muzio to provide a permanent home for the Esposizione Internazionale di Arti Decorative, held every three years. Since then, the Triennale has widened its scope to include architecture, urban planning, industrial design, fashion and audiovisual communications. As you wander through the park behind the building, you too might wonder what Giorgio De Chirico's bathers are doing in *Bagni misteriosi*. It was installed in 1973 along with Alberto Burri's *Il teatro continuo* and other works by 20th-century artists.

Porta Garibaldi, Isola & beyond

A stroll down **corso Garibaldi** will take you past enticing speciality shops, intriguing boutiques and the church of **Santa Maria Incoronata**. At the northern end is **Stazione di Porta Garibaldi**, designed by architects Gentili Tedeschi, Tevarotto and Associates (1960-63). With its simple lines, it's a perfect example of modern, functional architecture. For years, schemes have been afoot to transform the area around the station into an important cultural-financial zone.

To the east of station **Porta Garibaldi** (1826) rises the **Grattacielo Pirelli**. Erected between 1955 and 1960, the 'Pirellone' – Big Pirelli as locals calls it – is a tribute to post-World War II reconstruction, designed by a team of architects that included Giò Ponti, Pier Luigi Nervi and Arturo Danusso. The 1,000 square metres (10,753 square feet) it covers were once occupied by Pirelli's tyre factory. Until the end of the 1960s, it was the world's highest skyscraper in reinforced cement. It was also the first building in Milan to rise higher than the Madonnina (*see p57*) on top of the Duomo; to compensate, a small statue of the Virgin was installed on the roof. Further east still rises the massive bulk of Stazione Centrale, an overwhelming example of the heavy end of the Milanese Liberty style (*see p81* **Liberty**), built between 1912 and 1931. The city's inter-war Fascist leaders made it their own by applying the Fascist bundle-of-sticks symbol wherever they could; on the façade, Anno IX (year nine) refers to 1931, the ninth year of Mussolini's fascist regime, when the station was opened. A few blocks west of the station is the **Cimitero Monumentale**, a temple to Milanese art nouveau.

On the other side of the railroad tracks, across the via Farini bridge along the east side of the cemetery, is **Isola** (island), a *quartiere* that was once cut off from the rest of the city by *navigli* (canals) that have since been filled in; it is still isolated by the railway, however. Isola is traditionally an area of left-voting artisans and blue-collar workers (or petty criminals, depending on your point of view); the quarter still maintains something of its industrious flavour in the small workshops in via Pastrengo and via Borsieri, though it is now showing definite signs of edging towards trendiness. From piazza Segrino in the heart of this area, via Thaon de Revel leads to the church of **Santa Maria alla Fontana**, with a sanctuary that is attributed by different experts to both Leonardo and Bramante.

Sightseeing

The **Cimitero Monumentale** is an open-air museum of art nouveau.

West of here, the rundown industrial zone of Bovisa, too, is undergoing a minor renaissance, hinging on the creation of the **Museo del Presente** (*see p157* **Factories**) in its old gas works. To the north-east, on the other hand, a new university hub and the **Teatro degli Arcimboldi** (*see p176*) are injecting fresh cultural life into the Bicocca neighbourhood.

Cimitero Monumentale

Piazzale Cimitero Monumentale (02 659 9938). Bus 41, 51, 70, 94/tram 3, 4, 11, 12, 14, 29, 30, 33. **Open** 8.30am-5.15pm Tue-Sun. **Admission** free. **Map** p308 B2.

The cemetery was begun in 1866 by Carlo Maciachini (1866) and is 250,000 square metres (2,688,000 square feet) of pure eclecticism. It's virtually an open-air museum of art nouveau, though later major Italian artists – including Giacomo Manzù, Adolfo Wildt and Lucio Fontana – were also commissioned to produce monuments. The whole complex centres around the 'Temple of Fame' (Famae Aedes), where famous *milanesi* and other illustrious 'guests' are buried, including Manzoni (author of *I Promessi sposi, see p60* **Alessandro Manzoni**), Luca Beltrami (restorer of Castello Sforzesco and champion of the neo-Gothic movement), Arturo Toscanini and poet Salvatore Quasimodo. Non-Catholics are buried in separate sectors. A free map of the cemetery indicating the most noteworthy monuments is available at the entrance.

Santa Maria alla Fontana

Piazza Santa Maria alla Fontana 11 (02 688 7059). Metro Garibaldi or Zara/bus 82, 91, 92/tram 4, 11. **Open** *Church* 7.30am-7pm Mon-Fri; 8.30am-7pm Sat, Sun. *Sanctuary* 10am-noon, 3-5pm Sat; 9.30am-noon, 4-5pm Sun. **Map** p308 A2.

This church is essentially a modern structure in the neo-Renaissance style, with various nondescript additions. The presbytery, however, rests on a much older sanctuary, open at weekends. According to local tradition, French governor Charles d'Amboise was miraculously cured at a spring here, and so had an oratory built on the spot in 1506. The design for the building has variously been attributed to Leonardo and Bramante, but more rigorous scholarship attributes it to Amadeo, the genius behind the Certosa di Pavia (*see p254*) and much of Milan's Duomo (*see p57*). The original font is still inside the church.

Santa Maria Incoronata

Corso Garibaldi 116 (02 654 855/guided tours 02 607 1009/6900 0579). Metro Garibaldi/bus 94. **Open** 7.30am-1.30pm, 4-7.30pm daily. **Map** p308 B/C2.

This basically Romanesque church is, in fact, made up of two buildings erected by Guiniforte Solari and then united in 1468. The one on the left went up in 1451, and the one on the right followed shortly thereafter. In the apse are frescos from the 15th to 17th centuries. Frescos in the chapels in the left nave are attributed variously to the Leonardo-esque painter Zenale and Bergognone. Guided tours are arranged by appointment on Saturday.

San Babila & Eastern Milan

Aristocratic palazzi *and all the stars of the fashion firmament.*

If **via Manzoni**'s elegant *palazzi* make this busy thoroughfare the city's aristocratic core, the high-density designer boutiques in the streets to the south make what is known as the **Quadrilatero della Moda** (fashion quadrilateral) a world capital of couture. Similarly retail-oriented, **corso Venezia** starts out as the ultimate in snobbery at piazza San Babila only to end up in the long stretch of anything goes that is **corso Buenos Aires** on the other side of **Porta Venezia**.

Via Manzoni & piazza Cavour

Once a verdant haven due to the lush gardens that surrounded each of the villas along its length, **via Manzoni** (so named in 1865 after novelist, *see p60* **Alessandro Manzoni**) still has its elegant *palazzi* (*see p78* **Via Manzoni**)… though you may not notice them as you dodge screaming traffic.

Nestling between the impressive façades is the entrance to the **Museo Poldi Pezzoli**, a singular example of a late 19th-century Milanese noble residence, containing a wonderful treasure trove of a family collection.

Via Manzoni ends at the **Archi di Porta Nuova**. Begun in 1171 and heavily restored in 1861, this gate is one of only two surviving from the medieval walls; materials from the Roman gate that occupied the site previously were used in its construction. On the via Manzoni side are Roman inscriptions from the first century AD; the piazza Cavour side has a tabernacle with the Madonna, Child and saints Ambrose, Gervasius and Protasius (1330-39).

Beyond the gate is **piazza Cavour**, an attractive square with bookstalls near the tram stop in the centre and the welcome greenery of the **Giardini Pubblici** (*see p82* **All around the garden**) at its north-east corner. The massive grey hulk on the square's east side is the **Palazzo dei Giornali**, designed by Giovanni Muzio in 1942 as the headquarters for the daily newspaper *Popolo d'Italia*; it has reliefs by Mario Sironi. The monument to Unification thinker Camillo Cavour by Odoardo Tabacchi (1865) gives the square its name.

Museo Poldi Pezzoli

Via Manzoni 12 (02 794 889/02 796 334/www. museopoldipezzoli.it). Metro Montenapoleone/tram 1, 2/bus 61, 94. **Open** 10am-6pm Tue-Sun. **Admission** €6 (*see also p55*). **Credit** MC, V. **Map** p309 C1.

The museum was inaugurated in 1881 as a 'house-museum': an exploration of the Poldi Pezzoli is not exactly like any other gallery visit. The collection, begun in the 19th century by nobleman Gian Giacomo Poldi Pezzoli (1822-79), includes weapons, carpets, watches and fabrics, all interspersed among

Roman remains on the **Porta Nuova**.

Sightseeing

Home sweet home: the **Museo Poldi Pezzoli** is a house-museum. *See p77.*

Via Manzoni

For an idea of how aristocrats of the 18th and 19th centuries displayed their prosperity, take a walk along via Manzoni. Though none of the solid *palazzi* are open to the public (with the exception of one of the **Palazzi Poldi Pezzoli**, at No.12 and No.14, home of the eponymous museum, *see p77*), the façades of these lush pads exude self-confident wealth. At No.6, the **Palazzo Brentani** (19th century) has medallion-busts of famous Italian artists and scientists, including Alessandro Volta, Leonardo da Vinci, Cesare Beccari, Antonio Canova and Giuseppe Parini. This palazzo was the scene of Carlo Alberto's narrow escape in 1848, after turning Milan back over to Radetzky (*see p16*). **Palazzo Anguissola** (No.10; 1775-8) is now the Banca Commerciale Italiana archive. Its neo-Palladian façade hides a charming courtyard and gardens equipped with all the fake grottos, ornamental vases and fountains that a romantic garden should have. The composer Giuseppe Verdi died at the **Grand Hotel et de Milan** in 1901 (No.29; 1865). **Palazzo Gallarati Scotti** (No.30) dates from the early 18th century. (Across the road, a detour down via Pisoni leads to the remains of the 15th-century Humiliati convent of **St Erasmus**, which have been tastefully incorporated into a modern structure that echoes its graceful porticos.) Back on via Manzoni, the **Palazzo Borromeo d'Adda** at Nos.39-41 – with its neo-classical decorations and sumptuous courtyard with a view of the garden behind – was the haunt of artists and *letterati* when Stendhal called in 1800.

the many excellent works in the painting collection. Beyond Carlo Innocenzo Carloni's frescos and the textile collection with a cope embroidered with the Coronation of the Virgin to a design by Sandro Botticelli, the monumental staircase decorated with early 18th-century landscapes by Alessandro Magnasco leads to the first floor.

This houses the Lombard room, with Lombard painting from the 15th to 16th centuries, including Cristoforo Moretti's polyptych and Vincenzo Foppa's *Portrait of Giovanni Francesco Brivio*. There is also a room with works by non-Italian painters, including Lucas Cranach's *Martin Luther and His Wife* (1529). A glass case of precious porcelain ware separates these collections from the Salone Dorato, with Florentine and Venetian works from the early Renaissance: Piero della Francesca's *Madonna and Child* and *Lamentation* by Botticelli, *Portrait of a Woman* by Antonio Pollaiuolo, a *Madonna and Child* by Andrea Mantegna and a *Pietà* by Giovanni Bellini. Three rooms are dedicated to the Visconti Venosta collections, with portraits by Fra' Galgario (*Gentleman with a Unicorn*) and watches from the 16th to 18th centuries. Other rooms are dedicated to Murano glass and the life of Dante. In the last rooms is a collection of small bronzes, paintings by Tiepolo, a *Sacra Conversazione* by Lorenzo Lotto and a *Crucifixion* by Giovanni Bellini.

Quadrilatero della moda

There can be few places in the world with the designer boutique-density of Milan's *Quadrilatero della moda* (fashion quadrilateral, *see p132* **More stars than the Milky Way**). They're all there – Byblos, Cerruti 1881, Chanel, Etro, Fendi, Genny, Gianfranco Ferrè, Hermès, Jil Sander, Krizia, Laura Biagiotti, Mila Schön, Moschino, Prada, Romeo Gigli – in the golden square marked out by **via Montenapoleone**, **via Manzoni**, **via Sant'Andrea** and **via della Spiga**. Gold-card-toting hordes swan through portal after portal; wistful backpackers window-shop. But few notice the neo-classical façades and scenic courtyards of the homes of the aristocracy, like the *palazzi* **Taverna** and **Melzi di Cusano** at No.2 and No.18 via Montenapoleone respectively. Via Bigli, too, has delightful *palazzi* dating from the 16th to the 18th centuries.

The fashion zone also conceals two highly eccentric but rewarding museums, the **Museo Bagatti Valsecchi** and the **Civiche Raccolte Storiche**.

Museo Bagatti Valsecchi

Via Santo Spirito 10/via Gesù 5 (02 760 061 32/ www.museobagattivalsecchi.org. Metro Montenapoleone/tram 1, 2. **Open** 1-5.45pm Tue-Sun. **Admission** €6 (*see also p55*). **Credit** MC, V. **Map** p309 C1.

Opened in 1994, this neo-Renaissance palazzo with its two pretty courtyards – residence of the Bagatti Valsecchi brothers – is now a homage in museum form to the extraordinary tastes of these eclectic collectors from the late 19th century. Inside are works of art by masters of the Renaissance. But paintings are not the reason why you're here: it's collecting itself that counts. There's a demure *Santa Giustina* by Giovanni Bellini in Giuseppe Bagatti Valsecchi's room, but the tapestries, ceramics and arms are equally as fascinating. As are the rare manuscripts in the library. And the Valtellinese bedroom with a great 16th-century bed carved with the Passion of Christ and scenes from the Old Testament. Other curiosities include a richly decorated hand-carved wood-panelled room with a Valtellinese *stufa* (heater), and an ingenious piece of furniture that conceals a piano. There's also a collection of children's furniture from the 15th to 18th centuries (*see also p153*). If you don't feel one visit is enough, ask to have your ticket stamped when you enter, and it's good for two more visits over the following month.

Museo di Milano & Museo di Storia Contemporanea – Civiche Raccolte Storiche

Palazzo Morando Attendolo Bolognini, via Sant'Andrea 6 (02 7600 6245/www. museidelcentro.mi.it). Metro Montenapoleone/bus 61, 94/tram 1, 2. Closed for restoration as this guide went to press; due to reopen Dec 2002. **Map** p309 C1.

This 18th-century palazzo houses the city's historical collections, the Museo di Milano and the Museo di Storia Contemporanea. In the first, experience a quainter, more old-fashioned Milan in the private apartments of the Palazzo Morando Attendolo Bolognini, and in the documents and paintings relating to the city and its famous citizens. The second has relics from the two world wars.

From San Babila to Porta Venezia

Leading west from piazza del Duomo (*see p56*), Milan's main commercial artery **corso Vittorio Emanuele II** follows the route of a Roman road. It was once called corsia dei Servi: this is where the 1628 bread riots – recorded by Alessandro Manzoni (*see p60* **Alessandro Manzoni**) in *I promessi sposi* – took place. Standing under the arcades at No.13 is a Roman statue known – not very imaginatively – as the *Omm de preja* (man of stone). Milan's political satirists, unwilling to speak out loud against the city's ruler, would vent their spleens in pasquinades (written tirades) stuck to the statue in the dead of night.

After the church of **San Carlo**, the corso passes a surfeit of enticing stores and ends up in **piazza San Babila**, a post-war revamp

Sightseeing

A gold card is essential in the **Quadrilatero della moda**. *See p78.*

Alberto Villa
Marketing Manager
ore 18.00:
Full immersion

Harbour Club Milano, a perfect combination of nature, sport and relaxation. The regenerating contact with nature in the 70,000 sq. meters of luscious gardens, perfectly combined with sports facilities adapts to all needs: 16 tennis courts, 2 Olympic-size swimming pools, squash rooms, soccer fields, golf driving range, gym, aerobic studios and beauty farm.

The splendid Club House, with its spacious restaurant and terraces overlooking the garden park, is ideal for relaxation and also for business lunches. A qualified nursery and kindergarten offers a wide range of courses for your children.

Bring colour to your world, join us at Harbour Club to discover a new life style.

HARBOUR CLUB
MILANO
Your life style

Harbour Club Milano - Via Cascina Bellaria, 19 -20153 Milano
Tel. 02 452861 - Fax: 02 40910888 - Internet: www.harbourclub.it - Email: harbourclub@harbourclub.it

where eternally work-oriented *milanesi* bustle about. The brick faux-Romanesque façade of the church of **San Babila** meekly stands in the north-east corner of the square, dwarfed by the surrounding abundance of steel and cold stone.

Corso Venezia shoots straight as a die out of piazza San Babila and north-east to Porta Venezia. Elegant noble residences and posh shops line the thoroughfare. Starting from piazza San Babila, the late 15th-century **Casa Fontana Silvestri** at No.10 is one of the few remaining examples of a Renaissance residence in the city, possibly built to a design by Bramante; the terracotta decoration on the façade is typically Lombard. Across the street at No.11 is the **Seminario Arcivescovile** (seminary of the archdiocese), commissioned by Carlo Borromeo (*see p33*) in 1565, to implement the Council of Trent's regulations concerning the education of the clergy. The door, designed by Francesco Maria Richini, was added in 1652. The neo-classical **Palazzo Serbelloni** at the intersection with via San Damiano was constructed in 1793; it hosted Napoleon in 1796,

The **piazza San Babila**. *See p79.*

Liberty

The art nouveau ideas of the last years of the 19th century took a while to trickle down to Italy, caught up as this recently united nation was in providing itself with the pompous eclectic trappings that its new Torinese rulers felt essential to its dignity. The Milanese, however, were the Italians first to latch on and nowhere is their love affair with what was renamed *stile Liberty* (or *stile floreale*) more evident than in the network of streets (*vie Cappuccini-Barozzi-Vivaio-Mozart*) around piazza Duse (map p309 C2).

A short distance (north-east) from the quintessentially eclectic **Civico Museo di Storia Naturale** (*see p82*) on corso Venezia, a covered passageway leads (right) to via Salvini and piazza Duse. The architect Giulio Ulisse Arata is the genius behind three different *palazzi* built for the **Berri Meregalli** family in the area. One at via Barozzi 1 (1910) is decorated with animal heads that brighten up the solid structure. It's on the corner of via Mozart, and butts up against the other at via Mozart 21, with the same colour stone and animal-theme rams' heads, plus floral capitals and grotesque masks to hide the gutters; two nudes frescoed around the central balcony on the first floor heighten the grandiose tone of the architectural ornamentation. The third, at via Cappuccini 8

(1911-14), is a curious mix of just about every artistic style imaginable, from Gothic to Renaissance to Liberty. (Note the gloriously jungly garden nearby with its curious mix of birds, including a flock of flamingos.)

The **Palazzo Fidia** (via Melegari 2) is an even stranger combination of Liberty, *novecento*, Constructivist and Futurist styles by Aldo Andreani. **Casa Tensi** (1907; via Vivaio 4) by Ernesto Pirovano has round balconies, bow windows and ornate wrought-ironwork by Alessandro Mazzucotelli. Pirovano also designed the **Istituto dei Ciechi** (school for the blind) at via Vivaio 7 in 1890-92.

The offices of the Provincia di Milano in the neo-Renaissance **Palazzo Isimbardi** are also in via Vivaio (No.1); there are free guided tours on the first and third Fridays of every month to see Giambattista Tiepolo's *Apotheosis of Doge Morosini* on the ceiling of the Sala della Giunta (information and reservations at the APT, *see p290*).

Beyond traffic-packed Porta Venezia (*see p83*) lies another little Liberty enclave. Across piazza Oberdan in via Malpighi are two gems of art nouveau architecture by Giovanni Battista Bossi, the **Casa Galimberti** (1905; No.3) and the **Casa Guazzoni** (1903-06; No.12), with their colourful, exuberantly decorated façades.

Metternich in 1838, and King Vittorio Emanuele II and Napoleon III in 1859. It is now home to the journalists' club, the Circolo della Stampa. Check the newspapers for presentations of books or cultural debates, which are often held in the mirror-studded Salone dei Specchi. **Palazzo Rocca Saporiti** (No.40; 1812) was built to a plan by stage-designer Giovanni Perego in 1812; its imposing Ionic columns and cornice surmounted by statues of gods make it a perfect example of neo-Palladian architectural canons. The façade is decorated with a frieze with scenes from the history of Milan and was equipped with a loggia on the first floor so that its residents could watch parades from it. At No.47, the **Palazzo Castiglioni**, with its imaginative bronze and wrought-iron decoration in the art nouveau style, was built in 1904 by Giuseppe Sommaruga; the façade once contained sculptural decoration with statues of female nudes, which earned it the nickname *Ca' di Ciapp*, or Bun House. (For more art nouveau extravaganzas in the area, *see p81* **Liberty**.)

Corso Venezia ends in **piazza Oberdan**, where deafening, lung-challenging traffic screams around **Porta Venezia**. It's difficult

All around the garden: Giardini Pubblici & Villa Reale

Milan's oldest public park, the Giardini Pubblici covers a surface area of about 160,000 square metres. Designed in the 'English' style by Giuseppe Piermarini in 1786, the *giardini* were enlarged in 1857 to absorb the **Villa Reale** and the **Parco Dugnani**. The park's present arrangement – complete with 'natural' elements such as waterfalls and rocky outcrops – was the work of Emilio Alemagna for the international Expo of 1871.

Within the park is a host of sights. On the western via Manin side, the Palazzo Dugnani houses the **Museo del Cinema**. Further south-east, across via Palestra, are the **Padiglione d'Arte Contemporanea** (PAC) gallery (*see p158*) and the **Villa Reale**, with its modern art collection. North-east towards corso Venezia are the **Civico Museo di Storia Naturale** (Natural History Museum) and the **Planetario Ulrico Hoepli**. Deep in the heart of the *giardini*, the **Bar Bianco** (02 2952 3354, open 8am-7pm daily), with its outdoor tables, is a pleasant place for a coffee break, even though it lacks the elegance of the ex-Padiglione del Caffè (1863), now a nursery school. For transport to all sights, *see below*, **Giardini Pubblici**.

Giardini Pubblici

Metro Porta Venezia, Palestro, Repubblica or Turati/bus 94/tram 1, 9, 11, 29, 30. **Open** 6.30am-sunset daily. **Map** p309 C1.

Civico Museo di Storia Naturale (Natural History Museum)

Corso Venezia 55 (02 8846 3280/guided tours 02 783 528). **Open** 9am-6pm Tue-Fri; 9am-6.30pm Sat, Sun. **Admission** free.

Giovanni Ceruti's neo-classical building was put up in 1838 to house collections left to the city by aristocratic collector Giuseppe de Cristoforis. The museum's collections cover palaeontology, botany, mineralogy, geology and zoology. The rooms dedicated to palaeontology have life-size reconstructions of a triceratops and allosaurus. The old-fashioned dioramas are a real treat.

Museo del Cinema – Palazzo Dugnani

Via Manin 2 (02 655 4977). **Open** 3-6pm Fri-Sun. **Admission** €2.58. **No credit cards**.

Palazzo Dugnani was constructed at the end of the 17th century and remodelled in the 18th. In 1846 it became city property, its large estate incorporated into the Giardini Pubblici. A monumental staircase sweeps up to the great hall where there's a musicians' gallery, plus frescos (1731) by Giambattista Tiepolo: the Allegory of the Dugnani Family and Episodes from the Lives of Scipione and Massinissa. A Mafia bomb that exploded in nearby via Palestro in 1993 compounded damage from World War II bombardments and the private apartments usually open to the public were closed for restoration as this guide went to press. That part of the palazzo housing the cinema museum remains open, however: experiments in moving picture making from the 18th century, the Lumière brothers' efforts, and cameras with sound recording devices are all explained here. All your favourite stars feature in the collection of movie posters from 1905 to 1930. For information on film showings, *see p160*.

to imagine the area as sparsely inhabited and dotted with gardens, as described in *I promessi sposi*. When Renzo, that work's unfortunate hero, passed under here and into the thick of 17th-century bread riots, the gate was known as the Porta Orientale. One of the eight main entrances in the 16th-century Spanish fortifications, it was redesigned in the late 18th century when the city's Spanish walls were torn down to make way for tree-lined avenues. No longer defensive, the gate became a tollbooth. Giuseppe Piermarini's original neo-classical gate of 1787 was replaced in 1828 by the two

triumphal arches still standing today. Designed by Rodolfo Vantini, both elements have triple vantage points: toward the city, toward the country and toward the main thoroughfare viale Piave/bastioni di Porta Venezia.

San Babila
Piazza San Babila (02 760 02 877). Metro San Babila/bus 54, 61. **Open** 8am-noon, 3.30-6pm daily. **Map** p309 C1.
Standing out like a sore thumb in the midst of the post-war architecture and hectic traffic of piazza San Babila is the neo-Romanesque façade of the church that gives the square its name. The original fourth-

Planetario Ulrico Hoepli
Corso Venezia 57 (02 2953 1181/www.brera. mi.astro.it/~planet/). **Shows** 9pm Tue, Thur; 3pm, 4.30pm Sat, Sun. **Admission** €2.07. **No credit cards**.
Donated to the city by the publisher Ulrich Hoepli, the building was constructed in 1930 by Pietro Portaluppi in a faux-classical style. Projections take place in a great domed room, renovated in 1955.

Villa Reale & Galleria d'Arte Moderna
Via Palestro 16 (02 760 02 819). **Open** 9am-5.30pm Tue-Sun. **Admission** free.
The neo-classical Villa Reale was built by Leopold Pollack in 1790 for Count Ludovico Barbiano di Belgioioso. Napoleon lived there in 1802, and after him Marshall Radetzky (*see p17*). After the unification of Italy, ownership passed to the Italian royal family, who gave the palazzo to the city of Milan in 1921. Many Milanese have spoken their marriage vows under Andrea Appiani's frescos of Parnassus in the central hall.

The Galleria d'Arte Moderna occupies part of the central body and the first and second floors of the west wing of this U-shaped building, and is spread over 35 rooms (many closed for restoration as this guide went to press). The collections represent various currents in Italian painting in the 19th century from Francesco Hayez's historical Romanticism to 'Scapigliatura' and Divisionism. The main part of the surprisingly rich collections is in the west wing, accessed by a rather inconspicuous entrance staircase in a sad state of disrepair. Museum organisation is no better: there is neither museum plan, nor published guide. From the landing at the top of the stairs, the painting itinerary winds through a series of

rooms on the right; another of the collections, the Museo Marino Marini, is in the rooms on the left. It was opened in 1973 when the artist donated his own paintings and sculpture, including portraits of Arp, De Pisis, Carrà, Chagall and Stravinsky. Dominating the first room on the right as you start to make your way through the painting collection is Giuseppe Pelizza da Volpedo's *Quarto Stato* (1901), a monumental work of solidarity with the suffering poorer classes. The villa is also host to the Grassi (second floor, west wing) and Vismara (ground floor central core, accessible only when ceremonies are not being held) collections, with works by modern Italian and international masters including Van Gogh, Gauguin, Cézanne, Matisse, Picasso and Morandi.

century basilica was rebuilt in the 11th century, and further modified in the 16th century, only to have its Romanesque façade cack-handedly 'restored' in 1906 by Paolo Cesa Bianchi, who also did the main altar.

San Carlo al Corso
Corso Vittorio Emanuele II 14 (02 773 302). Metro San Babila or Duomo. **Open** 7.15am-12.15pm, 4-8pm Mon-Sat; 9am-1pm, 4-10pm Sun. **Map** p311 A1.
This neo-classical building was begun in 1839 and completed in 1847. The church is essentially a cylinder covered with a dome, recalling pantheons in Rome and Paris.

South of corso Monforte

Via del Conservatorio connects busy corso Monforte – with its city government offices and exclusive shops – to the Porta Vittoria zone and its law courts (*see p85*). Just past the political science department of the **Università di Milano,** which is located in the much-tampered-with late baroque Palazzo Resta-Pallavicino at No.7, is a little piazza with its south-east corner enclosed by **Santa Maria della Passione** and the **Conservatorio** (Conservatory).

Directly opposite the church is via della Passione, opened in 1540 to create a panoramic view of Santa Maria della Passione and to allow access from the church to the *navigli* (canals) that were once there.

On the corner of via della Passione and via Conservatorio is the neo-classical **Palazzo Archinto,** built from 1833-to 1847 by Gaetano Besia. It is still home to the Collegio delle Fanciulle (girls' school), an institution dating from Napoleonic times (1808). The art nouveau Liberty style (*see p81* **Liberty**) is not lacking here either: note in particular the **Casa Campanini** (via Bellini 11), from 1904. Via Conservatorio leads to via Corridoni and the church of **San Pietro in Gessate**.

Conservatorio Giuseppe Verdi
Via Conservatorio 12 (02 762 1101). Bus 54, 61, 77. **Open** for concerts only (*see p175*). Museum closed indefinitely for restoration. **Map** p311 A1/2.
The French dissolved religious orders when they ruled Milan in the early 19th century (*see p16*), freeing up prime real estate for ventures such as the Conservatory, which was founded in 1808 in what had previously been the Lateran convent. The prestigious institute still plays a fundamental role in Italian musical life. Many key figures in the history of Italian music studied in this institution; the young Giuseppe Verdi, however, was rejected. There are two concert halls, one for chamber music and one for symphonic and choral music. The library houses over 35,000 volumes and 460,000 musical works, including manuscripts by Mozart, Donizetti, Bellini and Verdi. There is also a little

museum (closed at the time of writing for restoration) with rare string instruments.

Santa Maria della Passione
Via Bellini 2 (02 7602 1370). Bus 54, 61, 77, 94. **Open** *Church* 7am-noon, 3.30-6.15pm daily. *Museum* closed for restoration as this guide went to press. **Map** p309 C2.
Construction of the church began in 1486 to a design by Giovanni Battagio. It was originally a Greek-cross church; one arm was lengthened to form a nave and six semicircular side chapels were added in 1573, making it the second-largest in Milan after the Duomo (*see p57*). The façade and the adjacent monastery – now the seat of the Conservatory (*see above*) – were added in 1692 by Giuseppe Rusnati, who kept the building low so as not to distract attention from the massive octagonal lantern of the dome (Cristoforo Lombardo, 1530).

The barrel vault of the church abounds with frescos of the Evangelists, St Ambrose, St Augustine, angels and allegories of the virtues by Giuseppe Galbesio da Brescia (1583); more intriguing are the paintings lower down in the church's three-aisled interior, a veritable picture gallery of works by many of the leading 16th- and 17th-century Lombard artists. On the pilasters of the nave are 14 canvases of saints of the Lateran order by Daniele Crespi. In the right-hand side chapels are Giulio Cesare Procaccini's *Scourging of Christ* (third chapel), and *Madonna di Caravaggio*, attributed to Bramantino (sixth chapel). The 16th-century wooden choir stalls are inlaid with mother of pearl. In the niches of the choir are two fabulous organs with 16th- and 17th-century carvings, both of which are still used for concerts; the shutters were painted by Crespi with scenes from the Passion. The church also has a little museum with access from the choir niche with the organ on the right. It contains even more paintings by Lombard schools from the 15th to the 17th centuries, along with 17th-century church furniture.

San Pietro in Gessate
Piazza San Pietro in Gessate/corso di Porta Vittoria (no phone). Bus 37, 60, 77, 84/tram 12, 23, 27. **Open** 8.30am-noon, 2-6pm daily. **Map** p311 A1.
The Florentine banker Pigello Portinari paid for San Pietro, built between 1447 and 1475 to a design by Pietro Antonio and Guiniforte Solari. Although heavily damaged during World War II, large parts of the pictorial decoration are still in place. The usual Lombards are here: Antonio Campi, Bergognone, Giovanni Donato Montorfano, Bernardino Butinone and Bernardino Zenale. The frescos were rediscovered under a layer of plaster in 1862: even works of art were subject to the mass paranoia caused by the fear of plague during the 16th and 17th centuries, and covered with fresh lime-based plaster in an attempt at disinfecting. The eight-stall choir is a reconstruction based on what was left of the one built in 1640 by Carlo Garavaglia: the original was used as firewood during World War II.

Porta Romana, the Navigli & Southern Milan

Martyrs, canals and shopping and nightlife meccas.

Until the 1930s, the area between piazza Santo Stefano (where fishmongers plied their trade) and today's irregularly shaped, traffic-congested Verziere was Milan's vast open-air food market; this was also the haunt of Carlo Porta, the city's great satirical dialect poet, immortalised in a monument in piazza Santo Stefano. Today the area's cheap eateries and bookstores serve the denizens of the Università degli Studi di Milano.

South from the university, corso di Porta Romana preserves something of an old-Milan flavour, with its muddle of little shops where purveyors of orthopaedic shoes sit cosily alongside gourmet food halls.

Until the advent of Napoleon and his anti-clerical policies at the beginning of the 19th century, the swathe of undeveloped territory to the west of corso di Porta Romana was awash with religious foundations. But with the suppression of orders and their monasteries, it fell prey to property developers. Corso di Porta Ticinese slices through a neighbourhood of early 20th-century working class *case di ringhiera*, so named for the railings (*ringhiere*) along the narrow balconies suspended on each floor around central courtyards. Many of these buildings have been converted into charming apartments or loft-type studios (peek into courtyards at No.64 or No.65). The *corso* is a fashion shopping and nightlife mecca (*see p142* **Corso di Porta Ticinese**); its boutiques, bars and nightclubs spill over into piazza XXIV Maggio, corso San Gottardo and into the watery, hopping Navigli district of canals (*see p92* **The Navigli**).

From the University to Porta Romana

Facing each other across piazza Santo Stefano are the churches of **San Bernardino** and **Santo Stefano**. East of the piazza, at corso di Porta Vittoria 6, **Palazzo Sormani** is a 17th-century building transformed in 1736 into one of the most splendid residences of the century, with a curving *barocchetto* façade. Restored after heavy damage in World War II,

it became the city library (*see p284*). A block further east stands the **Palazzo di Giustizia**, the hub of the *Mani puliti* investigations that rocked Italy's political and financial sectors in the 1990s (*see p22*). The law courts were built between 1932 and 1940 by Marcello Piacentini to take the place of the old Palazzo dei Tribunali in piazza Beccaria. The 65 courtrooms and 1,200 other rooms in this 300,000-square-metre (3,226,000-square-foot) space are decorated with mosaics by 20th-century artists including Mario Sironi.

Heading back towards corso di Porta Romana, the little **Giardino della Guastalla** is one of Milan's oldest public parks, and a refreshing place for a break.

Across via Francesco Sforza, the massive **Ca' Grande** – once a major hospital – is now the headquarters of the arts faculties of the **Università degli Studi di Milano**. The church of **San Nazaro Maggiore** at the corso

Top-heavy **Torre Velasca**. *See p86.*

di Porta Romana end of the Ca' Grande was a result of St Ambrose's fourth-century church-building programme.

Towering above them to the north, the unmissable **Torre Velasca** is the symbol and manifesto of post-war Milanese architecture. Designed by Studio BBPR and inaugurated in 1958, the colours and cantilevered upper section of the 26-floor tower are considered modern interpretations of medieval forms... though its shape depended to a large extent on the need to distribute a volume that was greater than the ground space available.

Further south off corso di Porta Romana, **San Calimero** is one of Milan's oldest churches. At the southern end of corso di Porta Romana in piazza Medaglia d'Oro stands the **Porta Romana** (Roman gate) itself, so-called not because it was built by the ancients (that one was nearer to present-day piazza Missori) but because it was where the road to Rome ended or started, depending on your point of view. The gate was constructed in 1598 to commemorate Austrian Archduchess Maria Margherita's stop in Milan on her way to Madrid to marry King Philip III of Spain. Dominating the south end of the square along via Sabotino and the beginning of via Filipetti

is the only remaining chunk of the Spanish walls built by Ferrante Gonzaga in 1545. Once among the most famous in Europe, the walls encircled the city for more than 11 kilometres (seven miles). They were torn down in 1889. The ancient portico-lined corso di Porta Romana was one of two main Roman streets, running from what is now via Paolo da Cannobbio to a triumphal arch further down the road at what is now the Crocetta.

Ca' Grande (Università degli Studi di Milano)

Via Festa del Perdono 5 (02 58 351). Metro Duomo or Missori/tram 12, 23, 27/bus 54, 60, 65. **Open** *7.30am-7.30pm Mon-Fri; 8am-11.30pm Sat.* **Map** *p311 A1.*

Now home to the arts departments of Milan university, Ca' Grande began its life as a hospital and hospice. It was Francesco Sforza who set out to consolidate Milan's 30 hospitals into one 'Casa Grande' or Ospedale Maggiore (Great Hospital) in 1456. His pet architect, Il Filarete, incorporated the idea into his plan for the grandiose transformation of Milan into an ideal Renaissance city. The building has a wing each for men and women – each subdivided into four inner courts – separated by the Cortile Maggiore (Great Court). Work continued on the project after Filarete's death (c1469), but ground

No longer reserved for chariots: 21st-century traffic on **largo Carrobbio**. *See p89.*

to a halt with the fall of Ludovico 'il Moro' (*see chapter* **History**), only to pick up from time to time through the 17th and 18th centuries. In 1939 the hospital was moved to its new headquarters at Niguarda in the northern suburbs. The university moved in the 1950s.

The façade, with its typically Lombard terracotta decoration, is one of the city's few to have been completed in the 15th century. The 15th-century courtyards were used for the women's baths and storing wood. The Cortile Maggiore, with its Renaissance portico and baroque loggia, is decorated with busts in the yellow-rose-grey stone from Angera on Lago Maggiore. The *cortile* was reconstructed after heavy damage during the war. The neo-classical Macchio wing – now home to university offices – once contained an art gallery. There's a canvas by Guercino (1639) in the 17th-century church of the **Annunciata** (02 583 074 65; open 7.30am-1.30pm Mon-Fri during university term) inside the courtyard.

San Bernardino alle Ossa

Piazza Santo Stefano (02 7602 3735). Metro Duomo or Missori/tram 12, 23, 27/bus 54, 60, 65. **Open** 7.30am-noon, 2.30-6pm Mon-Fri; 7.30am-noon Sat, Sun. **Map** p311 A1.

San Bernardino alle Ossa's ossuary chapel is decorated in macabre fashion with pictures and patterns picked out in human bones brought here from cemeteries suppressed in the 17th century. However, the gloom of the interior is enlivened by the bright colours of the illusionistic vault painted by Sebastiano Ricci (1659-1734), *Triumph of the Soul among the Angels*.

San Calimero

Via San Calimero 9 (02 5831 4028). Metro Crocetta/ tram 24/bus 94. **Open** 8.30am-noon, 4-6pm daily. **Map** p311 B1.

Of very ancient origins (perhaps contemporary with the four Ambrosian basilicas), the sacellum containing the body of San Calimero was restored by Bishop Lorenzo between 490 and 512. It was later redone in Romanesque form in the 12th century, and then again – both façade and interior – in 1609 by Francesco Maria Richini. Disastrous restoration work by Angelo Colla in 1882 wiped out any traces of earlier architecture. The terracotta façade, with its porch resting on two stately lion bases, dates from this last job.

San Nazaro Maggiore

Piazza San Nazaro (02 5830 7719). Metro Missori/ tram 4, 12, 15, 24, 27/bus 65, 94. **Open** 7.30am-noon, 3-6.30pm daily. **Map** p311 B1.

Situated on what was the ancient colonnaded corso di Porta Romana, San Nazaro was one of the four basilicas built during St Ambrose's evangelisation drive, between 382 and 386. Constructed to accommodate relics of the apostles Andrew, John and Thomas, and the first in the western world to be designed in the form of a cross, it was given

San Nazaro, outside the basilica.

the name Basilica Apostolorum. When Ambrose brought the remains of local martyr St Nazarus (died 396) here, the church was rededicated: you can see the saintly remains in the two altars of the choir, but the silver vessel holding them is a copy: the one St Ambrose commissioned is in the Duomo treasury (*see p57*). When it was built, the basilica stood outside the city walls in a Christian burial area, hence the sarcophagi behind the church. The church was destroyed by fire in 1075, but rebuilt using material from the original structure, including the pilasters holding up the central dome. The *basilichetta* of San Lino to the right of the altar dates from the tenth century. The octagonal Cappella Trivulzio, designed by Bramantino, was added to the church in 1512 as a mausoleum for the powerful Trivulzio family. Reworked in the late 16th century and given a neo-classical interior in the 1830s, the basilica suffered considerable damage during World War II and was stripped of many of its post-fourth-century trappings to restore a sense of its early Christian austerity between 1946 and 1963.

Santo Stefano Maggiore

Piazza Santo Stefano (Archivio storico 02 7600 6222). Metro Duomo or Missori/tram 12, 23, 27/bus 54, 60, 65. **Open** *Archivio storico* 9.15am-12.15pm Mon-Fri. Church closed. **Map** p311 A1.

Sant'Eustorgio. *See p91.*

Santo Stefano was originally built in the fifth century, but what you see today is a 1584 reconstruction with a baroque belltower added between 1643 and 1674 by Carlo Buzzi. The fragmentary pilaster just in front of the façade on the right is the only remnant of the medieval atrium where Galeazzo Maria Sforza (*see p15*) was assassinated on 26 December 1476. As this guide went to press, the church held the diocesan archives – a fascinating collection of ancient manuscripts – open to the public but in the process of moving to nearby via San Calimero near the church of the same name (*see p87*). Plans were afoot to reopen the church to the public in late 2002.

From via Torino to the Porta Ticinese

The great commercial artery of via Torino sweeps from the Duomo (*see p57*) to largo Carrobbio. The names of the narrow alleys on either side of via Torino – via Spadari (spear makers), via Cappellari (hatters) – are a reminder of the old artisan and merchant *contrade* (districts) that once occupied the area. Halfway along the street, **San Giorgio al Palazzo** was built in or near the Palatium, residence of the Roman emperor.

South off via Torino, via Soncino leads to the **Palazzo Stampa**. When the last Sforza (*see chapter* **History**) died in 1535, Massimiliano Stampa traded his city's independence for land and privileges for himself by raising the banner of Holy Roman Emperor Charles V over the Castello Sforzesco (*see p70*). The imperial eagle above a bronze globe, representing the dominion of Charles V, can still be seen on the tower of the palazzo.

Largo Carrobbio's name derives either from *quadrivium* (place where four roads meet), or *carrubium* (road reserved for chariots). The remains of the **Roman Porta Ticinese** (leading to the road to Ticinum, Roman Pavia) that once stood here can be seen on the corners of via Medici and via del Torchio. Bustling corsa di Porta Ticinese shoots south out of largo Carrobbio, passing by the church of **San Lorenzo**, with its 16 towering Roman columns, and the remains of the 12th-century Ticinese gate. At that time, a moat ran along the new walls along what is today's via Molino delle Armi (Weapons Mill), so called because of the waterwheels that powered the forges where arms were made. The *porta* was reworked after 1329, when it was decorated with a tabernacle showing St Ambrose giving a model of the city to the Madonna and Child by Giovanni di Balduccio. The two towers were restored in 1865.

Via E De Amicis leads west from here past the site of the Roman **amphitheatre** (at No.19, (scheduled to open in spring 2002 for visits by

appointment only; information 02 867 336, www.scaweb.net). Nearby, the little church of **San Vicenzo in Prato** stands in what was a pre-Christian necropolis.

A detour to the east of San Lorenzo along via Molino delle Armi and corso Italia leads to piazza Vetra, a name that probably derives from *castra vetera* (old barracks), an allusion to the fact that Roman soldiers defending the imperial palace camped here. In Roman days there was a port here, where the Seveso and Nirone rivers emptied into the navigable Vettabbia canal. (An alternative etymology claims that the piazza was named for the tanners – *vetraschi* – who had their shops along this canal.) Until 1840, lower-class ne'er-do-wells were hung here; nobles were decapitated at the Broletto (*see p64*). Cut through the pretty Parco delle Basiliche – from which there's a lovely view of the churches of Sant'Eustorgio and San Lorenzo from the back – to the church of **Santa Maria dei Miracoli**, also known as Santa Maria presso San Celso. Cutting back westwards, **Sant'Eustorgio** stands on the spot where the first Milanese Christians are reputed to have been baptised by the apostle Barnabus.

The *corso* ends in piazza XXIV Maggio, where the most recent **Porta Ticinese** – a neo-classical work by Luigi Cagnola (1801-14) – now stands.

The Darsena's **open-air market**. *See p90*.

Just west of the gate is the **Darsena**, confluence of the two **Navigli** (*see p92* **The Navigli**), artificial canals that connect Milan with the Ticino and Po rivers. Every Saturday, *milanesi* come here in droves to make the most of the great bargains, luscious foods and fresh produce at Milan's biggest open-air market.

Just past the church of **San Gottardo al Corso** (corso San Gottardo 6, 02 8940 4432, open 7am-noon, 4-7pm daily), with ornate 19th-century trappings that hide its third- and 16th-century past, the street widens into largo Gustav Mahler. Here stands the **Auditorium di Milano** (*see p173*), Milan's new temple of music, unveiled in 1999. Further on, approaching the outer ring roads, buildings become sparser and the landscape evolves into an indiscriminate mix of anonymous high-rise residential blocks, new housing developments and the occasional *cascina* (farmhouse), set against the vast backdrop of the Lombard plains.

Museo Diocesano

Corso di Porta Ticinese 95 (02 8940 4714/ bookings 02 8942 0019/www.museodiocesano.it). Tram 3, 9, 15, 20, 29, 30/bus 94. **Open** 10am-6pm Tue, Wed, Fri-Sun; 10am-10pm Thur. **Admission** €6; *see also p55.* **No credit cards. Map** p310 A/B2.

The Museo Diocesano – back in business after three years of renovations – contains religious art treasures culled from churches and private collections throughout Lombardy... and what a treasure trove it is. The new museum is a streamlined operation distributed over three floors of the former Dominican convent of Sant'Eustorgio. A slick entrance leads into a great hall; from here, the rooms are not numbered, but pamphlets with colour-coded ground plans abound, as do explanatory placards and computer points (in Italian).

On the ground floor are select pieces from St Ambrose's time (colour-coded ochre on the plan), followed by the first part of an itinerary (blue-green) with works from the 14th to 19th centuries, a multi-media room, and a collection of 17th- and 18th-century Italian paintings. Liturgical furniture (reliquaries, crucifixes, chalices and the like) is housed in the basement.

The first floor contains a space for temporary exhibitions as well as the bulk of the collections. The (blue-green) itinerary that began downstairs – which includes some works from the closed museum at Santa Maria della Passione, *see p84* – ends here with the latter end of the chronological timetable. This floor also houses the collections of several cardinals: Federico Visconti's (1617-1693) is contained in one small room, with copies of famous drawings, including portraits of Raphael and Titian by an anonymous Lombard painter of the 17th century;

San Lorenzo Maggiore and some of its columns. *See p91.*

Giuseppe Pozzobonelli's (1696-1783) has 17th century Italian landscapes; Cesare Monti's (1593-1650) has Lombard and Venetian works of the 16th and 17th centuries (don't miss Tintoretto's *Christ and the Adultress*, 1545-7). There is also a collection of 14th- and 15th-century altarpiece paintings with gold backgrounds, accompanied by an explanatory video – in Italian – on the gold-leafing process.

San Giorgio al Palazzo

Piazza San Giorgio 2 (02 860 831). Tram 2, 3, 14, 20. **Open** 9-11.30am, 3.30-6.30pm Mon-Fri; 9am-noon, 3.30-6.30pm Sat, Sun. **Map** p310 A2.
Founded in 750, San Giorgio was rebuilt in 1129 and heavily reworked in the 17th and early 19th centuries. Look hard amid the neo-classical trappings and you'll see a baptismal font fashioned out of a Romanesque capital and a couple of pilasters at the far end of the central nave from the original church. In the third chapel on the right don't miss the striking cycle of *Scenes from the Passion of Christ* by Bernardino Luini (1516).

San Lorenzo Maggiore (San Lorenzo alle Colonne)

Corso di Porta Ticinese 39 (02 8940 4129). Tram 3/ bus 94. **Open** *Church* 7.30am-6.30pm daily. *Cappella di Sant'Aquilino* 7.30am-6pm daily. **Admission** €2; *see also p55.* **No credit cards. Map** p310 A/B2.
Built at the end of the fourth century, San Lorenzo may have been the chapel of the imperial Roman palace. It is certainly one of the oldest centrally planned churches anywhere. Fires all but destroyed the church in the 11th and 12th centuries, but it was rebuilt to the original Roman model. When the cupola collapsed in 1573, the new dome – the tallest in Milan and a far cry from the original — brought cries of outrage from the local populace. Some traces of the original portals can be seen in the façade, which was heavily reworked in 1894.

On the backs of the two great arches that flank the main altar, columns were placed upside-down to symbolise the Christian religion rising up from the ruins of paganism. To the right, the octagonal Cappella di Sant'Aquilino may have been an imperial mausoleum. On its walls are fragments of the late fourth-century mosaics that once covered the entire chapel. Behind the altar, a passage leads under the church, where stones from pre-existing Roman structures used in the construction of San Lorenzo can be seen. There's a Byzantine sarcophagus down there too.

Outside the church stand 16 Corinthian columns from the second and third centuries. Where they came from is uncertain; they were, however, moved here from some unidentified temple in the fourth century, and topped with pieces of architrave, only some of which really belong. The 17th-century wings flanking the entrance to San Lorenzo were designed to link the columns to the church in a sort of pseudo-ancient atrium. In the centre, a bronze statue of the Emperor Constantine is a copy of one in Rome; it is a reminder that Constantine's Edict of Milan (313) put an end to the persecution of Christians.

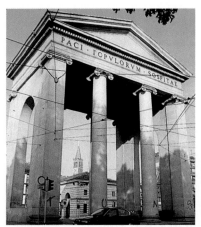

Porta Ticinese on pza XXIV Maggio. *See p89.*

Sant'Eustorgio

Piazza Sant'Eustorgio 1 (02 5810 1583/Cappella Portinari 02 8940 2671). Tram 3, 9, 15, 29, 30/ bus 59. **Open** *Church* 7.45am-noon, 3.30-6.30pm daily. *Cappella Portinari* 10am-6pm Tue-Sun. **Admission** *Church* free. *Capella Portinari* €6; *see also p55.* **No credit cards. Map** p310 B2.
The origins of this church are shrouded in legend – a favourite one is that Sant'Eustorgio, when still a bishop in the fourth century, had the place built to house relics of the Three Kings; the site was chosen when animals pulling the relic-laden cart reached this spot and refused to budge. That the relics were here was supposedly proved by the fact that Barbarossa (*see p11*) absconded with them in 1164; they were returned in 1903 and are venerated each Epiphany (6 January). The ceremony is timed to take place at the end of a mass with the arrival of a procession from piazza del Duomo; the procession is led by the Three Kings themselves, in costume.

Whatever its origins, the building has traces of seventh-century work, was rebuilt by the Dominican order in 1190 after being razed by Barbarossa, was restored and revamped on several occasions up to the 15th century, and had a new façade stuck on in faux-Romanesque style in 1865. (The little pulpit on the façade is a 16th-century substitution of the original wooden one where Dominican Inquisitor St Peter Martyr preached). Sant'Eustorgio was the first of Milan's churches to have a clock put in its belltower, in 1306.

Inside, the church is a treasure trove of works by Milanese and Lombard artists from the 13th to the 15th centuries: Giovannino di Grassi, Giovanni da Milano, Giovanni di Balduccio (see his Gothic funeral monument to Stefano Visconti, 1327, in the fourth chapel on the right), Bernardino Luini and the *maestri campionesi* all feature.

The main attraction, however, is the Cappella Portinari, built between 1462 and 1466 by Florentine banker Pigello Portinari for his own tomb as well as for a repository for the body of St Peter Martyr, murdered by heretics who had sunk a knife into his skull 200 years earlier. Perhaps the earliest truly Renaissance work in the city, the chapel unites the classical forms championed by Brunelleschi in Tuscany with typical Lombard fresco decoration by Vincenzo Foppa. Foppa's scenes from the life of the Virgin and St Peter Martyr's miracles (1466-8) is perhaps the painter's greatest masterpiece. In the centre of the chapel, the arc of St Peter Martyr, containing most of the saint's remains, is by Giovanni di Balduccio (1336-9). The rest of him – his skull – is in a silver urn in the little chapel to the left of the sacellum. The former monastery is now home to the Museo Diocesano (see p90).

Santa Maria dei Miracoli & San Celso (Santa Maria presso San Celso)

Corso Italia 37 (02 5831 3187). Tram 15/bus 65, 94. **Open** *Santa Maria* 7am-noon, 4-6.30pm daily. *San Celso* for exhibitions only. **Map** p310 A/B2.
Two little chapels once stood on this site where, according to legend, St Ambrose came across the bodies of martyrs Nazaro and Celso. The chapel of San Nazaro fell down long ago. But so great was the flow of pilgrims to the remaining chapel of San Celso – where, in the 15th century, the Virgin was said to be working miracles galore – that in 1493 contruction began on something bigger: Santa Maria dei Miracoli. Preceded by a fine early 16th-century quadriportico, this church has a lively façade from the same era, animated by sculptures by Stoldo Lorenzi and Annibale Fontana. The interior was decorated by the usual cast of Lombard Renaissance, mannerist and baroque artists.
A separate entrance through a gate and across a garden will take you to what remains of San Celso. Founded in the ninth century and rebuilt in the 11th, this little Romanesque church is decorated with frescos from the 11th to 15th centuries. The basilica is now also a venue for art exhibitions, theatrical performances and concerts. Entrance is free, but opening times vary.

San Vincenzo in Prato

Via Daniele Crespi 6 (02 835 7603). Tram 2, 14/ bus 94. **Open** 7.45-11.45am, 4.30-7pm daily. **Map** p310 B1.
Once an expanse of *prati* (fields), the area around this little church was used as a pagan, then a Christian, necropolis. Benedictine monks occupied the adjacent monastery in the ninth century and remained there until 1520; it's uncertain whether the present church dates from the ninth or 11th century. French occupiers turned it into a storehouse and then barracks in 1798. Later, it became a chemical factory, belching fumes that earned it the nickname the Magician's House. It was restored and reconsecrated in the 1880s.

The Navigli

Today Milan's watery Navigli (canal) zone begins at the Darsena (map p310 B2) between the *porte* Ticinese and Genova and extends through a limited area to the south and west that is dominated by boutiques, artists' studios, antique restorers, bookshops and the city's hottest nightspots (*see chapters* **Nightlife** and **Cafés & Bars**), plus a fair bit of picturesquely crumbling industrial plant. Until the 1930s, however, a dense network of waterways had covered much of the city, making landlocked Milan Italy's 13th-largest port by volume of trade. Then work began to fill in the historic canals. By 1979 not a single working boat broke the surface of what remained of the waters.

Excavations for the **Naviglio Grande** – which carries the waters of the diverted Ticino river from Lago Maggiore (*see* p187) to the Darsena – were begun in 1177. Canals for Bereguardo, the Martesana and Paderno followed, thus boosting Milan's already considerable commercial clout. Barges brought coal and salt (not to mention marble from Candoglia on Lago Maggiore used in the construction of the Duomo, *see p57*); they left laden with iron, grains, fabrics and other goods manufactured in the city. In the 15th century Leonardo da Vinci was called in by Ludovico 'Il Moro' Sforza to improve the system by creating a canal network within the city walls.

One major project got under way in 1359 when work began on the (still-extant) **Naviglio Pavese**. At first, the waterway was conceived merely to irrigate Gian Galeazzo Visconti's hunting reserve near Pavia. In 1597 a scheme to improve the canal was begun, but funds soon ran out, leaving what is still known as the *conca fallato* (failed sluice) in the southern suburbs. It wasn't, in fact, until the French applied themselves to the task that the canal was finished; after its inauguration in 1819, traffic soon outstripped that on the Naviglio Grande. In the late 19th century the area along the *navigli* Grande and Pavese was a thriving port; after World War II, building materials for the reconstruction of the badly bombed city were transported by waterway.

On the north bank of the Naviglio Grande, the little church of **San Cristoforoy** (open 7.30am-12pm, 4-7pm daily) is dedicated to the patron saint of boatmen. This is, in fact, two churches sandwiched together: the one on the left is the older of the two, and probably dates from the late 12th century. It was enlarged in 1398 when the adjacent Cappella Ducale was built by the relieved Milanese citizens at the end of a long famine; the portal and rose window on the older church was added at this time. The façade has traces of 15th-century fresco decoration. The belltower dates from the 15th century. Inside are frescos by 15th- and 16th- century Lombard painters.

On the eastern bank of the Naviglio Pavese, the **Chiesa Rossa** (not open to the public) was first mentioned in a document of 988 as an annexe of San Giorgio al Palazzo (see p91), under the name of Santa Maria di Fonteggio. In 1139 it was ceded to a nearby Benedictine monastery, then rebuilt over the next century. Restoration work in 1966 revealed the outer walls of a second-century church. Inside is the tomb of the nun Maria di Robacani (1333), who may have commissioned the faded frescos on the walls of the interior. Nearby in via Neera, the deconsecrated church of **Santa Maria Annunciata** holds the last work of American artist Dan Flavin (see p158).

The Associazione del Naviglio Grande, formed to protect the canal zone's cultural heritage, organises concerts, art exhibitions and antique markets. Check the website (www.navigliogrande.mi.it) for further details of upcoming events.

The Amici dei Navigli, an institution dedicated to research on the *navigli* environment, organises boat tours from the Darsena for a 20-kilometre (12.5-mile) round trip of the canals.

Amici dei Navigli tours

www.amicideinavigli.org. **Boat trips** *Apr-mid Sept* by appointment daily. **Rates** *Tours* 20.60; 10.30 concessions. *Boat hire* (4hrs) 387.30.
Tours of the Navigli and boat hire must be booked through Incoming Partners, see below.

Incoming Partners

Via Felice Casati 32, East (02 6702 0280/ www.incomingpartners.it). Metro Porta Venezia or Repubblica/tram 1, 2, 9, 11, 29, 30. **Open** 9.30am-1pm, 2-6.30pm Mon-Fri. **Credit** DC, MC, V. **Map** p309 B1/2.
Boat trips depart from the dock in piazza Cantore (map p310 B1) at the corner of viale G D'Annunzio.

Sightseeing

Sant'Ambrogio & Western Milan

Roman Milan, Christian Milan and of course, the *Last Supper*.

If you're passing through Milan quickly, chances are that, after your stopover at the Duomo (*see p57*), you'll head west – down via Meravigli and corso Magenta – into this area of imposing *palazzi*, antique shops, rare book dealers, stylish window displays and quiet, leafy residential streets, to reach the other best-known sight in this under-explored city: Leonardo da Vinci's *Last Supper*. But there is much more in this section of the city: the fourth-century basilica of Sant'Ambrogio – another emblem of the city and one of the world's finest examples of the Romanesque; a museum

that pays homage to science, technology and the great mind of Leonardo-as-inventor; and some captivating glances of what remains of Milan's ancient past.

Around Sant'Ambrogio

Milan's pivotal basilica of **Sant'Ambrogio** was built outside the Roman city walls, in an area of early Christian cemeteries and imperial buildings. Nine Italian kings were crowned in the church between the ninth and the 15th centuries, and four of them are buried here.

Milan's most-visited sight: Leonardo's **Last Supper**. See p98.

To maintain this tradition, Napoleon (1805) and Ferdinand of Austria (1838) came here after their coronations in the Duomo. Nowadays, the area around Sant'Ambrogio is crowded with students of the **Università Cattolica**, once a monastic complex.

By the basilica, the **Pusterla di Sant'Ambrogio** is a 1939 imitation of the medieval gate that once stood here. Some older materials, including a 14th-century relief by *maestri campionesi* showing saints Ambrose, Gervasius and Protasius, have been incorporated into the structure.

To the south, in via De Amicis, the crypt of **Santa Maria della Vittoria** contains artefacts from recent archeological digs around Lombardy. Beyond the Pusterla, the **Museo Nazionale della Scienza e della Tecnologia** is a magician's cave of technological wonders from all ages.

Next door, the church of **San Vittore al Corpo** stands on via degli Olivetani, where the prison of San Vittore – the temporary home to many of the businessmen and politicians caught up in the *Mani Puliti* corruption investigations of the 1990s (*see p22*) – looms threateningly.

Museo Nazionale della Scienza e della Tecnologia 'Leonardo da Vinci'

Via San Vittore 21 (02 485 551/www.museoscienza. org). Metro Sant'Ambrogio/bus 50, 54, 58, 94. **Open** 9am-4.50pm Tue-Fri; 9.30am-6.20pm Sat, Sun. **Admission** €6.20. **No credit cards. Map** p310 A1.

Milan pays homage to science and technology in the former convent of San Vittore, founded in the 11th century and rebuilt in the 16th. When the French suppressed religious orders in the early 19th century, the palazzo became a military hospital and then a barracks. Heavily damaged during World War II, it was restored and given over to its present role in 1947. The palazzo is built around two courtyards, where a section of the foundations of the Roman fort of San Vittore and the octagonal imperial mausoleum of Valentinian II are visible.

Few technical skills do not have a section devoted to them in this all-encompassing, labyrinthine museum, with displays dedicated to printing, metallurgy, bell-casting, minting, engines, watch making and timekeeping, as well as the sciences of physics, optics, acoustics and astronomy. An exhaustive computing section shows the evolution of calculating techniques from Pascal's abacus of 1642 to the first IBM processor.

There are areas devoted to the typewriter, cinema and photography, the history of the television and telephone, locomotion and aeronautics (in the via Olona pavilion). In the long first-floor Galleria di Leonardo da Vinci are faithful reproductions of the Renaissance genius's scientific, archaeological and

technical doodlings, including flying machines and impregnable city defences.

On the mezzanine, the Civico Museo Navale Didattico has a vast collection of model boats and ships from all over the world. As this guide went to press, the Museo Navale was due to be enriched with a collection donated by publisher Ugo Mursia of intrepid figureheads, decorated shells, wooden models of ships, compasses and whales' teeth.

The Museo is in the process of updating its display and security systems; you may not be able to see all of the collections, and the museum floor plan available free at the entrance may correspond only roughly to reality.

Santa Maria della Vittoria

Via E De Amicis 11 (329 966 5460). Metro Sant'Ambrogio/2, 3, 14 tram. **Open** 10am-5pm Mon-Fri. **Admission** free.

This new exhibition space, designed to house exhibits on recent archaeological research on pre-historical and Roman Lombardy, is located in the crypt of a 16th-century church built by Cardinal Luigi Omodeo in 1669 as a family mausoleum and now home to the Romanian Orthodox church (02 8940 7269, open for services only, 6.30-8pm Fri, 9.30am-1pm Sun). Displays planned for 2002 included eight medieval pirogues (canoes) dredged up from the Olona river (*see p108*) and latest findings on the columns of San Lorenzo (*see p91*).

Sant'Ambrogio

Piazza Sant'Ambrogio 15 (02 8645 0895/museum 02 8645 0895). Metro Sant'Ambrogio/bus 50, 54, 58, 94. **Open** *Church* 7am-noon, 2-7pm Mon-Sat; 7am-1.15pm, 2.30-7.45pm Sun. *San Vittore* 9.30-11.45am, 2.30-6.45pm Tue-Sun. **Admission** *San Vittore* €2. **No credit cards. Map** p310 A2.

The charismatic Bishop Ambrose (Ambrogio) – defender of orthodox Christianity against the Arian heresy (*see p13* **The Arian heresy**), later to become Milan's patron saint – had this *basilica martyrum* built between 379 and 386 over a cemetery that held the bodies of local martyr-saints Gervasius and Protasius (*see p11* **Milan's martyrs**). The remains of the martyrs still lie in the crypt.

The church was enlarged and the *campanile dei monaci* (monks' belltower) to the right of the façade was erected during the eighth century by the Benedictines. In the ninth century, under Archbishop Ansperto, the atrium preceding the façade was added. Ansperto's atrium – where the populace sought sanctuary in times of trouble – was remodelled in the 11th century, when a complete reconstruction of the church got under way. The *torre dei Canonici* (canons' tower) to the left of the façade was built in 1124. Further changes to the interior of the church were made in 1196 after the dome collapsed.

In 1492, Ludovico 'Il Moro' Sforza (*see p15*) called on Donato Bramante to remodel the eighth-century Benedictine monastery. The fall of Il Moro in 1499 put an end to Bramante's make-over, which was

Museo Nazionale della Scienza: a homage to technical skills. *See p95.*

limited to one side of the old cloister (the *portico della canonica*, accessible from the left of the nave). The church had a lucky escape from a planned remodelling job in the 17th century, but suffered severe air raid damage in 1943. The bombing destroyed Bramante's work, which was subsequently reconstructed using salvaged original materials.

In the atrium, capitals dating in part from the 11th century have carved scenes from Bible stories and mythical beasts symbolising the struggle between Good and Evil.

The interior has the sober proportions of the austere Lombard Romanesque, with its three aisles covered with ribbed cross-vaults and fake women's galleries to hold up the massive walls. Beneath the pre-Romanesque pulpit, reconstructed from the original pieces after the dome collapsed on it in 1196, lies what is known as the Stilicone sarcophagus, a fourth-century masterpiece traditionally believed to have been the burial place of the Roman general of that name who served the Emperor Honorius and died in 408. However, later research disproved this legend, and turned up something of more enduring importance: the sarcophagus is on the same axis as the original church, which indicates that it has not been moved since the fourth century. The 12th-century golden altar illustrated with scenes from the life of Christ on the front and of St Ambrose on the back once covered the porphyry casket commissioned to house the remains of Ambrose, Protasius and Gervasius when they were dug up in the ninth century; they now share an ornate glass coffin-for-three in the crypt. Suspended protectively above the altar, the tenth-century ciborium is in the form of a little temple; its four porphyry columns decorated in stucco are recycled Roman artefacts. To the right of the main altar, a series of chapels leads to the Sacello di San Vittore in Ciel d'Oro, part of the original fourth-century structure, clinically reworked in the 1930s, so that only its glorious, glowing golden fifth-century mosaic in the dome remains to remind us of its antique glory. St Ambrose stands between Gervasius and Protasius, with a sprinkling of other minor local martyrs looking on. This part of the church has been converted into a small museum (entrance through the 18th-century Cappella di Sant'Ambrogio Morente), consisting of the mosaics and precious church furnishings, including the silver and gold cross that was carried by St Charles Borromeo in 1576 in a procession of thanksgiving for the end of the plague.

There are more mosaics, from between the fourth and eighth centuries (though restored after extensive damage in 1943), in the apse of the main church. Christ sits enthroned between Gervasius and Protasius, while Ambrose performs miracles – including an interesting instance of bilocation, with the saint both in Milan and at the funeral in France of St Martin at the same time – all around.

The museum once housed in the cloisters has been split up and moved to the Museo Diocesano (*see p90*) and the San Vittore in Ciel d'Oro part of the basilica. The other remnant of the museum is an exhibition space opened in the Antico Oratorio della Passione (piazza Sant'Ambrogio 23A, opening times vary according to exhibition, admission free).

San Vittore al Corpo

Via San Vittore 25 (02 4800 5351). Metro Sant' Ambrogio/bus 50, 54, 59, 94. **Open** 7.30am-noon, 3.30-7pm daily. **Map** p310 A1.

The church and former monastery of San Vittore al Corpo grew up around the mausoleum of Emperor Valentinian II, who died in 392; parts of this ancient structure are now beneath the Museo Nazionale della Scienza e della Tecnologia (*see p95*). The complex was taken over in 1010 by Benedictine monks who got down to some serious rebuilding. It was given another overhaul in 1560, when it became one of Milan's most sumptuously decorated churches. Works by many local names of the late 16th and 17th centuries – Girolamo Quadrio, Camillo Procaccini, Giovanni Ambrogio Figino, Daniele Crespi – are still here. There are also choir stalls with wood-inlay intarsio work from the 1580s.

Università Cattolica del Sacro Cuore

Largo Gemelli 1 (02 72 341). Metro Sant'Ambrogio/ bus 50, 58, 94. **Open** *during university term* 8am-9.30pm Mon-Fri; 8am-4.30pm Sat. **Map** p311 A1.

Donato Bramante was called in in 1497 to redesign what was then a Cistercian monastery to the south-east of Sant'Ambrogio. Work had hardly even begun on his four-cloister plan before his patron Ludovico 'Il Moro' (*see p15*) was toppled from power. Two cloisters, one Ionic and one Doric, were completed in 1513 and 1630 respectively. Since 1921 the ex-monastery has been home to the Catholic university. Architect Giovanni Muzio overhauled the place through the 1930s and '40s in his usual dry, straightforward style (compare and contrast with the Palazzo dei Giornali, *p77*, in piazza Cavour, or the Palazzo dell'Arte, *p75*, in Parco Sempione).

Around Santa Maria delle Grazie

Corso Magenta is lined with sumptuous *palazzi*, shops purveying creature comforts and inviting bars and *pasticcerie*, including the charming Pasticceria Marchesi at the corner of the *corso* and via Santa Maria alla Porta that has been in operation since 1824. Just past the Marchesi, turn into via Brisa for a glimpse of the fenced-in ruins of the Roman imperial palace.

At corso Magenta 12 is the **Casa Rossi**, designed by Giuseppe Pestagalli around 1860 to simulate the superimposed loggias of Renaissance *palazzi*; sneak through the entrance for a peek at its octagonal courtyard. The **Palazzo Arese Litta** (No.24), now home to the Teatro Litta (*see p175*) and the headquarters of the Italian railway company, was begun in 1648. Its lively rococo façade is decorated with giant masks and two colossal telamons flanking the entrance. A monumental staircase built in the 18th century leads to the

Sala Rossa, with its red brocaded walls, where a pearl embedded in the floor recalls a tear shed by the awestruck Duchess Litta when she met Napoleon. Opposite Palazzo Litta, the little church of **San Maurizio** – once home to a powerful coven of Benedictine nuns – stands beside the **Museo Archeologico**. Past the art nouveau Bar Magenta (*see p130*) at largo d'Ancona, the brutally remodelled 16th-century **Palazzo dei Congressi** (No.61; commonly referred to by its older name Palazzo delle Stelline – little stars – after the little orphan girls it once gave a home to) is a venue for exhibitions and conferences.

But few visitors to Milan take much of this in during their headlong rush to piazza **Santa Maria delle Grazie**, further west along the *corso*. For in this square stands the church of the same name and the refectory of the adjoining monastery; and on one wall of the refectory is Leonardo's most famous work, the **Last Supper** (*Il Cenacolo*). There's another little-noticed Leonardesque memento across the way at corso Magenta 65-7: the Casa Conti (1919; not open to the public), which incorporates the 15th-century courtyard of an earlier construction on this spot, the **Casa degli Atellani**, where Leonardo stayed during his time in Milan.

Beyond, at No. 71, is the **Palazzo Busca**, future home of the Museo del Teatro della Scala (*see p63*). The original 16th-century edifice was reworked by Giuseppe Piermarini (1734-1808) and decorated with exuberant stucco by Giuliano Traballesi and Andrea Appiani.

Civico Museo Archeologico

Corso Magenta 15 (02 8645 0011). Metro Cadorna/bus 50, 54, 58/tram 18, 19, 24, 27. **Open** 9am-5.30pm Tue-Sun. **Admission** free. **Map** p308 C1/2.

The archaeological museum is conveniently situated over the only surviving stretch of Roman city walls, visitable along with the Etruscan, Pakistani and Greek sections in the basement beneath the second courtyard. In the first courtyard (once part of the Monastero Maggiore, home to the city's most influential order of nuns; see also San Maurizio, *p98*) stands a Bronze Age carved sacred stone from the Valcamonica (*see p269*). The itinerary starts on the ground floor, where a model gives an idea of how Mediolanum looked, and the sculpture collection in the room on the right is further testimony of Milan's Roman heritage.

Highlights of the sculpture collection include the portrait of Maximian (second century AD) and the bust of Hercules from the baths built by Maximian (286-305 AD) in the area that is now corso Europa. Among the Roman artefacts, note the Parabiago plate, a gilded silver platter from the middle of the fourth century AD showing Cibele and her followers,

Santa Maria delle Grazie.

and the coppa Trivulzio, a masterpiece of Roman glassmaking from the late fourth century AD bearing the inviting inscription *bibe vivas multis annis* (drink and you'll live long). A divider separates the model of Roman Milan from a section dedicated to the art of the Lombards and other assorted 'barbarians'. The stretch of Roman wall in the courtyard incorporates a defence tower known as the **Torre Ansperto**.

The Last Supper (Il Cenacolo)

Piazza Santa Maria delle Grazie 2 (02 498 7588/ reservations 02 8942 1146). Metro Cadorna, Conciliazione/tram 24. **Open** 8.15am-6.45pm Tue-Sun. **Admission** €7.24. **No credit cards**. **Map** p310 A1.

Note that reservations are obligatory for viewing the *Last Supper*, though if you are prepared to wait outside for a last-minute cancellation, you may be able to enter without one.

When Giorgio Vasari – painter, architect and biographer of Italian artists – saw the *Last Supper* in the 1550s, he complained that he could see nothing more than a 'magnificent blur'. Viewing this most famous of Milan's artworks today, the picture is a little clearer… though not much. Commissioned by Ludovico 'Il Moro' (*see p15*), Leonardo painted his *Last Supper* in 1495-7 while experimenting with a new method of working on dry plaster (true frescos were done on to wet plaster). He hoped this new method would give him the same flexibility as oil paints. It didn't, and the result was disastrous. Paint began peeling off almost immediately.

Already at the beginning of the 16th century, commentators noted that the *Last Supper* was fading fast, and 'touchings up' were not infrequent. Historical events conspired to worsen the situation: under French rule in the early 19th century, the monastery refectory where the painting is located was used as a stable. Drunken soldiers used Leonardo's faulty masterpiece for target practice.

Some nifty sandbagging during World War II, however, prevented the painting's final destruction in air raids that wreaked much serious havoc in the immediate vicinity.

Though the *Last Supper* has been more or less *in restauro* since it was made, the biggest, most definitive restoration got under way in 1977; layers of paint and detritus accumulated over the centuries were removed, some of the Renaissance master's luminous colours re-emerged, and the work – a bit gappy and somewhat lacking in definition – was unveiled in 1995.

The moment that is portrayed in this work is the intensely dramatic hiatus after Christ informed his companions that one of them was about to betray him. The apostles' gestures and facial expressions radiate out from the central figure of Christ in a sort of chain reaction, ripples from a stone dropped into a pond. The *Last Supper* was intended as more than a simple depiction of a Bible story; it's a study in human emotion ranging from surprise and disbelief to shock and hostility. This clinical psychological probing has earned Leonardo a special place in art criticism. On the opposite wall, Donato Montorfano painted his *Crucifixion* in 1495. Leonardo added the portraits of Ludovico 'Il Moro', his wife Beatrice and their children.

San Maurizio

Corso Magenta 15 (02 866 660). Metro Cadorna/ tram 18, 19, 24, 27/bus 50, 54, 58. **Open** 9am-noon, 2-5.30pm Tue-Sun. **Map** p308 C1/2.

San Maurizio was the church of the immense Monastero Maggiore (*see also* Civico Museo Archeologico, *p97*), the headquarters of a powerful community of Benedictine nuns. Much of the monastery was demolished after 1864. The structure of the church – begun in 1503 – reflects the needs of the closed order for which it was built. The rectangular space is divided in half across the centre by a partition in the middle of which stands the high altar. On one side sat the congregation; on the other the nuns. To the right of the altar is the *comunichino*, the opening through which the nuns received communion. In the nun's section is a rare 16th-century organ. Extensive fresco decoration by Bernardino Luini make the church a gem of 16th-century Lombard art.

Santa Maria delle Grazie

Piazza Santa Maria delle Grazie (02 4801 4248). Metro Cadorna or Conciliazione/tram 24. **Open** 7.30am-noon, 3-7pm daily. **Map** p310 A1.

The church of Santa Maria delle Grazie was begun in 1463 to a plan by Guiniforte Solari. Just two years after it was finished in the 1480s, Ludovico 'Il Moro' Sforza (*see p15*) commissioned architect Donato Bramante to turn the church into a family mausoleum that reflected the new styles of the Renaissance. (Some experts, it should be said, reject this theory, either doubting Bramante's involvement in the project at all, or otherwise ascribing a minor, preliminary planning role to him.) So down came

Solari's apse and up went a Renaissance tribune instead. At the same time, the *chiostrino* (small cloister) and a new sacristy were added to the adjoining Dominican monastery. The monks ran an active branch of the Inquisition in their monastery from 1553 to 1778, and continued to endow their church with decorative elements. The complex escaped the restorer's hand until the late 19th century, when some faux-Renaissance elements were added. World War II bombing in 1943 destroyed the great cloister of the monastery but spared the *chiostrino* and the refectory with Leonardo's *Last Supper* on its wall (*see p98*).

The terracotta façade of the church is in the best Lombard tradition; the portal is attributed to Bramante. Inside, Guiniforte's Gothic leanings in the three-aisled nave clash with the fresco-covered arches and the more muscular, massive style of Bramante (or whichever architect really was responsible for injecting a strong dose of Tusco-Umbrian Renaissance taste into the altar end of the church).

Standing out amid works by leading local artists from the 15th to 17th centuries is an altarpiece showing the *Holy Family with St Catherine* by the 16th-century Venetian painter Paris Bordone, which is in the sixth chapel on the left. The carved wooden choir stalls in the apse date from 1470. Entrance to the Bramantesque *chiostrino* is just before the main altar, where a door on the left takes you through the Cappella di Santa Maria delle Grazie e del Santissimo Sacramento and the old sacristy/bookstore, with 15th-century frescos (sometimes erroneously attributed to Leonardo) and huge cabinets with wooden inlay and painted Bible scenes. One cabinet hid a secret passage to the Castello Sforzesco (*see p70*), used by Ludovico. A door leads out into the *chiostrino*, also known as the frog cloister after the four bronze amphibians in the pool at its centre, from whose mouths water spouts. During mass, the cloisters can be accessed through a door in via Caradosso 1 (same opening times as the church).

Leonardo da Milano

If the name Leonardo da Vinci summons up visions of Tuscany, think again. As he was reaching his artistic prime – in 1482, aged 30 – Leonardo quit Florence to enter the service of Ludovico 'Il Moro' Sforza of Milan. In that city he remained for 17 years, returning for another seven-year stint in 1506.

The Renaissance all-rounder was sparing with his paintings in Florence; but he was even more so in Milan, where he completed fewer than ten works. The fact that one of these – the *Last Supper, see p98* – is generally acknowledged to be one of the western world's greatest masterpieces compensates to some extent. As does the extraordinary non-painting activity of this remarkable mind.

Leonardo was hired by Ludovico as *pictor et ingeniarius ducalis* (painter and engineer of the duke). It was the latter role that took up the lion's share of his time: he designed fortifications and worked on military strategy, engaged in hydraulic experiments of all kinds and beefed up the city's network of *navigli* (canals). What's more, in interminable notebooks and on countless scraps of paper, he jotted down his observations and ideas, which are all duly illustrated with sketches of striking beauty.

Beyond the *Last Supper* and the portraits of his ducal patron and his family on the wall opposite, there's little of Leonardo left in Milan. In the **Pinacoteca Ambrosiana** (*see*

p65) is a portrait of a musician; in the **Castello Sforzesco** (*see p70*), the much-restored ceiling frescos in the Sala delle Asse are attributed to him. Many of the genius's sketches were gathered together into what is now known as the Codex Atlanticus by 16th-century sculptor and art collector Leone Leoni (*see p63* **Casa degli Omenoni**); the codex is kept – under heavy lock and key, available only in facsimile form, even to scholars – in the **Biblioteca Ambrosiana** (*see p65*).

But there are reminders of Leonardo elsewhere in the city, too: he stayed, for example, at the **Casa degli Atellani** (*see p97*) while painting the *Last Supper,* and consorted with members of Ludovico's glittering court at the **Palazzo Carmagnola** (*see p69*). In the **Museo della Scienza e della Tecnologia** (*see p95*), there are reconstructions of the fabulous machines sketched in his notebooks. But perhaps the most bizarre tribute to the great man is in the **Ippodromo** (piazzale dello Sport 15) in the San Siro district (*see p100*): at the entrance to the racetrack stands a huge bronze horse, modelled on sketches made by Leonardo for a never-completed equestrian tribute to Ludovico. The statue was stuck at the racehorse track in 1999 by embarrassed city fathers who could think of no better place to put the unsolicited, outsized gift from the US-based Leonardo's Horse Foundation (www.leonardoshorse.org).

Sopranos run through scales in the **Casa di Riposo per Musicisti**.

The Fiera & San Siro

The **Fiera** – Milan's trade fair facility and temple to what the city is about: productivity and money-making – covers an immense territory extending from the post-war buildings of largo Domodossola, to piazzale Giulio Cesare and to viale Scarampo, the thoroughfare that leads to the motorways for Turin and the lakes. All around – with the exception of some art nouveau enclaves and the ultra-sleek new Portello pavilions – it's a sea of pretty, but soullessly uneventful, leafy residential districts. The **Casa di Riposo per Musicisti**, final resting place of composer Giuseppe Verdi, is a short walk down tree-lined via Buonarrotti from the piazzale Giulio Cesare side of the Fiera. Further south, yet another classy shopping drag – corso Vercelli – heads east from piazza Piemonte.

West of the Fiera is the **quartiere San Siro**, an unusually green area of Milan, with smart houses and numerous sports facilities, including the city's state-of-the-art **Stadio Giuseppe Meazza** football stadium.

If you tire of Milan's unending urban sprawl and relentless flatlands, take a breather in one of this suburb's parks: **Monte Stella** (via Cimabue or via Terzaghi, bus 68, an artificial hill created from World War II rubble, the **Parco del Trenno** (via Novara or via Cascina Bellaria, bus 64, 72, 80) or nearby **Bosco in Città** (via Cascina Bellaria or SS11, bus 420 Milano-Cuggiono from piazzale Lotto).

Casa di Riposo per Musicisti

Piazza Buonarroti 29 (02 499 6009). Metro Buonarroti. **Open** *Crypt* 10am-noon, 2.30pm-5pm daily. **Admission** free. **Map** off p310 A1.
A statue of composer Giuseppe Verdi presides over piazza Buonarrotti, where a neo-Romanesque palazzo designed in 1899 by architect Camillo Boito (the top floor is a post-war addition) houses a retirement home for musicians founded by Verdi himself. Across the courtyard – often filled with the sound of retired tenors or sopranos running through scales – stairs lead down to the crypt where Verdi and his wife Giuseppina Strepponi are buried.

Fiera di Milano

Largo Domodossola 1 (02 499 771/information desk 02 4997 7703/service centre 02 4997 7466/www. fieramilano.com). Metro Amendola-Fiera, Lotto-Fiera/ tram 19, 27/bus 48, 68/787shuttle from Lainate. **Open** varies according to exhibition. **Admission** varies according to exhibition. **Map** off p310 A1.
Milan's original trade fair was set up near Porta Venezia (*see p79*) in 1920 in an effort to kick-start an economy that was proving slow to recover from World War I. As fair events grew, the structure was moved to its current location, expanding as permanent pavilions were added over the years. Of the original structures, only the Palazzo dello Sport (1925) and a few art nouveau buildings near the beginning of via Domodossola survived wartime bombing. But reconstruction work was swift in the post-war period, and the Fiera is now among the largest trade structures in Europe. Its 375,000sq m are home to 26 exhibition pavilions. Each year it plays host to 31,000 exhibitors and millions of visitors.

Around Milan

There's green amid the industrial sprawl.

Milan's economic miracle has forced the city outwards, its suburbs and ugly industrial sprawl extending into what was once high-density agricultural territory.

Nowadays, much of it is breathtakingly ugly. But the occasional bout of far-sightedness has kept glorious pockets free from development (*see p102* **Parks of the Brianza** and *p106* **The Ticino Park Valley**). Rivers – the Lambro to the north, the Adda to the east, the Ticino to the west – and canals (the *navigli*, *see p92*) add a picturesquely watery element to the flat countryside, even though the parks created to protect these areas (such as the **Parco Naturale dell'Adda Nord**) are not always as well run as you might hope (the **Parco delle Groane**, *see p106*, is a case in point). Those bits of the rolling **Brianza** that haven't succumbed to industry are a pleasantly varied route into the foothills of the Alps (*see also chapter* **The Mountains**). Then there are abbeys and castles and fabulous *palazzi* and *ville* galore.

To the north-west, the province of Milan meets the province of Varese, a land of hills, lakes and an unexpected taste of Tuscany.

GETTING AROUND

Car is the simplest way to visit the area around Milan (for car hire, *see p279*). But there is efficient public transport to most of the destinations covered in this chapter (*see* individual destinations below). *See also p279* **Getting around Lombardy**.

Monza & the Brianza

The rolling hills that once made the Brianza district immediately north of Milan a favourite holiday mecca for the city's wealthier residents have long since been engulfed by a welter of ugly industry (furniture manufacturing being a chief occupation). But dotted amid the nightmarish industrial landscape are the lush villas to which relaxing *milanesi* once retired; and nick-of-time efforts have ensured that the occasional stretch of Brianza countryside has remained in some lovely protected areas (*see p102* **Parks of the Brianza**).

The Brianza's biggest draw is its main town, **Monza**. From the late fourth century, under the rule of the 'Barbarian' Lombards (*see p9*),

Heavenly ceilings at Monza's **Duomo**. *See p103*.

Monza was more important even than Milan. Emperor Frederick Barbarossa (see p11) kept up the tradition, favouring docile Monza over bolshy Milan. The city centre still maintains something of its medieval character in the 13th-century Arengario (town hall) and the magnificent **Duomo**.

Lombard Queen Theodolinda had a chapel dedicated to St John the Baptist built in the late sixth century where the Duomo now stands. Scant traces of this early Christian building still remain; the Duomo we see today is a mainly 14th-century structure with later additions. The lunettes above the door of the white marble Gothic façade show Theodolinda and her offspring can presenting what is known as the Iron Crown to John the Baptist.

Kept in the **Cappella di Teodolinda** to the left of the high altar, the gem-encrusted but subdued crown – probably dating from the fifth century and in fact made of gold, though believed to contain an iron nail from Christ's Cross – was used to crown Italy's kings from the Middle Ages up to Napoleon. Around this chapel's walls are 15th-century paintings by Franceschino, Gregorio and Giovanni Zavattari of scenes from the life of the queen. Her remains are in a sarcophagus behind the altar.

A door from the left nave leads to the cemetery and the **Museo Serpero**, containing treasures from the town's heyday, including articles donated to the original chapel by Theodolinda and Pope Gregory the Great; among the queen's gifts is a gilded, gem-studded missal. Theodolinda's crown – it's a little like a bejewelled pill-box hat – is kept here, as is a gilded silver hen with her seven chicks, probably made between the fourth and seventh centuries and said to represent Lombardy with its seven provinces.

To the north of the centre, the vast **Parco di Monza** (open 7.30am-6.30pm daily) contains the **Villa Reale** (1771-80) – now a space for temporary exhibitions, but once the summer residence of the archduke of Austria – a golf course and the **autodromo**, the renowned Formula One motor racing track. At weekends, you can take your own car up to the track and be Michael Schumacher for a hour or two.

North of Monza, **Biassono**'s town hall – Villa Verri – is a perfect example of the early 18th-century *barocchetta* style; its Museo Civico (open 2.30-7pm Sat; admission free) has reconstructions of farm life through the ages in the Brianza. In **Carate Brianza**, the Villa Cusani Confalonieri (not open to the public) is a 17th-century remodelling of a late 16th-century castle. The church of Santi Ambrogio e Simpliciano has outstanding canvases by Daniele Crespi and Francesco Hayez. In

Parks of the Brianza

Stretching north from the Parco di Monza (see p102) through forests of oak, ash, chestnut and conifers, the **Parco della Valle del Lambro** covers 65 square kilometres (25 square miles) along the banks of the River Lambro. Stop in at park headquarters at Triuggio for maps before starting out on a not-always-clearly-marked eight-kilometre (five-mile) hiking or mountain bike circuit cutting through the densely wooded valleys of the Lambro river. On a mixed route of dirt roads, trails and asphalt roads, you'll pass **Villa Jacini** (not open to the public), an 18th-century hunting lodge transformed into a neo-rococo villa by Antonio Citterio in the second half of the 19th century, the sprawling Renaissance complex of the Jesuit-owned **Villa Sacro Cuore** (not open to the public) near Zuccone Robasacco, and the old **Cascina Braghettone** farmhouse on the outskirts of the village. The stretch along the Cantalupo valley to Canonica passes by the 16th-century **Villa Taverna** (not open to the public).

North of Vimercate, the **Parco Regionale di Montevecchia e della Valle del Curone**, a weekend favourite with the Milanese, has a few short walks that wind through the hillside terraces planted with rosemary and sage. From the main square of the village of Montevecchia (the piazza is named after the mathematician Maria Gaetana Agnesi, 1718-99, whose villa is on its north-east side) a daunting stairway leads up to the village's 16th-century **Santuario della Beata Vergine del Carmelo** (open 3-7pm Sat; 8am-noon, 2-7pm Sun). From a landing halfway up, a Via Crucis (Stations of the Cross, open 2.30-6pm Sun) winds around the church on a lower terrace.

Back in the square, a stone path at the opposite end descends to several places for refreshment. The **Trattoria al Galeazzino** (via Galeazzino 4, 039 993 0850, closed Fri & Mon-Fri in Nov-Feb, average €15.50) serves simple food on a sunny terrace. The **Azienda Agricola Valcurone** (Cascina Casarigo, 039

Agliate, the basilica of Santi Pietro e Paolo (open 8am-1pm, 4.30-7pm daily) dates from the early 11th century. The church is built in river stone set in a herringbone pattern, as is its baptistery, a rare nine-sided structure.

To the east of Monza, **Arcore** is now indelibly linked in the Italian psyche to Prime Minister Silvio Berlusconi, who resides in a high-gated villa here. But there is also the 18th-century Villa Borromeo d'Adda (only the grounds are open to the public). The vast land holdings of these descendants of Milan's powerful cardinals (*see p16*) included a spread in **Oreno**, three kilometres (two miles) to the east, where the estate of the Villa Borromeo (via Piave 12, 039 669 004, open by appointment only) contains a hunting lodge with remarkable 15th-century frescos of hunting scenes.

Despite being a thriving manufacturing centre, **Vimercate** has preserved much of its original charm. In the town hall (Palazzo Trotti), an 18th-century fresco cycle stretches over 11 rooms. The basilica of Santo Stefano (open 8am-noon, 5-7pm daily) was built in the tenth to 11th centuries on earlier foundations. Along via Cavour, off the central piazza Roma, are several 15th-century *palazzi* and the little Romanesque Oratorio di Sant'Antonio, with frescos from 1450. At the end of the street, the San Rocco bridge, built from recycled Roman remains, was part of the medieval fortifications.

Autodromo di Monza
Parco di Monza (039 24 821/www.monzanet.it).
Open (for driving) 9am-12.30pm, 2-5pm Sat, Sun.
Admission driving €30 per hr. **Credit** AmEx, DC, MC, V.
Check the website for racing fixtures and details of how to reach the track.

Duomo & Museo Serpero
Piazza Duomo (039 323 404).
Open *Duomo* 9am-noon, 3-6.30pm daily.
Museum 9-11.30am, 3-5.30pm Tue-Sat; 10.30am-12.15pm, 3-5.45pm Sun. **Admission** *Duomo* free. *Museum* €2.50. *Chapel of Theodolinda* €1.
No credit cards.

Villa Reale
Viale Regina Margherita 2 (039 322 086/ guided tours 039 323 222). **Open** occasionally for exhibitions. **Admission** varies according to event.
Guided tours can be arranged by Villa Reale for groups of 20 and over several weeks in advance; €2.60 per person.

Getting there

By train
Mainline trains for Monza leave Stazione Centrale or Porta Garibaldi about every 15mins. Trains also leave hourly (every half hour during rush hours) from both stations for Arcore on the

993 0065, www.agriturismovalcurone.it, closed Mon & Tue, 3wks Jan, average €30) also arranges food, wine and nature tours of the area, as well as selling its own wine (9am-noon, 3-7pm Tue-Sun). The wine producer **Vitivinicola Cattaneo** (viale Palazzetto 8, 039 993 0043, 338 819 3970) offers tours of cellars and will arrange meals, but you must book.

Parco Naturale della Valle del Lambro
Park office: via V Veneto 19, Triuggio (0362 970 961/www.brianzainfo.it).
Open 8am-2pm Mon, Wed, Fri; 8am-noon, 1.30-6.30pm Tue, Thur.

Parco Regionale di Montevecchia e della Valle del Curone
Park office: via Donzelli 9, Montevecchia (039 993 0384). **Open** 9-10am Mon-Sat.
Call park volunteers (039 531 1275) on Friday after 9pm to arrange visits to the park museum or for information on excursions.

Trezzo's hydroelectric power plant.

Milan–Sondrio line. Triuggio, headquarters for the Parco Lambro, is on the Sesto–Lecco line, with trains every hour.

By bus
ATM buses 723, 724 and 727 from Stazione Centrale or 721, 820 and 821 from Sesto FS metro station cover the short hop to Monza, Vimercate and other Brianza destinations.

Tourist information

Pro Monza (IAT)
Palazzo Comunale, piazza Carducci, Monza (039 323 222/www.promonza.monza.net). **Open** 9am-noon, 3-6pm Mon-Fri; 9am-noon Sat.

Ufficio Cultura
Largo Vela 1, Arcore (039 6013 263). **Open** 9am-noon Mon, Wed, Fri, Sat.

The Valle dell'Adda

Work began on the **Naviglio Martesana** (*see also p92*), which runs from Milan to the River Adda, in 1457. Its waters were – and still are – used to irrigate the surrounding countryside, as well as providing a trade highway between the city of Milan and the neighbouring province of Bergamo. The spectacularly scenic banks of the River Adda, with their pretty little villages, are now protected areas in the Parco Naturale dell'Adda Nord. The Martesana canal reaches the river near the town of **Cassano d'Adda**,

where the magnificent Villa Borromeo (not open to the public) with its fine gardens was built in the first half of the 18th century but redone in neo-classical style after 1781 by Giuseppe Piermarini. In front of the U-shaped structure is a *cortile d'onore* (courtyard).

Further north in **Vaprio d'Adda**, the Villa Melzi d'Eril (1483; reworked in the 17th century and again in 1845; not open to the public) hosted such illustrious guests as Leonardo da Vinci, Austrian Empress Maria Teresa and Napoleon.

Continuing upstream, picturesque **Trezzo sull'Adda** is probably of Celtic origin. The towering *castello* that dominates the double-bend of the river here was – according to local lore – originally built for Lombard Queen Theodolinda (*see p8* **Theodolinda**). What remains today dates from the 13th and 14th centuries, erected by the Visconti family (*see chapter* **History**); the castle was already in ruins in the 18th century (much of its masonry was recycled in Milan's Arena, *see p74*, and the Villa Reale in Monza, *see p102*).

Almost as striking in its way as the castle, Trezzo's hydroelectric plant – the Centrale Elettrica Taccani (not open to the public) – was built in 1906 for industrialist Cristoforo Benigno Crespi, who commissioned architects Gaetano Moretti and Adolfo Covi to create a structure that would blend well with the landscape.

Il Castello
Via Valverde 33, Trezzo sull'Adda (information 02 909 0146/guided tours 02 909 2569). **Open** (by appointment only) *Mar-Oct* 2.30-6pm Sun. **Admission** €3.50. **No credit cards**.

Getting there

By metro & bus
You're almost there once you get to the end of the green line of the metro, Gessate. Buses 920, 921 and 922 provide a regular service from Gessate to Cassano d'Adda and Trezzo sull'Adda. SIA (02 8646 2350) operates four services daily from piazza Castello on its Milano–Brescia route, stopping on the motorway at Trezzo.

Tourist information

Pro Loco
Via Carlo Biffi 4, Trezzo sull'Adda (029 092 569/ www.ondavi.it/protre). **Open** 9am-noon Mon, Wed, Thur-Sat.

Parco Naturale dell'Adda Nord
Park office: via B Calvi 3, Trezzo sull'Adda (029 091 229). **Open** 9am-noon Mon-Sat.

North-west from Milan

The area north and west of Milan is no exception to the rule: there's little respite from the city's relentless, ugly industrial sprawl until you get past **Legnano** and **Saronno**. That said, there are some gems.

Near **Bollate**, the French- and Italian-style gardens of the **Villa Arconati** in Castellazzo di Bollate (1730, rebuilt over a medieval structure) are a delight, with their parterres, wooded groves, labyrinths, nymphea, hunting lodge, seraglio and hunting reserves.

Every Sunday in July, the towns of Bollate, Garbagnate and Arese organise a summer festival at the villa, when the gardens are open to the public.

Arese will be of little interest to anyone but car enthusiasts, who can revel in the **Museo Storico Alfa Romeo** with its collection of 110 of the manufacturer's most prestigious models, dating from 1910 to the present day.

In **Lainate**, the original **Villa Borromeo Visconti Litta** was built in the late 16th century, but much altered and added to in

Industrial paternalism

In the late 19th century, textile magnate Silvio Benigno Crespi decided to shift the family firm from Busto Arsizio west of Milan to a site on the banks of the River Adda that would provide the water needed for his manufacturing operations and the healthy environment he – with his Utopian vision of benign industrial paternalism – considered essential for combining his manufacturing with the well-being of his workforce.

From 1878 until 1910, architects were commissioned by the Crespi family to make their dream a reality on a site that was to become the town of **Crespi d'Adda**; few changes have been made since. By the river stands the cotton factory with its terracotta smokestack and an art nouveau clock with

motifs inspired by the Lombard Renaissance. On the other side of the main road, two-household workers' dwellings stand in neat rows, each with its own vegetable patch. More elaborate homes for management are located further from the factory. There's a church, designed by Luigi Cavenaghi (1893), who drew his inspiration from Bramante. Around this are clustered town services, including a theatre, a communal laundry house and a school. In the cemetery is the Crespi mausoleum, designed by Gaetano Moretti in 1907. Dominating the lot is the eclectic family *castello*, a wildly over-the-top affair complete with towers, crenellations and faux-Romanesque twirls by Ernesto Pirovano (1849-97). The village is now a Unesco World Heritage site.

The Ticino Valley Park

As the industrial horror of Milan romped over the surrounding countryside, some wise souls came up with the idea of saving the River Ticino – with its myriad branches, canals and banks rich in aquatic vegetation – from destruction. The result is a nature reserve, instituted in 1974, that spreads for 90,000 hectares (222,222 acres) across three provinces and through 46 municipal areas, from Sesto Calende in the north to Pavia (*see p259*) in the south.

Ancient farmhouses dot open fields; herons pick their way through rice paddies. Along each stretch of the river, the microhabitat is respected and preserved: the great woods in the north are all that remain of the forests that once covered the Po Valley; there are wetlands abounding in birdlife south of

Turbigo. Maps of the park's many trails can be obtained from the park office. To arrange guided tours contact the following:
Centro Agrituristico Caremma *via Cascina Caremma 1, Besate (02 905 0020).*
Open noon-1pm, from 8.30pm Thur-Sun).
TEA *via Bramante 29, Milan (02 3453 4147).*
Open 8.30am-12.30pm Mon-Fri.
Ditta Michele Maggi *via Don Verzini 16-18, Ozzero, 02 940 7573/338 326 7181.* Call any time. See also p110.

Parco Lombardo della Valle di Ticino

Park office: via Isonzo 1, Pontevecchia di Magenta (029 72 101/www.comunic.it/parks.html). **Open** 9am-noon, 2-5pm Mon-Thur; 9am-noon Fri.

the early 18th. The extensive gardens, with their fountains and water games designed as practical jokes on garden party guests, were completed in the late 18th century. Special summertime events include open-air cinema screenings and tours by guides in period costume.

Between Bollate and Saronno stretches the **Parco Regionale delle Groane**, 3,400 hectares (8,395 acres) of heathland (*groana* means heath in Milanese dialect) set aside in 1972 to protect the unique but dwindling flora and fauna of the district. The countryside is dotted with disused kilns in which local clay was baked into bricks. If you're prepared to go it alone – the park information office operates very restricted hours – take a train to Garbagnate (from Stazione Cadorna) and follow the cycle path past one of these kilns to Castellazzo di Bollate and Villa Arconati (*see above*). From there, more cycle tracks and dirt roads lead to sleepy Bollate, and a further two kilometres (1.25 miles) of paved road will take you to the town of Senago, from where the via Isolino leads to more kilns and the bike path along the canal back to Garbagnate.

Located just off the motorway (A9) to Lake Como (*see p194*), **Saronno** has been a place of commerce and religion since its earliest mention as 'vico Solomnio' in a document of 796. As early as 1301, a market was held there three times a week. The Franciscans and Humiliati (*see p110* **Humiliati**) had a foothold here from the 13th century; in 1458 there were 28 religious confraternities. The **Santuario della**

Madonna dei Miracoli (piazza Santuario 1, 02 960 3027, open 7am-noon, 3-7pm daily) was built in the early 16th century for the pilgrims who flooded to this spot where a miraculous cure reportedly took place in 1447. Partly mannerist, partly reminiscent of Bramante, the church was expanded into a Latin cross form in 1556-66. Inside are works by the best Lombard masters of the 16th century, including Bernardino Luini (*see p190* **Bernardino Luini**) and Gaudenzio Ferrari. Angelic musicians by the latter peer down cheekily from the cupola. Saronno's local specialities are the marzipan-flavoured Amaretto di Saronno liqueur, and matching biscuits, made by the Lazzaroni firm. The **Museo del Biscotto** charts the history of this treat.

Now an unprepossessing industrial hub, **Legnano** had its moment of glory in 1176, when the Lega Lombarda (*see p113*) caught the troops of Holy Roman Emperor Frederick Barbarossa offguard here and routed them, shaking up the political situation. Milan — the strongest faction in the Lega – established itself firmly as Lombardy's Top Dog and the empire was too weak to strike back. The event is commemorated on the last Sunday of May in the Sagra del Carroccio (fair of the old cart, symbol of the Lega). On the main square, the basilica of San Magno (1504-13) has frescos by Bernardino Luini and Bernardino Lanino. The **Museo Civico Guido Sutermeister** contains archaeological remains from the Bronze and Iron Ages, artefacts from the Lombard era and architectural fragments from the 15th century.

Museo del Biscotto presso il Museo delle Industrie e Lavoro Saronnese

Via Don Griffanti 6, Saronno (029 607 459).
Open 3-6pm Sun. By appointment at other times.
Admission free.

Museo Civico Guido Sutermeister

Corso Garibaldi 225, Legnano (033 154 3005).
Open 9am-12.30pm, 2.30-5pm Tue-Sat; 9am-12.30pm
Sun. **Admission** free.

Museo Storico Alfa Romeo

Via Alfa Romeo, Arese (029 392 9303). **Open** 9am-
12.30pm, 2-4.30pm Mon-Fri. **Admission** free.

Villa Arconati

*Via Fametta 1, Castellazzo di Bollate (festival
information 02 3500 5575).* **Open** *Gardens only*
9am-1pm, 3-7pm Sun in July. **Admission** €1.56;
guided tour €2.60. **No credit cards**.

Villa Borromeo Visconti Litta

*Piazza Vittorio Emanuele, Lainate (339 394 2466/
www.amicivillalitta.it).* **Open** *May, Oct* 3-6pm Sun.
June, July, Sept 9.15am-10.30pm Sat; 3-6pm Sun.
Closed Aug, Nov-Apr. **Admission** €5.16.
No credit cards.

Getting there

By train

Trains for Saronno leave Cadorna station every
10-15mins; Legnano is one (15min) stop along the
Domodossola or Lago Maggiore lines, with trains
leaving from Certosa or Garibaldi stations.

By bus

STIE (02 860 837) operates services for Saronno,
Legnano and Lainate that depart from via Paleocapa
near Cadorna station.

Tourist information

Parco Regionale delle Groane

*Park office: via della Polveriera 2, Solaro (02 969
8141).* **Open** 9am-1pm Mon-Fri.

Ufficio Sagra del Carroccio

*Piazza San Magno 6, Legnano (0331 471 258/
www.comune.legnano.it).* **Open** 9am-12.30pm,
2.30-5.30pm Mon-Thur; 9am-12.30pm Fri.

Varese & around

Equidistant between lakes **Como** (*see p194*)
and **Maggiore** (*see p187*), Varese is the capital
of the province of the same name.

The first recorded mention of **Varese** was in
the early Middle Ages, as a small village in the
diocese of Como; in the 13th century it became a
comune (self-governing town) in its own right,
though under the aegis of the archbishop of
Milan. All its feudal obligations were revoked

in 1538, leaving Varese independent until
1765, when Federico III d'Este established his
ducal court there.

The spreading parks of Varese's splendid *ville*
make the town one of Lombardy's greenest.
Palazzo Estense (via Sacco, now a municipal
complex including the town council offices and
library, 0332 255 272, open 10am-noon, 2-6.30pm
Mon-Sat) was built between 1766 to 1772 for
regional governor Francesco III d'Este by the
otherwise unknown architect Giuseppe Bianchi.
Its magnificent Italian gardens are accessible
from those of **Villa Mirabello**. This latter –
built in the 18th century and renovated in the
English style in 1843 with extensive gardens –
now houses the **Musei Civici**. The museum's
prehistoric and archeological section provides
an insight into life in the stilt-houses built on the
area's lakes by its earliest inhabitants. There's
also a tomb of an Italic warrior from the sixth or
fifth century BC, and a sixth-century BC menhir.

Fortified medieval Varese lay between
piazza del Podestà, corso Matteotti and via San
Martino. The **Santuario della Madonnina
in Prato** in piazza Madonnina at the end of
via Dandolo is a 17th-century reconstruction
of a late Gothic building, with massive
telemons (free-standing caryatids) shoring
up its dramatic entrance. Charming via San
Martino is lined with 16th- and 17th-century
buildings with lively courtyards, porticos
and communicating passageways. At corso
Matteotti 53 is a courtyard with a portico
that was once part of a Benedictine monastery
(1571-1606). In piazza San Vittore, the church
of San Vittore (open 8am-noon, 5-7.30pm) was
built between 1580 to 1615. Its neo-classical
façade is flanked by a high baroque belltower
(1617). Inside are works by 17th-century
Milanese artists. Behind the belltower, the
Battistero di San Giovanni is the oldest
building in the city. The great pool for baptism
by immersion dates from the seventh to eighth
centuries; the font was decorated by a *maestro
campionese* of the 13th or 14th century. The
14th- to 15th-century frescos represent the
Apostles and the Virgin Mary.

North of Varese, the **Sacro Monte** (*see
p108* **Holy Mountains**) in the Parco Regionale
Campo dei Fiori has long been a favourite
day trip for locals.

Still further north on the SS394, the **Villa
della Porta Bozzolo** in Casalzuigno is a
splendid frescoed 18th-century villa with
glorious baroque gardens.

To the west, the territory opens out into
gentle, rolling hills and little lakes: Varese,
Monate, Comabbio and the tiny Biandronno.
Prehistoric peoples built houses on stilts in
these lakes.

A ferry (operated by the Ristorante Isolino Virginio, 0332 766 268, €2.6 round trip, operates year-round with more frequent services at weekends) plies between the village of Biandronno and **Isola Virginia**, the area's most important prehistoric site. Digs here in the 1860s turned up neolithic and Bronze Age artefacts, many of which are displayed in the little museum. When the lake waters are very low, remains of the prehistoric pilings are visible in the mud.

South of Varese, **Castiglione Olona** is a little bit of Tuscany transported to the Lombard countryside. The exquisite village was the project of native Cardinal Branda Castiglioni, a papal legate who spent much of his career in Florence. At the beginning of the 15th century he returned to his home town – a village on the Olona river with Roman origins – with his head full of the ideas of the Renaissance. To appease local opinion, he began his rebuilding campaign with a Lombard-Gothic look for the **Collegiata** church. Then he let rip, imposing new Brunelleschian models on the **Chiesa di Villa** and his family's **Palazzo Branda Castiglioni**. As the icing on the cake, he brought Masolino da Panicale – teacher of Renaissance ground-breaker Massaccio – to the village to paint frescos in the palazzo and the baptistery.

Holy mountains

The Sacro Monte, so dear to northern Italians, is a 3-D version of the Via Crucis (Stations of the Cross)... or a religious Disneyland. The first one was built in the late 15th century in Varallo in the Piedmont region by a philanthropic monk called Fra Bernardino Caimi. Feeling sorry for the poor and lame who would never make it to the real Holy Places of the Holy Land, he came up with a facsimile version on a 'Holy Mountain'. Caimi's humble vision was given a garish turn the following century when Counter-Reformation and baroque ideas turned *sacri monti* into a series of diorama-style scenes from the life of Christ.

The Sacro Monte just north of Varese in the Campo dei Fiori nature reserve falls into the garish category, with 14 highly coloured scenes of the Passion of Christ eerily frozen in tableaux-filled chapels leading to the piazza of the village of Santa Maria del Monte. If the chapels don't grab you, the road leading up to the Sacro Monte – lined with faux-medieval, neo-Renaissance and art nouveau villas – might.

Further south along the Olona Valley, there's an abandoned village at the **Zona Archeologica di Castelseprio**, a couple of kilometres from the quaint inhabited town of the same name. Inside the site is the church of Santa Maria Foris Portas, a seventh- to eighth-century structure with rare Byzantine fresco remnants.

Chiesa di Villa
Piazza Garibaldi, Castiglione Olona (0331 858 048). **Open** 10am-noon, 2.30-5.30pm Tue-Sun. **Admission** €2.58. **No credit cards.**

Collegiata della Beata Vergine e dei Santi Stefano e Lorenzo
Via Cardinale Branda Castiglioni 1, Castiglione Olona (0331 858 048). **Open** 10am-noon, 2.30-5.30pm Tue-Sun. **Admission** €2.58. **No credit cards.**

Isola Virginia
Lago di Biandronno (0332 281 590). **Open** *Apr-Oct* 2-6pm Sat, Sun. Closed Nov-Mar. **Admission** €2.07. **No credit cards.**

Musei Civici
Villa Mirabello, piazza della Motta, Varese (0332 281 590). **Open** 10.30am-12.30pm, 2.30-5pm Tue-Sat; 9.30am-12.30pm, 2-5pm Sun. **Admission** *Museum* €2.06. *Gardens of Palazzo Estense & Villa Mirabello* free. **No credit cards.**

Palazzo Branda Castiglioni
Piazza Garibaldi, Castiglione Olona (0331 858 048). **Open** *Oct-Mar* 9am-noon, 3-6pm Tue-Sat; 3-6pm Sun. *Apr-Sept* 9am-noon, 3-6pm Tue-Sat; 10.30am-12.30pm, 3-6pm Sun. **Admission** €2.07. **No credit cards.**

Strong chiaroscuros at the **Abbazia di Chiaravalle**. *See p110.*

Villa della Porta Bozzolo

Viale C Bozzolo 5, Casalzuigno (0332 624 136). **Open** *House* Oct-mid Dec 10am-1pm, 2-5pm Tue-Sun; Feb-Sept 10am-1pm, 2-6pm Tue-Sun. *Garden* 10am-5pm Tue-Sun. *Park* 10am-6pm Tue-Sun. **Admission** €4.50. **No credit cards**.

Zona & Museo Archeologico di Castelseprio

Via Castelvecchio 58, Castelseprio (0331 820 438). **Open** *Feb-Oct* 8.30am-7.30pm Tue-Sat; 9.30am-6.30pm Sun. *Nov-Dec* 8.30am-4.30pm Tue-Sat; 9am-3pm Sun. **Admission** free.

Getting there

By train from Milan

Services to Varese run from Cadorna every 30mins and from Porta Garibaldi and Porta Venezia hourly. Journey time 25mins.

Getting around

GLC-Giuliani & Laudi (via Bainsizza 27, 033 228 1790) runs bus services to Castiglione Olona and Castelseprio from Varese.

Tourist information

APT

Via Carrobbio 2, Varese (0332 283 604/www. varesottoturismo.com). **Open** 9am-12.30pm, 3-6.30pm Mon-Fri; 9am-12.30pm Sat.

Ufficio Informazioni

Palazzo Branda Castiglioni, piazza Garibaldi, Castiglione Olona (0331 858 048). **Open** 9am-noon, 3-6pm Sat; 10.30am-12.30pm, 3-6pm Sun.

South of Milan

The area to the south of Milan is criss-crossed by *navigli* (canals), which were the city's main trade highways into the surrounding area and important sources of irrigation. It is punctuated by some of northern Italy's most important religious foundations.

Many orders, including the powerful Cistercians and the Humiliati (*see p110* **Humiliati**), built glorious structures from the 12th century onwards. The area was well chosen: in the midst of fertile terrain, the monks placed the Church at the centre of everyday life in a potent cocktail of prayer and agricultural labour. While winning over souls, the orders contributed greatly to farm technology by reclaiming land and improving the water management in this wet river plain.

The Cistercian **Abbazia di Chiaravalle** was built in 1135 according to the specifications of the order's founder, St Bernard of Clairvaux. Many alterations were made before the abbey fell into disrepair after French rulers dissolved religious orders in the late 18th century; reconstruction began in 1894 and Cistercian monks returned to the complex in 1952. Once inside the complex, a strong sense of its Romanesque-ness is apparent in the most painterly strong chiaroscuros of the church interior. The local inhabitants who come to buy fresh eggs at the little shop near the entrance to the complex enhance the country monastery experience of a visit here. Once outside, however, you're back in Milanoland: to get a decent view of the church and its striking tower, you have to cross the road, with its ATM bus stop and roaring commuter traffic.

The 13th-century **Abbazia di Viboldone** was built by the Humiliati, and is one of the most important Gothic monuments in Lombardy, with its *Last Judgment* by Giusto de' Menabuoi and frescos by followers of Giotto. Only the church remains of the original monastic complex.

The former **Abbazia di Mirasole** was another 13th-century Humiliati foundation, though it has been used as a hospital since the late 18th century. Beside the restored single-nave church is a pretty 15th-century cloister.

The two major *navigli* of the Milanese hinterland – the Pavese and the Grande – flow to the west of Mirasole. On the Naviglio Pavese

Humiliati

At the beginning of the 12th century, Holy Roman Emperor Henry V stomped down to Lombardy, quelled a rebellion there, and dragged the nobles behind the uprising back to Germany with him to keep them in line. The captives learned their lesson: they shunned the world's vanities, donned grey habits, took up charitable works and – after swearing fealty to the emperor – were allowed to return home to found monasteries.

Their order – the Humiliati – went on to become a driving force in the economic and civic life of the Milan area. But the considerable wealth and power the order accumulated over the centuries was to bring them into conflict with Church authorities. On orders from Rome, Milan's charismatic Cardinal Carlo Borromeo (*see p16*) got down to suppressing the Humiliati with a zeal that earned him considerable hostility. But the order sealed its own fate when one of its number, Girolamo Donati, made an unsuccessful assassination attempt on the cardinal's life. The order was dissolved by papal bull in February 1571.

is the town of **Binasco**, where the **Castello Visconteo** in the main piazza is a much-restored building of 14th-century origins. A rectangular structure with a moat – now dry – around it, this was where the jealous Filippo Maria Visconti had his hapless wife Beatrice di Tenda beheaded on suspicion of adultery. Rather more prosaically, the palazzo is now home to the town council. Just off the piazza, the church of **Santi Stefano e Giovanni** (1783; open 8am-noon, 4.30-7pm daily) has an altarpiece, *La Beata Veronica*, by Raphael's teacher Perugino.

The charming town of **Abbiategrasso** stands on the Naviglio Grande. Its church of **Santa Maria Nuova** (open 8.30am-1pm, 4.30-7pm daily) is thought to be the last Lombard work by Donato Bramante before he left for Rome (*see p28*).

Six kilometres (3.5 miles) south, the Cistercian **Abbazia di Morimondo** was built from 1100 onwards. From the road, it's difficult to imagine there could be anything behind that screen of humdrum residential buildings: but the monastery church is isolated in a broad meadow, and dominates this farmhouse-dotted terrain that slopes down into the *rogge* (little inland channels) of the Ticino river. Carriage tours of Morimondo can be arranged by calling Ditta Michele Maggi, via Don Verzini 16-18, Ozzero (02 940 7573/338 326 7181/www.carrozza.it) several days before you want to take your trip (minimum four people, €16 per hour each). Morimondo is in the heart of the Parco Ticino (*see p106*), and Maggi, a park guide, will also do tours of the surrounding park zone.

Abbazia di Chiaravalle
Via Sant'Arialdo 102, Chiaravalle Milanese (02 5740 3404). Metro Corvetto then bus 77. **Open** 9am-noon, 3-6.45pm Tue-Sun. **Admission** free.

Abbazia di Mirasole
Comune di Opera (02 5503 8311). Tram 15 almost to the southern terminus and then a long walk. **Open** 9am-12.30pm, 2.30-6pm Mon, Wed-Sun. **Admission** free.

Abbazia di Morimondo
Piazza San Bernardo 1 (02 9496 1919). Train from Porta Genova station to Abbiategrasso (departs hourly), then local bus. **Open** *Apr-Oct* 8.30am-noon, 2.30-6.30pm daily. *Nov-Mar* 8.30am-noon, 2.30-4.30pm daily. **Admission** free.

Abbazia di Viboldone
Via dell'Abbazia 6, San Giuliano Milanese (02 984 1203). Metro San Donato then bus for San Giuliano/train from Porta Garibaldi (Milano–Bologna line). **Open** 9-11.30am, 2.30-6pm daily. **Admission** free.

Eat, Drink, Shop

Restaurants

Italy's fashion capital still prefers neighbourhood *trattorie* and exotic imports over designer eating... just.

Despite being Italy's fashion capital, Milan is not big on designer eating. Even the city's trendsetters often prefer to eat in local *trattorie* – or places that were decorated last week to look like local *trattorie*. Some of these, like **Da Giacomo** (*see p117*), are in reality about as humble as Harry's Bar in Venice, and get packed with everyone who's anyone in Fashion Week. That said, there are now a few places with serious design credentials – including **La Terrazza** (*see p120*) and the Milanese offshoot of oriental superchef Nobu, housed inside the Armani superstore (*see p132*) in via Manzoni.

Milan is perhaps the only city in Italy to have welcomed outside influences with open arms. Successive waves of immigration, first from the south of Italy, later from North Africa and the Far East, have made the locals more receptive than most Italians to *cucina esotica* (in other words, anything that isn't Lombard). There's now a wide selection of ethnic restaurants, from Argentinian and Eritrean to Thai and Vietnamese.

EATING OUT

Eating out is very much a social event in Italy: the single diner is a rare beast. The standard meal consists of an *antipasto* (starter), followed by a *primo* (the first course, usually consisting of pasta or risotto) and *secondo* (the meat or fish course) accompanied by a *contorno* (vegetable side dish) and finally dessert, cheese, fruit, coffee and perhaps a *digestivo/amaro* or a grappa. But few manage four courses: the languid, three-hour lunchbreak is (almost) a thing of the past, and the workaholic Milanese will usually order a quick pasta dish and a side salad at lunchtime. You too should consider the standard menu sequence as a suggestion rather than a rule. Don't feel pressured into eating more than you want: even at dinner, a pasta course followed by a salad and/or a dessert is fine in most places.

Fixed-price meals are a rarity in Italy and especially so in untouristy Milan; anywhere that offers a *menu turistico* written in several languages is generally to be avoided. The more expensive restaurants sometimes offer a taster menu (*menu degustazione*), a good way of trying a bit of everything if you can't make up your mind.

For some of Lombardy's best and most famous restaurants, including Milan's **Il Luogo di Aimo e Nadia**, *see p37* **Food heaven**.

DRINKING

Italians are proud of their wines and will defend them furiously against foreign rivals. As a result, wine lists tend to be somewhat nationalistic. The good news is that Italy produces some first-class red and white wines – something that is not always obvious to outsiders, as few labels travel beyond the country's borders. The DOC (*denominazione di origine controllata*) seal of quality on the bottle is a reliable pointer to a good wine, but there are some equally wonderful *vini da tavola* (table wines) too – made under this humble guise because they do not conform to the stringent DOC regulations. *See also p231* **The Wines of Franciacorta** *and p258* **Milan's wine cellar**.

Cheaper eateries also offer *vino sfuso* (from the barrel), which can be ordered in quarter-, half- or one-litre carafes. It's cheap stuff and tends to range from mediocre to downright awful; don't be afraid of watering it down. For reasons known only to themselves, older Milanese men sometimes add a slice of lemon to their red wine. Note that pizza is traditionally accompanied by beer or soft drinks.

If you've ordered a full meal, you might be offered a *digestivo* or grappa on the house. The choice of *digestivi* is endless; Ramazzotti – a dark, syrupy liqueur made from herbs and spices – is a distinctly Milanese variant.

PRACTICALITIES

Nearly all eating establishments charge *coperto* (cover charge) for providing a tablecloth and bread. This should never be more than €2.50.

Tipping is a grey area. It's usually safe to assume that service is not included. Milanese, however, tend not to leave a tip unless they feel the food or service has particularly merited one. Tourists are generally expected to be more generous: anything between five and ten per cent will suffice, though bear in mind that you're under no obligation to leave anything, especially if you're dissatisfied with the service. It pays to check your bill: though most restaurateurs are scrupulously correct, there are those who will try to pull a fast one on first-time visitors.

Eat, Drink, Shop

All but the smallest *trattorie* and *pizzerie* accept credit cards. But Italy is still predominantly a cash society and many establishments will try to dissuade you from using plastic. Often this is in order to avoid issuing a proper receipt. Don't be fooled. By law you must be provided with an official receipt (*scontrino fiscale*) and you (and the restaurateur) will be fined in the unlikely event that a policeman catches you leaving a restaurant without one.

Italians like to eat at regular times and opening hours are fairly standard. The times listed in this guide refer to those when hot meals can be ordered, though the place may stay open much later. Normal eating hours are from around 12.30pm to 2.30pm and from 8pm to 10pm.

FULL MEALS, QUICK SNACKS

In theory, a *trattoria* is a cheap eaterie serving basic home cooking (*cucina casalinga*), while a *ristorante* is more refined. The division, however, is not always so clear-cut: there are plenty of upmarket *trattorie* that charge restaurant prices. The same goes for the *osteria*: originally the term was applied to workers' inns offering the most rustic of meals, but today it is often applied to *faux*-rustic establishments with serious prices. Authentic *trattorie* and *osterie* tend to have handwritten menus or even no menu at all; in the latter case, the day's fare is recited *a voce* (out loud).

Though McDonald's has made serious inroads, pizza remains the fast food of choice for most Italians. Most *pizzerie* worth their salt

in Italy (and all those listed below) use wood-fired ovens. Toppings are manifold but, in general, traditional: you won't find a Hawaiian pizza with pineapple, for instance, but you may find gorgonzola cheese with apple. The *margherita* – tomato and mozzarella – is the national favourite. In sit-down *pizzerie*, the thin Roman pizza is more fashionable nowadays than the thick, doughy Neapolitan variety.

For takeaway meals, go for a *pizza al taglio* (literally 'pizza by the slice') or something from a *rosticceria*. The latter is a kind of delicatessen serving spit-roast chicken, chips, stuffed vegetables and pasta dishes, either to eat in or take away. Many bars also serve excellent hot and cold sandwiches and filled rolls (*tramezzini* and *panini*); some also run a small *tavola calda* (hot buffet).

VEGETARIANS

Vegetarian restaurants are rare in Milan, as in the rest of Italy – though Joia (*see p119*), a temple to vegetarian haute cuisine – is an honourable exception. But don't despair: non-meat-eaters will find a host of tasty vegetable dishes and pasta sauces; main courses can often be replaced by a *contorno* or a vegetable *antipasto*. For snacking, bars offer a wide selection of vegetable- and cheese-based sandwiches. Though life will be harder for vegans, there is never any shortage of fresh fruit and vegetables.

Average restaurant prices in the listings below are based on three courses (two for *pizzerie*) and do not include beverages.

Table pitfalls

Milan's obsession with being seen to do the right thing extends to table manners too. Of course, foreigners are excused a great many sins, but to avoid possible embarrassment – or to score brownie points – you should take note of the following *faux pas*:

● Don't put parmesan on fish or seafood. Italians maintain that it ruins the flavour; shocked waiters may even refuse to bring it to your table.

● A *contorno* is emphatically a side dish: don't pile it on to your main course plate.

● It's perfectly acceptable to use toothpicks at the table, as long as you do it unobtrusively.

● Italians never use a spoon with their fork when eating spaghetti. If a waiter brings you one, give him a dark look.

● You can add water or ice to a cheap house wine, but never do the same with a good one.

● If Italians drink coffee after a meal, it is always espresso (referred to simply as *un caffè*). Asking for a cappuccino is like wearing a flashing neon 'I'm a tourist' sign.

● Pizza can be cut into slices and eaten with fingers. Bread can be used to mop up (*fare la scarpetta*) in all but the poshest restaurants.

● In image-conscious Milan, shorts and T-shirts do not go down well in restaurants, especially in the evening. *Pizzerie* and spit-and-sawdust *trattorie* have a more relaxed dress code.

● Children of all ages are welcome in restaurants, even late at night. This can make for noisy dining, but it's all part of the Italian experience.

Cucina aperta fino alle 00.30
Kitchen open until 12.30 am
Brunch Domenicale
Sunday Brunch
le biciclette
Ristorante > ArtBar
www.lebiciclette.com
Milano - Via Torti btw. Cso. Genova - tel +39 02 58104325 +39 02 8394177

Duomo & Centre

See also p142 **Peck**.

Italian

Bistrot Duomo

Via San Raffaele 2 (02 877 120). Metro Duomo/bus 54, 60/tram 2, 3, 13, 20. **Meals served** 7-10pm Mon; noon-2.30pm, 7-10pm Tue-Sat. **Credit** AmEx, DC, MC, V. **Map** p311 A1.

The place to come if you simply have to dine right in the centre and are willing to pay over the odds for it. From its location on the top floor of the Rinascente building you're at the same level as the gargoyles atop the Duomo (*see p57*), and the view is impressive – especially in summer, when the plexiglass roof is taken off. The pricey menu runs from traditional Italian to sushi; service is snootily efficient.

Don Lisander

Via Manzoni 12A (02 784 573). Metro Duomo or Montenapoleone/tram 1, 2, 20. **Meals served** 12.30-2.30pm, 7.30-10.30pm Mon-Sat. Closed 3wks Aug; 2wks Dec-Jan. **Average** €40. **Credit** AmEx, DC, MC, V. **Map** p311 A1.

In a prime location close to La Scala (*see p63*), this classic Milanese restaurant attracts lunching businessmen and well-to-do tourists. Try the *pesce spada marinato al pepe rosa* (swordfish marinated with red pepper) or *casoeüla con polenta* (pork and cabbage casserole with polenta). The cuisine, the service and the wine list are all outstanding, the waiters haughtily professional. There are tables outside in summer.

Cosy, rustic **L'Altra Pharmacia**.

Al Mercante

Piazza Mercanti 17 (02 805 2198). Metro Duomo/bus 54, 60/tram 2, 3, 12, 14, 24, 27, 20. **Meals served** Sept-July noon-2.30pm, 7-10.30pm Mon-Sat. Closed Aug, 1wk Jan. **Average** €40. **Credit** AmEx, DC, MC, V. **Map** p310 A1.

Tucked away in the medieval marketplace of piazza Mercanti, this tastefully understated restaurant serving safe pan-Italian cuisine seems to have more maître d's than waiters. Have your salad assembled from a selection of *pinzimonio* (raw vegetables, to be dipped in olive oil and balsamic vinegar). Tasty pasta dishes include home-made *tortelloni ai pinoli* (giant ravioli with pine nuts) and *tagliatelle ai carciofi* (with artichokes). There is a good selection of meat and fish main courses and a decent wine list – go for the robustly vivacious red Buttafuoco.

Sforzesco & North

See also p153 **Dulcis in Fundo**.

Italian

L'Altra Pharmacia

Via Rosmini 3 (02 345 1300). Metro Lanza/bus 57, 94. **Meals served** 12.30-2.30pm, 7.30pm-1.30am Mon-Sat. Closed 3wks Aug; 2wks Dec-Jan. **Average** €30. **Credit** AmEx, MC, V. **Map** p308 B2.

A cosily rustic eaterie in Milan's Chinatown, with simple paper place mats and modern art copies on bare brick walls. For a truly sublime culinary experience, try the delicious *risotto milanese mantecato in forma di grana* – risotto with saffron served in the hollowed-out rind of a parmesan cheese.

Centro Ittico

Via F Aporti 35 (02 2614 3774/ centroittico@acena.it). Metro Centrale FS or Pasteur/bus 90, 91, 92. **Meals served** 8-11pm Mon; 12.30-2.30pm, 8-11pm Tue-Sat. **Average** €40. **Credit** DC, MC, V. **Map** p309 A2.

The name – 'fishy centre' – sums this place up. The fresh and varied fish and seafood come straight from the fish market next door. If it's available, try the house speciality, *carpaccio di pesce* (thinly sliced raw fish served with salad vegetables). The decor is distinctly maritime, the atmosphere relaxed. Booking is a good idea – you can even do it by email.

Emilia & Carlo

Via Sacchi 10 (02 875 948/andreagalli.chef@tin.it). Metro Cairoli or Lanza/tram 3, 4, 12. **Meals served** Sept-July 12.30-3pm, 8-11pm Mon-Fri; 8-11pm Sat. Closed Aug, 2wks Dec-Jan. **Average** €35. **Credit** AmEx, DC, MC, V. **Map** p308 C2.

Creative Tuscan cuisine with a wide selection of starters from *pecorino* (goat's cheese) to fatty bacon and pickled vegetables. Second courses include the classic *bistecca fiorentina* t-bone steak. The wine-barrel arches are shamelessly kitsch, but the Brera location is good for sightseeing, and the wine list is extensive.

Eat, Drink, Shop

Delightful bolt-hole with lush garden: **Innocenti Evasioni**.

Franca, Paola & Lele
Viale Certosa 235 (02 3800 6238). Tram 19, 14.
Meals served *Sept-July* noon-2pm, 8-9.30pm Mon-Fri. Closed Aug; 1wk Christmas. **Average** €55.
Credit AmEx, DC, MC, V. **Map** off p308 A1.
A bit out of the way; but the superb Milanese and Lombard cuisine makes the trip into the northwestern suburbs worthwhile. Don't be fooled by the trattoria decor: quality (and prices) here are in the upmarket restaurant league. Go for the typically northern dishes such as *casoeûla* (pork and cabbage casserole) or *coniglio in salsa verde* (rabbit in parsley sauce). The wine cellar is excellent – but prices are high.

Innocenti Evasioni
Via privata della Bindellina (02 3300 1882/ innocentievasioni@libero.it). Bus 57/tram 1, 14.
Meals served *Sept-July* 8-11.30pm Tue-Sat. Closed Aug. **Average** €40. **Credit** AmEx, DC, MC, V.
Map off p308 A1.
A delightful bolt-hole in an unlikely part of town (near piazzale Accursio), with a young and adventurous chef-owner. The atmosphere is as understated as the waitresses' frumpy aprons. There is a choice of seasonal meat, fish or vegetarian menus. Unusual starters include *croccante di carciofi* (artichokes and mozzarella in a crispy pastry jacket); the *primi* include ravioli stuffed with polenta and toma cheese. The bread and desserts are homemade. There's a separate room with seating for couples and a lush garden with room for a few outside tables in summer. Despite its far-flung location, word is out, so book before making the trip out here.

Bar/restaurants

10 Corso Como Caffè
Corso Como 10 (02 2901 3581/info@10corsocomo. it). Metro Garibaldi/tram 11, 30, 33. **Meals served** 8pm-midnight Mon; 12.30-3pm, 8pm-midnight Tue-Sun. **Brunch served** 11am-5.30pm Sat, Sun.
Average €50. **Credit** AmEx, MC, V. Closed 2wks Aug. **Map** p308 B2.
This chic restaurant and designer store owned by fashion maven Carla Sozzani is arranged around the courtyard of a former car repair workshop. The restaurant serves a fusion of Mediterranean and Japanese recipes in nouvelle cuisine portions at outlandish prices; but it's still popular with the post-theatre and pre-nightclub crowd (it's close to both the Teatro Smeraldo, *see p176*, and a host of top nightlife venues). Great for a quiet midday coffee break; think twice before forking out for a full meal.

Tintero
Via Q Sella 2 (02 861 418). Metro Cairoli or Lanza/tram 3, 4, 12, 20. **Open** *Sept-July* 12.15-3pm, 7.45pm-1am Mon-Fri; 7.45pm-1am Sat, Sun. Closed Aug; 2wks Dec-Jan. **Average** €35 dinner. **Credit** AmEx, DC, MC, V. **Map** p308 C2.
A convenient spot for lunch after visiting the nearby Castello Sforzesco (*see p70*) or for cocktails on your way to the Brera district. This bar/restaurant has cool, minimalist decor, with a stainless steel bar counter. The restaurant – which stays open until late – does excellent *insalatone* (main course salads) and fish dishes, such as grilled *branzino* (sea bass). There are tables outside in summer.

Minimalist decor, very big salads at **Tintero**. *See p116.*

Ethnic

Serendib

Via Pontida 2 (02 659 2139). Metro Moscova/bus 41, 94. **Meals served** *Sept-July* 7.30pm-1am daily. Closed Aug. **Average** €25. **Credit** MC, V. **Map** p308 B2.

One of the best value of Milan's growing number of restaurants from the subcontinent (it's Sri Lankan). It's pleasantly low-lit with standard eastern decor; there's a choice of set menus based on vegetable, meat or fish main dishes. Wash that curry down with Three Coins lager, and finish off with ginger tea. At weekends it's a good idea to book.

San Babila & East

Italian

Da Abele

Via Temperanza 5 (02 261 3855). Metro Pasteur/bus 56. **Meals served** 8pm-midnight Tue-Sun. **Average** €20. **Credit** *Sept-July* AmEx, DC, MC, V. Closed Aug; 2 wks Dec-Jan. **Map** off p309 A2.

Abele is Milan's risotto king. The choice of variations on this Milanese staple is endless: from the classic *risotto milanese* (with saffron) to more imaginative concoctions such as *risotto cuneese* (with bacon and potatoes) and *risotto con spinaci e scamorza* (with spinach and smoked cheese). In the summer there are lighter recipes, such as *risotto di fragoline* (with tiny wild strawberries). If you've room for dessert, try the chocolate whisky cake.

Service is friendly and informal, and reservations are made on a same-day basis; so if you haven't booked, get there early.

L'Albero Fiorito

Via A Pellizzone 14 (02 7012 3425). Bus 38, 54, 61. **Meals served** noon-1.30pm, 7-8.30pm Mon-Fri; noon-1.30pm Sat. **Average** €12. **Credit** AmEx, MC, V. **Map** off p309 C2.

Run by gruff Giuseppe (who didn't want to appear in this guide, complaining he had too many customers already) and his Olive-Oyl-lookalike sister, this is the only place in Milan where you can eat a starter, first and second course for less than €15. At these prices there are no frills but the atmosphere is friendly and there's an eclectic mix of customers, ranging from brawny workmen to bespectacled students. On Fridays, try the delicious deep-fried sardines. Be prepared to share a table, and note the early evening closing.

Da Giacomo

Via P Sottocorno 6 (02 7602 3313). Tram 29, 30. **Meals served** 7.30-10.45pm Tue; noon-2.30pm, 7.30-10.45pm Wed-Sun. **Average** €50. **Credit** AmEx, DC, MC, V. Closed 3wks Aug; 2wks Dec-Jan. **Map** p309 C2.

It looks like nothing on the outside: an anonymous suburban trattoria with frosted windows in an anonymous suburban street. But Da Giacomo is one of Milan's most exclusive (though by no means most expensive) restaurants. In a series of bright and chatty rooms decorated by the late Renzo Mongiardino – interior designer to the rich and famous – major players from Milan's fashion and

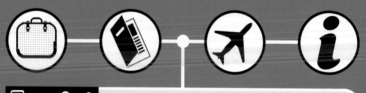

Da Abele, Milan's risotto king. *See p117.*

business worlds jostle for elbow room. Service can be uncertain, and the competent Mediterranean cuisine, with the emphasis on fish, would not win any prizes. But this is just what the city's captains of industry want: colour and comfort food in a 'trattoria' that is as difficult to book as the Ivy. Go with Giorgio, or book well ahead.

Da Ilia
Via Lecco 1 (02 2952 1895/ristdailia@tin.it). Metro Porta Venezia/tram 29, 30. **Meals served** *Sept-July* 12.30-2.30pm, 7.30-11pm Mon-Thur, Sun; 7.30-11pm Fri, Sat. Closed Aug; 2wks Dec-Jan. **Average** €35. **Credit** AmEx, MC, V. **Map** p309 B2.
Da Ilia is the sort of old-fashioned Milanese restaurant where starched waiters guide you to your table past a huge buffet of *antipasti*: but don't be put off; the prices are reasonable and the northern Italian cuisine first-rate. As a starter try the delicious *crostini con lardo* (super-fine slices of fatty bacon with olive oil and ground pepper on toast), followed by *agnolotti ripieni di zucca* (king-size ravioli stuffed with pumpkin). In summer, you can eat in the idyllic patio-garden.

Joia
Via P Castaldi 18 (02 2952 2124/www.joia.it). Metro Porta Venezia or Repubblica/tram 29, 30. **Meals served** *Sept-July* 12.30-2.30pm, 7.30-10.30pm Mon-Fri. Closed Aug. **Average** €50. **Credit** AmEx, DC, MC, V. **Map** p309 B/C1.
This sharp designer space just north of the Giardini Pubblici (*see p82*) is the Prada of vegetarian restaurants. Chef Piero Leeman exercises his considerable culinary (and literary) talents in dishes such as

Discovery: Variations on the Aubergine or *Asparagus Takes Form.* Zen menu pretension aside, this is high-level meatless cooking with plenty of hits and only a few misses. Ingredients vary from the homegrown to the exotic (Swiss-born Leeman has put in time in China and Japan), and there's hardly a pasta dish in sight. Book ahead, and definitely don't ask for nut roast. For hurried lunchers, there's a €15 special.

Masuelli San Marco
Viale Umbria 80 (02 5518 4138/www.masuelli-trattoria.com). Metro Lodi/bus 84, 90, 91, 92. **Meals served** 8-10pm Mon; 12.30-2.30pm, 8-10.30pm Tue-Sat. **Average** €40. **Credit** AmEx, DC, MC, V. **Map** p311 B2.
A Milanese institution that never fails to live up to its reputation. The atmosphere is warm, the service attentive, the cuisine stretches from Piedmont to Lombardy. Some of the dishes may not be to everyone's taste – such as the *filetti di aringhe* (herring fillets in milk), *bollito misto* (mixed boiled meats) or even tripe – but you won't find better versions of these classics in Milan. Start with the excellent choice of cured hams and salami, and order a good bottle of Barbera.

Milch
Via E Petrella 19 (02 2940 5870/milch2@inwind.it). Metro Caiazzo or Lima/tram 1. **Meals served** *Sept-July* 7.30-11pm Tue-Sun. Closed Aug. **Average** €40. **Credit** AmEx, DC, MC, V. **Map** p309 B2.
Situated close to Stazione Centrale, this former dairy outlet (hence the name) has now been converted into a chic little restaurant. The fusion cuisine is based

<table>
<tr><td>

The best

Places for...

Traditional Milanese cuisine
Masuelli San Marco (*p119*), **Franca, Paola & Lele** (*p116*), **Da Abele** (p117).

A romantic evening
Innocenti Evasioni (*p116*), **Osteria delle Vigne** (*p121*).

Pizza
Pizza OK (*p120*), **Super Pizza** (*p120*).

Something ethnic
Sukrity (*p120*), **Warsa** (*p120*), **Serendib** (*p117*), **Feijào Com Arroz** (*p123*).

Open-air dining
Tintero (*p116*), **Trattoria Madonnina** (*p122*).

Regional Italian cuisine
Emilio & Carlo (Tuscan, *p115*), **Al Merluzzo Felice** (Sicilian, *p121*).

Fish and seafood
Centro Ittico (*p115*), **Sushi-Kòboo** (*p124*), **Compagnia Generale dei...** (*p123*).

Seeing and being seen
Da Giacomo (*p117*), **Shambala** (*p124*), **Don Lisander** (*p115*).

Rustic Italian cooking
L'Altra Pharmacia (*p115*), **La Topaia** (*p122*), **L'Albero Fiorito** (*p117*), **Osteria delle Vigne** (*p121*).

Top-flight Italian cuisine
L'Ape Piera (*p121*), **Da Ilia** (*p119*), **Il Luogo di Aimo e Nadia** (*p37*), **Olivia** (*p121*), **Osteria Grand Hotel** (*p121*), **Cracco-Peck** (*see p142* Peck).

Fusion
10 Corso Como Caffè (*p116*), **Milch** (*p119*), **Joia** (*p119*).

</td><td>

On the top floor of an office block just outside Porta Nuova, this panoramic restaurant with summer terrace is one of the few with a sense of design to match Milan's reputation. The look is *Wallpaper** 1950s retro, with cherrywood consoles and chrome globe lights. Light, modern seafood dishes dominate the menu, beginning with the house speciality, 'Mediterranean sushi': a surprisingly successful attempt to use Italian fish, rice and pasta to recreate the spirit of Japan's top food export.

Ethnic

Sukrity
Via P Castaldi 22 (02 201 315). Metro Porta Venezia or Repubblica/tram 1, 11, 9, 29, 30. **Meals served** 12.15-2.30pm, 7.15-11pm daily. **Average** €25. **Credit** AmEx, DC, MC, V. **Map** p309 B/C1.
Milan's oldest Indian restaurant, Sukrity (its name in Sanskrit means 'good job') is a good-quality eaterie that stands out from the crowd. Its speciality is tandoori chicken or prawns, but it also serves excellent biryani and Madras curries accompanied by wine, Indian beers or tea. The decor is a bit on the sombre side; there's a no-smoking section.

Warsa
Via Melzo 16 (02 201 673). Metro Porta Venezia/ tram 29, 30, 23. **Meals served** noon-3pm, 7-10.30pm Mon, Tue, Thur-Sun. **Average** €15. **No credit cards. Map** p309 C2.
In the Porta Venezia area, home to much of Milan's large African community, Warsa offers Eritrean cooking and outstanding value for money. The menu includes dishes with veal, beef and chicken, plus plenty of vegetarian options – all eaten with your fingers. Try the *miès*, an aromatic wine.

Pizza & snacks

Pizza OK
Via Lambro 15 (02 2940 1272). Metro Porta Venezia/tram 5, 29, 30. **Meals served** noon-2pm, 7-11pm Mon-Sat. Closed 2wks Jan. **Average** €12. **No credit cards. Map** p309 C2.
Pizza OK serves the biggest, thinnest pizzas in town – so big they flop over the side of the plate. With over 120 varieties on the menu – including some strange ones like pear and gorgonzola – you're spoilt for choice. The interior is basic, but always packed.

Pizzeria 40
Via P Castaldi 40 (02 2940 0061). Metro Porta Venezia/tram 9, 29, 30. **Meals served** noon-2.45pm, 6.30-10.45pm Mon, Thur-Sun; noon-2.30pm Tue. **Average** €12. **Credit** MC, V. **Map** p309 B/C1.
If you've been shopping in corso Buenos Aires, this is an ideal place to stop for a quick lunch or snack. Although there are some pasta dishes on the menu, the house speciality is *pizza al trancio* – deep-pan pizza served in whopping big slices (real men ask for it *abbondante* – in an extra-large portion).

</td></tr>
</table>

almost exclusively on organic products: warm baby squid salad for starters, followed by fettucine with aubergine and ricotta, and loin of pork with sesame sauce. The service is low-key and friendly, the wine list short but select.

La Terrazza di via Palestro
Via Palestro 2, 4th floor (02 7600 2277/ terazzamilano@tiscalinet.it). Metro Turati or Palestro/bus 94. **Meals served** noon-2pm, 8.30-10.30pm Mon-Fri. Closed 3wks Aug; 2wks Dec-Jan. **Average** €45. **Credit** AmEx, DC, MC, V. **Map** p309 C1.

Milch: a chic former dairy. *See p119.*

Porta Romana & South

Italian

L'Ape Piera
*Via Ludovico il Moro 11 (02 8912 6060/www
.ape-piera.com). Bus 324, 325, 329, 351/tram 2.*
Meals served noon-2pm, 8-11pm Mon-Sat. Closed
3wks Aug; 2wks Jan. **Average** €50. **Credit** AmEx,
MC, V. **Map** off p310 C1.
A trad-look Naviglio *osteria*, complete with original
beams and cobbled paving. Specialities include
zuppetta di pomodorini con gamberi (cherry tomato
and shrimp soup), *risotto con mirtilli e coniglio*
(with blackcurrants and rabbit), *filetto con asparagi*
(fillet steak with aparagus). The wine list is select.
Finish off with the *millefoglie con zabaione all'aran-
cia* (a puff pastry dessert with orange-flavoured
zabaglione sauce).

Al Merluzzo Felice
*Via L Papi 6 (02 545 4711). Metro Lodi or Porta
Romana/bus 62, 77.* **Meals served** 12.30-2pm,
8-11pm Mon-Sat. **Average** €35. **Credit** AmEx,
DC, MC, V. **Map** p311 B2.
The lifeboat-sized 'Happy Cod' is always packed to
the gills, so book ahead. Shellfish risotto and pasta
with sardines make for tasty first courses, but the
speciality here is swordfish, prepared in a bewil-
dering variety of ways. There's also smoked tuna,
octopus and deep-fried breaded sardines. The
atmosphere is warm and welcoming, the service
friendly and attentive, and the cellar is chock-full
of good Sicilian wines.

Il Montalcino
*Via Valenza 17 (02 832 1926/ilmontalcino@tin.it).
Metro Porta Genova/tram 2.* **Meals served**
7.30pm-1am Mon-Sat. Closed 3wks Aug; 2wks Dec-
Jan. **Average** €35. **Credit** AmEx, DC, MC, V.
Map p310 B1.
In a rather sombre, wood-lined interior, Il
Montalcino serves predominantly Tuscan fare with
a countrified touch, with dishes such as *zuppa di
granaglie* (granary soup) or breast of duck ten-
derised in a red wine and *cinghiale* (wild boar) sauce.
There's an impressive selection of Tuscan wines,
including no less than 350 Brunellos. If you fancy a
canalside stroll afterwards, the restaurant is right
on the Naviglio Grande.

Olivia
*Viale G d'Annunzio 7/9 (02 8940 6052). Metro
Sant'Agostino or Porta Genova/bus 47, 59, 71,
74/tram 2, 3, 14, 20.* **Meals served** 12.30-3pm, 8-
10pm Mon-Sat. Closed 2wks Aug; 1wk Jan. **Average**
€32. **Credit** AmEx, DC, MC, V. **Map** p310 B2.
The unassuming entrance (it looks like someone's
front door; you'll have to ring the bell to enter) leads
into a small lobby and a split-level interior. There
are some mouthwateringly creative items on the
menu, including *strudel di verdura con crema
parmigiana* (vegetable strudel with parmesan white
sauce) or *tortelli della casa ripiene di pere e formag-
gio* (home-made pasta stuffed with pear and cheese).
There's always first-rate jazz on the sound system
and the service is polite and prompt. Great for a
romantic dinner.

Osteria Grand Hotel
*Via Cardinale A Sforza 75 (02 8951 6153). Bus 59,
71.* **Meals served** 8-11pm Tue-Sat; noon-2pm Sun.
Closed 3wks Aug; 2wks Dec-Jan. **Average** €35.
Credit AmEx, MC, V. **Map** p310 B/C2.
The cuisine is solidly Mediterranean, with fine
salami or hams to start, followed by meat or
vegetable main courses such as the baked potato
and artichoke *timbale*; portions, though, can be tiny.
Unusually for Italy, the extensive wine list has labels
from all around the world. The shady bower outside
is a welcome attraction in warm weather, as is the
live jazz at weekends. Parking, on the other hand,
is a nightmare.

Osteria delle Vigne
*Ripa di Porta Ticinese 61 (02 837 5617). Metro
Porta Genova/bus 47/tram 2.* **Meals served** *Sept-
July* noon-2pm Mon; noon-2.30pm, 8pm-1am Tue-Fri;
8pm-1am Sat. Closed Aug. **Average** €25. **Credit**
AmEx, MC, V. **Map** p310 B1.
This cosy, inexpensive *osteria* offers a surprisingly
good wine list and a highly varied menu. And
if that's not enough to tempt you, the ambience here
is decided laid-back... a plus in a district where the
eating places tend to be noisy and overcrowded. The
caramelle di ricotta e spinaci (sweet-shaped ravioli
stuffed with spinach and ricotta cheese) are a
delight. The tables are spacious, and it's a good place
to relax and chat.

Eat, Drink, Shop

Menu

Antipasti

antipasti di mare a selection of (usually) cold, cooked seafood, such as octopus, squid, clams, smoked swordfish, salmon, marinated sardines; **antipasti misti** (or **di terra**) a selection of salamis, hams, cheeses and olives; **funghi trifolati** cooked diced button mushrooms with garlic, chilli and parsley; **funghi pleos** grilled and dressed pleos mushrooms with oil, garlic and lemon; **alici marinate** sardines marinated in garlic, chilli and parsley; **saute di vongole** sautéd clams; **vitello tonnato** veal served with a tuna and mayonnaise sauce; **bresaola** cured horse meat or beef, served cold and thinly sliced with olive oil and lemon; **prosciutto e melone** parma ham and cantaloupe melon; **prosciutto e fichi** parma ham and figs; **mozzarella e prosciutto** mozzarella and parma ham; **peperoni ripieni** peppers cooked, rolled and filled with cheese and breadcrumbs; **bruschetta** toast, usually served with chopped tomatoes, garlic, basil and oil.

Pasta, polenta & risotto

al sugo with a simple tomato and basil sauce; **alla Genovese** with a thick onion and ham sauce; **alla Siciliana** with tomato, aubergine, basil and mozzarella; **alla Sorrentina** with tomato and mozzarella; **alla puttanesca, alla bella donna** with tomato, capers, black olives and a touch of chilli; **con fagioli e cozze** with beans and mussels; **al sugo di noci** with walnut sauce; **alla carbonara** with bacon, beaten egg and black pepper; **alle vongole** with clams; **al tartufo** with truffles, usually from Piedmont – served with pasta or as garnish; **con fiorilli** with courgette flowers; **alla Barese** with broccoli; **al pesto** with a Genoese sauce of basil, pine nuts and parmesan; **all'insalata** served cold; **pasta e fagioli** a dense pasta and bean soup; **pasta e ceci** the same, but with chickpeas; **ravioli di zucca** ravioli stuffed with pumpkin; **pizzoccheri** wholemeal pasta, usually served with potatoes, cabbage and Bitto cheese; **gnocchi** potato pasta; **polenta** a filling yellow cornmeal mash, served either semi-liquid or in harder, crumbly slices; **polenta fritta** fried polenta; **risotto milanese** a light risotto cooked in butter with white wine, beef marrow and saffron.

Carne (meat)

cotoletta milanese breaded veal cutlets; **busecca** a stew of tripe, lard, butter, beef, tomatoes and beans; **cassoeûla** a stew of pork cuts, sausage and cabbage; **ossobuco** beef bone marrow prepared as a stew with peas; **involtini** small rolls of beef or aubergine (*melanzane*) stuffed with ham and cheese;

La Topaia

Via F Argelati 40 (02 837 3469). Metro Romolo or Porta Genova/bus 47, 90, 91. **Meals served** 8-11.30pm Mon-Sat. Closed Aug. **Average** €25. **Credit** AmEx, DC, MC, V. **Map** p310 B1.
This delightful old-style restaurant, complete with candlelight and guitar-strumming crooners, is a short distance from the overcrowded, noisy dives of the Naviglio Grande. The menu is solidly traditional, with hearty dishes such as *minestrone d'orzo* (barley soup) and *stinco arrosto* (roast shin of pork). All the desserts are home-made, and the friendly atmosphere more than makes up for the indifferent wine list.

Trattoria Madonnina

Via Gentilino 6 (02 8940 9089). Bus 59, 7/tram 15. **Meals served** *Sept-July* noon-2.30pm, 8-11.30pm Mon-Wed; 8-11.30pm Thur-Sat. Closed Aug. **Average** €25. **Credit** MC, V. **Map** p310 B2.
Everything a trattoria should offer is here: wholesome food, an informal, cosy atmosphere, wooden tables, chequered napkins and a picturesque garden. As the name suggests (*The Madonnina* is the gold-en statue of the Madonna on top of the Duomo), the menu is typically Milanese, simple and filling. Meaty main courses include *ossobuco* (bone marrow stew) and *cotoletta milanese* (breaded veal).

Bar/restaurants

Tuberi Americani

Via Vetere 9 (02 8324 1152/www.tuberiamericani. com). Tram 2, 14. **Meals served** 7pm-2am Tue-Sun. Closed 1wk Aug. **Average** €25. **Credit** DC, MC, V. **Map** p310 B2.
A relatively recent arrival on the scene, this bar/restaurant is dedicated to that humble tuber, the potato, which is served with everything from the cocktail buffet to the main courses. Everything on the à la carte menu and the cheaper set menu is cooked to order, so be prepared to wait (a potato *timbale* takes about 20 minutes). Marble and steel surfaces provide a suitably stylish atmosphere for design-conscious Milanese diners. The restaurant is just next to the pretty Parco delle Basiliche behind the church of Sant'Eustorgio.

polpettone meat loaf; **polpette** meatballs, usually served in a thick tomato sauce; **carne al ragù** slow-cooked beef served in a tomato sauce; **carne alla pizzaiola** meat served with a tomato and basil sauce; **luganiga** pork sausage; **capriolo** mountain goat, usually braised; **cotechino con lenticchie** boiled pork sausage or pig's trotters served with lentils; **rane** frogs' legs, usually fried; **lumacche** snails; **mostarda** sweet 'n' sour fruit pieces preserved in oil and mustard – often served with lamb.

Pesce & frutti di mare (fish & seafood)

seppie in umido cuttlefish in tomato casserole; **musillo marinato** marinated fish of the cod family; **purpietielle/purpo/polpo/polipo** octopus; **pignatiello** seafood soup served with toast fingers; **mazzancolle** very large prawns; **totano** seafood similar to squid, often cooked with potatoes; **calamaro ripieno** stuffed squid; **lavarello** a freshwater fish from Lake Como; **persico** another freshwater fish from Lake Como; **missoltini** twaite shad; **pesciolini fritti** tiny fried sprats.

Contorni (vegetables)

fagiolini all'agro cooked green beans with garlic and lemon; **carciofi alla giudea**

artichokes cooked with olives and capers; **bietole** spinach beet; **melanzane al funghetto** diced aubergines cooked in tomato and basil; **melanzane alla brace** sliced aubergines, char-grilled and dressed with garlic, chilli and parsley; **funghi porcini** big mushrooms, usually prepared with parsley and garlic or as a pasta sauce; **chiodini** small mushrooms marinated in olive oil or prepared with parsley and garlic.

Formaggi (cheeses) & cheese dishes

mozzarella in carrozza deep-fried, traditionally on a small square of bread, but nowadays in breadcrumbs; **caprese mozzarella** tomato and basil salad; **provola** similar to mozzarella but with a smoky taste; **provola alla pizzaiola** smoky cheese cooked in a tomato and basil sauce; **taleggio** delicate, creamy cheese from the Lecco region.

Methods of cooking

all'acqua pazza baked with garlic, parsley and a touch of tomato – a method used for fish; **al sale** (fish) cooked under a huge pile of sea salt; **in bianco** without tomato; **lesso** boiled; **alla griglia/alla piastra** grilled; **al forno** baked in the oven; **al cartoccio** baked in aluminium foil; **macchiato** with a touch of tomato; **ripassato** (of vegetables) tossed in the frying pan with garlic and chilli.

Ethnic

Compagnia Generale dei Viaggiatori Naviganti e Sognatori

Via della Cascina di Cuccagna 4, off via Muratori (02 551 6154/www.trattoriagiapponese.com). Metro Porta Romana/bus 62, 90, 91. **Meals served** 8pm-midnight Tue-Sat; 8-11pm Sun. Closed 2wks Aug; 2wks Dec-Jan. **Average** €35. **Credit** AmEx, DC, MC, V. **Map** p311 B2.
This reasonably priced Japanese bar and restaurant is as remarkable for its delightful name – the General Company of Travellers, Navigators and Dreamers – as it is for its cooking. The decor is upbeat, all the more so when the restaurant is staging one of its regular art shows. Tables can be reserved online, although the wacky website is a bit confusing.

Feijào Com Arroz

Via Corrado II il Salico 10 (02 8951 2722). Tram 24. **Meals served** 8pm-2am Tue-Sun. Closed 2wks Aug. **Average** €25. **No credit cards.** **Map** p311 C1.

A fair hike from the centre, in the suburbs south-west of Porta Romana, this Brazilian diner provides a touch of Latin colour in fog-bound Milan – not least because it's popular with the city's South American transvestite community. The portions are generous and the Italo-Brazilian staff very friendly. Try the *frango a passarinho* (lemon-fried chicken pieces), followed by *picanha* (grilled beef with bean paste) and *bobo de camaráo* (shrimps in broth with cassava).

Seven

Corso Colombo 11 (02 5810 1669/www.sevengroup.it). Metro Porta Genova/tram 2, 14. **Meals served** 6pm-midnight Mon-Sat. Closed 3wks Aug; 2wks Dec-Jan. **Average** €20. **Credit** AmEx, MC, V. **Map** p310 B1.
This recently opened New York-style eaterie, with bright, squeaky-clean decor, spotlights the meatier edge of the American tradition: barbecued chicken wings, Aberdeen Angus steaks, New Zealand lamb. There are also various fish dishes and hefty quarter-pound hamburgers, accompanied by a wide-ranging (rather than outstanding) wine list from both the New and Old Worlds.

Eat, Drink, Shop

Seven spotlights meaty American traditions. *See p123.*

Shambala
Via Ripamonti 337 (02 552 0194). Tram 24. **Meals served** 8pm-1am Mon-Sat. Closed 3wks Aug; 2wks Dec-Jan. **Average** €45. **Credit** AmEx, DC, MC, V. **Map** p311 B/C1.
A new see-and-be-seen restaurant that deserves its reputation. The service is efficient and discreet, but the main reason for Shambala's success is the excellent Vietnamese/Asian fusion cuisine: stir-fry prawns with oyster sauce, seared tuna with coriander seeds, or house speciality, *kaeng kung* – steamed shrimps in coconut milk. There's an enormous terrace for open-air dining in the summer. Pricey but nice.

Sushi-Kòboo
Viale Col di Lana 1 (02 837 2608). Tram 15, 29, 30. **Meals served** 12.30-2.30pm, 7.30-11.30pm Tue-Sun. Closed 2wks Aug. **Average** €20. **Credit** AmEx, DC, MC, V. **Map** p310 B2.
A Japanese restaurant with a wide choice of fresh sushi and surprisingly reasonable prices. In the bright, clean interior, you can eat seated around the conveyor belt, or seated at a table.

Pizza & snacks

Super Pizza
Viale Sabotino 4 (02 5832 0410). Tram 9, 30. **Meals served** *Sept-July* noon-2pm, 7-10pm Tue-Sat; 7-10pm Sun. Closed Aug. **Average** €12. **No credit cards.** **Map** p311 B1.

Famous throughout the city for its wafer-thin, Roman-style pizzas, this no-nonsense pizzeria packs 'em in and moves 'em out (you're not encouraged to linger here). Besides the standard pizzas, there are also some more inventive toppings, such as salmon, or gorgonzola and bacon. No reservations accepted: just join the queue.

Sant'Ambrogio & West

Italian

Da Leo
Via Trivulzio 26 (02 4007 1445). Metro Piazza de Angeli or Gambara/bus 72, 80, 90, 91. **Meals served** 12.30-2.30pm, 7.30-10.30pm Tue-Sat. Closed 3wks Aug; 2wks Dec. **Average** €35. **No credit cards.** **Map** off p310 A1.
Giuseppe Leo, who is originally from Puglia, has been going to Milan's fish market at the crack of dawn for the past 30 years to select the freshest produce for his fish-only restaurant. The dishes served here are simple and wholesome: spaghetti (no other pasta is served) *in bianco* (without tomatoes) with tuna, clams, king prawns or calamari; and main course fish dishes (fried or grilled), with what's on offer depending on the catch of the day. The interior is unpretentious, the service friendly and efficient, the wine list extensive. It's best to book ahead for dinner.

Cafés & Bars

Quick-fire *caffè* and long lingering cocktails.

In this hyperactive, work-oriented city, coffee drinking is never seen as a time-killing activity that goes well with people-watching at the local street corner café. The Milanese enter a café, pay, head to the counter for their little brown pick-me-up, add sugar, shoot it, and then they're off. It takes two minutes… max. The average *milanese* will repeat this adrenalin-boosting ritual at least twice a day.

In fact, the bar as lingering place doesn't come into its own until after work: at that point the locals loosen their ties and head for their favourite *aperitivo* haunt (*see p129* **Aperitivi**).

Never a city to follow traditional Italian models, Milan has created unique grey areas in its café and bar scene. There are bar/restaurants (*see chapter* **Restaurants**), bar/discos (*see chapter* **Nightlife & Music**) and ice-cream parlours (*see p143* **Gelati**); and that same café where housewives natter over their morning cappuccino can turn into a wild and wonderful late-night venue later on.

WHERE TO DRINK WHAT

To the north of the centre, you'll find a hipper, more cosmopolitan bar scene, especially around Moscova at **Radetzky** (*see p127*) and **ATM** (*see p126*); if you're looking to take the weight off your feet for a bit over a cup of tea, **Caffè Letterario** (*see p126*) is another option. In Brera's pedestrianised streets, you'll find a bar behind practically every other door. If **Bar Brera**'s (*see p126*) *birreria*/café atmosphere doesn't grab you, try the **Pottery Café**'s (*see p153*) extensive coffee, cake and juice menu.

The neighbourhoods east of the centre harbour some of Milan's most historic, elegant cafés such as **Cova** (*see p128*) and **Sant'Ambroeus** (*see p129*), both of which are a must for anyone with a taste for classy cakes and ambience; and the hyper-trendy bar of the hotel **Sheraton Diana Majestic** (*see p45*).

In the south, the Navigli (canals; *see p92*) and the area around the Colonne di San Lorenzo (*see p91*) have become hubs for *aperitivi* bars.

Eat, Drink, Shop

Once a pool, now a seriously trendy bar at the **Sheraton Diana Majestic**. *See p45.*

PRACTICALITIES

In Italian, *caffè* generally means coffee, or, more specifically, espresso; the place where you drink it is sometimes a *caffè*, but more often a *bar*. And the counter you lean against as you do so is a *banco*. The word *locale* evokes something darker and smokier than *bar*.

The head of the coffee clan is the espresso. Its best-known relative is the cappuccino. There's also the *caffè macchiato* (spotted coffee) with a drop of steamed milk. For real caffeine fiends, there's the *caffè ristretto*, a tooth-enamel-removing brown syrup in the bottom of your cup. Its arch-enemy is the diluted *caffè lungo* (long coffee), which – though frowned upon – is still more acceptable to contemptuous Milanese bar staff than the *caffè americano*, an espresso in a teacup, filled to the brim with water. For a little more spice, there's the *caffè corretto* (corrected coffee), which includes a shot of liquor of your choice – usually grappa or sambuca.

Duomo & Centre

Café Vertigo
*Via San Vittore al Teatro 3 (02 7201 6462).
Metro Cordusio/bus 50, 58/tram 19, 20, 24, 27.*
Open 7am-2am daily. Closed 1wk Aug. **Credit** AmEx, MC, V. **Map** p310 A2.
A stone's throw from Milan's Fascist-era stock exchange, Café Vertigo is an old reliable of Milan's financial district. Businessmen and -women shoot their morning first *caffè* here, and their second after lunch. Come *aperitivo* time (happy hour 6.30-9pm;

The best **Bars**

For morning coffee
Radetzky (*p127*), Cigno Nero (*p128*).

For feeding your sweet tooth
Biffi (*p130*).

For writing your novel
Caffè Letterario (*p126*).

For seeing and being seen
Roialto (*p130*), 10 Corso Como (*p127*).

For drinking with the in-crowd
ATM (*p126*), 10 Corso Como (*p127*).

For serious *aperitivo* swilling
Morgan's (*p130*).

For *gelato*
Bastianello (*p128*).

---

cocktails €5), Vertigo attracts a diverse crowd. Everyone from stock traders to artists and students can be found drinking Negroni or prosecco.

Caffe Miani (Zucca)
*Piazza del Duomo 21 (02 8646 4435/
www.caffemiani.it). Metro Duomo/bus 50, 54/tram
8, 15, 19, 24.* **Open** Sept-July 7.30am-9pm Tue-Sun.
Closed Aug. **Credit** AmEx, MC, V. **Map** p311 A1.
Caffe Miani, or Zucca as it's known for the liqueur that was once unique to it, is a museum of 135 years of Milanese social history, and the mustachioed Orlando Chiari, the owner-historian-documentarian, is its curator. Stretching from piazza Duomo to the Galleria, this café, with its art deco mosaics, is a favourite *aperitivo* stop for Milan's opera *appas-sionati* en route to La Scala. A Campari *sceccherato*, Campari shaken with crushed ice and a squirt of lemon, is a classic.

Sforzesco & North

Try also **Casablanca Café** (*see p171*), **Pottery Café**, (*see p153*) and **Le Trottoir** (*see p170*).

ATM
*Bastioni di Porta Volta 15 (02 655 2365). Metro
Moscova/bus 51, 57/tram 3, 12, 14.* **Open** 11am-3pm, 6pm-2am Mon-Sat. **No credit cards.**
Map p309 B1.
Many consider this former tram station the *crème de la crème* of Milan's *aperitivo* bars. A twenty- and thirtysomething crowd heads for the rococo bar, but not to sit and chat: veteran ATM-ers – a mainly artsy, intellectual crowd – grab a drink and a plate of warm food and head outside to loiter. An hour or two – day or evening – at ATM offers a clear insight into more progressive Milanese fashions. Cocktails cost €4.

Bar Brera
*Via Brera 23 (02 877 091). Metro Montenapoleone
or Lanza/bus 61, 94.* **Open** Apr-Oct 7am-3am daily.
Nov-Mar 7am-3am Mon-Sat. **Credit** AmEx, MC, V.
Map p308 C2.
In the heart of Milan's quiet, pedestrianised old-bohemian-turned-affluent Brera zone, Bar Brera is a catch-all *locale*. Whether you want a coffee or beer, sandwich or cake, cigarette or cigar, inside or out, Bar Brera has it, and all year round. (There's no smoking inside from noon to 4pm, though.) The interior has an oak-panelled tavern feel, while the outside tables are warmed in winter by heaters.

Caffè Letterario
*Via Solferino 27 (02 2901 5119). Metro Turati/
bus 41, 43, 61.* **Open** 8am-1am Mon-Sat. Closed
2wks Aug. **No credit cards. Map** p308 B/C2.
If you fancy hours of coffee-sipping while you pen a chapter of your latest novel, the Caffè Letterario is the place for you. Milan's intelligentsia frequents it, as does anyone looking to sate a sweet tooth: the pastries are wonderful.

Eat, Drink, Shop

Exquisite chocolates at **Sant'Ambroeus**. *See p129.*

10 Corso Como

Corso Como 10 (02 2901 3581/
www.carlasozzani.com). Metro Garibaldi/tram 29,
30, 33. **Open** 11am-3pm, 6pm-2am daily.
Credit AmEx, MC, V. **Map** p308 B2.
Dieci Corso Como is *the* hotspot in Milan. The
creation of style guru Carla Sozzani, the bar and café
area has a vaguely oriental slant. Like the clothing
and accessories shops, luxury goods stores and
bookshops in the same complex, there's nothing
cheap about this bar (cocktails are €9). But a visit,
if not an *aperitivo*, is a must.

Good Fellas

Via Cusani 4 (02 869 0142). Metro Cairoli or
Lanza/tram 1, 3, 4, 12, 14, 27/bus 61. **Open** 8am-
2am Mon-Sat. **Credit** MC, V. **Map** p308 C2.
In the morning, Good Fellas offers great cappuccino and *brioche* to locals; at lunch it attracts a
professional crowd. But come *aperitivo* hour (cocktails €6), it exerts an irresistible pull on Milan's
fighetti (*see p172* **Fighetti**). Overlooked by a rather
obstreperous Armani billboard, this is the place to
come if you're looking to meet young *milanesi* on
the up and up.

Louisiana Bistro

Via Fiori Chiari 17 (02 8646 5315). Metro Lanza/
bus 61/tram 3, 4, 12, 14, 27. **Open** noon-4pm,
6pm-2am Tue-Sun. **Credit** AmEx, MC, V.
Map p308 C2.
This packed Brera-district bar is a good bet for
anyone seeking to strike up a conversation without
having to fumble through the phrase book. Expats
(as well as lots of young models in town for work)

congregate upstairs to drink beer, shoot pool and
watch sport on TV. It's easy to forget that you're in
Italy at all. Though it calls itself a bistro, the food is
not the high point.

Radetzky

Largo La Foppa 5 (02 657 2645). Metro Moscova/
bus 41, 43, 94. **Open** 7.30am-1.30am daily. Closed
2wks Aug. **Credit** AmEx, MC, V. **Map** p308 B2.
Radetzky offers morning coffee, afternoon tea or
evening cocktail drinkers a minimalist, white-
walled, marble-countered decor in which to imbibe
their tonic of choice. It's one of Milan's more modern cafés, where everyone from young professionals
to a chic, older crowd will meet for any type of drink
at any time of the day. There's one large round table,
where you can feel free to chat with your neighbour
or not, and two rows of tables where the same rules
apply. Cocktails cost around €6.

Victoria Café

Via Clerici 1 (02 805 3598). Metro Cordusio
or Duomo/bus 61/tram 1, 3, 12, 14, 20. **Open** *Bar*
5am-2am Mon-Sat. *Restaurant* noon-3pm, 7.30pm-
midnight Mon-Sat. Closed 3wks Aug. **Credit** AmEx,
MC, V. **Map** p308 C2.
Located in Milan's financial district, the Victoria
Café has become the after-work hub for a slew of
market movers. Stocks and bonds are left behind at
the door, however; Milan's financial circle heads here
to let off steam. The chandeliers and drapery create
a sort of decadent grandeur, but loud music adds a
touch of modernity. The food is abundant; so are the
people. There's a happy hour from 5pm to 8.30pm,
when cocktails cost €5; afterwards they're €7.

San Babila & East

Don't miss the bar at the **Sheraton Diana Majestic** (*see p45*).

Artdeco Café

Via Lambro 7 (02 2952 4760/www.artdecocafe.it). Bus 60/tram 5, 11. **Open** 6pm-2am daily. **Credit** AmEx, DC, MC, V. Closed 3wks Aug. **Map** p309 C2.
If the crowd at Lelephante (*see below*) is too flashy, head across the street to the Artdeco Café where the more subtle *milanesi* abscond for *aperitivi*. A DJ spins for a chic crowd seated around perspex tables with shells, flowers and toothbrushes embedded in them. Cocktails cost €5.16, 6-9pm, and €7.75 later.

Bastianello

Via Borgogna 5 (02 7631 7065/www.bastianello.com). Metro San Babila/bus 61, 54. **Open** 7am-9pm daily. Closed 3wks Aug. **Credit** AmEx, MC, V. **Map** p309 C1.
Bastianello's decor can't compete with the more elegant Cova (*see p128*) or Sant'Ambroeus (*see p129*), but then again, no one's hot chocolate can compete with Bastianello's. Moreover, the ice-cream here makes *gelato* elsewhere in Milan seem like an insult to the learned palate.

Cigno Nero

Via della Spiga 33 (02 7602 2620). Metro Montenapoleone, Turati or San Babila/bus 61, 94/tram 1, 2, 20. **Open** *Sept-July* 8am-8pm Mon-Sat. Closed Aug. **Credit** AmEx, MC, V. **Map** p309 C1.

If you're window-shopping in via della Spiga – and you inevitably will be – stop by Cigno Nero, where the confectionery and coffee are in a class of their own. A *caffè* and *brioche* at one of its elegant tables is the perfect way to begin your retail morning; a post-shopping tea or *aperitivo* won't disappoint either. The café's gourmet sandwiches are delicious, but get there early, as the bar draws more of the local professionals than it can reasonably hold between 1pm and 2pm.

Cova

Via Montenapoleone 8 (02 7600 0578/ www.pasteccriacova.it). Metro Montenapoleone or San Babila/bus 54, 61/tram 2, 20. **Open** *Sept-July* 9am-2.30am Mon-Sat. Closed Aug. **No credit cards**. **Map** p309 C1.
Founded in 1837, Cova is the classic Milanese café. In the designer label hub of luxurious via Montenapoleone, this *pasticceria* (pastry shop) and *confetteria* (confectioner's) makes all of its delights in-house. If you're up for a *panino* (filled roll), even the bread is home-made. You can shoot your coffee at the bar or nurse a cappuccino in one of the café's two sitting rooms adorned with paintings of Milan's historic sights.

Lelephante

Via Melzo 22 (02 2951 8768/www.lelephante.it). Metro Porta Venezia/bus 60/tram 5, 11. **Open** 6pm-2am Tue-Sun. Closed Aug. **No credit cards**. **Map** p309 C2.

The spacious **Roialto** screams new media. *See p130.*

Aperitivi

All Italians like their pre-meal *aperitivo*: it 'opens your stomach', they'll tell you. But in Milan it's more than a mere gastronomic curtain-raiser: it's a cultural institution.

For most, the point of having an *aperitivo* is *farsi vedere*, or being seen. Which also, naturally, implies seeing too.

At **Bar Magenta** (*see p130*), for example, clients eschew the seating and cram the bustling pavement; at **Good Fellas** (*see p127*), mobile phones squeal as often as ice clanks against glasses, as the Milanese check in with friends to make sure that the real action isn't happening elsewhere. For a more sophisticated aperitif, look no further than **10 Corso Como** (*see p127*) or **El Brellin** (*see p129*): the drinks are horribly expensive, but you're paying to exchange glances with a classier crowd.

There's nothing comfortable about the *aperitivo* ritual: trendy the verdant courtyard of the **Trattoria Toscana** (*see p130*) may be, for example, but you'll have to fight your way through a rib-crackingly packed crowd from 6pm to 9pm.

Unlikely as it seems, the *aperitivo* culture does have one advantage for budget travellers: finger food, or *stuzzichini*, comes gratis with aperitifs. At the **Tribeca Lounge** (*see p130*) there are quiches, pasta and vegetables to satisfy most appetites; **ATM** (*see p126*), too, has pastas, cold cuts, vegetables and even sauerkraut and wurstel, a tribute to Milan's years under Austrian rule.

The standard *aperitivo* is *spumante*, an Italian bubbly, either sweet or dry. The Puccini (dry *spumante* with mandarin juice) and the Rossini (dry *spumante* with strawberries) are so traditional that they're almost tacky.

And of course, there's Campari, the Italian bitter. Most Italians mix Campari with other spirits to sweeten the medicine. The Negroni – Campari, vermouth, dry gin and a slice of orange – is a classic with a quick kick.

Many *milanesi* will go for the latest Latin American fad, such as a Cuban Mojito. Mint Capriosca and blackcurrant Kir Royale are also firm favourites. Others will opt for a beer, or choose from the omnipresent array of red and white wines.

Known for the potency of its drinks (cocktails cost €5-€6) and its ever-changing interior design, Lelephant draws an eclectic crowd, from pit-bull-escorting university students to the avant-garde of Milan's underground fashion scene. There are snacks galore on the bar. It's also a hotspot for Milan's gay community.

Sant'Ambroeus

Corso Matteotti 7 (02 7600 0540). Metro Montenapoleone or San Babila/bus 61.
Open 7.45am-8.15pm daily. Closed 3wks Aug.
Credit AmEx, MC, V. **Map** p309 C1.
This café dates back to 1936, and the striking decor and feel of those heady years have been lovingly preserved. Everything from the chairs to the wood panelling, from the bar to the drapery, has been retained. Sant'Ambroeus's speciality chocolates – *ambrogetto* and *ambrogiotto* – are simply exquisite.

Porta Romana & South

Check out **Café l'Atlantique** (*see p170*), **Scimmie** (*see p168*) and **Cherubini** (*see p143*).

Le Biciclette

Conca del Naviglio 10 (02 5810 4325). Metro Sant'Ambrogio/bus 94/tram 20, 3, 14. **Open** 6pm-2am Mon-Sat; 12.30-4.30pm, 6pm-2am Sun. Closed 3wks Aug. **Credit** AmEx, MC, V. **Map** p310 B2.

With its monthly changing displays of contemporary artwork, Le Biciclette attracts everyone from Milan's young artists to successful thirtysomethings, models, would-be models and struggling journalists. It's the quintessential *aperitivo* hang-out, with a few south-after tables inside and outside, and twice as many people as chairs. The buffet of mortadella, cheese, carrots and olives is a classic. Cocktails cost €6.

El Brellin

Alzaia Naviglio Grande 14 (02 5810 1351). Metro Porta Genova/bus 59/tram 2, 9, 14, 15, 20, 29.
Open 12.30-2.30pm, 6.30pm-2am Tue-Sat; noon-3pm Sun. **Credit** MC, V. **Map** p310 B1.
El Brellin offers the most refined atmosphere to be found on the Naviglio Grande (*see p92*), Milan's *osteria*, pizzeria and *birreria* hub. To be fair, it's more of a restaurant that serves *aperitivi* than an *aperitivo* bar. But the building is the most charming around, and the *affettati* (cold cuts) are enticing more and more staunch *aperitivi* purists.

Cuore

Via G Mora 3 (02 5810 5126/www.cuore.it). Metro Sant'Ambrogio/bus 94/tram 2, 3, 14, 20. **Open** 6pm-2am daily. Closed 2wks Aug. **No credit cards**. **Map** p310 A/B2.
Dimmed lights and candles set the mood, while a DJ sets an electronic tone. Couches in the cosy interior

make it a winter favourite, though lack of outside seating and internal ventilation send the crowds seeking illusory cool elsewhere on muggy Milanese summer nights. Cocktails cost between €6.20 and €7.75; standard *stuzzichini* (appetisers) please those who aren't too hungry, while a piquant Indian dip offers a bit more.

Flying Circus

Piazza Vetra 21 (02 5831 3577). Metro Missori or Sant'Ambrogio/bus 94/tram 2, 3, 14, 20. **Open** 9.30am-2am Mon-Fri, Sun. Closed 3wks Aug. **No credit cards. Map** p310 B2.
Just off pretty. leafy Parco delle Basiliche (*see p89*) in the refreshingly quiet piazza Vetra, Flying Circus offers the perfect *aperitivo* for those looking for less of a scene. And if the laid-back atmosphere palls, it's a hop, skip and a jump from the Colonne di San Lorenzo (*see p91*), where there's always a crowd. The bar draws a packed house on Sundays, and is a civilised way to start off an evening or end a long day. Cocktails cost €4.

Indiana Post

Via Casale 7 (02 5811 2220). Metro Porta Genova/bus 47, 74/tram 2, 9, 14, 29. **Open** 6.30pm-2am daily. **Credit** AmEx, MC, V. **Map** p310 B1.
In other bars, it's the fad to down your *aperitivo* standing up; at Indiana Post you can rest your weary feet after a hard day's touring or shopping at tables and chairs galore. Located just off the Naviglio Grande (*see p92*), this American-themed bar is a little on the kitsch side, but spacious and friendly; it is also refreshingly free from pose-striking. Cocktails cost €6.50.

Trattoria Toscana

Corso di Porta Ticinese 58 (02 8940 6292). Metro Sant'Ambrogio/bus 94/tram 3, 20. **Open** 6pm-2am Mon-Sat. **Credit** AmEx, DC, MC, V. **Map** p310 A/B2.
The Trattoria Toscana fad has spread like wildfire, launching this bar/restaurant, with its verdant garden courtyard, into the first division of the city's *aperitivo* stops. Don't expect to find anywhere to sit… except, that is, in the restaurant inside, to which the management obviously hopes to lure sippers of Toscana's cocktails, which cost €4.50 before 9pm and €6 after.

Tribeca Lounge

Via Conca del Naviglio 22 (02 8942 0346/ www.tribecalounge.com). Metro Sant'Ambrogio/ bus 94/tram 2, 3, 14, 20. **Open** 6pm-2am Tue-Sat; noon-4pm Sun. Closed 3wks Aug. **Credit** AmEx, MC, V. **Map** p310 B2.
In warmer weather, get to Tribeca at the early end of happy hour (6-8.30pm; cocktails €5.16): the outside seating is spacious and quiet, but in high demand. There's a lounge-y feel to the winter seating downstairs, where there's attitude to spare – despite the name, Tribeca screams Milan. Local and international DJs are known to drop in for a spin; call ahead for information on special events. The bar's food ranks among the city's best.

Sant'Ambrogio & West

Biffi

Corso Magenta 87 (02 4800 6702). Metro Conciliazione/bus 18/tram 20, 24. **Open** 7.30am-8.30pm Mon, Wed-Sun. Closed 1wk Aug. **No credit cards. Map** p308 C1/2.
One of Milan's historic cafés, Biffi is located on the edge of one of the city's most affluent neighbourhoods. The counter is cosy but never overcrowded; the tearoom has a handful of tables for chatting and resting. The Biffi tri-chocolate, tri-layered cake will impress even the most seasoned chocoholic.

Colonial Fashion Café

Via de Amicis 12 (02 8942 0401). Metro Sant'Agostino/bus 94/tram 2, 3, 14, 20. **Open** 6.30pm-3am daily. **Credit** AmEx, MC, V. **Map** p310 A2.
Fashionable by name and by nature, the curbside summer seating and tables in the generic-ethnicky interior of the Colonial Fashion Café are a hive of people-watching activity well into the morning. Cocktails cost €5.

Magenta

Via Carducci 13 (02 805 3808/www.barmagenta. com). Metro Cadorna/bus 18, 94/tram 19, 20, 24, 27. **Open** 8am-3am daily. Closed 2wks Aug. **No credit cards. Map** p308 C2.
The Magenta is an institution, and has been for around 100 years. In spring and summer, the curb-side tables are a crucial Milanese meeting place. In the winter, the party moves inside. The bar is packed and thick with cigarette smoke from 6.30pm to 9pm. Cocktails cost €4-€5.

Morgan's

Via Novati (02 867 694). Metro Sant'Ambrogio/ bus 94, 58, 54, 50/tram 2, 14. **Open** *Sept-July* 6pm-2am Mon-Sat. Closed Aug. **Credit** AmEx, DC, MC, V. **Map** p310 A2.
A watering hole for Sant'Ambrogio locals and a favourite with *milanesi* from all spheres, Morgan's has become a classic. And unlike most *aperitivi locales*, Morgan's old-fashioned bar cosiness means it often retains the same crowd beyond the happy hour (6-8.30pm; cocktails €4).

Roialto

Via Piero della Francesca 55 (02 3493 6616). Bus 57, 94/tram 1, 19, 33. **Open** 6.30pm-2am Mon-Sat; 12.30-3.30pm, 6-9pm Sun. Closed 3wks Aug. **Credit** AmEx, MC, V. **Map** p308 B1.
Fashions come and go in Milan, and the long-running Roialto has become 'It' of late. Perhaps it's the cigar lounge; or maybe it's the spaciousness, which gives the *aperitivo*-sipper a choice of reclining on a sofa or propping up the enormous wooden bar imported (perhaps to enhance the cigary theme) from Cuba. Roialto has little time for the suit and tie type: it simply screams new media. Add a DJ spinning cool sounds and you get one of Milan's best *aperitivo* joints.

Shops & Services

Credit limit blow-outs or bargains galore: Milan – aka Pradaworld – is a shopper's delight.

Let's be honest. Most people come to Milan for two reasons: to catch a flight elsewhere or to shop. Even in a country where the police uniforms are designed by Valentino, the Milanese excel at being label conscious. Names like Versace and Cavalli attempt to shock with outlandish items, but those kind of pieces are really just eye candy worn mostly in export markets by people who think this is what Italian style is all about. The big surprise is how conservative the fashions can be in Milan (aka Pradaworld). The stoic look of minimalist chic is standard issue and most choices follow this fashion formula, interspersed with oddly polarised cheapo disco glam get-ups.

ALTA MODA, BASSA MODA

Most people, if pointed in the right general direction, will have no problem finding the modern altars of the ruling families of fashion (*see p132* **More stars than the Milky Way**). However, if your fashion radar is a bit dim, this guide will help you ferret out unique shops that offer an antidote to homogenous global style. Far beyond the black nylon and grey wool uniforms of via Montenapoleone (*see p78*), the avant garde hides out on the south side of town on corso di Porta Ticinese (*see p142* **Corso di Porta Ticinese**), where the creations of up-and-coming designers feature in small funky shops. If you've got D&G taste but a Benetton budget, trawl the mid-priced fashions on corso Buenos Aires, via Torino, Porta Vittoria and via Paolo Sarpi (map pp308-311 A/B2). For all kinds of clothes that are mainly affordable, load up your trolley on corso Vittorio Emanuele, or its condensed version on corso Vercelli.

Covert merchants dealing in the forbidden fruit of designer knock-off handbags can be found lurking around outside the Rinascente department store (*see p137*) or nestled between the fortune tellers on the narrow, cobbled via Fiori Chiari (map p308 C2) at night.

HARDLY MODA AT ALL

Old world atmosphere and modern retailing collide with a decidedly feminine focus in the Brera neighbourhood, where you'll find a preponderance of cosmetics shops, lingerie boutiques, candle and stationery stores and unique fashion shops lining via Solferino and via Fiori Chiari.

Antique furniture hunters go directly to the atmospheric neighbourhood surrounding the basilica of Sant'Ambrogio (*see p95*) on *vie* Lanzone, Caminadella and Santa Marta; modern furnishing design can be gazed upon in shop windows on corso Europa, via Monforte and corso Venezia.

THE SALES

Finding a bargain in Milan is not impossible (*see p146* **Bargain!**); seasonal markdowns are made in January (winter merchandise) and August (summer goods). At any point during the year, however, rest assured that the savvy locals, who know to shop in advance of the coming season, have already snapped up most of the good stuff before you've even disembarked from your plane.

THE APPROACH

A little respect on both sides of the cash desk can ensure that your shopping experience is an unencumbered jaunt through fashionland where money, merchandise and good humour flow freely. Don't interpret the *entrata libera* ('free entry', in other words 'come and browse') sign on the door as licence to barge in, paw the goods and then scram leaving a trail of rumpled clothing in your non-spending wake. You may have to brace yourself for the occasional death-ray stare from sullen shop assistants. It's nothing personal. It's just that tourists are generally browsers, rufflers and impulse buyers who don't know what they want until they see it (and feel it). If you just want to browse, offer the instant diffuser, *posso dare una occhiata?* (can I have a look around?) and you will most likely be left alone while the salespeople giggle in the corner over your atrocious accent. When you've spied something you like, alert a salesperson, especially if the item in question is currently neatly folded on a shelf. Don't be offended when barnacle personnel follow you from room to room and between floors. They are there to protect and serve.

OPENING HOURS

Generally speaking, Tuesday to Saturday retail hours are 9.30am to 12.30pm and 3.30pm to 7.30pm, with a half-day on Monday from 3.30pm to 7.30pm. The rule that everything is closed on Sundays still holds true for many

More stars than the Milky Way

The collection of shops located on the sizzlingly chic alleyways of via Spiga, via Montenapoleone (known as 'Montenapo' to insiders) and via Sant'Andrea reads like a design school's distinguished alumni list. The golden quadrilateral (*see p78*) is best reached from metro Montenapoleone or San Babila, by the 61 bus or the 2 tram. Most of its temples of design open between 3pm and 7pm on Monday, and 10am to 7pm Tuesday to Saturday (exceptions to this rule are given below). And all will accept any kind of plastic you flash at them. Here's a treasure map of the principals:

Alberta Ferretti
Via Montenapoleone 21A (02 7602 2780). **Open** 10am-7pm Mon-Sat.

Bruno Magli
Corso Vittorio Emanuele/corner via San Paolo 1 (02 865 695). **Open** 10am-7.30pm Mon-Sat, occasional Sun.

Cacharel
Via San Paolo 1 (02 8901 1127).

Chanel
Via Sant'Andrea 10/A (02 782 514). **Open** 10am-7pm Mon-Sat.

Dolce & Gabbana
Womenswear: via della Spiga 2 (02 7600 1155). Menswear: via della Spiga 26 (02 799 950). D&G: corso Venezia 7 (02 7600 4091). **Open** (all shops) 10am-7pm Mon-Sat.

Etro
Via Montenapoleone 5 (02 7600 5049). **Open** 10am-7pm Mon-Sat.

Exté
Via della Spiga 6 (02 783 050).

Fendi
Via Sant'Andrea 16 (02 7602 1617). **Open** 10am-7pm Mon-Sat.

Genny
Via della Spiga 4 (02 7602 3349).

GFF Gianfranco Ferrè
Corso Venezia 2 (02 7600 4072).

Giorgio Armani Superstore
Via Manzoni 31 (02 7231 8600). **Open** 10.30am-7.30pm Mon-Fri; 10am-7.30pm Sat.

Gucci
Via Montenapoleone 27 (02 771 271). **Open** 10am-7pm Mon-Sat.

shops. However, in a stunted and haphazard effort to cave in to the increasing demands of today's consumer cult, shops are slowly starting to extend their trading hours, be it to eliminate the midday closure or spurred by a seasonal impetus such as the December holidays. Most shops in downtown Milan no longer close for lunch and observe instead an *orario continuato*.

TAX REFUNDS
Non-EU residents can claim back the value added tax on purchases totalling over €154.94 from a single store that displays a 'Tax Free Shopping' sign.

Keep your receipts, have them stamped at customs when you leave Italy, don't wear your newly acquired stuff until you are well clear of customs, and don't forget to submit your 'VAT back' paperwork.

There are refund centres at Malpensa and Linate airports open 7am-11pm every day of the year. For more information, check the www.globalrefund.com website or phone 800 018 415 (from inside Italy only).

Antiques

Shops dealing in furnishings from the 16th to the 19th centuries are located along the ancient *vie* Lanzone, Caminadella and Santa Marta (map p310 A2). The pocket guide entitled *Milano Cultura & Shopping*, available free in any of the neighbourhood's antique shops, gives a brief history of the area that will enhance your walk through Milan's oldest quarter. Start your exploration from behind the basilica of Sant'Ambrogio.

Antik
Via San Giovanni sul Muro 10, North (02 8646 1448/www.antik.it). Metro Cairoli or Cadorna/bus 50, 58. **Open** *Sept-July* 3.30-7.30pm Mon; 10am-1pm, 3.30-7.30pm Tue-Sat. Closed Aug. **Credit** AmEx, DC, MC, V. **Map** p310 A2.
The shops on via Giovanni sul Muro are decidedly knick-knacky and deal in odds and ends that can easily be carried home, such as frames, vases, jewellery, and so on. Antik, for example, specialises in scientific objects, tools, compasses and brass measuring devices.

Helmut Lang
Via Sant'Andrea 14 (02 7631 8794).

Hermès
Via Sant'Andrea 21 (02 7600 3495).

Hugo Boss
Corso Matteotti 11 (02 7639 4667).

Max Mara
Corso Vittorio Emanuele (02 7600 8849).
Open 10am-7pm Mon-Sat.

Miu Miu
Corso Venezia 3 (02 7600 1799).
Open 10am-7pm Mon-Sat.

Moschino
Via Durini 14 (02 7600 4320).

Paul Smith
Via Manzoni 30 (02 7631 9181). **Open** 10am-
7pm Mon-Sat.

Philosophy by Alberta Ferretti
Via Montenapoleone 19 (02 7602 2780).

Prada
*Womenswear, menswear, shoes, sportswear:
Galleria Vittorio Emanuele II 63/65
(02 876 979).*

*Menswear: via Montenapoleone 6 (02 7602
0273). Womenswear: via Montenapoleone 8
(02 777 1771). Menswear, womenswear,
sportswear: via Sant'Andrea 21 (02 7600
1426). Accessories: via della Spiga 1
(02 7600 2019). Lingerie: via della Spiga 5
(02 760 4448).* **Open** (all shops) 10am-
7.30pm Mon-Sat.

Roberto Cavalli
Via della Spiga 42 (02 7602 0900).

Romeo Gigli
Via della Spiga 30 (02 7601 1983).
Open 10am-7pm Mon-Sat.

Trussardi
Piazza della Scala 5 (02 806 8821).
Open 10am-7pm Mon-Sat.

Gianni Versace
Via Montenapoleone 11 (02 7600 8528).
Open 10am-7pm Mon-Sat.

Louis Vuitton
Via Montenapoleone 14 (02 777 1711).
Open 9.30am-7.30pm Mon-Sat.

Ermenegildo Zegna
Via Pietro Verri 3 (02 7600 6437).
Open 9.30am-7pm Mon-Sat.

La Biscaglina
*Via Lanzone 27, West (02 805 7272). Metro
Sant'Ambrogio/bus 50, 58.* **Open** *Sept-July* 3.30-
7.30pm Mon; 9.30am-12.30pm, 3.30-7.30pm Tue-Sat.
Closed Aug. **No credit cards. Map** p310 A2.
The owner of La Biscaglina is a trained architect
with an eye for collecting pieces with rustic charm
and a country feel from throughout Italy. Painted
cabinets are a speciality.

Luigi Maccaferri
*Via Caminadella 17, West (02 7200 0118). Metro
Sant'Ambrogio/bus 50, 58.* **Open** *Sept-July* 4-7.30pm
Mon; 10am-12.30pm, 4-7.30pm Tue-Sat. Closed Aug.
No credit cards. Map p310 A2.
This is one of Milan's most important merchants
specialising in bronze statues from the Lombard
scapigliatura movement that started in Milan in
1875. The style emphasises a rough textural finish
and captures figures in daily routine activities.

Pit, 21
*Via Santa Marta 21, Centre (02 8901 3169/www.
pit21.it). Metro Cordusio/bus 50, 58, 94.* **Open**
10am-7pm Tue-Sat. Closed 3wks Aug. **Credit** DC,
MC, V. **Map** p310 A2.

Contemporary design sits alongside period antiques
in this well-curated store. Pit, 21 seamlessly blends
the old with the new, East with West, humour and
elegance into one coherent story.

Understate
*Via Varese 20 (enter from viale Crispi), North
(02 6269 0435). Metro Moscova/bus 94/tram 3, 4.*
Open 10am-1pm, 3-7.30pm Tue-Sat. **Credit** MC, V.
Map p308 B2.
On one side of the shop are 'really old' antiques; on
the other, reproductions and originals of the greatest furniture hits from the 20th century. Understate
is a lovely spacious showroom, but the real action
takes place in the overstuffed basement. Make sure
you ask to see it.

Artists' supplies & stationery

Fabriano
*Via Verri 3, Centre (02 7631 8754). Metro
San Babila/bus 61.* **Open** 3-7.30pm Mon; 10am-
7.30pm Tue-Sat. **Credit** AmEx, DC, MC, V.
Map p309 C1.

Eat, Drink, Shop

anelli NUDO

Pomellato

www.pomellato.it

Milano - Via S. Pietro all'Orto, 17 - tel. 02 76006086

OTT? Nah – **Understate**. *See p133.*

Eat, Drink, Shop

Mastri Cartai e Dintorni: paper so fine it's a shame to write on it.

This exceptional quality papermaker dates back to the 1200s, yet Fabriano is totally up to date, offering a complete range of paper specifically for digital printing. Luxury class products are guaranteed to satisfy the most discriminating taste.

Mastri Cartai e Dintorni

Corso Garibaldi 26/34, North (02 805 2311/www. mastricartai.com). Metro Moscova/bus 41, 43, 61, 94/tram 3, 4, 12, 14. **Open** 3.30-7.30pm Mon; 11am-7.30pm Tue-Sat. Closed 3wks Aug. **Credit** DC, MC, V. **Map** p308 B/C2.

The texturally rich, handmade paper sold here sparks the imagination and begs the question of where paper stops and fine art begins. Products run the gamut from thick marbled card stock up to fine jute netting.

Ordning & Reda

Via Formentini 5/via Fiori Chiari 7, North (02 8699 6630). Metro Lanza/bus 61/tram 3, 4, 12, 20. **Open** 1.30-8pm Mon; 10am-8pm Tue, Wed; 10am-11pm Thur-Sat. **Credit** AmEx, MC, V. **Map** p308 C2.

True to its Swedish roots, this ultra-urbane selection of stationery items – including agendas, pens and paper – has a utilitarian feel, but it's all executed in beautifully saturated colours. Legend has it that a CV printed on O&R lavender-coloured vellum landed its sender a coveted position at Dolce & Gabbana.

Pellegrini

Via Brera 16, North (02 805 7119). Metro Lanza/ bus 61/tram 3, 4, 12, 20. **Open** 8.30am-7pm Mon-Fri; 8.30am-1pm, 2.30-7pm Sat. Closed 2wks Aug. **Credit** AmEx, DC, V. **Map** p308 C2.

One of Italy's leading book chains, this very central store has lots of titles in English, including the city's best selection of English-language travel books.

Libreria Internazionale Ulrico Hoepli
Via Ulrico Hoepli 5, Centre (02 864 871/www. hoepli.it). Metro Duomo/bus 61/tram 1, 2, 20. **Open** 10am-7.30pm Mon-Sat. **Credit** AmEx, DC, MC, V. **Map** p311 A1.
Swiss-born publisher Ulrico Hoepli established this bookstore in 1870, originally specialising in scientific and technical books. Today it is the most complete source in Milan for books in any language, on any subject. There is even an extensive selection of English-language books on a variety of topics within each subject heading.

Department stores

Coin
Piazza Cinque Giornate 1/A, East (02 5519 2083). Bus 60, 73/tram 9, 12, 20, 23, 27, 29. **Open** 9.30am-8.30pm Mon-Sat; 10am-8pm Sun. **Credit** AmEx, DC, MC, V. **Map** p311 A2.
A retail focal point on the mid-priced shopping street of corso di Porta Vittoria, this multistorey department store caters to the refined Milanese taste for classical, high-quality, good-value clothing and accessories for men, women and children, plus housewares, cosmetics and shoes. A restaurant and two bars – one macrobiotic – occupy the upper floor. A second branch of Coin anchors the slightly upmarket boutique-y shopping streets of corso Vercelli and via Belfiore.
Branch: corso Vercelli 30/32, West (02 4399 0001).

La Rinascente
Piazza Duomo, Centre (02 88 521). Metro Duomo/ tram 1, 2, 3, 14, 19, 20, 24. **Open** 9am-10pm Mon-Sat; 10am-8pm Sun. **Credit** AmEx, DC, MC, V. **Map** p311 A1.
This six-floor colossus is distinguished by a sporty actionwear department at the back of the first and second floors, reached by a well-hidden indoor bridge that also houses terminals for free internet access. On the top floor there is a tax-free shopping information point, an Estée Lauder Spa, plus an indoor and outdoor café where you can wave to visitors walking the Duomo's roof. Under the same management is an economically priced, scaled-down version of itself called Upim.

Fashion: accessories

Most designer brands and fashion boutiques will offer a selection of accessories in their shops, and are sometimes the best source for fashionable bits and pieces, including bags, belts, jewellery, shoes and underwear.The range of classically chic accessories at **Plus** (*see p140*) is definitely worth checking out.

Ordning & Reda. *See p135.*

Any international artist worth their salt will make an obligatory stop at this venerable shop to peruse its vast assortment and unique selection of fine art products. Prices are competitive, service competent and courteous. Strategically located near the Brera Fine Arts University and Pinacoteca (*see p70*).

Bookshops

Also worth a browse is the bookshop in the **FNAC** megastore (*see p150*).

The English Bookshop
Via Mascheroni 12 (entrance via Ariosto), West (02 469 4468). Metro Conciliazione/bus 68/tram 29, 30. **Open** 9.30am-8pm Mon-Sat. Closed 3wks Aug. **Credit** AmEx, DC, MC, V. **Map** p308 C1.
This shop has the most varied English-language fiction and non-fiction selection in the city. There are also English-language videos, audio books and an extensive children's section, plus a noticeboard with expat community postings.

Libreria Feltrinelli
Via Ugo Foscolo 1/3, Centre (02 8699 6903). Metro Duomo/bus 61/tram 1, 2, 3, 4, 20. **Open** 10am-11pm Mon-Sat; 10am-8pm Sun. **Credit** MC, V. **Map** p310 A2.

Eat, Drink, Shop

Bizarre bazaar

Forget Versace and Armani. The true arbiter of Milanese style is Carla Sozzani. Formerly a fashion editor for Italian *Vogue* – a post her sister currently holds – Sozzani opened the groundbreaking retail concept store, **Corso Como 10** (*see p140*), ten years ago, armed with a fascination for bazaars and very little cash. A pioneer in multi-product merchandising, Carla reckoned that if you appreciate the style of a pair of trousers or a blouse, there's no reason why you wouldn't adore a teapot or candle of related taste and style. The merchandise mix has grown to include men's and women's ultra-hip fashions, accessories, shoes, bags, CDs, housewares, an indoor/outdoor café (*see p127*), a bookshop and a contemporary art exhibition space (*see p155*).

The common denominator throughout is the doyenne's unmistakable penchant for the thoroughly modern with a hint of the rough-hewn. The taste level: elevated. The median price point: sky high.

But Ms Sozzani was not the first – and neither is she the last – to build her emporium on the bazaar strategy. When Elio **Fiorucci** opened his eponymous store at galleria Passarella 2 (02 7602 2452) in 1970 it was regarded as the epicentre of kitschy cool – a galaxy of gadgets and funky fresh fashion. Three decades later it is still a crazy retail carnival ride. Newcomers include **Zap!** (*see p140*), which like Fiorucci is based on a franchising model that leases 'corner' space to various labels so there's a constant turnover of choices. **2Link** (*see p140*) has a small but excellent selection of things that have a raw, arty, deconstructed air about them. **No Season** (*see p140*) is a museum-quality centre of slick, sleek urban fashions and furnishings. But perhaps the quirkiest selection of products and services – from exotic plants to Asian-style massage – is to be found at **360°** (*see p147*), located in an up-and-coming neighbourhood around via Tortona, where the nuts and bolts of fashion and journalism grind daily.

Jewellery & watches

Donatella Pellini

Via Manzoni 20, Centre (02 7600 8084). Metro Montenapoleone/tram 1, 2, 20. **Open** 3.30-7.30pm Mon; 9.30am-7.30pm Tue-Sat. **Credit** AmEx, DC, MC, V. **Map** p309 C1.

Ms Pellini augments her own signature synthetic resin jewellery designs with baubles and bangles that she collects during her worldwide travels. Not a shy piece among them.

Era L'Ora

Corso Magenta 22, West (02 8645 0965). Metro Cadorna/bus 54/tram 19, 20, 24, 27. **Open** Sept-July 10am-7.30pm Tue-Sat. Closed Aug. **Credit** AmEx, DC, MC, V. **Map** p308 C1/2.

This time-oriented shop specialises in rare, vintage wrist and pocket watches and clocks. Sales, repairs and restoration of the utmost quality are all done in-house.

La Gioielleria del Corso Vercelli

Corso Vercelli 2, West (02 469 4169). Metro Pagano or Conciliazione/tram 24. **Open** 9am-1pm, 3-7pm Tue-Sat. Closed 3wks Aug. **Credit** AmEx, DC, MC, V. **Map** p308 C1.

Authorised dealer of Tag Heuer, Piaget, Breitling and Baume & Mercier, with a fine jewellery selection from Tiffany, Damiani and others. The atmosphere is relaxed but professional, and there's an on-site repair facility.

Shoes

Les Amis

Corso Garibaldi 127, North (02 653 061). Metro Moscova/bus 94/tram 3, 4. **Open** 3.30-7.30pm Mon; 10am-7.30pm Tue-Sat. Closed 3wks Aug. **Credit** AmEx, MC, V. **Map** p308 B/C2.

This is a tiny shop that packs a punch. There's always something out of the ordinary at Les Amis, but it offers enough jazzed-up basics to keep the bills paid too. Boots are its strong suit. Women's shoes only.

Pollini

Piazza Duomo 31, Centre (02 875 187). Metro Duomo. **Open** 2.30-7.30pm Mon; 10am-7.30pm Tue-Sat; 10am-1pm, 2-7pm Sun. **Credit** AmEx, DC, MC, V. **Map** p311 A1.

Pollini is a leading name in sombre yet razor-sharp footwear style for men and women. Nobody will doubt that these shoes were made in Italy; add a matching belt and bag and you almost qualify for national citizenship.

Le Solferine

Via Solferino 2, North (02 655 5352). Metro Moscova/bus 94/tram 11, 29, 30, 33. **Open** 3-7.30pm Mon; 10am-7.30pm Tue-Sat. Closed 2wks Aug. **Credit** AmEx, DC, MC, V. **Map** p308 B/C2.

A choice selection of shoes for men and women that is just slightly offbeat. Vivienne Westwood is a star here… plain Jane shoes are anathema.

Eat, Drink, Shop

Twinkly toes at **Le Solferine**. *See p139.*

Fashion: boutiques

If you can't be bothered to trudge the streets to each individual designer's shop (*see p132* **More stars than the Milky Way**), check out some of the following multi-label boutiques, where the buyers have cherrypicked items from the designer collections to create their own edited version of the fashion world for you to enjoy.

Biffi

Corso Genova 6, South (02 831 1601/www.biffi. com). Metro Porta Genova/bus 94/tram 2, 14. **Open** 3-7.30pm Mon; 9.30am-1.30pm, 3-7.30pm Tue-Sat. Closed 1wk Aug. **Credit** AmEx, DC, MC, V. **Map** p310 B2.
A Milan institution for men's and women's classic designer choices, Biffi also stocks the mildly wild trend pieces of the season.

Bipa

Via Ponte Vetero 10, North (02 878 168). Metro Cairoli/bus 61/tram 1, 3, 4, 12, 14. **Open** 3-7.30pm Mon; 10am-7pm Tue-Sat. Closed 3wks Aug. **Credit** AmEx, DC, MC, V. **Map** p309 C1.
Bipa offers fashion forward-picks of the daring designers. It-girls will delight in the fashion lunacy, but be warned: most of the garments at this boutique will not outlive their sell-by date.

Corso Como 10

Corso Como 10, North (02 2900 2674). Metro Garibaldi/bus 94/tram 11, 29, 30, 33. **Open** 3-7.30pm Mon; 10.30am-7.30pm Tue; 10.30am-9pm Wed, Thur; 10.30am-7.30pm Fri-Sun. **Credit** AmEx, DC, MC, V. **Map** p308 B2.
A true emporium (*see p139* **Bizarre bazaar**) dedicated to the philosophy 'the only thing constant is change'. Prices are not for the faint at heart, but this place is a must see for the neophyte and seasoned fashionista alike. The merchandise mix includes men's and women's fashions, accessories, shoes, bags, housewares, books and CDs; there's an indoor/outdoor café (*see p127*) and a contemporary art exhibition space (*see p155*).

No Season

Corso di Porta Ticinese 77, South (02 8942 3332). Metro Porta Genova/tram 3, 9. **Open** 3.30-8pm Sun; 10.30am-1pm, 3.30-8pm Tue-Sat. Closed 3wks Aug. **Credit** MC, V. **Map** p310 A/B2.
Men's and women's fashions and shoes, along with the music, books, stationery and gadgets to fill in the spaces of modern urban living. An oasis of cool and calm in a happily chaotic shopping street.

Plus

Piazza Missori 2, Centre (02 8646 1820). Metro Missori/bus 54, 60/tram 12, 24. **Open** 3-7pm Mon; 10am-7pm Tue-Sat. Closed 3wks Aug. **Credit** AmEx, DC, MC, V. **Map** p310 A2.
Clothes, shoes and accessories that are designed to enhance your own unique personality without being overtly unique themselves. Women's modern classics come in fine fabrics and beautiful knits, and shoes are comfy but fashionable.

2Link

Largo La Foppa 4, North (02 6269 0325). Metro Moscova/bus 94. **Open** 3-8pm Mon; 10.30am-8pm Tue-Sat; 3-8pm Sun. Closed 3wks Aug. **Credit** AmEx, DC, MC, V. **Map** p308 B2.
A decidedly avant-garde selection of men's and women's clothing, plus accessories with a deconstructionist essence. The experimental style flows into related merchandise like speciality chopsticks, ponderous personal gadgets, and CDs. Duck across the street for coffee and a slice of something sweet at Radetzky Café (*see p127*).

Zap!

Galleria Passarella 2, Centre (02 7606 7501). Metro San Babila/bus 54, 61. **Open** 1-7.30pm Mon; 10am-7.30pm Tue-Sat. Closed 1wk Aug. **Credit** AmEx, DC, MC, V. **Map** p311 A1.
Reflecting the caprice of fashion and a label franchising technique modelled after the Fiorucci department store (*see p139* **Bizarre bazaar**), this shop's merchandise mix is constantly evolving. Currently, there is a second-hand section and a block of vintage wedding dresses, plus funky trims and ribbons sold by the metre that augment the consistently cutting-edge choice of women's fashion, shoes and accessories.

No Season is firmly in fashion at all times of year. *See p140.*

Fashion: designer boutiques

Anybody who is a fashion anybody has an outlet in Milan: just slink around the fiercely chic alleyways of high fashion along via Montenapoleone and via Spiga (*see p132* **More stars than the Milky Way**) and you'll see what we mean.

Big-name stars aside, the following are Italian designers who may not have a global marketing team that places their products in the suburbs of Tokyo, but do have their own following of fashion insiders.

Lorella Braglia
Via Solferino at via Ancona, North (02 2901 4514). Metro Moscova/bus 94/tram 11, 29, 30, 33. **Open** 3-7.30pm Mon; 10am-2pm, 3.30-7.30pm Tue-Thur; 10am-7.30pm Fri, Sat. Closed 3wks Aug. **Credit** AmEx, DC, MC, V. **Map** p308 C2.
Perfectly balanced lines, luxurious fabrics and a young quirky attitude sum up this very feminine, modern line of women's clothing, in which fashion acumen is expressed with sufficient subtlety to allow the wearer's own personality to shine through.

Luisa Beccaria
Via Formentini 1, North (02 863 807). Metro Lanza/ bus 61/tram 4, 12, 14. **Open** 3-7.30pm Mon; 10am-7.30pm Tue-Sat. Closed 1wk Aug. **Credit** AmEx, MC, V. **Map** 308 C2.
With a gentle nod to the classic ladylike lines of yesteryear and a couture sensibility, Ms Beccaria offers impeccable suits and feminine dresses that would

make Audrey Hepburn swoon. A selection of adorable children's clothing is also available in the same, finely executed style – at a price.

Martino Midali
Via Ponte Vetero 9, North (02 8646 2707). Metro Cairoli/bus 61/tram 4, 12, 14. **Open** 3-7pm Mon; 10am-2pm, 3-7pm Tue-Sat. Closed 3wks Aug. **Credit** AmEx, DC, MC, V. **Map** p309 C1.
Work at Martino Midali is characterised by its use of rich colours, and by texturally interesting knits. It's popular with modern, stylish women who have discovered the comfort and ease of knitwear and are never turning back.

Fashion: leatherwear

You're better off shopping in Florence if you're looking for a concentrated selection of good-quality leather products. Aside from the pieces offered in the designer lines, there's only one specialist shop that stands out in Milan for handcrafted leather garments.

Cut
Corso Porta Ticinese 58, South (02 839 4135). Metro Porta Genova/tram 3, 9, 15, 29, 30. **Open** Sept-July 3-7.30pm Mon; 10.30am-1.30pm, 3-7.30pm Tue-Sat. Closed Aug. **Credit** AmEx, DC, MC, V. **Map** p310 A/B2.
Cut is certainly not stocked with the ubiquitous Brad Pitt leather blazers. Instead you'll find a range of uniquely designed, high-quality leather garments for both men and women.

Corso di Porta Ticinese

When you tire of the repetitious trendsville of the city centre, jump on the No.3 tram and head for corso di Porta Ticinese.

The shops on this street are refreshingly unique and offer genuinely authentic, one-of-a-kind or offbeat fashions. The urban lifestyle temple **No Season** (*see p140*) is about as commercial as it gets here, and is certainly no slouch. At **B-Fly** (No.46; 02 8942 3178), stylists featured in the shop are selected during the owner's frequent trips to headhunt emerging talent from European fashion schools. The artistically wrinkled women's clothing at **Fashion Plissé Store** (No.46; 02 8942 2151) is a suitcase stuffer's dream and the perfect fashion statement for contrarians. The upmarket **Martino Midali** (No.60; 02 8940 6830) offers sumptuous knits that attract an international following. The name **Fatto A Mano** (handmade; No.76; 02 8940 1958) says it all for this intimate shop known for its hand-loom silk fabrics that are stitched up into beautiful dresses, scarves and accessories. When well-known mono-label stores **Stüssy**, **Carhartt** (both at No.103; 02 8942 7499) and **Fornarina** (No.78; 02 8320 0759) moved into the neighbourhood, the *corso*'s edgy streetwear theme was definitively underscored.

Give your fashion feelers a rest and get some aural pleasure at the two notable CD shops: **Supporti Fonografici** (*see p149*) and the no name/no phone micro-sized used CD shop next to Eco Pizza at No.76 (it specialises in techno grooves). For unexpected gift ideas check out the vintage objects at **Studio 1950** (No.68; 02 836 0304). Each piece has such a strong personality, it is sure to bring a friend or loved one to mind. Lastly, the grand merchant of 'stuff you didn't know you needed but is so cheap you can't live without it is certainly **Paradiso delle Sorprese** (No.62; 02 835 7187).

Shops on corso di Porta Ticinese generally follow similar trading hours (3.30-7.30pm Mon; 9.30am-12.30pm, 3.30-7.30pm Tue-Sat) and accept, at a minimum, MasterCard and Visa. **Map** p310 2AB.

Fashion: lingerie

Christies

Corso Vercelli 51, West (02 4802 2152). Metro Pagano/bus 61/tram 24. **Open** 3-7pm Mon; 10am-2pm, 3-7pm Tue-Sat. Closed 3wks Aug. **Credit** AmEx, DC, MC, V. **Map** p308 C1.

Clean, unfussy but super-sexy lingerie, swimwear and a small selection of ready-to-wear pieces. The smooth Tatto line comprises bras and knickers with absolutely no stitching. Extra-large sizes too.

Kristini Ti

Via Solferino 18, North (02 653 379). Metro Moscova/bus 41, 42, 94/tram 11, 29, 30, 33. **Open** 3-7pm Mon; 10am-7pm Tue-Sat. Closed 3wks Aug. **Credit** AmEx, DC, MC, V. **Map** p308 B/C2.

The best thing to come out of Turin since the Fiat Cinquecento: lingerie so delicate, it's almost fragile. Also a micro-line of super-feminine ready-to-wear.

La Perla

Via Monte Napoleone 1, East (02 7600 0460). Metro San Babila/bus 61/tram 1, 2. **Open** 3-7pm Mon; 10am-7pm Tue-Sat. Closed 3wks Aug. **Credit** AmEx, DC, MC, V. **Map** p309 C1.

The words sultry, sophisticated and sexy made manifest in lingerie, swimwear and ready-to-wear gear. How can something so small cost so much? Well, only the finest fabrics are used, manufactured into garments of outstanding quality in Bologna.

Fashion: mid-range

For self-directed bargain shoppers: withdraw your cash limit from an ATM and head straight for the plethora of econo-chic shops that line the streets of via Torino, corso Buenos Aires, via Paolo Sarpi (Chinatown) and Porta Vittoria. The rest of you, read on.

Avant

Corso Buenos Aires 39, East (02 2951 1115). Metro Lima/bus 60/tram 33. **Open** 2.30-7.30pm Mon; 10.30am-7.30pm Tue-Sat. **Credit** AmEx, DC, MC, V. **Map** p309 B2.

An enormous shop for men and women where the merchandise is so close to being ugly that it's fabulous. Dress like a rockstar in clothing that screams 'I'm unique' – but is also cheap.

Nadine

Corso Vittorio Emanuele 34, Centre (02 7600 9028). Metro San Babila/bus 61. **Open** 1-7.30pm Mon; 9.30am-7.30pm Tue-Sat; 10am-7.30pm Sun. Closed 3wks Aug. **Credit** AmEx, DC, MC, V. **Map** p311 A1.

Savvy city gals know they can pick up sexed-up basics at commodity prices plus the occasional directional piece that can instantly update a tired wardrobe. Prices are at the top of the mid-price range but happily allow multiple-item sales. If you can't find anything here, better have another espresso before moving on.

ProMod

Corner via Mazzini & via Torino, Centre (02 7208 0009). Metro Duomo/tram 1, 2, 3, 14, 19, 20, 24. **Open** 10am-8pm daily. **Credit** AmEx, MC, V. **Map** p310 A2.

ProMod has cornered the cute and affordable casualwear market for young women. Clothing, accessories and lingerie are styled with a French sensibility for colour, pattern and cut that is *très chic*.

Food & drink

See also p148 **Markets**.

Peck

Via Spadari 9, Centre (02 802 3161). Metro Duomo/ bus 18/tram 2, 3, 4, 12. **Open** 3-7.30pm Mon; 8.45am-7.30pm Tue-Sat. **Credit** AmEx, DC, MC, V. **Map** p310 A2.

A temple of fine food and wine for more than 100 years, Peck was founded in 1883 by a humble pork butcher from Prague, Franz Peck. These days, the main action is in the three-floor flagship shop on via Spadari where there is a butcher, bakery, dazzling delicatessen, smallish selection of wines, prepared foods, oils and bottled sauces, plus a lovely tearoom. But that's definitely not the whole story as most of a city block has now become Peck-land. Around the corner at via Victor Hugo 4 is the wine cellar, which is considered one of the best in the world, and the sit-down restaurant Cracco-Peck (closed Saturday lunch and all Sunday, average €95) which has confirmed Carlo Cracco as one of Italy's most promising young chefs. If your budget doesn't quite stretch to such gourmet excesses, remember that steps away is a hot-food takeaway (via Cantù 3). Peck is the first and last word on bacchanalian and gastronomic delights in Milan.

Confectionery & cakes

California Bakery

Via Solferino 12, Centre (02 659 9236). Metro Moscova/bus 41, 42, 94/tram 11, 29, 30, 33. **Open** 9am-7.30pm Mon-Sat. Closed 3wks Aug. **No credit cards**. **Map** p308 B/C2.

If you're hankering for Anglo-Saxon sweets or want to delight your Italian hosts with an exotic cheesecake, bag of chocolate chip cookies, brownies, muffins or – gasp – bagels, this is the only place in town you're gonna find 'em done right.

Cherubini

Via Trincea della Frasche 2, South (02 5410 7486). Metro Porta Genova/tram 3, 9, 15, 29, 30. **Open** 7am-10pm daily. Closed 3wks Aug. **No credit cards**. **Map** p310 B2.

Although this is a full service bar and café, it is best known for its delicious home-made pastries and brioche breakfast rolls, all made fresh daily on the premises. Polite service in an old world atmosphere. Located on a tiny street on the south-east side of piazza XXIV Maggio.

Ethnic food

Superpolo

Largo La Foppa 1, North (02 657 1760). Metro Moscova/bus 94. **Open** 9am-1pm, 3.30-7.30pm Mon-Sat. **Credit** MC, V. **Map** p308 B2.

This international food market has a little bit of everything from many countries around the world, as well as the basics. A large selection of frozen goods, dry goods, some produce and dairy, plus soya-based products too.

Zhou Supermarket

Via Canonica 54, North (02 312 371). Bus 57/tram 1. **Open** 9am-7.30pm Mon, Sat; 9am-12.30pm, 2.30-7.30pm Tue-Fri. **Credit** MC, V. **Map** p308 B1/2.

Located in the heart of Milan's Chinatown district, Zhou Supermarket is a massive store that stocks strictly Asian fare. China, Japan and Korea are the countries best represented.

Gelati

Ice-cream lovers should also find room for some of the delicious delights on offer at **Bastianello** (*see p128*).

Il Gelato Ecologico

Via Ravizza 5, West (02 4801 0917). Metro Wagner/bus 90, 91/tram 24. **Open** 2pm-1am Mon-Wed, Fri-Sun. Closed 1wk Aug. **No credit cards**. **Map** off 310 A1.

All natural ingredients and the freshest, most flavourful fruits make this *gelateria* stand head and shoulders above the rest. The *granite* (chunky sorbet), *frullati* (blended fruit shakes) and frozen yogurt are mouth-watering, and there are kosher varieties too.

Viel

Via Paolo da Cannobio 9, Centre (02 805 5508). Metro Missori/bus 65/tram 12, 20, 27. **Open** 9am-midnight Mon-Sat. Closed 3wks Aug. **No credit cards**. **Map** p311 A1.

An all-time Milanese favourite, Viel serves up some tasty, straightforward *gelato* not to mention an utterly tempting range of excellent fresh-fruit *frullati* blended drinks.

Healthfood

Centro Botanico

Piazza San Marco 1, North (02 2901 3254/ www.centrobotanico.it). Metro Lanza/bus 61/tram 3, 4. **Open** 3.30-7.30pm Mon; 10am-2.30pm, 3.30-7.30pm Tue-Fri; 10am-7.30pm Sat. Closed 3wks Aug. **Credit** AmEx, DC, MC, V. **Map** p308 C2.

A true centre for health products in the city, this place stocks organically grown produce, macrobiotic groceries, vitamin capsules, pure fibre clothing, baked goods and more. There's also a juice bar and-café on site.

Eat, Drink, Shop

timeout.com

The online guide to the world's greatest cities

Feeling peckish? Enjoy the gorgeous gastronomy at **Peck**. *See p143.*

Eat, Drink, Shop

IKOS-Il Circolo della Natura
Via Boccacio 4, West (02 460 616). Metro Cadorna/ bus 94/tram 1, 19, 27. **Open** 7.30am-8pm Mon-Sat. Closed 3wks Aug. **Credit** AmEx, DC, MC, V. **Map** p308 C1.
A light and airy space that houses a bar, restaurant and self-service lunch buffet as well as a small market offering a selection of groceries, produce and beauty items. All the products and menu items on sale are either all-natural, organic or macrobiotic.

Supermarkets
Esselunga
Viale Papiniano 27, West (02 498 7674/www. esselunga.it). Metro Sant'Agostino/bus 50/tram 20, 29, 30. **Open** 9am-10pm Mon; 8am-9pm Tue-Sat. **Credit** MC, V. **Map** p310 A/B1.
A large, modern supermarket stocking all major food brands plus an extensive line of biologically pure products and organically grown produce. There's a complete deli counter with catering services and some takeaway choices.
Branches: viale Piave 38 (02 204 7871); viale Certosa 59 (02 3300 3711).

Wine
For a real treat, don't miss the wonderful wine cellar at **Peck** (*see p143*).

L'Altro Vino
Viale Piave 9, East (02 780 147). Metro Porta Venezia/bus 54, 61/tram 9, 20, 29, 30. **Open** *Sept-July* 11.30am-7.45pm Tue-Sat. Closed Aug. **Credit** AmEx, DC, MC, V. **Map** p309 C2.

Extremely knowledgeable and approachable proprietors make this a very pleasant shop. There's a vast selection of national and international bottles, with regular tastings organised on the first and third Thursdays of the month.

Health & beauty
Besides its gym facilities, **Downtown Spa & Fitness** (*see p180*) offers beauty treatments for men and women.

Univers Beauté
Via Conca del Naviglio 18, South (02 8940 0850). Metro Porta Genova/bus 94/tram 2, 9, 14. **Open** 9.30am-6.30pm Mon-Sat. Closed 3wks Aug. **Credit** MC, V. **Map** p310 B2.
Facials, body treatments, massage, waxing and more *pour femme*, from a team of caring professionals. Indulge in the glorious *pedicure estetico e curativo* with rose petals floating in the foot bath.

Cosmetics & perfumes
Madina
Via Meravigli 17, Centre (02 8691 5438). Metro Cordusio/bus 18/tram 12, 19, 20, 24. **Open** 3-7.30pm Mon; 10am-7.30pm Tue-Sat. Closed 3wks Aug. **Credit** AmEx, DC, MC, V. **Map** p308 C2.
Products carrying the name Madina Milano become coveted souvenirs not only for their high quality but their international cachet. The line has a strong following in the beauty trade and colours galore: 400 lipstick shades, 250 eyeshadows and 300 foundation, blusher, bronzer and face powder tones.

Bargain!

The main goal of any shopping pilgrimage to Milan is to leave better dressed than when you arrived. At designer prices, buying one key piece a season can be an extravagance and consume a precious shopping budget quickly. There are, however, shopping alternatives that can keep you in the fashion loop without draining your wallet entirely.

Stock houses

This roughly translates as a place to sell off surplus odds and ends from last year's runs, or merchandise gathered from boutiques going out of business. Some are shams, but not **Salvagente**, which truly is a shopping maven's lifesaver. There's a constant turnover of goods due to a high volume of dedicated customers on the prowl. Pick through an ever-changing kaleidoscope of designer goods for men and women; for children there's a separate location ten blocks away called **Salvagente Bimbo**.

With a sneaky name and a cryptic location (just off corso Vittorio Emanuele), your sleuthing efforts will be well rewarded when you step into **Diffusione Tessile** (textile warehouse). This shop deals exclusively in all the womenswear brands under the Max Mara umbrella, including Sport Max, Marina Rinaldi and Marella. There is a vast selection of clothing and shoes, tidy racks, plus friendly and helpful staff. Celebrate your financially efficacious score by busting a move with the breakdancers benignly grooving on the smooth marble sidewalk outside the shop.

Diffusione Tessile
Galleria San Carlo 6, East (02 7600 0829).
Metro Duomo or San Babila/bus 61, 73.
Open 3.30-7.30pm Mon; 10am-7.30pm Tue-Sat. **Credit** AmEx, DC, MC, V. **Map** p311 A1.

Salvagente
Via Fratelli Bronzetti 16, East (02 7611 0328). Metro Lima/bus 54, 60, 61, 62/ tram 12, 27. **Open** *Sept-July* 3-7pm Mon; 10am-12.30pm, 3-7pm Tue, Thur, Fri; 10am-7pm Wed, Sat. Closed Aug. **Credit** AmEx. **Map** p311 A2.

Salvagente Bimbo
Via Balzaretti 28, East (02 2668 0764).
Metro Piola/bus 62/tram 11, 23.

Pharmacies

See also p283.

Antica Farmacia di Brera
Via Fiori Oscuri 13, North (02 8646 1949).
Metro Lanza/bus 61/tram 3, 4, 12, 20. **Open** 8.30am-1pm, 3.30-7.30pm Mon-Fri; 9.30am-12.30pm Sat. Closed 3wks Aug. **Credit** AmEx, MC, V. **Map** p309 C1.
Founded in 1699, this is the oldest pharmacy in Milan. It stocks everything you'd expect from a modern pharmacist, but you'll also find homeopathic products and natural cosmetics.

Farmacia Santa Teresa
Corso Magenta 96, West (02 4800 6772).
Metro Conciliazione/bus 68/tram 20, 24, 29, 30. **Open** 8.30am-12.30pm, 3.30-7.30pm Mon, Tue, Fri; Sat; 8.30am-12.30pm Thur; 8.30am-1pm, 3.30-8pm Sun. **Credit** DC, MC, V. **Map** p308 C1/2.
The art nouveau interior alone warrants a visit to this well-run, modern pharmacist's, where you'll also find traditional and homeopathic cures. Another bonus: after closing time, ring the bell and someone will pass your medicine through a little hole in the shutter. This service is available every night of the year from 8pm until 8.30am the following morning.

Great gadgetry at **High Tech**. *See p147.*

Eat, Drink, Shop

Open *Sept-July* 3-7pm Mon; 10am-1pm, 3-7pm Tue, Thur-Sat; 10am-7pm Wed. Closed Aug. **No credit cards**. **Map** off p309 C2.

Clothing previously worn by...

Consignment shops are a burgeoning trend in Milan. **Il Nuovo Guardaroba** offers the biggest selection of women's second-hand clothing and accessories, with a small selection of men's items too; a separate shop nearby called **Il Guardarobino** has children's clothing and baby hardware such as strollers and highchairs.

High-end designer duds swiped from the closets of socialites and TV personalities who wouldn't be caught dead in the same outfit twice are regular stock at **Tè con Le Amiche** (tea with the gals). Although the name suggests an easygoing oasis, the atmosphere a bit chilly and the owner is strictly business.

At **L'Armadio di Laura** there's good reason for the sign reading 'please don't ask for further discounts'. The prices in this thriftstore-like shop are low enough already.

At **Centoborse** it's difficult to decide what to choose: rent a glitzy, glam evening clutch, select a brand new one-of-a-kind cloth bag by a local designer, or go straight for the consignment leather handbags, wallets and belts whose prices are so low that you could easily take two.

For vintage clothing from old hands in the business the clear choice is **Cavalli & Nastri**. Each piece in this tidy collection is in mint condition and selected with a razorsharp eye that weeds out obvious and dowdy 'period' pieces, leaving only the crème de la crème of vintage chic.

Fashion looks that were pioneered in the 1960s, '70s and '80s can be bought in their original retro form or in reinterpreted, brand-new versions at **Docks Dora**. Merchandise here includes a well-tended selection of vintage coats and jackets, plus men's ruffled tuxedo shirts in a rainbow of colours. Lemon yellow, anyone?

L'Armadio di Laura

Via Voghera 25, South (02 836 0606). Metro Porta Genova/bus 68/tram 14. **Open** *Sept-July* 10am-6pm Tue-Sat. Closed Aug. **Credit** MC, V. **Map** p310 B1. ▶

Home design & accessories

Il Centro Tavolo

Via Spadari 11, Centre (02 866 641). Metro Duomo/tram 1, 2, 3, 14, 19, 20. **Open** *Sept-July* 3-7pm Mon; 10am-7pm Tue-Sat. Closed Aug. **Credit** AmEx, DC, MC, V. **Map** p310 A2.

Aspiring dinner party hosts and hostesses will delight in the array of well-appointed table linens and place settings at Il Centro Tavolo – as well as revelling in the sheer beauty of this very special store. Nothing is stodgy or over-starched here – you'll just find elegant dining accessories that range from casual to formal.

High Tech

Piazza XXV Aprile 12, North (02 624 1101/ www.high-techmilano.com). Metro Garibaldi/bus 94/tram 11, 29, 30, 33. **Open** 10.30am-7.30pm Tue-Sun. **Credit** AmEx, DC, MC, V. **Map** p308 B2.

High Tech is a veritable shopping labyrinth of nooks and crannies packed to the rafters with every imaginable item and gadget for the design-conscious homeowner. All sorts of goodies are available here, from housewares to beauty and bath products, to office accessories. Hours and hours can evaporate wandering in a daze from room to room or simply trying to locate the exit. A new branch of the High

Tech firm has recently opened in the eastern suburbs. It's called Cargo and sells cut-price merchandise. There's also a bar for the adults and a kids' play area on site.
Branch: Cargo via Meucci 39, East (02 2722 1301).

Penelopi 3

Via Palermo 1, North (02 7200 0652). Metro Moscova/bus 41, 43, 94/tram 3, 4. **Open** 3-7.30pm Mon; 10am-7pm Tue-Fri; 10.30am-7.30pm Sat. Closed 3wks Aug. **Credit** AmEx, DC, MC, V. **Map** p308 C2.

Desirable small furnishings, tempting design objects and an eclectic mix of decorative pieces with a faintly exotic, international flavour are all up for grabs at Penelopi 3.

360°

Via Tortona 12, South (02 835 6706). Metro Porta Genova/bus 68/tram 14. **Open** *Sept-July* 11am-7pm Tue-Sun. Closed Aug. **Credit** MC, V. **Map** p310 B1.

This multifaceted design space is dedicated to well-being and soothing the senses through simplicity. It deals in an odd mix of exotic plants, food, young designer furniture and oriental-style massage to create an unique shopping environment. A small kitchen turns out a mainly vegetarian buffet lunch and weekend brunch.

► Bargain! (continued)

Cavalli e Nastri

Via Brera 2, North (02 7200 0449).
Metro Cairoli/bus 61/tram 3, 4, 12, 20.
Open *Sept-July* 3.30-7pm Mon; 10.30am-7pm
Tue-Sat. Closed Aug. **Credit** AmEx, DC, MC, V.
Map p308 C2.

CentoBorse

*Via Gian Giacomo Mora 9, South (02 8942
0877). Metro Sant'Ambrogio/bus 94/tram
2, 3, 14.* **Open** *Sept-July* 4-7.30pm Tue-Fri;
10.30am-1.30pm, 4.30-7.30pm Sat. Used
clothes accepted by appointment 11am-2pm
Tue-Fri. Closed Aug. **Credit** MC, V.
Map p310 A/B2.

Docks Dora

Corso Garibaldi 127, North (02 2900 6950).
Metro Moscova/bus 41, 94/tram 3, 4, 11.
Open 3-8pm Mon; 11am-8pm Tue-Sat.
Credit AmEx, DC, MC, V. **Map** p308 B/C2.

Il Guardarobino

Via Washington 5, West (02 4801 5802).
Metro Wagner/bus 61, 67/tram 24. **Open**
10am-1pm; 3-7pm Tue-Sat. Closed 4wks July-
Sept. **No credit cards**. **Map** off p301 A1.

Il Nuovo Guardaroba

*Via Asti 5A, West (02 4800 1678). Metro
Wagner/bus 61, 67/tram 24.* **Open** 10am-
1pm, 3-7pm Tue-Sat. Closed 3wks Aug.
No credit cards. **Map** off p310 A1.

Tè con Le Amiche

*Via Visconti di Modrone 33, East (02 7733
1506). Metro San Babila/bus 61, 94/tram
12, 20, 27.* **Open** *Sept-mid June* 3-6.30pm
Mon; 10am-12.30pm, 3-6.30pm Tue-Sat.
Closed mid June-Aug. **Credit** AmEx, MC, V.
Map p311 A1.

Outlet malls

Forget the high prices of downtown, but don't
forget your passport. The originator in factory
outlet shopping is **Fox Town Factory Stores**,
located just over the border in Switzerland.
There are 80 international shops housed
inside a three-storey mall with two
restaurants, free parking, a kids' playground,
a florist, currency exchange and postal
counter. The other choice is the exceptionally
popular **Serravalle Outlets** located between
Milan and Genoa in the city of Serravalle

Fabric

Le Mercerie

*Via San Vittore 2, West (02 8645 4338). Metro
Sant'Ambrogio/bus 50, 58, 94.* **Open** 3-7pm Mon;
9.30am-1.30pm, 3-7pm Tue-Sat. Closed 3wks Aug.
Credit AmEx, MC, V. **Map** p310 A1.
A treasure trove for all sorts of textiles and accessories. A system of sliding walls reveals buttons, ribbons and passementerie three shelves deep, and
fabrics in virtually every colour or pattern, plus
cross-stitch and embroidery kits.

Silva

*Via Olona 25, West (02 8940 0788). Metro
Sant'Agostino/tram 20, 29, 30.* **Open** 9am-12.30pm,
3-7pm Mon-Fri. Closed 3wks Aug. **Credit** MC, V.
Map p310 A1.
An insane selection of upholstery fabrics and groovy
wallpaper. Located in the building's courtyard.

Markets

Mercato Communale

*Piazza Wagner, West (no phone). Metro Wagner/bus
67/tram 24.* **Open** 8.30am-1pm Mon; 8.30am-1pm, 4-
7.30pm Tue-Sat. **No credit cards**. **Map** off p310 A1.

A permanent covered food emporium where you can
shop the old-fashioned way: visiting stalls for produce, deli, dairy, groceries, dry goods and plants,
and having a chat with each proprietor.

Ever-eclectic **360°**. *See p147.*

Scrivia. With more than 100 shops carrying international brands for clothing, sport and housewares, plus three restaurants, it aims to become the largest shopping centre in Europe. Both are open Sundays.

For winter sports enthusiasts, **Samas** is a factory outlet on the SS38 near Chiuro (*see p267*) selling discounted skiwear. It's also popular on rainy summer days when snappy *signore* fight over sportsgear, knits and kids' clothes. **Skitrab** in Bormio (*see p267*) sells discounted skis and equipment for cross-country and *sci alpinismo* (that's the one where really keen skiers glue artificial skins to their skis, head uphill to a mountain peak and free-ski down). You'll also find skiwear and some downhill stuff here too.

Fox Town Factory Stores

Via A Mapsoli 18, Mendrisio, Switzerland (00 41 848 828888/www.foxtown.ch). **Open** 11am-7pm daily. **Credit** AmEx, DC, MC, V. From Milan, take the A7 motorway; after the border take the Mendrisio exit and turn left. If you're travelling by train, go from Stazione Centrale to Chiasso. A bus departs from the station to Foxtown every 15 minutes.

Papiniano

Viale Papiniano, West (no phone). Metro Sant' Agostino/tram 20, 29, 30. **Open** dawn-1pm Tue; dawn-5pm Sat. **No credit cards**. **Map** p310 A/B1. The city's most popular open-air market, with food, plants, clothing, shoes, housewares and textiles. It's fun, but ripe for pickpockets.

San Donato Flea Market

Around metro San Donato, South (no phone). Metro San Donato. **Open** 8am-1pm Sun. **Map** off p311 C2. Chase the Sunday blues with yet more spending therapy. As in any universal souk, gadgets, junk and hidden treasures abound if you're willing to dig a bit. And there are plenty of international food stalls to keep your energy up and tastebuds tingling. Local police reckon this is a good place to locate your stolen bicycle. Stalls shut down around 1pm.

Music: CDs, records & instruments

Ricordi Media Store

Galleria Vittorio Emanuele, Centre (02 8646 0272). Metro Duomo/tram 2, 3, 20. **Open** 10am-11pm Mon-Sat; 10am-8pm Sun. **Credit** AmEx, DC, MC, V. **Map** p311 A1.

Samas

Via Stelvio, Chiuro (0342 485 011). **Open** 9am-12.30pm, 3-7pm Mon, Wed-Sat. **Credit** AmEx, DC, MC, V. For details of how to get to Samas by private and public transport, *see p264*.

Serravalle Outlet

Strada statale 35 bis, Serravalle Scrivia (0143 609 000/www.mcarthurglen.com). **Open** 10am-9pm daily. **Credit** MC,V. From Milan, take the A7 Milan–Genoa motorway; exit Serravalle Scrivia, at the roundabout take the road toward Novi Ligure. The mall is 1km (half a mile) from the motorway exit. If you're travelling by train, go from Stazione Centrale to Serravalle Scrivia. The mall is a 15km (nine-mile) taxi-ride from the train station; there's no public transport.

Skitrab

Via Tirano 6, Bormio (0342 901 650). **Open** 8am-12.30pm, 2.30-7.30pm Mon-Sat; 8.30am-noon, 4-6.30pm Sun. **Credit** AmEx, MC, V. For details of how to get there by private and public transport, *see p264*.

A subterranean media emporium beneath the glass-covered Galleria. Ricordi stocks a varied selection of CDs in all categories plus instruments, sheet music, games, personal electronics and concert/theatre tickets. Enter the connecting Feltrinelli bookstore (see p137) in one seamless step.

Supporti Fonografici

Corso di Porta Ticinese 100, South (02 8940 0420/ www.supportifono.com). Metro Porta Genova/tram 3, 9, 15, 29, 30. **Open** 3-7.30pm Mon; 9am-7.30pm Tue-Sat. **Credit** AmEx, DC, MC, V. **Map** p310 A/B2. Some customers never set foot in the store but lurk, chat and buy only at the shop's website. Listening samples and recommendations are provided by a staff of genuine enthusiasts well versed in the niche markets of indie, new wave, Brit pop and electronica.

Services

Dry-cleaning/laundry

Onda Blu

Via Savona, opposite No.1, South (no phone/ www.ondablu.com). Metro Genova/tram 29. **Open** 8am-10pm daily. **Map** p310 B1. Coin-operated launderette with washers and dryers.

Eat, Drink, Shop

Hairdressers & beauticians

Antica Barbiera Colla
Via Gerolamo Morone 3, Centre (02 874 312).
Metro Montenapoleone/tram 1, 2, 20. **Open** *Sept-July* 8.30am-12.30pm, 2.30-7pm Tue-Sat. Closed Aug.
No credit cards. Map p311 A1.
Going for that groovy Giacomo Puccini look? The barbers in this shop have been shearing since 1904 and proudly display the scissors used to keep the composer's locks properly coiffed. Call for an appointment. Men only.

Intrecci
Via Larga 2, Centre (02 7202 2316). Metro Missori/tram 12, 20, 27. **Open** 10am-11pm Tue-Fri; 9am-10pm Sat. **Credit** MC, V. **Map** p311 A1.
Cutters, stylists and make-up artists blur the line between male and female, making this a unisex salon in more ways than one. Music blares, impromptu dances are performed and the phone doesn't ring: it flashes a ring of blue neon light. Hair and make-up services to get you club-ready.

Marchina
Corso Venezia 3 (2nd floor), East (02 799 636). Metro San Babila/bus 61. **Open** 9am-6.30pm Tue-Sat; 9am-10pm Thur. **Credit** DC, MC, V. **Map** p309 C1.
Expert haircutter Pino Marchina lords it over a busy staff of master colourists, cutters and beauticians in a clean, modern salon just a hop, skip and a jump from San Babila. It's a full-service salon for hair, nails and body for men and women, and everybody sails out looking far better than when they walked in. Mary speaks perfect English and all the employees are efficient and friendly.

Opticians

Salmoiraghi & Vigano
Corso Matteotti 22, East (02 7600 0100). Metro San Babila/bus 61. **Open** 3.30-7pm Mon; 10am-7pm Tue-Sat. **Credit** AmEx, DC, MC, V. **Map** p309 C1.
A solid optician's with 11 branches in Milan, well known throughout Italy for its professionalism, expertise and quality selection of frames.
Branches: throughout the city.

Photocopy/fax/photo developers

Almost any stationery store (*cartoleria*) will offer a fax and photocopy service: just ask. If you've got 24 hours, Esselunga supermarket (*see p145*) does photo processing, and its rates are much cheaper than the 30-minute specialist photo places.

Mail Boxes Etc.
Via del Torchio 12, South (02 7200 2932). Bus 94/tram 2, 3, 9, 14. **Open** 9am-6.30pm Mon-Fri. Closed 3wks Aug. **Credit** MC, V. **Map** p310 A2.

Photocopying and fax facilities, DHL courier pick-up, business card printing, Western Union point, internet access, document plastification, postbox rental, packaging and office supplies sales.
Branches: throughout the city.

NE.CA Fiera
Via Giovanni da Procida 29, West (02 317 465). Tram 1, 19, 33. **Open** 8.30am-7.30pm daily.
Credit AmEx, DC, MC, V. **Map** p308 B1.
Develops any kind of film in 30 minutes. Specialises in digital printing and image manipulation. Top-name cameras for sale as well.

Ticket agencies

There is no single source for concert and event tickets and information. However, if one ticket agency is sold out, another may still have tickets available. Tickets for **Teatro alla Scala** must be purchased through the theatre (*see p177*).

Messaggerie Musicali: Box Tickets
Corso Vittorio Emanuele, Centre (ticket counter 02 795 502). Metro Duomo/tram 12, 20, 27. **Open** 1-7pm Mon; 10am-7pm Tue-Sat. **No credit cards.**
Map p311 A1.
This service provides tickets for a range of performances, such as concerts and theatrical and sporting events.

FNAC
Via Torino at via della Palma, Centre (ticket counter 02 720 821). Metro Duomo/tram 2, 3, 9, 14.
Open 9am-8pm Mon-Sat; 10am-8pm Sun.
No credit cards. Map p310 A2.
This megastore, a recent arrival from France, has books, records, a photo developing service, electronic gadgets, a café and an exhibition space. It also sells tickets for concerts, theatre and sporting events.

Travel agencies

CIT (Compagnia Italiana Turismo)
Galleria Vittorio Emanuele, Centre (02 8637 0226/www.cititalia.net). Metro Duomo/tram 1, 2, 20.
Open 9am-7pm Mon-Fri; 9am-1pm, 2-6pm Sat.
Credit AmEx, DC, MC, V. **Map** p311 A1.
A full-service agency for all travel needs; package holidays, air and train tickets on the spot, plus currency exchange and money transfer.

Video rental

Blockbuster
Via Mario Pagano 31A, West (02 4801 3664). Metro Pagano/bus 61, 68/tram 1, 19, 27, 29, 30.
Open 11am-11pm Mon-Thur; 11am-midnight Fri-Sun. **Credit** MC, V. **Map** p308 C1.
Multiple city branches and a selection of English-language titles make this international conglomerate hard to ignore.
Branches: throughout the city.

Eat, Drink, Shop

Arts & Entertainment

Children

Milan has culture, fashion and designer food for kids.

Until recently, Milan suffered from the usual Italian contradiction: though children of all ages are universally adored, child-friendly facilities and activities were non-existent. Slowly but surely, things are changing. That doesn't mean you'll find state-of-the-art, hands-on attractions on every street corner, but most museums lay on children's activities, several restaurants offer kid-friendly menus and a (toddler-sized) fistful of books present a child's-eye view of the city.

GETTING AROUND

Family-friendly improvements have yet to reach public transport. There is no space to store pushchairs on trams, buses and metro trains; stroppy tram/bus drivers occasionally yell over the loudspeaker at parents who fail to collapse prams; some underground stations don't have escalators. So if your baby still fits in a sling or backpack, forget the other options.

On the upside, Italian kid-worship means you'll never be short of people willing to help you clamber on or off transport or to give up their seats. And while ticket barrier inspectors are supposed to charge the standard €1 fare for children over one metre (three and a half feet) tall, they frequently look the other way, especially at weekends.

SIGHTSEEING IN THE CITY CENTRE

The best bet for kids under 12 is a sprint around the fun bits of sights in the extensive central pedestrianised area. Parents can walk from piazza San Babila, east of the Duomo, to Parco Sempione, north of Castello Sforzesco without ever (well, hardly ever) having to worry about little Johnny (or Jemima) ending up under a tram. That said, one or two well-trafficked thoroughfares do still cut through this pedestrian paradise, so watch out.

A sure-fire first port of call for those unencumbered by prams is the **Duomo** roof (*see p57*). The 150-odd steps leading to the top are do-able for anyone in good health over the age of four; otherwise it's best to take the lift. Once up on the well-barricaded roof, kids can clamber along little parapets, pick out the weirdest of the 3,500 sculptures or simply pretend that they're drifting around on a pink marble wedding cake.

Back on terra ferma, look for the shiny leg on the Duomo's early 20th-century brass door: though the leg belongs to a macabre figure in

The **Duomo**, a sure-fire hit with kids.

the act of flagellating Christ, superstitious Milanese say that touching it brings good luck and kids are rarely perturbed.

Next, nip inside the Duomo to check out the sundial (on the floor behind the entrance). Children can spot the hole in the roof through which a beam of light shines on non-grey days, hitting the metal timeline at midday. More determined parents can always point out a couple of the Duomo's serious artworks before their offspring start edging towards the exit.

Past the street performers pretending to be sculptures in piazza del Duomo, accumulate more good luck by emulating the Milanese practice of spinning your heels on the nether regions of the mosaic bull on the floor beneath the central dome of the **Galleria Vittorio Emanuele** (*see p60*). Kids too cool to perform such antics may be happy to peer through the windows of the world's oldest Prada store (founded in 1913 and containing many original fittings) at Galleria Vittorio Emanuele 63-5.

After lunch at **Coco**'s (*see p153*), head up via Dante. This pedestrian-only street offers plentiful opportunities for chasing pigeons, grabbing an ice-cream or shopping for kids' clothes (designer togs at Petit Bateau and L'Angelo; cheap and chic outfits at Du Pareil au Même) before braving the museum at the **Castello Sforzesco** (*see p70*). Ignore the sterile displays on the top floors (no need to feel guilty; admission is free) and make for the armoury room (Hall XIV). A knight on horseback, two-metre long guns and a selection of vicious-looking swords and spears will get youngsters in the mood to spot the severed arm on the *Pietà Rondanini* – Michelangelo's last sculpture – conveniently located in Hall XV. The great artist died before removing the stray limb from this massive block of marble.

With culture well and truly done for the day, parents can sink gratefully on to a park bench while younger kids romp around the small but well-appointed play area in the **Parco Sempione** (*see p74* **All around the garden**) behind the castle. Offspring aged three to ten can burn off any lingering signs of energy on the nearby bumper cars and/or the mini-train (mid Feb-Oct 10am-dusk Sat, Sun; Nov-mid Feb 2.30pm-dusk Mon-Fri, 10am-dusk Sat, Sun; fare 80¢). If that doesn't suffice, there's always the **Acquario Civico**, a teeny aquarium housing shoals of fish and other slippery creatures, also in the park (*see p74*).

Milanese families at a loose end trail past the stuffed animals and dinosaur skeletons at the **Museo Civico di Storia Naturale** (*see p82*); an alternative is to check out the massive ship and Leonardo inventions at the **Museo Nazionale della Scienza e della Tecnologia** (*see p95*). Better than these are two residence-turned-museums where kids can imagine that they're honoured guests in a rich family's home. The **Museo Poldi Pezzoli** (*see p77*) has a room ticking with watches, little pull-out drawers filled with ancient textiles and lace and – for those whose bloodthirsty instincts weren't satisfied at the Castello – another collection of vicious antique arms. At the **Museo Bagatti Valsecchi** (*see p78*) look out for the 400-year-old high chair-cum-potty and 17th-century baby walker. Kids may also appreciate the **Museo del Giocattolo e del Bambino**, which houses antique toys and a mock-up of a 19th-century classroom in a scruffy ex-orphanage. All these museums host workshops and guided tours, some of them in English. Call for details.

The city council has also woken up to the needs of local kids. There are workshops and guided visits for children aged three to 12 during major art shows at the **Palazzo Reale**

(*see p61*), action-packed storytelling sessions at the **Biblioteche Comunali** (*see p284*) and activities and shows at the Castello Sforzesco. Children's events are also held in the summer and on traffic-free 'ecological' Sundays. For information call 02 8846 3700. Ask about English-speaking guides/workshop leaders.

Museo del Giocattolo e del Bambino

Via Pitteri 56, East (02 2641 1585/www. museodelgiocattolo.it). Metro Lambrate/bus 54, 75. **Open** 9.30am-12.30pm, 3-6pm Tue-Sun. **Admission** €4.10; €3.10 concessions; free under-14s Sun. **No credit cards. Map** off p309 B2.

Food

Though Anglo-Saxon parents have a hard time believing it, most *pizzerie*, *trattorie* and restaurants here actually welcome children. It's not unheard of for waiters to whisk Baby off for a tour of the kitchen while Mum and Dad tuck in, and even the most terrifying table manners will be met with indulgent smiles from fellow diners. To make life even sweeter, Milan's kiddie eating scene has undergone a mini-revolution in recent years. Many eateries will drag out highchairs on request and some even offer kids' menus, though changing facilities in eateries – as in museums and galleries – are still almost non-existent.

Coco's

Via San Prospero 4, Centre (02 4548 3253/ www.cocos.it). Metro Cordusio/bus 50, 54/tram 1, 2, 3, 4, 12, 14, 19, 20, 24, 27. **Open** 11am-11pm daily. **Average** €7.50. **Credit** AmEx, DC, MC, V. **Map** p310 A2.
A New Age fast-food joint serving dinosaur-, tapir- and penguin-shaped pasta and teddy-bear veggie burgers. It's guaranteed to get the most diehard veggiephobes begging for more.

Dulcis in Fundo

Via Zuretti 55, North (02 6671 2503/dulcissimi@ libero.it). Metro Centrale FS/bus 42, 43, 53. **Open** 10.30am-7.30pm Tue, Wed, Fri, Sat; 10.30am-12.30pm Thur. Closed Aug, 2wks Dec-Jan. **Average** €13 brunch/lunch, €30 dinner. **Credit** MC, V. **Map** p309 A2.
A child-friendly restaurant with home-made, health-conscious savouries, irresistible cakes, a children's play area and designer chairs (this is Milan after all). Saturday brunch is a highlight on the kiddie calendar. Book in advance.

Pottery Café

Via Solferino 3, North (02 8901 3660/fax 02 7201 3385/www.bridgewater.it). Metro Lanza/bus 41, 43, 61. **Open** 10am-8pm Tue-Thur; 10am-midnight Fri, Sat; 10am-8pm Sun. Closed Aug, 1wk Jan. **Ceramic fee** €15. **Credit** DC, MC, V. **Map** p308 C2.

Arts & Entertainment

Milan's restaurants welcome children. *See p153*.

Kids aged four and over can create colourful and cheerful ceramics in this café-cum-art lab while Mum and Dad relax over cappuccino and cakes. Crafty parents drag kids round the nearby Pinacoteca di Brera gallery first (*see p70*), using this pricey pottery stopover as a bribe.

Entertainment & babysitting

Nano Gigante

Via Lambrate 18, East (02 2682 6650). Metro Loreto or Pasteur/bus 55, 62/tram 33. **Open** 9am-7pm Mon-Fri; 10am-7pm Sat, Sun. **Admission** Membership fee €15.50, then €5-€10.50 per visit (membership fee includes 1 free entry). **Credit** MC, V. **Map** off p309 A2.

One of city's many newish play centres with the usual ball pools, bouncy castles and the like. Parents will be pleased to hear of the 'parking' service for children aged zero to three (9am-1.30pm Monday to Friday); kids aged three to 12 are welcome 9am-7pm Monday to Friday. Book in advance.

Teatro delle Marionette

Via degli Olivetani 3, West (02 469 4440/fax 02 481 8490/gianniecosettacolla@tin.it). Metro Sant'Ambrogio/bus 50, 58, 68/tram 29, 30. **Tickets** €12; €8 concessions. **No credit cards.** **Map** p310 A1.

The Teatro is Milan's longest-established puppet theatre. Book in advance.

Shopping

Milan is a paradise for design-conscious families on a budget. For listings of 20 bargain clothing outlets for kids, pick up *La Guida Agli Spacci*, by Marina Martorana (Sperling and Kupfer, 2001). It's in Italian, but you don't need to be a language genius to decipher the addresses (*see* **Bookshops** *p137*). Top outlets include Il Salvagente Bimbi (via Balzaretti 28, East, 02 2668 0764), which stocks designer returns by top labels, and Il Guardarobino (via Washington 5, West, 02 4801 5802), selling barely worn designer cast-offs.

Publications

Two fun guides for kids, both in Italian but with pretty pictures, are *VivaMilano* by Daniela De Rosa and Paola Scibilia (Elzeviro, 2000) and *I Bambini alla Scoperta di Milano* by Monica Buraggi (Fratelli Palombi, 1999). *Happy Kids* by Silvia Colombo (Proedi, 2001) contains detailed listings of schools and attractions in Italian. Children's events are listed in the *ViviMilano* supplement (Wednesday) of the *Corriere della Sera* daily under '*Ottogiorni Bambini*', and in the *Tutto Milano* supplement (Thursday) of *La Repubblica* under '*Bimbi*'.

Don't miss Highlights outside Milan

Archeopark, Boario Terme
How the ancients lived: this archaeological theme park has reconstructions of thatched stilt-houses perched around a lake. *See p271*.

Villa Pallavicino, Stresa
Zebras, llamas and kangaroos roam the beautiful gardens of this villa on the shores of Lago Maggiore. *See p190*.

Gardaland, Peschiera del Garda
Italy's answer to Disneyland. Steer clear of weekends and holidays to avoid the queues. *See p207*.

Museo della Bambola e della Moda Infantile, Rocca d'Angera
Hundreds of antique dolls hold court in a medieval fortress. *See p193*.

Arts & Entertainment

Contemporary Art

Milan's galleries, like its catwalks, have all the big names.

The pulse of the Italian contemporary art scene is in Milan… and it's racing. Like the glasses of prosecco at the openings that are certain to fill the diary of any art lover on every day of his or her stay, the city overflows with contemporary art spaces. If you can drag yourself away from Dolce&Gabbana for long enough, you'll find a veritable aesthetic feast. Like its catwalks, Milan's galleries have all the big names… and it's all for sale.

It's only really in the last decade that Milan has come into its own. The arrival here of important collectors such as Lia Rumma and Karsten Greve inspired the city with lashings of artistic self-confidence, resulting in a proliferation of private galleries through the 1990s and beyond.

THE SCENE

While contemporary art in Rome is defined by the *Transavanguardia* and in Turin by its Arte Povera movement, Milan – with no defining art movement of its own – is a melting pot. the city is not obsessed with its own history; it is, on the other hand, infatuated with industry, fashion and getting things done. As a result, beautiful, stylish exhibitions take place here, organised with an energy that is unparalleled elsewhere in the country.

Step one in blitzing this effervescent contemporary art scene is to pick up the free monthly *Artshow* booklet (www.artshow.it) the moment you arrive, available at the APT office (*see p290*) near the Duomo or from most galleries. Always up to date, it lists over 100 exhibition spaces and, more importantly, points you to all the *vernissages*.

There is no central art area. However, there is a concentration of galleries as you head north of the Duomo, and there are clusters in via Solferino (map p308 B/C2) and via Farini (map p308 B2). Many galleries are in apartments: ring the bell and you'll be buzzed in.

Private galleries

Antonio Colombo Arte Contemporanea

Via Solferino 44, North (02 2906 0171/fax 02 2906 0171/www.colomboarte.com). Metro Moscova/bus 94/tram 11, 30, 33. **Open** 4-7.30pm Tue-Sat. Closed 2wks Dec-Jan. **No credit cards.** **Map** p308 B/C2.

This two-level space hosts interesting exhibitions that are usually dominated by Italian modernists. Note the silver ashtrays. The catalogues are brief, bilingual and beautiful.

B & D Studio Contemporanea

Via Calvi 18, Centre (02 5412 2563/fax 02 5412 2524/www.bnd.it). Metro Porta Venezia/bus 60/tram 12, 27. **Open** 10am-7.30pm Tue-Sat. **No credit cards.** **Map** p311 A2.

Director Tommaso Renoldi Bracco has a fascination with the possibilities offered by art in the age of technological proliferation. So this very cool space hosts shows ranging from digital photography to video art, light installation and any new media that revolves around man's place in the electronic era. The website is as sexy as the gallery.

Ca' di Fra'

Via C Farini 2, North (02 2900 2108/fax 02 2900 2108/composti@inwind.it). Metro Garibaldi/bus 94/tram 4, 12, 14. **Open** Sept-July 3-7pm Mon; 10am-1pm, 3-7pm Tue-Sat. Closed Aug. **No credit cards.** **Map** p308 B2.

Past a labyrinth of books and a spiral staircase, this charming, cosy space has old red velvet flip-down cinema seats from which to enjoy exhibitions featuring young Italian and foreign artists. The library – a favourite with art students – is open for consultation from 10am to 1pm Tuesday to Sunday.

Carla Sozzani

Corso Como 10, North (02 653 531/fax 02 659 2015/www.galleriacarlasozzani.org). Metro Garibaldi/bus 33/tram 11, 29. **Open** 3.30-7.30pm Mon; 10.30am-7.30pm Tue, Fri-Sun; 10.30am-9pm Wed, Thur. **Credit** AmEx, MC, V. **Map** p308 B2.

Part of the Corso Como 10 concept store (*see p140*) created by a former fashion editor of Italian *Vogue*, this gallery translates magazine into space: pages become art works; readers become customers. Don't even attempt to attend an exhibition opening unless you're clad in full Fendi armour.

Galleria Blu

Via Senato 18, East (02 7602 2404/fax 02 782 398/www.galleriablu.com). Metro Turati/bus 94/tram 1, 29, 30. **Open** 9.30am-12.30pm, 3.30-7.30pm Mon-Fri, Sun; 3.30-7.30pm Sat. Closed 2wks Dec-Jan. **No credit cards.** **Map** p309 C1.

Founded in 1957, this is Milan's oldest and most prestigious venue for post-war art. It was the first to showcase the likes of Lucio Fontana, Alberto Burri and Emilio Vedova. Crowding the archives are works by Braque, Balla, Basquiat, Chagall, Ernst, Giacometti, Kandinsky, Klee and Manzoni.

Magic mushrooms hang out in the ultra-trendy **Fondazione Prada**. *See p158.*

Galleria Emi Fontana

Viale Bligny 42, South (02 5832 2237/fax 02 5830 6855). Metro Porta Romana/bus 24/tram 30. **Open** 11am-7.30pm Tue-Sat. **No credit cards.** **Map** p311 B1/2.

Since opening this gallery in 1992, Emi Fontana has been showing the hottest international contemporary artists working in all media – including Turner Prize winner Gillian Wearing.

Giò Marconi

Via Tadino 15, East (02 2940 4373/fax 02 2940 5573/www.thegallerynet.com/marconi). Metro Porta Venezia/tram 1, 11. **Open** 10am-1pm, 4-7.30pm Tue-Sat. **No credit cards.** **Map** p309 B2.

Giovanni Marconi has created a fantastic space on three levels: it's immaculate, interesting, welcoming and at the cutting edge of contemporary art. The gallery caters to all tastes, exhibiting everything from Italian post-war art to the latest in video.

Karsten Greve

Via Santo Spirito 13, East (02 783 840/fax 02 783 866). Metro Montenapoleone or San Babila/bus 94/tram 1. **Open** 10am-1pm, 2-7pm Tue-Sat. **No credit cards.** **Map** p309 C1.

With galleries already established in Cologne, Paris and St Moritz, Karsten Greve has now expanded into Milan. It's a stylish space on a very stylish street, but this gallery is about much more than finding

something to match the couch. As well as showing a vast spectrum of art – from Joseph Cornell to Louis Bourgeois, William de Kooning to Cy Twombly – Karsten Greve publishes stunning catalogues.

Laura Pecci

Via F Bocconi 9, South (02 5843 0047/fax 02 5843 4287/www.gallerialaurapecci.com). Tram 30. **Open** 3-7pm Tue-Sat and by appointment. **No credit cards.** **Map** p311 B/C1.

Any artist showing in this space can (and inevitably does) indulge his or her whims in projects on a grand scale. Wim Delvoye turned the gallery into a sty for his live tatooed pigs.

Lia Rumma

Via Solferino 44, North (02 2900 0101/fax 02 2900 3805/www.gallerialiarumma.com). Metro Moscova/bus 94/tram 11, 30, 33. **Open** 11.30am-1.30pm, 3.30-7.30pm Tue-Sat. **No credit cards.** **Map** p308 B/C2.

The sister space of the Lia Rumma gallery in Naples, this long narrow corridor should not be overlooked. A clear case of less is more, with meticulously presented shows by established and emerging artists.

MC Magma

Via Tortona 4, West (02 832 1280/fax 02 832 1280/www.mcmagma.com). Metro Porta Genova/tram 9, 14. **Open** 3-7pm Wed-Sat. Closed 3wks Dec-17 Jan. **No credit cards.**

Opened in 1999, this small project space functions as a launch pad for young international artists and keeps the local art scene up to date on less-known though critically acclaimed 'minor' figures.

1000 Eventi

Via del Lauro 3, Centre (02 805 3920/fax 02 805 3923). Metro Cairoli/tram 1, 4, 12. **Open** *Sept-July* 10am-1pm, 3.30-7.30pm Tue-Sat. Closed Aug. **No credit cards. Map** p308 C2.

Mille Eventi is big on video and multimedia, with up-and-coming Italian artists well represented.

Salvatore & Caroline Ala

Via Monte di Pietà 1, Centro (02 890 0901/ fax 02 8646 7384). Metro Montenapoleone or Cairoli/bus 50, 58, 61/tram 1, 2, 3, 4, 12, 14, 20, 24, 27. **Open** *Sept-July* 10am-7pm Tue-Sat. Closed Aug. **No credit cards. Map** p309 C1.

The Alas are excellent at providing exhibition space for young artists, both in solo and group shows.

Studio Guenzani

Via Eustachi 10, East (02 2940 9251/fax 02 2940 8080). Metro Porta Venezia/tram 11/bus 60. **Open** *Sept-July* 3-7.30pm Tue-Sat. Closed Aug. **No credit cards. Map** p309 B/C2.

Under the direction of distinguished art collector Claudio Guenzani, Studio Guenzani has shown Cindy Sherman, Hiroshi Sugimoto and Joseph Kosuth. There's also a strong link with Milanese artists including photographer Gabriele Basilico and painter Margherita Manzelli.

Zonca & Zonca

Via Ciovasso 4, Centre (02 7200 3377/fax 02 7200 3369/www.zoncaezonca.com). Metro Cairoli, Montenapoleone or Lanza/tram 1, 12, 14. **Open** 3.30-7.30pm Mon; 10am-1pm, 3.30-7.30pm Tue-Sat. **No credit cards. Map** p308 C2.

This father-and-daughter-run space merges the super-contemporary with Italian modernism in six annual exhibitions. Selections by Gianfranco Zonca, which have included work by Fontana and Mimmo Rotella, are balanced by Elena Zonca's predilection for cutting-edge installation and photography.

Photography

Also look out for shows by local photographer Gabriele Basilico at **Studio Guenzani** and the avant garde photography at **Zonca & Zonca** (for both, *see above*).

Factories

'The museum', said Josef Beuys, 'is only a building. It could be a church or a station. It depends on what we put inside it.' If London has added 'power station' to that list with the opening of Tate Modern, Milan is doing its bit with a tram factory and a decommissioned gasworks. Industrial wasteland and skeletons of old factories are being brought back to life with the **Fabbrica Eos**, the **Fabbrica del Vapore** and – most recently and excitingly – the **Museo del Presente**.

The Museo del Presente — due to open in June 2002 - will occupy 4,700 square metres (50,540 square feet) of space around two gas storage tanks in the dreary northern suburb of Bovisa. It was against this background that Luchino Visconti set his dramatic neo-realist film, *Rocco e i suoi fratelli* (1960). Futurist painter Mario Sironi (1885-1961) depicted the Bovisa plant as an icon of gas-powered modernity. Now the buxom furnaces that once supplied Milan with light, electricity and heat will be reigniting a hot new contemporary scene, with site-specific shows by up-and-coming European artists.

La **Fabbrica del Vapore** (Steam Factory) is a converted tram manufacture and repair plant in which the city council collaborates with local businesses to provide creative

space for the city's youth. Still getting off the ground, the initiative is oozing with potential. Focusing on the fusion of photography, music, design and fashion, **Fabbrica Eos** – housed in a disused warehouse – functions as an interdisciplinary space with the primary objective of 'eliminating all superficiality to reach the seed of art'. The gallery was inaugurated in 1987 by Peter Gabriel.

Fabbrica Eos

Piazza Baiamonti 2, North (02 659 6532/ www.inforel.it/fabbricaeos). Metro Garibaldi/ bus 94/tram 12, 14, 30, 33. **Open** *Sept-July* 10am-1pm, 4-7pm Tue-Sat. Closed Aug. **Admission** free. **No credit cards. Map** p308 B2.

La Fabbrica del Vapore

Via Procaccini 4, North (02 8846 4102/fax 02 8846 4117/www.fabbricadelvapore.org). Bus 94/tram 12, 14, 30, 33. **Open** varies according to exhibition. **Admission** free. **No credit cards. Map** p308 B1/2.

Museo del Presente

Officine del gas di Bovisa, Via Giampietrino 24, North (www.milano.arte contemporanea.org). Metro Bovisa/ bus 82/tram 1, 12. **Map** off p308 A1.

Arts & Entertainment

Museo di Fotografia Contemporanea

Villa Ghirlanda, via Frova 10, Cinisello Balsamo (02 6602 3550/fax 02 6602 3503/www.museo fotografiacontemporanea.com). Bus 727 from Stazione Centrale. **Open** 3-7pm Tue, Thur, Fri; 3-10.30pm Wed; 10.30am-7.30pm Sat, Sun. **Admission** €2.60. **No credit cards. Map** p307.

A visit to this museum of contemporary photography entails a short trip out of town, but if you're an avid fan of the medium, it's well worth it. Even if you're not, the 17th-century Villa Ghirlanda is gorgeous enough to warrant the 30-minute bus ride.

Photology

Via della Moscova 25, North (02 659 5285/fax 02 654 284/www.photology.com). Metro Moscova/bus 94/tram 11, 30. **Open** 10am-1pm, 3-7pm Mon-Fri. **Credit** MC, V. **Map** p308 B2.

If a print by Ansel Adams or Robert Mapplethorpe tops your shopping list, head for Photology. This is one of the most prestigious galleries on the international photographic arts circuit. But it's also an exhibitor of the established and the up-and-coming in photography.

Spazio Erasmus Brera

Via Formentini 10, North (02 8646 5075/fax 02 8691 3653). Metro Cairoli or Lanza/tram 3, 12, 14. **Open** 11.30am-1pm, 4-7.30pm Tue-Sat. **No credit cards. Map** p308 C2.

A relatively small space hidden away in the pebbled maze of streets off via Fiori Chiari in the Brera neighbourhood, the Spazio Erasmus is worth checking out for its contemporary photography exhibitions, and for its representation of interesting young artists, Italian and otherwise.

Public spaces

Art-lovers should also check out the exhibitions at **CIMAC** (*see p57*) and **Palazzo dell'Arte-Triennale** (*see p74* **All around the garden**).

PAC Padiglione d'Arte Contemporanea

Via Palestro 14, East (02 7600 9085/fax 02 783 330/www.pac-milano.org). Metro Palestro/tram 1, 9, 29/bus 60, 61. **Open** 9.30am-6pm Tue-Sun. **Admission** €5.16; €2.58 concessions. **Credit** MC, V. **Map** p309 C1.

In 1947 Milan's city council began casting about for a space in which to hold contemporary art shows. Having rejected Villa Reale (*see p83*), the council commissioned architect Ignazio Gardella to design a space next door. Completed in 1954, PAC presents consistently high-quality temporary shows.

Viafarini

Via Farini 35, North (tel/fax 02 6680 4473/ www.viafarini.org). Metro Porta Garibaldi/bus 70, 90, 91, 92/tram 3, 4, 11. **Open** Sept-July 3-7pm Tue-Sat. Closed Aug. **Admission** free. **No credit cards. Map** p308 B2.

More than just a gallery, this space – run in conjunction with the city council – provides facilities for research on contemporary art in Milan. There's an art library, a data bank and an archive on young working artists. Viafarini also runs the C/O (Care Of) space on the outskirts of Milan (tel/fax 02 619 7359/www.careof.org), which organises and hosts conferences, workshops and external projects.

Private foundations

Fondazione Nicola Trussardi

Palazzo Marino alla Scala, piazza della Scala 5, Centre (02 806 8821/fax 02 8068 8281/www. fondazionenicolatrussardi.com). Metro Duomo/ tram 1, 20. **Open** 10am-8pm Tue-Sun. **Admission** €6.20. **No credit cards. Map** p311 A1.

Don't be daunted by the window display or the high security at Palazzo Marino alla Scala, HQ of the designer label Trussardi. Through the doors (and up in the lift) is a serious exhibition space dedicated to the promotion of contemporary culture. From installation works to fashion, director Beatrice Trussardi's multi-disciplinary approach focuses on the aesthetic advances of the visual arts in all forms. There's a reading room, and all the latest arty catalogues are on sale.

Fondazione Prada

Via Fogazzaro 36, East (02 5467 0515/fax 02 5467 0258/www.fondazioneprada.org). Metro Porta Venezia/tram 9, 29, 30/bus 37, 45, 60, 73. **Open** varies according to exhibition. **Admission** free. **Credit** MC, V. **Map** p311 B2.

Situated in a former bank archive, Fondazione Prada boasts an archive of a very different nature: the hottest names in international contemporary art. Miuccia Prada and spouse Patrizio Bertelli have remodelled 1,000sq m (3,500sq ft) into the cleanest, coolest space, which hosts only two exhibitions a year: from land art to light, sculpture to installation (previous shows ranged from Michael Heizer to Anish Kapoor, Marc Quinn to Carsten Höller), this is definitely the residence of the art star. If the shows themselves don't appeal, go just to purchase one of the ultra-classy coffee-table catalogues. Oh, and take a look at the guards' feet: yes, those are Prada shoes.

Progetto Chiesa Rossa, Dan Flavin, Untitled 1996

Via Neera 24, South (02 5467 0216/ www.fondazioneprada.org). Tram 3, 15. **Open** 4-7pm daily. **Admission** free. **Map** off p310 C2.

Dedicated to the worship of light, this permanent installation by American minimalist Dan Flavin was created specifically for the nearby Chiesa Rossa (*see p93*), in conjunction with Fondazione Prada (*see above*). It was Flavin's last work, completed two days before his death in 1996. An aesthetic and spiritual experience, the fluorescent light piece is site-specific art at its best. Best after dark; try to avoid arriving during mass (4.30-5pm daily).

Film

Little-filmed but good for film going... though the dubber reigns supreme.

Lacking the charm of Venice, the brashness of Naples and the history of Rome, Milan is perhaps the least-filmed Italian city. Bad weather and a comparatively bleak cityscape haven't done much for its celluloid career either. Over 90 per cent of Italian film production takes place in Rome, though Milan is gaining in popularity for commercials. The city does, however, have a few gems to its credit (*see p160* **Milan in the movies**).

MOVIE-GOING

With 113 cinemas dotted around the city – the big, most central and most commercial ones are concentrated around corso Vittorio Emanuele immediately to the east of the Duomo – you'll have no trouble finding a flick to focus on... if you're into dubbed films, that is.

In Milan the dubber reigns supreme: there's no cinema that shows only undubbed films, though a handful have one *versione originale* (original language) day each week. (Look for 'VO' beside the name of films in programmes.) Milan comes up trumps, however, for film festivals (*see p160*); and the decent fare on offer at the city's cineclubs should keep serious cinephiles busy.

At most cinemas, tickets cost between €3.61 and €5.16 for the first afternoon screening at around 1pm, and from €6.70 to €7.25 for later showings. Times of screenings vary wildly from cinema to cinema, though in most the last one begins at 10.30pm.

First-run cinemas

Arcobaleno Film Center

Viale Tunisia 11, East (02 2940 6054/reservations 02 2953 6368/www.milanoalcinema.com). Metro Porta Venezia/tram 1, 5, 11. **Tickets** €4.65; €6.15. **No credit cards. Map** p309 B1/2.
This clean and colourful cinema shows the latest releases in their original languages on Tuesday.

Ariosto

Via L Ariosto 16, West (02 4800 3901). Metro Conciliazione/tram 1, 24, 29. **Tickets** €5.20. **No credit cards. Map** p308 C1.
This is the place to catch a first- or second-run Spanish or French film. Recent international and independent films are screened here in Italian at 5pm, 7.30pm and 10pm Tuesday to Sunday, and in *lingua originale* on Monday.

Odeon

Via Santa Radegonda 8, Centre (02 874 547). Metro Duomo/bus 60/tram 1, 2, 12, 14, 27, 24. **Tickets** €4.13; €7.25. **Credit** MC, V. **Map** p311 A1.
Once a bustling production house, the Odeon is now a cineplex with ten screens. It's not all dubbed blockbusters, however: as well as first-run features, it shows second-runs and classics. VO films are shown on Monday.

Art-house cinemas

Anteospazio Cinema

Via Milazzo 9, North (02 659 7732/ www.anteospaziocinema.com). Metro Moscova/bus 41, 43, 94/tram 11, 29, 30, 33. **Tickets** €3.65; €6.70. **Credit** shop & restaurants only MC, V. **Map** p308 B2.
With its restaurant, bookshop, exhibition space, film courses, children's programme and conferences – not to mention three screens showing everything from classics to avant-garde films to independent contemporary flicks (and even the occasional live international football match) – the Anteospazio offers something for just about everyone. Original language films are on Monday.

Centro Sociale Barios – Cineclub Simone Signoret

Corner via Barona & via Boffalora, South (02 8915 9255). Metro Romolo/bus 71, 74. **Film shows** 9pm Thur. **Admission** free. **Map** off p310 C1.
At the Centro Sociale Barios, you can check your email, run the gauntlet of some harmless Italian stallions and watch a short film on Thursday evenings.

Cineteatro San Lorenzo alle Colonne

Corso di Porta Ticinese 45, South (02 5811 3161). Metro Porta Genova/tram 3. **Tickets** €4; membership €1. **No credit cards. Map** p310 A/B2.
As well as its usual roster of independent film showings, this art-house cinema runs special weekend sessions in which two international films by the same director are screened each evening in their original language.

Cineteca Italiana

Spazio Oberdan, viale V Veneto 2, East (02 7740 6300/www.cinetecamilano.it). Metro Porta Venezia/ tram 29, 30. **Tickets** €5; 10 shows €30; membership €5. **Credit** MC, V. **Map** p309 B/C1-2.
The Cineteca has been restoring, lending and promoting films since 1947; its archive now runs to 15,000 titles. Film screenings take place in the Spazio

Oberdan, a 193-seat space revamped by architect Gae Aulenti in 1999. The programme ranges from presentations by directors such as Abbas Kiarostami to seminars, debates and screenings on themes that have included the origins of pornography in film. The website has details of events. The cinema is closed on Monday.

Mexico

Via Savona 57, South (02 4895 1802). Metro Sant'Agostino/bus 61, 68, 90, 91/tram 14. **Tickets** €3.62; **No credit cards. Map** p310 B1.

The Cinema Mexico has been screening the *Rocky Horror Picture Show*, accompanied by live performances with lots of audience participation, for the past 16 years, but you still need to book to be sure of a place (tickets €5.68). During the winter, the cinema organises the Revolution Music Film Festival where everything from *A Hard Day's Night* (1963) to *Pink Floyd in Pompeii* (1972) makes its way on to the screen. Undubbed films are shown on a Thursday.

Museo del Cinema

Palazzo Dugnani, Via D Manin 2B, North (office 02 799 224/02 7602 2847/info 02 655 4977/www.cinetecamilano.it). Metro Turati/tram 1.

Open 3-6pm Fri-Sun. **Admission** to museum €2.59. **Tickets** for films €1.50; €2.50. **No credit cards. Map** p309 C1.

Besides cabinets full of cinematographic curiosities, the Museo has screenings at 4pm and 5pm of obscure Italian titles.

Festival del Cinema Africano a Milano

Centro Orientamento Educativo, via G Lazzaroni 8, North (02 6671 2077/02 669 6258/www.festival cinemaafricano.org). Metro Centrale FS/bus 60/ tram 2. **Dates** end Mar. **Tickets** prices vary. **Map** p309 B1.

This seven-day festival of works by African filmmakers (working both inside and outside Africa) screens its films and videos in four cinemas around the city. The 2001 festival included a special section on the African musical, while in 2002 the festival focused on both the cinema of the Ivory Coast and African cartoons.

Street Film Festival

Fax 02 7639 8540. **Dates** early-mid July. **Tickets** prices vary. **No credit cards.**

Milan in the movies

Milan has never been a great favourite with film makers, though Milan native Luchino Visconti, one of the founders of neo-realism, set his heart-wrenching *Rocco e i suoi fratelli* (*Rocco and his Brothers*, 1960; pictured p161) – the tale of a Sicilian family that leaves its impoverished farming community to eke out a living in the harsh city – against

the industrial backdrop of the northern suburb of Bovisa (*see p76*). In Vittorio De Sica's urban tragedy *Miracolo a Milano* (*Miracle in Milan*, 1950; pictured), the city is peppered with the fantastic: boys are born beneath cabbages and fairy godmothers send magic doves to grant wishes to the poor.

The 1980s brought a minor resurgence of interest in Milan as a backdrop… though a depressing number of films showed just brief glimpses of the city as protagonists struggled to get away from it to something 'better'. Another *milanese*, Gabriele Salvatores, filmed *Kamikazen. Ultima notte a Milano* (*Kamikazen. Last Night in Milan*, 1987) here, though mostly inside a theatre. And in his *Marrakech Express* (1989) there are fleeting shots of the city as a group of old friends speed out of Milan on their way to Morocco to rescue another mate. The tit-and-bum films of Carlo Vanzina – *Sotto Il Vestito Niente* (1985), *Yuppies* (1986) and *Monte Napoleone* (1986) – contain a crude dollop of insight into the Milan rag trade.

For an alternative view of the city, try awardwinning *Princesa* (Henrique Goldman, 2000), a provocative film dealing with transvestite prostitution in Milan's red-light districts.

Arts & Entertainment

Milan certainly puts on a show for the outdoor Street Film Festival. It's not just a time-killer, however, but one of the most important festivals of independent film production in Italy. The audience votes for the festival's main prizewinner.

Milano Film Festival

Piccolo Teatro Strehler, largo Greppi, North (02 8942 1256/fax 02 4548 0168/www.milano filmfestival.it). Metro Lanza/tram 3, 4, 12, 14/bus 43, 57, 70. **Dates** mid-late Sept. **Tickets** €5.20 daily pass; €12.95 weekly pass. **No credit cards.** **Map** p308 C2.

Young organisers and filmmakers unite to give an equally young audience the chance to see contemporary developments in international cinematography from 30 countries. The Festival is a superbly organised, interdisciplinary affair that includes art exhibitions, live music, performances and workshops. Take your pillow along for the movie marathon, where some 300 Italian short films are screened.

Film Festival Internazionale di Milano

Various venues (02 8918 1179/02 5740 3738/ www.miffmilano festival.com). **Dates** mid-late Oct. **Tickets** prices vary. **No credit cards.**

This festival, established in 2000, is driven by the concept of film as art and provides an international platform for experimental and independent filmmakers to strut their stuff.

Sport Movies & TV International Festival

Via E de Amicis 17, South (02 8940 9076/ fax 02 837 5973/www.ficts.com). Metro Sant'Ambrogio/bus 94/tram 3. **Dates** end Oct-early Nov. **Admission** free. **Map** p310 A2.

Into its 19th year in 2002, this is one of the most important festivals dedicated to sports films, documentaries and television programmes. It's organised by the International Federation of Sport in Cinema and Television and recognised by the IOC.

Filmmaker International Documentary Festival

Spazio Oberdan, viale Vittorio Veneto 2, East (02 331 3411/www.cinetecamilano.it). Metro Porta Venezia/tram 30. **Dates** end Nov-early Dec. **Admission** free. **Map** p309 B/C1-2.

Run by *Filmmaker* magazine, this event pools international documentaries focusing on a different theme each year: the 2001 theme was the human landscape. Twelve finalists are selected from over 400 entries.

Gay & Lesbian

From *fashionista* locales to gay tea dances, Milan's cool, chic fashion sector makes the gay scene hot.

Italy is no Promised Land for lesbians and gays. The watchful eye of the Vatican and a culture heavily centred around the 'traditional' family make for a cool (though generally cool-indifferent, rather than cool-hostile) reception for homosexuals, while Italy lags far behind its northern neighbours in safeguarding gay rights. The brouhaha in 2000 over the staging of Italy's World Pride parade in Rome – in the same year as the Catholic Church's Jubilee Holy Year celebrations – illustrates how divisive the issue remains for many Italians.

But Milan – far from the shadow of the dome of St Peter's and with a large and variegated international community – is distinctly on the open-minded side of this divide. The percentage of Milan's population that is gay and lesbian is second only to Bologna's. And while public displays of affection may remain rare and gays and lesbians may tend to keep their sexual orientation hidden under a bushel, Milan is nonetheless a mecca for homosexuals from all over the country. It is also a magnet for transvestites, who frequent the area around Stazione Centrale.

The rag trade helps make the city more open. The fashion sector throngs with young gays working in the trade, and the international success of high-profile gay designers such as Giorgio Armani, Gianni Versace, Domenico Dolce and Stefano Gabbana has helped the average Milanese get used to the concept. The fashion sector is a *zona franca*, where homosexual couples are as accepted as hetero ones. What's more, this superabundance of gays of the coolest, chicest type has made the club scene hot.

PRACTICALITIES

More and more of Milan's gay clubs require clients to have an ArciUno Club card, issued by **Arcigay**, Italy's leading gay and lesbian organisation (*see p165*); you'll need it to get into certain saunas, discos and bars – we've indicated which ones in listings below. The card can be bought in any club that requires it. Annual membership costs €13.

Another indispensable tool for clubbing in Milan is the free map found at most clubs and at Milan's leading gay and lesbian bookstore,

Get up close and personal at Milan's gay venues.

Libreria Babele Galleria (*see p166*). The map has a comprehensive list of clubs, shops, saunas and cruising areas with phone numbers and addresses. It also includes briefer listings for Bologna and Verona.

Like just about everything else in the city, most gay and lesbian venues close for a good part of July and/or August, as well as up to two weeks around Christmas. The annual closure can vary from year to year; it pays to call ahead to check that venues are open.

Many predominantly straight clubs have gay nights (*see chapter* **Nightlife**). These can change from time to time; once again, it pays to phone ahead to make sure you're going to the right place on the right night.

Venues

Milan's gay venues offer something for everyone. Obviously, there are the *fashionista* locales where designer duds are the rule and you're there to see and be seen: good looks, a hot body and the fanciest of clothes are essential for these clubs. But there's plenty of scope for mere mortals too, including those with a penchant for leather and/or dark rooms.

Bars & clubs

After Line
Via Sammartini 25, North (02 669 2130/ www.afterline.com). Metro Centrale FS/bus 42, 53, 60, 90, 91/tram 2. **Open** 9pm-2am Mon-Sat; 6pm-2am Sun. **Admission** free. **Credit** MC, V. **Map** p309 A4.
Located on what's known as 'Gay Street', After Line is one of Milan's oldest gay clubs, frequented by an easygoing mix of habitués. Thursday is singles night; on Fridays there are go-go boys and strip men.

Ricci Bar
Piazza della Repubblica 27, North (02 6698 2536). Metro Repubblica/bus 2, 11, 30/tram 29. **Open** 8pm-2am Tue-Sun. Closed 3wks Aug, 2wks Dec-Jan. **Admission** free. **Map** p309 B1.
This is one of Milan's most famous gay clubs, but you'd never know it if you passed by during the day, when office workers flock to it – in its guise of local café – for their shots of caffeine. Only after dark does it blossom into a trendy bar and Milan's fashion set and beautiful people replace the hassled workers.

Discos

Gay Tea Dance
Via Bonnet 11, North (347 220 1024/www. teadance.it). Metro Garibaldi/bus 94. **Open** *Sept-May* 5-10pm Sun. Closed June-Aug. **Admission** €1 before 5.30pm; €7.50 after 5.30pm. **No credit cards. Map** p308 B2.

This Sunday afternoon club is housed in the Gasoline Club disco (*see p171*) and caters to a good-looking crowd of 16- to 30-year-olds. Cube dancers provide entertainment for the largely male crowd, with happy hours and a sushi bar for sustenance. On the colourful Tea Dance website you can sign up for updates on special theme parties, or send messages to someone you spotted on the dancefloor.

Jet Lag
Via Pietrasanta 14, South (02 5521 1313). Bus 90, 91/tram 24. **Open** *Sept-May* 11.30pm-4.30am Fri. Closed June-Aug. **Admission** (includes 1st drink) €16. **No credit cards. Map** p311 C3.
Friday night is gay and lesbian night at Magazzini Generali (*see p168*), one of Milan's biggest straight discos, when the cavernous, two-floor club goes by the name of Jet Lag, drawing a mixed crowd of under-40s who dance until nearly dawn to thumping house music. In the summer, the entire scene decamps to the Idroscalo (map p307), when it's renamed Billy.

Segreta
Piazza Castello 1, North (02 8699 7142/335 808 5169/www.segreta.com). Metro Cairoli/bus 57/tram 1, 27. **Open** 11pm-4am Thur-Sat. **Admission** (includes 1st drink) €8 Thur; €13 Fri; €16 Sat. **No credit cards. Map** p308 C2.
Tight jeans and toned pecs are the rule for the good-looking muscle crowd that populates what is one of Milan's best-known discos. Segreta spreads over three floors inside a medieval palazzo, and comes complete with a labyrinth and suspended dancers. The largely male clientele ranges in age from twentysomethings to 40-pluses.

Saunas

Metro
Via Schiapparelli 1, North (02 6671 9089/www. metroclub.it). Metro Centrale FS/bus 42, 53, 60, 90, 91/tram 2. **Open** 1pm-2am Mon-Fri, Sun; 1pm-3am Sat. **Admission** (with ArciUno card) €13 Mon-Sat; €16 Sun and holidays; €10.50 after 10pm daily. **Credit** MC, V. **Map** p309 A2.
Definitely one of Milan's choicest gay saunas, having undergone a top-to-toe renovation just two years ago. Spread out over two floors, it has jacuzzis, a nice bar with snacks and drinks, a steam bath, a massage room and a Finnish sauna. The clientele tends towards the young and the fashionable. For your private viewing pleasure, there are videos in the 'relax' rooms, as well as an internet hook-up. Free condoms are handed out at the door. There are discounts for under-26s.

Thermas
Via Bezzecca 9, East (02 545 0355). Bus 37, 45, 73/tram 12, 23, 27. **Open** noon-midnight daily. Closed 2wks Aug. **Admission** €13 Mon, Wed, Fri, Sat; €11 Tue, Thur; €14 Sat; €11 after 8pm daily. **No credit cards. Map** p311 A2.

Arts & Entertainment

Spartan but clean, Thermas serves a very diverse crowd ranging from corporate executives to designers of most age groups. There's a steam bath, a very small body-building room, television, a cooling-off area, a jacuzzi tub and red leather beds in the changing rooms for close encounters.

Miscellaneous

American Contourella
Piazza della Repubblica 1/A, North (02 655 2728/ www.contourella.it). Metro Repubblica/tram 11, 30, 29. **Open** 8am-10pm Mon-Fri; 8am-8pm Sat; 10am-6pm Sun. **Admission** €15. **Credit** AmEx, MC, V. **Map** p309 B1.
Definitely less flash than Downtown (*see below*), American Contourella – again, not exclusively gay – is another well-known meeting place for gay men (who tend to be less flash than Downtown clients). The gym offers all of the standard physical fitness services, from free weights to an 18m pool.

Company Club
Via Benadir 14, East (02 282 9481). Metro Cimiano/bus 53, 56. **Open** 10pm-3am Tue-Thur, Sun; 10pm-9am Fri, Sat. **Admission** free with ArciUno card only. **No credit cards**. **Map** off p309 A2.
A fair hike from the centre, near the Parco Lambro in the north-eastern suburbs, this leather club is the place for anyone looking for a quick hook-up. There's a dark room and a video room.

Cruising Canyon
Via Paisiello 4, East (02 2040 4201). Metro Loreto/ bus 90, 91, 92. **Open** 24hrs daily. **Admission** €7. **No credit cards**. **Map** off p309 B2.

This enormous venue is a sex club pure and simple, open 24/7. A one-stop shop with indoor reproductions of cruising areas, the Canyon has a mock-up park, a cinema and a labyrinth. Definitely for those looking for a quick but close encounter.

Downtown
Piazza Cavour 2, North (02 7601 1485/www. downtownpalestre.it). Metro Turati/bus 61, 94/tram 1, 2, 20. **Open** 7am-midnight Mon-Fri; 10am-9pm Sat, Sun. **Admission** €41 per day; €155 per mth. **Credit** MC, V. **Map** p309 C1.
This (by no means exclusively gay) gym is one of the trendiest in Milan and is a well-known magnet for some of the best-looking gay men in the city. The crowd is a mix of fashion types, managers and executives, some of whom spend as much time checking out their prospects as toning their pecs. The gym itself is top class with great equipment, saunas, steam rooms and a good array of aerobics classes. Its restaurant – which serves a Sunday brunch – is great for scoping out new prospects.

Organisations & shops

The best source of information on gay events, clubs and publications throughout Italy is to be found on the website, **www.gay.it**. Information is broken down by region and the site also offers a multitude of links to other organisations, chatrooms and venues as well as updates on special events.

Newsstands that stock gay pornography include the one in **piazza Oberdan** (map p309 C2) at the corner of **via Tadino**, as well as the one on **corso Buenos Aires** (map p309 C2),

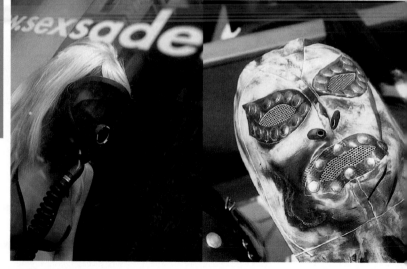

Cruisin'

So packed with gay bars and clubs is **via Sammartini** (map p309 A/B2) – the street hugging the western side of Stazione Centrale – that it's known as 'Gay Street'. While the area around the station can be dodgy and a little caution is needed, keep to the bits that are hopping and you shouldn't have any security problems.

In general cruising in Milan is safe and hassle-free, particularly because most of it is done by car. The one exception is the area behind **Cadorna station** (map p310 A2) – known as *la fossa*, the ditch – which is mainly pedestrian and rather too close for comfort to Parco Sempione (map p308 C12), an after-dark haven for drug users.

The **Orto Mercato** (in the south-eastern suburbs, and along via Monte Cimino in particular; map off p311 B2) and **Parco Nord** (along via Fulvio Testi in the northern Sesto San Giovanni suburb; map off p309 A1) usually have the friendly feel of an open-air party. The former attracts a smartish young Milanese crowd, mostly in cars; the latter a decidedly more blue-collar bunch of out-of-towners, both on foot and motorised.

close to Porta Venezia. You can also find some steamy stuff at the newsstands in and around **Stazione Centrale**. Most mainstream bookstores don't stock gay and lesbian literature or publications. **Libreria Babele Galleria** (*see p166*), on the other hand, offers a wide selection of gay and lesbian titles.

Arcigay

Via Bezzecca 3, East (02 5412 2225/helpline 02 5412 2227/www.arcigaymilano.org). Bus 37, 45. **Open** 10am-1pm, 2-8pm Mon-Fri; 3-7pm Sat, Sun. Closed 1wk Aug; 1 wk Dec. **Map** p311 A2.
The Bologna-based Arcigay and ArciLesbica (*see p166*), Italy's main gay and lesbian associations, are important sources of information on gay and lesbian life, both in Milan and throughout Italy. The Arcigay website is excellent and it also runs a telephone service for those looking for services or in need of help. The association also issues the ArciUno card (*see p162*), ever more essential for getting into gay venues. The Milan office of Arcigay is open on Sunday afternoons to welcome new members and answer questions. The group also hosts occasional members' dinners (call for times and dates). The cultural office organises film festivals and debates. There is a small library stocked with gay-related books, magazines and videos.

Castro Market

Via San Rocco 5, South (02 5843 0898/www. castromarket.it). Metro Porta Romana/tram 29, 30. **Open** 9.30am-7.30pm Tue-Sat. **Credit** AmEx, MC, V. **Map** p311 B1.

Arts & Entertainment

Latex and leather at **Sex Sade**. *See p166.*

This shop is totally dedicated to lesbian and gay products, offering gay videos, magazines, books and gay pride T-shirts and baseball caps. Many of its products are available online. It's also open 10am-7pm on Sundays in November, December and June.

Libreria Babele Galleria

Via San Nicolao 10, West (02 8691 5597/ www.libreriababele.it). Metro Cadorna/bus 43, 70, 94/tram 1. **Open** 2-7pm Mon; 10am-7pm Tue-Sun. Closed 2wks Aug. **Credit** MC, V. **Map** p310 A2.

Milan's main bookstore for gays and lesbians. In addition to its 7,000 books, it sells foreign and Italian magazines, videos, posters, postcards and a variety of gadgets. It also hosts cultural events and exhibitions and houses a gay and lesbian travel agency, Arcoturismo. Many of its products are also on sale via the internet.

Sex Sade

Via Santa Maria Valle 1, South (02 804 880/ www.sexsade.it). Metro Missori/bus 94/tram 2, 14. **Open** 10am-1pm, 2.30-7.30pm Tue-Sat. **Credit** AmEx, MC, V. **Map** p310 A2.

If you're into S&M, this is the place for you. Latex and leather clothing, accessories and underwear are here in abundance.

Lesbian Milan

While gay clubs are relatively plentiful in Milan, the city offers much less for lesbians, with just a handful of long-standing bars and discos geared towards women seeking women.

If you read Italian, pick up a copy of the bimonthly magazine *Towanda* for information on lesbian life in Milan. A highbrow publication with book reviews, political commentary and art critiques, it also contains advertisements for lesbian-only vacation spots and news on events organised by Italy's main lesbian group, **ArciLesbica** (*see below*). Milan's gay and lesbian bookstore, **Libreria Babele Galleria** (*see above*), also has updated information on clubs, events and film series. Finally, a good resource for events, chatrooms and even job listings is the Lista Lesbica portal at **www.listalesbica.it**.

Bars & clubs

Oca Dipinta

Statale Paullese, km 17.3, Zelo Buon Persico, Lodi (02 906 5027/www.ocadipinta.com). Tram 12 or 27 to viale Umbria, then bus Q8 or 12B from via Cena on the Milan–Melzo–Comazzo route. **Open** 8pm-3am Thur. Closed Jan, 2wks Aug. **Admission** €8. **Credit** AmEx, MC, V.

A relatively recent addition to Milan's lesbian circuit, the Oca Dipinta is 15km (9.5 miles) outside the city, but it's well worth making the trip. A disco and restaurant are housed in a renovated farmhouse,

and the place is open throughout the summer, when the action moves out to the garden. Thursday night is lesbian night.

Recycle

Via Calabria 5, North (02 376 1531/www. associazionerecycle.it). Bus 90, 91, 92. **Open** 9pm-1am Wed, Thur, Sun; 9pm-2am Fri, Sat. Closed Aug; 2wks Dec-Jan. **Admission** €2.60; annual membership €10.20. **No credit cards.** **Map** p308 A1.

A bit out of the way, and with decor that is ultra-simple, Recycle is a lively joint, with cabaret, live music or a DJ, depending on the evening, as well as the odd cultural event such as a book presentation or lesbian film festival. You can also grab a bite to eat at the bar. The clientele – from the city and the hinterland – is friendly. There's a wide age range, though Fridays tennd to draw a slightly younger crowd. Friday, Saturday and Sunday evenings are women-only.

Sottomarino Giallo

Via Donatello 2, East (339 545 4127/www. sottomarinogiallo.it). Metro Piola/tram 11/bus 90, 91. **Open** 11pm-3am Wed, Sun; 11pm-4am Fri; 11pm-5am Sat. Closed 3wks Aug. **Admission** (includes 1st drink or 1st 2 if you enter before midnight) free Wed; €13 Fri, Sat; €10 Sun. **No credit cards.** **Map** off p309 B2.

One of Milan's long-established lesbian clubs, the Yellow Submarine has a cosy lounge-like bar upstairs and a disco downstairs, which features mainstream dance music. The place is popular with a range of age-groups, though most those who come here are in the thirtysomething band. Saturday nights are women-only; gay men or male friends of regulars are admitted on other nights.

Organisations

ArciLesbica

Corso Garibaldi 91, North (02 6311 8654/ http://women.it/arcles). Metro Moscova/bus 41, 94. **Open** for events only. **Map** p308 B2.

While Arcilesbica is much less active than its brother group Arcigay (*see p165*), it is nevertheless Italy's main political organisation for lesbians. Its website contains a calendar of activities, which range from long weekends in Naples to political workshops and film screenings. The group also runs a helpline at the number given above, open 7-9pm on Thursdays.

Collettive Donne Milanese

Corso Garibaldi 91, North (347 451 2456). Metro Moscova/bus 41, 94. **Open** for events only. **Map** p308 B2.

CDM is one of the most active lesbian associations in Milan and works in close association with Arcilesbica (*see above*). It organises everything from brunches to lesbian-themed film screenings to political debates. Some events are held at the Libreria Babele Galleria (*see p166*), where calendars of the group's activities can also be found.

Nightlife & Music

Smoky late-night bars, and seriously trendy clubs.

The Milanese (or, more specifically, the people who happen to live in Milan) are known as the national workhorses, but that doesn't mean that they're early to bed, early to rise types. After office hours is when the real work gets done.

Milan considers itself a centre for all things stylish and trendy. Its residents, therefore, are particularly susceptible to the Latest Thing, whether it's an authentic-tasting *mojito* or high-tech furnishings worthy of a photo shoot. People in Milan expect a lot from their clubs and, for the most part, the clubs deliver, attracting their fair share of headliner foreign DJs. Milan is also a regular stopover for touring bands – from the biggest to the most underground.

On Saturdays many of the more commercial clubs fill up early with out-of-towners on a Big Night Out. Sundays are gaining in popularity too, with dancing starting in the early evening. On any other night, arriving before 11.30pm is almost certain to ensure you a good hour to yourself… the only advantage being that you'll battle less to get the barman's attention.

PROTOCOL

More and more clubs are introducing a pay-as-you-leave system. Where this is the case, you'll be given a ticket (*tessera*) at the door; this will be punched when you use the cloakroom, buy drinks, and so on. Drinks usually cost around €7; it's often the same whether you order soft drinks, spirits or beer. Hang on to that card: the fine for losing it is exorbitant.

Most nightclubs serve dinner before the business of the night begins in earnest: while the food is unlikely to be memorable, it certainly will be more than adequate, and there is often live jazz music during dinner hours. Taking a table usually ensures access to the *privé* (which is just a fancy term for a restricted chill-out room).

Evergreen **Magazzini Generali**...

INFORMATION

ZeroDue (which of course refers to Milan's phone prefix, 02) is a free mini-sized bimonthly magazine that is an indispensable tool for finding out what's going on where, when. Look for it in those little orange racks with the free advertising postcards in cafés and bars catering to the hip crowd. It includes everything from art exhibitions to concerts to clubs (in Italian). The **www.milanoin.it** website has events listings; again, only in Italian.

ON THE TOWN

For loud and smoky late-night bars (*locali*), the **Brera**, **corso Como**, **Porta Ticinese** and **Navigli** districts are hopping: head for one of these neighbourhoods in the evening and you're guaranteed to find a place with good drinks, a good crowd and good music. Closing time for most bars is around 2am, whereas clubs usually stay open until at least 4am.

Live music

As well as hosting bands, most of the following venues double up as dance clubs.

Mega-venues

Really big headlining bands generally play at the **FilaForum** (via di Vittorio) and the **PalaVobis** (via Elia 33), two immense venues in immensely inconvenient locations in the southern Assago and the western San Siro suburbs respectively. If there's a show you just can't miss, tickets can be bought in central record shops, including Messaggerie (*see p150*), Ricordi (*see p142*) or FNAC (*see p150*).

Medium-to-large venues

Alcatraz

Via Valtellina 25, North (02 6901 6352). Bus 82, 90, 91, 92/tram 3. **Open** *Club* 10pm-3.30am Fri, Sat. *Concerts* check local press for dates and times. **Admission** *Club* (includes 1st drink) €14. *Concerts* prices vary. **Credit** MC, V. **Map** p308 A2.
As a concert venue, Alcatraz is definitely on a par with the world's best. This ex-industrial building holds around 2,000 people. During the week it hosts Italian and foreign bands that are big, but not big enough to fill an entire stadium (think Faithless, Coldplay, Air, and so on). On weekends, it turns into a dance club: Friday nights feature house and 'revival' music; Saturdays are all rock 'n' roll.

Leoncavallo

Via Watteau 7, North (02 670 5185/www. leoncavallo.org). Bus 43/tram 1. **Open** 8.30pm-1am Mon-Thur, Sun; 8.30pm-4am Fri, Sat. **Admission** varies. **No credit cards. Map** off p309 A2.

The 'Leonka' (as locals call it) is an institution for the city's (politically and musically) left-wing youth. A very active *centro sociale* (squat), it hosts talking shops and protest meetings in the afternoon and more underground entertainment at night. Concerts range from hip hop to punk to rock, and DJs play sets until the wee hours. Drinks are cheap, as is the late-serving cafeteria. Check the website for events. The last Friday of the month is a must for fans of anything electronic: swarms of blithely spacey people pack four separate rooms throbbing with house, techno and drum 'n' bass.

Magazzini Generali

Via Pietrasanta 14, South (02 5521 1313). Bus 90, 91/tram 24. **Open** *Sept-June* 11pm-4am Wed-Sat. Closed July, Aug. **Admission** *Club* free Wed, Thur; €15 Fri, Sat. *Concerts* prices vary. **No credit cards. Map** p311 C1.
It's hard to define Magazzini: as a concert venue, disco, party space and/or art gallery, this has been one of the In Places in Milan since it opened in 1995. With a capacity of about 1,000, Magazzini hosts musical acts of every genre – from Pavement to the Black Crowes to Wyclef Jean. Wednesday is to be avoided unless you're after a student crowd. Jet Lag on Friday is a Milanese classic: heavily gay but not exclusively so, with muscular go-go dancers and house music. Saturday is more commercial and attracts a younger set.

Small-to-medium venues

Also check out **La Banque** (*see p170*).

Rolling Stone

Corso XXII Marzo 32, East (02 733 172/www. rollingstone.it). Bus 73/tram 12. **Open** *Club* 11pm-4am Tue, Thur-Sat. *Concerts* (occasionally) Mon, Wed, Sun; check local press for dates and times. **Admission** *Club* (includes 1st drink) €18 Tue; €6 Thur; €13 Fri, Sat. *Concerts* prices vary. **Credit** AmEx, MC, V. **Map** p311 A2.
This is Milan's leading rock venue, with concerts during the week and dancing on Fridays and Saturdays. If rock isn't your bag, however, try it on Tuesday for Fidelio: the venue transforms itself into a softly lit restaurant/nightclub with tables and chairs around the periphery of the dancefloor (dinner is served from 8pm, average €35). If you don't want to eat, get there around 11pm and stake out a good vantage point: at midnight, a ring of cloaked and masked girls re-enact the 'ritual' scene from Stanley Kubrick's *Eyes Wide Shut*. And yes, the cloaks do come off. Afterwards, all the pretty people get up and shake to grooveable, but fairly mainstream vibes.

Scimmie

Via Ascanio Sforza 49, South (02 8940 2874/ www.scimmie.it). Metro Romolo or Porta Genova/bus 59/tram 3. **Open** 8pm-3am daily. **Admission** free. **Credit** AmEx, MC, V. **Map** p310 B/C2.

... bar, club, live music venue, art gallery... you name it. *See p168.*

One of the first places in Milan to introduce the now-popular bar and entertainment combo, this canal-side hotspot is a great place for eating, drinking, listening to live music (jazz, Dixieland, blues, rock and reggae). It's an especially pleasant destination in the summer months, the only problem being the Navigli's infamous mosquitos. Music starts at 10.30pm nightly. Come earlier to eat; reservations are recommended, especially at weekends and in the summer, when food is served on a barge-type platform on the canal.

Le Trottoir

Corso Garibaldi 1, North (02 801 002).
Metro Lanza/tram 3, 4, 12, 14. **Open** 11am-3am daily. **Admission** free. **Credit** MC, V.
Map p308 B/C2.

A throwback to Milan's more bohemian days, this tiny, narrow place in the heart of Brera is packed almost every night, with people spilling on to the street and loud, live music. Upstairs, you might get lucky and find a place to sit down. But for the most part the clientele is happy to stand pressed together and bop. Worth a trip just to see how a postage stamp-sized stage can accommodate a five-person band. A good place to meet people, even if it's usually too noisy and cramped to make much conversation.

Tunnel

Via Sammartini 30, North (02 6671 1370/www.
uscitanuovisuoni.com). Metro Centrale FS/bus
43/tram 2, 33. **Open** *Club* Oct-May 10pm-3am Fri, Sat. Closed June-Sept. *Concerts* Oct-May check local press for dates and times. Closed June-Sept.
Admission *Club* €5-€10. *Concerts* prices vary.
No credit cards. **Map** p309 A2.

This ex-warehouse beneath the Stazione Centrale has been transformed into an alternative live music space and dance club for emerging Italian bands and house DJs. The line-up is consistently interesting.

Clubs & discos

La Banque

Via B Porrone 6, Centre (02 8699 6565). Metro
Cordusio/tram 1, 3, 12, 19, 24. **Open** Sept-July 6pm-2am Tue-Thur; 6pm-4am Fri, Sat; 7pm-midnight Sun. Closed Aug. **Admission** (includes 1st drink) €11 Tue-Thur; €16 Fri; €18 Sat; €11 Sun. **Credit** AmEx, MC, V. **Map** p310 A2.

An aesthetically pleasing spot (and fantastically central), La Banque's the kind of place that attracts guys who go out in suits. On Thursday there's live music from 11pm; Friday night pulls a younger crowd; Sunday is popular for its early *aperitivi* (with generous free buffet) and dancing to house and hip hop. On weekdays La Banque opens for *aperitivi* at 6pm, and serves an elegant dinner nightly from 8pm to midnight. No trainers, please: you'll be turned away if you're not turned out appropriately.

Café L'Atlantique

Viale Umbria 42, South (02 5519 3925/www.
cafeatlantique.com). Bus 90, 91. **Open** Sept-June 9pm-4am Tue, Wed, Fri, Sat; 7.30pm-4am Thur, Sun. Closed July, Aug. **Admission** (includes 1st drink) €7-€15. **Credit** MC, V. **Map** p311 B2.

Duelling DJs rip it up at **Tunnel**.

Summer in the city

As the weather heats up, many Milanese residents head out of the city on Friday nights, not to return until late Sunday. But there's still plenty of nightlife options for those who are left. While some clubs and discos close between June and August, many stay open, and others change location to less central spots where it's cooler (supposedly) and there's space for dancing under the stars.

Public transport has a nasty habit of drying up just when you're heading for *locali estivi* (summer night spots). But if you can get a lift or spare the taxi fare, try the **Idroscalo** – a huge man-made lake near Linate airport – for the nearest thing that land-locked Milan has to a beach disco. At *entrata sud, porta sette* (southern entrance, gate seven) **Café Solaire** is one of the most popular summer party places, where much tanned, sweaty flesh is exposed, to the joy of hordes of nuclear mosquitos. South-east of the centre, **Borgo del Tempo Perso** is another summer hangout, with DJs, drinks and dancing in its two gardens and two inside spaces. Once there, head for the club **Karma**: it's newer, less well known and attracts an in-the-know crowd.

Staying in the city can be fun too. In the summer, the **Navigli** area is closed to traffic after 8.30pm, and canal-side bars and cafés stay open until late. The nightlife neighbourhoods of **Brera**, **corso Como** and **Porta Ticinese** come out of their shells and on to the pavement with the arrival of warm weather: seven nights a week, there's scope for endless curbside table-hopping.

Borgo del Tempo Perso/Karma

Via Fabio Massimo 36 (02 569 4755/www. borgodeltempoperso.com). Metro Corvetto or Porto di Mare. **Open** *May-Sept* 11.30pm-4am Thur-Sat. *Oct-Apr* 11.30pm-4am Wed-Sat. **Admission** (includes first drink) €15. **Credit** AmEx, M311 C2C, V.
Borgo's restaurant is open 9.30-11.30pm (average €5).

Café Solaire

Idroscalo, Segrate, southern entrance, gate 7 (02 5530 5169/www.cafesolaire.it). **Open** *May-Sept* 11pm-5am Thur-Sun. **Admission** (includes first drink) €15. **Credit** MC, V. **Map** p307.

As this guide went to press, L'Atlantique was The Place To Be in Milan: if you don't seriously dress up, you'll never get through the door. Positioned beneath an enormous and truly incredible modern chandelier, the circular bar in the centre of the main room is one of the best places in the city to do some *fighetti*-spotting (*see p172 **Fighetti**).* There's hip-hop/house in two different rooms on Thursday and Friday; Saturday's attracts a younger crowd and is more commercial; on Thursday and Sunday the action begins at 7.30pm for *aperitivi* and early dancing. New York Bar – an especially exclusive (read: especially expensive – €25) night with the world's top DJs – takes place on the first and third Sunday of each month.

Casablanca Café

Corso Como 14, North (02 6269 0186). Metro Garibaldi/tram 11, 33, 29, 30. **Open** *Sept-July* 6pm-3am Tue-Sun. Closed Aug. **Admission** free Tue-Fri, Sun; €8 Sat. **Credit** AmEx, MC, V. **Map** p308 B2.
This disco-bar and restaurant has a DJ (music tends towards commercial house) and dancing, but that's not what the Casablanca Café is really about. People come here to watch each other and to sip cocktails in the hiatus between exiting from restaurants and heading out to other, more serious, clubs in the neighbourhood.

De Sade

Via Piazzi 4, North (02 688 8898). Bus 82, 90, 91, 92/tram 3. **Open** *Sept-May* 9.30pm-3am Thur-Sun. Closed June-Aug. **Admission** (includes 1st drink) €10. **Credit** MC, V. **Map** p308 A2.
Every second and fourth Sunday of the month De Sade hosts Pervert, and the name says it all: dress as wildly as you dare and don't be surprised if the most glamorous women head for the men's loo. The music, obviously, is hard house. Thursday, on the other hand, is when those sleek-haired, well-heeled Italians come to dance to hip hop and R&B. Fridays are geared towards the university crowd; Saturdays feature house and dance music from the 1970s and '80s.

Gasoline Club

Via Bonnet 11A, North (02 2901 3245/ www.discogasoline.it). Metro Garibaldi/tram 11, 29, 30, 33. **Open** *Sept-June* 10.30pm-4am Tue-Sat; 5-9.30pm Sun. *July* 10.30pm-4am Sat. Closed Aug. **Admission** (includes 1st drink) €7-€15. **Credit** MC, V. **Map** p308 B2.
Situated in the Bermuda Triangle of nightlife around hip corso Como, this small club features everything from '80s pop to deep house. For those who crave something a little different, try the Gasoline Club's Sunday afternoon gay tea dance (*see p163*), with sushi and Go-Go Boys.

Fighetti

Fighetti lurk just about everywhere in Milan: they're the guys leaning nonchalantly against a particularly fine scooter, talking on a tri-band cellphone the size of their palm; or the girls with the perfectly blown-out, highlighted hair negotiating cobbled streets effortlessly in pointy-toed high-heels, while swinging Gucci bags off their perfectly manicured fingers.

Derived from figo (cool), the term – naturally – originated in image-obsessed Milan. It's not a classist word – though without plenty of disposable income, it's well-nigh impossible to perfect the look. Nor is it a term that anyone would ever apply to themselves: use it, and you'll never be a true fighetto or fighetta.

While fighetti can be spotted in daylight hours in some of the city's swisher neighbourhoods, they come into their own after dark, flocking to particular bars and discos. Popular watering holes include **Café L'Atlantique** (especially the New York Bar on the first and third Sundays of every month, see p170), **De Sade** (Thursdays; see p171), **Hollywood** (Fridays; see p172) and **Toqueville 13** (Sundays; see p172).

Hollywood

Corso Como 15, North (02 659 8996). Metro Garibaldi/tram 11, 29, 30, 33. **Open** *Sept-June* 10.30pm-4am Tue-Sun. Closed July, Aug. **Admission** (includes 1st drink) €13 Tue; €16 Wed-Sun. **Credit** AmEx, DC, MC, V. **Map** p308 B2.
A prominent feature on the nightlife scene since 1986, there's a high model-to-mortal ratio in this locale, especially on Friday nights: suck in your cheeks and look bored if you want to fit in. The music is definitely commercial: this is not a cutting-edge place. It's somewhere you go in order to say you've been there. Which is not necessarily a bad thing.

Old Fashion

Viale E Alemagna 6, North (02 8056 2317/www. oldfashion.it). Metro Cadorna/bus 61/tram 1, 27, 19. **Open** 8.30pm-4am daily. **Admission** (includes 1st drink) €12-€15. **Credit** AmEx, MC, V. **Map** p308 C1.
Central and hip, Old Fashion draws a good crowd throughout the year. Wednesday is student night, so steer clear unless that's your cup of tea. If *bella gente* (beautiful people) are what you're after, Mondays and Saturdays are best. The restaurant serves dinner ever night from 8.30pm to midnight (average €42). It also opens for a nice Sunday brunch, noon-4pm, €18.

Plastic

Viale Umbria 120, East (02 733 996). Bus 92/ tram 12. **Open** *Sept-June* midnight-4am Thur-Sat; 8pm-2am Sun. Closed July, Aug. **Admission** (includes 1st drink) €15-€20. **No credit cards.** **Map** p311 B2.
At this enduringly trendy spot (be sure to dress to impress or you'll never make it past the bouncers) you can dance 'til late to a agreeable mix of house and hip hop. It's a popular gay destination and a prime place to spot some of the city's lovely drag queens. The atmosphere is a touch mellower in the Juke Box Hero Room where you can play billiards as you down your drinks. Sunday *aperitivi* at Plastic is an industry standard: hard-working creative folk flock here to bid the weekend goodbye, getting their groove on and then getting to bed early.

Shocking Club

Bastioni di Porta Nuova 12, North (02 8645 4630). Metro Garibaldi/tram 11, 29, 30, 33. **Open** 11pm-4am Tue-Sun. Closed Aug. **Admission** (includes 1st drink) 12- 17. **Credit** AmEx, MC, V. **Map** p309 B1.
Reopened in February 2002 after a two-year hiatus, 'Lo Shocking' is back with a vengeance. During the 1990s this was a bastion of Milanese nightlife and now, following a refurbishment, its new modern/ minimalist decor will see it well into the 21st century. Located right by the beginning of trendy corso Como, this is the hub of the *locale* zone and should not be missed.

Soul To Soul

Via San Marco 33A, North (02 2900 6350). Metro Moscova/bus 41, 43. **Open** 9pm-3am daily. **Annual membership** €18. **No credit cards.** **Map** p308 B/C2.
Playing exclusively hip hop and R&B, this small basement disco with a chill-out room is an refreshing antidote to Milan's racially homogenous dancing scene. Soul To Soul gets pretty hot and sweaty and it's definitely a long way from chic, but if commercial house music is wearing you down, give this place a go.

Tocqueville 13

Via A Tocqueville 13, North (02 2900 2973/ www.tocqueville13.com). Metro Garibaldi/tram 11, 29, 30, 33. **Open** *Sept-June* 10pm-3am daily. Closed July, Aug. **Admission** (includes 1st drink) €15. **Credit** AmEx, MC, V. **Map** p308 B2.
This place is a classic on the nightlife scene, with 1970s-inspired decor. The music varies from night to night, with the emphasis on fairly commercial house and some Latino dance grooves. Tocqueville attracts footballers, models and local VIPs on Sunday nights (they're likely to be tucked away in the *privé*, however); Mondays and Thursdays are popular with a more sophisticated, well-dressed crowd. Dinner is served in the evenings from 9.30pm until midnight (average €35); if you eat, you too can be privy to the *privé*.

Performing Arts

La Scala is Milan's prima donna but it's not the whole story.

Milan's performing arts scene does not begin and end with *La Bohème* at La Scala (though if you get a chance, don't pass it up). Industrial, parochial but prosperously elegant, eternally contradictory Milan has Italy's liveliest theatre by far, and is no slouch compared with Vienna or Paris either.

La Scala, Milan's cultural prima donna, holds centre stage. But all around, the tricks of the city's thriving fashion trade seem to have been applied successfully to the theatre. Productions are catwalk-perfect, as aesthetically pleasing as they are entertaining, with lashings of the city's unabashed exhibitionism. And as Milan effortlessly absorbs all ages, classes, orientations and clichés, so its stages cater for all comers.

CLASSICAL MUSIC AND OPERA
The **Teatro alla Scala** is out of action until 2004 (*see p176* **La Scala moves north**), and in its place the **Teatro degli Arcimboldi** – where the La Scala company has taken up temporary residence – has become the city's opera mecca. The *teatri* **Smeraldo** and **Carcano** stage lighter operatic offerings. The recently renovated **Auditorium di Milano** is the city's main venue for classical music.

THEATRE
Milan's 35-plus theatres offer a vitality and richness that no other Italian city can match. The three theatres of the Piccolo group (*see p174* **The Strehler legacy**) are unquestionably the cherry on the cake. But the **Arsenale** and **Manzoni** are reliably top-notch too. For something less mainstream, check out the **CRT**, the two **Teatrithalia** venues, **Teatro Litta** and the **Teatro Out Off**: the latest productions from up-and-coming directors, hyper-contemporary pieces, avant-garde reinterpretations and the occasional well-performed modern classic fill their programmes. The *teatri* **Ciak**, **Smeraldo** and **Nuovo** churn out musicals, cabaret and variety.

DANCE
The **Centro di Ricerca per il Teatro (CRT)** is Milan's main purveyor of contemporary dance, organising festivals (*see p177*) in which dance plays a key role. The **Teatro Carcano** and **Teatro Out Off** also schedule interesting international

choreographers into their programme. **La Scala** (now at the **Teatro degli Arcimboldi**; *see p176* **La Scala moves north**) is the city's main classical ballet venue.

THE SEASON
Most theatres launch their season at the beginning of October and carry through until the end of May, although some start performances halfway through September, and carry on into June, when the festivals get going.

The opera season – for which read La Scala – stages its be-furred and bejewelled opening night on 7 December.

INFORMATION AND TICKETS
For all but the most prestigious big-name performances, tickets can be purchased at individual theatre box offices prior to shows. Alternatively, many venues accept phone bookings with credit cards; tickets should be picked up an hour before the curtain rises.

For the majority of theatres listed below you can check programmes and buy tickets online through www.ticketweb.it, www.ticketone.it, www.ticketitalia.it and www.prenofacile.it, all of which accept all major credit cards.

Fifteen theatres – including the ones marked * below – participate in the **Invito a teatro** scheme, in which a €62 pass allows access to eight shows over the space of the season. The pass can be purchased from participating theatres or from the online box offices mentioned above.

Venues

Auditorium di Milano
Theatre: largo Mahler 1, South (02 8338 9225/ www.auditoriumdimilano.org/ www.orchestrasinfonica.milano.it). Metro Duomo/tram 3, 15. **Performances** 8.30pm Tue-Sat; 4pm Sun. *Chamber music* 11am Sun. **Map** p310 B2. *Box office: corso San Gottardo 42A, South (02 8338 9201). Metro Duomo/tram 3, 15.* **Open** 10am-7pm daily. **Credit** AmEx, MC, V.

The Cinema Massimo, built in 1939 and left empty for several decades after World War II, burst back into life in 1999 as home to Milan's Orchestra Sinfonica Giuseppe Verdi, directed by *maestro* Riccardo Chailly. In a massive restoration project, the old cinema was gutted, then provided with 1,400 seats, state of the art technology and an excellent acoustic.

The Strehler legacy

Giorgio Strehler (1921-97).

The combination of a steaming Milanese summer evening and the beckoning 'air-conditioning' sign outside the Teatro Odeon seduced a young Giorgio Strehler into watching his first performance of Carlo Goldoni's *Una delle ultime sera di Carnovale*. The man who was to become the most influential Italian theatre director of the second half of the 20th century was hooked.

Though Strehler was responsible for introducing the rest of the world (and many Italians) to the prolific 18th-century Venetian playwright Goldoni, his name is little known internationally outside drama circles. Not so in Italy – and especially in his home town of Milan – where there's no escaping his legacy. 'Giorgio has long been and still is theatre in Italy,' popular actor Paolo Villaggio said of him.

Strehler studied at Milan's Accademia dei Filodrammatici drama school, where he hatched grandiose plans with his friend and fellow-student Paolo Grassi. Disillusioned by the hidebound Italian theatre scene, they formed the Piccolo company and opened the Piccolo Teatro in 1947, launching with Maxim Gorky's *The Lower Depths* and continuing with Goldoni's *Servant of Two Masters*, a neglected play that went on to become one of Italian theatre's longest-running productions. In the same year, Strehler began his opera-directing career with a production of *La Traviata* at La Scala (*see p176* **La Scala moves north**). All this when he was barely 26.

In the early years of the Piccolo Teatro, Strehler directed 12 productions per season. Seeking to make theatre culturally relevant to a broad public, he staged plays by TS Eliot, Buzzati, Pirandello, Ibsen, Flaiano and Calderón; he was also responsible for bringing Bertold Brecht's works to Italy. But all didn't run smoothly for the irascible director, who left the Piccolo to form the Teatro d'Azione in 1968, only to return to the Piccolo in 1972 after Grassi was named manager of La Scala.

By this time the diminutive Piccolo Teatro was way too small for Strehler's grand plans. In the late 1970s, work began on the Nuovo Piccolo to a design by Marco Zanuso. Another of his projects, the experimental Teatro Studio – a highly controversial conversion of the old Teatro Fossati, also by Zanuso – opened in 1987. But it took 20 years, a sky-rocketing budget and many court cases before the lights went up in the Nuovo (now Teatro Strehler). A year later, the still-embittered Strehler was dead.

Today the Piccolo company is under the artistic direction of Luca Ronconi, a highly regarded veteran of the Italian stage, and the management of impresario Sergio Escobar. The original 500-seater Piccolo Teatro – now known as the Teatro Grassi – is still one of Italy's foremost repertory theatres, offering high culture at low prices to a very broad church.

Teatro Grassi (Piccolo Teatro)

Via Rovello 2, Centre (02 7233 3222/www. piccoloteatro.org). Metro Cordusio/bus 54, 58, 70, 43/tram 1, 3, 4, 12, 14, 19, 24, 27. **Open** *Box office* 10am-6.45pm Mon-Sat; 10.30am-6.30pm Sun. *Performances* 8.30pm Tue-Sat; 4pm Sun. **Credit** AmEx, MC, V. **Map** p308 C2.

Teatro Strehler (Nuovo Piccolo)

Largo Greppi, North (02 7233 3222/www. piccoloteatro.org). Metro Lanza/bus 43, 57, 61, 70/tram 1, 3, 4, 12, 14. **Open** *Box office* 10am-6.45pm Tue-Sat; 10.30am-6.30pm Sun. *Performances* 8.30pm Tue-Sat; 4pm Sun. **Credit** AmEx, MC, V. **Map** p308 C2.

Teatro Studio

Via Rivoli 6 (02 7233 3222/ www.piccoloteatro.org). Metro Lanza/bus 43, 57, 61, 70/tram 1, 3, 4, 12, 14. **Open** *Box office* 10am-6.45pm Sun; 10.30am-6.30pm Sun. *Performances* 8.30pm Tue-Sat; 4pm Sun. **Credit** AmEx, MC, V. **Map** p308 C2.

Conservatorio Giuseppe Verdi
Via Conservatorio 12, East (02 762 1101/
www.conservatorio-milano.com). Metro San
Babila/bus 94. **Open** *Box office* 1hr before concerts.
Performances 9pm Mon-Fri. **No credit cards**.
Map p311 A1/2.
Conservatorio students and travelling ensembles
play favourites such as symphonies by Mozart and
violin concertos by Bach and Paganini.

*CRT Teatro dell'Arte
Viale Alemagna 6, West (02 8901 1644/www.
teatrocrt.org). Metro Cadorna/bus 61/tram 1, 29, 30.
Open *Box office* 11.30am-7pm Mon-Fri; 3-7pm Sat.
Performances 8.30pm Tue-Sat; 4pm Sun. **Credit**
AmEx, MC, V. **Map** p308 C1/2.
Established in 1974, the Centro di Ricerca per il
Teatro (CRT) is Italy's leading forum for theatrical
experimentation, organising themed programmes
that blend music, theatre, dance and cinema. A lively mix of contemporary drama and opera, classical
theatre, and dance – from ballet to the latest
European developments in choreography – is staged
at the Teatro dell'Arte and the smaller CRT Salone
(via Dini 7, same phone number and box office). The
CRT is also responsible for some of the city's most
exciting arts events and festivals (*see p177*).

*Teatridithalia Elfo
Via C Menotti 11, East (02 716 791/
www.elfo.org). Metro Porta Venezia or Palestro/
bus 60, 62, 92/tram 5, 11. **Open** *Box office* 10am-
6.30pm Tue-Fri. *Performances* 8.45pm Tue-Sat;
4pm Sun. **No credit cards**. **Map** p309 C2.
The Elfo sprang irreverently to life in 1973, the
brainchild of film director Gabriele Salvatores (of
Nuovo Cinema Paradiso fame) and Ferdinand Bruni,
when they were still in their early 20s. It still shakes
a fist at convention, with productions such as
Federico Tiezzi's pop adaptation of Goldoni's classic *Due gemelli veneziani* in 2001. Tickets can be
booked by phone and picked up on the day of the
show at 6.30pm.

*Teatridithalia Portaromana
Corso di Porta Romana 124, South (02 5831 5896/
www.elfo.org). Metro Porta Romana/bus 62, 77/tram
9, 29, 30. **Open** *Box office* 11.30am-6.30pm Mon-Sat.
Performances 8.45pm Tue-Sat; 4pm Sun. **Credit**
AmEx, MC, V. **Map** p311 A/B1.
Established in 1979, and under the Teatridithalia
umbrella since 1992, the Portaromana is as radical
as Milanese theatre gets, eschewing any attachment
with bourgeois 'entertainment'. Recent treats have
included a fantastic adaptation of Shakespeare's
sonnets in song, music and dance by the Virus
String Quartet.

*Teatro Arsenale
Via C Correnti 11, South (02 832 1999/www.
teatroarsenale.org). Metro Missori or
Sant'Ambrogio/bus 94/tram 2, 3, 14. **Open**
Box office 3-7pm Mon-Fri; 30mins before
performances. *Performances* 9.15pm Tue-Sat;
4.30pm Sun. **No credit cards**. **Map** p310 A2.

Housed in a 13th-century church, this theatre now
has a stage where the pulpit once was; TS Eliot,
Banana Yoshimoto or Luigi Pirandello will move
you to spiritual (or theatrical) reverence. There's
everything from plays to poetry, plus some chamber music thrown in for good measure.

*Teatro Carcano
Corso di Porta Romana 63, South (02 5518
1377/www.teatrocarcano.com). Metro Crocetta/bus
77, 94/tram 4, 23, 24. **Open** *Box office* 10am-
6.30pm Mon; 10am-8pm Tue-Sat; 1-6.30pm Sun.
Performances 8.30pm Tue-Sat; 4pm Sun. **No credit
cards**. **Map** p311 A/B1.
Established in 1803 and once the home of grand
opera, the Carcano has been under the artistic control of renowned director Giulio Bosetti since 1997.
It presents a diverse range of genres, from puppetry
to operetta, plus an eclectic mix of plays from writers as diverse as Luigi Pirandello and Woody Allen.

Teatro Ciak
Via Sangallo 33, East (02 7611 0093/02 3932
2737/www.teatrociak.com). Bus 93/tram 5. **Open**
Box office 11am-6.30pm Tue-Sat; 3-6.30pm Sun.
Tickets also sold at Teatro Smeraldo (*see p176*).
Performances 9pm Wed-Sun. **No credit cards**.
Map off p311 A2.
The former Cinema Goddess was transformed into
the Teatro Ciak in 1977 by Leo Wachter, the man
responsible for organising the Beatles' first Italian
performance. There's variety, which can be side-
splitting if you're into Italian humour; the occasional interesting Italian or international band plays;
there's some decent contemporary theatre and
cabaret, and the occasional mime show.

Teatro Dal Verme
Via San Giovanni sul Muro 2, North (02 8790 5201/
www.dalverme.org). Metro Cairoli/tram 1, 27. **Open**
Box office 11am-9pm Tue-Sun. *Performances* 9pm
Tue-Sun; 5pm Sat, Sun. **No credit cards**.
Map p308 C2.
Inaugurated in 1872, the Dal Verme was transformed from theatre to cinema after World War II.
In April 2001 it reopened its doors as a concert hall
after 20 years behind scaffolding. Besides a variegated evening programme by visiting orchestras,
the Orchestra I Pomeriggi Musicali plays classical
music in this spacious wood-floored venue on weekends at 5pm.

*Teatro Franco Parenti
Via Pier Lombardo 14, East (02 545 7174/
www.teatrofrancoparenti.com). Metro Porta
Romana/bus 62/tram 9, 29, 30. **Open** *Box office*
10am-Mon-Sat; 11am-12.30pm Mon-Sat.
Performances Sala Grande 8.30pm Tue-Sat; 4pm
Sun. Sala Piccola 9pm Tue-Sat; 4.30 or 5pm Sun.
Credit DC, MC, V. **Map** p311 B2.
Modern classics by the likes of Beckett, Brecht,
Chekov and Thomas Bernhard are brought to life
by the Franco Parenti company and other presti-
gious Italian groups.

Arts & Entertainment

La Scala moves north

For sheer flashy opulence, few events can beat the opening night of the La Scala season, held each year on 7 December, the feast of the city's patron saint, Ambrose. Flashes pop as actors rub designer-clad shoulders with politicians and judges bestow self-satisfied smiles on elegant industrialists whom earlier in the week they were sentencing for cooking company books. Animal rights activists are so bewildered by the zoo of fur that they hardly know where to aim their rotten eggs; mere mortal onlookers wonder how many lottery wins it would take to amass jewellery in these quantities.

*Teatro Litta

Corso Magenta 24, West (02 8645 4545/www. teatrolitta.it). Metro Cadorna/bus 50, 54, 58/tram 18, 19, 24. **Open** *Box Office* 2.30-7pm, Mon-Sat. *Performances* 9pm Tue-Sat; 4.30pm Sun. **Credit** MC, V. **Map** p308 C1/2.

Located in the sumptuous Palazzo Arese-Litta (*see p96*) a stunning baroque structure which is also home to the Italian state railways headquarters, the Teatro Litta has thrown off its former aristocratic connections and become a favourite with younger theatre buffs, hosting lectures, workshops, a pretigious drama school and great productions of contemporary works.

Teatro Manzoni

Via Manzoni 42, Centre (02 763 6901/www. teatromanzoni.it). Metro Montenapoleone/bus 61, 94/tram 1, 2. **Open** *Box office* 10am-7pm Mon-Sat; 10am-5pm Sun. *Performances* 8.45pm Mon-Sat; 3.30pm, 11am Sun. **Credit** AmEx, MC, V. **Map** 309 C1.

This elegant venue, which stages good classic and contemporary Italian productions, has pepped up its act with *Aperitivi in concerto*, a series of top-class contemporary jazz concerts held each Sunday at 11am. (Get there at least an hour before to beat the crowds.) For €10.34 you get music and a wake-you-up cocktail. The theatre's website has the full programme.

Teatro Nuovo

Corso Matteotti 20, Centre (02 7600 0086/www. teatronuovo.it). Metro San Babila/bus 37, 54, 61, 65, 73. **Open** *Box office* 11am-6pm Mon-Sat; 11am-1pm, 4.30-6pm Sun. *Performances* 8.45pm daily. **Credit** AmEx, MC, V. **Map** p309 C1.

Established in 1938 in a building that is a monument to the architectural tastes of the Fascist era, the Nuovo is the place to come should you be gripped with a burning desire to see musicals such as *Grease* or *Little Shop of Horrors* in Italian.

*Teatro Out Off

Via Dupré 4, West (02 3926 2282/www. teatroutoff.it). Metro Lotto/bus 90, 91/tram 12. **Open** *Box office* 9am-6pm Mon-Fri. *Performances* July-May 9pm Tue-Sat; 4pm Sun. June 9pm Tue-Sat; 4pm, 9pm Sun. **Credit** AmEx, MC, V. **Map** p308 A1.

The Out Off often works in tandem with the transgressive Teatridithalia group (*see p175*) staging – among other things – some interesting contemporary dance performances. Its Contrasti Poetici poetry festival is held annually from mid-May to mid-June. Under-25s get a 30 percent discount; over-60s get in for half price.

Teatro Smeraldo

Piazza XXV Aprile 10, North (02 2900 6767/ www.smeraldo.it). Metro Moscova or Garibaldi/bus 94/tram 11, 29, 30, 33. **Open** *Box office* 11am-

But there's another group of Scala-frequenters who shun the see-and-be-seen frenzy, though they're no less dedicated to opening nights for all that. The theatre's *loggionisti* grab the cheapest tickets, high up in the gods, and are the true arbiters of what goes and what doesn't in the theatre. They're as ready to respond with a hiss or a whistle (the Italian equivalent of a 'boo') as with applause; and even sacred cows of the opera world risk a shower of paper planes (or even bunches of turnips) should they miss a note or turn in a second-rate performance. They love opera classics, but they're willing to accept the new or experimental too... as long as the singing's up to scratch.

The 2001-2 season opened with Placido Domingo in Verdi's *Otello*. Shortly afterwards, scaffolding went up around the historic theatre, and operations moved way out into the new Teatro degli Arcimboldi, in the up-and-coming Bicocca neighbourhood in the northern suburbs. In a project that has aroused much controversy, the Teatro alla Scala is due to remain closed until 2004,

during which time its ageing fittings are to be restored and its security arrangements brought up to 21st-century standards.

Tickets – notoriously difficult to obtain – should be slightly easier to get hold of for the Arcimboldi, which has 2,400 seats against La Scala's 2,015. The new theatre was designed by Vittorio Gregotti, who is also responsible for office blocks and housing developments in Bicocca. The new university campus is also located here, in what City Hall hopes will become a buzzing cultural zone.

Teatro alla Scala

Piazza della Scala, Centro (02 7200 3744/ www.teatroallascala.org). Metro Duomo or Cordusio/bus 43, 54, 58, 70/tram 1, 3, 4, 12, 14, 19, 24, 27. **Map** p311 A1.

Teatro degli Arcimboldi

Viale dell'Innovazione, North (02 7200 3744). Metro Precotto then shuttle bus. **Open** *Box office at La Scala 10am-6pm daily; at theatre 2hrs before performances.* *Performances 8pm Tue-Sun.* **Credit** AmEx, DC, MC, V. Map p307.

6.30pm Mon-Sat; 11am-1pm Sun. *Performances* 8.45pm Tue-Sat; 4pm Sun. Also some 8.45pm performances Sun. **No credit cards.** Map p308 B2. It's not much to look at from the front, but this block of cement conceals a huge plush theatre where all your favourite musicals – from *Evita* to *Cats* – are staged, and where big musical names – including David Bowie, BB King, Paolo Conte and even Miles Davis – have performed.

Festivals

Festival dei Bambini

Teatro Strehler, Largo Greppi, North (02 7233 3222/www.piccoloteatro.org). Metro Lanza/bus 43, 57, 61, 70/tram 1, 3, 4, 12, 14. **Box office** 10am-6.45pm Tue-Sat; 10.30am-6.30pm Sun. **Credit** AmEx, MC, V. **Map** p308 C2.
Children aged four to 14 can enjoy seeing theatre, mime, music, puppetry, circus and dance as well as taking part themselves in workshops at this festival of children's theatre.

Festival Milano OLTRE90

Various venues (02 5831 5896/www.elfo.org). **Box office** at venues 2hrs before performances. **Dates** end Sept-end Oct. **Credit** AmEx, MC, V.
Billed as an 'inferno of the contemporary', this festival of theatre, dance, poetry, new media and music has been gathering strength since 1986, with offer-

ings from international directors as diverse as Jan Fabre, Nigel Charnock, Krypton, Koeja, Motus, Nekrosius, Santagata and many others. Festival events take place in 12 theatres around town. Tickets can be bought online on the www. ticketone.it website.

Short Formats Festival

CRT Teatro dell'Arte, viale Alemagna 6, West (02 8901 1644/www.teatrocrt.org). Metro Cadorna/bus 61/tram 1, 29, 30. **Box office** 10am-6.45pm Tue-Sat; 10.30am-6.30pm Sun, and before performances. **Dates** mid-late May. **Credit** AmEx, MC, V. **Map** p308 C1/2.
Coordinated by the ever-active Centr di Ricerca per il Teatro (CRT, *see p175*), this festival is an investigation into all the latest European trends in dance. Fourteen Italian and international dance companies and 12 European research centres collaborate in a grand spectacle of contemporary dance.

Tramedautore: Festival della nuova drammaturgia italiana

Various venues (information 02 3925 7055/www. manifatturae.it/tramedautore.htm). **Box office** at venues before events. **Dates** mid-end Sept. **No credit cards.**
This ten-day festival of performances, studies, readings, writing, workshops and encounters with Italian writers got off the ground in 2001.

Arts & Entertainment

Sport & Fitness

The Milanese tone beautiful bodies in state-of-the-art gyms.

The Milanese feel under pressure to look good, but their office-job lifestyle makes keeping themselves in trim a challenge. This explains, perhaps, their higher-than-(Italian)-average rate of sporting activity.

For men, playing soccer in the evenings and skiing or cycling at weekends is a must. And while women are just as likely to be found on the slopes, they tend to trade in cycles and soccer balls for swimming and aerobics.

The two worlds meet in the fitness centres around the city. As men jockey for workout bikes with the best view, women pretend not to notice the stares as they prance on treadmills or the aerobics floor.

Evenings and lunchtime at the gym are more social than mornings, when the dedicated few have the machines and squash courts to themselves. In recent years, however, free weights and Nautilus equipment have yielded space to 'relax rooms', where 'wellness' is achieved through colour therapy and soothing aromas.

When the weather is good in Milan – a rare event – cycling or jogging along the canals (see p179 **On yer bike**) provides a chance for free sun and exercise, though paying for a treadmill and solarium has the added perk of not inhaling the city's notorious pollution.

Smog and spectator sport come together in a roaring crescendo in the neighbourhood of San Siro, at the Stadio Giuseppe Meazza.

Football

Stadio Giuseppe Meazza, more commonly known as San Siro, is to football what La Scala is to theatre. Both are Milanese institutions with long traditions and immense funds at their disposal, both are the centre of endless political bickering and both have provided high-profile stages for generations of *prime donne* of all imaginable ilks. San Siro is home to two rival teams.

AC Milan (www.acmilan.com) was created by a group of expatriate Brits, led by one Herbert Kilpin. Herbert and his drinking buddies found themselves with few outlets for English sports in a cycling-mad city, hence the Milan Cricket and Football Club was born in 1899. Only one team – Genoa, also founded by the English – claims to be older.

So successful was AC Milan that in 1908 the Italian Football Federation meanly decided to exclude foreign players from the national championship. The internationals of AC's roster marched off in dissent, forming their own club and calling it Football Club Internazionale (**Inter**). Eventually, they won the right to compete in the championship.

Over the years, the clubs evolved into two very different political animals. Until media magnate and soon-to-be prime minister Silvio Berlusconi bought a nearly bankrupt AC in 1986, *milanisti* were known as *cacciavite* (screwdrivers), a reference to the club's exclusively blue-collar fan base. In the tumultuous '70s, the club represented the hard left, and the red of their red and black strip signalled their Communist leanings.

Inter (www.inter.it), on the other hand – with regal blue and black stripes – has always been associated with the bourgeoisie. The Moratti family of oil barons presided over a decidedly aristocratic club for most of the 20th century. Inter's headquarters near the Duomo is in a historic palazzo with Homeric frescos.

Fiercely antagonistic, fans shun each other except for twice-yearly encounters at San Siro. The first derby was held there in 1945 – for three decades before that, the teams played at the Arena in Parco Sempione (*see p74*) – drawing a crowd of 35,000. These days, more than 80,000 spectators turn out twice a year for the match. It's a finely balanced thing: since the first derby in 1908, each team has won about 100 games, with nearly 80 draws.

Third-ring seats are pretty far away from the pitch, but unlike Rome's Stadio Olimpico, for example, the field is not surrounded by an athletics track, which means the stands are closer to the action. San Siro's other attraction is ease of exit: it is said that no stadium in the world can fill up or empty out as quickly. More facts and figures on this remarkable building and the fabled personalities associated with it can be found at the **Museo Inter e Milan**.

Museo Inter e Milan

Gate 4, Stadio Giuseppe Meazza, via Piccolomini 4, West (02 404 2432/02 4879 8253/fax 02 404 2251/ 02 4879 8251/onarisi@tin.it). Metro Lotto/tram 24. **Open** 10am-5pm Mon-Sat; 10am-20 mins before kick-off on match days (usually Sun). **Admission** €10; €7 concessions. **No credit cards.**

On yer bike

With its cobbled streets, treacherous tram tracks and snarling traffic, Milan might seem the least promising place to enjoy a bike ride. But the city is blessed with a few remaining canals (many more have been filled in over the centuries) and a cycle path runs alongside each one.

There are three that are worth the trip, each passing historic sites and rare patches of natural beauty, though the riding surfaces vary greatly.

The longest path, which runs along the Martesana canal for much of its route, crosses the whole city, from the far north-east – where it connects with a lovely track to the suburb of Gorgonzola – to Porta Genova in the south-west. Pick up this bike track at the Gioia metro station on the green line (you can take bikes on the metro if you buy an extra ticket). For Gorgonzola and a suburban experience, head north-east along via Melchiorre Gioia – a smooth, red-painted surface occasionally obstructed by parked cars – and you will eventually see the waterfalls of the canal. For something more urban, follow blue signs with a bicycle on them pointing south-west; don't despair when the signs disappear – only briefly – round about Parco Sempione, and be prepared for a bumpy ride over cobbles, particularly in the Brera district.

At its south-west end at Porta Genova (another metro station and potential starting

point), the Martesana track joins separate paths running along Milan's two biggest canals: the Naviglio Grande and the Naviglio Pavese. It's impossible to get lost on these tracks: they are both straight shots leading to the towns of Abbiategrasso (see p110) and Pavia (see p253) respectively.

The path to Pavia, with its Carthusian monastery (see p256 **For Caterina, with love**), is rough riding: you'll need a mountain bike to handle the bumps. It passes locks designed by Leonardo da Vinci.

The path that follows the Naviglio Grande is the most pleasant of all, often consisting of finished jogging surfaces and populated mostly by fellow cyclists and runners. Abbiategrasso, which is just an hour away at racing speed, is bland enough. But the path continues up past verdant villas with views of the Alps; a further 15 kilometres (9.5 miles) down the road is the stunning medieval centre of Vigevano.

For bike hire, see p279.

The admission price includes a guided tour of the stadium. On match days, a ticket for the game allows entrance to the museum until 20 minutes before kick-off.

Tickets

Note that games against the rival home team or against Juventus are generally sold out far in advance, though if you're determined to get in to a match, the ticket touts around the stadium before the game will be happy to help you... at a price.

Milan Point

Via San Gottardo 2, piazza XXIV Maggio entrance, South (02 8942 2711/fax 02 839 3192). Metro Porta Genova/tram 29. **Open** 10am-7.30pm Mon-Sat. **Tickets** €11-€108.50. **No credit cards**. This is the place to come to purchase tickets for AC Milan home games.

Ticket One/Spazio Oberdan

Viale Vittorio Veneto 2, East (02 2953 6577). Metro Porta Venezia/tram 29. **Open** 10am-9pm Tue-Sun. **Tickets** €11-€58. **No credit cards**. For Inter home games.

Golf

The countryside around Milan has some of the most beautiful courses in the country. However, almost all require membership. The one exception is Golf Le Rovedine: the only public course in Lombardy. It is situated, appropriately, on via Karl Marx in the Milanese suburb of Opera.

Golf Le Rovedine

Via Karl Marx 18, Noverasco di Opera (02 5760 6420/fax 02 5760 6405/www.rovedine.com). Metro Porta Romana then walk to via Ripamonti and take bus 24 to end of line. **Open** 8am-7pm daily.

Rates *for 18 holes* €30.98 Mon-Fri; €51.65 Sat, Sun & holidays. **Credit** AmEx, DC, MC, V.

This basic, par-72 course is 7km (4.5 miles) outside the city. Given the increasing popularity of the sport in Italy, Le Rovedine can draw a crowd in good weather, especially at weekends, so booking is always advisable.

Gyms

Much of Milanese fitness revolves around gyms, or *centri di benessere* (wellness centres) as they are more often termed. There is much more to these temples of body worship than workout equipment: facilities commonly include dance studios, tanning beds, nutritionists, hairdressers, pools, saunas, squash courts, boxing rings, restaurants, travel agencies, climbing walls, sports equipment stores not to mention the suddenly ubiquitous 'relax rooms'.

Downtown Palestre

Piazza Cavour 2, North (02 7601 1485/fax 02 7639 4283/www.downtownpalestre.it). Metro Turati/bus 61, 94/tram 1, 2, 20. **Open** 7am-midnight Mon-Fri; 10am-9pm Sat, Sun. **Rates** €41 per day; €155 per mth. **Credit** MC, V.

Downtown's clientele consists of the rich, the famous and the very beautiful, including models keeping cat-walk-trim for the spring and autumn fashion shows. There are postmodern workout services such as Watsu and water massage, Tantsu Thai treatments and kick boxing, plus two floors of gym equipment, including treadmills and stair-climbers. The spa and beauty centre, at the same address (02 7631 7233), offers all kinds of pampering.

Skorpion Club

Corso Vittorio Emanuele 24, East (02 781 424/fax 02 782 753/skorpioncenter@tin.it). Metro San Babila/bus 60, 65, 70, 73/tram 15, 19, 23. **Open** 7am-11pm Mon-Fri; 10am-9pm Sat, Sun. **Rates** €40 per day; €80 per wk. **Credit** AmEx, MC, V.

Steps from the Duomo, the less sweat, more relaxation Skorpion is the most centrally located gym in Milan and is consequently pricey. It offers a full range of activities, including Turkish baths for men and women. The 11th-floor solarium has a sweeping view of the city.

Pools

While most private gyms have their own pools, many Milanese opt for a pay-as-you-go plan. Public pools are much cheaper, though the open-access swimming schedules can be baroque to say the least. Remember your bathing cap: you will not be allowed in the water without one. Times given below are for open-access swimming: at other times, pools are usually used for swimming classes.

Parco Solari

Via Montevideo 20, West (02 469 5278). Metro Sant'Agostino/bus 50/tram 14, 20, 29, 30. **Open** 7.15-9am, noon-3.30pm Mon; 10.30am-2.30pm, 6.30-10.30pm Tue; 7.15-9am, noon-2.30pm, 7.30-10.30pm Wed; noon-3.30pm Thur; 7.15-9am, noon-2pm, 6.30-9.30pm Fri; noon-6pm Sat; 10am-7pm Sun. **Rates** €3.60 Mon-Fri; €4.13 Sat, Sun. **Credit** MC, V.

One of the city's more modern-looking public pools is housed in a saddle-shaped building with floor-to-roof windows looking out on to the park, but there are few frills and the staff can be surly. Swimming, water aerobics and scuba courses are available.

Piscina Cozzi

Viale Tunisia 35, North (02 659 9703). Metro Repubblica/tram 1, 11, 29, 30. **Open** noon-10pm Mon; 10am-1.30pm Tue, Thur, Fri; 10am-8.30pm Wed; 10am-4.30pm Sat, Sun. **Rates** €3.60 Mon-Fri; €4.13 Sat, Sun. **No credit cards**.

Built in 1934, with a Fascist exterior and Soviet interior, this is one of Milan's most popular and populist pools. It's Olympic-size, but often crowded. Opening hours are extended during the hottest months.

Squash

Although old-school *milanesi* still opt for tennis in clubs that require year-long memberships, squash is increasingly popular with go-getters. You can see why in rainy, workaholic Milan: it's quick, played indoors and has a northern European feel. Slower outdoor sports, Milan's *squashisti* feel, are best left to the Romans.

Tonic Club

Via Mestre 7, East (02 2641 0158/fax 02 2641 2295/www.newtrefor.it). Metro Udine/bus 55, 75. **Open** 7am-midnight Mon-Fri; 9am-7.30pm Sat, Sun. **Rates** €20.70 per day; €160.10 for 10 sessions; €377 for 30 sessions. **Credit** AmEx, MC, V.

Tonic is large, refreshingly industrial and generally devoid of the glamour of the clubs closer to the centre. In 2001 the management attempted to turn it into an all-purpose wellness centre; the clientele remains the same, however. It has four squash courts and racket rental. But the highlight is a boxing ring built in 2000 for Mike Tyson's bout-that-never-was against Lou Savarese. Day passes and multiple entries are valid for all equipment.

Vico Squash

Via GB Vico 38, West (02 4800 2762/ 02 4801 0890/viavicocity@tiscalinet.it). Metro Sant'Agostino/bus 50. **Open** 7am-11pm Mon, Wed; 8.30am-11pm Tue, Thur, Fri; 10am-9pm Sat, Sun. **Rates** €36.15 per mth; €7.75 single session for non-members. **No credit cards**.

With a dozen squash courts, this is the place for Milan's favourite New Economy sport. Ironically, Squash Vico is located opposite an Old Economy monument: the San Vittore prison, where many of the city's former elite did time during the Clean Hands probe (*see p24*).

Lakes & Cities

HOTEL VILLAMARIE

Lakes & Cities of Lombardy

From ski resorts to lakes and rice paddies.

Nature

Some 5,000 square kilometres (1,900 square miles) of Lombardy – over 20 per cent of the region's territory – are protected, in national, regional and local parks and reserves. For more information, consult **www.parks.it**, or the WWF's Italian site at **www.wwf.it**. Parks covered in this guide include:

Parco delle Incisioni Rupestri (Grosio), *p266*.
Parco Lombardo della Valle di Ticino, *p106*.
Parco Naturale dell'Adda Nord, *p104*.
Parco Naturale della Valle del Lambro, *p103*.
Parco Naturale Regionale di Montevecchia e della Valle del Curone, *p103*.
Parco Nazionale delle Incisioni Rupestri, *p272*.
Parco Nazionale dello Stelvio, *p268*.
Parco Nazionale della Val Grande, *p189*.
Parco Regionale Adamello, *p269*.
Parco Regionale delle Groane, *p107*.
Parco Regionale dell'Oglio, *p240*.
Parco Regionale delle Orobie Valtellinesi, *p263*.
Riserva Piramidi di Zone, *p220*.

Beyond Italy's financial and industrial powerhouse – Milan – lies a region of almost infinite variety. In the far north, the Alps and Alpine foothills (*see chapter* **The Mountains**) swarm (in an empty, wild kind of way) with summer hikers; ski resorts, while perhaps not as chic as those of the Veneto region next door, are well equipped and family-oriented, with slopes for all tastes and levels of expertise.

The southern reaches of the region, on the other hand, are bound by the Po, Italy's largest river, which meanders its stately way through interminable flatlands punctuated by rice paddies, stands of poplars and villages that for millennia have been home to the tillers of these fertile plains.

In between are towns large and small: their pretty centres palimpsests of moments of indigenous glory and foreign domination; their outskirts scarred by the trappings of the industries that have made this region one of Italy's most prosperous. There are wheat-growing regions and wine-growing regions (*see p231* **The wines of Franciacorta**, *and p258* **Milan's wine cellar**), natural parks (*see above* **Nature**), theme parks (Archeopark; *see p272*) and amusement parks (Gardaland; *see p208*). There are some of Italy's finest gardens here too (*see p183* **Gardens** *and* **Less-secret gardens**) and restaurants (*see p36* **Food heaven**).

And of course there are the lakes, Lombardy's most visited attraction. For ease of use, each of the major lakes – **Maggiore**, **Como** and **Garda** (plus **Orta**, which is in fact in the neighbouring Piedmont region but far too beautiful and easily reached to omit from this guide) – has been dealt with in separate chapters: itineraries begin at a southern point and continue in a clockwise direction around each lake's shores.

Each chapter in this section contains information on getting there – both by car and by public transport – from Milan, and on getting around the area covered. For information on getting around Lombardy in general, *see p279*.

Less-secret gardens

The majority of Italy's most beautiful gardens are still in private hands, and getting to see them has always depended very much on the availability of their aristocratic owners, or, worse still, on the whims of a caretaker, installed by the banks or insurance companies that have acquired many properties as investments.

But things are getting easier, thanks to an indefatigable Como-based Englishwoman, Judith Wade Bernardi, who in 1995 set up **Grandi Giardini Italiani**, a voluntary association that acts as a quality controller, a marketing company, a press office and a forum for exchanging ideas. Thanks to GGI, dozens of Italian garden owners now throw their gates open to the public, some every week or every month, some on annual open days; consult the organisation's website (*see below*) for openings.

Also intrumental in opening Italian stately homes and gardens is the **Fondo per l'Ambiente Italiano** (FAI), Italy's answer to Britain's National Trust, which administers – among many other places – the **Villa del Balbianello** (*see p202* **Como's gardens**) on Lake Como. Besides acquiring, restoring and opening properties to the public on a permanent basis, FAI also organises *Giornate FAI*, when long-locked homes, gardens, churches and many other hidden treasures are opened to the public over a weekend; consult FAI's website (Italian only; *see below*) for information.

Fondo per l'Ambiente Italiano

Viale Coni Zugna 5, South, Milan (02 467 6151/www.fondoambiente.it). Metro Sant'Agostino or Porta Genova/tram 20, 29. **Open** *9am-1pm, 2-8pm Mon-Fri.*
Though not an information office as such, FAI's headquarters in Milan will dispense printed information in English on the Fondo's properties and activities.

Grandi Giardini Italiani

Piazza Cavour 6, Cabiate (031 756 211/ fax 031 756 768/www.grandigiardini.it).

Gardens

Garden lovers are spoilt for choice in Lombardy, where the interplay of lakes and mountains creates microclimates galore. Note, however, that most gardens are open only for limited periods, when their blooms are at their best. *See also above* **Less-secret gardens** *and p202* **Como's gardens**.
Giardini Botanici Hruska (Gardone Riviera), *p212*.
Giardino Alpinia (Alpino), *p189*.
Palazzo Borromeo, Isola Bella (Stresa), *p189*.
Palazzo Borromeo, Isola Madre (Stresa), *p189*.
Palazzo Estense & Villa Mirabello (Varese), *p107*.

Parco Botanico di San Pancrazio (Brissago), *p192*.
Villa Arconati (Castellazzo di Bollate), *p107*.
Villa del Balbianello (Lenno), *p202*.
Villa Borromeo Visconti Litta (Lainate), *p107*.
Villa Carlotta (Tremezzo), *p202*.
Villa d'Este (Cernobbio), *p201*.
Villa Melzi (Bellagio), *p202*.
Villa Pallavicino (Stresa), *p190*.
Villa Passalacqua (Moltrasio), *p199*.
Villa Serbelloni (Bellagio), *p202*.
Villa Taranto (Pallanza), *p190*.
Il Vittoriale (Gardone Riviera), *p208*
The child of pleasure.

Lago d'Orta

Charming villages and quirky museums in a lakeside setting of bewitching loveliness.

Located west of Lago Maggiore in the Piedmont region, diminutive Lake Orta trumps its blowsier neighbour easily in beauty and atmosphere. Charming villages, quirky museums and bewitching panoramas dot its shores, which measure just 13 kilometres (eight miles) in length and three kilometres (two miles) across. You'll have to immerse yourself in the lake's beauty rather than its waters, however: the International Lake Environment Committee classifies the water quality as having 'serious' levels of toxic contamination and acidification.

Getting there

By car
Take the A4 towards Turin. Exit at Novara Ovest and take the SS229 towards Borgomanero, Omegna and Gravellona.

By train
Mainline service to Novara, then local service stopping at Orta/Miasino, Pettenasco and Omegna. Note: all stations except Omegna are located up steep hills above the towns, 15-20mins walk from the lake.

Getting around

By car
The two-lane road that circumnavigates the lake is 33km (21 miles) long, with only slight variations in altitude and a smooth surface. A car is more or less essential for visiting the towns above the lake shore.

By boat
Navigazione Lago d'Orta (0322 844 862) operates a boat service around the lake, stopping at Orta, Isola San Giulio, Pettenasco, Gozzano and elsewhere. (Daily Easter-mid Oct; Sat and Sun in Oct & Nov; Sun only in Jan). The best departure points are Pella, where there's ample parking and Omegna. A full day's ticket costs €6. No credit cards.

By bike
Lago d'Orta Autonoleggio (338 986 4839) rents mountain bikes with pick-up in Orta San Giulio: €4 per hour, €10 per half-day, €15 per day. No credit cards.

Orta San Giulio

The medieval lakeside town of **Orta San Giulio** has enough charm and quiet natural beauty to melt the heart of any city slicker. The main via Olina winds past cream-coloured houses to piazza Motta, where the frescoed 16th-century Palazzo della Comunità perches on elegant loggia-stilts. Cafés and shops line the square: at No.26, **Penelope** sells locally made hand-loomed kitchen linens colourfully printed using antique wooden stamps and natural dyes.

A labyrinth of narrow cobbled alleyways radiates from piazza Motta. Four hundred metres offshore, the Isola San Giulio (see p185) completes the fairytale panorama.

Perched above the town in the wooded **Sacro Monte** nature reserve are 20 small chapels (1591-1770) containing life-size and remarkably lifelike terracotta tableaux depicting scenes from the life of St Francis. A semi-strenuous but very pleasant pilgrims' path (30 minutes) departs from piazza Motta and leads up the steep street towards the 15th-century Chiesa dell'Assunta, from where signs point to Sacro Monte. Alternatively, you can drive to the top.

Loggia-stilts in **Orta San Giulio**.

Note that the town centre is closed to traffic and cars must be left in the pay parking lots at the edge of town.

Where to stay & eat

For a light snack and some local grape, **Osteria al Boeuc** (via Bersani 28, 0322 915 854, closed Mon & Tue from Oct-Feb, average €7) serves bruschetta, cheese and cold cut plates to accompany a vast selection of wines. Check your email and have a snack at the town's only internet café, **La Sibilla Cusiana** (via Giovanetti 27, 0322 905 117, www.orta.net/sibillacusiana, closed Mon-Wed and 2wks Dec-Jan, average €6.50). For an intimate dinner in a cosy setting, the **Taverna Antico Agnello** (via Olina 18, 0322 90 259, closed Tue and Dec-Jan, average €36) serves creative regional cuisine and seasonal specialities. The four-star **Hotel San Rocco** (via Gippini 11, 0322 911 977, www.hotelsanrocco.it, double room €165.26-€201.41) offers lakeside rooms and dining (average €40), as does the three-star **Leon d'Oro** (piazza Motta 43, 0322 911 991, www.orta.net/leondoro, closed Jan, double room 96), where tables are spread on an outdoor terrace (average €25). Alternatively, the **Contrada Dei Monti** (via Contrada dei Monti 10, 0322 905 114, www.orta.net/contradadeimonti, closed Jan, double room €77.47) has heaps of charm.

Tourist information

Distretto dei Laghi
Via Panoramica, Orta San Giulio (0322 905 614/fax 0322 905 800/www.orta.net). **Open** 9am-1pm, 2-6pm Mon-Fri.

Isola San Giulio

According to legend, St Julius (San Giulio) water-skied on his cloak to the island that now bears his name, then got down to banishing its thriving population of snakes and dragons. These days you can reach the enchanting island and its lovely seventh-century basilica by taxi boat (€2.50 round-trip). If you're feeling sporty, row yourself across (boat hire €7.50 per hour, contact Piero Urani, 333 605 0288, who's always to be found on the dock).

Inside the basilica, a dark green marble pulpit has rare Saxon-influenced carvings; frescos from many centuries battle for space around its party-coloured walls. From the Benedictine monastery, the via del Silenzio runs down to the island's villa-lined shores: along the way, signs offer thoughts such as 'In silence you hear and understand' to make your *passeggiata* truly contemplative.

St Julius water-skied to **Isola San Giulio**...

If you arrive on or around the saint's feast day (31 January), rap on the old seminary door to obtain a bag of *pane San Giulio* (dried fruit and nut bread) from the nuns for a small donation. (You can find this bakery treat in mainland bakeries throughout the year.) The island has one restaurant (**Ristorante San Giulio**, via Basilica 4, 0322 90 234, www.orta.net/sangiulio, closed Mon in Apr-Oct, Mon-Sat in Jan-Mar, all Nov-Dec, average €25), where atmosphere outstrips quality; there's no hotel.

Around the lake

Perched on the hill above Orta San Giulio, **Vacciago di Armeno** is home to the **Collezione Calderara di Arte Contemporanea**. Antonio Calderara (1903-78) transformed his late 17th-century home and studio into a museum; of the 327 paintings and sculptures, 56 are by Calderara himself and are by no means amateurish dabblings. The collection documents the international avant-garde from the 1950s and '60s, with an emphasis on geometric abstractionism, kinetic art, op art and visual poetry. Calderara selected contributing artists on the basis of friendship and common interests: given this fact, the collection is of a surprisingly impressive standard.

Pettenasco stands on the lake shore north of Orta San Giulio. Its Romanesque church tower started life attached to the church of Sant'Audenzio, who was a pal of San Giulio and Pettenasco's town prefect in the fourth century. The church was rebuilt in 1778 and dedicated to St Catherine. A postage stamp-sized public beach is accessible behind the Dolphin Bar, located on the north end of via Unità d'Italia.

Trips Out of Town

... but it's simpler by boat.

The intricate woodwork for which the town was once famous is commemorated at the **Museo dell'Arte della Tornitura del Legno**, where tools and machines collected from the town's old factory are on display.

Confronted by the pre-Roman defences of **Omegna**, at the northern tip of the lake, Julius Caesar exclaimed, 'Heu moenia!' (woe to you, oh walls!) – and eventually ploughed through them. Known as Voemoenia, then Eumoenia and finally Omegna, it was the site of tremendous battles from autumn 1943 to April 1944. Today the town – the biggest on the lake – specialises in manufacturing kitchenware products. In the **Forum Di Omegna** cultural centre a museum documents the area's industrial history. The Forum, with its park and bar/restaurant, is reachable on foot from the town centre. A gift shop sells kitchen items from local manufacturers Alessi, Bialetti, Calderoni, Lagostina and others.

Seven kilometres (4.5 miles) west and up from Omegna, **Quarna Sotto** offers stupendous views of Lake Orta from a height of 800 metres (2,667 feet), plus one of the area's wildest museums.

Three industrious local lads – two brothers by the name of Forni and a Signor Rampone – brought the craft of making wind instruments back to Quarna after an apprenticeship in Milan. By the second half of the 19th century, the town was famous around the world for its wood and metal wind instruments. The **Museo Etnografico** honours this tradition with graphic explanations of manufacturing methods. But that's not all: in this lovingly curated gem are displays on housing design, local costume, domestic arts, and regional natural history as well as a refurbished water mill.

From **Pella**, on the lake's western shore, a signposted road climbs precipitously uphill for ten kilometres (six miles) to the church of Madonna del Sasso. En route, the hamlet of **Artò** has antique wash houses, sundials and a 16th-century fresco adorning a local house, **Centonara** has an ancient millstone for

processing hemp, and **Boleto** is a picture with its cobbled lanes and church. At the top, the **Madonna del Sasso** church (0323 896 229; open irregular hours daily) was built between 1730 and 1748 and sits 638 metres (2,127 feet) above the lake on a granite outcrop. In thanks for some miracle, a successful local cobbler had an earlier chapel reconstructed in 1730-48, and arranged for the bones of San Donato to be transferred there from the San Callisto catacombs in Rome. The holy skeleton, resting oddly on its side, lies in a crystal coffin to the left of the altar. The frescos, plus a painting above the casket, are the work of local artist Lorenzo Peracino. The skill of this probably self-taught dabbler is highlighted by the *Pietà* (1547) framed in pink marble above the high altar: studying under Caravaggio did little to enhance the talents of its author, Fermo Stella.

Collezione Calderara di Arte Contemporanea

Via Bardelli 9, Vacciago di Armeno (0323 89 622/ 0322 998 192). **Open** *mid May-mid Oct* 10am-noon, 3-6pm Tues-Sun. *Mid Oct-mid May* by appointment. **Admission** free.

Forum di Omegna

Parco Rodari 1, Omegna (0323 866 141/guided tours 0323 883 120/www.forumomegna.org). **Open** 10am-12.30pm, 3-7pm Tue-Sat; 3-7pm Sun. **Admission** €2.50; €1.50 concessions. **Credit** AmEx, DC, MC, V.

Museo dell'Arte della Tornitura del Legno

Via Vittorio Veneto, Pettenasco (0323 89 622). **Open** *June-Sept* 10am-noon, 2-6pm Tue-Sun. **Admission** free.

Museo Etnografico e Dello Strumento Musicale a Fiato

Via Roma, Quarna Sotto (0323 826 001/0323 89 622). **Open** *July-Sept* 10am-noon, 3-7pm Tue-Sun. *Oct-June* by appointment. **Admission** €2.50; €1.50 concessions. **No credit cards**.

Where to eat & stay

The **Hotel Restaurant Panoramico** in Boleto (via Frua 31, 0322 981 312, www.hotelpanoramico.it, closed Nov and mid Jan-Mar, double room €61.97-€77.46) has plain but comfortable rooms and a restaurant (average €25) with an outdoor terrace and wonderful lake views.

Tourist information

Pro Loco di Omegna

Piazza XXIV Aprile 17, Omegna (tel/fax 0323 61 930/www.proloco.omegna.vb.it). **Open** *Apr-Sept* 9am-noon, 3-6pm Mon-Sat.

Lago Maggiore

Gentrified lakefront hotels hide humble fishing villages.

Straddling Lombardy, Piedmont and the Swiss Ticino canton, Maggiore is Italy's second-largest lake. It could as easily have been called 'Lake Eden' or 'Lake Charm', or any of the superlatives gushed by John Ruskin, Stendhal, Gustave Flaubert or the many other artists and writers who found inspiration here.

Sparsely settled since prehistoric times, fought over by the Romans, then a fief of Milan's ruling families, the lake was on the Grand Tour map by the end of the 18th century. From the 19th century, its mild climate and enchanting position, with the Alps as a backdrop, attracted Italian nobility, wealthy foreigners and the budding industrial bourgeoisie, who built spacious, sometimes quirky, villas with sumptuous gardens. This still continues: Aldo Rossi's villa in Suna for the Alessi family is an example.

Originally fishing villages, the lake's towns were gentrified when elite tourism took them by storm. Lakefront hotels and landscaped promenades were conceived to protect the delicate sensibilities of the upper class visitors. Behind the fashionable façades, the jumble of small houses and winding streets attest to humbler beginnings.

Getting there

By car
The A8 merges with the A26 Genova–Gravellona Toce to the Piedmont shore. For Luino, take the A8, to Varese and local roads for the remaining 25km (15 miles) to Luino. For Locarno, exit the A9 at Bellinzona.

By train
Trains run regularly from Milan's Centrale and Garibaldi stations for the Piedmont shore and Locarno; services for Luino depart from Stazione Garibaldi; services for Laveno leave from Cadorna.

By bus
Autoservizi Nerini (0323 552 172) provides a twice daily bus service for the Piedmont shore (8.30am and 5.50pm); Baldioli (0332 530 271) also runs services (5.30pm Mon-Fri, 2.30pm Sat, 9.15am & 8.30pm Sun) to the Lombard shore. All leave from piazza Castello.

The Piedmont shore

Lake Maggiore's western shore is in the Piedmont region, but has strong historical and cultural ties with Lombardy. From Arona to Cannobio, small towns alternate with majestic

Fishy business on the **Isola dei Pescatori**. *See p188.*

villas (around 350), nestled in vibrant gardens with dozens – in some cases thousands – of varieties of plants, colourful microcosms in the study of biodiversity. Most of the villas are still in private hands and best visible from the boats (see p191) that regularly criss-cross the lake.

At the southern tip of Lago Maggiore where the Ticino river winds from the lake is **Arona**, a lively commercial town where San Carlo Borromeo (see p16) was born. The climb to the 17th-century, 35-metre (117-foot) copper statue of the saintly local hero high on a rock above the town – built using the same technique later used for the Statue of Liberty – is rewarding. The **Statua San Carlo** is next to the ruins of a 13th-century Visconti fortress.

A few kilometres north, the smaller town of **Meina** has some of the lake's prettiest private residences: Villa Faraggiana (1855) and the 17th-century Villa Eden (both closed to the public). But a dark chapter of Italian history mars the town's apparent serenity. In September 1943, 16 Jewish guests at a local hotel were taken by Nazi troops and shot in Italy's first pogrom. The hotel was abandoned 20 years ago and now stands in ruins.

Belgirate has a collection of mementos of author Alessandro Manzoni's (see p65) stay here in its **Museo Manzoniano**. Above Belgirate's tiny historic centre – a network of narrow lanes, porticos and variegated façades – is the so-called **Chiesa Vecchia** (Santa Maria del Suffragio, open Sat & Sun), with frescos by the school of Bernardino Luini, the local 16th-century artist (see p190). In Massino Visconti, four kilometres (two and a half miles) uphill from Belgirate, is the 13th-century **Castello Visconti di San Vito** (visible from outside).

Stresa stands on the Golfo Borromeo, which, with its islands, is the heart of the lake. The town became famous after receiving rave reviews from Dickens and Byron; Hemingway set chapters of *A Farewell to Arms* here. During the belle époque, Stresa's grandiose hotels, refined attractions and casino rivalled those of Montecarlo and Venice's Lido.

The **Villa Pallavicino** has an English garden where kids can enjoy close encounters with llamas, kangaroos and zebras. Along the road climbing to the top of the Montagna Mottarone is the **Giardino Alpinia**, with 700 species of plants. The hike from Stresa takes about five hours, but the lazy can opt for a cable car to the 1,491-metre (4,970-foot) summit, where the world's first international giant slalom was held in 1935. On a clear day, you can see seven lakes.

Facing Stresa are the **Isole Borromee**. The Borromeo family took possession of the islands in the 16th century. **Isola Inferiore**, or **Isola**

Bella, was named in honour of Isabella d'Adda, whose husband, Carlo Borromeo III, began transforming the island in 1632. *Bello* indeed is the island's grandiose baroque **Palazzo Borromeo** (where there's a bed slept in by Napoleon and Josephine after the former had conquered northern Italy) and its stately Italian-style garden occupied by albino peacocks.

The **Isola Superiore** – more often called **Isola dei Pescatori** – is one long strip of narrow lanes and whitewashed houses, ending in a tongue-shaped park with benches and shady trees. There are several restaurants, and a little grocery store that makes sandwiches.

The 16th-century **Palazzo Borromeo** on **Isola Madre** has an 18th-century puppet theatre and is surrounded by an English-style garden where roaming peacocks hold court.

Beyond Stresa, **Baveno** is home to the tenth-century church of **Santi Gervasio e Protasio** (open daily, hours vary). A charming dock café juts out over the water.

Feriolo, three kilometres (two miles) further on, maintains the quaint characteristics of a fishing village. For fans of contemporary architecture, the industrial area designed by Aldo Rossi (1931-97) in the hinterland between Feriolo and **Fondotoce** is a must-see. The reed thickets in Fondotoce's **Riserva Naturale** (information 0322 240 239, office open 9am-noon, 2-5pm Mon-Fri, 9am-noon Sat), at the mouth of the Toce river, are a nesting ground for many birds. Several hiking and bike trails are marked, some leading to the smaller **Lago Mergozzo**.

Verbania, the provincial capital, is made up of several towns unified in 1939. **Suna** has an unusually high concentration of good eateries as well as the little lakefront church of **Santi Fabiano e Sebastiano** (closed), with a Romanesque apse and belltower. A Roman settlement, **Pallanza** is renowned for its gardens, though unfortunate landscaping has ruined its original lakeside promenade. The **Museo del Paesaggio** houses a rich collection of Piedmontese and Lombard art. One branch of the museum has paintings, sculptures and archaeological finds; the other, devoted to popular piety, gives a unique perspective of centuries of homegrown religious art with its collection of 5,000 votive offerings. A winding lane leads to the poorly signposted Romanesque church of **San Remigio** (closed to the public except with tours of the **Villa San Remigio**, next door). The villa, now government offices, boasts a beautiful park, fruit of the romantic fancies of love-struck cousins who met as children, fell in love as teenagers and married. They spent 50 years landscaping a monument to their love for each other. For guided visits, contact the Verbania tourist office (see p191).

Lakes & Cities

More spectacular is the **Villa Taranto** between Pallanza and Intra, laid out by retired Scottish captain Neil McEarcharn and famous for its garden with over 20,000 species of plants. **Intra**, which has seen the proliferation of charming boutiques and speciality stores in recent years, fills up on Saturdays when a large market draws shoppers eager to find a bargain.

One of Europe's largest wilderness areas, the **Parco Nazionale della Val Grande** (information 0323 557 960, www.parks.it/parco.nazionale.valgrande, office open 8.30am-1pm, 2.30-6pm Mon-Fri) stretches behind Verbania and is reached from the town of **Cicogna** in the hills above. Dozens of hiking and bike trails lead to meadows, gorges, and peaks where chamois far outnumber hikers.

Heading towards Switzerland, **Ghiffa** was once famous for its felt hats (there's even a museum, the **Museo dell'Arte del Cappello**). It's now better known for two nearby sights, the church of **Santa Maria Assunta** at **Susello** (open 6pm Sun), a 12th-century church with 15th- and 16th-century frescos, and the **Riserva Naturale Sacro Monte della Santa Trinità** (information 0323 59 870, office open 8.30am-1pm, 1.30-6pm Mon, Wed, 8.30am-1pm Tue, Thur, Fri), a 200-hectare (494-acre) protected area. Hiking trails are well marked and lead past three 17th-century chapels to a rebuilt sanctuary.

The belltower in **San Pietro in Gonte** is the highest on the lake (42 metres/140 feet). Further north, **Cannero Riviera** is so-called because its climate and vegetation – lemons and olive trees – are distinctly Mediterranean. On three small islands here are the ruins of the Malapaga castles originally inhabited by the Mazzarditi family, local pirates who terrorised locals for some three centuries until Filippo Maria Visconti (see p14) laid siege in 1414.

Cannobio is the last town before the Swiss border, and was once an important centre of transit and commerce, as its large medieval **Palazzo della Ragione** suggests. The palace is closed to the public though exhibitions are sometimes held under its portico. Nearby, the **Orrido di Sant'Anna** is a dramatic gorge plunging into dark depths and crossed by stone bridges. The 17th-century church of **Sant'Anna** (open in summer only, hours vary) totters over one edge.

Giardino Alpina

Montagna Mottarone, Località Alpino (0323 20 163). **Open** *Apr-mid Oct* 9am-6pm Tue-Sun. **Admission** free.

Museo Manzoniano

Villa Stampa, via la Fontana, Lesa (0322 76 421). **Open** *July, Aug* Sat, Sun, hours vary. **Admission** €2. **No credit cards**.

Bernardino Luini

Though his expressive, luminous works are a common feature in many of the churches of Lombardy, Bernardino Luini's origins remain obscure.

He was born sometime around 1480. In his *Lives of the Artists* (1550), Giorgio Vasari apparently ignored Bernardino's lake connection, referring to him as 'del Lupino' and again as 'di Lupino'. Though the citizens of Luino (*see p193*) happily claim him as a native son, recent scholarship suggests that the painter's name might actually have been Bernardino Scapi and that his family hailed from the small inland town of Dumenza, some seven kilometres (4.5 miles) from Luino. Bernardino gave little away himself, signing his works with the Latin *Lovinus*.

Museo dell'Arte del Cappello

Corso Belvedere 279, Ghiffa (0323 59 174).
Open *Apr-Oct* 3.30-5.30pm Sat, Sun; groups at other times by appointment. **Admission** free.

Museo del Paesaggio

Palazzo Viani Duniani, via Ruga 44, Pallanza (0323 556 621). **Open** *Apr-Oct* 10am-noon, 3.30-6.30pm Tue-Sun. **Admission** €2. **No credit cards.**

Museo del Paesaggio

Palazzo Biumi Innocenti, Salita Biumi 6, Pallanza (0323 556 621). **Open** *Apr-Oct* 10am-noon, 3.30-6.30pm Tue-Sun. **Admission** €2. **No credit cards.**

Palazzo Borromeo

Isola Bella (0323 30 556). **Open** *Apr-Oct* 9am-noon, 1.30-5.30pm daily. **Admission** €8.50. **No credit cards.**

Palazzo Borromeo

Isola Madre (0323 31 261). **Open** *Mar-Oct* 9am-noon, 1.30-5.30pm daily. **Admission** €8. **No credit cards.**

Statua San Carlo

Piazzale San Carlo, Arona (no phone). **Open** *Apr-Oct* 9am-12.30pm, 2.30-6pm daily. *Nov-Mar* 9am-12.30pm, 2.30-5pm Sat, Sun. **Admission** €2.50. **No credit cards.**

Villa Pallavicino

Strada Statale 33, Località Stresa (0323 31 533/ www.parcozoopallavicino.it). **Open** *Mar-Oct* 9am-6pm daily. **Admission** €6.40. **No credit cards.**

Villa Taranto

Via V Veneto 111, Pallanza (0323 556 667/ www.villataranto.it). **Open** *Apr-Oct* 8.30am-6.30pm daily. **Admission** €7. **No credit cards.**

Where to eat

A short detour east of the southern tip of the lake leads to Soriso, where the three-Michelin-starred **Al Sorriso** (via Roma 18-20, 0322 983 228, closed Mon, lunch Tue, average €125) has food critics choking on superlatives.

More affordable and immersed in the countryside four kilometres (2.5 miles) from Arona, **Campagna** (via Vergante 12, San Carlo, frazione Campagna, 0322 57 294, closed Mon dinner & Tue, 2wks Jan, 2wks June and 2wks Nov, average €38) serves *pasta e fagioli* (bean soup) and fresh home-made pasta with herbs.

In a villa just outside Lesa, the elegant **Antico Maniero** (via alla Campagna 1, Lesa, 0322 7411, closed Mon and Nov, average €65) serves both lake and sea fish. **Al Camino** (via per Comnago 30, 0322 7471, closed Wed and 4wks Dec-Jan, open weekends only in Jan, average €35) serves local cuisine on a pretty terrace. In Stresa, the **Triangolo** (via Roma 61, 0323 32 736, closed Tue in Oct-May, average €35) has no view but the fish ravioli is superb.

There are two restaurants of note in Verbania-Suna. The lively **Osteria Boccon Di Vino**, (via Troubetzkoy 86, 0323 504 039, closed Sun, dinner Mon and Nov-Mar, average €28) serves local fare and fine wine, while the cuisine at elegant **Monastero** (via Castelfidardo 5-7, 0323 502 544, closed Mon and 2wks Aug, average €46) draws diners from miles around.

In Pallanza, **Milano** (corso Zanitello 2, 0323 556 816, closed dinner Mon, all Tue and 6wks Jan-Feb, average €60) serves classic dishes and excellent lake fish, on its terrace overlooking the lake. In Intra, the **Osteria del Castello**, (piazza Castello 9, 0323 516 579, closed Sun, 1wk Oct & 1wk Feb, average €25) has homier fare: cold cuts and local cheeses and wines.

In the village of Bee in the hills behind Verbania, the **Piazzetta** (via Maggiore 20, 0323 56 430, closed Wed, 2wks Nov, 3wks Jan & Tue in Sept-June, average €30) has a terrace where local delicacies such as crayfish are served.

In Cannobio, **Lo Scalo** (piazza Vittorio Emanuele II 32, 0323 71 480, closed Mon, Tue lunch and 5wks Jan-Feb, average €45) serves fresh market produce and home-baked bread.

Where to stay

At the pleasant **Hotel Giardino** (corso della Repubblica 1, Arona, 0322 45 994, www.giardinoarona.com, double room €56.81-€82.63) half of the rooms have lake views.

In Lesa, the **Villa Lidia** (via Giuseppe Ferrari 7/9, 0322 7095, 02 5810 3076, patrizia.lanfranconi@consultami.com, double room €70) is a charming three-room B&B.

Lakes & Cities

Statua San Carlo above Arona. *See p188.*

Staying at the five-star belle époque hotels in Stresa or Baveno may involve a second mortgage, but does give a sense of what brought the *beau monde* to the lake. Among the most sumptuous are the **Grand Hotel des Iles Borromées** (corso Umberto I 67, 0323 938 938, www.stresa.net/hotel/borromees, double room €269.50-€352) and the **Hotel Regina Palace** (corso Umberto I 33, 0323 936 936, closed 2wks Dec-Jan, double room €250-€330).

The **Lido Palace Hotel Baveno** at SS Sempione 30, 0323 924 444, www.lidopalace.com, closed Nov-Feb, double room €155) has an enviable view over the Borromeo islands. The **Hotel Verbano** on the Isola dei Pescatori (via U Ara 2, 0323 30 408, www.verbaniahotel.it, closed Jan-Feb, double room €135) has 12 charming rooms and a restaurant.

In Pallanza, the **Hotel Villa Azalea** (salita San Remigio 4, 0323 556 692, double room €64.50-€67) is small and high in the hills. On the waterfront, the **Hotel Pace** (via Cietti 1, 0323 557 207, double room €83) has ten comfortable rooms. In Intra, the **Hotel Ancora** (corso Mameli 65, 0323 53 951, double room €135) and the **Hotel Intra** (corso Mameli 133, 0323 581 393, www.verbaniahotel.it, double room €80-€130) are both delightful.

In Cannobio, the **Hotel Pironi** (via Marconi 35, 0323 70 624, closed mid Nov-mid Mar, www.pironihotel.it, double room €98-€126) is a 16th-century house with frescoed ceilings. Two kilometres south, the **Hotel Del Lago** (via Nazionale 2, Carmine, 0323 70 595, www.enoteca lago.com, closed Nov-Mar, double room €93-€109) has ten rooms, a private beach and a restaurant serving classic cuisine (average €62). In Cannero Riviera, **La Rondinella** (via Sacchetti 50, 0323 788 098, www.hotel-la-rondinella.it, double room €73-€86) is in an art deco villa with antiques.

Getting there & around

By car
The SS33 winds along the Piedmont shore from to Fondotoce where it becomes the SS34 to Cannobio.

By train
Most trains from Milan for Domodossola, Paris or Geneva stop in Arona, Stresa and Verbania. Local services stop at all towns in between.

By bus
Trasporti Nerini (0323 552 172/www.saf2000.com) runs buses between Arona and Verbania. VCO Trasporti (0323 518 711) takes over from Verbania to Brissago in Switzerland.

By boat
Navigazione Lago Maggiore (0322 46 651/www.navigazionelaghi.it/www.navlaghi.it) operates boats, from paddlewheels to hydrofoils, to most of the towns around the lake. Schedules are seasonal.

Tourist information

For full, regularly updated information on lake sights and events, see www.lagomaggiore.it.

APT
Piazza Duca d'Aosta, Arona (tel/fax 0322 243 601). **Open** *Apr-Sept* 9am-12.30pm, 3-6pm Mon-Sat. *Oct-Mar* 9am-noon, 3-6pm Mon-Fri.

IAT
Piazza Marconi 16, Stresa (0323 30 150/fax 0323 32 561). **Open** *Nov-Feb* 10am-12.30pm, 3-6.30pm Mon-Sat. *Mar-Oct* 10am-12.30pm, 3-6.30pm daily.

IAT
Corso Zanitello 6-8, Verbania (0323 503 249/fax 0323 507 722). **Open** *Apr-Sept* 9am-12.30pm, 3-6pm Mon-Sat. *Oct-Mar* 9am-12.30pm, 3-6pm Mon-Fri.

Pro Loco IAT
Viale Vittorio Veneto 4, Cannobio (tel/fax 0323 71 212). **Open** *Apr-Sept* 9am-noon, 4-7pm Mon-Sat; 9am-noon Sun. *Oct-Mar* 9am-noon, 4.30-7pm Mon-Wed, Fri, Sat; 9am-noon Sun.

The Swiss shore

Crossing from Italy into Switzerland has a certain *Alice Through the Looking Glass* feel to it, like crossing over into a parallel universe where everything looks the same but is undeniably sprucer and more organised.

Brissago's reputation rests on its production of fine cigars. The 16th-century **Madonna del Ponte** church (open daily in summer, hours vary), just south of the town on the lake, has a fresco of the Assumption. During the summer, small boats (operated by Navigazione Lago Maggiore, *see p191*) leave Porto Ronco for the **Brissago islands**. One – the **Isola di San**

Pancrazio – has a **Parco Botanico**, created in 1885. The other island, with the remains of a 12th-century church, is not accessible.

An ancient fishing village, **Ascona** is now a fashionable resort with chi-chi boutiques and art galleries. For years, the town's hills have come alive with the sound of music, as Ascona plays host to an important European jazz festival (end June-early July, information www. jazzascona.ch) and, from August to October, more highbrow classical tunes (information www.settimane-musicali.ch). Behind the lakefront's hotels and cafés, the 16th-century church of **Santi Pietro e Paolo** (open 9am-noon, 4-6.30pm daily) has 17th- and 18th-century frescos. On **Monte Verità**, a hike from the centre, is a little museum documenting a Utopian vegetarian community dating from the end of the 19th century.

Cosmopolitan **Locarno**, at Maggiore's northern tip, hosts a prestigious film festival (information www.pardo.ch) each August. The piazza Grande, a porticoed square lined with cafés and boutiques, is transformed into an open-air cinema for first-rate first-run films. The remains of a 14th-century tower recalls Visconti rule until the 15th century; in the jumble of streets of the old centre churches and noble *palazzi* alternate with more plebian dwellings. The city **Pinacoteca** (art gallery) in the 17th-century Casa Rusca owns an original collection donated by Hans and Margherita Arp. There's a **Museo Archeologico** and a collection of costumes and porcelain inside what remains of the (much-rebuilt) 14th-century **Castello Visconti**. The art-filled **Madonna del Sasso** church (open 7am-6pm daily), founded in 1480 but rebuilt in the 17th century, can be reached by funicular or by walking up a steep hill flanked by the Stations of the Cross.

Note: to dial a Swiss number from outside the country, prefix it with international code 00 41.

Monte Verità
Strada della Collina 76, Ascona (91 791 0181/ www.csf-mv.ethz.ch). **Open** *end Mar-Oct* 2-6pm Tue-Sun. *July, Aug* 3-7pm Tue-Sun. **Admission** SF6. **No credit cards**.

Museo Archeologico
Castello Visconteo, piazza Castello 2, Locarno (91 756 3180). **Open** *Apr-Oct* 10am-6pm Tue-Sun. **Admission** SF7. **No credit cards**.

Parco Botanico del Canton Ticino
Isola di San Pancrazio (91 791 4361). **Open** *Apr-Oct* 9am-5.30pm daily. **Admission** SF7. **No credit cards**.

Pinacoteca
Casa Rusca, piazza Sant'Antonio/via Collegiata 1, Locarno (91 756 3185). **Open** *Apr-mid Dec* 10am-5pm Tue-Sun. **Admission** SF7. **No credit cards**.

Where to eat, drink & stay

In Brissago, there's a pleasant feel to the family-run **Hotel Eden** (via Vamara 26, 91 793 1255, www.hotel-eden-brissago.ch, closed Nov-mid Mar, double room SF156-SF204).

In Ascona, the **Romantik Castello-Seeschloss** (piazza Motta, 91 791 0161, www. castello-seeschloss.ch, double room SF248-SF548) is in a 13th-century castle. Charming **Albergo Al Porto** (lungolago G Motta, 91 785 8585, www.alporto-hotel.ch, double room SF187-SF285) has 36 rooms; though larger, **Hotel Tamaro** (piazza Motta 35, 91 791 0282, www.hotel-tamaro.ch, closed Nov-Mar, double room SF190-SF290) has a homey feel.

In Locarno, the lakefront **Treff Hotel Beau Rivage** (viale Verbano 31, 91 743 1355, www.treff-hotels-ticino.com, closed Nov-Feb, double room SF200-SF260) is modern and attractive. For a more historic stay, the **Schlosshotel** (via Rusca 9, 91 751 2361, www.ticino.com/schlosshotel, closed Dec-mid Mar, double room SF154-SF208) occupies part of the Visconti castle (*see above*). **Centenario** (lungolago Motta 17, 91 743 8222, closed Sun, Mon, 3wks Jan and 3wks July, average SF80) is an elegant eaterie in Locarno.

In the Valle Maggia, 11 kilometres (seven miles) north of Locarno, **Uno Più** (Gordevio, 91 753 1012, closed Dec-Mar, average SF30) serves local seasonal delicacies; it rents out six rooms too (double room SF110-SF168).

Getting there & around

By car
The road that meanders along the lake starts as the via Cantonale 13, becoming 22 on the eastern side.

By train
Trains run from Locarno (towards Domodossola) along the northern shore, and all along the eastern shore (from Domodossola).

By bus
FART Viaggi (91 751 8731/viaggi@centovalli.ch) runs a regular service between Brissago and Locarno.

By boat
Navigazione Lago Maggiore (*see p191*; 91 751 6140/ www.navigazionelaghi.it) also operates services on the Swiss side of the lake.

Tourist information

Ente Turistico Lago Maggiore
Via B Luini 3, Locarno (91 751 0333/www.maggiore. ch). **Open** *Apr-Oct* 9am-5.30pm Mon-Fri; 10am-5pm Sat; 10am-noon, 1-3pm Sun. *Nov-Mar* 9.30am-12.30pm, 2-5.30pm Mon-Fri; 9.30am-12.30pm Sat.

The Lombardy shore

After bustling Locarno, Maggiore's more sparsely inhabited eastern (Lombard) shore is decidedly low key. Of Roman origin, **Luino** has been a tourist haven since the 1880s when it became a stop on the Milan–Lugano railway. Every Wednesday since 1541 a market has taken over the streets of the centre. The church of **San Pietro** (open daily, hours vary) has frescos attributed to local artist Bernardino Luini (*see p190*) and a Romanesque belltower.

Laveno is a busy port, with ferries to Intra. In 1856 the Richard Ginori ceramics company was founded here; the 16th-century Palazzo Perabo houses the **Museo di Design Ceramico-Civica Raccolta di Terraglia**.

A 20-minute walk from the lake road near Leggiuno leads to the 12th-century sanctuary of **Santa Caterina del Sasso Ballaro**, perched on a rock 18 metres (60 feet) above the lake. Most of the sanctuary can be visited; the cells on the second floor of the monastery are occupied by Dominican monks.

Angera is best known for its **Rocca**, a towered and crenellated fortress built in the 11th century and expanded and fortified until the 17th. In Visconti family hands from the 13th century, it was added to the Borromeo family's estates in 1449. One wing has a rare cycle of 14th-century frescos by local Lombard artists; another houses a collection of dolls and children's toys dating from the 17th century. The Borromeo wing has frescos removed from the family's Milanese palazzo, including rare works attributed to Giovanni Zenone.

Despite its good **Museo Archeologico**, **Sesto Calende**, at the lake's southern tip, is usually bypassed for the nearby ninth- to 12th-century abbey of **San Donato** (0331 924 692, open 8am-noon, 5-6.30pm daily), or the Iron Age tombs at **Golasecca** dating from between the ninth and fifth century BC. These large rocks are scattered through a field and are freely accessible from the road between Sesto and Golasecca.

The wetland area, **Parco dei Lagoni di Mercurago** (information 0322 240 239, office open 9am-noon, 2-5pm Mon-Fri) has interesting marsh and acquatic vegetation.

Museo di Design Ceramico-Civica Raccolta di Terraglia
Frazione Cerro, Laveno (0332 666 530). **Open** 2.30-5.30pm Tue-Thur; 10am-noon, 2.30-5.30pm Fri-Sun. **Admission** €2.70. **No credit cards**.

Rocca di Angera
Via alla Rocca 10, Angera (0331 931 300). **Open** *Apr-Oct* 9.30am-6pm daily. *Oct-Nov* 9.30am-5pm daily. **Admission** €6. **No credit cards**.

Santa Caterina del Sasso Ballaro
Via Santa Caterina 5, Leggiuno (0332 647 172). **Open** *Nov-Feb* 9am-noon, 2-5pm Sat, Sun. *Mar* 9am-noon, 2-5pm daily. *Apr-Oct* 8.30am-noon, 4.30-6pm daily. **Admission** free.

Where to eat & stay

Don't miss the fish at **Il Sole di Ranco** (*see p36* **Food heaven**).

In Luino, the **Camin Hotel Luino** (viale Dante 35, 0332 530 118, www.caminhotelluino. com, closed 5wks Dec-Jan, double room €115-€150) is a 19th-century villa with a garden, decorated with art deco furniture. **Giardinetto** restaurant (via Rossini 6, 0332 537 882, average €25) serves simple, traditional fare.

South of Laveno in Mombello, the **Hotel Porticciolo** (via Fortino 40, 0332 667 257, www.ilporticciolo.com, closed 1wk Nov and 2wks Jan-Feb, double room €92-€144) is a charming hotel and good restaurant (average €45, closed Tue) serving lake fish and snail salad. A less expensive option is the lakefront **Hotel Moderno** (via Garibaldi 15, Laveno, 0332 668 373, meublemoderno@libero.it, closed Jan & Feb, double room €63-€73), which has simple, clean rooms.

In Angera, the pleasant **Hotel Dei Tigli** (via Paletta 20, 0331 930 836, www.hotel deitigli.com, closed 4wks Dec-Jan, double room €100) has period furniture.

In Sesto Calende, the seven-room **Locanda Sole** (via Ruga del Porto Vecchio 1, 0331 914 273, double room €87.47) is in a very central 18th-century house, and has a restaurant.

Getting there & around

By car
The SS629 hugs the lake's shores.

By train
Local trains stop at most towns on the eastern shore.

By bus
Autolinee Nicora e Baratelli (0332 668 056/www.sila.it) operates regular services between Luino and Laveno.

By boat
See p191.

Tourist information

IAT
Via Piero Chiara 1, Luino (0332 530 019/www. luino-online.it). **Open** 9am-noon, 3-6.45pm Mon-Sat.

IAT
Via de Angeli 18, Laveno-Mombello (0332 666 666/www.laveno-online.it). **Open** *Apr-Sept* 9am-noon Mon-Sat. *May-Aug* 9am-noon, 3-6pm Mon-Sat.

Lakes & Cities

Lago di Como

Be inspired by enchanting lakeside scenery and luscious villa gardens.

'It surpasses in beauty everything I have ever seen hitherto,' gasped the poet Percy Bysshe Shelley when he first laid eyes on Lake Como. For centuries before – and ever since – this sparkling sapphire body of water has bewitched writers and composers, artists and lovers… and the package tourists who crowd its picture-postcard shores from early spring to late autumn.

Of glacial origin (but warm enough today), the lake stands at an altitude of 198 metres (660 feet), and stretches for 46 kilometres (29 miles) in an inverted Y shape from rocky Alpine peaks in the north to the foggy, soggy plain around Milan in the south. At 410 metres (1,367 feet), it is Europe's deepest lake. The largest of the 37 rivers that flow into Como is the Adda, which splashes down from the Valtellina (*see p263*) in the north and exits southward at Lecco (*see p204*).

Etruscans, Celts and even a few wandering Greeks put in time around the shores of Lario, as the lake is also known. But it was the Romans who colonised it systematically. Pliny the Younger (*see p196*) wrote ecstatically of

the 'several villas' that he possessed on the lake, singling out two (which he called Comedy and Tragedy) as his special favourites. One was on the hill, the other by the shore. From the latter, 'you can quite simply cast your line out of the window without getting out of bed'.

Even Ostrogoth and Lombard kings built houses in Bellagio, their rough Barbarian edges smoothed away by all this beauty. Later, crowned heads, Napoleonic henchmen and wealthy bankers joined the fray, building sumptuous villas such as the **Villa d'Este** in Cernobbio (now a hotel, *see p201*) or the **Villa del Balbianello** (*see p202* **Como's gardens**) near Lenno. The central section of the lake, based around the triangle of Bellagio, Menaggio and Varenna, is where the scenery is at its most spectacular. The town of Como itself (*see p197*), to the south, is busy, industrialised and built-up: its proud civic buildings and commercial nous make it seem a mini-Milan. The northern lake – known as the Alto Lario – is quieter, and the sharp edges of the central section dissolve in places into reed beds; but there are rewards here too for the discerning traveller.

Lakes & Cities

Lake Como is of glacial origin but warm enough today.

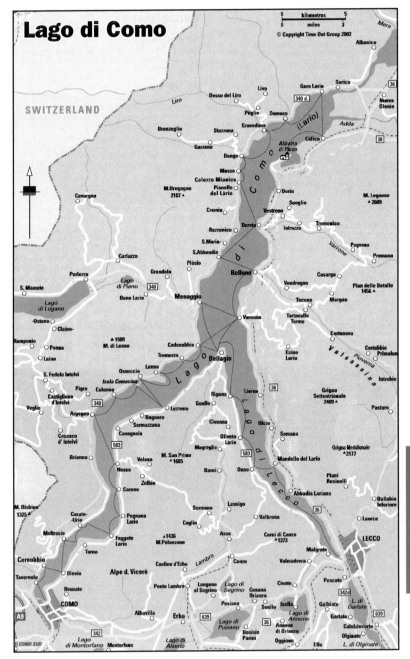

Lago di Como

0 kilometres 5
0 miles 3
© Copyright Time Out Group 2002

SWITZERLAND

Lakes & Cities

HISTORY

Como's strategic position at the crossroads between central Europe and the Mediterranean made it a highly sought-after possession. It came under Roman control in 89 BC, after which the lake's two most famous ancients – historian and scientist Pliny the Elder (AD 23-79), and man of letters and jurist Pliny the Younger (AD 64-114) – spread its fame. Huns and Goths overran the area as Rome tottered; they in turn were defeated by the Lombards whose redoubtable Queen Theodolinda (*see p8* **Theodolinda**) had the **via Regina** (Queen's Road) built linking the town of Como to Colico at the northern end of the lake. Through the Middle Ages Como battled with arch-rival Milan, signing a peace treaty in 1186 and bowing to inevitable Milanese rule. Milanese territory, however, bowed to *comasco* style: throughout medieval Lombardy, northern Italy and far beyond, Como's itinerant stonemasons – *maestri comacini* – embellished their characteristic brick- and stone-faced walls and façades with their exquisite carvings.

The lake area was impoverished by crippling taxes when the Spanish took over in 1535. But by that time Como's reputation as a centre for woodworking and textiles (especially dyeing and silk) was already firmly established; periods of hardship alternated with rapid recoveries due to this fundamentally healthy manufacturing sector. The same industries are still the mainstay of Como's economy.

Getting there

By car
Take the A8 motorway west out of Milan and fork on to the A9 after Lainate. The SS35 and SS36 head north from Milan to Como and Lecco respectively.

By train
Services for Como depart about every 30mins from Milan's Stazione Centrale and Cadorna. Services for Lecco depart about once an hour from Stazione Centrale. Either trip takes 40mins.

By bus
Autostradale (information 02 801 161/www. autostradale.it) runs infrequent services from Milan to lakeside towns.

Getting around

By car
The SS340 and SS583 around the lake's shores are very scenic but very heavily trafficked, especially in summer and at weekends. On the western and southern shores there is no alternative to these roads; on the eastern shore, your progress will be quicker, if less picturesque, on the SS36. Minor roads up into the surrounding hill villages can be challenging, to say the least.

By bus
Società Pubblici Trasporti (031 247 247/ www.sptcomo.it) runs services from piazza Matteotti in Como to towns around the lake and throughout the region.

The 13th-century **Broletto**. *See p197.*

Lakes & Cities

By boat

Navigazione Lago di Como (via per Cernobbio 18, Como, 031 579 211, www.navigazionelaghi.it, office open 8am-noon, 1-5pm daily) operates ferry and hydrofoil services year-round. Timetables change frequently. Services link Como (Dock 1) with: Tavernola, Cernobbio, Moltrasio, Torno, Urio and Pognana Lario at the southern end of the lake; Colico at the lake's northern tip; and with intermediate towns such as Bellagio, Varenna, Cadenabbia and Menaggio. Longer routes are also covered by car ferry.

Como

On the lakeside by the busy ferry jetty, piazza Cavour is a bustling meeting point for the *comaschi*. The pompous neo-classical **Mausoleo Voltiano** (aka Tempio Voltiano, open Apr-Oct 10am-noon, 3-6pm Tue-Sun, Nov-Mar 10am-noon, 2-4pm Tue-Sun) in the **Giardini Pubblici** west of the square was erected in 1927 to mark the centenary of the death of physicist Alessandro Volta, the man who invented the battery and gave us the volt. Still further west in via Sinigaglia, the **Novocomum** apartment block (1927-9), designed by Giuseppe Terragni, is a prime example of rationalist architecture.

Arcaded via Plinio leads south from piazza Cavour to piazza del Duomo, home to the **Duomo** – a late Gothic wonder with equally spectacular Renaissance additions – and the **Broletto**, the 13th-century town hall, which over the ages has done service as a theatre and a record office. It's now used for exhibitions.

At the apse end of the Duomo in piazza Verdi stands the 19th-century **Teatro Sociale**, its neo-classical façade adorned with six mighty Corinthian pillars. The theatre had its moment of glory at the end of World War II when its opera season outshone Milan's, if only because La Scala (*see p63*) had been badly bombed. Further east in piazza del Popolo is another of Giuseppe Terragni's visionary creations, the ex-Casa del Fascio, now known as **Palazzo Terragni** (1932-6).

Via Vittorio Emanuele leads southwards out of piazza del Duomo. At the far end is the church of **San Fedele** in the piazza of the same name. It was once Como's cathedral. Further on, in piazza Medaglie d'Oro Comasche, are the **Museo Storico** and the **Museo Archeologico**.

From here viale Battisti leads south-west along one of the few remaining stretches of Como's 12th-century walls to the imposing **Porta Torre** gate (1192). A few blocks north of here is the **Pinacoteca Civica** (via Diaz 84, closed for restoration until 2003), with a collection of 18th- and 19th-century works

The **Duomo**, a late-Gothic wonder.

by lake artists that will be of interest only to very dedicated seekers of local colour. Continue south-west into the areas of town that sprang up around the old walls in the Middle Ages to reach the breathtaking Romanesque church of **Sant'Abbondio**.

Head east on viale Battisti, which becomes via Grossi, to find the steep path leading up to **Brunate** (about an hour and a half), a Como suburb with a superb view, perched on a hill 720 metres (2,400 feet) above the city centre. (Alternatively, return to piazza de Gaspari on the eastern side of the lakefront and take the funicular.) On the road up to Brunate, with its luscious art nouveau villas, the **Sagrario degli Sports Nautici** (031 305 958, open 2.30-6pm Sun) is a parish priest's slightly dotty tribute to the lake's strapping young water-sportsmen, in a dinghy-shaped chapel.

It's no easy task locating the **Museo Didattico della Seta** (silk museum) in Como's southern suburbs, but the effort is well worth it.

Duomo

Piazza del Duomo (031 265 244). **Open** 8am-noon, 3-7pm daily.

A meld of Romanesque, Gothic, Renaissance and baroque, Como's cathedral is not only unique but spectacularly beautiful. It was begun in 1396 on the

Sant'Abbondio: Romanesque jewel.

site of the Romanesque basilica of Santa Maria Maggiore, growing in fits and starts and eating into the Broletto, which sacrificed a wing to the nave. The late-Gothic façade (1455-86) is striking enough, with its host of sculptures, many of them by the local Rodari family of stonemasons; the fact that sculptural pride of place is given to two renowned pagans – the Plinies, Older and Younger – makes it even more so. Note also Tommaso Rodari's intricate Frog Door leading into the left side of the nave.

In the Latin-cross interior, the three-aisled nave is Gothic, the transept Renaissance, while the great octagonal dome was designed by Filippo Juvarra in 1744. The lions holding up holy water bowls by the main portal came from the original basilica; the tapestries lining the central nave date from the 16th century. More sculptural extravaganzas from local masters including the Rodaris mingle with mostly Renaissance paintings of varying quality by lake artists, plus a lovely *Holy Family* by Bernardino Luini (*see p190* **Bernardino Luini**) over the fourth altar on the right and several other works by the same artist elsewhere. By the second altar on the right is the sarcophagus of Bishop Bonifacio of Modena (1347), another relic from the old church. Also from Santa Maria Maggiore is the relief of *Mary Enthroned* (1317) on the pulpit in the apse.

Funicolare Como-Brunate
Piazza de Gaspari 4, (no phone/www.geocities.com/funicolarecomobrunate). **Open** 6am-10.30pm daily. **Ticket** €2.12. **No credit cards**.
Built in 1894, the funicular takes six and a half minutes to cover 1,084m at gradients of up to 55%.

Museo Archeologico & Museo Storico
Piazza Medaglie d'Oro Comasche (031 271 343). **Open** 9.30am-12.30pm, 2-5pm Tue-Sat; 10am-1pm Sun. **Admission** €2.50. **No credit cards**.
The city's archaeological and historical museums occupy *palazzi* Giovio and Olginati respectively. The former, with a collection begun in the late 19th century, contains artefacts – kitchenware, crockery and accessories – left behind by the lake shore's earliest prehistoric inhabitants, as well as some Egyptian, Roman and later pieces.

The history museum, on the other hand, focuses to a large extent on unification hero Giuseppe Garibaldi (*see p18*) who spent some time in Como, and on the struggle against the Austrians. There's some World War II memorabilia too.

Museo Didattico della Seta
Via Valleggio 3 (031 303 180/museoseta@libero.it). **Open** 9am-noon, 3-6pm Tue-Fri. By appointment Sat. **Admission** €7. **No credit cards**.
This lovingly curated museum inside Como's silk-making school brings the city's main industry – silk – to life. Displays range from the life cycle of the silkworm (which is no longer raised on the lake; raw thread is imported from the Far East) to the earliest and more modern silk looms, printing equipment, dyeing processes and numerous examples of the luxurious endproduct.

San Fedele
Piazza San Fedele (no phone). **Open** 8am-noon, 3-7pm daily.
This basilica – built some time between the tenth and 12th centuries – is named after the saint who brought Christianity to Como in the fourth century, and was Como's cathedral until the Duomo (*see p197*) was built. It was constructed over the sixth-century church of Sant'Eufemia; an eighth-century lion from the portal of that earlier church holds up the holy water stoop in the left-hand bulge of the oddly shaped transept. Also odd are the almost unique five-sided apse and the 13th-century rear door, with its presiding monsters. The rose window over the reconstructed main entrance is from the 16th century; the majority of the decorations inside are uninspiring baroque.

Sant'Abbondio
Via Sant'Abbondio (no phone). **Open** 8am-6pm daily.
It may have been visiting monks from northern Europe who were responsible for the innovative design of this Benedictine abbey church – including the twin belltowers, a Norman touch – built to replace

an earlier structure in the 11th century. Wherever the inspiration came from, this remains one of the greatest jewels of the Lombard Romanesque, its five aisles separated by slim columns of granite, and its starkly simple walls broken by bands of intricate carving around the windows of the apse, which also contains 13th-century frescos.

Where to eat & drink

Run by the same family for three generations, **Sant'Anna 1907** (via Turati 3, 031 505 266, closed Sat lunch, Sun and 4wks Aug, average €40) serves a delicious fish risotto. **Breeze Inn Ristorante** (via Natta 29, 031 242 320, closed all Sun & Mon lunch, Aug & 1wk Dec, average €30) serves local specialities in a pleasant setting. Good pizza makes up for lack of atmosphere at **Le Colonne Ristorante Pizzeria** (piazza Mazzini 12, 031 266 166, closed Tue, average €25). **Visini** (via Ballerini Francesco 9, www.visini.it, closed Sun, average €40) is a wine bar and restaurant with an excellent choice of local delicacies. Housed in a converted barn, **Il Solito Posto** (via Lambertenghi 9, 031 271 352, www.bsur.it/solitoposto, closed Mon, average €40) does creative things with local stalwarts.

Shopping & services

Marco Polo is said to have introduced silkworms to Como after his jaunt to China. There are no silkworms here now – raw thread is imported from the Far East – but silk textile manufacturing and printing remains one of the city's key industries, much favoured by fashion designers from Italy and further afield. Factories with retail outlets include **Binda** (viale Geno 6, 031 303 440, www.gbinda.it, open 8.30am-noon, 2-6.30pm Mon-Sat) and **Martinetti** (via Torriani 41, 031 269 053, open 2.30-6pm Mon, 8.30am-noon, 2.30-6pm Tue-Fri, 8am-noon Sat).

Where to stay

The **Barquetta Excelsior** (piazza Cavour 1, 031 3221, www.hotelbarquetta.com, double room €180-t223) is located right on the lakefront with rooms that make up for in facilities what they lack in charm. In the same lakeside square, the characterful **Metropole & Suisse** (piazza Cavour 19, 031 269 444, www.hotelmetropolesuisse.com, closed 3wks Dec-Jan, double room €116-€155) has been going strong since 1892; its restaurant, **L'Imbarcadero** (average €50) is highly regarded. **Le Due Corti** (piazza Vittoria 12/13, 031 328 111, hotelduecorti@virgilio.it, double room

€130-€181) is a romantic spot with beauty treatments available; **Posta** (via Garibaldi 2, 031 266 012, www.hotelposta.net, double room €67.14-€82.63) is comfortable and central; the rooms at **Tre Re** (piazza Boldoni 20, 031 265 374, www.hoteltrere.com, double room €96-€112) have been renovated recently but retain their olde worlde atmosphere.

Tourist information

APT
Piazza Cavour 16 (031 269 712/fax 031 240 111/ www.lakecomo.com/www.lakecomo.org). **Open** 9am-1pm, 2.30-6pm Mon-Sat.

The western shore

The via Regina, the road commissioned by Lombard Queen Theodolinda (*see p8* **Theodolinda**), heads along the western shore out of Como town, the suburbs of which merge into **Cernobbio**. This town of magnificent villas and private boat jetties is dominated by the **Villa d'Este**, built in 1565-70, possibly to a design by Pellegrino Tibaldi. In 1814, the villa became the lush and riotous home of Princess Caroline, estranged wife of Britain's Prince Regent; it is now a luxurious hotel (*see p201*). The 16th-century Italian garden (not open to the public) has fountains, grottos, stretches of 'wilderness' and some imposing statues. **Villa Bernasconi** (via Regina 7, open for exhibitions only) is a stunning example of Liberty (art nouveau) style, complete with colourful ceramics and beautiful wrought iron.

The via Regina continues to **Moltrasio**, where a type of grey stone popular with sculptors and church builders is quarried. The 18th-century **Villa Passalacqua** (closed indefinitely for restoration) has another stunning Italian garden.

From the little resort of **Argegno**, a **cable car** (031 821 344, operates Apr-June 8am-noon, 2-6pm daily, July & Aug 8am-noon, 2-7pm daily, return ticket €2.90) runs up to **Pigra** (literally 'lazy'), a lofty hamlet with superb views across the lake to Isola Comacina and the Bellagio promontory.

Boats depart from **Sala Comacina** (338 459 9492, www.boatservices.it, operates Mar-Oct 9am-midnight daily) for **Isola Comacina**, the lake's only island. Its air of utter peace is deceptive: the island was fought over from Roman times; in 1169 the *comaschi* razed it, forcing the inhabitants – who had unwisely allied themselves with Milan – to flee to Varenna (*see p203*) on the eastern shore. Bought in 1918 by the king of Belgium, who later

Lakes & Cities

Severe, stunning **Santa Maria del Tiglio**.

donated it to Milan's fine arts academy, the island is now home to a bizarre restaurant (*see p201*), a handful of ancient ruined churches and the baroque oratory of San Giovanni.

LA TREMEZZINA

The stretch of shore from Lenno to Menaggio – known as *La Tremezzina* – is lakeland *per eccellenza*, awash with the camelias and azaleas for which Como, with its balmy micro-climate, is famed, and home to any number of extravagant holiday villas. It also has a few faded reminders of an age when British dowagers came to winter (and summer) here: an Anglican church (in Cadenabbia), a Victorian tearoom, even a crazy golf course.

Lenno may have been the site of Commedia, one of Pliny the Younger's (*see p196*) villas; the baths of a sumptuous Roman villa were unearthed in the crypt beneath Lenno's 11th-century parish church of **Santo Stefano** (open 8am-noon, 3-6pm daily).

A turn-off to the left just south of Santo Stefano leads to the 12th-century abbey of **Acquafredda** (0344 55 208, open 9am-4.30pm daily), built by Cistercian monks but now home to some Capuchins. The remains of an earlier pre-Romanesque chapel are still visible below the campanile.

Another road left out of Lenno leads up to **Giulino Mezzegra**, where a plaque on the gate of via XXIV Maggio 14 recalls that this was the spot where Partisans executed Mussolini and his mistress Clara Petacci on 28 April 1945.

Lenno's jetty is the departure point for boats to the picture-postcard **Villa del Balbianello** (*see p202* **Como's gardens**).

In **Tremezzo**, the neo-classical **Villa Carlotta** (*see p202*) boasts swathes of statues by Antonio Canova and, more impressively, 5.5 hectares of spectacular garden.

Cadenabbia stands where the lake forks; ferry services (*see p197*) ply between here and Bellagio across the water. Konrad Adenauer, the first chancellor of post-war Germany, took his R&R here in the **Villa Margherita Ricordi** (not open to the public), where, years before, Verdi had composed much of *La Traviata*.

Long a bustling commercial town and now an equally bustling resort, pretty pink- and ochre-tinted **Menaggio** has a ruined castle and lovely views across to Bellagio and the eastern shore.

THE NORTHERN REACHES

Continuing north towards the towering heights of the Valchiavenna (*see p261*), the road passes through tunnels and past campsites to the *Tre Pievi* (three parishes) – Dongo, Gravedona and Sòrico – which formed an independent community in the Middle Ages.

For Italians, the former steel-manufacturing town of **Dongo** is inevitably associated with Mussolini, who was captured here with Clara Petacci as they tried to escape to Switzerland, before being shot near Lenno (*see above*). A much earlier killing took place in the town in 1252, when St Peter Martyr (*see also p91*) was finished off with a hatchet through the head by Cathar heretics; the subject is a favourite one in the devotional iconography of his order, the Dominicans.

A manufacturing town and popular water sports centre, **Gravedona** was the most important of the *Tre Pievi* and a key ally of medieval Milan – hence it was razed by Como in the 12th century. Romanesque **Santa Maria del Tiglio** (via Roma, open 3-5pm Mon-Fri, 10am-6pm Sat, Sun) is simple, severe and stunning. Though it is unlikely that it was built for Queen Theodolinda, as local lore would have it, the church – in grey and white stone with a distinctive campanile – is certainly ancient, with traces of fifth-century mosaic paving.

The fishing village of **Domaso** still produces a white wine mentioned by Pliny the Elder. In fortified **Sòrico**, tolls were extracted from travellers arriving on the lake's shores from the Valchiavenna (*see p261*) and Valtellina (*see p263*).

Where to eat

In Moltrasio, the **Crotto Valdurino** (via Besana 37, 031 290 101, closed Tue, average €20) and the **Imperialino** (via Antica Regina 26, 031 346 600, closed Mon, Oct-Mar & 5wks Jan-Feb, average €55) are both reliable.

On the island, the **Locanda dell'Isola Comacina** (0344 55 083/0344 56 755, closed Nov-Mar, Tue in Apr, May & Oct, set meal €45) offers a truly bizarre dining experience. Host Benvenuto entertains guests with his very own 'fire ceremony' designed to exorcise a curse supposedly put on the island in the 12th century – a useful distraction from the mundanity of the set menu, which revolves around lake trout and non-lake chicken, and from the relatively steep final bill.

In Sala Comacina, the **Alessio** (via Statale 14, 0344 55 035, closed Mon and Nov, average €25) offers filling, hearty pasta dishes, while **La Tirlindana** (0344 056 637, piazza Matteotti 5, closed Mon in Mar-Oct, Mon-Fri in Nov-Feb, average €45) is renowned for its delicious home-made ravioli stuffed with lemon-flavoured cheese.

In Lenno, the family-run **Santo Stefano** (piazza XI Febbraio 3, 0344 55 434, closed Mon, Nov & Jan, average €25) serves the hard-to-find local delicacy *missoltini* (dried twaite shad) and other lake fish.

Tremezzo has various restaurants linked to the **Grand Hotel** (*see below*), but for a change of pace (and price), try the **Trattoria del Rana** (via Monte Grappa 27, 0344 40 602, closed Tue and 3wks Oct, average €20), a laid-back trattoria serving good lake standards.

Where to stay

For unbeatably elegant luxury – at bank-loan prices – the **Grand Hotel Villa d'Este** (via Regina 40, Cernobbio, 031 3481, www.villadeste.it, closed mid Nov-Feb, double room €560-€645) is the place. In Tremezzo, the splendid art nouveau **Grand Hotel Tremezzo Palace** (via Regina 8, 0344 42 491, www.grandhoteltremezzo.com, closed mid Nov-Feb, double room €200-€280) is another luxury option, with spectacular lake views.

In Moltrasio, **Albergo Posta** (piazza San Rocco 5, 031 290 444, closed Jan & Feb, double room €85-€125) is a reliable bet, while Lenno's **San Giorgio** (via Regina 81, 0344 40 415, closed Oct-Mar, double room €100-€115) is modest but pleasant, in a modern building with a garden.

Menaggio's **Grand Hotel Victoria** (via Lungolago Castelli 9, 0344 32 003, www.palacehotel.it, double room €155-€187) was

Hiking

The mountains that encircle Lake Como are a hiker's paradise: spectacular, well watered, served by a network of footpaths, and provided with a number of mountain refuges, some open year-round.

Opportunities for shorter hikes are legion; the following long-distance trails allow for some more demanding excursions. Both are at their best in late spring and early autumn, away from the heat of summer and the rigours of winter.

Dorsale del Triangolo Lariano

Bellagio is the luxurious tip of the rocky Triangolo Lariano, which rises to 1,685 metres (5,617 feet) at the peak of Monte San Primo. Those tired of the pool at the Grand Hotel Villa Serbelloni (*see p205*) might want to head out of town on this 30-kilometre (20-mile) trail to Como, best split into two equal stages with an overnight stay at Pian del Tivano (five apartments are available year-round at the **Azienda Agricola Valsecchi**, 031 677 019, rates €62-€52 per person). Walkers heading in the other direction can pick up the signposted trail at Brunate, a funicular ride up from Como (*see p197*). Maps and details of the trail can be had at the main Como tourist office.

Information APT in Como (*see p199*) or Comunità Montana Triangolo Lariano (031 672 000).

Via dei Monti Lariani

The spirit of the Como region is as much in mountains and chestnut groves as in lemons and windsurfing. And one of the best ways to get in touch with the secret, highland soul of the area is to take this well-marked long-disance footpath that leads from Cernobbio to Sòrico at the northern end of the lake. Running for 130 kilometres (81 miles) at an average height of 1,000 metres (3,500 feet), the trail uses the network of old mule tracks that criss-cross the mountains on the west side of the lake. There is enough walking here for a whole week – broken up into six easy stages, with overnight stays in mountain refuges. The Como tourist office and the local section of CAI can provide a map, details of refuges and other information.

Information APT Como (*see p199*) or Club Alpino Italiano (via Volta 56, Como, 031 264 177, open 5.30-7.30pm Tue, Thur).

Lakes & Cities

Como's gardens

See also p183 **Gardens** *and* **Less-secret gardens**.

Cradled among protective mountains, exposed to the soft-but-warm rays of the pre-Alpine sun, the shores of Lake Como constitute a balmy, heady micro-climate in which flora flourishes. These special conditions have been exploited by generations of garden-loving patrons who have made the lakeside a series of little Edens.

The gardens of the **Villa del Balbianello** tumble down a headland protruding into Lake Como just south of Lenno. The house itself – two square-set blocks, one above the other, with a stately loggia on higher ground still – occupies the very tip of the promontory. Built in the 16th century, extended in the 18th, the house itself is visitable by appointment only. The library and map-room in the loggia – packed with the travel-oriented collections of the villa's last private owner, polar explorer and scaler of Everest Count Guido Monzino – are open. It is the gardens, however, that are the real reason for coming here. Amid centuries-old holm oaks and plane trees, perfectly groomed lawns edged with perfectly clipped box hedges surround bursts of vibrant azaleas and rhododendrons through the spring and early summer.

Rhododendrons are very much in evidence, too, among the 500-plus species present in the eight hectares of garden at **Villa Carlotta** (*pictured*) in Tremezzo. Built in resoundingly neo-classical style in the early 18th century for the Marquis Giorgio Clerici, the villa passed to the Sommariva family, who laid out

Italian gardens in the 18th century, and then in the 1850s to Princess Carlotta of the Netherlands, who had yet more of the extensive grounds planted in the English style. The gracious, terraced result is a riot of colour through the flowering season. Inside the house, there's little colourful about the collection of sculptures by Antonio Canova, including his well-known *Cupid* and *Psyche*.

Superlatively pretty Bellagio is beautified still further by the *ville* Melzi and Serbelloni. The former is a neo-classical pile that has hosted Metternich, Stendhal, Francis I of Austria and Franz Liszt among many others. The latter dates from the 17th century and is now owned by the Rockefeller foundation.

The gardens of the **Villa Melzi** slope gently up the hill from the lakeside, dotted with exotic trees. There's a pretty Japanese garden, some splendid water lilies and a lapis lazuli-blue Moorish-looking coffee house. The house itself is not open to the public.

Villa Serbelloni, high on the point above Bellagio's town centre, may be on the site of one of Pliny the Younger's villas (*see p196*). Its gardens, the biggest on the lake, are a verdant mass of trees – magnolias, oleanders, palms and cedars – which now seem to blend effortlessly into the landscape; in fact, they were among the first examples of these 'exotic' species ever planted in Italy, in the 19th century. Close to the house (which is closed to the public), close-clipped hedges of box and yew alternate with glorious expanses of roses.

---

built in 1806 and retains much of its old world charm; what's more, its private beach is great for windsurfing.

Tourist information

APT
Via Regina 33B, Cernobbio (tel/fax 031 510 198). **Open** *Feb-Dec* 9.30am-12.30pm, 2.30-5.30pm Mon-Sat.

Pro Loco
Via Regina 3, Tremezzo (0344 40 493). **Open** *May-Sept* 9am-noon, 3.30-6.30pm Mon-Wed, Fri, Sat.

IAT
Piazza Garibaldi 3, Menaggio (tel/fax 0344 32 924). **Open** *mid June-Sept* 9am-noon, 3-6.30pm Mon-Sat. *Oct-mid June* 9am-noon, 3-6pm Mon-Sat.

The eastern shore

Mountains plunge precipitously into the lake waters along much of Como's eastern shore, making for considerably lower-density tourist development than across the water.

At the far north-eastern end of the lake, **Colico** is an unprepossessing port town built rather too close to unhealthy swamps. From here the dual-carriageway SS36 plunges through tunnels on its swift way south towards Lecco (*see p204*) and Milan. Opt for the slower lakeside road if you want to see the sights.

On a small promontory separating Lake Como proper from the oddly green Laghetto di Piona is the dramatic **Abbazia di Piona** (open 8.30am-12.30pm, 1.30-7pm daily), consecrated

Villa del Balbianello
Via Commedia 8 (0344 56 110/
02 469 3693/www.fondoambiente.it).
Open *Apr-Oct* 10am-12.30pm, 3.30-6.30pm
Tue, Thur-Sun. Closed Nov-Mar. **Admission**
€5. **No credit cards**.
Boats depart every half hour from the jetty
at Lenno (*see p200*) between 9.45am and
3.45pm on open days. In March you can
approach from the land side at weekends.

Villa Carlotta
Via Regina 2 (0344 40 405/www.
villacarlotta.it). **Open** *Mar, Oct* 9-11.30am,
2-4.30pm daily. *Apr-Sept* 9am-6pm daily.

Closed Nov-Feb. **Admission** €6.50.
No credit cards.

Villa Melzi
Lungolario Marconi (031 950 318).
Open *Mar-Oct* 9am-6pm daily. Closed
Nov-Feb. **Admission** €5.16. **No credit cards**.

Villa Serbelloni
Piazza della Chiesa (031 950 204).
Open (guided tours of garden only) *Apr-Oct*
11am & 4pm Tue-Sun. Closed Nov-Mar.
Admission €5.50. **No credit cards**.
Tours should be booked at the Pro Loco
in Bellagio (*see p204*).

as a Cluniac house in 1138 and now home to
Cistercians. The complex has a 13th-century
cloister with Romanesque and Gothic columns
and fragments of earlier frescos lining its walls,
and the abbey-church of San Nicolao, with 13th-
century frescos and a couple of marble lions
that used to hold up the raised pulpit. Groups
seeking to meditate in peace can rent rooms in
the monastery (information 0341 940 331).

The Pioverna river thunders down the
Orrido (gorge) **di Bellano** at the town of
Bellano, providing the driving force for the
hydroelectricity that has long powered the
area's textile industry.You can feel the force
for yourself by braving the **bridge** (0341 821
124, open Oct-May 10am-1pm, 3-6pm Mon-Sat,
10am-6pm Sun, June-Sept 10am-10.30pm daily,
admission €2.60) suspended above the torrent.

There's something magical about **Varenna**,
the most sedately elegant of the lake's resorts,
with its little rock-hewn footpath skirting the
steep lake shores to join the scattered parts of
the town. The **Villa Monastero** (gardens open
Apr-Oct 9am-7pm daily) began life as a 13th-
century convent, whose rather too worldly nuns
were evicted in the 16th century. The ruined
Castello di Vezio on the road out of Varenna
towards Esino Lario (open weekends Feb,
Mar, Oct, daily Apr-Sept, Sun in Nov, Dec) may
have been built for Queen Theodolinda (*see p8*
Theodolinda). A path leads from Varenna,
past the village cemetery, to the **Fiumelatte**
(River of Milk), Italy's shortest (250 metres/833
feet), most mysterious and most predictable
river. From the end of March to the end of
October each year, frothy water tumbles into

Lakes & Cities

the lake. Leonardo da Vinci clambered down its chasm in an attempt to find out what happened to it the rest of the year, but neither he nor anyone else has ever discovered the secret.

Bikers may want to stop off in **Mandello del Lario**, a sprawling town that cowers beneath the wild and woody Grigna mountain range. Once a silk centre, the town began producing MotoGuzzi motorbikes in 1921, as lovingly documented in its **Museo del Motociclo**.

Museo del Motociclo

Via Parodi 57 (0341 709 111/www.motoguzzi.it). **Open** 3-4pm Mon-Fri. **Admission** free.

Where to eat & stay

In Varenna, romantic **Vecchia Varenna** (contrada Scoscesa 10, 0341 83 0793, closed Mon and Jan, average €40) serves excellent fish fresh from the lake on a lovely terrace in summer or in its cosy interior in the cooler months. Equally romantic, the **Hotel Du Lac** (via del Pristino 4, 0341 830 238, www. albergodulac.com, double room €140-€207) has 19 pretty rooms in a 19th-century palazzo. The **Royal Victoria** (piazza San Giorgio 5, 0341 815 111, double room €150-€181) has period furniture in its public rooms; its restaurant, the **Victoria Grill** (closed Mon, average €25), is known for its good-value delicate cuisine.

In Mandello, delicious food is served in an intimate atmosphere at **Il Ricciolo** (via Statale 165, 0341 732 546, closed dinner Sun, all Mon, 3wks Sept & 2wks Dec-Jan, average €35).

Tourist information

The APT in Lecco is a good source of information (*see p205*).

Lecco, Bellagio & the southern shore

Stunningly located but grimly overshadowed by its iron and steel industry, the city of **Lecco** signifies just one thing to the vast majority of Italians: *I promessi sposi* (*The Betrothed, see p64* **Alessandro Manzoni**). For this was the birthplace of Alessandro Manzoni (1785-1873), author of that seminal novel, and this was the background against which he set the adventures of Renzo and Lucia.

Settled from prehistoric times, Lecco and its tribes were brought to order by the Romans in 195 BC. The town stood on key trading routes, and was an important link in the defences of Milan's Visconti family (*see chapter* **History**). Azzone Visconti had an eight-arch bridge (three more arches were added later) built

over the River Adda in 1336; it still bears his name. And central piazza Manzoni boasts an impressive statue of the town's most famous son. That's about it for Lecco's attractions, with the exception of the basilica of **San Niccolò**, the city's cathedral in piazza Cermenati. Local lore attributes the original church to the Lombards in the seventh century. The current building owes more to 19th-century make-overs, though there are remnants of a 12th-century church in the Cappella del Battistero.

To find out more about the author Italian schoolchildren love to hate, visit Alessandro's birthplace, the **Villa Manzoni** (via Don Guanella 1, 0341 481 247, open 9.30am-5pm Tue-Sun, admission €4.13), which houses a collection of memorabilia and manuscripts, as well as a small collection of works by local artists.

Just south-west of Lecco on the SS36, **Civate** is home to the charmingly simple 11th-century church of **San Pietro al Monte** (0341 551 576, open 9am-3pm Sun), with striking 11th- and 12th-century frescos inside.

The SS583 hugs the shore of the lake's V-shaped central promontory. High above (reachable via Bellagio) is the little **Madonna di Ghisallo** sanctuary (always open), a temple to the heroic days of cycling adorned with the jerseys and bicycles of Italian champions, from Coppi to Moser.

Perched at the tip of the southern promontory, **Bellagio** is simply glorious, with its peach and yellow houses tumbling down to the sapphire water. Narrow streets zigzag up the hill from a port lined with the impressive reminders of a more elegant age of tourism. Two villas (*see p202* **Gardens**) provide the icing on the cake: the **Villa Serbelloni** – crowning the hill where one of Pliny the Younger's villas stood – and the **Villa Melzi**, a Napoleonic pile surrounded by lush gardens where azaleas and rhododendrons run riot.

Swinging back towards Como town, the 16th-century **Villa Pliniana** (not open to the public) in **Torno** is a gloomy pile, reportedly haunted by the ghost of Count Giovanni Anguissola from Piacenza. This aristocrat took refuge in the building after having taken part in a conspiracy that led to the murder of powerful Count Pier Luigi Farnese. Perhaps it was this that attracted Byron, Stendhal, Liszt and many others to the place; Rossini composed his opera *Tancredi* here.

Where to eat

For first-rate fish (at top prices) in Lecco, head for **Al Porticciolo** (via Valsecchi, 5, 0341 498 103, closed Mon, Tue, lunch Wed-Sat, 2wks Jan & all Aug, average €45). Nicolin (via Ponchielli

54, 0341 422 122, closed Tue and Aug,
average €45) is a lively father-and-son
operation offering meaty Lombard specialities
if the appeal of lake fish has worn thin.

In Bellagio's outskirts, heading towards
Como, the family-run **Silvio** (via Carcano 12,
031 950 322, closed mid Nov-mid Feb, average
€25) offers lake fish and beautiful views; it
also has good-value rooms available (double
room €70-€80).

In Bellagio itself, **Barchetta** (salita Mella 13,
031 951 389, closed Dec-Feb, average €35) is a
romantic location for an intimate dinner under
a pergola; the desserts are out of this world.

The best of Torno's restaurants is the
Belvedere (piazza Casartelli 3, 031 419 100,
closed Tue and Jan-mid Mar, average €30),
which serves typical lake dishes including a
delicious fish risotto.

Where to stay

Silvio, just outside Bellagio is also a good
bet (*see above*). In Bellagio itself, the lakefront
La Pergola (piazza del Porto 4, 031 950 263,
closed Nov-Mar, double room €125-€180) is
decorated in old-fashioned rustic style and has
a restaurant (closed Tue, average €30) serving
lake fish; both rooms and cuisine are somewhat
lacklustre, however. In an 18th-century palazzo,
the **Florence** (piazza Mazzini 46, 031 950 342,
www.bellagio.co.nz, closed Nov-Easter, double
room €125-€175) has charming rooms, and jazz
in its cocktail bar each Sunday; book well in
advance. The well-appointed **Hotel du Lac**
(piazza Mazzini 32, 031 950 320, www.
bellagiohoteldulac.com, closed Nov-Easter,
double room €93-€206) has been welcoming
travellers for 150 years. For real luxury, follow
in the footsteps of Winston Churchill and John
F Kennedy and make for the **Grand Hotel
Villa Serbelloni** (via Roma 1, 031 950 216,
www.villaserbelloni.it, closed Nov-Mar, double
room €296-€738).

For something less expensive, try Torno's
Villa Flora (via Torazza 10, 031 419 222,
closed Nov-Feb, double room €80), which
has rooms with period furniture.

Tourist information

APT

*Via Nazario Sauro 6, Lecco (0341 362 360/fax 0341
286 231/287 402/www.aptlecco.com).* **Open** 9am-
12.30pm, 2.30-6pm daily.

IAT

*Piazza Mazzini/Pontile Imbarcadera, Bellagio
(031 950 204/fax 031 950 204/prombell@tin.it).*
Open *April-Oct* 9am-noon, 3-6pm daily. *Nov-Mar*
9am-noon, 3-6pm Mon, Wed-Sat.

Bellagio is simply glorious.

Lakes & Cities

Lago di Garda

Miniature castles meet amusement parks on the shores of Italy's largest lake.

Map p207.
Stretching between Verona and Brescia
(*see p225*), Lago di Garda is Italy's largest lake:
53 kilometres (33 miles) long, and from three
to 18 kilometres (two to 11 miles) wide. Its
broad southern basin is flanked by gentle hills
that rise into steep mountains further north.

Tourism is the lake's main source of income.
The south is an unbroken string of campsites,
hotels, discos and amusement parks. The
geography of the northern shores – mountains
rising sheer from the water – has saved them
from this fate. Whichever end you choose, you'll
find few villages without a picturesque
medieval *centro*, often guarded by miniature
castles. Many of the villages also boast fine
Romanesque churches. There are significant
Roman remains at **Desenzano** and **Sirmione**.

During the summer months, Garda can feel
like a little bit of Germany south of the Alps.
But despite the northern invasion, the lake
remains a favourite weekend haven for the
inhabitants of nearby Verona and Brescia.
Landlocked as they are, Garda is their
alternative to the sea; and with the possible
exception of golden sand and crashing breakers
(these latter rare, anyway, in the languid
Adriatic), Garda has as much to offer in the
way of watersports as any sea beach. With
sharp breezes blowing off the mountains, the
northern lake is particularly good for windsurfing. Anyone wanting to commune with

nature, however, would do well to come in
winter, when services are scant but the shores
full of the charm of emptiness.

Getting there

By car
The Milan–Venice A4 motorway has exits at
Desenzano, Sirmione and Peschiera .

By bus
SAIA (030 738 022/www.infopoint.it) operates hourly
Brescia–Verona services, calling at Desenzano,
Sirmione and Peschiera.

By train
Many trains on the Milan–Venice line from Stazione
Centrale stop at Desenzano and Peschiera. Journey
time around 1hr 30mins.

Getting around

By car
The lake itself is encircled by the Gardesana road,
an incredible – if not entirely admirable – feat of
engineering completed in 1931; on the north-western
shore the road bores its way through many miles
of solid mountain, with nearly 80 tunnels, connecting
a number of villages which were previously only
accessible by boat. Their economies and gene
pools have undoubtedly benefited; their charm
and tranquillity less so. In summer expect heavy
traffic, particularly around the Gardaland
amusement park (*see p208*).

In winter, **Lake Garda**'s shores are charmingly empty.

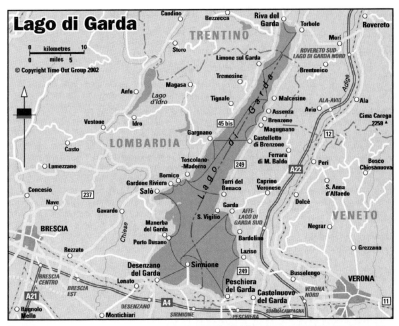

By bus

The southern shore (Desenzano–Sirmione–Peschiera) is served by buses from both Brescia and Verona (see *p206* **Getting there**). SAIA (030 738 022/www. infopoint.it) runs buses from Desenzano to Riva along the western shore; APT of Verona (045 805 7911/www.apt.vr.it) operates services from Peschiera to Riva along the eastern shore.

By boat

Hydrofoil and steamer services are frequent in the summer, connecting most important points on the lake. Throughout the year there is a regular car ferry service (roughly every 40mins) between Maderno and Torri del Benaco. All boat services are operated by Navigazione sul Lago di Garda (030 914 9511/fax 030 914 9520/www.navigazionelaghi.it) .

The southern shore

Nestling in Garda's south-western corner, **Desenzano** is the largest of the lakeside towns, with a thriving tourist industry. Behind the quaint old port is the arcaded piazza Malvezzi with its statue of St Angela, and the church of **Santa Maria Maddalena** (open 9am-noon, 4-6pm daily). Inside the church is a striking *Last Supper* signed by Giambattista Tiepolo, but painted in a style more reminiscent of his son, Giandomenico, who may have restored papa's work extensively. To the west,

along via Crocefisso, is the **Villa Romana**. The remains of the large third century AD **Villa Romana** were dug up in 1921. Note the lively fishing scenes in the splendid mosaic floors.

Six kilometres (3.5 miles) east, perched at the end of a three-kilometre (two-mile) lizard-tongue promontory, the medieval town of **Sirmione** is the lake's main tourist magnet, protected by the supremely picturesque 13th-century **Rocca Scaligera**. This moat-girdled castle contains little of major interest, but there are wonderful views of the lake from its battlements.

Sirmione's other attraction is the **Grotte di Catullo**, the extensive ruins of a colossal first-century villa – in fact unlikely to have belonged to a mere poet like Catullus. There is a good museum at the entrance. But the main pleasure of the site is its magnificent setting amid sloping olive groves at the tip of the peninsula. Whether or not the villa was his, Catullus was spot-on when he described the place as 'jewel of all islands and all almost-islands…'.

Peschiera, at the south-eastern corner of the lake, has a decidedly military feel to it. It has been fortified since Roman times; in the 19th century the Austrians rebuilt and strengthened the 16th-century Venetian defences. The town now provides equally important, if less picturesque, environmental defence, thanks to a huge purifying plant.

Trips Out of Town

Just to the north of the town is **Gardaland** – Italy's answer to Disneyland – which draws more than three million visitors each year. Since 1975 it has continued to grow, its Dinosaur Islands, Dolphinariums and Jungle Rapids engulfing ever more of the lakeside, and its traffic queues strangling the road system. In high season expect a one-to-three ratio of active fun to passive queueing. The success of the park has spawned a number of imitators nearby.

Gardaland
SS 249 Gardesana Orientale, Castelnuovo del Garda (045 644 9777/www.gardaland.it). **Open** *late Mar-late June* 9.30am-6.30pm daily. *Late June-early Sept* 9am-midnight daily. *Last 3wks Sept* 9.30am-6.30pm daily. *Oct* 9.30am-6.30pm Sat, Sun. Closed Nov-late Mar. **Admission** €20.50; €17.25 children over 1m & under 10; free children under 1m. **Credit** AmEx, DC, MC, V.

Grotte di Catullo
Piazza Orti Manara, Sirmione (030 916 157). **Open** *Mar-mid Oct* 8.30am-7pm Tue-Sat; 9am-6pm Sun. *Mid Oct-Feb* 8.30am-4.30pm Tue-Sat; 9am-4.30 Sun. **Admission** €4; €2 concessions. **No credit cards.**

Rocca Scaligera
Piazza Castello, Sirmione (030 916 468). **Open** *Apr-Oct* 8.30am-6.30pm Tue-Sun. *Nov-Mar* 8.30am-4.30pm Tue-Sun. **Admission** €4; €2 concessions. **No credit cards**.

Villa Romana
Via del Crocefisso 22, Desenzano (030 914 3547). **Open** *Mar-mid Oct* 8.30am-7pm Tue-Sun. *Mid Oct-Feb* 8.30am-sunset Tue-Sun. **Admission** €2; €1 concessions. **No credit cards**.

Where to stay & eat

In Desenzano, the **Hotel Tripoli** (piazza Matteotti 18, 030 914 1305, double room €88-€104) has lake views and comfortable if anonymous rooms. The restaurant **Il Molino** (piazza Matteotti 16, 030 914 1340, closed all Mon & Tue lunch, average €45) does good fish dishes.

In Sirmione, luxury is available at non-luxury rates at **Hotel Fonte Boiola** (viale Marconi 11, 030 990 4922, closed 2wks Jan, double room €100-€200 per person, half board). It's in the heart of the old town , and has a spa, a restaurant and a wonderful garden on the lake.

The child of pleasure

Much can be guessed about the personality of Gabriele D'Annunzio from his obsessively over-the-top villa, **Il Vittoriale**. It doesn't, however, tell the whole story.

For by the time the poet, playwright and novelist retired here in 1921 at the age of 58, his creative life was pretty well over. The villa and its magnificent grounds were a gilded prison for a man whose life had been one of restless movement – forever shifting from home to home, from one literary and political trend to another, and from one mistress to the next.

Two years before he settled into the villa, D'Annunzio had taken it upon himself to 'liberate' the city of Fiume (Rijeka), which had been ceded to Yugoslavia in 1918. The following year, the embarrassed Italian government had had to send a contingent to drive out Fiume's self-styled 'dictator' and his band of ex-combattant followers.

When Mussolini came to power in 1923, he recognised D'Annunzio as perhaps Italy's only other megalomaniac capable of upstaging him. 'If you have a rotten tooth,' said Il Duce of the popular poet and hero, 'either you have it pulled out or you cover it with gold.' To keep D'Annunzio at bay,

Il Vittoriale was made into a national monument and D'Annunzio remained there in comparative tranquillity until his death in 1939. (Incidentally, while D'Annuzio remained in his luxury cage, Mussolini took a leaf out of his book and extended his hold over the Balkans.)

D'Annunzio passed his final years redesigning – with his friend, the architect Gian Carlo Maroni – the villa and grounds. Despite its patriotic name, Il Vittoriale degli Italiani is essentially a monument to its owner, in which no aspect of his character or achievements is uncelebrated. The villa's interior, with its claustrophobia-inducing clutter, reveals his numerous rampant enthusiasms: music, literature, art, the Orient and – most rampant of all – sex. The grounds celebrate his more extrovert passions, from theatre (his most celebrated love affair was with actress Eleonora Duse) to bellicose heroics: where other people might have garden gnomes, D'Annunzio erected the prow of the battleship *Puglia* to commemorate the death at sea of two companions from his Fiume exploit.

The one thing that this extraordinary jumble of memorabilia fails to reveal, however,

The **Osteria Torcol** (via San Salvatore 30, 030 990 4605, closed Wed, average €25) serves home-made pasta and hot and cold snacks.

Tourist information

IAT
Via Porto Vecchio 34, Desenzano (030 9141 510/ fax 030 9144 209/www.bresciaholiday.com). **Open** 9am-noon, 3-6pm Mon-Fri; 9am-12.30pm Sat.

IAT
Viale Marconi 2, Sirmione (030 916 114). **Open** *Apr-Oct* 9am-12.30pm, 3-6pm daily. *Nov-Mar* 9am-12.30pm, 3-6pm Mon-Fri; 9am-12.30pm Sat.

IAT
Piazzale Betteloni 15, Peschiera (045 755 1673 /fax 045 755 0381). **Open** *Nov-Feb* 8am-1pm, 3-6pm Tue, Thur, Fri; 8am-1pm Wed, Sat. *Mar-Oct* 8am-1pm, 3-6pm Mon-Sat; 8am-1pm Sun.

The western shore

Garda's western shore is more magnificently rugged than the eastern one, particularly in its northern reaches. It was here that lakeside tourism really began: splendid villas built from the 18th century onwards dot its shores. Two of these were home to a pair of major (if somewhat hammy) actors on the world stage of the 20th century: Gabriele D'Annunzio (*see p208* **The child of pleasure**) and Benito Mussolini.

The lakeside road leads north from Desenzano (*see p207*) to **Salò**, the Roman Salodium, set in a deep bay. The town's name is irrevocably linked with the puppet republic set up here by the Nazis in 1943 for Mussolini after he had been ousted from power in Rome (*see p211* **Salò**). But Salò's other, happier, claim to fame is as the birthplace of Gasparo da Salò (1540-1609), generally agreed hereabouts to have invented the violin (but *see also p244*).

The fine art nouveau hotels along the lake front were built after an earthquake in 1901. The many medieval and Renaissance *palazzi* in the centre, however, show that the town was important well before then. In piazza del Duomo, the cathedral of the **Annunziata** (open 9am-noon, 3.30-6.30pm daily) has a Renaissance portal in its unfinished façade and a splendid Venetian-Gothic interior. On the high altar is a

is that D'Annunzio was a significant writer. For all his posturing, his contribution to literature was an important one. His early novel, *Il Piacere* (*The Child of Pleasure*, 1898), with its unrestrained sensuousness, is a key text in European Decadence. His poetry, strongly influenced by symbolism and the Pre-Raphaelites, shows a genuine lyrical gift.

Il Vittoriale degli Italiani
Via Vittoriale, Gardone di Sopra (036 529 6511/www.vittoriale.it). **Open** *Garden* Apr-Sept 8.30am-8pm daily. Oct-Mar 9am-5pm daily. *House* Apr-Sept 10am-6pm Tue-Sun. Oct-Mar 9am-1pm,2-5pm Tue-Sun. **Admission** *Garden* €5. *Garden & house* €10. **No credit cards**.

Trips Out of Town

Prehistoric lake-dwellers built houses on stilts.

Gothic altarpiece with gilded statues of saints, while the walls and chapels of the left aisle contain two paintings by Romanino and a polyptych by Paolo Veneziano. Around the cathedral is the oldest part of the town, with fine *palazzi* from the 15th to the 18th centuries lining the main streets parallel to the lake.

Four kilometres (2.5 miles) further north is **Gardone Riviera**. It was here, in the 1880s, that the peaceable German occupation of the lake began when scientist Ludovic Rohden noted the mildness of the climate. The town dates from that period; cosmopolitan hotels were set up and holiday villas constructed, including Villa Alba, built for (though never used by) the Austrian emperor.

Gardone's main attraction is the **Giardini Botanici Hruska**. Laid out from 1910 to 1971 by Arturo Hruska, a dentist and naturalist, it contains a host of tropical plants but is mainly notable for its rock gardens and Alpine flora.

From Gardone there is a good view of **Isola di Garda**. In the ninth century this island was given by Charlemagne to Verona's archbishop – later saint – Zeno. It remained in ecclesiastical hands until 1798. The present extraordinary villa – in Venetian Gothic style – was built by the noble Borghese family in 1900-3 and is still privately owned (not open to the public).

On the hill above Gardone Riviera is the old town of **Gardone di Sopra**, notable mostly as the site of the grandiose **Vittoriale degli Italiani**. This presumptuously named villa was the residence of poet, novelist, dramatist, man-of-action and *grand poseur* Gabriele D'Annunzio (*see p208* **The child of pleasure**). The word 'restraint' was missing from D'Annunzio's personal dictionary, as the villa and its grounds bear witness: highlights

include the the spare bedroom with the coffin in which D'Annunzio would meditate Bela Lugosi-fashion; the dining room complete with pet tortoise embalmed in bronze after it died from over-eating; and his monstrous wedding-cake mausoleum.

Continuing north, **Toscolano-Maderno** is a resort with a good beach. Maderno – the more touristy of the two connected villages – was Benacum, the most important Roman town on the lake, which sank into its waters after an earthquake around the year AD 243. Roman and Byzantine traces can be found in the 12th-century Romanesque church of **Sant'Andrea** (piazza San Marco, open 9am-noon, 3-6pm daily), particularly in the pillar-capitals; the church is a miniature version of Verona's San Zeno Maggiore.

Bogliaco, the next village, is home to the grandiose 18th-century **Villa Bettoni** (closed to the public), the largest villa on the lake after Isola di Garda. It was here that the ministers of the Salò republic (*see p211* **Salò**) would meet; the villa was damaged during over-enthusiastic celebrations after the Liberation. The Gardesana road has severed the villa from its magnificent formal garden (also closed).

DH Lawrence lived in nearby **Gargnano** in 1912-13; *Twilight in Italy* contains – amid reflections on Italian phallocentricity – some of the finest descriptions of the lake ever written. Gargnano's fine 13th-century church of **San Francesco** (open 9am-noon daily) has cloisters in Venetian Gothic style; note the pillar-capitals with carved lemon leaves. Looking on to the lake by the jetty is **Palazzo Feltrinelli** (not open to the public), built in 1894 for a wealthy industrialist family; during the Republic of Salò, this was Mussolini's administrative headquarters, where the Nazis allowed him to play at being in charge. *Il Duce*'s private residence was in the larger **Villa Feltrinelli**, set in a large garden to the north of the town. This has recently been restored as a luxury hotel (www.villafeltrinelli.com).

Beyond Gargnano, the lake narrows and the mountains rise sheer out of the water. The Gardesana continues as a series of tunnels driven through solid rock, with only occasional openings for tiny hamlets on the lakeside. During World War II the tunnels were used as bomb-proof factories for weapons (Breda and Beretta), car-engines (Fiat) and aeroplane engines (the Luftwaffe).

Larger than most of the northern villages, **Limone sul Garda** has a small port and an attractive medieval centre with steep, narrow streets and staircases. There's also a two-mile beach. It's unclear whether the town's name derives from the Latin *limen* (border) or from its extensive lemon plantations, said to have been the first in Europe. After Italian unification in the 1870s, the Garda citrus industry couldn't compete with Sicily's. The bare pillars that used to support protective greenhouse cover during the winter months now stand like 'ruined temples... forlorn in their colonnades and squares... as if they remained from some great race that had once worshipped here', as DH Lawrence fancifully put it.

The parish **church** (open 9am-6pm daily) in the main square has pretty patterns picked out in cobbles; it contains a fine late 16th-century wooden crucifix. At the northern end of the village, at the top of a steep staircase, is tiny 14th-century **San Rocco** (often closed but viewable through the window), with a frescoed altar-piece inside a *trompe-l'oeil* frescoed frame.

Through yet more tunnels, the Gardesano leads to **Riva del Garda**, the largest town in the northern half of the lake. It stands between Monte Brione to the east and the sheer cliffs of Monte Rocchetta to the west, which bring early dusk to the town. Once a major port, from 1813 until 1918 it lay in Austrian territory, and saw fighting during the World War I.

Though it's now a prosperous tourist resort, Riva still has some of the feel of a lively trading centre. The centre of the town is piazza III

Salò

By the time northern Italy's Nazi occupiers installed Mussolini in Villa Feltrinelli (*see p211*) in Gargnano on the shores of Lake Garda, the Fascist leader had been humbled and overtaken by history. Most of his Fascist Grand Council had voted to remove him from power on July 25 1943, by which time Anglo-American forces were firmly installed in Sicily and inflicting crushing blows up the boot of Italy. The king had defected to the Allied side and had Mussolini imprisoned in a mountain fastness in Abruzzo; it had taken an SS commando team to get him out and whisk him off to an illusion of power in the north.

Il Duce's comeback took the vicious, squalid form of the Repubblica di Salò. Mussolini did not choose the place from which he was to 'govern' northern Italy for the next 18 months: he would have preferred to return to Rome for a bloody settling of accounts. But the more pragmatic Germans put their jack-booted feet down, keeping Mussolini in the more easily controllable north. Just to make sure he was under no illusions of his administration being anything but a puppet, the Germans spread ministries haphazardly around lakeside towns and made no secret of the fact that everything – including Mussolini's letters to his lover

Clara Petacci, who had been set up in an ex-convent in Gargnano – was checked over by the SS.

Holed up in Villa Feltrinelli, Mussolini was a pathetic parody of his former strutting self. He drew up futile plans for the war effort, refusing to face the fact that the Nazis and/or uncontrolled bands of thugs and sadists were running the show. His family squabbled around him as amused Nazi troops looked on.

The Salò Republic's one memorable act was to put on trial and subsequently execute five members of the Grand Council that had voted Mussolini out of office, including his son-in-law, Galeazzo Ciano. Mussolini went to great lengths to pretend that the malevolence of others had prevented him from signing a pardon. When his daughter refused to believe his version of events, he whinged that it was his 'destiny to be betrayed by everyone, including my own daughter'.

The beauty of the setting in which these sordid events took place was of little consolation to Mussolini. 'Lakes are a compromise between river and sea,' he moaned, 'and I don't like compromises'. As it turned out, it was beside another lake – Como (*see p194*) – that he was to be executed by uncompromising Partisans.

Novembre, with the imposing 13th-century **Torre Apponale**, the 14th-century **Palazzo Pretorio** (not open to the public) and picturesque medieval porticos. An archway beneath the Palazzo Pretorio leads to tiny piazza San Rocco, where the surviving apse of a church destroyed in the World War I has been converted into an open-air chapel. Eastwards from piazza III Novembre is the moat-encircled **rocca** (castle), containing a **Museo Civico** with collections of archaeology and armour. North through porta San Michele, viale Roma leads to the **Chiesa dell'Inviolata** (open 8.30am-noon, 4-6pm daily), an octagonal church of the 17th century, the work of a Portuguese architect whose name local history has failed to record and who saw no reason to stint on stucco and gilt, covering every surface inch with decoration; paintings by the prolific Palma il Giovane adorn the chapels.

More baroque splendour can be found in the Madonna chapel of the **Chiesa dell'Assunta** in via Mazzini (open 8.30-noon, 3-6.30pm daily), with cavorting *putti* and lavish carved marble drapery. The energetic can follow a zig-zag path up to the **Bastione**, a cylindrical tower built by the Venetians in 1508, commanding a splendid view (212 metres, 707 feet) over the town.

Giardini Botanici Hruska

Via Roma, Gardone Riviera (no phone).
Open *Mar-Oct* 9am-6.30pm daily. Closed Nov-Feb.
Admission €3. **No credit cards**.

Rocca & Museo Civico

Piazza Battisti 3, Riva del Garda (0464 573 869).
Open *Mid Mar-mid June, mid Sept-Oct* 9.30am-12.45pm, 2.15pm-5.30pm Tue-Sun. *Mid June-mid Sept* 9.30am-6pm daily. Closed Nov-mid Mar.
Admission €3. **No credit cards**.

Where to eat & stay

In Salò, the **Gallo Rosso** (vicolo Tomacelli 4, 0365 520 757, closed 1wk Jan & 1wk June, average €20) offers good fish dishes at reasonable prices. **Pignino Sera** (via Panoramica 13, Salò, 036 522 071, rates €21-€21.50 per person) is a farm situated about a kilometre from the centre of Salò in olive groves, with a splendid lake view, offering basic accommodation to groups of six people. For an exhaustive list of *agriturismo* (farm holiday) accommodation around the lake, consult the website www.gardalake.it/contiterzi.

In Gardone di Sopra, **Agli Angeli** (piazza Garibaldi 2, closed mid Nov-mid Feb, 036 520 832, average €35) was the restaurant Gabriele D'Annunzio advised his friends to try, although he himself always ate at home. The home-made pasta is good.

In Limone, the **Hotel Bellavista** (via Marconi 20, 0365 954 001, www.gardalake.it/hotelbellavista, closed Nov-Mar, double room €96) is situated on the lake and has a pretty garden. It has been run by the same family for nearly a century.

The **Grand Hotel Riva** (piazza Garibaldi 10, Riva del Garda, 0464 521 800, grandhotelriva@gardaresort.it, double room €75-€140) is a large and comfortable hotel in a fine central position by the lake.

Tourist information

IAT

Lungolago Zanardelli, Palazzo Municipale, Salò (036 521 423/www.comune.salo.bs.it). **Open** *Apr-June* 9am-12.30pm, 3-6pm Mon, Tue, Thur-Sat; 9am-12.30pm Wed. *July-Sept* 9am-12.30pm 3-6pm Mon-Sat; 9am-12.30pm Sun. *Oct* 9am-12.30pm, 3-6pm Mon, Tue, Thur, Fri; 9am-12.30pm Wed. *Nov-Mar* 9am-12.30pm, 3-6pm Mon-Fri; 9am-12.30pm Sat.

IAT

Corso Repubblica 8, Gardone Riviera (tel/fax 036 520 347). **Open** *Apr-Sept* 9am-12.30pm, 3-6.30pm Mon-Sat; 9am-12.30pm Sun. *Oct-Mar* 9am-12.30pm, 3-6pm Mon-Wed, Fri, Sat; 9am-12.30pm Thur.

IAT

Via Lungolago 18, Toscolano-Maderno (tel/fax 036 564 1330). **Open** *Apr-Sept* 9am-12.30pm, 3-6.30pm Mon-Sat; 9am-12.30pm Sun. *Oct-Mar* 9am-12.30pm, 2.30-6pm Mon, Tue, Thur-Sat; 9am-12.30pm Wed.

IAT

Piazza Feltrinelli, Gargnano (036 571 222/www.prolocogargnano.com). **Open** 3.30-6.30pm Mon; 9am-noon, 3.30-6.30pm Tue-Sat; 9am-noon Sun.

Ufficio Informazione

Via IV Novembre (0365 954 720). **Open** *Oct-Mar* 8.30am-noon, 1.30-5.30pm daily. *Apr-Sept* 8am-10pm daily.

APT

Giardini di Porta Orientale 8, Riva del Garda (046 455 4444/fax 046 452 0308/www.garda trentino.com). **Open** *Apr-Oct* 9am-noon, 3-6.30pm Mon-Sat. *Nov-Mar* 9am-noon, 2.30-5.15pm Mon-Fri.

The eastern shore

Steep shores and magnificent views on the stretch from Torbole in the north give way to relentless camp-sites and amusement parks further south, with only the occasional small medieval town to provide aesthetic relief.

A short tunnel beneath the massive wedge of Monte Brione joins **Riva** (*see p212*) to **Torbole** on the lake's north-eastern corner. It is here that the River Sarca, the lake's main feeder, flows in. Torbole's port is extensive. In 1439 it witnessed the launching of a fleet of 26 Venetian ships that had been dragged, *Fitzcarraldo*-fashion, over the mountains for a surprise attack on the Milanese rulers, the Visconti.

Malcesine (15 kilometres south) is unquestionably the eastern shore's most delightful town, with one of its finest castles, on a craggy promontory looming over the medieval quarter. The castle has a small **museo** with sketches done by Goethe in 1786. The poet was nabbed by a suspicious local as he sketched and arrested for spying.

Close to the Gardesana road is the church of **Santo Stefano** (open 9am-noon, 4-6.30pm daily). In via Capitanata del Lago, alongside the lake, the **Palazzo dei Capitani del Lago** (not open to the public) has a fine frescoed lion of St Mark on the ceiling of the entrance hall and frescoed coats-of-arms of the Captains of the Lake (local administrators from the 16th to the 18th century) upstairs. There is also a garden-courtyard overlooking the lake.

As this guide went to press the cable car from Malcesine to Monte Baldo was closed, due to re-open in July 2002. Consult the website www.malcesinepiu.it/funivia for information.

In **Torri del Benaco** are a few remnants of the ancient town walls and the 14th-century **Castello Scaligero**, built, like many in the region, by Verona's ruling Della Scala family (the adjective of which is *scaligero* – hence the name). Inside is a small museum with worthy but unthrilling displays on local crafts. In piazza **Santissima Trinità** the church of the same name (open 9am-noon, 4-6pm daily) contains 15th-century frescos, including a splendid *Christ Pantocrator* in gleaming hippy-style flowered garb.

The town of **Garda** lies on a deep bay with Monte Garda behind. It was in a no-longer-extant castle on this hill that Queen Adelaide was imprisoned by Berenger II, after he had murdered her husband and she had refused to marry his son Adalberto (*see p10*). The centre of Garda has several notable Renaissance *palazzi*. For more, take the magnificent (but unshaded) path north along the curving shore towards **Punta San Vigilio**, lined with villas, hotels, and gardens rolling down to the lake. At the tip of the headland is a harbour, with a tiny chapel dedicated to **San Vigilio** (erratic opening times); a path leads up to the 16th-century **Villa Guarienti**; it's privately owned but a glimpse can be caught of its splendid formal gardens, much loved by Winston Churchill and Laurence Olivier among others. On the other side of the promontory is the tiny **Baia delle Sirene**, with a beach. South of Garda, the waterside footpath is a pleasant and mostly pine-shaded walk as far as Bardolino.

Bardolino – of wine fame – has two fascinating churches. **San Zeno** (open 9am-6pm daily) is reached by turning eastwards off the Gardesana road along the suburban-looking via San Zeno; the tiny church, standing in a rustic courtyard, is a ninth-century building with faint traces of fresco. **San Severo** (open 9am-6pm daily), a well-preserved 12th-century building with a fine campanile, contains notable 12th- and 14th-century frescos. The town is flanked by fine gardens giving on to the lake.

In **Lazise** is another **Castello Scaligero** (now incorporated into the garden of a privately owned villa); an arcaded 16th-century Venetian custom-house shows how important the place once was. South of here lie the delights of **Gardaland** (*see p208*) and its tacky imitators.

Castello Scaligero

Viale Fratelli Lavanda 2, Torri del Benaco (tel/fax 045 629 6111). **Open** *late Mar-Oct* 9.30am-1pm, 4.30-7.30pm daily. *Dec-Mar* 2.30-5.30pm Sun. **Admission** €3; €1 concessions. **No credit cards**.

Castello Scaligero & Museo

Via Castello, Malcesine (045 740 0837). **Open** *mid Mar-Oct* 9am-8pm daily. *Dec-mid Jan* 10am-5pm daily. *Mid Jan-mid Mar* 11.30am-5.30 Sat-Sun. **Admission** €4; €3 concessions. **No credit cards**.

Where to eat & stay

In Malcesine, **Hotel Malcesine** (piazza Pallone 2, 045 740 0173, double room €58-€138 half board) is situated on the lakefront.

The **Albergo Gardesana** in Torri del Benaco (piazza Calderini 20, 045 722 5411, www.hotel-gardesana.com, closed Jan, double room €80-€136) has a fine lakeside location; such personalities as Winston Churchill and Kim Novak have stayed in the 34 rooms.

In Garda, away from the lake, the **Stafolet** (via Poiano 9, 045 725 5427, closed Wed & Nov, average €25) does good grilled dishes and pizza. In Bardolino, the **Ristorante Aurora** (piazza San Severo 1, 045 721 0038, closed Mon, average €35) serves reliable local dishes.

Tourist information

IAT

Piazzale Aldo Moro 5, Bardolino (045 721 0078/fax 045 721 0872). **Open** *Apr-Oct* 9am-1pm, 3-6pm Mon-Sat; 9am-1pm Sun. *Nov-Mar* 9am-1pm, 3-6pm Tue, Thur, Fri; 9am-1pm Wed, Sat.

APT

Lungolago Regina Adelaide 13, Garda 045 627 0384/fax 045 725 6720/www.aptgardaveneto.com). **Open** *Apr-Oct* 9am-noon, 3-6.15pm Mon-Sat; 10am-noon Sun. *Nov-Mar* 8.30am-1.30pm, 3-6pm Tue, Thur, Fri; 8.30am-1.30pm Wed-Sat.

Bergamo & Around

Bergamo province strives to preserve the good things of life.

Ask an Italian for a description of the *bergamaschi*, and you'll probably hear 'closed', 'stubborn' and/or 'provincial'. The locals, needless to say, see things differently. They see themselves as preservationists – of the commerce and industry that made Bergamo wealthy, of the mountains and valleys that shape the *bergamasco* soul, of the small villages and hamlets, of the often unintelligible local dialect, of a way of life. The Milanese may flock to the valleys and lakes of Bergamo because the air is cleaner; they also come because they find something that Milan lost long ago.

Bergamo

Elsewhere in Italy, a walled medieval city on a hill would soar majestically over its surroundings. But majestic soaring is not in keeping with the *bergamasco* character, so Bergamo's **Città Alta** presides more in solid reassurance, a link in the chain of the way things have always been.

The turning point in Bergamo's history came in 1428, when it became part of the Venetian Republic, gaining protection against Milan's Viscontis (*see p13*), who had been ruling and attacking Bergamo off and on for almost 200 years. And while the arrival of *La Serenissima* did not guarantee peace in their times – the fighting in Bergamo didn't stop until 1516 – it did mark the beginning of a 350-year relationship between Venice and its small border town.

Even before the Viscontis, Bergamo had been a popular target, attacked by Goths, Huns, Vandals, Lombards and Franks, as well as the Spanish, the French and the Holy Roman Empire. Its position made it a valuable prize: the city commands a good portion of the fertile plains of the Po river, as well as the entrance to two river valleys – the Serio and the Brembo.

Bergamo still reflects the influences of Venice, commerce and industry. The massive *mura* (defensive walls) of the Città Alta were built by the Venetians: the lion of St Mark – the symbol of Venice – shows up throughout the

Bergamo's **Città Alta** viewed from San Vigilio. *See p215.*

Bergamo

city. Today the city on the hill, or **Città Alta**, remains the heart of Bergamo. Below, in the more modern **Città Bassa** (lower city), affluent shoppers stroll along Sentierone and via XX Settembre, pausing to contemplate exorbitantly priced accessories in shop windows.

Sightseeing

Città Alta

The main road (viale Vittorio Emanuele II) up to Città Alta passes through *le mura*, the city's defensive walls, at Porta Sant'Agostino, which was built in 1575 by the Venetians (though Venice's rule of Bergamo ended in 1797, St Mark's lion still holds pride of place above the arch). The Venetians were not the first to build walls in Bergamo; there is evidence that the Etruscans had fortified sites on the hills, and there are remnants of earlier defences, including la Rocca (*see p217*) and la Cittadella (*see p216*).

The walls defended Bergamo, but they also limited its growth. It was not until 1430, when the Venetians built a further stretch of wall (torn down in 1902), that the *bergamaschi* felt safe enough to spread into the Città Bassa.

Accessible from Porta Sant'Agostino, the viale Mura promenade – built in the 1880s – follows a good portion of the walls, passing by two more of Città Alta's four extant gates: San Giacomo and Sant'Alessandro. (The fourth – San Lorenzo, or Garibaldi – is a bit more rustic and off the tourist track at the end of via della Fara.) Besides a pleasant tree-lined stroll and soulful views of Città Bassa and the plains, viale Mura offers an insight into just how tight space is in Città Alta.

Just inside the Porta Sant'Agostino stands the 13th-century ex-convent of Sant'Agostino. Opposite, via Porta Dipinta leads up to the heart of Città Alta. The gate guarding the street is long gone, but one of its towers – called Sub Foppis – remains, a piece of the pre-Venetian defensive

Lakes & Cities

system. Further up the street to the left is the church of **San Michele al Pozzo Bianco**.

Via Porta Dipinta climbs to piazza Mercato delle Scarpe, passing impressive *palazzi* built in the 16th and 17th centuries by successful *bergamaschi*. About halfway up the street there is also a small tablet marking the spot where Porta Sant'Andrea stood; called *porta dipinta* (painted gate) because of its pre-1500 frescos, it was torn down in 1815 in an unfortunate fit of urban development.

At the end of via Porta Dipinta, piazza Mercato delle Scarpe is an important hub in Città Alta. On the southern side of the square is the *funicolare*, the cable car from Città Bassa. Stretching to the north-west is via Gombito, Città Alta's main drag. A few steps into via Gombito, via Rocca (right) leads up to the **Rocca**.

Via Gombito was the main *decumanus* (north–south axis) of Roman Bergamo; today it's a narrow street lined with small shops and bars. At the intersection with via Lupo stands the Torre Gombito (not open to the public), dating back to the Guelph-Ghibelline struggles of the 12th century (*see p13*). Across the street from the *torre*, the romantic houses of piazza Mercato del Fieno are overshadowed by Città Alta's main parking lot.

Via Gombito opens out into piazza Vecchia. Stunningly lovely, piazza Vecchia is also an utterly functional part of 21st-century Bergamo. The medieval buildings on the eastern side of the square house offices of Bergamo University. The magnificent **Palazzo della Ragione** is used as an exhibition space. The neo-classical Palazzo Nuovo is home to the municipal archives and library. And the bells in the **Torre del Campanone** still toll 100 times each evening at 10pm, a reminder of the city's historical curfew.

A passage through the loggia of the Palazzo della Ragione leads to piazza Duomo, which houses some of Bergamo's most important buildings: the **Duomo**, the basilica of **Santa Maria Maggiore** and the **Cappella Colleoni**. Behind Santa Maria Maggiore, via Arena leads to the **Museo Donizetti**, dedicated to Bergamo-born composer Gaetano Donizetti.

Past piazza Vecchia, via Gombito becomes via Colleoni and leads to piazza Mascheroni, home to La Cittadella. Built in the 14th century to defend Città Alta from an attack from the west, the Cittadella was adapted to more peaceful uses by the Venetians. Beyond piazza Cittadella, historic Città Alta ends at Colle Aperto, an open space just inside the porta Sant'Alessandro, with views across to the foothills of the Alps.

Cappella Colleoni

Piazza Duomo (035 210 061). **Open** *Nov-Mar* 9am-12.30pm, 2.30-4.30pm Tue-Sun. *Apr-Oct* 9am-12.30pm, 2.30-6.30pm Tue-Sun.

As a *capitano generale* or *condottiere* (mercenary captain) in the Venetian army, Bartolomeo Colleoni (1400-75) was the man responsible for the defence of *bergamasco* territory. This did not stop him from occasionally changing sides in Venice's conflicts with Milan, but the Venetians and *bergamaschi* focused on his attributes rather than his perfidy, rewarding him with land and fame. Colleoni had the old sacristy in Santa Maria Maggiore demolished to make way for his mausoleum, which was finished one year after his death. His tomb – a late Gothic work – and that of his daughter Medea – whose serene-looking statue lies on top of the sarcophagus – grace the chapel, as do frescos (1733) by Gianbattista Tiepolo. On the gate outside the chapel, the Colleoni coat of arms has been polished to a bright sheen by hands rubbing it for luck. The coat of arms bears three testicles – as did Colleoni, so legend has it. Italians rub testicles where Anglo-Saxons knock on wood: which leads one to think of one song that wouldn't translate well into Italian.

Duomo (Cattedrale di Sant'Alessandro)

Piazza Duomo (035 210 223). **Open** 7.30-11.45am, 3-6pm daily.

Building began on the Duomo – to a design by Il Filarete (*see p32*) – in 1459, on a spot previously occupied by an early Christian church. The project passed through the hands of several other architects before completion in 1886. In the first chapel on the left is an interesting *Madonna e santi* by Moroni (1576); among the mainly 18th-century works surrounding the main altar is Gianbattista Tiepolo's *Martyrdom of St John the Bishop*. The 17th-century wooden choir is by Johann Karl Sanz. A larger-than-life statue of Pope John XXIII at the Duomo's entrance is a reminder of the importance of the *bergamasco* pope to the city (*see p222* **Il Papa Buono**).

Funicolare al Mercato delle Scarpe

Piazza Mercato delle Scarpe/viale Vittorio Emanuele II (035 364 222). **Open** *Mid Sept-mid June* 7am-midnight Mon-Fri; 7am-midnight Sat, Sun. *Mid June- mid Sept* 7am-1.30am daily. **Tickets** 85¢. **No credit cards**.

A crucial link between Città Alta and Città Bassa, the funicular inspires justifiable pride in local breasts. Built in 1887, it travels 240m (800ft) at angles of up to 52 degrees – a remarkable feat of Italian engineering.

Museo Donizettiano

Via Arena 9 (035 399 269). **Open** *Oct-Mar* 10am-1pm Tue-Fri; 10am-1pm, 2.30-5pm Sat, Sun. *Apr-Sept* 10am-1pm, 2.30-5pm Tue-Sun. **Admission** free.

Located in a palazzo that also houses Città Alta's music school, this one-room museum is dedicated to Gaetano Donizetti (1797-1848), composer of such

Lakes & Cities

operas as *Anna Bolena* and *Lucia di Lammermoor*. The museum contains a number of manuscripts and musical instruments.

Palazzo della Ragione

Piazza Vecchia (035 399 203). **Open** exhibitions only, times vary.

Originally constructed in the 12th century, the Palazzo della Ragione has seen many changes. The covered staircase leading to the principal meeting room was added in 1453, and the street-level loggia was a 1520 addition. Inside, the *sala superiore* provides an impressive backdrop for temporary exhibitions, its walls covered in frescos dating back to the 13th century. Also here are frescos of three *filosofi* (1477) by Donato Bramante; the *filosofi* were removed from the Palazzo del Podestà on the north-west corner of the square. Named for the *podestà* – the Venetian governor of Bergamo – the palazzo was built in 1340.

La Rocca

Piazzale Brigata Legnano (035 224 700). Closed for restoration; due to reopen some time after Dec 2002.

Construction began on La Rocca, part of Bergamo's pre-Venetian defences, in 1331 on the site of the Roman capitol. It was finished under the Viscontis (*see p13*). The Venetians added the Sala dei Bombardieri; the Austrians turned it into a key fort of the Risorgimento (*see p17*). It has also been used as a barracks and a prison; these days its grounds are a public park.

San Michele al Pozzo Bianco

Via Porta Dipinta (035 247 651).
Open 8am-6pm daily.

Set off the street on a little square and hemmed in by its neighbours, this church seems almost inconsequential. But the neighbours actually came later than the church: it dates back to the eighth century. It has been revamped and rebuilt a number of times: the façade is less than a century old, though most of the interior is from the 1400s. Inside, the walls of the single-naved church are covered in magnificent frescos, including scenes from the life of Mary by Lorenzo Lotto (*see p224* **Lorenzo Lotto**) in the chapel to the left of the high altar. In the crypt are more frescos, some dating from the 13th century.

Santa Maria Maggiore

Piazza Duomo (035 223 327). **Open** *Nov-Mar* 9am-12.30pm, 2.30-5pm Mon-Sat; 9am-12.45pm, 3-6pm Sun. *Apr-Oct* 9am-12.30pm, 2.30-6pm Mon-Sat; 9am-12.45pm, 3-6pm Sun.

Santa Maria Maggiore outshines the Duomo (*see p216*) as piazza Duomo's most impressive edifice. Begun in 1157 on the site of an earlier church, construction did not end until 1521, when the Porta della Fontana was completed. Each period of construction offers something of beauty, from the presbytery (1187), to the prothyum (1350), to the new sacristy (late 15th century). The most impressive aspect, however, is the stunning series of intarsia (wooden

inlay) works on the presbytery stalls. These exquisite woodcarvings, designed by Lorenzo Lotto (*see p216*), not only tell stories from the Old Testament: they also contain detailed comments in the form of alchemical symbols.

Torre del Campanone

Piazza Vecchia (035 224 700). **Open** *Nov-Feb* 10.30am-4pm Sat, Sun. *Mar, Apr* 10am-12.30pm, 2-6pm Tue-Fri; 10am-6pm Sat, Sun. *May-Sept* 10am-8pm daily. *Oct* 10am-6pm Sat, Sun. **Admission** €1. **No credit cards**.

The *torre civica*, or torre del Campanone, was built by the Suardi family in the 12th century as a Ghibelline counterbalance to the Guelph Torre Gombito (*see p216*). Climb to the top for a different view of Città Alta. (The Palazzo del Podestà was also built by the Suardis.)

Outside the walls

Historic (and touristic) Città Alta occupies the first of seven hills. On the other hills are woods with trails, and residential Città Alta. Far from the madding crowds, this part of Città Alta is an Eden of villas, gardens and vineyards.

Outside Porta Sant'Alessandro, via San Vigilio leads up to piazza San Vigilio and via Castello (for the less fit, there's the San Vigilio funicular). At the top is **Il Castello**, another part of the city's defences. Now a public park, il Castello offers views of Città Alta and a swathe of the Apennines and Alps including, on a clear day, Monte Rosa.

Città Bassa

There are more office buildings and apartment blocks than historical monuments in busy, hard-working Città Bassa, but this doesn't mean that there's nothing to see. In piazza G Carrara, the **Pinacoteca Accademia Carrara**, with its collection stretching from Raphael to Rubens, is a case in point.

From the piazza, via San Tomaso leads to via Pignolo, one of the old approaches to Città Alta. After 1430, when the Venetians constructed a wall for Città Bassa, Bergamo's merchants felt safe from attack. The result of their new-found security was this narrow street lined with substantial *palazzi* and churches, which adds a distinctly medieval touch to modern Bergamo.

Moving towards the modern centre, via Tasso leads to Sentierone, a tree- and portico-lined avenue. Sentierone ends in Bergamo's modern centre, which owes its looks to one man, architect Marcello Piacentini. Starting in 1914, Piacentini began a lengthy process of giving a homogenous appearance to the

A ride in the *pianura*

The Middle Ages saw the development of an intricate defence system in the vast plains that stretch away from Bergamo towards the River Po far to the south. Small towns with circular fortifications were built at short distances, both to protect the people working the plains and to keep a lookout for threats approaching the city. The following 50-kilometre (30-mile) drive (or bike ride: there's not a hill in sight) provides a good introduction to the towns of the *pianura*.

South of Bergamo on the SS591, **Urgnano** has a 14th-century *rocca* (fort). Built by the Viscontis (*see p13*), it now serves as the town hall. South of Urgnano at **Cologno al Serio**, where little remains of the medieval walls, the road for Treviglio (follow signs) leads past family farms to **Brignano Gera d'Adda**, where there is another Visconti castle. The prolific family also built a castle (complete with drawbridge) at **Pagazzano** (SP128 from Brignano). After Pagazzano, SP129 goes through Morengo, on to the SS591 and thence to the SP130, which

crosses the Serio river and leads to **Romano di Lombardia**. This town boasts a rectangular castle built by the Viscontis and piazza Roma – a marvellous square typical of the towns of the Po plains, with Renaissance porticos and character in buckets, marred only by the hulking, out-of-place medieval Palazzo della Comunità. From Romano, the SS498 marks the return leg to Bergamo, stopping first in **Martinengo**, a town with Roman origins that offers a distinctive *centro storico* with porticoed streets and decorative frescos.

Nearing Bergamo, the SS498 passes through **Ghisalba**, where via Malpaga leads to the **Castello di Malpaga**, the home and headquarters of Bartolomeo Colleoni (*see p216*). With its history of intrigue, lost corpses and hidden tunnels, the castle (open Feb-Nov 2.30-6.30pm Sun & public holidays, admission €4.13) is well worth touring. The road to Seriate (SP96) returns to the SS498, which ends in the centre of Seriate. From there, via Dante points the way back to Bergamo.

buildings and *piazze* of the centre. He later became a darling of the Fascist regime; the imposing faux-classical feel of his designs makes it easy to see why.

Via XX Settembre is Bergamo's high-fashion shopping strip, filled with examples of Italy's well-maintained teenagers. Moving away from piazza Matteotti, it leads to piazza Pontida, the centre of medieval Città Bassa. From piazza Pontida, the ancient via Sant'Alessandro begins its ever-steeper ascent toward Città Alta. Along the final stretch stands a viaduct built on triumphal arches in the late 1500s.

Pinacoteca Accademia Carrara

Piazza G Carrara 82A (035 399 643/www. accademiacarrara.bergamo.it). **Open** *Oct-Mar* 9.30am-1pm, 2.30-5.45pm Tue-Sun. *Apr-Sept* 10am-1pm, 3-6.45pm Tue-Sun. **Admission** €2.58. **No credit cards.**

The Pinacoteca's permanent collection is concentrated on the second floor, with the tour starting in earnest with a couple of Botticellis – note the wonderfully smug contentment in the portrait of Giuliano de' Medici in sala II. The focus of the Accademia's collection is on Lombard painters, and while they may not be as famous as other Italian artists, this only adds to the joy of discovering the quality of their works: Vincenzo Foppa's *I tre*

crocifissi in sala IV, Lorenzo Lotto's *Nozze mistiche di Santa Caterina* in sala VI and Moroni's *Ritratto di bambina di casa Redetti* in sala IX are world-class works. (French soldiers in the 1520s were so charmed with the view of Mount Sinai seen through a window in the Lotto that they took it home with them – hence the missing panel.)

Where to eat & drink

Bergamasco cuisine is for hearty appetites. *Antipasti* focus on cold cuts, particularly home-made salami and *lardo*, creamy white slices of pork fat (it's better than it sounds). *Casoncelli*, Bergamo's contribution to the pasta canon, are meat-filled *ravioli* in a sage and butter sauce. Main courses tend to roasts and braised dishes, invariably served with *polenta* (cornmeal porridge). *Polenta taragna* is a speciality of the valleys and is made with the addition of buckwheat, rich cheese and occasionally cream.

Antica Trattoria la Colombina

Via Borgo Canale 12 (035 261 402). **Meals served** 12.15-2.15pm, 7.45-10.15pm Wed-Sun. Closed 3wks Jan, 3wks June. **Average** €22. **Credit** AmEx, DC, MC, V.

Impeccable food and a marvellous view from the terrace outside this welcoming, historic trattoria.

Bar Pizzeria Martiriggiano Teresa

Via Pignolo 92 (035 234 822). **Open** *Bar* 9.30am-midnight. *Meals served* noon-2pm, 6.30-11.30pm Mon, Tue, Thur-Sun. *Both* Closed Aug. **Average** €15. **No credit cards**.
Not far from the Accademia Carrara (*see p218*) is this small pizzeria. The sign on the outside says 'Bar Genie' – a remnant of past ownership – and the inside is casual, bordering on funky. The pizzas are baked in a wood-fired oven and the *fritto misto* is far better than it has any right to be.

Borgo San Lazzaro

Via San Lazzaro 8 (035 242 452). **Meals served** noon-2.30pm, 7.30-11pm Mon-Sat. **Average** €22. **Credit** DC, MC, V.
In a small *vicolo* (alley) off piazza Pontida, this restaurant offers stylish takes on *bergamaschi* stalwarts like the cold-cut *antipasto* and *coniglio e polenta* (rabbit with polenta).

Cavour Pasticceria

Via Gombito 7A (035 243 418). **Open** 7.30am-midnight Mon, Tue, Thur-Sun. Closed 3wks Aug. **Credit** MC, V.
There is nothing more civilised than a morning cappuccino and *brioche* in the slightly Austrian elegance of Cavour's dining room, nor more inviting than a hot chocolate in the afternoon. Just the displays of chocolates can occupy the sweet-toothed for hours.

Cooperativa Città Alta

Vicolo Sant'Agata 19 (035 218 568). **Open** 8.30am-2am Mon, Tue, Thur-Sun; 11am-2am Wed. **Average** €15. **Credit** MC, V.
Known to *bergamaschi* as il Circolino, this rambunctious restaurant, bar and beer hall offers a wide menu and a social conscience. Meals are available for most of the day.

La Marianna

Largo Colle Aperto (035 237 027). **Open** *Bar* 8am-midnight Tue-Sun. *Meals served* 12.30-2pm, 7.30-10.30pm Tue-Sun. Closed 1wk Aug, 2wks Jan. **Average** Bar €7; restaurant €40. **Credit** DC, MC, V.
The restaurant is a current favourite of *bergamasco* gastronomes but the bar is a better bet, offering some of the best *gelato* in Bergamo and, at lunchtime, a variety of tasty sandwiches.

Da Ornella

Via Gombito 15 (035 232 736/www. paginegialle.it/trattoriadaornella). **Meals served** noon-3pm, 7-11pm Mon-Wed, Fri-Sun. **Average** €22. **Credit** AmEx, DC, MC, V.
Large servings of traditional food are Ornella's mainstay. The main course of mixed grilled meats comes on a big platter made for sharing.

Vineria Cozzi

Via B Colleoni 22 (035 238 836). **Open** 10.30am-2am Mon, Tue, Thur-Sun. Closed 2wks Aug. **Average** €20. **Credit** AmEx, MC, V.

The bar is open all day for a reviving coffee or glass of wine. At lunch and dinner, the back room fills with *bergamaschi* looking for a civilised repast, and Cozzi becomes one of the better restaurants in Bergamo. Food is served for most of the day.

Where to stay

In Città Alta, the reception area of the **Agnello d'Oro** (via Gombito 22, 035 249 883, www.agnellodoro.it, double room €85) is a mind-boggling bazaar; the location is as central as it gets, the building dates back to the 16th century and the 20 rooms are small but comfortable.
   In Città Bassa, the **Capello d'Oro** (viale Papa Giovanni XXIII 12, 035 232 503, www.hotelcapellodoro.it, double room €190) was recently restored by Best Western and strives – with some success – to combine modern convenience with tradition. On the outskirts of town, **Una Hotel** (via Borgo Palazzo 154, 035 308 111, double room €220) is run by an Italian chain, and offers large, modern rooms and easy access to Orio al Serio, the local airport (*see p274*).

Essentials

Getting there

By car

Take the A4 autostrada from Milan towards Venice; exit at Bergamo.

By train

Services run from Milan's Stazione Centrale via Treviglio and from Stazione Porta Garibaldi via Carnate. The Carnate service is more regular and crosses the Adda river on the dramatic ponte di Paderno (information 848 888 088).

By bus

Autostradale buses leave Milan's piazza Castello for Bergamo every 30mins (information 035 244 354).

Getting around

City buses are operated by ATB (information 035 364 222). Tickets, which cost 85¢, must be bought before boarding buses. They can be obtained at tobacconists and some newsstands. Destinations outside the city are served by SAB (information 035 289 011).

Car hire

Avis

Central Parking, via Paleocapa 3 (035 271 290). **Open** 8.30am-12.30pm, 2.30-6.30pm Mon-Fri. **Credit** AmEx, DC, MC, V.

Lakes & Cities

Little lakes

Explore Lombardy's less well-known watery delights.

Lago d'Iseo

Nestled in the mountains of eastern Bergamo and western Brescia (it forms part of the boundary of the two provinces), **Lago d'Iseo** lacks the cachet (and size) of lakes Como, Maggiore and Garda, but boasts the same sterling panoramas and weekend recreation opportunities, not to mention two names (the other is Sebino). Fed by the Oglio river, the waters of the lake not only mirror majestic mountains and host determined fishermen and boaters; they also hold one of the jewels of Lombardy, Monte Isola, the largest lake island in Italy.

THE BERGAMO SHORE

Sarnico (*pictured*), at the south-western tip of the lake, has been inhabited since prehistoric times. These days, particularly in summer, 'occupied' might be a better word. The lakefront gets crowded with campers in town for supplies and *gelato* and weekend water-skiers, windsurfers and motor-boaters in for the measured mile on the lake. Off the water, the winding streets of the medieval centre offer picturesque window-shopping.

At the other end of the lake is **Lovere**, which was originally settled by Celts and Ligurian tribesmen who had come to the region in search of metals and minerals. Strategically important because it guards the passage from the lake to the Valcamonica (*see p269*), Lovere traditionally played a big role in the trade and industry – particularly textiles – of the region. Today, its lakefront *piazze* offer outdoor cafés and people-watching in abundance. Fine palazzi along the shore bear witness to the prosperity Lovere has enjoyed over the centuries. Behind, the different levels of the medieval *borgo* (village) run along the hillside, connected by a series of stairs and alleys. On the first level is piazza Vittorio Emanuele. The tower in the square is a much-modified remnant of the old fortifications.

THE BRESCIA SHORE

Across from Lovere sits Pisogne. Though there are few ancient remains – just a few pieces of wall – Pisogne owes its existence to its iron ore deposits, worked by the Romans, and the via Valeriana, the Roman road linking Brescia with the Valcamonica (*see p269*). The

uncrowded lakefront piazza del Mercato contains the 13th-century torre del Vescovo. The relative lack of tourists in the small, melancholy medieval *borgo* behind the tower makes it easy to feel transported back in time.

From Marone, a narrow road (SP32) climbs through a series of hairpin turns to **Zone**, a small hamlet surrounded by mountain peaks and glimpses of the lake. In Zone's small nature reserve, erosion has left boulders stranded atop towering pinnacles called *piramidi di terra* (earth pyramids). Trails allow visitors to get close to the 'pyramids' and see what wind and water can create over the aeons. At the entrance to the park, the isolated 15th-century church of San Giorgio nonchalantly offers a series of stunning frescos on its walls. A boat service runs to the island (*see below*) from **Sulzano**, six kilometres (3.5 miles) south of Marone.

Further south, **Iseo** is the lake's principal town, a more cosmopolitan affair than its lacustrine neighbours, with bigger shops and better restaurants. But despite its focus on modern-day tourism, it manages to retain its ancient air and convey a peculiar timelessness, with a labyrinth of narrow streets and alleys, the 12th-century pieve di Sant'Andrea church (open 7.30am-12.30pm, 3-6.30pm daily), and the 14th-century Castello Oldofredi, which is now the town library.

THE ISLAND

The ferry (*see p221*) from Sulzano to **Peschiera Maraglio** on **Monte Isola** only takes a few minutes, but carries visitors to a very different world. There are no cars, and the paths up and down the mountain are filled with the most unfamiliar sounds of silence. Besides Peschiera Maraglio, the island is home to a number of other small villages. Thanks to the microclimate, olives grow at **Sensole**, at the south-western corner of the island. Along the western coast, **Menzino**, **Sanchignano** and **Siviano** each keeps at least one foot firmly planted in the past. And at the top of the mountain, the Madonna della Ceriola sanctuary (open access) offers unparalleled views of the lake. Bicycles can be rented near the ferry dock from Easter to September (information 030 982 5228/ 5144): two wheels and a picnic lunch make a wonderful way of passing a summer's day.

Where to eat & stay

In Iseo, **Il Volto** does a wonderful blend of haute cuisine and lake comfort food (via Mirolte 33, 030 981 462, closed Wed & Thur lunch, average €40). The **Relais Mirabella** (via Mirabella 34, Iseo, 030 989 8051, www.relaismirabella.it, closed Jan-mid Mar, double room €115) is a new hotel with lake views.

Getting there

By car
From Bergamo, take the A4 towards Brescia; exit at Grumello del Monte and follow signs for Lago d'Iseo.

By bus
From Bergamo, SAB (035 289 011/sab@sab-autoservizi.it) runs frequent services to Lovere and Sarnico.

By train
From Bergamo, take the Brescia train and change at Palazzolo; 6 trains a day run each way between Palazzolo and the Paratico line (summer only). Brescia–Iseo trains leave regularly from Brescia's Stazione Centrale.

Getting around

By boat
The ferry (information 035 971 483/www.navigazionelaghi.it) from Sulzano to Peschiera Maraglio costs €2.80 round-trip; from Iseo to Peschiera costs €4.10 round-trip.

Tourist information

APT Bresciano
Lungolago Marconi 2C, Iseo (030 980 209/fax 030 981 361/www.bresciaholiday.com). **Open** *Oct-Easter* 9am-12.30pm, 3-6pm Mon-Fri; 9am-12.30pm Sat. *Easter-Sept* 9am-12.30pm, 3-6pm Mon-Fri; 9am-12.30pm, 3-6pm Sat; 9am-12.30am Sun.

Lago di Endine

A few kilometres to the west of Lago d'Iseo, unspoilt Lake Endine mirrors woods and far-off mountains. Small (only 2.3 square kilometres, one square mile), the lake has migrating birds, good fishing and picturesque **San Felice al Lago**, with its parish church looking out over the lake. Down the road, **Monasterolo del Castello** is another small lakefront *borgo* with two small *piazzette*.

Across from Monasterolo, **Bianzano** sits some 300 metres (1,000 feet) above the lake. Here, the Castello Suardo (information 035 210 204, reservations 039 380 374, open July & Aug 5.30-6.30pm Thur & Sat, otherwise by appointment) guards the road to **Clusone** in Val Seriana. Built in the 13th or 14th century, the castle was one of the few in Val Cavallina to survive the Venetian policy of dismantlement, and it remains one of the best preserved in Bergamo province. Nearby, **Ranzanico**'s medieval tower was part of the town's fortifications; in the parish church (open 8.30am-6pm daily) are two paintings by Palma il Giovane. The road back down to the lakeside offers idyllic views; if you're sightseeing by car, be prepared to pull over... locals have little patience with slow-moving tourists.

Getting there

By car
Take the SS42 from Bergamo.

By bus
SAB (035 289 011/sab@sab-autoservizi.it) runs services from piazza Marconi in Bergamo.

Tourist information

Contact the APT in Bergamo (*see p222*).

Tourist information

APT
Viale Vittorio Emanuele 20 (035 210 204/fax 035 230 184/www.apt.bergamo.it). **Open** 9am-12.30pm, 2-5.30pm Mon-Fri.

Ufficio IAT
Vicolo Aquila Nera 2 (035 242 226/fax 035 242 994). **Open** 9am-12.30pm, 2-5.30pm daily.

Around Bergamo

The province of Bergamo offers a little of everything. There are the valleys and mountains of the **Alpi Orobie**, the plains between the Adda and Oglio rivers, and the waters of lakes **Endine** and **Iseo** (for both, *see p220* **Little lakes**). Most of all, the province offers a sense of timelessness. Not only in the sense that history has been preserved – though the intactness of the medieval *borghi* (hamlets) and art collections in obscure churches bears witness to that – but in the sense of things being much the same as they always were. Notwithstanding satellite dishes and BMWs, a twilight stroll through any valley hamlet will give you the definite feeling that nothing – or at least nothing important – has changed. And, indeed, that nothing needs to.

Getting there from Bergamo

By car
See individual destinations for routes.

By bus
All destinations covered in this section can be reached by SAB buses (information 035 289 011) that depart from the bus terminus in piazza Marconi.

By train
Trains are singularly un-useful for travel around Bergamo: if you're using public transport, opt for a bus.

Valle Brembana

The mouth of Valle Brembana, closed and severe, kept the valley isolated until the 16th century. Even today, with a revamped highway (SS470) designed to speed tourist euros from Milan to the valley's upper reaches, Valle Brembana – which is narrow and lined with domineering crags – retains a sense of aloofness.

By far the most famous name in the Valle Brembana, San Pellegrino is now synonymous with its bottled water, but **San Pellegrino Terme** was known for its waters long before

the current fad: it has been a spa since the 1700s, and enjoyed a spell as a jet-set destination in the early 1900s. Today the abandoned and slightly decrepit remains of the Grand Hotel hulks on the far side of the river, and the old casino is used as a conference centre. But the baths (via Taramelli 2, 0345 22 455, closed Oct-Apr) still offer mud and hot-water treatments in season, the many Liberty-style buildings continue to please the eye, and the main viale Papa Giovanni XXIII still fills with strollers on summer evenings.

A small road on the right just beyond the town of San Giovanni Bianco brings you to **Camerata Cornello**, the home of the Tasso (or Taxis) family, who founded a courier company in the Middle Ages that operated through much of Europe (the plot of Thomas Pynchon's *The Crying of Lot 49* hinged to a large extent on the firm). Today a few people continue to live in the small village – accessible on foot only, about a kilometre (half a mile) from the parking lot – which contains the ruins of the Tassos' ancestral home and a marvellous series of porticoed streets.

Where to eat

In San Pellegrino Terme, the **Ristorante Tirolese** (via de' Medici 3, 0345 22 267, closed Tue and 2wks June or Sept, average €17) offers honest takes on valley cuisine and, when the mood strikes, surprisingly good fish.

Il Papa Buono

No one is more important to the *bergamaschi* than Angelo Giuseppe Roncalli, the second Pope John the 23rd (the first was a 15th-century anti-pope, never recognised by Rome), who was born in the small peasant community of Sotto il Monte in 1881. Though only pope for five years (1958-63), *Il Papa Buono* (the good pope) gave the Catholic Church a much-needed shake, launching it into the modern world through his master work, the Second Vatican Council: the complacent hierarchy was revamped and vernacular replaced Latin as the language of mass, among other innovations.

The *bergamasco* penchant for preservation extended to his corpse as well, which was found in surprisingly good shape when it was exhumed at the time of his beatification in September 2000.

The **funicular** links uptown and downtown Bergamo. *See p216.*

Getting there from Bergamo

By car
The SS470 follows the valley.

Tourist information

IAT
Viale Papa Giovanni XXIII 18, San Pellegrino Terme (0345 23 344). **Open** *June-Sept* 9.30am-12.30pm, 3-5pm daily. *Oct-May* 9.30am-12.30pm, 3-5pm Mon-Wed, Fri-Sun.

Valle Imagna

Almenno San Bartolomeo offers one of the jewels of Bergamo province, **San Tomé** (via San Tomé, open 2-4pm Sun), a romanesque church dating from the 11th century. Circular and utterly simple, San Tomé continues to offer a sense of tranquillity some 900 years after its construction.

Further up the valley, the **Fonte della Salute** (in the hotel Villa delle Ortensie; *see p223*) in **Sant'Omobono** (St Good Man) provides mud therapy and a number of other spa treatments in a discreet, pine-scented setting.

Where to eat & stay

Sant'Omobono offers fine dining with an interesting mix of tradition and exploration at **Posta di Frosio** (via Vittorio Veneto 169, 035 851 1341, closed Tue and 2wks July, average €40). Also in Sant'Omobono, **Villa delle Ortensie** (viale alla Fonte 117, 035 851 114, www.villaortensie.com, closed mid Jan-Feb. double room €75) is an elegant hotel attached to the spa with plenty of late-1800s charm and personal attention.

Getting there from Bergamo

By car
Take the SS471; at Almè, fork left for Valle Imagna.

Tourist information

Pro Loco
Viale Vittorio Veneto 99, Sant'Omobono Imagna (035 852 457). **Open** 9.30am-12.30pm Mon-Fri.

West of Bergamo

If it weren't for Pope John XXIII (*see p222* **Il Papa Buono**) the small farming community of **Sotto il Monte** would still be an obscure hamlet in the *bergamasco* foothills. Pilgrims flock, however, to the **casa natale**, the house where Angelo Roncalli was born (open 8.30am-5.30pm daily) and to his summer residence, which is now a museum (open 8.30-11.30am, 2.30-6.30pm daily).

In the hills above Sotto il Monte, the beautiful **abbazia di Fontanella** (in frazione di Fontanella), with its romanesque church and sarcophagus-filled cortile, offers another reason to visit.

Getting there from Bergamo

By car
Take the SS342; at Ponte San Pietro, take SP166 for Sotto il Monte.

Tourist information

Pro Loco
Via Privata Bernasconi 7 (035 792 922). **Open** 9.30am-12.30pm Mon-Fri.

Lorenzo Lotto

Why would an artist who came from culturally renowned Venice and had painted for the pope in Rome spend many of his most productive years in provincial Bergamo? When Lorenzo Lotto (c1480-1557) arrived in Bergamo he was already 30 years old, and had been on the road for years. But while he had made something of a name for himself (he was already referred to as a *pictor celeberrimus* in 1505), he had never found a stable audience.

And so he followed commissions from town to town. In fact, it was a commission from Bartolomeo Colleoni (*see p216*) that brought Lotto to Bergamo in 1513. In all, Lotto spent 13 years in and around the city, painting not only religious works but portraits of important

merchants and their families. The works are obsessively detailed, but therein lies his symbolism. In the portrait of Lucina Brembatti (in the **Accademia Carrara**; *see p218*), for example, the sitter's character is found in her stole, and her identity in a puzzle located in the upper left-hand corner. With Lotto, it always pays to look twice.

Works by Lotto can also be seen in the churches of **San Michele al Pozzo Bianco** (*see p217*); **Santa Maria Maggiore** (*see p217*); **San Bartolomeo** (*Madonna col Bambino e santi*; on the pedestrianised Sentierone); **Sant'Alessandro in Colonna** (a *Deposition*; via San Alessandro 34); and **Sant'Alessandro della Croce** (a *Trinity*; via Masone 23).

Brescia & Around

Wealthy industrial Brescia has an ancient Roman heart.

The **Castello** towers above Brescia's ancient centre.

Map p229.

Industrial Brescia, Lombardy's second-largest city, can – at first sight – appear distinctly unprepossessing. But get past its steel, arms and precision tool factories and Brescia's well-hidden gems reveal themselves. As does the city's enormous wealth, evident in its luxury shops and excellent restaurants.

The province of Brescia holds further attractions: as well as lakes **Garda** (*see p206*), **Iseo** (*see p219* **Little Lakes**) and **Idro**, there are **Val Trompia** and **Val Sabbia**, both with excellent skiing and hiking, and some excellent wine is produced in splendid **Franciacorta**.

Brescia

The Roman colony of Brixia was established on the site of a Gallic settlement in 89 BC. The city was one of the 36 northern Italian duchies under Lombard rule from the sixth to eighth centuries, and joined the Milan-led Lega Lombarda (*see p24*) in the 11th century to liberate itself from the yoke of the Holy Roman Empire. By the 15th century, however, it had fallen to the Venetians, and remained under their control for 350 years; during this period it

was endowed with the usual plethora of Venetian-style *palazzi* on which the lion of St Mark – the symbol of Venice – is proprietorially much in evidence.

Sightseeing

Roman Brixia extended in grid form around what is now via dei Musei (the *decumanus maximus*) and via Gallo (the *cardus*). At the junction of these two streets stood the forum, built AD 69-96. Buried until the early 19th century, the ruins of the **Tempio Capitolino** and **Teatro Romano** that surrounded the forum have since been brought to light: the towering columns of the temple give some idea of the building's former splendour. In piazzetta Labus, to the south of piazza del Foro, the building at No.3 has parts of the ancient curia or basilica incorporated into its façade.

Towering above the forum on Colle (hill) Cidneo – site of Bronze Age settlements – the massive **Castello** (open 8am-8pm daily) is a mainly 16th-century construction containing elements from previous centuries. The view over Brescia and the surrounding countryside is striking. Inside the castle are a history museum and the **Civico Museo delle Armi Luigi**

Marzoli (open Oct-May 9.30am-1pm, 2.30-5pm Tue-Sun, June-Sept 10am-5pm Tue-Sun, admission €2.50), which pays tribute to the area's flourishing arms industry with a collection of 1,000 weapons dating from the 15th to 18th centuries.

East of the forum along the via dei Musei, the **Monastero San Salvatore** complex was begun in the eighth century. It now houses the **Museo della Città**.

West from the forum, via dei Musei opens out into piazza Paolo VI (formerly piazza del Duomo and still referred to as such), a medieval square where all the symbols of religious and political power are concentrated. The **Broletto** has housed town council offices since its completion at the end of the 13th century. Next door, the Duomo Vecchio – better known as **La Rotonda** – is an 11th-century structure built over a paleo-Christian church; it stands well below the current piazza at the level of the Roman road that passed here. The **Duomo Nuovo** is a 'recent' 17th-century addition.

Via Beccaria leads to piazza dell'Loggia, a magnificent example of Renaissance town planning dominated by the **Loggia** itself, a quintessentially Venetian structure built between 1492 and 1574. The Venetian influence is equally visible in the Monte di Pietà, a two-part palazzo joined by an arch and constructed between 1484 (Monte Vecchio, on the right) and 1600 (Monte Nuovo, on the left). The collection of Roman epigraphs set into the façade of the

Very Venetian **piazza della Loggia**.

Monte Vecchio in 1485 may have been Italy's first ever municipal archeological collection. Opposite the Loggia, the **Torre dell'Orologio** (clock tower) is a mid 16th-century structure with a clock dating from the same era. The memorial next to the fountain in front of the clocktower honours the victims of a terrorist bombing that took place here on 28 May 1974. Eight people died when the explosive device went off during a trade union demonstration.

The city expanded into the area north and west of piazza della Loggia in the late 12th century, when new walls were built to take account of the town's growing population. The **Torre di Palata** (1248) at the junction of via della Pace and corso Garibaldi was part of these fortifications.

Across via dei Musei from the piazza, the convent attached to the church of **San Giuseppe** (vicolo San Giuseppe, open 6-11am, 3-5.45pm Mon-Sat, 6-11am Sun) houses a small **Museo Diocesano di Arte Sacra** (via Gasparo di Salò 13, open 10am-noon, 3-6pm daily, admission €3) with artefacts and vestments from churches around the city. Further west, **San Giovanni Evangelista** (contrada San Giovanni, open 7-11am, 4-6.30pm daily) is a 16th-century church built over a fourth-century one, with some Romanesque touches in its pretty cloister.

Moving south from piazza della Loggia, the contrast with piazza della Vittoria couldn't be more striking. A swathe of ancient Brescia was razed to allow space for Marcello Piacentini, darling of the inter-war Fascist regime, to let rip with this strong-but-sterile glorification of the second Roman Empire that was believed to be at hand. The **Palazzo delle Poste** (main post office) is a veritable extravaganza.

In the mid 13th century, still greater population growth meant Brescia's walls had to be extended again; though the fortifications were torn down from 1875, the shape of the walls is clearly visible on a map (they follow via XX Settembre, via Fratelli Ugoni, via Leonardo da Vinci, via Pusterla, via Turati, and so on).

Piazza del Mercato, a 16th-century reconstruction, marked the southern extent of the earlier medieval walls; it is dominated by the Venetian baroque **Palazzo Martinengo Villagana** (No.13). To the south-west, on corso Martiri della Libertà, stands **Santa Maria dei Miracoli** (open 6am-noon, 3-6pm Mon-Sat), with its richly decorated Renaissance façade. A detour to the right along vicolo San Nicola before reaching Santa Maria dei Miracoli leads to **San Francesco d'Assisi** (church open 7-11.30am, 3-6pm daily, large cloister open 8am-noon, 2.30-6.30pm Mon-Sat), a splendid Romanesque-Gothic church of the 13th century.

Piazza della Vittoria. See p226.

Of the 13th- to 15th-century frescos that once covered the whole church, those on the right wall of the nave survive; the smaller of the church's two cloisters has 13th-century frescos. Two streets beyond Santa Maria, turn left for the 15th-century church of **Santi Nazaro e Celso** (open 2-4pm daily or by appointment, phone 0303 754 387), where the Averoldi polyptich (commissioned by a member of the Averoldi family, 1522) is by a young and inexperienced Titian.

Corso Zanardelli – Brescia's chicest shopping boulevard – runs east out of piazza del Mercato, changing its name to corso Magenta further along, and following the line of the first set of medieval walls. Designer boutiques cluster beneath porticos built in bits and bobs up until the late 18th century. On corso Zanardelli, the plush **Teatro Grande** (box office and information via Paganora 19A, 0302 979 333) was built in 1739, refitted by Luigi Canonica in 1811, and underwent further redecoration in 1862-3; it is home to an international piano festival held each spring.

South off corso Magenta, via Crispi leads to the **Pinacoteca Civica Tosio Martinengo**. At the eastern end of corso Magenta stands **Sant'Afra** in **Sant'Eufemia** (open 7-11am, 4-7pm Mon-Sat, 7.30am-1pm, 3.30-7pm Sun), where an 18th-century church conceals a 15th-century crypt. In the first chapel on the left are a *Martyrdom of St Afra* by Veronese and other works by Palma il Giovane.

Broletto

Piazza Paolo VI (030 2977 7300). **Open** 8.30am-1.30pm Mon-Fri; 8.30am-12.15pm Sat.
The Broletto, a Romanesque-Gothic building, was built in the 12th century as the seat of the local government. There's a 17th-century fountain at the centre of its pretty coat-of-arms-filled courtyard. The 12th-century Torre del Popolo towers above the building. Now the local records office, you can wander in while it's open for business.

Duomo Nuovo

Piazza Paolo VI (030 42 714). **Open** 7.30am-noon, 4-7.30pm Mon-Sat; 8am-1pm, 4-7.30pm Sun.
The Duomo was built between the 17th and early 19th centuries on the site of a paleo-Christian basilica. The Greek-cross interior houses a very Venetian-looking *Arc of SS Apollonio and Filastrio* (1510; third chapel on the right), and, over the altar, a copy of Titian's dramatic *Assumption of the Virgin* by Giacinto Zoboli (1733).

Duomo Vecchio – La Rotonda

Piazza Paolo VI. **Open** *Apr-Oct* 9am-noon, 3-7pm Tue-Sun. *Nov-Mar* 9am-noon, 3-6pm Sat, Sun.
The Duomo Vecchio is an 11th-century structure built over the sixth-century church of Santa Maria Maggiore (it's built at the same level, well below the modern road). Locals call it La Rotonda for obvious reasons. In the vast, stark interior, stairs lead up to a circular ambulatory, at the far end of which is a sarcophagus in red Verona marble with sculptures by *maestri campionesi* of Bishop Berardo Maggi (d1308). Central sections of the ambulatory floor contain mosaics from the sixth-century church. Also from the ambulatory, more stairs lead down into the ninth- to 11th-century crypt of San Filastrio, with columns taken from Roman ruins, and some remains of Byzantine frescos. Over the high altar is an *Assumption* (1526) by Moretto da Brescia.

La Loggia

Piazza della Loggia 1 (030 297 7300). **Open** 7am-8pm Mon-Fri; 7am-1pm Sat.
Begun in 1492 but not completed until 1574, the imposing Loggia, with its ground-floor porticos, dominates the city centre. Many leading architects – including Jacopo Sansovino and Andrea Palladio – had a hand in the ever-changing blueprint, though Lodovico Beretta was probably responsible for its final shape. The ship's-hull-shaped cupola was added in 1914 after the removal of an attic floor that had been added in 1769 by Luigi Vanvitelli. The upper octagonal room – named after Vanvitelli – has a striking wooden ceiling. The Loggia now houses city council offices.

Monastero San Salvatore & Museo della Città

Via dei Musei 81B (0302 977 834/www.asm.brescia.it/musei). **Open** *Oct-Mar* 9.30am-5pm Tue-Sun. *Apr-July* 9am-7pm Tue-Thur, Sat, Sun; 9am-9pm Fri. *Aug, Sept* 10am-8pm Tue-Thur, Sat, Sun; 10am-10pm Fri. **Admission** €5.10. **No credit cards**.
This huge Benedictine monastery complex was begun in 753 by Queen Ansa, wife of Lombard King Desiderius. Besides the monastery of San Salvatore itself, the complex includes the churches of San Salvatore, Santa Giulia and Santa Maria in Solario.

The monastery proper houses the Museo della Città (museum of the city), a superbly curated museum documenting Brescia's history and pre-history from the Bronze Age, through the Romans (digs in the Tempio Capitolino, *see p228*, and forum area yielded up many treasures) and the Lombards, to Venetian rule. Among the Roman works, note the Winged Victory, a first-century AD bronze statue that was originally gilded.

Across the courtyard, the basilica of San Salvatore is one of Lombardy's most stunning medieval churches. Built by Desiderius and overhauled in the ninth century, its three-naved interior contains columns dating from the sixth century and sections of ninth-century fresco in the central aisle. There are more frescos – dating from the eight and ninth centuries – in the exquisite crypt that was built in 762-763 to house the relics of St Julia and other martyrs.

The church of Santa Giulia, which is attached to San Salvatore, is used as an exhibition space.

The church of Santa Maria in Solario – perhaps named after the pre-Christian altar to the sun god incorporated into the church's lower room – was built in the 12th century. The upstairs oratory is a riot of wall-to-wall 16th-century frescos by local artist Floriano Ferramola and his workshop. The late eighth-century Cross of Desiderius, inlaid with gems and cameos, is housed here, with other pieces from the monastery's treasury.

Pinacoteca Civica Tosio Martinengo

Piazza Moretto 4 (0303 774 999). **Open** *Oct-May* 9.30am-1pm, 2.30-5pm Tue-Sun. *June-Sept* 10am-5pm Tue-Sun. **Admission** €2.50. **No credit cards**.

Housed in a 15th-century palazzo, this *pinacoteca* (art gallery) contains works of the Renaissance and after. In Room II are a Christ (1505) and the head of an angel (1501) by Raphael and important works by François Clouet. In Room IV are four saints by Paolo Veneziano (1350-60). There's a *Shepherds in*

Cross of Desiderius.

Adoration (1518) by Lorenzo Lotto (*see p224* **Lorenzo Lotto**) in Room IX. Elsewhere, Lombard artists, including Vincenzo Foppo, Moretto da Brescia and Romanino, prevail.

Tempio Capitolino & Teatro Romano

Via dei Musei 57A (030 297 7834).

The Capitoline temple was built under Emperor Vespasian in AD 73 but left to crumble and gradually concealed by landslides from Colle Cidneo above. Digs began in 1835 to uncover the temple; some areas of the complex were dug out and reconstructed – not entirely faithfully – in the 1930s. The *pronao* (steps) and 11m (36ft) columns of the temple convey an idea of the area's former grandeur. To the left of the temple, the theatre has been excavated only in part. Much of it was incorporated into the Renaissance Palazzo Gambara, now semi-abandoned. As this guide went to press the complex was closed indefinitely for excavations. The ruins are visible from outside and important works have been moved to the Museo della Città (*see p227*).

Where to eat

The romantic **Vasco da Gama** (via dei Musei 4, 030 375 4039, closed Tue and 2wks Sept, average €30) serves Brescian specialities such as *casonei* (ravioli) and game, while **La Sosta** (via San Martino della Battaglia 20, 030 295 603, closed dinner Sun, all Mon, 3wks Aug & 1wk Jan, average €40) offers classic local cuisine in a more stately ambience as befits its palazzo location. What the **Trattoria al Frate** (via dei Musei 25, 030 377 0550, closed Mon and 3wks Aug, average €30) lacks in atmosphere it makes up for with great renditions of local treats. The **Trattoria Mezzeria** (via Trieste 66, 030 40 306, closed Sun, July & Aug, average €25) serves great home cooking at fair prices. At **Il Pentalaccio** (via Paganora 6A, 030 292 454, closed Tue, average €15) you'll have to brave clouds of cigarette smoke to enjoy delicious pasta and a fine choice of wine.

Where to stay

The five-star, art nouveau **Vittoria** (via X Giornate 20, 030 280 061, www.hotelvittoria. com, double room €217) is the only top-notch hotel in the centre. The **Park Hotel Ca' Noa** (via Triumplina 66, 030 398 762, double room €134.29) is more modern and has a highly regarded restaurant (average €30) attached. Located near the station, the **Jolly Hotel** (viale Stazione 15, 030 44 221, www.jollyhotels.it, double room €145-€181) is anonymous but convenient; the **Hotel Cristallo** (viale Stazione 12A, 030 377 2468, closed 2wks Jan, double room €103) is a cheaper option in the same area.

Brescia

Essentials

Getting there

By car

Take the A4 Milan–Venice motorway and exit at
Brescia Ovest or Brescia Centro.

By train

Brescia is on the main Milan–Venice line. Fast
Intercity and/or Eurostar trains run approximately
once an hr.

By bus

SIA (030 44 061) runs infrequent services from
Milan's piazza Castello.

Getting around

The centre of Brescia is small enough to
negotiate on foot. Alternatively, Brescia
Trasporti (030 355 3700, www.asm.brescia.it)
runs an efficient service (tickets valid for 1hr
cost 85¢ and should be bought from *tabacchi*
shops or newsstands before boarding). Linea C
runs from the station to via Zanardelli. Or grab
one of the bicycles provided free by the city
council at car parks, including the ones in via
Ugoni, and via L Gambara by the Palagiustizia
(law courts).

Tourist information

APT

*Corso Zanardelli 34 (030 43 418/fax 030 293 284/
www.bresciaholiday.com).* **Open** 9am-12.30pm, 3-6pm
Mon-Fri; 9am-12.30pm Sat.

Servizio Turismo
Comune di Brescia

*Piazza della Loggia 6 (030 377 3773/www.comune.
brescia.it/musei).* **Open** *Apr-Sept* 9.30am-6.30pm
Mon-Sat. *Oct-Mar* 9.30am-12.30pm, 2-5pm Mon-Fri;
9am-12.30pm Sat.

Trips Out of Town

Around Brescia

North from Brescia

For Brescia province's most northerly area, the Valcamonica, *see chapter* **The Mountains**. For the area along the shores of Lake Iseo, *see p219* **Little Lakes**. For the area along the shores of Lake Garda, *see chapter* **Lago di Garda**.

The area north of Brescia is a land of contrasts, with glorious countryside and soaring mountains alternating with ugly heavy industry. The locals have a reputation for being hard-working folk, who can turn their hand to traditional crafts and cheese-making, as well as precision instruments manufacturing.

In an area of high per capita income, the wealthy and not-so-wealthy share a consuming passion for hunting, perhaps tied up with the area's historic industry. Locals in their thousands converge on the **Val Trompia** each weekend in the hunting season to wreak carnage on the valley's fauna.

The town of **Gardone Valtrompia** has been famous for its weapons for over 500 years: the Beretta firm has its headquarters here. East of Gardone, **Lumezzane** puts its steel to more peaceful purposes: cutlery and saucepans.

Further still up the valley, the little resort town of **Bòvegno** is a great base for hiking; for a relatively easy jaunt, limit yourself to climbing Colle San Martino for a look at theruins of the castle and Romanesque-Gothic chapel (always open) at its summit. For more strenuous treks, try Monte Muffetto, Monte Ario or Colmo di Marcuolo. There's some skiing in Bòvegno, but even more at **Collio**, which was once an iron- and silver-mining town.

To the east of Val Trompia, **Val Sabbia** runs from Brescia to little Lake Idro and beyond. Marquetry was the traditional industry of this less bellicose area, as beautiful and intricate intarsio work in the little churches along the valley show.

At 370 metres (1,233 feet), **Lago di Idro** is one of Lombardy's highest bodies of water. Less well known than its larger counterparts, the lake has fewer tourist facilities and less pollution. The towns of **Idro** on the eastern and **Anfo** on the western shore are popular for sailing and windsurfing… and swimming if you can take the cold. Above Anfo looms the Rocca D'Anfo (closed to the public), a fortress built in 1450 and rebuilt on numerous occasions, including in 1796 by the French to keep the Austro-Hungarians on the other side of the border marked by the lake. North west of the lake, the rural hamlet-cum-resort of **Bagolino** (altitude 800 metres, 2,667 feet) is famous for its rambunctious carnival: on each Monday and

Tempio Capitolino. *See p228.*

Tuesday from 6 January to Ash Wednesday anyone dressed up as an elderly peasant can play tricks on anyone who isn't… and they do.

Getting there from Brescia

By car
The SS345 from Brescia runs the length of Val Trompia. The SS237 from Brescia follows the Val Sabbia.

By bus
SIA (030 44 061) operates buses for Val Trompia and Val Sabbia every 30mins from via Stazione.

Tourist information

Pro Loco
Via Trento 25, Idro (0365 83 224). **Open** *Oct-May* 9am-12.30pm Mon-Sat. *June-Sept* 9.30am-12.30pm, 3-5pm Mon-Sat.

Franciacorta

Between Brescia and Lago Iseo, the rich Franciacorta area has become famous for more than its churches and cuisine. In the 1960s the Berlucchi wine producer shook up the area's lacklustre grape-growing sector, making a much-praised *spumante* (sparkling wine). Other producers rose to the challenge (*see p231* **The wines of Francia corte**).

The Cluniac **Abbazia Olivetana di San Nicola** (via Brescia 83, 030 610 182, church always open, phone ahead for guided tours at weekends) on the outskirts of **Rodengo-Saiano** was recorded in documents in the 11th century, though its church was built in the late 15th century. The complex is constructed around three lovely cloisters, the oldest of which has Gothic capitals to its columns. The wine-making centre of **Erbusco** is Franciacorta's capital. It has a quaint medieval sector along via Castello and a two-Michelin-starred restaurant, the modestly named Gualtiero Marchese, where G Marchese himself – guru of Italy's new gastronomic age – holds court, serving up his own, very particular, takes on local specialities (*see p36* **Food heaven**).

Pretty medieval **Capriolo** is home to the **Museo Agricolo e del Vino Ricci Curbastro**, with tools and equipment used in wine-making. There's another 11th-century Cluniac foundation, the monastery of **San Pietro in Lamosa** (open May-Sept 9am-noon, 2.30-6pm daily, Oct-Apr 9am-noon, 2.30-6pm Mon-Sat), in Provaglio d'Iseo.

Museo Agricolo e del Vino Ricci Curbastro

Villa Evelina, via Adro 3, Capriolo (030 736 094/www.riccicurbastro.com). **Open** 8am-noon, 2-6pm daily. **Cellar visit/wine tasting** €4.50. **Credit** MC, V.
The friendly Ricci Curbastro family also has seven apartments available for rent, costing from €45 for two per night.

Getting there

By car
Exit the A4 motorway at either Palazzolo sull'Oglio, Rovato or Ospitaletto.

By bus
SIA (030 44 061) runs services approximately hourly between Brescia and Erbusco.

Tourist information

See p229.

The wines of Franciacorta

Vines have been grown for centuries in this exceptional territory, with east- and west-facing hills, great drainage and a lake nearby to soften any climactic extremes. **Cabernet Franc**, **Cabernet Sauvignon**, **Barbera**, **Nebbiolo** and **Merlot** varieties have long clothed the hillsides and are used in the DOC Terre di Franciacorta vintages – the classic still reds and whites of the area. But in 1995, with the focus having shifted resoundingly to bubbly, the efficiently organised Consorzio per la Tutela del Franciacorta gave its 170-odd members rigid new production rules, and obtained a DOCG Franciacorta appellation for its *spumanti*. **Pinot bianco**, **Pinot nero** and **Chardonnay** grapes go into the sparkling brew, which has to remain in the bottle for 25 months, 18 of which must be spent in contact with yeast. Franciacorta produces some 7,500,000 bottles of wine a year, half of which is sparkling.

All Italian producers sell direct to the visiting public, who are not obliged to buy after touring the cellars but rarely (out of politeness) leave completely empty-handed. If you'd prefer the wine without the tour, try the shop below:

Cantine di Franciacorta
via Iseo 56, Erbusco (030 775 1116/ www.cantinefranciacorta.com). **Open** 9.30am-1pm, 2.30-7pm Mon, Wed-Sun. **Credit** AmEx, DC, MC, V.

The producers

Bellavista
Via Bellavista 5, Erbusco (030 776 2000/ 030 776 0761). **Open** 9am-noon, 2-6pm Mon-Fri. **Credit** AmEx, DC, MC, V.

Ca' del Bosco
Via Case Sparse 20, Erbusco (030 776 6111/www.cadelbosco.it). **Open** by appointment only. **Credit** AmEx DC, MC, V. Wines from here can also be bought at Cantine di Franciacorta (*see above*).

Fratelli Berlucchi
Via Broletto 2, Borgonato di Cortefranca (030 984 451/www.berlucchi.it). **Open** 8.30am-5.30pm Mon-Fri. **Credit** DC, MC, V. Phone ahead to arrange tours of the cellars.

Trips Out of Town

Mantova & Around

Visionary rulers and pumpkin-filled *tortelli*.

Nestling in the south-eastern corner of Lombardy, Mantova (Mantua) province was for long an independent duchy under the control of the Gonzaga family, whose power and patronage turned their fortified capital into one of Italy's great Renaissance cities. To this day Mantovans feel little affinity for their regional capital, Milan. Distance and a spirit of individualism nurtured some curious outbreaks of regional autarchy, as at **Sabbioneta** (*see p239* **Little Athens**) – a sleepy village that became, for the lifetime of a single visionary prince, a new Athens.

Elsewhere, though, it is the Po, northern Italy's old man river, that dominates the scene, determining the climate (cold and foggy in winter, hot and sticky in summer), the flat landscape and also the area's agricultural vocation, which revolves around the cultivation of rice and pumpkins.

Politically, the province has long been one of the reddest in Lombardy, but it is also a centre of support for Umberto Bossi's right-wing regionalist Northern League (*see p24* **Northern League**).

Art and architecture aside, one of the main reasons to make the time-consuming detour here is to eat. Mantovan cuisine is complex and refined, with sweet-and-sour flavours predominating in its flagship pasta dish, *tortelli di zucca* (pasta filled with pumpkin).

Mantova

Though a small piece in the patchwork of medieval and Renaissance Italy, the Duchy of Mantova enjoyed three centuries of unbroken prosperity and freedom between 1328 and 1629. Some of this had to do with the canny diplomacy of the city's ruling Gonzaga family, traditionally allied with the Holy Roman Emperor (*see p10* **Popes & Emperors**), yet careful to keep on the right side of the papacy. The city's position helped: halfway between Milan and Venice, it acted as a mutually respected buffer zone between these two northern Italian giants. Successive dukes of Mantova – notably Gianfrancesco II (1484-1519) and his son Federico II (1500-40) – won

Piazza della Erbe. *See p234.*

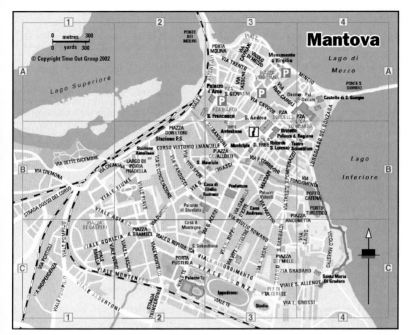

reputations as military commanders: in fact, after agriculture, soldiering was the leading Mantovan export for many years.

The good years came to an end in 1630, when the city was sacked by Habsburg troops; a minor branch of the Gonzagas presided over a depopulated, plague-ridden shadow of the former duchy until the Austrians put an end to their misery in 1707.

The *centro storico* of Mantova offers a unified example of medieval to Renaissance urban planning. The ruling Gonzaga clan dictated every aspect of the city's life and growth, hiring the best artists and architects. Gonzaga patronage began in earnest under Gianfrancesco I (ruled 1404-44): Pisanello painted chivalric frescos inside Palazzo Ducale; educational theorist Vittorino da Feltre set up a school in the city where ducal heirs mixed with the plebs. Ludovico III (1444-78) was one of his pupils; immersed in the new humanist culture, he invited artist Andrea Mantegna and architect Leon Battista Alberti to make Mantova a city worthy of a scholar-prince. Ludovico's son, Gianfrancesco II, was more into war than art; he left the latter to his wife, Isabella d'Este, whose court sparkled with creativity. But by this time Gonzaga patronage had become more inward-looking, more of a family affair: nowhere was

this more evident than in the decadent pleasure palace of Palazzo Te, designed and frescoed by mannerist painter Giulio Romano for Duke Federico II in 1524. Later dukes continued the tradition in a minor key. Claudio Monteverdi's *Orfeo*, the first modern opera, was composed for Vincenzo I in 1607.

Today the city has sprawled beyond the now-demolished town walls to the south to occupy the low-lying area that was once a lake, drained in the 18th century. Parts of the centre – especially around the railway station – are blighted by post-war reconstruction, but the nucleus of the medieval and Renaissance city, which centres on the interlinked *piazze* delle Erbe and Sordello, is gloriously intact. To see it at its buzzing, cultural best, come to Mantova at the beginning of September, when the **Festivaletteratura** literary festival comes to town (for dates, consult www.festivaletteratura.it).

Sightseeing

Mantova's *centro storico* occupies a squarish promontory surrounded on three sides by freshwater lakes. Busy roads separate the town from a series of waterside gardens, popular with Sunday cyclists and evening snoggers. The old town expanded from the north-eastern corner of the promontory, and this area – occupied by the **Palazzo Ducale** (*see below*) and a series of interlocking *piazze* – is still the city's civic, commercial and religious hub.

Mantova's two main shopping streets, via Roma and the arcaded corso Umberto I, converge on piazza Mantegna, dominated by the audacious triumphal arch façade of Leon Battista Alberti's basilica of **Sant'Andrea**. Around the corner to the right, charming piazza delle Erbe – site of a Thursday morning market – is surrounded on three sides by Gothic and Renaissance loggias. The castellated 13th-century **Palazzo della Ragione** on the east side ends in the **Torre dell'Orologio** (1473), a tower crowned by a little classical temple. The astrological clock on the façade was designed to tell not just the time, but whether the time was right. Below the tower stands the pretty circular church of **San Lorenzo**, Mantova's oldest.

The 15th-century **Palazzo del Podestà** (governor's palace) divides piazza delle Erbe from tiny piazza Broletto. Here, at the base of the **Torre Civica**, a covered passage leads into the palace's court of honour, dominated by an arcaded late-Gothic external staircase that looks like just the sort of place where Romeo might have dawdled during his exile in Mantova. On the north side of piazza Broletto, via Cavour, and its eastward extension via Accademia, mark the line of the moat that guarded the *civitas vetus* – the original nucleus of the town.

Via Accademia offers a worthwhile diversion in the form of the pretty 18th-century interior of the **Teatro Accademico Bibiena**, near the end of the street on the right. From piazza Broletto, an archway leads into the vast cobbled expanse of piazza Sordello, the result of a huge clearance of the medieval town, carried out by the Gonzagas in the 13th and 14th centuries. To the right is the forbidding castellated façade of **Palazzo Ducale**, where the Gonzagas slept, ate, partied and wove intricate diplomatic webs. Opposite, **Palazzo Castiglioni** was probably built by the Gonzagas before their rise to power. The north end of the square is closed off by Mantova's fiddly baroque **Duomo**, officially known as the cattedrale di San Pietro. On the corner with vicolo Gallo is a 15th-century house known as the **Casa del Rigoletto** – not

Palazzo Ducale

A city within the city, the vast, sprawling Gonzaga power base takes up two-thirds of the area occupied by Roman and early medieval Mantova. When the Gonzagas took over from the Bonacolsi clan in 1328, they also inherited the fortified palazzo that the Bonacolsis had built on this site in the 1290s. This 'Corte Vecchia' formed the nucleus of the Gonzagas' diplomatic and residential headquarters, which mushroomed over the next four centuries to include gardens, galleries, bedrooms, state rooms and private chapels.

Visitors follow a rigid one-way itinerary through around 100 of the palace's 500 rooms. The first big treat comes almost immediately, in the Sala del Pisanello. Long thought lost, Pisanello's frescos, based on episodes from the courtly epic *Lancelot*, came to light in 1972. Though painted over 500 years ago, around 1442, when the first stirrings of the Renaissance were animating the Mantovan court, their style is deliberately retro-medieval. In some cases, only the sinopia (preparatory drawing in red ochre) remains; but Pisanello's hastily sketched scenes of knights and damsels are just as evocative as the finished frescos.

A series of neo-classical rooms just beyond house a collection of 16th-century Flemish tapestries based on Raphael's cartoons of the Acts of the Apostles. The rococo Sala dei Fiumi looks over a pretty, porticoed hanging garden; in the long, barrel-vaulted Sala degli Specchi (mirror room), composer Claudio Monteverdi organised musical soirées, including the very first opera performances. The Salone degli Arcieri has a pious family portrait (1605) by Rubens, sliced through the middle by Napoleon's kleptomaniac troops. More 16th- and 17th-century art, of varying quality, fills the ducal apartments that follow. Rooms decorated with mythological subjects lead into the long Galleria della Mostra, which overlooks the large, oblong courtyard of the Prato della Mostra. Gods and heroes spill over into the Sala di Troia, frescoed by assistants of Giulio Romano in 1536-9.

Just as all this gilded pomp is beginning to drag, we enter the Gonzaga's austere fortress, the Castello di San Giorgio, erected between 1390 and 1406 but substantially modified by Luca Fancelli in the 1470s, when it became the residence of Ludovico II. A horse-friendly spiral ramp leads up to the first-floor star turn: Andrea Mantegna's frescos in the Camera degli Sposi, painted some time

because Verdi's hero was supposed to have lived here, but because it was once used as a backdrop for open-air stagings of the opera.

The area to the west of piazza Sordello and piazza delle Erbe is full of medieval, Renaissance and baroque houses and *palazzi*, dotted among the more anonymous parts of the urban fabric. From piazza Mantegna, arcaded via Verdi leads past the late 17th-century Palazzo Canossa – home to the descendants of powerful medieval countess Matilda of Canossa – to piazza d'Arco. **Palazzo d'Arco**, which dominates the square, is the only one of the city's aristocratic townhouses that is open to the public – worth a visit for the vivacious 16th-century frescos in the Sala dello Zodiaco. The church of **San Francesco**, just south of here, has some good (though fragmentary) frescos by Tommaso di Modena from the 1370s.

Mantova's other sights lie in the 'third circle', south of the Rio (canal) that formed the boundary of the medieval city. The main north–south axis is via Principe Amedeo and its continuation, via Acerbi, which ends in front of the extravagant mannerist **Palazzo Te**.

Romano's frescos in **Palazzo Te**. *See p236.*

Fun-loving artist Giulio Romano put heart and soul into the construction and decoration of this ducal love-nest; but he also found time to build himself the house that can be seen at via Poma 18. Another, earlier, artist's house stands near the Palazzo Te end of via Acerbi (No.47): the cube-shaped **Casa di Mantegna**, dating from 1496, which may or may not have been designed by Andrea himself. Opposite is Leon Battista Alberti's often-overlooked second Mantovan church, **San Sebastiano**. Its façade was messed around with in 1925, when the two flights of stairs were added; but Alberti's penchant for classical mix-and-match is still evident, with its clutter of doors that run the gamut of architectural history. The Greek cross interior is permanently closed.

Fans of the Romanesque may want to trek out to the mid 13th-century church of **Santa Maria del Gradaro**, in the south-eastern suburbs: a barn-shaped brick structure with a good rose window, it conserves traces of Byzantine frescos, including a charming *Last Supper*.

Duomo
Piazza Sordello (0376 320 220). **Open** 7am-noon, 3-7pm daily.
Behind the rococo façade is an uncharacteristically austere interior designed by Giulio Romano in 1545. The five-nave plan harks back to Rome's early Christian basilicas. Off the left-hand nave is the Cappella dell'Incoronata, an ensemble of stonework and frescos, commissioned by Ludovico II Gonzaga in 1480.

between 1465 and 1474. The episodes depicted on the two frescoed walls took place on 1 January 1462: Ludovico II receives news of the illness of his ally, Francesco Sforza of Milan, then meets his son Francesco, recently created cardinal, while hurrying to Milan to lend his aid. But more than the historical details, it is the unshakeable self-confidence of these Renaissance men (and women) that makes the scenes so compelling. Beyond, the set of rooms occupied by Isabella d'Este after the death of her husband, Gianfrancesco II, are charming enough, but fail to resurrect the spirit of one of Italy's greatest cultural movers and shakers. The paintings by Mantegna, Perugino and others that formerly hung here are now in the Louvre, and all that remains of Isabella's Wunderkammer – the collection of natural curiosities, cameos, medals and antiquities that were displayed in the Grotta – are six intarsia cabinet doors.

Palazzo Ducale
Piazza Sordello (0376 382 150).
Open 9am-6.30pm Tue-Sun (ticket office closes 1hr earlier). **Admission** €6.50; €3.25 concessions. **No credit cards**.

Palazzo d'Arco

Piazza d'Arco 4 (0376 322 242). **Open** *Nov-Feb* 10am-12.30pm Sat, Sun. *Mar-Oct* 10am-12.30pm, 2.30-6pm Tue-Sun. **Admission** €3. **No credit cards**.

The noble d'Arco family had this elegant neo-classical townhouse built in 1782-4. When the last descendant died in 1973, the house became a museum of itself – a provincial aristocratic residence after two generations of minor art collecting and furniture rearrangement. The real treat comes right at the end, when the obligatory guided tour crosses the garden and climbs the stairs of a 15th-century building to enter the Sala dello Zodiaco, its walls covered in lively *trompe-l'oeil* frescos (1509) by Giovanni Maria Falconetto. The scheme is that of a loggia, whose 12 arches open on to allegorical scenes based on the signs of the zodiac; all around, Roman and heraldic motifs run riot on the painted masonry.

Palazzo Te

Viale Te (0376 323 266). **Open** 1-6pm Mon; 9am-6pm Tue-Sun. **Admission** €8; €5.50 concessions. **No credit cards**.

Mannerism is the Renaissance gone decadent; and Palazzo Te is the apotheosis of mannerism. Of course, Giulio Romano's tumbling artistic excess had not a little to do with the function of this pleasure dome: it was, essentially, a love-nest, built for Federico II's mistress, Isabella Boschetti, on a (then) rural site far away from the disapproving eyes of his mum, Isabella d'Este. The name apparently derives from *tejeto*, a place of reed huts; a more fanciful etymology has it punning on the two meanings of *te* in Italian: 'tea' and 'you'.

Romano was one of Raphael's most talented apprentices. In 1524 he relocated from Rome – where a series of erotic prints had almost landed him in jail – to Mantova; a year later he secured this major commission, which would occupy the next ten years of his life. Both architect and artist, he based the whole project on the concept of variety, change, instability. Gods, heroes and transformations are the subjects of the frescos that decorate most of the rooms on the ground floor. Giulio really gets into his stride in the Sala di Psiche, with its scenes of Bacchic revelry, adapted from Apuleius' *Golden Ass*. In the vertiginous Sala dei Giganti, a huddle of hammy Titans cowers amid broken columns from the wrath of Jove. Upstairs is a display of Mesopotamian and Egyptian antiquities. The Palazzo often organises temporary exhibitions.

San Lorenzo

Piazza Erbe (no phone). **Open** 10am-noon, 2.30-4.30pm daily. **Admission** free.

A surviving testimony of early medieval Mantova, the Rotonda is modelled on the Church of the Holy

The mother of all battles

The Battle of Solferino, which took place in the flatlands north of Mantova on 24 June 1859, was one of the main engagements in the war for Italian independence. On one side were the troops of King Vittorio Emanuele II of Sardinia-Piedmont, and those of his French ally, Napoleon III. On the other were the Austrians – up to then uncontested masters of Lombardy and the Veneto – commanded by Emperor Francis Joseph I.

Disorganisation and a lack of clear information about the other side's movements turned what might have been a minor skirmish into one of the bloodiest battles fought anywhere in the world before World War I. Neither the Franco-Italians nor the Austrians had anticipated a full-scale engagement; and both sides were so evenly matched that a victory could only be secured through messy man-to-man combat. By the end of the day, 38,000 men lay dead or severely wounded. Though the French and Italians had won the day – and secured Lombardy for the Kingdom of Savoy – they were too tired even to pursue the retreating Austrians. Shocked by the extent of his losses, Napoleon III soon made peace with Austria, leaving Vittorio Emanuele to fight his own battles.

Another man who was shocked by the bloodshed was Swiss humanitarian Henri Dunant, who happened to be in the nearby town of Castiglione dello Stiviere when the battle broke out. He worked alongside local people to treat the wounded, and the experience – narrated in his pamphlet *Un Souvenir de Solférino* – led to his foundation in 1863 of the world's first volunteer-based, non-aligned relief and medical agency: the International Red Cross. Dunant's work, and the courage of the townspeople, is remembered at **Museo Internazionale della Croce Rossa** in Castiglione dello Stiviere.

In Solferino itself, the **Museo Risorgimentale** – with material on the battle and the movement for Italian independence – is housed in the town's heavily restored 11th-century castle, Rocca Spia d'Italia. Same times and entrance fee apply to the **Ossuario** behind the church of San Pietro, with its rather macabre accumulation of the skulls and bones of thousands of combatants.

Trips Out of Town

Sepulchre in Jerusalem. Built towards the end of the 11th century, it was later swallowed up by Mantova's Jewish ghetto. Inside, an ambulatory supports a matroneum (women's gallery); there are also traces of frescos from the 11th to the 13th centuries.

Sant'Andrea

Piazza Mantegna (0376 328 504). **Open** 7.30am-noon, 3-7pm daily.

This mighty basilica, based on a design by Renaissance wunderkind Leon Battista Alberti, is closer to the heart of most *mantovani* than their official cathedral. In 1470 Ludovico II Gonzaga asked Alberti to design a temple for his family's number one relic: a phial of Christ's blood. Alberti was a visionary architectural theorist who had problems finishing the few real buildings he was asked to design. At least he had a good excuse here: he died two years into the project, and his plan, based on Vitruvius' drawing of an Etruscan temple, was watered down by his successor, Luca Fancelli, and again in 1765, when the baroque dome was added. But the bizarre triumphal arch entrance and the lofty, barrel-vaulted nave are pure Alberti. It's worth wading through the rich, overladen decoration of the interior to find Andrea Mantegna's tomb, in the first chapel on the left, and the Mausoleo Strozzi (1529), in the left transept, whose elegant caryatids were inspired by classical statues in the Gonzaga collection.

North of here is the **torre** (tower) of San Martino della Battaglia, built in 1893 on the site of the battle. If the musty display of battle relics that punctuate the climb to the top don't do it for you, the view across Lake Garda (*see p206*) should compensate.

Museo Internazionale della Croce Rossa

Via Garibaldi 50, Castiglione dello Stiviere (0376 638 505/www.micr.it). **Open** Apr-Sept 9am-noon, 3-6pm Tue-Sun. Oct-Mar 9am-noon, 2-5pm Tue-Sun. **Admission** €1.50.

Museo Risorgimentale

Rocca Spia d'Italia, Solferino (0376 854 068). **Open** Mar-Oct 9am-12.30pm, 2.30-6.30pm Tue-Sun. Nov-Feb 9am-noon, 2-5pm Sat, Sun. **Admission** €1.50.

Torre

Via Torre 2, San Martino della Battaglia (030 991 0370). **Open** Apr-Sept 9am-noon, 2-6.30pm Tue-Sun. Oct-Mar 9am-noon, 2-5.30pm Tue-Sun. **Admission** €3.60.

Teatro Accademico Bibiena

Via Accademia 47 (0376 327 653). **Open** 9.30am-12.30pm, 3-6pm Tue-Sun. **Admission** €2.07; €1.03 concessions. **No credit cards.**

An under-publicised jewel, the Teatro Accademico is one of Europe's most perfect late baroque theatres. In the 18th century, three successive generations of the Bibiena family delighted the courts of Europe with their theatrical set designs, wedding pageants and festive tableaux. Some – such as Antonio Galli Bibiena – also designed more permanent structures, like the present theatre (also known as the Teatro Scientifico), built in 1769. A cadenced curve of arched boxes undulates around the auditorium and continues in an arcade behind the stage. The 14-year-old Mozart played here in 1770, and was enchanted by the backdrop.

Where to eat & drink

Aquila Nigra

Vicolo Bonacolsi 4 (0376 327 180). **Open** noon-2pm, 8-10pm Tue-Sat. Closed 1wk Jan, 3wks Aug. **Average** €50. **Credit** AmEx, DC, MC, V.

In a late Gothic townhouse near the Palazzo Ducale, this is currently Mantova's best, most elegant restaurant. The cuisine – like the decor – combines respect for tradition with a light, creative touch. Game dishes, such as pigeon cooked in honey and balsamic vinegar, or guinea fowl with carrot purée, are a speciality. Also opens for Sunday lunch in April, May, September and October.

Bar Venezia

Piazza Marconi 9/10 (0376 363 499). **Open** 7am-9pm Mon-Sat. **Credit** AmEx, MC, V.

Mantova's most celebrated *caffè letterario* dates from the end of the 18th century. The decor has changed a few times since then, but it still takes its literary vocation seriously, with shelves of books available for browsing – though one should take care not to do this while indulging in the house speciality, *fondu du chocolat*. There are tables outside, and a good range of lunchtime snacks and pizzas on offer.

Buca della Gabbia

Via Cavour 98 (0376 366 901). **Open** 11am-3pm, 6pm-1am Mon-Wed, Fri-Sun. **Average** €14. **Credit** AmEx, DC, MC, V.

For a quick lunch, or simply a glass of wine, head for this cellar winebar that does a range of good salads, *crostini* and cheese or salami selections.

Il Cigno – Trattoria dei Martini

Piazza d'Arco 1 (0376 327 101). **Open** 12.20-1.45pm, 7.30-9.45pm Wed-Sun. Closed Aug, 1wk Jan. **Average** €35. **Credit** AmEx, DC, MC, V.

This place was a trailblazer of new Mantovan cuisine in the 1970s – which is where some of Il Cigno's decor is stuck. The Swan recently changed course by bringing its dishes – and its prices – closer to the people; luckily, its trademark dish, *cappone in agrodolce* (sweet-and-sour capon), survived the downsizing.

Ochina Bianca

Via Finzi 2 (0376 323 700). **Open** 12.30-2pm,
7.30-10.30pm Mon, Wed-Sun. Closed 1wk Jan,
3wks Aug. **Average** €25. **Credit** AmEx, DC, MC, V.
The best of a new breed of Mantovan restaurant, this
bright, modern *osteria* combines local specialities
(including *asino* – donkey meat – and pike) with
good creative turns, including a delicious leek and
prawn risotto.

Where to stay

San Lorenzo

*Piazza Concordia 14 (0376 220 500/fax
0376 327 194/www.hotelsanlorenzo.it).*
Rates €140 single; €165 double; €196 suite.
Credit AmEx, DC, MC, V.
Mantova's best hotel is located right in the centre.
Rooms are mostly large and comfortable, and there
is a terrace with views over piazza delle Erbe and
San Lorenzo.

Broletto

Via Accademia 1 (0376 326 784/fax 0376 221 297).
Rates €68 single; €113 double. Breakfast €6 extra.
Credit AmEx, MC, V.
Just off piazza Broletto, this small, neat two-star is
a good budget option. All rooms have en suite
bathrooms, air-conditioning and satellite TV.

Villa Bogoni

*Via Veneto 19A, Sorgà (tel/fax 045 737 0129/
www.villabogoni.it).* **Rates** €70-€90 single;
€118.79 double. **Credit** AmEx, DC, MC, V.
Sleep in a sight: a 16th-century Gonzaga villa decorated with frescos by a follower of Giulio Romano.
In the village of Sorgà, 18km (11 miles) east of
Mantova, the Villa's bedrooms bristle with antiques,
including charming *baldacchino* canopy beds.

Essentials

Getting there

By car
From the A4 Milan–Venice motorway take the A22
and exit at Mantova Nord.

By train
Take the high-speed mainline train service from
Milan to Verona and change to a slow *interregionale*
for Mantova.

Getting around

All the main sights are within easy walking
distance. Local bus company **APAM** (0376
327 237/www.apam.it) runs both city and
country routes. The bus station is at via
Mutilati e Caduti del Lavoro 4, five minutes
south of the train station. Bus 1 (tickets 55¢)
runs from the station to the centre.

Tourist information

APT
*Piazza Mantegna 6 (0376 328 253/fax 0376 363
292/www.aptmantova.it).* **Open** 8.30am-12.30pm,
3-6pm Mon-Sat; 9.30am-12.30pm Sun.

Around Mantova

Rice paddies, pumpkin and melon fields and long
lines of poplars; crumbling castles and grand,
depopulated villages with ideas beyond their
station; rustic *trattorie*, a stuffed crocodile and
an unexpected art nouveau café: welcome to the
province of Mantova. Outside of **Sabbioneta** –
the short-lived ideal city of a Renaissance
scholar-prince (*see above* **Little Athens**) –
this is one of the least-visited rural areas in Italy.
It rewards those visitors who have time on their
hands and no particular place to go.
  The stretch of countryside between Mantova
and Lake Garda (*see p206*) around Solferino (*see
p236* **The mother of all battles**) had more
blood shed on it in 1859 than in any other battle
anywhere prior to World War I.

Getting around

By train
Four rural train lines radiate from Mantova, one
for every point of the compass. Few, though, stop
anywhere useful; in fact, of the towns and villages
mentioned below, only Piadena and Suzzara are
worth approaching by train rather than bus.

A traditional wooden pontoon bridge
crosses the Oglio. *See p240.*

Little Athens

When **Vespasiano Gonzaga** was born in the 16th century, his family – a cadet branch of the Gonzagas – had been ruling the medieval village of Sabbioneta for around 70 years. His predecessors had been content to build up the walls and collect the tithes, but cultured Vespasiano was determined to turn this sleepy Po valley community into the ideal city of a scholar-prince.

In less than 40 years, beginning in 1556, Vespasiano gave his *principato* (the title was conferred on Sabbioneta in 1574) most of the appendages of the Renaissance city-state: a castle (since demolished), a garden palace, an academy, a long gallery to display the requisite collection of classical statues, a theatre, a library, a mint and a printing press. The leading artists and architects of the day were summoned to paint, sculpt and build; scholars – especially Jewish scholars – were drawn here by the climate of enlightened tolerance. But when Vespasiano died without an heir in 1591 (apparently of syphilis), so did his dream of a 'Little Athens'. The town reverted to the main Gonzaga line, its inhabitants went back to growing their pumpkins (they'd never really stopped, to tell the truth), and Sabbioneta became what it is today: a historical curiosity, frozen in time.

By bus

APAM (0376 327 237/www.apam.it) runs services to most towns and villages in Mantova province, and also offers long-distance routes to Brescia, Parma and Peschiera sul Garda. Buses depart from and arrive at the bus station in via Mutilati e Caduti del Lavoro 4. Services to Sabbioneta run hourly during rush hour, and every two hours at other times.

Tourist information

The **APT** in Cremona (*see p245*) can also provide a range of useful tourist information, maps and other details about the region.

Pro Loco

Via Marta Tana 1, Castiglione dello Stiviere (0376 944 061/fax 0376 948 940/info.tur. castiglione@tin.it). **Open** *Apr-Sept* 10am-1pm, 2-4.45pm Tue-Sat; 9am-noon Sun. *Oct-Mar* 9am-1pm Tue-Sat; 9am-noon Sun.

The Oglio Valley

Four kilometres west out of Mantova on the Cremona road, the **Santuario di Santa Maria delle Grazie** (0376 349 002, open 7.30am-noon, 2.30-7pm daily) was founded by Francesco I Gonzaga in the early 15th century. Surrounded by reed beds, it's a lonely and atmospheric place, which comes to life on 15 August each year, when the huge square in front of the church fills up with *madonnari* (pavement artists who specialise in religious subjects) and their works. The interior of the church is truly surreal: a stuffed crocodile, supposedly caught in one of the Mincio lakes thanks to the intercession of the Virgin Mary, hangs from the ceiling, and the walls are surrounded by naïve ex-voto statues – including one of a local executioner, brandishing the tools of his trade.

The entire course of the River Oglio, which flows from Lago d'Iseo (*see p220*) and the Po, is a regional park. Perhaps the best place to appreciate its lazy, reedy charm is from the garden of Dal Pescatore, just outside **Canneto sull'Oglio** – one of the best restaurants in this, or indeed any, part of the world (*see p36* **Food heaven**). There's little to see in Canneto itself; better to head north to **Asola**, for a long time a Venetian bulwark against the local Gonzaga hegemony. The Venetian influence is felt in the church of **Sant'Andrea** (open 8.30am-noon, 5-6.30pm daily), which has a remarkable cycle of paintings dating from 1525-1536 by Il Romanino, and in **Caffè Liberty** in piazza XX Settembre – an incongruous art nouveau jewel in the middle of Mantova's combine harvester belt.

Across the Oglio from Canneto, **Piadena** was the birthplace of Platina – assumed name of Bartolomeo Sacchi (1421-81), Renaissance humanist, Vatican librarian and another contender (*see also p35*) for the title of author of the first printed cookery book, *De Honesta Voluptate*. Platina lifted most of his recipes from the *Libro di Arte Coquinaria*, a vernacular manuscript collection of recipes committed to paper by a certain Maestro Martino of Como.

Sabbioneta

Note that one ticket covers all Sabbioneta's main sights. The ticket, which can be bought from the Ufficio di Turismo del Comune (*see p240*), comes in two versions: with guided tour (Italian only, lasting around 90 minutes; €7.20); or without (€5.70). Under-sixes are admitted free and children aged seven to 18 pay €3.10. A ticket for one single sight costs €2.60. All the sights are open 10am to 1.15pm and 3pm to 5.45pm from Tuesday to Saturday, and 10am to 1.15pm and 3pm to 6.45pm on Sunday.

The private residence of Vespasiano Gonzaga (*see p239* **Little Athens**), **Palazzo del Giardino** takes up most of the southern part of Sabbioneta's main piazza d'Armi (also referred to as piazza Castello), just inside the main town gate, Porta Vittoria. Its façade and much of the interior decoration have seen better days, but there is still plenty left to marvel at: the rooms are an intricate hive of fresco, stucco and grotesque, all on mythological and Arcadian themes. A pretty ivy-frescoed staircase leads into the Galleria degli Antichi. Truncated – like Sabbioneta itself – this ornate gallery once displayed Vespasiano's collection of classical sculpture, filched by Maria Teresa of Austria in 1774.

The two other big sights lie north of via Gonzaga, the main central axis of the Vespasian town. Easily the most charming is Vincenzo Scamozzi's **Teatro Olimpico**, designed in 1588 and opened for a single, brief season before the prince's demise brought an end to masques and revels. Scamozzi was a pupil of Palladio, and the latter's Teatro Olimpico in Vicenza is the obvious model. Note the 12 statues of divinities on top of the semicircular colonnade – part of Vespasiano's personal campaign for New Caesar status. Restoration of the sadly decayed theatre brought to light the Venetian-style frescos at the side of the stage; in one, a barber leans out of a window, wielding a pair of scissors. The under-stage dressing rooms – no longer visitable – were similar to those that would be incorporated into Shakespeare's Globe a few years later.

Just down the road in piazza Ducale (or piazza Garibaldi – most squares around here have at least two names) is Vespasiano's official seat, the imposing **Palazzo Ducale**, one of the few buildings that was finished in time for him to enjoy it. Traces of frescos by Bernardino Campi and others remain inside, but the real treats are the polychrome wooden equestrian statues of the prince and four of his ancestors in the Sala delle Aquile; and the Galleria degli Antenati, with more ancestors – this time in stucco bas-relief. In the **Museo dell'Arte Sacra** at via Pesenti 6 (0375 52 035, closed Mon & Fri pm), a rather desultory collection of art and artefacts belonging to Vespasiano's branch of the Gonzagas is enlivened by the Golden Fleece awarded to the prince in 1585 by Philip II of Spain in reward for his services as a military engineer.

Where to stay & eat

The only hotel worth considering in Sabbioneta itself is the three-star **Al Duca** (via della Stamperia 18, 0375 52474, double room €60), a family-run place with a touch of class.

The same hotel's restaurant is the best of the town's uninspiring eateries; if you have a car, head for Saltini in Pomponesco (*see below*).

Tourist information

See also **APT** (*p245*) in Cremona.

Ufficio di Turismo del Comune

Piazza d'Armi 1, Sabbioneta (0375 221 044/ fax 0375 222 119/www.unh.net/sabbioneta or www. sabbioneta.org). **Open** *Apr-Sept* 9.30am-12.30pm, 2.30-6pm Tue-Sat; 9.30am-12.30pm, 2.30-7pm Sun. *Oct-Mar* 9.30am-12.30pm, 2.30-5pm Tue-Sat; 9.30am-12.30pm, 2.30-6pm Sun.

Basso mantovano

Viadana has little to show for its millennium of history; it's famous today for melons and duvets. Far more interesting is **Pomponesco**, a tiny village with a huge porticoed central square – a gift of Giulio Cesare Gonzaga at the end of the 16th century – which ends rather incongruously in one of the high banks that protect the area from flooding. Underneath the arches is the **Trattoria Saltini** (piazza XXIII Aprile 10, 0375 86 017, closed Mon and mid July-mid Aug, average €23), an excellent, cheap local hostelry that does good local pasta staples like *tortelli di zucca* and *tagliatelle al sugo di anatra* (with duck sauce), to be washed down with a glass or two of honest Lambrusco. Covering one wall is a curious mock-Egyptian mural from the 1920s.

North from Viadana, the road between Villastrada and Cesole crosses the River Oglio on a wooden pontoon bridge – once a common sight around these parts. There is little but pumpkins and tractors to detain one until Borgoforte, where the main Mantova–Parma road crosses the Po.

On the southern bank, at **Motteggiana**, a road heads east along the top of one of the Po flood banks, past floating riverhouses and flapping egrets – one of the few roads that could be described as picturesque in this landscape of flatness. It ends up at **San Benedetto Po**, a dozy brick village that is dominated by the **Abbazia di Polirone** (0376 615 124, open 7.30am-noon, 2.30-7.30pm daily) – a Benedictine abbey founded in 1007. The rambling complex – mostly dating in its present form from the 16th century – is worth a visit for the sacristy, an exuberant Mannerist *concerto* with frescos by the school of Giulio Romano, and for the 12th-century Oratorio di Santa Maria, which harbours a charming medieval mosaic of a black St George manfully taming a dragon. Also inside the church look out for the tomb of medieval power-broker Matilde of Canossa.

Cremona, Lodi & Around

Pretty churches, charming piazzas and castles dot the *bassa pianura*.

The harsh-sounding place names of the *bassa pianura* (flatlands) around Cremona, Lodi and Crema and the northern physiognomies of the area's inhabitants are the legacy of the ferocious Lombards (*see chapter* **History**), who doggedly conquered an area that had previously been home to Byzantines, Romans and Celts.

The Germanic invaders took a full 34 years of siege to bring Cremona to heel (then demolish it) in 603. Having settled, then taken up farming, the Lombards kept their hand in with an informal regional league of inter-municipal warfare. Fixtures became particularly lively with the intervention of Holy Roman Emperor Frederick Barbarossa in the 12th century; Lodi and Crema's turns to be dismantled came in 1158 and 1160 respectively. The participants still bear grudges, but the medieval traces left by the subsequent reconstruction work are an integral part of the towns' appeal.

Though the rebuilding was done with considerable style – Cremona provided itself with one of Italy's most remarkable towers, the **Torrazzo** – the *bassa pianura* has never quite made it on to the tourist map. On the surface, you can see why: the landscape is a monotonous maize monoculture punctuated only by the occasional stand of poplars, the bright braziers of roadside prostitutes and exotic road-kill in the shape of coypus, endemic in the area's wetlands.

But the *bassa pianura*'s towns and villages have any number of charming *piazze* and churches. The rivers that cross it – the Adda, Po, Oglio and Serio – provide more redeeming features in the shape of parks preserving last vestiges of the swamps that, with vigorous reclamation from the 13th century onwards, were converted into one of the world's most productive agricultural regions.

Cremona

Cremona is known as city of the Three Ts – *torri, tette e torrone* (towers, tits and nougat) – but despite its sweet tooth and famously pneumatic womenfolk, this elegant provincial

Piazza del Comune. *See p242.*

capital is sleepy rather than racy. Its heyday was in the 15th century, when a major building programme followed the marriage in October 1441 of Bianca Maria Visconti, the illegitimate daughter of the Duke of Milan, to Francesco Sforza, her father's chief mercenary. The marriage is commemorated annually in a festival of *torrone*, which according to legend was invented for the event.

From then on, however, plague, foreign domination and economic crises drove things downhill. The city did produce at least one world-changing masterpiece in the age of the baroque: the violin, which emerged in its modern form here in the workshop of Andrea Amati (*see p244* **Fiddles**). The same period in Cremona also produced the divine tunesmith Claudio Monteverdi and the artistic superstar

Sofonisba Anguissola, both of whom, however, moved away from Cremona to achieve fame and fortune.

The medieval **piazza del Comune** is the city's hub. The **Duomo** is flanked by Europe's highest belltower, the **Torrazzo**, and the **baptistery** (0372 273 86, open irregularly; ask for times in the sacristy of the Duomo), which dates from 1167 but was spruced up with marble in the 16th century. Facing it, the **Loggia dei Militi** was a clubhouse for the aristo faction in the Middle Ages. The two moody chaps with cudgels are both Hercules, the city's mythical founder, said to lie under the Duomo. In the courtyard of the **Palazzo del Comune** is the Bookshop (open 9am-6pm Tue-Sat, 10am-6pm Sun), for museum tickets. Leading north towards piazza Roma, narrow medieval via Solferino is a good place to pick up local delicacies: *torrone* and *mostarda cremonese*, translucent pickled fruit to be eaten with roast meat or cheese. (Beware of the oranges; eating them is like snorting curry powder.) North of the well-kept patch of green in piazza Roma (the statue is of violin-maker Stradivarius, *see p244* **Fiddles**) lie the **Museo Civico** and the **Museo Stradivariano**.

A couple of streets west, in corso Garibaldi, the pointed medieval arches of the **Palazzo Cittanova** (new city, not open to the public)

mark what was once an alternative town centre. This was the power base of the *popolari*, who were at daggers drawn with the Duomo-based nobs for most of the 12th and 13th centuries. So fierce was the strife that Cremona's patron saint Omobono won instant canonisation for trying to keep the peace. His Romanesque statue stands outside the nearby church of **Santi Egidio e Omobono** (only used for weddings), surveying a cobbled-over plague pit.

From corso Garibaldi, via Trecchi leads south to the tiny church of **Santa Margherita** (open 7.45am-6.30pm Mon-Sat, 7.45am-noon Sun) with its mannerist frescos, and to **Sant'Agostino**. In nearby via Ponchielli, the resoundingly baroque church of **Santi Marcellino e Pietro** (open 8am-noon daily and occasionally for concerts) has paintings by Angelo Massarotti depicting the saints galloping forth to wallop the hated Milanese.

From piazza Roma, corso Mazzini leads to the eastern part of the centre. The corso soon forks: veer right into via Gerolamo da Cremona for Cremona's oldest church, **San Michele** (open 7.30am-noon, 4-7.30pm daily), an 11th-century structure. In the crypt are remains of a seventh-century church, including Lombard capitals, one of which shows a very oddly shaped St Michael. A left fork into corso Matteotti, on the other hand, leads past the elegant Renaissance

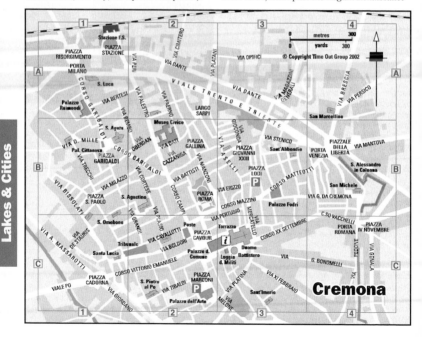

Palazzo Fodri (No.17, open 8.30am-12.30pm, 2-6.30pm Mon-Fri), which has a collection of violins inside and a striking terracotta frieze in its courtyard. Nearby **Sant'Abbondio** (via Lauretano, open 7am-noon, 3-7pm daily) is late mannerist in style; there's a stately cloister and a 17th-century replica of the Virgin Mary's 'home': the original, brought 'miraculously' to Italy by angels in 1294, is in Loreto in east-central Italy.

Cremona's most spectacular church, **San Sigismondo**, is two kilometres (1.25 miles) down the road to Parma (bus 2 goes to the church; bus 1 stops at the nearby hospital).

It's a good idea to buy a *biglietto cumulativo* (cumulative ticket), which is valid for all of Cremona's paying attractions. It costs €10 and can be purchased at the Bookshop in the Palazzo del Comune (*see below*).

Duomo

Piazza del Comune (0372 22 582). **Open** 7.30am-noon, 3.30-7pm Mon-Sat; 7.30am-1pm, 3.30-7pm Sun. Consecrated in 1190, Cremona's magnificent cathedral is a high point of the Lombard Romanesque, with Gothic, Renaissance and baroque elements tacked on over centuries of (mostly) splendid development. On the elaborately sculpted marble façade – begun in the 13th century but not completed until well into the 16th – are medieval peasants going about their bucolic tasks (1220-30), Byzantine-style prophets, and Madonnas from various periods. Inside, a fresco cycle of scenes from the life of Christ and his mother starts (first left-hand arch of the central aisle) in Renaissance restraint with Boccaccio Boccaccino's *Apparition of the Angel to St Joachin* (1514) and ends (facing the altar) with Pordenone's luridly mannerist *Crucifixion*. The inlaid choir stalls (1490) have views of Cremona; the two pulpits were pieced together in 1813 from 15th-century fragments.

Museo Civico Ala Ponzone

Via Ugolini Dati 4 (0372 407 770/31 222). **Open** 9am-6pm Tue-Sat; 10am-6pm Sun. **Admission** €7; €4 concessions. **No credit cards**. The grand setting for Cremona's art gallery is the Renaissance Palazzo Affaitati. It contains works by those responsible for embellishing the region's churches (the presence of the Campi and Boccaccini families made for very respectable Renaissance and mannerist periods) and a *San Francesco in Meditazione* by baroque superstar Caravaggio (whose light effects clearly influenced the Campis). Cremonese noblewoman Sofonisba Anguissola (1532-1625), the first female Italian artist to win international fame, contributes a family portrait; a cack-handed *San Francesco* by her sister Anna Maria reassures those happier with a man at the easel. There's also a curious portrait by Giuseppe Arcimboldo that transforms into a bowl of salad if you stand on your head.

Francesco Sforza. *See p241.*

Museo Stradivariano

Via Ugolini Dati 4 (0372 407 770/31 222). **Open** 9am-6pm Tue-Sat; 10am-6pm Sun. **No credit cards**. The contents of Antonio Stradivari's workshop were disposed of by his son Paolo, but by graft and good fortune many of his models, forms and tools have now been brought back to his home town and are displayed here along with historic instruments. *See also p244* **Fiddles**.

Palazzo del Comune

Piazza del Comune 8 (0372 40 71). **Open** 8.30am-6pm Tue-Sat. **Admission** €6; €4 concessions. **No credit cards**. The figure that greets you at the foot of the stairs is (putatively) local hero Baldesio, who won the city a tax rebate in single combat with an emperor's son. The first-floor Salone dei Quadri contains vast 17th-century canvases by Genovesino; the Sala dei Violini's glass cases hold the world's most precious fiddles; some are played each morning (call 0372 22 138 to book a place).

San Sigismondo

Largo Bianca Maria Visconti (0372 437 357). **Open** *Apr-Oct* 9am-noon, 3-6pm daily. *Dec-Mar* by appointment. Love them or loathe them, you will not be indifferent to the mannerist frescos on this 15th-century church. It was an older church on this site – a low-key venue outside the city walls – that hosted the epochal marriage of Bianca Maria Visconti and Francesco Sforza in 1441 (*see p241*). Afterwards the church was rebuilt and embellished at Bianca Maria's behest. Frescos of *Christ and the Adulteress*

San Sigismondo. *See p243.*

come back) shines in this rather gloomy showcase for 15th- to 16th-century local artistic talent. The Cavalcabò chapel contains important works by Bonifacio Bembo.

Torrazzo
Piazza del Comune 1 (0372 27 633). **Open** *Apr-Oct* 10.30am-noon, 3-6pm Mon-Sat; 10.30am-12.30pm, 3-7pm Sun. *Nov-Mar* by appointment. Closed for restoration until late 2002.

At 111m (370ft), this is Europe's tallest belltower; it has a stupendous view. The astrological clock dates from 1583 and still works with the original mechanism, marking lunar and solar eclipses as well as the time. Before being executed in 1424, evil local overlord Cabrino Fondulo claimed his life's one regret was inviting the pope and the Holy Roman Emperor to the top of the tower in 1413, and not chucking them off. It is currently undergoing restoration.

(featuring bizarrely pupil-less eyes) by Camillo Boccaccino in the presbytery, and of various breeds of small dogs in Biblical scenes, are particularly odd.

Sant'Agostino
Piazza Sant'Agostino (0372 22 545). **Open** 8am-noon, 3.30-6pm daily.

A *Madonna Enthroned with Saints* (1494) by the Umbrian Perugino (one of many paintings pilfered by Napoleonic troops, and one of the very few to

Where to eat & drink

Centrale
Via Pertusio 4 (0372 28 701). **Open** *Bar* 9.30am-11pm Mon-Wed, Fri-Sun. *Meals served* noon-3.30pm, 8-10pm Mon-Wed, Fri-Sun. **Average** €20. **Credit** AmEx, DC, MC, V.

The Centrale serves unpretentious traditional home cooking in an unpretentious traditional atmosphere. It is also a bar, where oldsters cluster round the TV for crucial matches. An ideal place to try the Cremonese speciality *marubini in brodo*, a variety of ravioli in broth.

Il Centrale della Birra
Viale Trento Trieste 62A (0372 33 267). **Meals served** 7.30pm-midnight Tue-Sun. **Average** €10. **Credit** AmEx, DC, MC, V.

This lively micro-brewery with a capacious beer garden serves its own lager (hence no additive-enhanced hangovers) and pizzas cooked in a wood oven to a young clientele.

Fiddles

Around Lake Garda (*see pp206-213*), they'll tell you that one Gasparo da Salò invented the violin. Wherever it originated, the violin undoubtedly hit top form in Cremona, in the workshop of Andrea Amati (c1511-76), whose grandson Nicolò carried on the tradition. Nicolò's pupils included Andrea Guarini (who established a rival dynasty) and, possibly, the greatest violin-maker of them all, Antonio Stradivari (c1644-1737). Stradivari experimented with form, making his instruments longer, narrower, larger or shallower in his search for perfect pitch. The secret of his success was long believed to lie in his thick varnish, the recipe for which is still unknown, though it is rumoured to include virgin's wee. But according to the head of Cremona's Scuola di Liuteria – the violin-making school set up in 1938 to revive the craft, in decline since the late 18th century – today's instruments may sound just as impressive after a few centuries' use.

There are violin collections for public viewing in the **Palazzo del Comune** and the **Palazzo Fodri** (for both, *see p243*). Cremona APT (*see p245*) will provide a list of violin workshops. Also, don't miss the **Museo Stradivariano** (*see p243*).

Martinelli

Palazzo Cattaneo, via degli Oscasali 3 (0372 30 350/ www.ristorantemartinelli.it). **Open** 12.30-2.30pm, 8-10pm Mon, Tue, Thur, Fri; 12.30-2.30pm Wed. Closed 2wks Aug. **Average** €30. **Credit** DC, MC, V.
Offering possibly the poshest ambience in Cremona – the neo-classical opulence of Palazzo Cutaneo-Ala Ponzone – Martinelli nevertheless serves up food that consists of hearty regional favourites such as risotto and pumpkin *tortelli*. There is also a good choice of Cremonese salami.

Osteria Porta Mosa

Via Santa Maria in Betlem 11 (0372 411 803). **Meals served** *Sept-July* 12.30-2pm, 7.30-10pm Mon-Sat. Closed Aug. **Average** €35. **Credit** AmEx, DC, MC, V.
In this small (so make sure you book) rustic *osteria*, the owner is out front and his mother is in the kitchen. The cuisine is strictly seasonal and includes specialities like truffle and snails. The cheeses, which are personally chosen by the proprietor in France, are remarkable.

La Sosta

Via Sicario 9 (0372 456 656). **Meals served** noon-3pm, 7.30-10.30pm Tue-Sat; noon-3.30pm Sun. Closed 3wks Aug, 1wk Jan. **Average** €35. **Credit** AmEx, DC, MC, V.
This bright restaurant draws theatrical types with its Cremonese specialities, including *gnocchi alla Vecchia Cremonese*, which are still prepared according to a 17th-century recipe.

Taverna La Botte

Via Porta Marzia 5 (0372 29 640/www. tavernalabotte.com). **Meals served** *Sept-July* noon-3pm, 8pm-midnight Tue-Sun. Closed Aug. **Average** €30. **Credit** AmEx, DC, MC, V.
This trattoria for the in-crowd is located in the enormous front room of an ancient palazzo near the Duomo. Cosy and intimate, La Botte serves good fish and solid traditional fare.

Where to stay

The **Continental** (piazza della Libertà 26, 0372 434 141, www.hotelcontinentalcremona.it, double room €110) is a long-established four-star hotel and generally considered the best in the city. Alternatively, the unfussy little **Duomo** (via dei Gonfalonieri 13, 0372 35 242, double room €56.81) is a decent choice that, as the name suggests, is centrally located by the Duomo.

Getting there

By car

Take the A1 motorway from Milan to Piacenza Sud; change on to the A21 and exit at Cremona. The single-lane SS415 is a slower, more scenic, route from Milan via Crema.

By train

Services leave from Milan's Stazione Centrale. Few trains are direct; you will probably have to change at Codogno.

By bus

STAR (0371 51 011) provides direct morning and evening commuter services (journey time 1hr30mins) between San Donato metro station in Milan and Cremona; during the day, change at Crema.

Getting around

Cremona is best explored on foot. However, KM (0372 442 011) operates buses around the city (one-hour tickets 80¢). Bikes can be hired from the car park in via Villa Glory or from the APT (*see below*).

Tourist information

APT

Piazza del Comune 5 (0372 23 233/www. aptcremona.it). **Open** 9am-12.30pm, 3-6pm Mon-Sat; 9am-12.30pm Sun.

Crema

Crema was originally an island in a swamp. Today the enterprise and industry of the famously self-satisfied *cremaschi* lend this attractive little town a lively feel. From 1449 to 1797 it was part of the Venetian republic.

Crema's **Duomo** and **Torrazzo**. *See p246.*

(The lion of St Mark – the symbol of Venice – struts on façades all around piazza del Duomo.) Now it belongs to the province of Cremona, which joined Emperor Frederick Barbarossa in the 12th century to raze Crema to the ground. (In an act of singular ferocity, *cremaschi* hostages perished tied to a siege engine.)

Dominating Renaissance piazza del Duomo is the **Duomo** itself, a 13th- to 14th-century building with a spartan interior heavily reworked in 1780. In the crypt are traces of the eighth-century cathedral destroyed during Barbarossa's rampage. The terracotta decoration of the asymmetric façade (full of arcane numerological significance) and the form of the belltower sent British visitor John Addington Symonds into ecstasies when he visited a century ago. (He was also delighted to pick up an unusual crucifix from a local monastery that handily transformed into an assassin's dagger).

In the badly lit fourth niche on the right is the last unfinished work of Guido Reni, the darling of Victorian Grand Tourists. At the far end of the left nave, the feet of Christ on the 14th-century crucifix raised themselves – according to local lore – in 1448 to avoid scorching when a local heretic hurled it into a fire.

The town hall – **Palazzo del Comune** (1525) – occupies the side of the square opposite the Duomo; a passage beneath its **Torrazzo** (tower) leads west to pedestrianised via XX Settembre, past the almost parodically baroque church of the **Santissima Trinità** (open 7am-noon, 4-7pm daily) – note the works by the Grand Tourists' favourite portraitist Pompeo Batoni) – to the Porta Ombriano gate. In nearby via Fino, the church of **Madonna delle Grazie** (open 7am-noon, 4-7pm daily) has frescos by Giangiacomo Barbelli, Crema's top 17th-century artist.

There's more Barbelli south of the Duomo along via Matteotti in the church of **San Giovanni Battista** (open 7am-noon, 4-7pm daily). A left turn here (via del Ginnasio) leads to the early 18th-century **Palazzo Terni de Gregory** (not open to the public) with its statue-topped wavy baroque wall, one of the town's most striking noble residences. Opposite stands the 15th-century ex-convento di Sant'Agostino, home to the **Museo Civico**. With accidental long-sightedness, Napoleonic troops preserved colourful 16th-century frescos with a coat of quicklime when the refectory was converted into a stable. The museum is home to local archaeological finds and some local art, much of it singularly unmemorable.

At the end of via Mazzini stands the city's eastern gate, the neo-classical **Porta Serio**. From here it's a short trot of a kilometre to

Crema's architectural jewel, the Bramantesque basilica of **Santa Maria della Croce**. In 1490 local noblewoman Caterina degli Uberti was attacked here by her husband and left for dead. The Virgin Mary kept her alive just long enough to see her kids and shop her spouse; in no time there was a shrine here. Circular in plan, the church's interior is richly decorated by Carlo Urbino and Bernadino and Antonio Campi. Beneath the altar a tableau depicts Caterina with Mary.

Duomo
Piazza del Duomo (0373 256 218). **Open** 7am-noon, 4-7pm Mon-Sat; 7am-1pm, 3.30-8pm Sun.

Museo Civico
Via Dante 39 (0373 257 161). **Open** 2.30-6.30pm Mon; 9am-noon, 2.30-6.30pm Tue-Fri; 10am-noon, 4-7pm Sat, Sun. **Admission** free.

Santa Maria della Croce
Via Santa Maria della Croce 25 (0373 259 597). **Open** 7.30am-noon, 2.30-7pm Mon-Sat; 7.30am-noon, 2-7pm Sun.

Where to eat, drink & stay

Il Ridottino (via A Fino 2, 0373 256 891, closed Sun dinner & all Mon, 1wk Jan and 3wks Aug, average €50) is a lively place in the ornate rooms of an 18th-century aristocrat's pad; the innovative cuisine includes lots of fish and poultry. **Mario** (via Stazione 118, 0373 204 708, closed Tue dinner & Wed, average €38) is a spacious restaurant in an ex-warehouse, serving traditional fare. In a cellar with vaulted ceiling near the Duomo, **Enoteca** (piazza Trento e Trieste 14, 0373 84 339, closed lunch, closed Mon & Tue, average €25) serves a huge range of wines and alcohol-absorbing snacks. A cosy trattoria down a country lane two kilometres (1.25 miles) north-west of the centre, **Il Fante** (via Fante 23, Santo Stefano Vairano, 0373 200 131, closed Tue, Wed, 2wks Jan and 3wks Aug, average €35) serves local specialities such as *lonza affumicata* (smoked loin), duck and *tortelli cremaschi* (marrow-stuffed pasta).

Just outside Porta Serio – Crema's liveliest area – the **Ponte di Rialto** (via Cadorna 5-7, 0373 82 342, closed 3wks Aug, double room €88) has been a hotel since Venetian times; it has since been rebuilt almost out of recognition, but retains touches of character.

Getting there

There are hourly train services to Crema from Cremona during the week. For details of travelling to Cremona and Crema by car or bus, *see p245.*

Tourist information

Pro Loco

Via Racchetti 8 (0373 81 020). **Open** 9.30am-
12.30pm Tue-Sat; 10am-noon Sun.

Around Crema

The countryside of Cremona province can be
bleak, to say the least, but a clutch of pretty
towns around Crema offers relief. To the east,
on the banks of the River Oglio, **Soncino** is
particularly picturesque, with a formidable
brick **Rocca** (fortress) erected in 1473
but immediately rendered obsolete by the
development of gunpowder. A bridge hidden
by the moat's stagnant waters led via a secret
passage to the church of **Santa Maria delle
Grazie** (via Fontane Sante, open 10am-noon,
3-6pm daily; ring bell next door to get a nun
to open it), which bursts with vivid mannerist
frescos. The **Museo della Stampa** in the
fortress commemorates an important 15th-
century printing works that was based here.
Attached to the church of **San Giacomo**
(via IV Novembre, open 9-11.30am, 3-6pm
daily) is a rare seven-sided tower.

South of Crema on the Cremona road,
Castelleone is less attractive, but it does
have a 47-metre (157-foot) tower – the **Torre
Isso** – in its centre and (a kilometre north of
town) the delightful church of **Santa Maria**
di Bressanoro, built in the ninth century,
then rebuilt in Renaissance style in 1461. On
the wall on your right as you enter a fresco
depicts a delightfully multicultural *Last
Judgment*, with black Africans and white
Italians being resurrected on their respective
sides of the Mediterranean. Castelleone holds
a lively antiques fair on the second Sunday
of each month.

Twelve kilometres (7.5 miles) south of
Castelleone, on the banks of the River Adda,
Pizzighettone's massive defence system
was designed with gunpowder in mind
(but proved no match for Napoleon's guile). The
unique barrel-vaulted *casematte* – embryonic
pillboxes where the town's defenders and
their animals took refuge – have recently been
restored (for tours contact Gruppo Volontari
delle Mura, *see p248*). The French king Francis
I was imprisoned in a tower here in 1525. In the
church of **San Bassiano** hangs a mammoth
rib, said to be from the Tarantasio dragon
that haunted the swampy vicinity until St
Christopher slew him on New Year's Day 1300.

Rocca & Museo della Stampa

*Largo Salvini & via Lanfranco 6, Soncino
(Rocca 0374 84 883/Museo 0374 83 171).*
Open *Both* Oct-Mar 10am-noon Tue-Fri;
10am-12.30pm, 2.30-5.30pm Sat, Sun; Apr-Sept
10am-noon Tue-Fri; 10am-12.30pm, 3-7pm Sat, Sun.
Admission €2.55; €2.05 concessions.
No credit cards.

Crema's Bramantesque **Santa Maria della Croce**. *See p246.*

Lakes & Cities

The ticket allowing access to both of Soncino's main monuments can be purchased at the Pro Loco (*see below*).

Where to eat, drink & stay

In Soncino, **I Cinque Frati** (via de Baris 11, 0374 85 560, closed Mon and 2wks Jan, Feb, average €20) is an *enoteca* with a roaring fire in winter; nibbles are available to go with your wine.

North-west of Crema in Trescore, the **Trattoria del Fulmine** (via Carioni 12, 0373 273 103, closed Sun dinner & Mon, Aug, average €50) serves elegant takes on local staples. Still further west in Nosadello, **Volpi** (via Indipendenza 34, 0373 90 100, closed lunch Sat, dinner Sun, all Mon, 2wks Jan and 2wks Aug, average €37) is a simple family-run trattoria serving unpretentious *cremaschi* dishes.

Due south of Crema, Ripalta Cremasca's suburb of Bolzone is home to **Via Vai** (via Libertà 18, 0373 268 232, www.trattoriaviavai. com, closed lunch Mon & Thur-Sat, all Tue & Wed, 2wks Jan and 4wks July-Aug, average €35), famous for its take on the local speciality *tortelli cremaschi* (sweet ravioli filled with amaretto, lime, peppermint, raisins, nutmeg and grana cheese).

In Offanengo, four kilometres (2.5 miles) from Crema on the Soncino road, **Villa Mantovani** (circonvallazione Sud 1, 0373 780 213, double room €82.63) has a swimming pool and pretty garden. West of Crema on the SS415 to Milan, Spino d'Adda is a good base for exploring the Parco Adda Sud (*see p250* **Parco Adda Sud**); **Cascina Fraccina** (0373 965 166, www.fraccina.it, closed Jan, Feb and Aug, apartments €155 per weekend) is a farm holiday centre in a 16th-century farmhouse. In Castelleone, the central **City Hotel** (via Cavour 54, 0375 43 424, closed 2wks Dec-Jan, double room €67.14) is in a converted stable with wooden ceilings.

Getting there & around

By car

Car is by far the best way to explore this region's well-kept by-ways.

By train

Most trains on the Milan–Codogno–Cremona line stop at Pizzighettone.

By bus

AGI (02 5540 0298/0373 257 948) runs services from Milan and Crema to Soncino. There is also a route from Lodi via Crema to Soncino run by SISA and AGI (0371 44 911/0373 84 887).

Tourist information

Gruppo Volontari delle Mura
Piazza d'Armi, Pizzighettone (0372 730 333). **Open** 10am-noon Thur, Sat; 10am-noon, 2-6pm Sun. There are guided tours (Italian only) of the walls on Saturday, Sunday and public holidays; call ahead to book your place.

Pro Loco
Via IV Novembre 14, Soncino (0374 84 883/ 84 499). **Open** 8.30am-12.30pm Tue-Sat.

South & east from Cremona

For details of **Piadena**, *see p240*.

Mantova's Gonzaga dynasty (*see p232*) imposed its style on what are now the eastern reaches of Cremona province. The best example is **Isola Dovarese**, east of Cremona via the SS10, where the extraordinary piazza Matteotti was remodelled between 1587 and 1590 by Giulio Cesare Gonzaga. Locals in period costume re-enact a 1322 Gonzaga wedding here on the second Sunday of each September. The piazza's former garrison building is a historic ice-cream parlour, bar and restaurant (**Crepa**, piazza Matteotti 14, 0375 396 161, open 8am-3pm Mon, 8am-3pm, 6pm-1am Wed-Sat, 8am-1pm, 4.30pm-1am Sun).

Castles abound between Casalmaggiore and Cremona; a *sentiero dei castelli* (castle trail; contact the APT in Cremona for information, *see p245*) runs from **Cicognolo** – on the SS10 – to **Torre de' Picenardi**, passing by mainly 18th- and 19th-century aristocratic residences. Further south in **San Giovanni in Croce**, **Villa Medici del Vascello** is a much-reworked 15th-century structure with a glorious park in faux-Gothic style. All of these, however, can only be glimpsed from outside. To get inside one of the local piles, head east from San Giovanni to **Casteldidone** where the towered and turreted **Villa Mina della Scala** has 18th-century furniture, frescos and gardens.

The province's third town, **Casalmaggiore**, stands scenically on the banks of the Po. Its unusual **Museo del Bijou** contains 20,000 geejaws produced by a local firm between the late 19th century and 1970 and provides an eye-opening insight into changing fashions. More conventional attractions include the neo-classical **Duomo di Santo Stefano** (open 4-6pmTue-Sun and other times if the priest is feeling like it); beneath it lie the remains of a Romanesque church and a nuns' graveyard (visible from outside), and the bas-relief-adorned façade of **Palazzo Mina Tentolini** (not open to the public). Both are in central piazza Garibaldi.

Lakes & Cities

Two kilometres (1.25 miles) north-west of town, the **Santuario della Madonna della Fontana** (open 9am-noon, 3-6.30pm Mon-Sat, 7.30am-noon, 3-6.30pm Sun) houses a 'miraculous' spring and the mortal remains of the mannerist painter Parmigianino.

Museo del Bijou
Via Porzio 9, Casalmaggiore (0375 43 682). **Open** 10am-noon, 3-7pm daily. **Admission** €1.5. **No credit cards**.

Villa Mina della Scala
Via E Montale 6, Casteldidone (0375 91 105). **Open** *late Mar-mid Nov* 3-6pm Sun by appointment; during the week for groups of more than 10 by appointment. Closed mid Nov-mid Mar. **Admission** €7.75. **No credit cards**.

Where to eat & stay

In Cicognolo, **Umbreleer** (via Mazzini 13, 0372 830 509, closed dinner Tue & all Wed, 4wks Aug-Sept, average €25) is a rustic trattoria with a truly vast choice of cheese and cold cuts and a great wine cellar.

In Torre de' Picenardi, **Italia** (via Garibaldi 1, 0375 394 060, closed dinner Sun, all Mon and Aug, average €30) is a restaurant with cosy bar in a historic palazzo, offering traditional dishes with a touch of innovation. In the nearby hamlet of San Lorenzo di Torre de' Picenardi, **Azienda Cantonazzo** (via Verdi 44, 0372 33 507, double room €35.15-€41.32) is an *agriturismo* (farm holiday centre) with apartments where you can cater for yourself, or eat with the owner's family.

Stagno Lombardo, five kilometres (three miles) south-east of Cremona, is home to another, rather superior, little *agriturismo*, **Lo Stagno** (Cascina Gerre del pesce, book through Caffelletto, 02 331 1814, www.caffelletto.it, double room €103.40). Accommodation is housed in a former Benedictine monastery and doesn't accept children under seven.

Getting there & around

By car
The SS10 and a host of well-maintained smaller roads shoot through the flat countryside between Crema and the provincial villages.

By train
Some trains on the Cremona–Mantova line stop at Torre de' Picenardi.

By bus
Saia Trasporti (030 242 7812/www.saiatrasporti.it) operates bus services from Cremona and Mantova to Casalmaggiore.

Maria Cosway

Santa Maria delle Grazie (*see p250*) attracts two very different kinds of pilgrim. Some come for the image of Judas Thaddeus, patron saint of lost causes. Others come to visit the tomb of the artist, musician, *salonière*, educator and all-round Enlightenment babe Maria Cosway (1760-1838). Brought up in Florence by her British parents, Maria Hadfield married the English miniaturist and socialite Richard Cosway in 1781. Four years later – her talents and morale oppressed by an envious and unfaithful husband – she had a fiery affair with US president-to-be Thomas Jefferson in Paris (as portrayed in the aptly named 1995 film *Jefferson in Paris*). In her lower-profile later life Maria moved to Lodi and set up an innovative school for girls in the palazzo next to the church.

Tourist information

Pro Loco
Piazza Garibaldi 6, Casalmaggiore (0375 40 039). **Open** 9.30am-noon, 4.30-7pm Mon-Sat; 9am-noon Sun.

Lodi

The old town of Lodi (Lodi Vecchio, *see p252*), of Celtic origin, was razed by the Milanese in 1158, after which Emperor Frederick Barbarossa (*see p11*) had a new town built nearby. There was little love lost between the *lodigiani* and the *milanesi*, who continued to lord it over Lodi. After centuries of thralldom, Lodi finally became a provincial capital in 1992.

The town of Lodi and its province are overwhelmingly agricultural, and produce cheeses – *grana padana*, the region's take on parmesan, which can be served *a raspadura* (in slithers); *pannerone*; and creamy *mascarpone* – which can be purchased at the market in piazza Mercato (Tuesday, Thursday, Saturday and Sunday mornings).

Central piazza della Vittoria is dominated by the **Duomo** – one of the first things to be rebuilt after the old town was destroyed – and the 18th-century **Palazzo Comunale** (town hall). Under the pleasantly varied arches of the piazza are bars with pavement tables.

Through the arcades next to the church, triangular piazza Broletto has a fountain fashioned from the Duomo's 16th-century ex-font. At the apse end of the Duomo in piazza Mercato is the **Palazzo Vescovile** (bishop's palace, 1730), now home to the **Museo Diocesano**.

Via Incoronata leads north from piazza della Vittoria to Lodi's chief treasure, the **Tempio dell'Incoronata**. Corso Umberto, on the other hand, leads north-east to the **Museo Civico** and the imposing baroque church of **San Filippo** (open 9am-noon Mon-Sat, 9am-1pm Sun). This road continues to the bridge over the Adda, where Napoleon routed an Austrian army in 1796 to conquer Italy. The area along the riverbanks had an unsalubrious reputation and is still picturesquely *popolare*. Via Maddalena heads north before the bridge, leading to the 18th-century church of **Santa Maria Maddalena**, a single-nave church highly reminiscent of a railway terminus, with a 'miraculous' flood-predicting crucifix.

South of corso Umberto are the church of **San Francesco** and the **Ospedale Vecchio**. A delightful Renaissance cloister in the latter leads to the **Museo Paolo Gorini**. The town's monument to embalming genius Gorini was erected in the teeth of fierce opposition by local God-botherers; its grisly embellishment of corpses did nothing to placate them; the statue's inverted coat pockets were Gorini's signal to the city's poor that he had no cash left to distribute.

Via XX Settembre leads west back to the centre. On the corner with via Volturno, **Palazzo Mozzanica** (not open to the public) has elaborate Renaissance terracotta decorations, possibly including portraits of Bianca Maria Sforza (*see p241*) and other VIPs. Napoleon and several monarchs stayed in the baroque **Palazzo Modegnani** (not open to the public) on the corner with via Roma. At the southern end of corso Roma is the church

of **Santa Maria delle Grazie** (*see also p249* **Maria Cosway**), which is open 9am to noon and 3pm to 6pm daily.

Further down via XX Settembre, turn north into via Marsala for the 14th-century church of **Sant'Agnese** (open 8-11.30am daily), a fine example of Lombard Gothic. At the end of the street, via Garibaldi runs south past the recently restored church of **San Lorenzo** (open 9am-noon, 4-6pm daily), a 12th-century structure much revamped over the centuries; this is Lodi's second-oldest church and has some serious stucco, frescos and a *St Catherine* by Callisto Piazza. At the end of the street is what is left of Lodi's castle.

Duomo & Museo Diocesano

Piazza della Vittoria (Duomo 0371 511 341/Museo 0371 410 512). **Open** *Duomo* 8am-noon, 3-6.30pm daily. *Museo* 3-6pm Sun; by appointment at other times. **Admission** donation of at least €1 expected.

Built over a century from 1160, the Duomo underwent a controversial revamp in 1956 when later accretions inside were hacked away and the building was 'restored' to how the original Romanesque church may (or may not) have looked. The columns

Parco Adda Sud

The River Adda flows from Lake Como at Lecco (*see p204*) to the River Po at Cremona (*see p241*), forming the border between Cremona and Lodi provinces in its southern section. Along its whole length is a regional park (divided for administrative purposes into Parco Adda Nord and Parco Adda Sud) set up in the 1980s with the aim of protecting the river environment, the few remaining stretches of undrained wetlands and the unique flora and fauna (over 200 species of bird have been counted here).

A cycle track follows the river for much of its length. On track or road, this is ideal cycling territory: dead flat and sparsely trafficked. Information on routes can be obtained from the Parco Adda Sud office (*see below*) or the park's website. The APT in Lodi (*see p252*) dispenses cycling itineraries and plans to rent bikes.

Consorzio Parco Regionale Adda Sud

Via A Grandi 6, Lodi (0371 45 081/ www.parcoaddasud.lombardia.it). **Open** *Office* 9am-12.30pm Mon; 9am-12.30pm, 2-4pm Tue-Fri.

of the entrance porch rest on marble lions believed to come from the old town of Lodi. The main entrance is 12th century, the rose window 16th century. Inside, the bas-relief of the *Last Supper* above the entrance to the crypt is from the 13th century, as is the frescoed *Last Judgment* (fourth chapel on the right) showing bishops being dragged to their doom by hook-wielding devils. Note the marble figure of a cobbler on the sixth pillar on the left: evidence of the contribution of the guilds to reconstruction efforts. The blocked-off window to the left of the main entrance was once used by the local powers in the comune to spy on who was going to church.

The Museo Diocesano (entrance from inside the Duomo) in the sumptuous 18th-century Palazzo Vescovile has a selection of religious art and church trappings from around the province.

Museo Civico

Corso Umberto I 63 (0371 420 369). **Open** 9.30am-12.30pm Sat; 3.30-6.30pm Sun. **Admission** free.
Housed in a Counter-Reformation monastery, the museum has three sections: locally produced ceramics going back to the 15th century; archaeology, including scant remains from the old town of Lodi; and the Pinacoteca (picture gallery), where there are yet more examples of the works of Lodi's omnipresent Piazza dynasty. The former monastery's fine library, with many ancient documents including the 12th-century charter for the rebuilding of Lodi, is open to bona fide scholars only.

Museo Paolo Gorini

Ospedale Vecchio, piazza Ospedale 4 (0371 372 986). **Open** by appointment only. **Admission** free.
This museum contains macabre examples – adults, babies, animals and even a penis – of embalmings by scientist Paolo Gorini (1813-81). Gorini was also a pioneer of cremation and is famed in local folklore for his amorous exploits, ribald wit and eating breakfast and lunch in one sitting to save time.

San Francesco

Piazza San Francesco (0371 420 019). **Open** 6.30am-noon, 4-6.30pm Mon-Sat; 7am-noon Sun.
Observing the flat rectangular brick façade of this 13th-century Gothic church, you might think the builders had stopped halfway. You'd be right. Inside, the church preserves its original interior to a unique extent and is a treasure trove of colourful 14th- and 15th-century frescos. In the third chapel on the left are remarkably cartoon-like frescos of the life of San Bernardino from 1477.

Tempio dell'Incoronata

Via dell'Incoronata (0371 56 055). **Open** 9-11.20am Mon; 9-11.20am, 3.30-6pm Tue-Fri; 9-11.20am Sat, Sun.
This ornate octagonal building was built in Bramantesque style in 1488-9 to commemorate an appearance by the Virgin Mary. Her image (now behind the altar) was outside a brothel where, after the umpteenth brawl, she put in a personal appearance. In the San Paolo chapel is *Christ being Presented at the Temple* by Bergognone. The prolific Piazza brothers – Antonino, Callisto and Fulvio – were responsible for much of the mid 16th-century fresco decoration.

Where to eat

La Cittadella

Bipielle City, via Polenghi Lombardo (0371 428 457/ www.korso.it). **Meals served** noon-2.30pm, 8-10pm Mon-Wed, Fri-Sun. Closed 1wk Aug. **Average** €35. **Credit** AmEx, DC, MC, V.
Intimate, bright and cheerfully decorated, the Cittadella is in a spanking new complex near the railway station, conceived by architectural wunderkind Renzo Piano. The clientele is young and smart; the food is more traditional.

La Quinta

Viale Pavia 76 (0371 35 041). **Meals served** Sept-July noon-2.30pm, 7-10pm Tue-Sat; noon-2.30pm Sun. Closed Aug. **Average** €45. **Credit** AmEx, DC, MC, V.
Local specialities and fish are served in a somewhat stuffy exposed beam and brick sort of space.

Tre Gigli all'Incoronata

Piazza della Vittoria 47 (0371 421 404). **Meals served** 12.30-2pm, 8-9.45pm Tue-Sun. Closed 1wk Dec-Jan, Aug. **Average** €50. **Credit** AmEx, DC, MC, V.
Lodi's top eaterie is a stone's throw from the Duomo: there's a relaxed family atmosphere despite its smart clientele, and great fish is served in summer.

Where to stay

Anelli

Viale Vignati 7 (0371 421 354/fax 0371 422 156). Closed 2wks Aug, 2wks Dec-Jan. **Rates** €65-€70 single; €85-€90 double; breakfast €10 extra. **Credit** AmEx, DC, MC, V.
This small, family-run hotel is conveniently situated within easy walking distance of the centre; free use of bicycles.

Europa

Viale Pavia 5 (0371 35 215/fax 0371 136 281/www. italiaabc.it). Closed 2wks Aug, 2wks Dec-Jan. **Rates** €62 single; €99 double. **Credit** AmEx, DC, MC, V.
This well-kept three-star has a soothing ambience.

Getting there

By car
From Milan, take the A1 motorway towards Bologna; exit at Lodi.

By train
Trains to Lodi leave regularly from Milan's Stazione Centrale, Lambrate and Rogoredo (journey time from Milan 40mins).

Lakes & Cities

By bus

STAR (0371 51 011) operates a more or less hourly service between San Donato metro station in Milan and Lodi.

Getting around

Lodi is small enough to negotiate on foot. As this guide went to press, the APT (*see below*) was planning to set up a bike-hire operation.

Tourist information

APT

Piazza Broletto 4 (0371 421 391/www.apt.lodi.it). **Open** 9am-12.30pm, 3-6pm Mon-Fri; 9am-1pm Sat.

Around Lodi

The towns of the Lodigiano are strictly one-horse. They are also one-*campanile*, with belltowers marking each of around 60 little communities, most of which could be given a miss in favour of the delights of the **Parco Adda Sud** nature reserve (*see p250*).

Six kilometres (3.5 miles) west of Lodi, **Lodi Vecchio** is where the town stood until the Milanese razed it (*see p241*). In **St Bassiano** (0371 752 900, open 3.30-4.30pm Mon-Wed, Fri, 3-5pm Sat, 9.15-11.30am, 3.30-5.30pm Sun), monstrous animals and stylised vegetation on the capitals date from the 11th century, while the frescos, including a homely labourer with his cart, are from a 14th-century rebuilding.

The austere **Abbazia del Cerreto** (0371 72 219, open by appointment) in the hamlet of Abbadia Cerreto, just across the Adda from Lodi, is a late Romanesque abbey surrounded by flatlands drained by its Cistercian inhabitants.

South of Lodi at Ospedaletto Lodigiano is the **Abbazia dei Gerolomini** (0377 86 622, open by appointment). It's a 16th-century complex; the gorgeous monastic church has Leonardesque paintings and a pile of skulls in the porch.

The River Lambro marks the Lodigiano's western border. On the riverbanks, **Sant' Angelo Lodigiano** is home to the imposing medieval **Castello Bolognini**, which is the province's largest castle and one of very few open to the public: inside is a museum of agriculture and bread, and 27 rooms with antique furnishings. In neighbouring **San Colombano** are the remains of a castle where the poet Petrarch once kipped. But the town is best-known for its vineyards, which occupy the province's only hills, and produce sparkling reds. The **Consorzio Volontario Vino DOC San Colombano** will organise cellar visits.

Castello Bolognini

Piazza Bolognini 2, Sant'Angelo Lodigiano (0371 211 140/http://fmb.supereva.it). **Open** *Mar-July, Sept-mid Nov* 3-5.30pm Sun; groups with bookings only 8.30am-12.30pm, 2-6pm Tue-Sat. **Admission** €6.50. **No credit cards.**

Consorzio Volontario Vino DOC San Colombano

Via Ricetto 3, Castello Belgioioso (0371 898 830/ www.sancolombanodoc.it). **Open** 8.30am-1pm, 2-4pm Mon-Fri.

Where to stay & eat

For B&B accommodation in San Colombano, look no further than the **Associazione Barbarossa** (0371 897 998/0347 866 4843, rates vary), which has establishments for all tastes on its books. On a steep track among vineyards outside San Colombano, **La Caplania** (strada Serafina 11, 0371 897 097, closed Mon, 2wks Jan and 2wks Aug, average €40) is a family-run haven of local specialities such as duck, risotto and gnocchi; the converted farmhouse is more atmospheric than the glassed-in extension.

There's a clutch of good eating and sleeping bets heading south-east from Lodi, along the River Adda. In Cavenago, the **Antica Barca** (piazza Carabinieri d'Italia 12, 0371 701 385, closed Fri, dinner Sun and Aug, average €25) has been run by the same family for 50 years; there are wooden ceilings, old codger card-players round the fireplace, and local treats such as *brasato d'asino* – sliced ass in gravy. In Maleo, **Il Sole** (via Trabattoni 22, 0377 58 142, closed Jan & Aug, double room €134.50) is a 15th-century inn with a restaurant (closed Sun dinner & all Mon, average €45) that has long been among the province's best, though **Il Leon D'Oro** (via Dante 69, 0377 58 149, closed Wed, 3wks Aug and 2wks Jan, average €50) has arguably nudged ahead, with its excellent cellar. In Maccastorna, **Il Cavallino** (via Roma 7, 0377 700 367, closed Tue, average €19) has decor sure to appal (note the waterfall with moving water effect in the bar) but solid home cooking that will delight gourmets. The village has a fine 13th-century moated castle full of wailing ghosts.

Getting there & getting around

By bus

STAR (0371 51 011) operates bus services thoughout the Lodigiano.

Tourist information

The APT in Lodi is the best source of information about the surrounding area (*see above*).

Pavia & Around

Rice, vines and the spectacular Certosa.

Map p254.
There's nothing of the prima donna about this hard-working, unassuming province to the south of Milan. But Pavia was once northern Italy's most important city and it has significant landmarks – including its spectacular **Certosa** (*see p256* **For Caterina, with love**) – to prove it. Moreover, there is a host of bucolic pleasures close at hand, in the rice-growing Lomellina or the rolling, vine- (and winery-) filled Oltrepò Pavese.

Pavia

The Romans began their turn at lording it over Pavia (which they called Ticinum) in the third century BC, having been preceded by the ancient Ligurians and Celts. Spreading along the Roman *cardus* (now Strada Nuova) and *decumanus* (now corso Cavour and corso Mazzini), Pavia was resplendent in the grim Dark Ages: the Goths took a liking to it, but it was another Germanic tribe – the Lombards – who really put the city on the map, making it their command centre in 564.

Pavia has long been an attraction. Some of the first (non-belligerent) foreigners to traipse through were pilgrims travelling the via Francigena that joined the great Christian shrines at Canterbury and Rome; Archbishop Siric of Canterbury made the journey in 990. Others came for ceremonies at the San Michele basilica in which Pavia elders patiently crowned a revolving door of Italian kings.

THE SIGHTS
Pavia's railway station, bus station and pay parking lot are all located within steps of one another on the eastern edge of the city. With the transit stations at your back, enter the city from the roundabout where a statue of Minerva has been stalwartly welcoming and watching since 1939 in all her amazon, Fascist glory.

From here, via Scopoli becomes corso Mazzini – the Roman *decumanus* – leading to central piazza della Vittoria. The main attraction here – apart from one of Lombardy's earliest examples of Romanesque architecture in the 12th-century **Broletto** (town hall); its façade is a 19th-century reconstruction – is

Morning mist in Pavia's **piazza della Vittoria**.

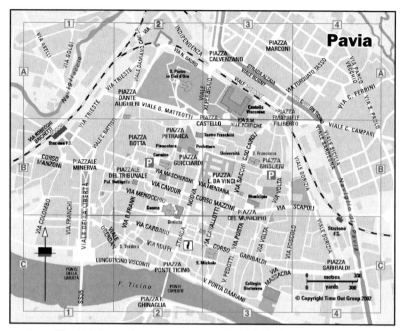

Pavia

people-watching. This is most fun during the
early evening *passeggiata*, when the *pavesi*
stroll here en masse.

A narrow street exits south from the piazza
towards the **Duomo** (open 7.30am-noon, 3-7pm
daily), a chunk of a cathedral started in 1488.
Masters including Leonardo da Vinci and local
boy Giovanni Antonio Amadeo tried and failed
to lend it some elegance. Bramante is to thank
for its best feature, the octagonal cupola, which
was finally completed in 1884, and is Italy's
third tallest. Perhaps weary of surveying its
unattractive neighbour for so long, the 11th-
century **Torre Civica** collapsed in 1989
without warning, killing five people; a pile
of masonry now marks the spot.

The medieval heart of the city, with its
narrow cobbled streets and ancient buildings,
stretches between the Duomo and the river.
At its heart, the brick church of **San Teodoro**
(open 7.30am-noon, 3-7pm daily) was originally
erected in the eighth century but rebuilt in
its present Romanesque style during the 12th.
Inside is an intricate fresco by Bernardino
Lanzani of the town as it appeared in the
early 16th century, with its 100 towers (five
remain) and original covered bridge. The
Ponte Coperto that now spans the Ticino
river is a post-war affair, a much-contested
liberal interpretation of the bomb-damaged

14th-century original. Across the bridge is
the Borgo Ticino, a pleasant fisherman's village
of little houses and old inns: a pleasant spot
for lunch at a riverside *osteria*.

Back on the north side of the bridge, at
the end of via Capsoni, stands the basilica of
San Michele Maggiore (open 7.30am-noon,
3-7pm daily), founded in 661 but rebuilt in
the 12th century after it was either struck by
lightning or ruined in the earthquake of 1117,
depending on which act of God you subscribe
to. San Michele is the only church in Pavia
made of sandstone, which has a dual effect: it
makes it a lovely honey colour, but erosion of
the soft stone has given some of the fantastical
animals that adorn the façade a melting look.
Charlemagne (*see p18* **Popes & emperors**)
celebrated his defeat of the Lombards and
assumed the crown of Italy here. Frederick
Barbarossa (*see p11*) followed suit in 1155.

Further north along the Strada Nuova stands
one of the oldest (1361) and most respected
European schools of law and medicine, the
Università di Pavia. Busts and statues of
the institute's alumni in the cloistered hallways
(courtyards open 7am-8pm daily) read like a
Who's Who of great Italian minds: among the
distinguished are Alessandro Volta, noted for
his electrifying experiments and invention of
the battery (*see also p197*), and Camillo Golgi,

who won the Nobel Prize in 1906 for his strides in understanding malaria. Three medieval towers loom in piazza Leonardo da Vinci, reminders of the time when 100 towers bristled above the city's *palazzi,* serving not only as vantage points but symbols of the owners' wealth and power.

The **Castello Visconteo**, at the northern end of the Strada Nuova, was built between 1360 and 1365 and dryly described as 'most notable' by Florentine poet Petrarch, who was summoned to the hulking fortress in the mid-14th century by the Viscontis to catalogue the family's vast collection of manuscripts. The **Museo Civico** is housed in the castle. The archeological and medieval sculpture sections contain artefacts from Gaulish, Roman and Lombard Pavia. The picture gallery has a memorable *Portrait of a Man* by Antonello da Messina among its works by a host of Lombard and Venetian masters.

East of the castle in a quiet pedestrian zone stands the lovely basilica of **San Pietro in Ciel d'Oro** (St Peter in the Golden Sky; open 7.30am-noon, 3-7pm daily), founded in the first half of the seventh century and rebuilt in 1132 in its present glory (though *sans* the golden ceiling that supposedly gave it its name). The mortal remains of three unlikely bedfellows rest here. First is St Augustine, whose bones were transported here in 772 by Lombard King Liutprando; the marble structure over the main altar carved by *campionesi* (*see p26*) stonemasons in the saint's honour is lovely. Second is Liutprando himself, who tried in vain to unite his Lombard population with that of the declining Romans; he lies near a pillar to the right of the presbytery. The third is of another would-be unifier: philosopher Severino Boezio

(Boethius), the persuasive orator who played matchmaker between the Goths and Romans but was ultimately imprisoned and tortured by jealous Goth officials and later murdered by Emperor Theodoric of Ravenna in 524. While in prison he wrote his famous work *De Consolatione Philosophiae*.

Pavia's magnificent **Certosa** (*see p256* **For Caterina, with love**) is located nine kilometres (5.5 miles) north of the city centre.

Castello Visconteo & Museo Civico

Piazza Castello, viale Febbraio XI (0382 304 816). **Open** *July, Aug, Dec-Feb* 9am-1.30pm Tue-Sun. *Mar-June, Sept-Nov* 9am-1.30pm Tue-Fri; 10am-7pm Sat, Sun. **Admission** 4.13. **No credit cards**.

Where to eat & drink

Antica Osteria del Previ

Via Milazzo 65 (0382 26 203). **Meals served** 12.30-2pm, 8-11pm Mon-Sat. Closed 2wks Jan, 3wks Aug. **Average** €35. **Credit** MC, V.
Three generations of family recipes ensure that each plate is tied to tradition. Ingredients are fresh, seasonal and bought from local producers; the simple dining room is warm and inviting.

Bar Bordoni

Via Bordoni/via Mentana 26 (0382 21 652). **Open** 7am-7.30pm Mon-Sat. **No credit cards**.
Come and swap philosophy with the university students who hang out here.

Caffè Janko

Via Riboldi 48 (0382 21 365). **Open** 7.30am-1pm Mon; 7.30am-7pm Tue-Sat. Closed 2wks Aug. **No credit cards**.
The golden ceiling here recalls what San Pietro in Ciel d'Oro (*see above*) used to look like. Enjoy a cup of the house coffee or pick up a bag of local or international chocolates. The aroma alone is to die for.

Locanda Vecchia Pavia al Molino

Via al Monumento 5 (0382 925 894). **Meals served** 12.30-2pm, 7.45-10.30pm Tue, Thur-Sun; 7.45-10.30pm Wed. Closed 3wks Jan, 2wks Aug. **Average** €45. **Credit** AmEx, DC, MC, V.
This restaurant close to the Certosa offers delicious local favourites according to whatever is seasonally available. The *risotto alla Certosina* is the monks' traditional recipe and is made with frogs' legs and river shrimp.

Osteria della Madonna da Peo

Via Cardano 63 (0382 302 833). **Meals served** 12.30-2pm, 7.45-10pm Mon-Sat. **Average** €25. **Credit** MC, V.
Located in a 16th-century wine cellar in the medieval neighbourhood between San Teodoro and the Duomo, this warm, cosy restaurant specialises in regional specialities and home-made pasta.

The **Ponte Coperto**. *See p254.*

Lakes & Cities

Osteria della Malora

Via Milazzo 79 (0382 34 302). **Meals served** 12.30-
2pm, 8-10pm Tue-Sat; 12.30-3pm Sun. Closed 3wks
Jan, 2wks July. **Average** €25. **Credit** AmEx, DC,
MC, V.
A mecca for locals who come for the solid cooking
and friendly atmosphere. The owners take pride in
serving the freshest local produce.

Where to stay

Pavia's newest hotel, the **Ritz** (via dei
Longobardi 3, San Genesio ed Uniti, 0382 580
280, www.hotelritzpavia.com, double room €83)
offers more facilities than you would expect for
the price; it's three kilometres (two miles) from
the city centre but there are shuttle services into
town. The **Excelsior** (piazzale Stazione 25,
0382 28 596, www.hotelritzpavia.com, double
room €73), on the other hand, is right across
from the station: nothing to write home about,
but rooms are pleasant and clean.

Getting there

By car

From Milan, take the A7 motorway; exit at
Bereguardo-Gropello.

By train

Many trains on the Genova, La Spezia, or Ventimiglia
lines from Milan's Stazione Centrale stop in Pavia.

By bus

SGEA (02 8954 6132/www.infopoint.it) runs buses
every 15mins between Milan's Famagosta metro
station and Pavia, stopping en route at the Certosa.

Getting around

Pavia is best covered on foot. The APT (*see
p257*) provides a list of walking guides. Bikes
can be rented from AL Service (Bar Gra-Car,
piazza del Monumento, 348 490 6190, open 8am-
7pm Tue-Sun) for €2.58 an hour or €18 a day.

For Caterina, with love

In a prenatal vision in 1390, Caterina Visconti
dreamt that a new monastery must be built
for the Carthusian monks of Siena. She
begged her husband, Gian Galeazzo (*see
p14*), to have it done should she die in
childbirth. She survived, but the duke got
to work on the **Certosa di Pavia** anyway: in
1394 he instructed architect Bernardo da
Venezia (who had been busy tinkering with
Milan's Duomo since 1390) and draftsmen
Cristoforo Conigo and Giacomo da Campione
to come up with 'something great'.

Gian Galeazzo wanted the monastery's
church – situated on the northern fringes
of the Visconti's Pavia estate – to serve as
a family mausoleum, and indeed the duke's
body was brought here in 1474 and lies
buried in a sepulchral extravaganza in the
right transept. But the fame of this religious
foundation was to come from achieving a
position as one of northern Italy's wealthiest
and most powerful – a renowned centre for
prayer, learning and art. The structure that
housed it grew gradually over the years,
a record in stone and fresco of the stylistic
shift from Gothic to the Renaissance and
on to mannerism.

The Pavian complex is a typical *certosa*
(charterhouse – in other words, a Carthusian
monastery) in plan: individual monks' cells
around a great cloister; a smaller cloister
adjoining the church where monks met and

talked business; pilgrim accommodation
(now housing a museum, closed indefinitely
for restoration); a cavernous refectory; and
cells for staff and lay brothers.

Beyond the frescoed entrance vestibule
(note the inscription 'Gra-Car', *Gratiarium
Charusia* or Charterhouse of Grace, which is
repeated all over the complex) lies the grassy
great courtyard and the church's façade, a
masterpiece of Renaissance art completed
after the interior was finished. The lowest,
earliest decorations date from 1473 and
were designed by Guiniforte Solari. Who
was responsible for the rest of the exuberant
sculpture added over the ensuing century
and more is the topic of hot debate; the
portal, however, dates from 1501 and is
by Benedetto Briosco.

The roof vaults of the *certosa*'s three-aisled
interior were frescoed by – among others
– Bernardino Bergognone, whose works are
dotted all over the *certosa*. In the second
chapel of the left aisle is a polyptich by
Perugino (1499); Bergognone's *St Ambrose
with Four Saints* (1490) graces the sixth
chapel on the left. Funerary statues of
Ludovico Il Moro (*see p15*) and Beatrice
d'Este by Cristoforo Solari stand in the
transept, though neither the Milanese
ruler nor his wife are buried here. In the
fourth chapel of the right aisle is a moving
Crucifixion by Bergognone (1490).

Tourist information

APT del Pavese
Via Filzi 2 (0382 22 156/www.apt.pv.it).
Open 8.30am-12.30pm, 2-6pm Mon-Sat.

La Lomellina

La Lomellina lies north-east of Pavia, bound to the south by the River Po and the north by the River Ticino. Known for its thriving shoe manufacturing sector, and for the beauties of the **Parco Ticino** (*see p106*), this area has another, less likely speciality. In springtime, don't mistake the glassy stretches across the plains for lakes: they're rice paddies, shimmering with the *arborio, rosa marcheti, ribe, originario* and *carnaroli* varieties so dear to Lombard cooks.

The hub of La Lomellina, **Vigevano** is Sforzatown East. Multiple generations of this Milanese ruling family (*see chapter* **History**) took a loving interest in it, making it their summer playground. The city's greatest patron Ludovico 'Il Moro' Sforza (1451-1508) was born here. Ludovico brought Donato Bramante to design the **piazza Ducale** and expand and complete the **castello**, started in 1345 by Luchino Visconti. The piazza was completed in glowing Renaissance splendour in 1494. The squiggly sunbursts that radiate from the lightposts are in white stone taken from the Ticino river. Finishing touches to the castle included the **Torre del Bramante**, a *falconeria* (falcon roost) and *scuderie* (stables). In 1532 Francesco Sforza commissioned the **Duomo** (piazza Ducale, open 8am-noon, 3-7pm daily), dedicated to Milan's patron saint, Sant'Ambrogio. It was consecrated in 1612 and the baroque façade added in 1684; there's a small **museo** attached (0381 690 370, open 3-6pm Sun or by appointment, closed Aug).

The small cloister (c1462) may have been designed by Guiniforte Solari. It is a delightful place with lively terracotta decorations around columns with elaborate capitals.

The *certosa* today is occupied by Cistercian monks, who run a gift shop to the right of the entrance vestibule where they do a sprightly business in herbal tinctures and liqueurs, honey, calendars and chocolates. Put your camera away and enjoy the quiet beauty of this spot secure in the knowledge that you can pick up a lovely book of hand-rendered images of the *certosa* from local printer **Torchio De'Ricci**.

Certosa di Pavia
Via del Monumento 5, Pavia (0382 925 613).
Open *May-Sept* 9-11.30am, 2.30-6pm Tue-Sun. *Oct-Mar* 9-11.30am, 2.30-4.30pm Tue-Sun. *Apr* 9-11.30am, 2.30-5.30pm Tue-Sun.

Torchio De'Ricci
Viale Partigiani 74, Pavia (0382 933 566).
Open *Sept-July* 9am-1pm, 3-6.30pm Mon-Fri. Closed Aug. **No credit cards.**
This shop is a master of incognito book sales. There's nothing on display: ask for the books of drawings of the *certosa*.

Getting there

By car
The *certosa* is 9km (5.5 miles) north of Pavia on SS35. Binasco is the nearest exit from the A7 autostrada.

By bus
Buses depart about every 20mins from Pavia bus station (toll-free 800 014 401/ www.asm.pv.it).

Lakes & Cities

Vigevano's **Museo della Calzatura** houses a presentation of footwear from around the world as well as from its own backyard. A shoe worn by Ludovico's wife, Beatrice d'Este, confirms her famous penchant for fashion; a reproduction of Charlemagne's foppish slippers seem more suited to Beatrice.

To the south-west, **Mortara** is known for its *salame di oca* (goose salami). Production dates back to the 11th century, when Mortara's large Jewish community, avoiding pork products, took the preparation of goose meat to new heights. The **Collegiata di San Lorenzo** (via San Lorenzo, open 8am-noon, 3.30-6.30pm daily) is a Gothic construction (1375) with a Romanesque belltower, all heavily reworked in the 19th century. There's an early 14th-century fresco on the arch above the altar.

Sartirana Lomellina is home to La Lomellina's largest **castello** (0384 800 804, open 11am-6pm Sat, Sun, or by appointment), which now houses collections of contemporary silver and gold objects, textiles and graphic art. It was given by Francesco Sforza to his trusted counsellor Cico Simonetta, who is best remembered for irrigation projects and for being beheaded in 1480 by Francesco's second son, Ludovico, who then took possession of the castle.

A prestigious goldsmith school is **Mede**'s claim to fame today, but the town traditionally owes its fortunes to rice. The oldest producer in the area, Riseria Masinari, got started in 1750 (via Molino 4, 0384 820 445, guided visits by appointment). A gushing letter from Queen Elizabeth II, dated 1955, hangs in the office, thanking the Masinari family for the rice sample they graciously sent her.

Lomello – the place that gave its name to the area – is a small town with a big church: a Romanesque complex comprising the basilica of **Santa Maria Maggiore**, first built in 1025 over the site of a paleo-Christian chapel; and the fifth- to seventh-century **Battistero di San Giovanni ad Fontes**, which lay buried for centuries below street level. It has an oversized full-immersion font. According to local lore, Lombard Queen Theodolinda (*see p8* **Theodolinda**) married Duke Agilulf in this church in 590, after which the devil inflicted considerable damage on the edifice

Milan's wine cellar

The Oltrepò is Italy's third-largest producer after Chianti and Asti, with vineyards covering 16,000 hectares (39,500 acres) and annual production of DOC wines totalling 550,000 hectolitres (over 12 million gallons). Yet Oltrepò wines are little known beyond the borders of Lombardy. Producers find a ready market in the region; some happily report that their 'export' market is Milan.

Such loyal regional support doesn't really encourage the Oltrepò's predominantly small producers to scale oenological heights. There are some good to excellent labels among the middle-of-the-road plethora, however. And if the DOC (*denominazione di origine controllata*) certificates held by 20 local wines are a fair guarantee of their quality, there are as many *vini da tavola* (table wines) that are just as good, despite – or maybe because of – the fact that they are blended without observing the strict rules governing local DOC and DOCG (*denominazione di origine controllata e garantita*) production.

The area is noted for reds: Bonarda, Barbera, Buttafuoco and Sangue di Giuda. But there's a large quantity of (rather bland) Riesling turned out too, and *spumante* (sparkling white) made from Pinot noir grapes.

Wine tasting (and buying) can be approached in two ways: the one-stop method by visiting one of the regional *cantine* (the outlets of producers' co-operatives), or pre-booked visits to the individual wineries.

Cantine

Cantina Cooperativa Canneto Pavese

Frazione Camponoce 27, Canneto Pavese (0385 60 078/www.cantinacanneto.it). **Open** 9am-noon, 2.30-6pm daily. **Credit** MC, V.

Cantina Sociale La Versa

Via Crispi 15, Santa Maria della Versa (0385 798 411/www.laversa.it). **Open** 9am-12.30pm, 3-7pm Tue-Fri; 9am-7pm Sat, Sun. **Credit** MC, V.

Wineries

Call at least one day in advance to advise the owners of your intended visit. Though you are under no obligation to buy, it is courteous not to leave empty-handed. Six apartments are available to rent at €25 per person per night.

when Agilulf refused to embrace his new
wife's Roman Catholicism. The town's other
Romanesque church, **San Michele** (open
8am-12.30pm, 2.30-7pm daily), houses a chip
from the True Cross. Originally constructed
in the tenth century, the **castello** in the centre
of town is now the site of municipal offices
but has, over the centuries, been home to
several noble families including the Visconti
and the Sforzas.

South-east of Vigevano, across the Ticino
river, **Bereguardo** is in the heart of the **Parco
Lombardo della Valle di Ticino** (*see p106
The Ticino Valley*), a nature reserve crossed
with well-maintained walking paths. A pontoon
bridge joins the town with the south bank.

Museo Civico della Calzatura Pietro Bertolini

Corso Cavour 82, Vigevano (0381 690 370).
Open 10.30am-12.30pm, 3-6pm Sun. By appointment
Mon-Sat. **Admission** €1.30. **No credit cards**.

Santa Maria Maggiore

Via Castrovecchio, Lomello (0384 85 542). **Open**
Easter-Oct 9am-noon, 3pm-sunset daily. *Nov-Easter*
by appointment.

Castello & Torre del Bramante

Piazza Ducale, Vigevano (no phone). **Open** *Torre*
Apr-Sept 10am-12.30pm Tue, Fri; 10am-6pm Sat,
Sun. Oct-Mar 10am-6.30pm Sat, Sun. *Castello* Apr-Oct
8.30am-7pm Mon-Fri; 8.30am-8pm Sat, Sun. Nov-Mar
8.30am-6pm Mon-Fri; 8.30am-7pm Sat, Sun.
Guided tours of the castle 2.30-6.30pm Sat, Sun.
Admission €1.30. **No credit cards**.

Where to eat

In Vigevano, the **Ristorante Marmonti**
(via del Popolo 13, 0381 690 968, closed
Mon, 1wk Jan & Aug, average €30) excels
at both traditional dishes and daring modern
interpretations; the wine list is excellent. The
Pasticeria Dante (piazza Ducale, 0381 83 776,
closed Tue and Aug, average €6) has delectable
home-made pastries and *brioche* at all times,
and bar snacks at lunchtime.

Getting there & around

By car

Car is the best way to visit La Lomellina. The SS494
runs from Vigevano through the area.

Azienda Agricola Castello di Luzzano

*Località Luzzano 5 (0523 863 277/www.
castelloluzzano.it).* **Open** 8.30am-noon,
2.30-6pm Mon-Sat. **Credit** AmEx, MC, V.
This winery occupies a whole *borgo* (walled
hamlet) complete with castle and medieval
cellars, a small collection of first-century
Roman artefacts excavated from the property,
a neo-classical church, plus an old customs
house delightfully converted into an inn
(double room €88). Approach the winery from
the SS10, turning right at the town of Castel
San Giovanni.

Azienda Agricola Martilde

*Frazione Croce 4, Rovescala (0385 756
280/www.martilde.it).* **Open** Mon-Sat by
appointment only. **No credit cards**.
Located in the heartland of Bonarda, this
producer (a former city slicker) succeeds
in taming the fickle grape with all the skill
of an old-timer.

Azienda Agricola Montelio

*Via Mazza 1, Codevilla (0383 373 090/
montelio.g@virgilio.it).* **Open** 8.30am-noon,
2.30-6pm Mon-Sat. **Credit** MC, V.

Documented vine cultivation here dates back
to the late 1200s; the estate occupies what
was once a farm run by Benedictine monks.

Isimbarda Santa Giulietta

*Frazione Castello, Cascina Isimbardi (0383
899 256).* **Open** 9am-noon, 3-7pm Mon-Fri;
10am-noon Sat. **No credit cards**.
Tradition and technology are this winery's
strong suits; it also maintains a rigorous
respect for the environment.

Tenuta Il Bosco

*Località Il Bosco, nr Zenevredo (0385 245
326/www.ilbosco.com).* **Open** 10am-noon,
3-6pm Mon-Fri; 9am-noon Sat. **Credit** MC, V.
Award-winning wines with well-tended
vineyards and super-high-tech winemaking
processes. The winery works magic with the
local red Croatina grape.

Tenuta Mazzolino

*Via Mazzolino 26, Corvino San Quirico (0383
876 122).* **Open** 9am-noon, 3-6pm Mon-Fri;
10am-noon Sat. **Credit** AmEx, MC, V.
The owners here are Pinot noir specialists
who age their wines in small French oak
casks with great skill.

Lakes & Cities

By train

Local trains run from Milan's Porta Genova station to Vigevano and Mortara; trains from Pavia stop in Lomello and Mede.

By bus

All buses from Pavia to surrounding towns depart from the bus station (toll-free 800 014 401/www. asm.pv.it) on via Trieste. STAV (0381 23 725) runs services from Vigevano to Pavia and Mortara. Cuzzoni Gilona (0382 84 025) runs services between Pavia and Lomello and Mede.

Tourist information

IAT Pro Loco

Corso Vittorio Emanuele 29, Vigevano (0381 299 282/hwsci@tin.it). **Open** 10am-noon, 4-7pm Mon-Fri; 10am-noon, 4-6pm Sat.

Oltrepò Pavese

Situated, as its name says, *oltre il Po* – beyond the River Po – south of Pavia, this area of splendid rolling hills is shaped (with a little bit of imagination) like a bunch of grapes, which is fitting, given that it is home to 500 producers of some very drinkable wine (*see p258* **Milan's wine cellar**).

The area's main town, **Voghera**, is an industrial hub and wins no prizes for beauty or charm. But the brick church of Sant'Ilario (via Tempio Sacrario della Cavalleria, open 10am-noon Sun) – known as the **Chiesa Rossa**, the red church – is a pretty Romanesque structure with a shrine to the Italian cavalry; the cavalry's former barracks now houses the **Museo Storico** (via Gramsci 1B, 0383 43 636, open by appointment).

There's a curious continuation of the horsy theme at the **Cowboys Guest Ranch**, an anomalous but totally authentic American Wild West-style dude ranch that hosts monthly rodeos, courses in cattle roping, a lively saloon, a Western duds store, hotel (€97 per person per day including horse) and a hugely popular restaurant specialising in steaks the size of Texas (via T Morato 18, Voghera, 0383 364 631, www.cowboys.it, closed Tue, open for dinner only, average €20).

Heading south from Voghera, **Salice Terme** (willow spa) sounds charming but is, in fact, populated by serious water-takers at hospital-like treatment-hotels.

At **Ponte Nizza** a road forks east towards the village of **Pizzocorno**. Just beyond the village is the abbey of **Sant'Alberto di Butrio** (open 7am-noon, 3-7pm daily), a medieval gem built by the noble Malaspina family as thanks to the local grotto-dwelling hermit, Alberto, who cured their mute son.

Alberto died in 1073 and was canonised six years later. The complex consists of three interconnected churches – Sant'Antonio, Santa Maria Genitrice and Sant'Alberto – this last containing relics of the saint as well as traces of 15th-century frescos.

Back on the main road, a minor road just south of Ponte Nizza leads west to **San Ponzo Semola**, another village with hermit credentials. A 45-minute walk from this tiny, perfectly preserved medieval village is the grotto where San Ponzo lived while converting the locals to Christianity, an activity that got him beheaded; the easy stroll leaves from in front of the church and is signposted *Sentiero del Giubileo*. The 11th-century church of **San Ponzo** (0383 59 266, open 10.30-11.15am, 2-5pm Sun, or by appointment) houses the saint's remains and a statue in his honour.

The main road swings east towards **Varzi**, with its low-hanging medieval porticos, narrow, twisting alleys and looming towers. The **Chiesa dei Cappuccini** (open 8.30am-7pm daily) stands guard at the entrance to the village. A Romanesque facelift hides its true age: the church dates back to 448, when it was dedicated to St Germain. Capuchin monks were its longest-standing tenants, hence the church's name; but in 1802 it was deconsecrated and rented out to local families as a barn. Fortunately, in 1971 it was restored to its former Romanesque beauty.

Getting there & around

By car

Car is the best way to visit the Oltrepò. The SS35 leads from Pavia to Casteggio from where minor roads fan out.

By train

Services run from Pavia to Voghera every 20mins.

By bus

Autoservizi Voghera-Varzi (0383 41 268) runs services from Voghera to Salice Terme and Varzi. STUMP (0383 365 111) runs a Milan–Pavia–Salice–Ponte Nizza–Stradella–Broni route. For general information about buses departing from Pavia call (toll-free) 800 014 401 or consult www.asm.pv.it.

Tourist information

IAT Pro Loco

Via Marconi 8, Salice Terme (0383 91 207). **Open** 9am-12.30pm, 2.30-6pm Mon-Sat.

IAT Pro Loco

Piazza della Fiera, Varzi (tel/fax 0383 545 221/ www.varziviva.net). **Open** *Sept-May* 9.30am-noon, 4-6pm Mon-Fri; 9am-noon Sat, Sun. *June-Aug* 9am-noon, 4-7pm daily.

The Mountains

Lombardy's little-known mountains have spectacular scenery and great snow.

Though they contain some of Italy's most spectacular Alpine terrain, the Valtellina, Valchiavenna and Valcamonica valleys are not exactly household names. But those who have yet to discover these valleys don't know what they're missing. Between them, they contain just about everything needed for a perfect Italian sojourn... apart from the sea. With winter and summer sports, inspiring mountain scenery, abundant flora and fauna, plenty of art and architecture and a unique culinary tradition (*see p264* **Mountain fare**), what more could a holidaymaker want?

So, do these valleys have any faults? Well, yes, of course they do. In many towns, the line between development and speculation has been sadly blurred, resulting in some hideous modern constructions, particularly in the ski resorts; and the people, like all true mountain types, can be diffident, even gruff. But for every taciturn *orso* (bear), you'll find two or three friendlier souls who are dying to let you in on the secrets of their valleys.

For information on all public transport to and between the locations covered in this chapter, consult the website www.infopoint.it.

Valchiavenna

Valchiavenna is heavily influenced by the microclimate of **Lake Como** (*see p194*), making it warmer and wetter than its sister valleys. Where the Mera and Adda rivers enter the lake lies the Riserva Naturale del Pian di Spagna e del Lago di Mezzola, a protected wetland zone. Slightly further north along the SS36, the open Piano di Chiavenna plain is more reminiscent of the balmy lakeland zone at the valley's feet than of the hostile mountains that lie to the north.

Valchiavenna's strategic position attracted the canny Romans, who built its first road. And the coming and going of merchants, pilgrims and travellers over the centuries gave **Chiavenna** an international touch that remains today.

The city's most important monument is the **Collegiata di San Lorenzo**, a fifth-century complex whose church, baptistery, cloisters and tower were largely rebuilt between 1537 and 1719. Its most jealously guarded artwork, a jewel-studded gold gospel cover known as

the *Pace*, is housed in the nearby **Museo del Tesoro di San Lorenzo**. Dating from the 11th or 12th century, this breathtaking piece of medieval gold work is encrusted with 97 pearls and 94 rubies, emeralds and opals, a spectacular filigree cross and gold bas-relief symbols of the evangelists. San Lorenzo's other major work – a six-metre circumference Romanesque font sculpted from a single chunk of *pietra ollare* – is tucked away in the **Battistero** (baptistery). Carved around this 950-year-old monolith are figures taking part in an Easter baptismal ceremony, including an incense-swinging priest, a nobleman on horseback clutching a falcon, and a blacksmith busily bashing away at his anvil.

Locate your *valle*

Each of Lombardy's major mountain valleys follows the course of a river. The River Mera cascades north–south from the Swiss border through the mountainous **Valchiavenna** (*see above*) before plunging into the top of Lake Como.

Valtellina (*see p263*) runs west–east, perpendicular to Valchiavenna, with the glinting waters of the River Adda flowing through it. The valley's south-facing northern edge is flanked by the sunny Alpi Retiche, while the wilder Orobie chain lines its north-facing, southern side. Two-thirds of the way down, the valley turns abruptly north-east, its northern limit blocked by the semicircular Ortlès-Cevedale group.

South-east of Valtellina is **Valcamonica** (*see p269*). At its northern extreme is the Adamello group (3,554m/11,846ft), but the valley is dominated by mounts Concarena (2,549m/8,496ft) and Pizzo Badile Camuno (2,435m/8,116ft), which loom over the prehistoric area of Capo di Ponte (*see p272*) halfway down. The River Oglio snakes its way between the flanking mountains before joining Lago d'Iseo (*see p220* **Little Lakes**) in the south. Note that names of valleys are preceded by 'Val'. You will come across variant spellings, either as one word or two; both are valid.

The locally crafted, grey-green *pietra ollare* stone on doorways, portals and fountains along via Pedretti and via Dolzino testifies to the large number of stonemasons in previous centuries; this tradition has all but died out.

At Chiavenna the SS37 forks east from the SS36 towards **Prosto di Piuro** and its tiny sub-hamlet of **Cortinaccio**, where the noble **Palazzo Vertemate Franchi** (0343 36 384, opening times vary, closed Nov-Feb) was the only building to survive the landslide that buried this wealthy area and its 1,000 inhabitants in 1618. The 16th-century interior contains some of the region's best Renaissance frescos, including the Salone dello Zodiaco inspired by Ovid's *Metamorphoses* and a traditional *stua* (wood-panelled room with wood stove). Two 17th-century paintings showing what Piuro looked like before and after the landslide. The garden has orchards, chestnut trees and frescoed walls.

North from Chiavenna, the SS36 winds up through some wild, steep mountainside to the ski resort of **Madesimo** (*see p270* **Snow good**) and the Spluga Pass (2,115m/7,050ft).

Battistero
Piazza Bormetti 3, Chiavenna (0343 32 117). **Open** *Jan-Mar* by appointment. *Apr, May* 2-6pm Sat, Sun. *June-Sept* 9am-noon, 2-6pm daily. *Oct-Dec* 2-5pm Sat.

Collegiata di San Lorenzo
Piazza Bormetti 3, Chiavenna (0343 32 117). **Open** 7.30-11.45am, 2-6.30pm daily.

Museo del Tesoro di San Lorenzo
Piazza Bormetti 3, Chiavenna (0343 37 152). **Open** *Mar-Oct* 3-6pm Tue-Fri, Sun; 10am-noon, 3-6pm Sat. *Nov-Feb* 2-4pm Tue-Fri; 10am-noon, 2-4pm Sat; 2-5pm Sun. **Admission** €3. **No credit cards**.

At Villa di Chiavenna on the SS37, the **Ristorante Lanterna Verde** (via San Barnaba 7, 0343 38 588, closed Wed, 2wks Jan, 4wks Nov-Dec, average €35) is the only restaurant in Sondrio province with a Michelin star. Similarly priced, and one of Chiavenna's classiest restaurants, is **Passerini** (via Dolzino 128, 0343 36 166, closed Mon, 1wk June & 2wks July, average €35), which serves local dishes and fresh fish in the elegant, 18th-century Palazzo Salis.

Chiavenna is best known for its *crotti*, cavities formed during ancient landslides whose steady air flow makes them perfect larders. Over time, many have morphed into *trattorie*. Among the best is the **Crotto Refrigerio** (via Pratogiano 56, 034 334 175, closed Mon and 2wks June, average €20).

Up the mountain at Montespluga, the 17th-century **Hotel Vittoria** (via Dogana 12, 0343 54 250, www.passospluga.it, double room €70, closed Nov and during heavy snow) has been in business since 1847.

Shops & services

The valley's ancient *pietra ollare* stone-carving tradition (*see above*) rests exclusively in the hands of artisan **Roberto Lucchinetti** in the hamlet of Prosto di Piuro (via alla Chiesa 5, 034 335 905, call for appointment). Lucchinetti's traditional stone cooking pans (*laveggi*) are coveted by chefs everywhere. His wife also recently opened a workshop next door selling hand-woven linen.

The Alpine allure of **Valchiavenna**.

Trips Out of Town

Pietra ollare carved by **Roberto Lucchinetti.** *See p262.*

Essentials

Getting there

By car
From the north of Milan, follow signs for the
superstrada 'I Laghi', then Lago di Como and Lecco.
Take the SS36 along the eastern shore of Lake Como
and on to Chiavenna (journey time around 1hr 40mins).

By train
Local services run from Milan's Stazione Centrale
to Colico, Sondrio or Tirano; change at Colico for
Chiavenna. Journey time to Chiavenna is 2hrs 40mins.

By bus
Autostradale (02 801 161/www.autostradale.com)
runs bus services from Milan's piazza Castello to
Madesimo (*see p262*) in season.

Getting around

By car
The main road links in Valchiavenna are the SS36
(*see above*) and the SS37 (open all year), which passes
through Piuro, before winding up the mountain to
San Moritz in Switzerland.

By train & bus
Although it's generally much easier to get around
by car, in heavily trafficked periods (Sun evenings,
holidays), the train can be much quicker. Trains
go no further north than Chiavenna. There are buses
from Chiavenna to Madesimo, Samolaco, Villa
di Chiavenna and Sondrio.

Tourist information

APT
*Corso Vittorio Emanuele II 2, Chiavenna (034
336 384/www.valchiavenna.com).* **Open** 9am-
12.30pm, 2.30-6pm Mon-Sat; 9am-12.30pm Sun.

APT
*Via alle Scuole, Madesimo (034 353 015/www.
madesimo.com).* **Open** *Dec-Apr* 9am-12.30pm, 3-
6.30pm Mon-Sat; 4-6pm Sun. *May-mid June, Sept-Nov*
9am-12.30pm, 2.30-6pm Mon-Sat; 9am-12.30pm Sun.
Mid June-Aug 9am-12.30pm, 3-7pm daily.

Valtellina

'The Valtellina', wrote Leonardo da Vinci in
the 1480s, 'is a valley surrounded by lofty and
terrible mountains; it produces a great quantity
of strong wine, and has so great a stock of cattle
that the peasants say that it produces more
milk than wine'.

While the valley bottom, dominated by
the River Adda, is now splattered with patches
of ugly ribbon development, Leonardo's

description still holds true for the upper
reaches. Valtellina's east–west direction has
created two contrasting microclimates: the
south-facing Alpi Retiche are covered with
terraced vineyards and apple plantations and
dotted with ancient stone villages, churches
and castles, while the north-facing Orobie chain
is altogether wilder. Snow sticks around for
longer here, and there are forests and pastures
where small herds of Alpine dairy cattle graze.
A regional park, the **Parco Regionale delle
Orobie Valtellinesi**, protects the slopes
above 1,000 metres (3,500 feet).

Valtellina's strategic position has meant a
chequered history for the 119-kilometre (74-mile)
valley. Celts, Romans, Lombards, Franks,
Milan's Visconti and Sforza families, Swiss
Grigioni, French, Spaniards and Austrians have
all held sway here, each leaving their mark in
historical structures. The valley's relatively
unspoilt environment is partly responsible for
its above-average per capita income. Tourism
– with its resulting demand for local food
products – is one of the valley's main industries.

Getting there

By car
From the north of Milan, follow signs for the
superstrada 'I Laghi', then Lago di Como and Lecco.
Take the SS36 along the eastern shore of Lake Como;
after Colico take the SS38, which runs the length of
the Valtellina and over the Stelvio Pass (open May-
Nov, snow permitting). Journey time to Morbegno
is 1hr 20mins.

By train
Trains run from Milan's Stazione Centrale to Sondrio
or Tirano every couple of hours. Journey time to
Sondrio is 2hrs; to Tirano, 2hrs 30mins.

Trips Out of Town

Mountain fare

Limited agricultural potential and restricted access to outside food supplies for many snowed-in months of the year made the mountain people of Valcamonica and Valtellina canny with the raw materials they had. Don't miss the following regional treats.

Bisciola: dried fruit bread stuffed with walnuts, chestnuts or figs.

Bitto: Valtellina's most prestigious cheese, from the Valgerola (*see p264*), which gets its sharp bite from a blend of cow and goat milks.

Braulio: a medicinal-tasting alcoholic *amaro* (after-dinner drink) made with mountain herbs, roots and berries, from Bormio (*see p267*).

Bresaola: salt-dried beef.

Casoncelli: Valcamonica's half-moon pasta shapes, with fillings that vary from village to village.

Cuz: a salty, fatty, mutton stew from Corteno Golgi, Valcamonica.

Pizzoccheri: buckwheat noodles cooked with potatoes, greens and melted casera cheese drenched in butter. Valtellina's trademark dish.

Polenta taragna: polenta made from buckwheat and maize flour.

Sciàt: deep-fried cheese balls covered in crispy buckwheat batter.

By bus

Autostradale (02 801 161/www.autostradale.com) operates services from Milan's piazza Castello to major ski resorts in season.

Getting around

By car

Car provides the best way of exploring the Valtellina and its offshoots. The SS38 is a fast-moving route; the panoramic drives from Monastero to Sondrio, and from Sondrio to Tirano are a slower, pleasurable alternative. Pick up 'Strada del Vino e dei Sapori della Valtellina' leaflet from most tourist information offices, or see www.valtellinavini.com.

By train

FS (state railway) trains go no further than Tirano. From here, a small tourist railway, the Bernina Express (information 0342 701 353), winds its way into Switzerland and San Moritz, with views of the Morteratsch Glacier and the Bernina chain. Journey time 2hrs 20mins.

By bus

Buses meet trains to link Tirano to Bormio and Livigno. An extensive, if somewhat irregular, network connects most towns in the valley.

Bassa Valtellina

Morbegno (alt. 262m/873ft) is a bustling place with a sprawling modern zone. Impressive churches and *palazzi* in the old centre reflect the strategically placed town's former importance. Sadly, many of these buildings are now much the worse for wear. The **Palazzo Malacrida** (via Malacrida 6, 0342 611 480, open by appointment) is the valley's best example of 18th-century rococo, with frescos by Valtellinese artist Cesare Ligari (1716-1770). On via Garibaldi, baroque *palazzi* with wrought-iron balconies and frescos now house alternative boutiques, antique and food shops, and cafés.

From Morbegno, the SS405 heads south along Valgerola, one of Valtellina's most unspoilt valleys, where *bitto* cheese (*see above* **Mountain fare**) is made. In the village of **Sacco**, the mythical *uomo selvatico* (wild man) – a hairy, bearded figure wielding a vicious-looking club – is portrayed in a rare 15th-century fresco in the former hayloft that is now home to the **Museo dell'Homo Salvadego** (località Sacco, 0342 617 028, open by appointment). Also at Sacco is the newly converted **Museo Vanseraf**, small museum of peasant culture in a working flour mill. But this tiny hamlet's main claim to fame is as the birthplace of goatherd-turned-mercenary Bona Lombarda (*see p265*). Inside the church is a peeling 17th-century portrait of the feisty lady (Signor Vaninetti, the museum guide, will help you get inside). A marked footpath (No.3) leads from the road below Sacco, past Bona Lombarda's birthplace, and back to Morbegno.

East of Morbegno on the SS36 is the turn-off for **Valmasino** and **Val di Mello**. These two valleys are a paradise for mountain climbers, containing the Pizzo Badile (3,308m/11,026ft), Pizzo Cengalo (3,367m/11,223ft) and Monte Disgrazia (3,678m/12,260ft).

Museo Vanseraf

Località Rasura (0342 610 460/www.museovanseraf. com). **Open** *Easter-Nov* 2.30-5.30pm Sat, Sun and by appointment. Closed Dec-Easter.

Where to stay & eat

Morbegno's best restaurant is the **Vecchio Ristorante Fiume** (contrada di Cima alle Case 1, 0342 610 248, closed dinner Tue & all Wed, average €30), though locals also recommend the newly renovated **Antica Osteria Rapella** (via Margna 36, 0342 610 377, average €20). The **Hotel Trieste** is located in a recently renovated palazzo in the centre (via San Rocco 3/5, 0342 610 259, double room €58).

Shopping

If you do nothing else in Morbegno, visit the fabulous **Fratelli Ciapponi** gourmet store (*pictured p264*; piazza III Novembre 23, 0342 610 223, open 8.30am-12.30pm Mon, 8am-12.30pm, 3.30-7pm Tue-Sat), where most of Valgerola's *bitto* cheese ends up. Don't miss the 500-year-old cheese cellars beneath the main shop. In Sacco, snap up a pot of genuine mountain honey from the **Associazione Produttori Apistici della Provincia di Sondrio** at a tiny store next to the museum (località Sacco, 0342 617 028, open 9am-noon, 2-6pm daily).

Media Valtellina

Sondrio (alt. 307m/1,023ft) is Italy's second-least-populated province capital; its territories encompass Valchiavenna and Valtellina (but not Valcamonica). The town's main square, piazza Garibaldi, is dominated by a statue of the ubiquitous Italian hero (he spent a night in Sondrio, at via del Gesù 7). The 16th-century **Palazzo Comunale** is in piazza Campello. In the same square is Sondrio's main church, the **Collegiata dei Santi Gervasio e Protasio** (0342 514 510, open 9am-noon, 3-7pm daily) based on 18th-century plans by Pietro Ligari, but completed by Swiss architect Pietro Taglioretti after Ligari fell out with the powers that be. Close by is the recently restored **Museo Valtellinese di Storia e Arte**, with works by the Ligari family. The museum also has some interesting women's art, including sketches by Pietro Ligari's daughter, Vittoria, and a portrait attributed to the Swiss artist Angelika Kaufmann. Via Scarpatetti winds up past rustic stone dwellings to the medieval **Castello Masegra**. The central shopping streets – the pedestrian-only via Dante and via Beccaria – are lined with some great little fashion, food and flower shops.

The road to **Valmalenco** leads north from Sondrio. Most people head up this valley to admire, walk, hike, ski (*see p270* **Snow good**) or climb on the spectacular Bernina group, capped by Valtellina's highest peak, Piz Bernina (4,049m/13,496ft). Other impressive peaks include Monte Disgrazia (3,678m/12,260ft) and Pizzo Scalino (3,323m/11,076ft). Rock freaks can admire some of the 261 types of mineral from the valley in the church of **Santi Giacomo e Filippo** attached to the Museo della Valmalenco, in the hamlet of **Chiesa Valmalenco** (for information call APT Chiesa Valmalenco; *see p267*).

From Sondrio, the SS38 continues to **Tirano**. Running more or less parallel is the aptly named Strada Panoramica, a more winding

Bona Lombarda

Bona Lombarda (1417-68) was a female soldier of fortune who started life as a humble goatherd. Her unlikely adventures began when a dashing horseman named Pietro Brunoro abducted her as she was tending her animals near her birthplace in the village of Sacco (*see p264*). Mercenary captain Brunoro had been fighting for the Milanese against the Venetians at the Battle of Delebio (1432) in the valley bottom. Why he chose to make off with Bona is unclear: her earliest chronicler describes her as *bruta, nera, picola* (ugly, dark and small). But despite its dubious beginnings, the relationship endured.

Catholic versions of the story maintain that Bona and Brunoro married in secret; it seems more likely that she was Brunoro's own private joy division, following him around until he was thrown into jail after a disagreement with King Alfonso of Naples. Here, Bona showed her true mettle. She convinced the noble and powerful of the land to bombard the king with letters begging for Brunoro's release; and, knowing Alfonso's weakness for falcons, she showered him with gifts of precious hunting birds, along with sparrowhawks, horses and dogs. Eventually, the captain was released, and it is at this point that they married, according to most accounts. The couple had three children, but motherhood did not stand in the way of Bona, who continued to fight as a mercenary alongside her husband. She died and was buried at Modon (Methoni) in Greece, aged 51, on her way back from fighting against the Turks.

alternative, passing vineyards and orchards. Pick up this road (signposted to Montagna) before Sondrio hospital, east of the town centre.

At **Montagna** (alt. 567m/1,890ft), the ruined 14th-century **Castel Grumello** has been recently restored.

Ponte in Valtellina (alt. 485m/1,616ft) is one of the best-preserved medieval/Renaissance towns in the Alps. Its principal monument is the church of **San Maurizio** in piazza Luini (0342 482 158, open by appointment only), a combination of Romanesque, Gothic and Renaissance styles, crowned by a 15th-century fresco, *Madonna and Child with San Maurizio* by Bernardino Luini.

Teglio (alt. 851m/2,837ft) is home to Valtellina's most important Renaissance residence, the noble **Palazzo Besta** (1433). Its courtyard contains frescos of scenes from Virgil's *Aeneid*.

At Tresenda is the turn-off for **Aprica** (alt. 1,172m/3,907ft) and the pass to Valcamonica. Hurriedly constructed in the 1960s, '70s and '80s, Aprica is not the classiest of the valley's resorts (*see p270* **Snow good**). But its splendid position – wedged on a sunny pass between the Valtellina and Valcamonica valleys and surrounded by national parks – almost makes up for its aesthetic defects.

The SS38 continues to **Tirano** (alt. 441m/1,470ft), a market town and home to one of the valley's most successful baroque constructions, the **Santuario della Madonna di Tirano** (piazza Basilica, opening times vary, call the UIT Tirano for information, *see p268*). The highlight is its 17th-century hand-carved organ sound box, festooned with flowers, fruit and religious scenes, played during 11am mass each Sunday. Nearby is the **Museo Etnografico Tiranese**, with well-organised displays of rural implements. The spectacular Bernina Express train to San Moritz, Switzerland, departs from Tirano.

Just before **Grosio** (alt. 653m/2,177ft) on the SS39 is an entrance to the (open-access) **Parco delle Incisioni Rupestri** (guided tours 0342 847 454), containing the Rupe Magna, the most-engraved rock in the Alps, with over 5,500 prehistoric carvings. Also in the park are the ruins of two medieval castles, the Castello Vecchio and the Castello Nuovo, both of which you can wander round.

Castel Grumello

Montagna (0342 380 994). **Open** *Oct-Dec* 10am-5pm Sat, Sun; by appointment Tue-Fri. *Feb-Sept* 10am-6pm Sat, Sun; by appointment Tue-Fri. Closed Jan. **Admission** €1.50.

Museo Etnografico Tiranese

Piazza Basilica 30, Tirano (0342 701 181). **Open** *June-Sept* 10am-noon, 3.30-6.30pm Tue-Sun. *Oct-May* 10am-noon, 2.30-5.30pm Sat; or by appointment. **Admission** €1.50.

Museo Valtellinese di Storia e Arte

Palazzo Sassi de' Lavizzari, via Quadrio 27, Sondrio (0342 526 269). **Open** *mid Sept-May* 9am-noon, 3-5pm Tue-Sat. *June-mid Sept* 10am-noon, 3-6pm Tue-Sat. **Admission** €4.

Palazzo Besta

Via Besta 7, Teglio (0342 781 208). **Open** *May-Sept* 9am-noon, 2-5pm Tue-Sat, 1st & 3rd Sun of mth. *Oct-Apr* 8am-2pm Tue-Sat, 1st & 3rd Sun of mth, 2nd & 4th Mon of mth.

Where to eat & drink

In Sondrio, the **Terra di Mezzo** serves pizzas and pasta dishes to Sondrio's younger crowd (via Bonfadini 14/16, 0342 212 902, closed Wed, average €17).

As befits a route that winds through vineyards, the Strada Panoramica (*see p264*) offers plentiful opportunities to eat and drink. At Montagna is the **Ristoro Castel Grumello** (0342 380 994, closed Mon, 3wks Jan, 3wks June & July, average €35), a stylish restaurant at the

Fauna-spotting

No time to go wildlife spotting? There's a one-stop shop at the **Osservatorio Eco-Faunistico Alpino**, a 20-hectare park where many native species are kept. Otherwise, search for these animals in the following natural habitats.

Red deer: Vezza d'Oglio, Sonico, Saviore.
Chamois: Parco Adamello in Val Malga (Sonico), Val Salarno, Valle Adamè near Cimberga and Paspardo, Parco dello Stelvio in Val Zebrù.
Ibex: as for chamois. Also Val Grosina and Val di Lei.
Mouflon (introduced species): Val Belviso.
Marmot: anywhere in the region above 2,000m (6,665ft).
Roe deer: keep your eyes peeled.
Capercaillie: woodlands above Albosaggia, Faedo and Piateda during mating season. Forests in Parco delle Orobie.

Osservatorio Eco-Faunistico

Office: corso Roma 150, Aprica (0342 745 153). **Open** *Park* Easter-Oct daily by appointment, snow permitting. Nov-Easter appointments may be possible; phone to check. **Admission** €9.30. **No credit cards**.

Impossibly scenic **Bormio** attracts the Milan jetset. *See p268*.

foot of the ruined castle, serving freshly prepared, unusual dishes. At Tresivio is the not-to-be-missed **Jom-Bar** (via Chioso 42, 0342 430 609, closed Mon and all lunchtimes), an old stone house with a bright orange interior, a 1,000-strong cocktail list and easy-listening jazz. From 6pm until 9pm, the bar is laden with free snacks, and cocktails are half price (€3.50).

At Ponte in Valtellina, the historic **Ristorante Cerere** (via Guicciardi 7, 0342 482 294, closed Wed, 3wks July & 2wks Jan, average €30) serves local dishes in a refined, traditional interior, while the rougher-and-readier **Osteria Sole** (via Sant'Ignazio 11, 0342 565 298, closed Tue, 1wk Feb, 1wk July, 3wks Sept, average €20) dishes up platters of steaming *pizzoccheri* and *sciatt* (*see p264* **Mountain fare**).

Shopping

In Sondrio, the **Libreria del Viaggiatore** (via Angelo Custode 3, 0342 218 952) offers a vast array of informative travel books in English and Italian.

At Lanzada in Valmalenco, Valtellina's most respected bee-keeper, **Walter Nana** (via Spini 316, 0342 453 053), has a shop selling his unbelievably delicious honey and own-brand cosmetics. At Ponte in Valtellina is **Pezzotti della Valtellina** (via Nazionale 2, 0342 482 232), which sells Valtellina's traditional, multi-coloured rag rugs (*pezzotti*); ask to see the workshop where owner Cristina Toppi weaves her creations on a hand-loom.

Further along the SS38 at Chiuro is the ski and knitwear factory outlet, **Samas** (*see p146* **Bargain!**). Also at Chiuro is Valtellina's most prestigious vineyard, **Nino Negri** (via Ghibellini 3, 0342 482 521). Call for an appointment to tour, taste and buy.

On a winding track off the SS39 just west of Aprica, local character Luigi della Moretta makes fresh goat's cheese at **Li Spondi** (via Sponde, 0342 745 212). It's best to arrive after 5pm; Luigi doubles as the village bus driver.

Where to stay

Sondrio's oldest and poshest hotel is the 165-year-old **Hotel della Posta** (piazza Garibaldi 19, 0342 510 404, double room €106). It also has a well-known restaurant (closed Sun).

In the old centre of Tirano is the friendly **Casa Mia** (via Arcari 6, 0342 705 300, double room €40-€60), a B&B offering three clean, if slightly fussy, rooms and big breakfasts.

In Aprica, the family-run **Kinderheim Biancaneve** has rooms for families and unaccompanied kids (via Italia 33, 0342 746 521, double room €40-€80) and a babysitting service.

Tourist information

APT Valtellina
Via Trieste 12, Sondrio (0342 512 500/www.valtellina online.com). **Open** 9am-12.30pm, 2.30-6pm Mon-Fri.

APT
Corso Roma 150, Aprica (0342 746 113/www. valtellinaonline.com). **Open** *Dec-Mar* 9am-12.30pm, 3-6.30pm Mon-Sat; 9am-12.30pm, 4-6pm Sun. *Apr-June, Sept-Nov* 9am-12.30pm, 2.30-6pm Mon-Sat; 9.30am-12.30pm Sun. *July, Aug* 9am-12.30pm, 3-7pm Mon-Sat; 9am-12.30pm, 4-6pm Sun.

APT
Piazza San Giacomo e Filippo, Chiesa in Valmalenco (0342 451 150/www.valmalencofree.com). **Open** *Dec-Apr* 9am-12.30pm, 3-4.30pm daily. *Apr-mid June, mid Sept-Nov* 9.30am-12.30pm, 2.30-6pm Mon-Sat; 9.30am-12.30pm Sun. *Mid June-mid Sept* 9am-12.30pm, 3-7pm Mon-Sat; 9am-12.30pm, 4-6pm Sun.

Trips Out of Town

UIT
*Piazza Stazione, Tirano (0342 706 066/www.
valtellinaonline.com).* **Open** *mid Sept-mid June*
9.30am-12.30pm, 2-5pm Mon-Sat; 10am-12.30pm
Sun. *Mid June-mid Sept* 9am-1pm, 2-7pm Mon-Sat;
9am-1pm, 2-5pm Sun.

Alta Valtellina

Bormio (alt. 1,225m/4,083ft) has it all. One
of the oldest settlements in the valley, it boasts
a well-preserved old centre and an impossibly
scenic position at the foot of the Ortlès-Cevedale
range. Bursting with hotels, restaurants and
sporting facilities – not to mention a Roman
spa – it is fast becoming a favourite haunt for
Milan's fashion set… which doesn't mean that
ordinary mortals can't join in the fun.

Bormio's most imposing church is **Santi
Gervasio e Protasio** (piazza Cavour, open
8am-noon, 3-6pm daily), a baroque edifice with
a candy-pink striped spire. Across the piazza
from the church is the squat **Kuèrc**, a 14th-
century building with a slate-tiled roof and cut-
away walls, where justice was administered in
warmer weather. Just off the via della Vittoria is
the **Museo Civico**, where highlights include
ancient wooden skis and reconstructions of a
carpenter's and a cobbler's workshop.

Across the bridge at the end of via Morcelli
is the rustic Combo neighourhood. At via
Sant'Antonio 3, Bormio's most photographed
house has roof-props and beams carved like
twisted ropes. Nearby, the house at via Zuccola
5 has an external 15th-century fresco of the
Madonna and Child attended by angels in well-
preserved floral frocks. The heart of Combo is
the church of **Santo Crocefisso** (piazza del
Crocefisso, open 8am-noon, 2-6pm daily), which
contains a gruesome 15th-century crucifix, said
to have healing and miraculous powers.

The recently restored **Bagni Vecchi
Bormio** (0342 910 131, admission €15-€30)
is three kilometres (two miles) north of town on
the SS38. This Roman spa has waters flowing
from nine hot springs at temperatures of 36-
43°C; it includes a long, hot-water tunnel carved
from a cave, hot waterfalls, a natural steam
bath and an outdoor thermal pool with
spectacular views of the surrounding
Alps, and offers around a dozen beauty
and relaxation treatments.

The SS38 continues to the Stelvio Pass and
the **Parco Nazionale dello Stelvio**, Italy's
largest protected natural area, covering 134,000
hectares in the Lombardy and Trentino Alto-
Adige regions. The park contains the entire
Ortlès-Cevedale massif, 110 glaciers, 2,000 plant
species and a huge variety of mammals and
birds. The Consorzio del Parco Nazionale

dello Stelvio visitors' centre (via Roma 26,
Bormio, 0342 910 100, www.stelviopark.it)
dispenses information and maps.

The SS301 branches off the SS38 east of
Bormio, and leads to **Livigno** (alt. 1,816m/
6,053ft). Until 1951, when its access road was
first opened year-round, Livigno was completely
cut off for nine months of the year; going there
still feels like driving to the edge of the world.
To compensate, the town was granted duty-free
status in the 16th century, a privilege it still
enjoys. These days people head here to ski (*see
p270* **Snow good**), or shop. Bargain-hunters can
pick up designer clothes, perfume and electronic
goods at discounts of around 30 per cent.

Museo Civico

Via Buon Consiglio 25, Bormio (0342 912 216).
Open *Jan-Easter* 3-7pm Mon-Sat. *Mid June-mid Sept*
3-7pm Mon; 10am-12.30pm, 3-7pm Tue-Thur, Sat,
Sun; 9-11pm Fri. *Easter-mid June, mid Sept-mid Dec*
3.30-6.30pm Tue, Thur, Sat.

Where to stay & eat

Bormio's restaurant-of-the-moment is **Al Filò**
(via Dante 6, 0342 901 732, closed all Mon &
Tue lunch, 2wks May & 2wks Oct, average
€25), where Valtellinese dishes are served in
a 17th-century stable. Also in Bormio, the
Vecchia Combo (via Sant'Antonio 6, 0342
901 568, closed Sun in Sept-July, average €22)
serves traditional food in an ancient building.

The bar of the friendly **Ristorante Bar
Kuérc** (piazza Cavour 7, 0342 904 738, closed
Tue, 2wks May-June & 4wks Sept-Oct, average
€20) is another local hotspot. The restaurant
upstairs serves hearty traditional dishes.

At the newly revamped **Bar Braulio**
(via Roma 27, 0342 902 726), customers pick
at snacks in a contemporary stone-and-wood
salon. The bar is owned by the makers of
Bormio's famous herbal post-prandial *amaro*;
pick up a bottle of the stuff while you're here.
The recently reopened **Chateau Les Bains**
(Strada Statale dello Stelvio, Bagni di Bormio,
0342 910 131, www.bagnidibormio.it, double
room €75-€152) is attached to the Roman
baths; prices include entry to the spa.

Tourist information

APT

*Via Roma 131B, Bormio (0342 903 300/www.
valtellinaonline.com).* **Open** *Dec-Apr, July, Aug* 9am-
12.30pm, 3-6.30pm daily. *Apr-June, Sept-Nov* 9am-
12.30pm, 2.30-6pm Mon-Sat, 9.30am-12.30pm Sun.

APT

*Via dala Gesa 65, Livigno (0342 996 379/www.
aptlivigno.it).* **Open** 9am-12.30pm, 2.30-6.30pm daily.

Valcamonica

Situated in the province of Brescia (*see p225*), Valcamonica is very different from the neighbouring Valtellina, and the two valleys have a long tradition of rivalry, even hatred. The *camuni* will proudly tell you that they have one of Europe's longest documented histories, thanks to over 300,000 pictorial rock carvings dating back 10,000 years; and unlike Valtellina, Valcamonica enjoyed a long period of stability as part of the Venetian Republic (1428-1796). Their economies differ too: Valcamonica's is primarily industrial and the 80-kilometre (50-mile) valley bottom is scarred with textile, steel and lingerie factories. But head up any of the minor valleys and you'll find treasures that anywhere else would have herds of tourists trampling over them; here they are undisturbed.

The SS39 swirls down the mountainside from Aprica, past the **Riserva Naturale Regionale delle Valli di Sant'Antonio**, a popular area for walks and picnics. At **Edolo** (699m/2,230ft), a pleasant market town with some attractive, rustic dwellings, the SS41 heads north to Ponte di Legno, or south to Darfo Boario Terme. The SS42 runs the length of the valley; some of the minor roads leading off it are a challenge.

Getting there

By car

From Milan, take the A4 motorway east; exit at Seriate and follow the SS42 through Lovere to Darfo Boario Terme. Journey time to Darfo around 1hr 40mins.

From Valtellina, take the SS38 to Tresenda, then the SS39 to the Aprica Pass (open all year). At Aprica, continue east to Edolo. Alternatively, the scary Passo di Gavia road (open June-Oct, snow permitting) goes from Bormio to northern Valcamonica.

By train

Railway connections are slow and irregular. Take a mainline train from Milan to Brescia, from where a branch line winds its interminable way through spectacular countryside up the valley to Edolo. You may have to change en route.

By bus

SAB (035 289 000) runs services from piazza Castello, Milan to Ponte di Legno via Edolo. Journey time 4hrs. There are irregular services from Aprica to Edolo.

Tourist information

Ufficio Turistico IAT

Piazza Martiri di Libertà 2, Edolo (0364 71 065). Open mid June-mid Sept 9am-12.30pm, 3.30-6.30pm Tue-Sat; 9am-12.30pm Sun. Mid Sept-mid June 9am-12.30pm, 3.30-6.30pm Tue-Sat.

North from Edolo

The northern reaches of Valcamonica are more spectacular by far than the southern stretches. Factories give way to rocky mountain slopes, pine forests and the occasional *baita* (stone farm buildings traditionally used during summer grazing).

At **Temù** (alt. 1,144m/3,813ft) is the **Museo della Guerra Bianca**, with photographs, documents and artefacts from the dramatic 'White War' fought between the Austrians and Italians on the nearby mountains during World War I.

Ponte di Legno (alt. 1,257m/4,190ft) is best-known as a ski resort (*see p270* **Snow good**) but is also a good departure point for summer hiking and mountain biking in the nearby Stelvio (*see p268*) and Adamello (*see below*) parks. The town centre – razed during World War I and rebuilt in the early 20th century – is blissfully closed to traffic making it a pleasant place to stroll.

Just outside the village is the **Scuola Italiana Sleddog** (località Case Sparse 10, 0364 922 31/www.scuolaitalianasleddog.it), which organises courses for mushers, plus sled dog rides (Dec-Easter, €38 for 2hr beginner course) and husky trekking (Apr-Sept, €18 per hr).

The 50,000-hectare **Parco Regionale Adamello** runs the eastern side of Valcamonica from Breno to Ponte di Legno, where it borders with the Parco dello Stelvio. Within its confines are the Lombardy slopes of the Adamello group, Italy's largest glacier, and one of the last habitats of the Alpine brown bear. The **Comunità Montana della Valle Camonica visitors' centre** in Breno will provide information and maps about this beautiful region.

Comunità Montana della Valle Camonica visitors' centre

Piazza Tassara 3, Breno (0364 324 011/ www.parcoadamello.it). Open 9am-noon, 2-5pm Mon-Thur; 9am-noon Fri.

Museo della Guerra Bianca

Via Adamello, Temù (0364 94 617/www. museoguerrabianca.it). Open Mid June-mid Sept 5-7.30pm daily. Mid Sept-mid June by appointment.

Tourist information

Ufficio Turistico IAT

Corso Milano 41, Ponte di Legno (0364 91 122). Open Sept-June 9am-12.30pm, 3.30-7pm Mon-Sat; 9.30am-12.30pm Sun. July, Aug 9am-12.30pm, 3-7pm daily.

Snow good

Chiesa Valmalenco

See p267.
Chiesa has (a few) older, rustic buildings interspersed with modern constructions clinging to the mountainside. But no one comes here for the architecture: the ski slopes overlook the spectacular Bernina range and include Valtellina's only peak over 4,000m (13,330ft). Winter skiing.
Vital statistics: 35km (22 miles) of pistes; 3 black runs, 7 red runs, 6 blue runs; 1 cableway, 5 chair-lifts, 4 ski-lifts; snowboard park, 37km (23 miles) of cross-country tracks, outdoor ice rink.
Daredevil dive: To turn the view to a blur, dive down the Thoeni black run, which drops 1,400m (4,670ft) from Alpe Motta, losing 50 per cent of its height on the final, heart-stopping stretch.

Ski hire

Pircher Sport
Via Roma 150 (0342 451 301).
Rates *Skis & boots* €5.50 per day.
Credit AmEx, DC, MC, V.

Ski school

Scuola Italiana Sci Valmalenco
Alpe Palù (0342 451 409). **Rates** €26.
Credit MC, V.

Aprica

See p265.
Small, quiet and not exactly hot on *après-ski*, Valtellina's Aprica is an ideal spot for families and beginners, who will have the slopes pretty much to themselves during the week. Winter skiing.
Vital statistics: 40km (25 miles) of pistes; 2 black runs, 6 red runs, 7 blue runs; 2 cableways, 5 chair-lifts, 8 ski-lifts; 9.5km (6 miles) of cross-country tracks, outdoor ice rink.

Ski hire

Larino
Corso Roma 127 (0342 745 434). **Rates** *Skis & boots* €12.40 per day. **Credit** MC, V.

Ski schools

Scuola Italiana Sci Aprica
Piazza Palabione 46 (0342 746 004).
Rates €25.82 per hr. **No credit cards**.

Bormio

See p268.
Valtellina's classiest ski resort, Bormio is the best bet for anyone who wants to punctuate their skiing with history, art and culture. Winter skiing.
Vital statistics: 50km (31 miles) of pistes; 2 black runs, 5 red runs, 4 blue runs; 3 cableways, 7 chair-lifts, 7 ski-lifts; 7.5km (4.5 miles) of cross-country tracks, indoor ice rink.
Daredevil dive: Test your stamina on Europe's longest slope, which plunges 1,800m (6,000ft) from Monte Vallecetta directly into the town.

Ski hire

Celso Sport
Via Vallecetta 5 (0342 901 459).
Rates *Skis & boots* €12.90 per day.
Credit AmEx, DC, MC, V.

Ski school

Scuola Nazionale Sci Bormio
Via Funivia 6 (0342 901 553/www. scuolascinazionale.bormio.it). **Rates** €26 per hr. **Credit** AmEx, DC, MC, V.

Livigno

See p268.
Sunny Livigno's extensive network of pistes runs down six different mountain slopes in Valtellina, mostly across open, unforested land. The town's altitude means it often has snow long after it has melted in rival resorts. Livigno compensates for its deficiency on the style front with a lively, youthful atmosphere. Winter skiing.
Vital statistics: 150km (94 miles) of pistes; 9 black runs, 37 red runs, 29 blue runs; 3 cableways, 13 chair-lifts, 15 ski-lifts; 2 snowboard parks, 50km (31 miles) of cross-country tracks, outdoor ice rink.

Daredevil dives: snowboarders seek their thrills in the snow parks on the Mottolino and Vetta Blesaccia mountains.

Ski hire & school

Scuola Italiana Sci Livigno
Via Saroch 180 (0342 970 300). **Rates** *Skis & boots €15.50 per day.* **Lessons** *€27 per hr.* **Credit** AmEx, DC, MC, V.

Passo dello Stelvio

See p268.
At 2,758m (9,193ft), Valtellina's Passo dello Stelvio is Europe's largest summer ski area, in full swing from May until October, when most other resorts are taking a break. In the winter months, the Stelvio Pass is closed. The Associazione Operatori Stelvio (0342 903 300/www.passostelvio.com) will provide information on other ski schools in the area.
Vital statistics: 20-25km (12-16 miles) of pistes, 2 cable railways, 8 ski-lifts, 2 cross-country tracks.

Ski hire & school

Pirovano
Corso Vittorio Veneto 7, Sondrio (summer 0342 904 421/winter 0342 210 040). **Rates** *Skis & boots €15 per day.* **Lessons** *€28 per hr.* **Credit** AmEx, DC, MC, V.

Ponte di Legno & Tonale

See p269.
Not so much a ski resort as a whole stack of them piled up alongside the Stelvio and Adamello national parks in Valcamonica. Ponte di Legno is a modern resort, with the usual outsized-chalet buildings around a more stylish centre. Higher up are the Tonale pass (1,800m/6,000ft) and the Presena glacier (3,100m/10,330ft), where ski addicts can slip down the slopes year-round.
Vital statistics: 80km (50 miles) of pistes; 4 black runs, 17 red runs, 7 blue runs; 1 cable car, 11 chair-lifts, 14 ski-lifts; 16.5km (10 miles) of cross-country tracks; ice rink, sledge dog school at Tonale (*see p269*).
Daredevil dives: only tackle the resort's most famous run – the Pista Paradiso – if you're up to it. Italy's national ski team train here.

Ski hire

Le Ski Lab
Via Corno d'Aula 21 (0364 900 393). **Rates** *Skis & boots €14 per day.* **Credit** MC, V.

Ski school

Scuola di Sci Pontedilegno-Tonale
Corso Milano 6 (0364 913 01/0364 903 943). **Rates** *€27 per hr.* **Credit** MC, V.

Information

Call 848 077 for snow and weather reports in Italian, or see www.valtellinaonline.com. Call 118 for Soccorso Alpino (Alpine Rescue).
For factory outlets selling discounted skiwear, *see p146* **Bargain!**

Trips Out of Town

South from Edolo

Valcamonica's most visited town is **Capo di Ponte**, home to the **Parco Nazionale delle Incisioni Rupestri**, a Unesco World Heritage site. Spread over 300,000 square metres (3,226,000 square feet) are over 100 rocks with carvings dating back 10,000 years, depicting everything from antler-headed deer-gods to primitive carts. The **Centro Camuno di Studi Preistorici** (0364 42 091) organises archaeological summer courses.

Capo di Ponte also boasts two of the most atmospheric Romanesque churches you'll ever see. To reach the 11th-century monastery church of **San Salvatore** (0364 42 389, open by appointment), follow the signs from the SS42 just north of Capo di Ponte. This privately owned church, with its octagonal dome, sits in a little park where the only sounds are the trickle of water and the occasional peacock screech. The simple, austere interior has pillars carved with eagles, imaginary beasts and mermaids. The floor laid in the church 1,000 years ago is still here. The first pillar on the left has a base that rests on live rock, as, indeed, does the church itself. To visit the 12th-century **Pieve di San Siro** (at Cemmo, near Capo di Ponte) leave a document with the Pro Loco at Capo di Ponte (*see below*) in exchange for the keys. The church's exterior has an arched doorway; the stone portal is carved with mythical fauna, enhanced with well-preserved scales, feathers and fur. The no-frills interior has a zen-like baptismal font carved from a single block of stone, a huge stone altar platform, some 15th-century frescos, and a crypt partly carved from the rock below the church. Just above Capo di Ponte, **Pescarzo** is one of the best-preserved medieval villages in the valley.

At **Cerveno** (alt. 500m/1,667ft) is one of the valley's most surprising works of art. Attached to the church of **San Martino** (0364 434 014, open Oct-May 8am-noon, 2.30-5pm daily; June-Sept 8am-noon, 2.30-6pm daily) is the via Crucis (Stations of the Cross), a closed-in flight of steps lined with 14 chapels containing 198 life-size 18th-century sculptures. To find it, walk through the church and unbolt the main door. The best of these lifelike tableaux (chapels I-VII, XI-XIII) are by the Brescian sculptor Beniamino Simoni (1720-1800), and show the agony of Christ before, during and after the crucifixion.

Bienno's (alt. 445m/1,483ft) well-preserved medieval/Renaissance centre has a network of narrow, cobbled streets with arches, towers and frescoed *palazzi* at every turn. The town has a working flour mill, the **Mulino Museo**, and there's a thermal spa at **Darfo Boario Terme**

(alt. 218m/726ft). Housed in an art deco structure, the **Terme di Boario** (viale Igea 3, 0364 5391, www.termediboario.it, closed mid Dec-mid Jan) has water that is reputed to do great things for liver complaints. For the hale and hearty there are saunas, Turkish baths and the like.

Just north of Darfo Boario Terme on the SS42, the **Archeopark** has reconstructions of a prehistoric farm (complete with wild boars), an artisan's village and traditional *camuni* houses on stilts around a lake.

Archeopark

Località Gattaro (0364 529 552/www.archeopark. com). **Open** *Mar-Nov* 9am-5.30pm. Closed Dec-Feb. **Admission** €8.

Mulino Museo

Via Glere, Bienno (0364 300 307). **Open** 8.30-11.30am Mon-Sat. **Admission** free.

Parco Nazionale delle Incisioni Rupestri

Località Naquane (0364 42 140). **Open** *Mar-Oct* 8.30am-7pm Tue-Sun. *Nov-Feb* 8.30am-4.30pm Tue-Sun. **Admission** €4.

Where to eat & stay

In the medieval centre of Bienno is the **Hostaria Vecchia Fontana** (via Fontana 3, 0364 300 849, closed all Mon & Sat lunch, closed 1wk Mar & 2wks Sept, average €25), located in a colourful ex-stable and serving local fare. At Ponte di Legno **La Cantina** (corso Trieste 55, 349 602 9580, closed Mon in off-season) serves wine and snacks at large wooden tables.

Shopping

If you run out of clean knickers, call in at the **Cotonella** factory outlet in Malonno (via Nazionale 135, 0364 759 311, open 3-7pm Mon, 8.30am-12.30pm, 3-7pm Tue-Sat) for underwear with discounts of 30 per cent. At Ponte di Legno, you'll find **Antonio Sandrini** (via Nino Bixio 27, 0364 92 526), one of the valley's last woodcarvers, who fashions exquisite little frogs, grasshoppers and snails.

Tourist information

Pro Loco

Via Briscioli 42, Capo di Ponte (0364 42 080/ 0342 426 619). **Open** 9am-noon Mon; 9am-noon, 2.30-4.30pm Tue-Sat.

Ufficio Turistico IAT

Piazza Einaudi 2, Darfo Boario Terme (0364 531 609). **Open** *Mid Sept-June* 9am-12.30pm, 3-6pm Mon-Fri; 9am-12.30pm Sat. *July-mid Sept* 9am-12.30pm, 3-6pm Mon-Fri; 9am-12.30pm Sat, Sun.

Directory

Features

Directory

Getting Around

Aeroporto di Malpensa

02 7485 2200/www.sea-
aeroportimilano.it. **Map** p307.
Milan's main airport is in Somma
Lombarda, 50km (30 miles) from the
city centre in the province of Varese.
Malpensa has two terminals:
Terminal 1 is for intercontinental,
international and domestic flights;
Terminal 2 is mostly for charter
flights, although it's also used by a
few international services.

Aeroporto di Linate

02 7485 2200/www.sea-
aeroportimilano.it. **Map** p307.
Milan's national airport is in Segrate,
part of the city's straggling suburbs,
about 7km (4.5 miles) from the centre
of town. It handles domestic and
continental flights.

Aeroporto di
Orio al Serio

035 326 323/flight information 035
326 111/www.milanoorio-airoport.it.
Bergamo's airport is in Orio al Serio,
about 45km (28 miles) from Milan
and 5km (3 miles) from Bergamo. It
handles national, continental,
intercontinental and charter flights.
When Milan's airports are fog-bound,
flights are often rerouted here.

On from Malpensa

FNME (Ferrovie Nord
Malpensa Express)

02 20 222 (7am-8pm)/recorded
information in English 02 27
763/www.ferrovienord.it. **Tickets**
€9; €4.50 4-12s; free under-4s.
The Ferrovie Nord's Malpensa
Express train runs every 30mins
from around 6am to 10pm daily
between Malpensa Airport
(Terminal 1) and Cadorna metro
station (journey time 40mins),
stopping at Bovisa/Politecnico and
Saronno. This is replaced by a bus
service (50mins) until around 1am
in both directions. A free shuttle bus
runs at 10min intervals between
Malpensa's terminals 1 and 2.
Tickets can be bought at the
Ferrovie Nord desks in the airport
and at stations where the Malpensa
Express stops as well as all FN
stations. Note that there's a hefty

surcharge for buying tickets on the
train/bus. Tickets should be stamped
in the machines on the station
platform before boarding.

Malpensa Bus Express

Information 02 9619 2301 (8am-
12.20pm, 2-6pm Mon-Fri)/
www.ferrovienord.it. **Tickets** €5.06;
€2.53 3-12s; free under-3s.
Services depart every 20mins
(6.30am-11.50pm Malpensa Terminal
1 to Stazione Centrale; 5.10am-
10.30pm from Stazione Centrale to
Malpensa) and take approximately
1hr. All services make intermediate
stops at Malpensa Terminal 2 and,
on request, Milano Fiera. Tickets are
available in the arrivals terminals at
the airport, at the SAP office at
piazza Luigi di Savoia by Stazione
Centrale, at the APT office (*see p290*)
near the Duomo, or on the bus.

Malpensa Shuttle

Information 02 5858 3202/
recorded information in English
02 5858 3185/www.malpensa-
shuttle.com. **Tickets** €4.13; €2.07
2-12s; free under-2s.
Services depart every 20mins
(3.15am-12.15am from Malpensa;
4.30am-10.30pm from Stazione
Centrale) and take approximately
50mins. Buses will stop on request
at Fiera. Tickets can be purchased in
the arrival arrivals halls, at the SAP
office at piazza Luigi di Savoia by
Stazione Centrale or on the bus.
Malpensa Shuttle also runs 7 shuttle
bus services a day each way between
Malpensa and Linate (journey time
1hr10mins). Tickets, which can be
bought on the bus, cost €7.75.

By taxi

See also p277.
A taxi from Malpensa to Milan costs
approximately €68. Journey time is
around 45mins. Beware of rush-hour
traffic, which can lengthen the trip
substantially. Use only white or
yellow taxis lined up at the ranks
and avoid all drivers who solicit
business as you exit the terminal.

On from Linate

By bus

There is no train service into Milan
from Linate but there is the excellent
ATM bus 73, which departs every

10mins from Linate Airport and San
Babila metro station. Travel time is
around 25mins, rising to 40mins at
rush hour. An ordinary €1 city bus
ticket is valid for the airport service.

By taxi

See also p277.
A taxi to or from Linate will cost
approximately €15-€20, depending
on what part of town you are
travelling from or to.

On from Orio

Trains depart hourly from Orio al
Serio Airport for Milan's Stazione
Centrale. **Autoservizi Zani** (035
678 611/www.zaniviaggi.it) runs
buses every half hour from 5.50am to
9.15pm between Bergamo railway
station and the airport (98¢) .
Travelling time is about 1hr by train
and 10mins by bus.
Autostradale (information 035
318 472/www.autostradale.com) runs
six buses daily (with more services in
high season) in each direction
between Orio al Serio Airport and the
air terminal at Milan's Stazione
Centrale. Tickets can be bought on
board and cost €6.71 (€3.36
concessions). Autostradale also has
half-hourly bus links between
Bergamo bus terminus and Milan's
piazza Castello. When fog closes
Milan's airports, airlines provide
buses to ferry stranded passengers to
and from Orio al Serio.

Airlines

Alitalia

Domestic flight information & ticket
sales 848 865 641/international
flight information & ticket sales 848
865 642/www.alitalia.it. **Phone**
lines open 24hrs daily. **Credit**
AmEx, DC, MC, V.
Via Albricci 5, Centre (02 2499
2700). Metro Duomo/bus 54, 65/
tram 12, 23, 27. **Open** 9am-6pm
Mon-Fri. **Map** p311 A1.
Piazzale Cadorna 14, West (02 2499
2500). Metro Cadorna/bus 50, 58,
94/tram 1, 27. **Open** *For ticket*
purchase, check-in and connection to
Malpensa Express train service (see
above) 7am-8.30pm Mon-Sat. *For*
frequent flyer ticket pick-up and
assistance 9am-6pm Mon-Fri; 9.30am-
5pm Sat. **Map** p308 C2.

Malpensa Airport Terminal 1, 2nd floor (domestic ticket office 848 865 643/international ticket office 848 865 643). **Open** 5.30am-11pm daily. **Map** p307.

British Airways
Flight information & ticket sales 848 812 266/www.britishairways.com/italy. **Phone line open** 8am-8pm Mon-Fri, 9am-5pm Sat. **Credit** AmEx, DC, MC, V.
Corso Italia 8, South (02 724 161). Metro Missori/bus 65/tram 4, 23, 24. **Open** 9am-5pm Mon-Fri. **Map** p310 A/B2.
Malpensa Airport Terminal 1, 2nd floor (02 7486 6596). **Open** 9am-5.30pm daily. **Map** p307.

Arriving by bus

The long-distance bus companies that serve Milan use piazza Castello (map p308 C2) as a terminus.

Arriving by train

Long-distance, international and Eurostar trains arrive at and depart from Milan's Stazione Centrale. (The station is a pickpocket's paradise, so watch your wallet and luggage carefully.) Trains arriving at night may stop at Lambrate or Rogoredo stations. If you arrive late in the evening, it is advisable to take a taxi to your destination; the metro stops shortly after midnight (*see p275*). For information on buying train tickets, *see p276*.

Public transport

See transport map, *p312*. The services operated by the Azienda Trasporti Milanesi (ATM) are the mainstay of Milan's transport system, serving both the inner-city *rete urbana* (urban network) and the Greater Milan area (for details of the system, *see p276* **Greater Milan**).

ATM manages a public transport network of three metropolitan railway lines and 120 tram, trolley-bus and bus lines, covering nearly 1,400km and reaching 86 municipalities.

Public transport is fairly safe, even at night. Watch out for pickpockets in packed buses and subways.

Most ATM buses, trams and metro trains are orange, though you will see an occasional green one – the new supertram 24 or the turn-of-the-century service tram.

The transport system is easy to use once you've got the hang of it. There are three **metro lines** (MM1/red, MM2/green, MM3/yellow) that connect to **buses** and **trams** throughout the city.

The city centre is circled by three concentric ring roads, each of which is covered by public transport offering handy routes between inner and outer suburbs avoiding the traffic chaos of the centre. Buses 50, 58, 61 and 94 travel (portions of) the inner circular route, which passes close to the centre. Trams 29 and 30 circle the city along the middle circular route. Buses 90, 91 and 92 travel the outer circular route. Many trams cut across the city, connecting ring roads and continuing into outlying or suburban areas.

The newly built **Passante Ferroviaria** (rail throughway) connects Porta Venezia, Repubblica, Garibaldi (FS), Lancetti, Bovisa (FNM) and Certosa (FS) metro and train stations.

Metro trains run every 4-5 mins from 6am until midnight daily; after 9pm, services run only every 10-12mins. All ATM bus and tram services – except night services, *see below* – also run between 6am and midnight daily, departing every 5-20mins, depending on the route and time of day. The doors for boarding are clearly marked *entrata*; doors for alighting are marked *uscita*. Some new buses require that you push a button to open the doors. If you wish to alight from a bus, make sure you have pushed one of the red

buttons alerting the conductor that the next stop is requested. The conductor will speed by without stopping if there's no request and he sees no passengers waiting at the stop.

At each bus stop a sign shows all stops made along the route and includes a timetable for weekdays (*feriale*), Saturdays (*sabato/pre-festivi*) and Sundays and holidays (*domenica e festivi*).

Radiobus (02 4803 4803) is a request-only bus service that operates within the innermost ringroad. Call to communicate your route and the time you want to travel. Radiobus can be reserved days in advance or at short notice. Tickets are sold at all ATM sale points and on the bus. They cost €1.50 if bought at a sale point, €2 if bought on the bus, plus the cost of a regular single ticket (or season ticket) for the urban network; if you board the bus without a ticket or season ticket, you'll be charged €3.

Night services

The three metro lines are closed from midnight; buses then ply the same routes until about 1.30am. There are also 55 night bus and tram routes, which run from 12.30am to 2.30am. There is no service between 2.30am and 6am.

Tourist services

See also p290. **Tours**. The ATM Ciao Milano tourist tram 20 (information 02 7200 2584) departs from Castello Sforzesco (*see p70*). Tickets are €15.50; passengers can get off to investigate sights en route and then pick up a later tram.

Tickets & fares

ATM tickets can be bought at metro stations (6am-8pm at staffed desks; from ticket machines at other times), *tabaccai* (*see p288*) and most

Directory

newsstands as well as Lampugnano, Bisceglie and Famagosta station car parks.

The same tickets are valid on all ATM bus, tram and metro lines operating within the inner-city *rete urbana* (urban network). Travel to and through other zones requires appropriate tickets.

Tickets must be bought before boarding. When you board you must stamp tickets in the machines by the rear and/or front doors. If travelling without paying looks an easy option, bear in mind that there are ticket inspectors around: if you are caught you will be fined €100 on the spot.

Children less than one metre in height travel free of charge. Students, pensioners and the disabled pay lower rates for monthly and yearly tickets.

Biglietto singolo (€1)

Valid 75mins from when it's stamped for use on unlimited ATM trams and buses on the *rete urbana* (inner-city network), plus one trip on the metro. This ticket is also valid on the rail throughway and on the urban sections of the Ferrovie del Nord and Ferrovie dello Stato mainline railways.

Biglietto giornaliero (€3)

Valid 24hrs for unlimited use on all transport in the *rete urbana* area.

Abbonamento due giorni (€5.50)

Valid 48hrs for unlimited use on all transport in the *rete urbana* area.

Abbonamento settimanale (€16.75)

Valid seven days for unlimited use of all transport in the *rete urbana* area.

Abbonamento mensile (€37.75)

Valid one calendar month for unlimited use of all transport within the *rete urbana* area.

Transport information

Bus and tram routes and numbers change with some regularity. If you plan to use public transport, it's a good idea to consult www.atm-mi.it

or pick up a copy of *City*, a free daily published by *Corriere della Sera* (*see p285*), in any metro station. This has a full page of ATM transport updates, areas under construction or renovation and route changes. The ATM Point (*see p276*) dispenses a free detailed map of the public transport system; the same map can be purchased (€2.58) at most newsstands.

ATM Point

Galleria del Sagrato, mezzanine floor, inside Duomo metro station, Centre (tollfree 800 016 857). **Open** 7.45am-8.15pm Mon-Sat. The main ATM information desk has English-speaking staff, although its phone line (7.30am-7.30pm daily) is Italian-speaking only.

Greater Milan services

ATM manages a Greater Milan fare system called SITAM (Sistema Integrato Trasporti Area Milanese; Milan Area Integrated Transport System). Many extra-urban transport operators with routes running into the city participate in this system. Beyond the *rete urbana* (*see p275*), the area is divided into concentric coloured outer zones – yellow, green, red, blue, brown, orange, purple and grey; fares depend on the number of zones travelled through.

The ATM Point (*see above*) in the Duomo metro is the best place for information on travel to Greater Milan destinations.

TICKETS

To travel from what Milanese call 'l'hinterland' into the city, or from one town to another in the hinterland, *biglietti interurbani* (inter-urban tickets) and *biglietti cumulativi* (combined tickets) are available. The former can be used exclusively on routes outside the *rete urbana*; the latter can be used both in the hinterland and on the *rete urbana*.

Abbonamento un giorno cumulativo Area Grande (€6.90)

Valid 24hrs on all ATM routes and on inter-urban SITAM routes within almost all the colour-coded zones.

Rail services

Milan's metropolitan rail network (*see p275*) is useful and heavily used. Regular bus/tram/metro tickets are valid on trains as far as the stations marked *limite tariffe urbane* (urban tariff limit) in red on the map on p312.

For train travel in the Lombardy region, check individual destinations in the Lakes & Cities section of this guide.

Mainline train services are operated by the Ferrovie dello Stato (FS, state railways; aka Trenitalia). The FS website, ww.trenitalia.com, is well organised and in English, though reservations and payment on the internet are still a challenge. The following phone lines provide information on services:

FS Informa (information on routes and prices, open 7am-9pm; not reachable from mobile phones) 848 888 088.
FS Client Assistance 02 6371 2016/02 670 4818.
FS Disabled Passengers 02 6707 0958.
FS Lost and Found office 02 6371 2667.

TIMETABLES/TICKETS

Train timetables can be purchased at any *edicola* (newsstand). The easiest to read is *Nuovo Grippaudo Orario*: all Milan hinterland train timetables are included here as well as boat schedules for Lago Maggiore (*see p187*).

Mainline train tickets can be bought at stations or travel agents with an FS sign, or online by credit card on the FS website. Children under 12 pay half-fare; children under four travel free. For information on taking wheelchairs on trains, *see p281*.

Slower trains (*diretti, espressi, regionali* and *interregionali*) are very cheap; a system of supplements means that faster services – InterCity (IC), EuroCity (EC), Eurostar (ES, not to be confused with Channel tunnel trains) – are closer to the European norm.

Advance reservation is obligatory and free on ES trains on Fridays and Sundays, and all week at certain peak times of year. An R inside a square on train timetables indicates this; check when purchasing your ticket. Booking a seat on IC and internal EC routes costs €3 and is well worth it even when not obligatory to avoid standing at peak times. If your ES, IC or EC train arrives more than 30 minutes late and you have a seat booking, you can have the supplement reimbursed at the booth marked *rimborsi*.

Larger stations and ticket machines accept all major credit cards. Most travel agents accept them for train tickets too.

You must stamp your train ticket – and any supplements you have – in the yellow machines by each platform before boarding the train: failure to do so can lead to a hefty fine. Being foreign and looking forlorn can get you off the hook.

The principal stations in Milan are listed below. For information on which stations to use for destinations in Lombardy, *see p279*.

Stazione Centrale

Piazza Duca D'Aosta, North. **Map** p309 B1/2.
Connects with MM2 and MM3.

Stazione di Cadorna (Milano Nord)

Piazzale Cadorna, West.
Map p308 C2.
Connects with MM1 and MM2.

Stazione Porta Garibaldi

Piazza Freud, North. **Map** p309 B1.
Connects with MM2.

Taxis

Licensed taxis are white (a few old yellow ones remain), and are meter operated. If anyone comes up to you at Stazione Centrale or any of the other major tourist magnets muttering 'Taxi?' always refuse, as they are likely to charge you up to 400 per cent more than the normal rate.

Most of Milan's taxi drivers are honest; if, however, you suspect you're being ripped off, make a note of the driver's name and number from the metal plaque inside the car's rear door. The more ostentatiously you do this, the more likely you are to find the fare returning to its proper level. Report complaints to the drivers' co-operative (its phone number is shown on the outside of each car) or, in serious cases, the police.

Fares & surcharges

When you pick up a taxi at a rank or hail one in the street (no easy task), the meter should read zero. As you set off, it will begin to indicate the minimum fare – €3 at the time of writing – for the first 200 metres, after which the charge goes up according to time and distance. There are surcharges on Sundays, public holidays and for trips to and from the airport, plus €1.03 for each item of luggage placed in the boot. €2.58 is added to the basic fare between 10pm and 7am. The supplement from town to Malpensa airport is €7.49; from the airport to town it's €5.94; to and from Linate airport, it's €5.16.

Taxi ranks

Ranks are indicated by a white sign with 'Taxi' written in black. In the city centre there are ranks at piazza Duomo, piazza Scala, piazza San Babila, piazza Fontana, piazza Diaz, piazza Beltrade, largo Cairoli, piazza Cavour, largo Carrobbio, via Manzoni, largo Augusto, piazza Cadorna and largo Greppi.

Phone cabs

You can phone for a taxi from any of the following companies. When your call is answered, name the street and number, or the name and location of a bar, club or restaurant where you wish to be picked up. You will then be given the taxi code-name (always a location followed by a number) and a time, as in 'Bahama 69, *in tre minuti*' (Bahamas 69, in three minutes). A radio taxi will start the meter from the moment your call is answered.

If you wish to pay by credit card, say so when you order your taxi. You must ask which credit cards are accepted as not all vehicles are equally equipped, even within the same taxi company. Usually AmEx, MC and/or V are accepted. Taxis can be ordered well in advance, a precaution that is strongly recommended if you intend to use one at rush hour, during a major city event, or in inclement weather.
Taxi Blue 02 4040.
Radio Taxi 02 8585.
Taxi Subito (recorded message in Italian asks you to digit the taxi stand nearest to you) 848 814 781.

Driving

Having a car in Milan can be great fun, or a huge liability. At first glance, Milanese driving resembles a Formula One race; in fact it's a high-speed conversation, with its own language of glances and light flashing.

If you do use a car in the city, some tips to be borne in mind are listed below. Short-term visitors should have no trouble driving with their home licences, although if they are written in different scripts or less common languages, an international licence can be useful. EU citizens must take out an Italian driving licence after being resident for one year. Remember the following:

● You are required by law to wear a seat belt at all times, and to carry a warning triangle in your car.

● Keep your driving licence, Green Card, vehicle registration and personal photo ID documents on you at all times.

● Do not leave anything of value (including a car radio) in your car. Take all your luggage into your hotel when you park.

● Flashing your lights in Italy means that you intend to pass the driver in front of you, so you want him to pull over into the supposedly slower right lane. It doesn't mean you will slow down (contrary to British practice).

● If traffic lights flash amber, stop and give way to the right.

● Watch out for death-defying mopeds and pedestrians. By local convention, pedestrians usually assume they have the right of way in the older, quieter streets without clearly designated pavements.

Restricted areas

Large sections of the city centre are closed to non-resident traffic during business hours, and sometimes in the evening. You may be fined if you are caught trying to get in; your vehicle may be wheel-clamped if you do manage to slip in and park – you'll have to pay a fine and a charge to have the clamp removed. If you are in a hired car or have foreign plates and are stopped, mention the name of your hotel, and you will probably be waved on. Occasional Sundays are designated no-car days: this is rigidly enforced in the city centre, but there are exceptions for moving around outside the inner ring road.

Breakdown services

It is advisable to join a national motoring organisation, like the AA or RAC in Britain or the AAA in the US, before taking a car to Italy. They have reciprocal arrangements with the Automobile Club d'Italia (ACI).

If you require extensive repairs and do not know a mechanic, pay a bit more and go to a manufacturer's official dealer, as the reliability of any garage depends on long years of building up a good client-mechanic relationship. Dealers are listed in the Yellow Pages under *auto*, along with specialist repairers such as *gommista* (tyre repairs), *marmitte* (exhaust repairs) and *carrozzerie* (bodywork and windscreen repairs). The *English Yellow Pages*, available from most English bookshops (*see p137*), has a list of garages where English is spoken.

Automobile Club d'Italia (ACI)

Corso Venezia 43, East (02 77451/ emergencies & information 803 000/24hr traffic information line 02 774 5355). Metro Palestro. **Open** 8.30am-12.45pm, 2.15-5pm Mon-Fri. **Map** p309 C1.

The ACI has English-speaking staff and provides a range of services for all foreign drivers, free or at low prices. Members of associated organisations are entitled to basic repairs free, and to other services at preferential rates. This is still the best place to call in the event of a breakdown even if you are a non-member. You will be charged, but prices are generally reasonable.

Touring Club Italiano (TCI)

Corso Italia 10, South (members' information line 02 535 9973/ bookshop 02 852 6304/travel agency 02 852 676/www.touringclub.it). *Metro Missori/bus 65/tram 15.* **Open** *Bookshop* 9am-7pm Mon-Sat. *Travel agency* 9am-7pm Mon-Fri, 9am-12.30pm Sat. **Credit** AmEx, DC, MC, V. **Map** p310 A/B2.

The Milan office has a bookshop with an English-language section and a travel agency. English is spoken and there are discounts on books, and varying discounts on travel packages for members, including those from international sister clubs.

Parking

Parking is a nightmare in Milan: the best solution is to leave your car in one of the 20-odd guarded car parks (*see below*) in the downtown area. Alternatively, use the Sosta Milano parking system: buy tickets (€1.30 for an hour) at newsstands, *tabaccai* (*see p288*) or from some parking attendants, and scratch them to indicate the day and time. Leave them on the dashboard.

Watch out for signs by entrances saying *Passo carrabile* (access at all times), *Sosta vietata* (no parking), and disabled parking spaces marked by yellow stripes on the road. The sign *Zona rimozione* (tow-away area) means no parking, and is valid for the length of the street, or until you come to a tow-away sign with a red line through it. If a street or square has no cars parked in it, you can safely assume it's a seriously enforced no-parking zone. In some areas, self-appointed *parcheggiatori* will 'look after' your car for a small fee; although it is illegal, it's worth coughing up to ensure that your tyres remain intact.

Garage Meravigli

Via Camperio 4, North (02 8646 1784). Metro Cairoli/bus 54, 58/ tram 1, 19, 24. **Open** 7am-midnight Mon-Sat; 7-10am, 8pm-midnight Sun. **Rates** €4 per hr; €24.80 24hrs. **No credit cards**. **Map** p308 C2.

Rinascente

Via Agnello, Centre (02 885 2419). Metro Duomo/bus 60, 61/tram 1, 2, 15. **Open** 7am-1am daily. **Rates** €9.30 3hrs; €11.36 4hrs; €1.03 each subsequent hr. **Credit** AmEx, DC, MC, V. **Map** p311 A1.

Autosilo Diaz

Piazza Diaz, Centre (02 8646 0077). Metro Duomo/bus 54/tram 15. **Open** 7am-2am daily. **Rates** €2.07 per hr; €28.92 24hrs. **No credit cards**. **Map** p311 A1.

Car pounds

If you can't find your car, it has probably been towed away. Phone the municipal police (*Vigili urbani*) on 02 77 271 and quote your number plate to find out which car pound it has been taken to.

Petrol

Petrol stations sell unleaded petrol (*senza piombo* or *verde*) and regular (*super*), though this latter will be phased out. Diesel is *gasolio*. Liquid propane gas is GPL. Most stations offer full service on weekdays; pump attendants do not expect tips. At night and on Sundays many stations have self-service pumps that accept €5 or €25 notes in good condition. Sometimes unofficial 'assistants' will do the job for you for a small tip (50¢).

Car hire

To hire a car you must be over 21 – in some cases 23 – and have held a licence for at least a year. You will be required to leave a credit card as security. It's advisable to take out collision damage waiver (CDW) and personal accident insurance (PAI) on top of basic third party insurance. Companies that do not offer CDW are best avoided.

Avis

National booking line *199 100 133*. **Credit** AmEx, DC, MC, V. **Open** 24hrs daily.
Linate airport (02 717 214). **Open** 7.30am-11.30pm daily.
Malpensa airport (02 585 8481). **Open** 7.30am-midnight daily.
Galleria delle Carrozze, Stazione Centrale, North (02 669 0280). **Open** 7.45am-8pm Mon-Fri; 8am-4pm Sat. **Map** p309 B2.
Piazza Diaz, Centre (02 863 494). *Metro Duomo/bus 54/tram 15.* **Open** 8am-7pm Mon-Fri. **Map** p311 A1.

Hertz

Linate airport (02 7020 0256). **Open** 7.30am-11.30pm daily.
Malpensa airport (02 5858 1137). **Open** 7.30am-midnight daily.
Galleria delle Carrozze, Stazione Centrale, North (02 669 0061). **Open** 8am-7pm Mon-Fri; 8am-2pm Sat. **Map** p309 B2.
Via Solferino, North (02 657 5726). *Metro Moscova/bus 41, 43, 94.* **Open** 8am-1pm, 2-7pm Mon-Fri; 8am-1pm Sat (later pick-ups can be arranged). **Map** p308 B/C2.
All **Credit** AmEx, DC, MC, V.

Bicycles & motorbikes

This city isn't kind to bikes or bikers, due to aggressive drivers, numerous tram tracks and cobbled streets. There are some cycle paths, however, around the grounds of the Milano Fiera (see *p100*) and the Parco Sempione (see *p74*).

The Ciclobby club (02 6931 1624/www.provincia.milano.it/associazioni/ciclobby) organises bike tours in cultural and/or environmentally interesting areas every Sunday for members and non-members.

Bike hire

To hire a **scooter** or **moped** (*motorino*) you'll need a credit card, an identity document and/or a cash deposit. Helmets are required on all kinds of motorbikes, scooters or mopeds; the police are very strict about enforcing this. For bicycles, it is normally sufficient to leave an identity document rather than pay a deposit. For mopeds up to 50cc you need to be over 14; a driver's licence is required for anything over 50cc.

AWS Bicimotor

Via Ponte Seveso 33, North (02 6707 2145). Metro Centrale FS or Sondrio/bus 90, 91, 92/tram 2. **Open** 9am-1pm, 3-7pm Tue-Sat. **Credit** MC, V. **Map** p309 A2.
City and mountain bike rental.

Biancoblu

Via Gallarate 33, West (02 308 2430/www.biancoblu.com). Tram 14, 19, 33. **Open** 9am-6pm Mon-Sat; 8-10am, 6-8pm Sun for pre-booked bikes only. **Credit** AmEx, DC, MC, V. **Map** off p308 A1.
Bikes and electric bikes for rent.

Motorcycle Tours & Rentals

Via del Ricordo 31, East (02 2720 1556/www.mototouring.com). Metro Cresenzago or Cimiano then bus 53. **Open** Oct-Apr 9am-6pm Mon-Sat. *May-Sept* 9am-6pm daily. **Credit** AmEx, DC, MC, V. **Map** off p309 A2.
Bikes, motorbikes and scooters.

Getting around Lombardy

For public transport in the Greater Milan area, see *p276*. For general train information, see *p276*. For travel between Milan and destinations covered in this guide, see chapters in the Lakes & Cities section. **Long-distance bus services** are run by Autostradale (piazza Castello 1, 02 801 161).

The regional council's website www.infopoint.it has a handy journey-planner.

Regional rail services

Regional train services start at Milan's numerous stations (*see p277*). The fastest trains leave from Stazione Centrale; regional and inter-regional trains from other stations:
● **Cadorna** for commuter trains to northern suburbs, Meda–Canzo–Asso, Saronno–Varese–Laveno Monbello, Saronno–Como.
● **Porta Garibaldi** for Rho, Novara, Vercelli, Chivasso.
● **Lambrate** for Pavia, Tortona, Treviglio, Brescia, Desenzano and Sirmione.
● **Lambrate & Rogoredo** for Lodi.

Driving

For general driving information, see *p277*. Once you have negotiated Milan's *Tangenziale* ring road and exited from the city, you can opt for excellent *autostrade* (motorways) that will whisk you efficiently from A to B but may be short on atmosphere.

Alternatively, there is a far-reaching and, on the whole, well-maintained network of *strade statali* (SS; state highways), which provide a more picturesque view of the region. *Strade provinciali* (SP; provincial roads) are not always in tip-top condition, and don't always take the straightest route from A to B, but will undoubtedly provide some memorable Lombard driving moments.

Directory

Resources A-Z

Accommodation

It's always wise to have a hotel reservation before arriving in Milan. If you don't, the following phone/online booking agencies will help you.

Associazione Provinciale Albergatori di Milano

www.traveleurope.it. **Open** 9.30am-6pm Mon-Fri. **Credit** AmEx, DC, MC, V.

Centro Prenotazione Hotel Italia

Tollfree 800 015 772/02 2940 4616/ 02 2940 4616/fax 02 2953 1586/ www.hotelmi.it. **Open** 9am-8pm Mon-Fri; 2am-5pm Sat. **Credit** varies depending on hotel booked.

Milano Hotels Central Booking

02 805 4242/fax 02 805 4291/ www.hotelbooking.com. **Open** 9am-6pm Mon-Fri. **Credit** AmEx, DC, MC, V.

Age restrictions

Cigarettes and alcohol cannot legally be sold to under-16s. Beer and wine can be consumed at bars from the age of 16, spirits from 18. Anyone aged 14 or over can ride a moped or scooter of 50cc; no licence is required. You must be over 18 to drive and over 21 to hire a car.

Business

If you're doing business in Milan, a call or visit to the commercial section of your embassy or consulate (*see below*) is a good first move. As ever in Italy, any personal recommendations will smooth your way immensely: use them shamelessly and mercilessly.

American Chamber of Commerce

Via Cantù 1 (02 869 0661/fax 02 805 7737/www.amcham.it). **Open** 9am-12.30pm, 2-5.30pm Mon-Fri.

British Chamber of Commerce

Via Dante 12 (02 877 798/fax 02 805 6094/www.britchamitaly.com). **Open** 9am-1pm, 2-5pm Mon-Fri.

Business centres

Conservatorio 22 Business Center

Via Conservatorio 22 (02 77 291/ fax 02 772 940/www.cogesta.it).

Executive Service

Via V Monti 8 (02 467 121/ fax 02 4801 3233/www. executivenetwork.it).

Tiempo Nord

Via Giovanni da Udine 34 (02 3809 3456/fax 02 3809 3305/ www.tiemponord.it).

Conference organisers

There are excellent conference facilities of all kinds and locations in this city, which moves and shakes with over 900 conventions held each year at the Fiera di Milano (*see p100*). Company conferences can be held in magnificent historic buildings such as the Milan Chamber of Commerce's very central Palazzo Affari Ai Giureconsulti (02 8515 5873/ fax 02 8515 5885) or in the very modern Magna Pars (via Tortona 15, 02 8940 1384/fax 02 5810 4760) located near the fashion-shoot Navigli district (*see p92*). Alternatively, most of the major hotels can cater for events (*see chapter* **Accommodation**). If you don't wish to handle the details yourself, there are a number of agencies that will smooth the way for you. Two conference organisers who've been in the business for over 20 years are Viaggiando-Promoconvention (02 837 2396/fax 02 5810 1302) and MGR Srl Socio Italcongressi (02 4800 6110/ fax 02 4800 8471).

Interpreters

Connor Language Services

Piazza Piemonte 8 (02 469 5819/ fax 02 469 5807/www. connorlanguage.com).

Communication Trend Italia

Via Palestrina 31 (02 669 1338/ fax 02 669 7335/info@cti- communication.it).

Executive Service Network

Via V Monti 8 (02 467 121/fax 02 4801 3233/www.executivenetwork.it).

Couriers (international)

There are no problems at all in Milan with courier services and pick-up at your doorstep is reliable. Make sure the driver/company provides you with a company envelope or box: if you courier documents in a plain envelope (to the US), the receiver will be charged customs duty upon arrival.
DHL 02 575 721/199 199 345/ www.dhl.it.
Federal Express 02 218 81/ tollfree 800 123 800/www.fedex.com.
TNT 02 982 0471/fax 02 9822 5555/ www.tntitaly.it.
UPS tollfree 800 877 877/ www.ups.com.

Couriers (local)

Two local courier services deliver extremely quickly. If you're planning a lengthy stay, get a subscription to either.
Pony Express 02 8441/www.pony.it.
Rinaldi L'Expresso 02 760 311.

Consulates & embassies

Listed below are the Milan consulates of the main English-speaking countries. A full list is found under *Consolati* in the phone book.

Australia
*Via Borgogna 2, Centre (02 7712
1120). Metro San Babila/bus 54, 60,
61, 65, 73.* **Map** p309 C1.

Britain
*Via San Paolo 7, Centre (02 723
001). Metro Duomo or San
Babila/bus 60, 65, 73.* **Map** p309 C1.

South Africa
*Vicolo San Giovanni sul Muro 4,
Centre (02 809 036/saconsulate
@iol.it). Metro Cairoli/tram 20.*
Map p310 A2.

US
*Via Principe Amedeo 2/10, North
(02 290 351). Metro Turati/tram 1,
2, 20.* **Map** p309 C1.

Embassies in Rome

Australia 06 852 721/
www.austrade.gov.au.
Britain 06 4220 0001/www.britain.it.
Canada 06 445 981/www.canada.it.
Ireland 06 697 9121.
New Zealand 06 441 7171/
www.tradenz.govt.nz.
South Africa 06 852 541.
US 06 46 741/www.usembassy.it.

Customs

EU citizens do not have to
declare goods imported into or
exported from Italy for their
personal use, as long as they
arrive from another EU
country. For non-EU citizens,
the following limits apply:
400 cigarettes or 200 small
cigars or 100 cigars or 500
grams (17.64oz) of tobacco; one
litre of spirits (over 22 per cent
alcohol) or 2 litres of fortified
wine (under 22 per cent alcohol);
50 grams (1.76oz) of perfume.

There are no restrictions on
the import of cameras, watches
or electrical goods. Visitors are
also allowed to carry up to
€10,329.14 in cash.

Disabled travellers

Information

The best source of information
for the disabled is offered by
AIAS. This non-profit group is
working with City Hall to offer
its information in English, but
for the moment most

brochures, maps and booklets
are in Italian. Check the
website (*see below*) for updated
information, or send a specific
request to aiasmivacanze@
tiscalinet.it and you will
receive information on Milan
and Lombardy in English.
The city council also runs a
sportello disabili (disabled
desk), where helpful
information is dispensed in
Italian only.

The **www.asphi.it/
english** website provides
information in English on
hearing and vision impaired,
Down's Syndrome, autism,
specialised teachers and
therapists, aids and prostheses,
sport and leisure time,
alternative communication and
other associations.

AIAS Milano Onlus group
*Via San Barnaba 29 (02 5501
7564/fax 02 5501 4870/www.
milanopertutti.it).*

Sportello disabili
*Via Fabio Filzi 22 (02 6765
4740/fax 02 6765 5898).*

Transport

Some but not all city transport
lines are equipped for the
disabled. See **www.atm-mi.it**
for a full listing, or visit the
ATM information point inside
the Duomo metro station
(*see p276*). AIAS (*see above*)
provides up-to-the-minute bus,
tram and metro information.

The newer Yellow metro line
is fully accessible with
elevators. The older red and
green Lines were being
brought up to scratch as this
guide went to press.

The Ferrovie dello Stato
(FS, state railway) is phasing
in easy-access carriages but
don't expect miracles. Trains
with wheelchair facilities are
indicated by a wheelchair
symbol on official timetables.
The *Centro assistenza disabili*
(CAD, disabled assistance;
information 02 6707 0958) at

Centrale, Cadorna or Garibaldi
stations will arrange help for
boarding or alighting from
trains; 24 hours prior to
departure, the disabled
traveller or someone
representing him/her must go
to the CAD in the appropriate
station to fill in a form
requesting assistance.

Transport to both Linate
(bus 73) and Malpensa
(Malpensa Express) airports
(*see p274*) is wheelchair-
accessible. Both airports have
sala amica waiting areas for
handicapped persons. Inform
your airline when you book
that you would like assistance.

Book **taxis** in advance,
specifying if you need a car
large enough to cope with a
wheelchair (*una carozzella*).
Alternatively, the following
services use small vans and
seating for up to eight; book at
least 48 hours in advance.
Missione Handicap 02 4229 0549/
fax 02 4895 8413.
CTA 02 355 9360/02 357 4768/
fax 02 3320 0456.

Sightseeing

Like most Italian cities,
pavements in Milan's centre
are narrow, and negotiating
cobbled streets is a challenge
(though many have been
covered in asphalt over the last
five years). On the upside,
most street corners have
pram/wheelchair ramps, and
well-designed ramps and lifts
and toilets have been installed
in many museums.The AIAS
website (*see above*) provides
updated information.

Where to stay & eat

AIAS (*see above*) keeps an
updated list of hotels that are
wheelchair accessible: see the
website for listings. *See also
chapter* **Accommodation**
where disabled facilities are
listed. Few restaurants or bars
are fully accessible, though in
most staff will be more than
willing to help you overcome

Directory

barriers. The situation improves in summer months when tables are placed outside.

Toilets

While the law requires all public facilities to have bathrooms for the disabled, many of those in old buildings haven't yet faced the music. The more modern looking the bar, restaurant, convention facility or museum, the more likely it is to have renovated and appropriately adapted all of its public facilities.

Wheelchair hire

Farmacie (pharmacies) either rent wheelchairs or can direct you to specialised wheelchair rental services.

Drugs

If you are caught in possession of drugs of any type, you will be taken before a magistrate. If you can convince him or her that the tiny quantity you were carrying was for purely personal use, then you will be let off with a fine or ordered to leave the country.

Habitual offenders will be offered rehab. Anything more than a tiny amount will push you into the criminal category: couriering or dealing can land you in prison for up to 20 years. It is an offence to buy or sell drugs, or even to give them away. Sniffer dogs are a fixture at most ports of entry into Italy; customs police take a dim view of visitors entering with even the smallest quantities of narcotics, and they are nearly always refused entry.

Electricity

Most wiring systems work on 220v, which is compatible with British-bought appliances. With US 110v equipment you need a current transformer. A few systems in old buildings

are 125v. Two-pin adaptor plugs (*adattatore*) can be bought at any electrical shop (*Casalinghi* or *Elettricità*).

Emergencies

See also **Safety & security** *p288*, **Health** *p282*, **Police** *p286*, **Money** *p286*.
Thefts or losses should be reported immediately at the nearest police station (*see p286*). You should report the loss of your passport to your consulate or embassy (*see p280*). Report the loss of a credit card or travellers' cheques immediately to your credit card company (*see p286*).

National emergency numbers

Police Carabinieri (English-speaking helpline) 112; Polizia di stato 113.
Fire service Vigili del fuoco 115.
Ambulance Ambulanza 118.
Car breakdown Automobile Club d'Italia, ACI 116.

Domestic emergencies

If you need to report a malfunction in any of the main services, these emergency lines are open 24 hours a day.
Electricity AEM 02 2521; Enel 16 441.
Gas Italgas 800 900 700; AEM 02 5255.
Telephone Telecom Italia 188.
Water 02 412 0910.

Health

Emergency health care is available for all travellers through the Italian national health system and, by law, hospital accident and emergency departments (*see below*) must treat all emergency cases free. *See also* **Insurance** *p284*.

Accident & emergency

If you need urgent medical care, go to the *Pronto soccorso*

(casualty department) of one of the hospitals listed below, all of which offer 24-hour casualty services. If you have a child needing emergency treatment, head for the casualty department of **Ospedale dei Bambini Vittore Buzzi**.

Ospedale dei Bambini Vittore Buzzi

Via Castelvetro 32, North (02 5799 5363). Metro Bullona/bus 57, 94/tram 14. **Map** p308 B1.
Obstetric as well as paediatric casualty departments.

Ospedale Maggiore di Milano

Via F Sforza 28/35, South (02 5503 3209/switchboard 02 55 031). Metro Crocetta or Missori/bus 77, 94/tram 4, 24. **Map** p311 A1.

Ospedale Niguarda

Piazza Ospedale Maggiore 3, North (02 64 441/poison centre 02 6610 1029). Bus 40, 51, 83/tram 4. **Map** off p308 A2.
Also has a department for severe burns and a poison centre hotline.

Ospedale Fatebenefratelli

Corso Porta Nuova 23, North (02 63 631). Bus 43. **Map** p309 B/C1.

Ospedale Mangiagalli

Via della Commenda 12, South (02 57 991). Metro Crocetta/bus 77/ tram 4. **Map** p311 B1.
Obstetrics and sexual violence casualty department (02 5799 2489).

Complementary medicine

A wide range of homeopathic remedies is available from most chemist's shops.

Contraception & abortion

Condoms are on sale near checkouts in supermarkets, or over the counter in pharmacies.

The contraceptive pill is available on prescription. The morning-after pill can be obtained at hospital casualty departments; the doctor on duty will write a prescription that you take to the chemist's. Abortion is available on financial hardship or health grounds, and legal only when performed in public hospitals.

Each district has a *Consultorio familiare* (family-planning clinic), run by the local health authority, and EU citizens with an E111 form are entitled to use them, paying the same low charges for services as locals. They also give advice and help on contraception, abortion and gynaecological problems. They are listed in the phone book under *Consultori*; or consult www.didael.it/comestai/ Consulto.htm.

Gynaecological advice can also be had at the following women's clinics, or at the international health centres listed below.

AIED

Via Vitruvio 43, North (02 6671 4156). Metro Lima/bus 60/tram 5, 20, 33. **Map** p309 B2.

Centro Azione Milano Donne

Via S Pellico 8, Centre (02 7201 1787). Metro Duomo/tram 1, 2, 20. **Map** p311 A1.

Dentists

Most dentists (see *Dentisti* in the Yellow Pages) in Italy work privately. You may wait for months for a dental appointment in a public hospital. Dental treatment in Italy is not cheap and may not be covered by your health insurance. For serious dental emergencies, make for the hospital casualty departments listed above. Check with your consulate for international health clinics where English-speaking dentists can help you. The *English Yellow Pages* lists English-speaking dentists.

Doctors

EU nationals with an E111 form (obtain this before leaving home from your local health authority) can consult a national health service doctor

free of charge. Drugs that he or she prescribes can be bought at chemists at prices set by the Health Ministry. If you need tests or specialist out-patient treatment, this too will be charged at fixed rates (*il ticket*). Non-EU nationals who need to consult health service doctors will be charged a small fee at the doctor's discretion.

Pharmacists are generally useful sources of information: they will recommend local doctors and provide you with addresses of recommended laboratories to have tests done. Milan's long-established international health clinics have highly qualified medical staff, will do tests and deal with emergency situations.

AIMC American International Health Center

Via Mercalli 11, South (02 5831 9808). Metro Missori/bus 94/tram 15. **Map** p311 B1.

International Health Center

Via San Paolo 15, Centre (02 7200 4080). Metro Duomo or San Babila/bus 61. **Map** p309 C1.

The Milan Clinic

Via Cerva 25, Centre (02 7601 6047). Metro San Babila/bus 60, 65, 73. **Map** p311 A1.

Helplines & agencies

See also **Ospedale Mangiagalli** *p282.*

CADMI

02 5501 5519/http://web.tiscali.it/ cadmi/guida. **Open** 10am-1.30pm Mon-Thur.
Sexual violence and rape helpline. There is normally an English-speaking volunteer available.

ALA

02 8951 8046/02 8951 6464. **Open** 10am-3.30pm Mon-Fri.
STD, HIV and AIDS helpline.

Hospitals

Milan's public hospitals (see **Accident & emergency** *p282*) offer good-to-excellent treatment for most ills.

Opticians

See p149.

Pharmacies & medicine

Pharmacies (*farmacia*, identified by a red or green cross) give informal medical advice for straightforward ailments, as well as making up prescriptions from a doctor. Most pharmacies also sell homeopathic and veterinary medicines, and all will check your height/weight/ blood pressure on request.

Over-the-counter drugs such as aspirins are considerably more expensive in Italy than in the UK or US. Anyone who requires regular medication should bring adequate supplies of their drugs with them. Also, take care to know the chemical (generic) name of medicines you need. They may only be available in Italy under different names.

Normal opening hours are 8.30am-12.30pm and 3.30-7.30pm Mon-Sat. Outside of normal hours, a duty rota system operates. Night service typically operates between 9pm and 8am. A list by the door of any pharmacy indicates the nearest open ones; this is also published in the local paper. At duty pharmacies there is a surcharge of €3.87 per client (but not per item) when the main shop is shut.

The following chemist's have night services (usually 9pm-8am); more pharmacies are listed on p145.

Stazione Centrale

Stazione Centrale, North (02 669 0935). **Map** p309 B2. **Open** 24hrs.

Carlo Erba

Piazza del Duomo 21, Centre (02 878 668). Metro Duomo. **Map** p311 A1.

Formaggia

Corso Bueno Aires 4, North (02 2951 3320). Metro Porta Venezia. **Map** p309 B2.

Directory

ID

You are required by law to carry photo ID with you at all times. You will be asked to produce this if you are stopped by traffic police (who will demand your driving licence, which you must have on you whenever you are in charge of a motor vehicle). ID will also be required when you check into a hotel.

Insurance

See also **Health** *p283*; **Police** *p286*.

EU nationals are entitled to reciprocal medical care in Italy, provided they have an E111 form, available in the UK from health centres, post offices and social security offices. This will cover you for emergencies, but using an E111 involves having to deal with the intricacies of the Italian state health system, and for short-term visitors it's better to take out health cover under private travel insurance. Private insurance allows you to choose your health care provider. Non-EU citizens should take out private medical insurance for all eventualities before setting out from home.

If you rent a vehicle, motorcycle or moped, make sure you pay the extra charge for full insurance cover, and sign the collision damage waiver when hiring a car.

Internet & email

Most hotels – even budget ones – will allow you to plug your modem into their phone system; more up-market establishments should have PC points in bedrooms.

Italian providers offering free internet access include: **Caltanet** (www.caltanet.it), **Libero** (www.libero.it), **Tiscali** (www.tiscalinet.it), **Kataweb** (www.kataweb.com) and **Wind** (www.inwind.it).

Checking email or surfing the net is no problem in Milan and larger Lombard towns, where there are internet cafés galore. There is also an internet corner in the very central Galleria Vittorio Emanuele II (*map p311 A1*) Telecom centre (open 8am-9pm daily), where you can use a regular phone card (*see p289*).

Left luggage

Most hotels will look after your luggage for you, even after you have checked out. The left luggage depot at **Stazione Centrale** (02 6371 2667) operates from 3am-1am daily; at **Malpensa airport** Terminal 1 from 6am-10pm daily – Terminal 2 was closed indefinitely at the time of writing; **Linate airport** from 7am-9.30pm daily (if you find it closed during these hours, ring the bell and someone will turn up, though it may take ten minutes).

Legal help

The first stop if you find yourself in need of legal help should always be your consulate; *see p280*. You may be directed to local law firms with mother-tongue English-speaking staff. Milan is also home to numerous branches or associates of English and American law firms.

Libraries

Milan has some 40 libraries with public access, the most useful/central of which are listed below. Other specialist libraries can be found under *Biblioteche* in the phone book. It is always useful to take an identity document with you.

Archivio Storico e Biblioteca Trivulziana

Castello Sforzesco, North (02 8645 4638). Metro Cairoli/tram 1, 27. **Open** 9am-noon, 1.30-4.30pm Mon-Fri. **Map** p308 C2.

The historical archives cover Milanese and Lombard history, art and local traditions. The historical library specialises in history, literature, philology and miniatures.

Biblioteca Ambrosiana

Via P Pio XI 2, Centre (02 806 921). Metro Duomo or Cordusio/tram 2, 3, 4, 12, 14, 24, 27. **Open** 9.30am-5pm Mon-Fri. **Map** p310 A2.

One of Italy's oldest libraries, the vast collection includes many codices dating back to the fifth century.

Biblioteca del Conservatorio G Verdi

Via Conservatorio 12, East (02 7600 3097). Metro San Babila/bus 54, 61. **Open** 8am-7.30pm Mon-Fri; 8am-1pm Sat. **Map** p311 A1/2.

Attached to Milan's conservatory, this library has a huge collection of music-related books and manuscripts. Requests for books must be made from 9am-noon, 3-6pm.

Biblioteca Nazionale Braidense

Via Brera 28, North (02 8646 0907/ www.cilea.it/braidens). Metro Montenapoleone/bus 61/tram 12, 14. **Open** 8.30am-6.15pm Mon-Fri; 9am-1.45pm Sat. **Map** p308 C2.

The Braidense contains 1,000,000 books, plus manuscripts, periodicals, 19th-century prints and antique books, microfilms and CDs.

Biblioteca Sormani

Corso di Porta Vittoria 6, South (02 7600 1555). Metro Missori/bus 94/tram 12, 27. **Open** 9-7.30pm Mon-Sat. **Map** p311 A1/2.

Milan's largest library, with over 580,000 works, including Stendhal's library, a great collection of daily newspapers, and an audio collection of recordings.

English-language libraries

British Council

Via Manzoni 38, Centre (02 772 221). Metro Montenapoleone/tram 1, 2. **Open** 9am-1pm, 2-6pm Mon-Fri. **Map** p309 C1.

There's a yearly fee of €56.81.

CSSU

Istituto di Anglistica, piazza Sant' Alessandro 1, Centre (02 5835 3593/ cssu@mailserver.unimi.it). Metro Missori/bus 65/tram 2, 3, 14. **Open** 10am-5pm Mon-Thur. **Map** p310 A2.

Housed in Milan University, the library hosts a collection of over 10,000 volumes in English, focusing particularly on social and political issues, literature and history.

Lost property (Lost & found)

Ufficio Oggetti Rinvenuti

Via Friuli 30, East (02 546 8118). Bus 62, 90, 92/tram 4. **Open** 8.30am-4pm Mon-Fri. **Map** p311 B2. This is Milan city council's lost property office.

Ufficio Ferrovie dello Stato

Via Sammartini 108, North (02 6371 2667). Metro Centrale/bus 53/tram 2. **Open** 7am-1pm, 2-8pm daily. **Map** p309 A2. Anything lost on trains should end up here.

Media

Magazines

With the naked, glistening female form emblazoned across their covers most weeks, Italy's serious news magazines are not always immediately distinguishable from the large selection of soft porn on newsstands. But *Panorama* and *L'Espresso* provide a generally high-standard round-up of the week's news, while *Sette* and *Venerdì* – colour supplements of *Corriere della Sera* (Thur) and *La Repubblica* (Fri) – have nice photos, though the text can leave much to be desired.

For tabloid-style scandal, try *Gente* and *Oggi*, or the execrable *Eva 3000*, *Novella 2000* and *Cronaca Vera*. But the biggest-selling magazine of them all is *Famiglia Cristiana* – from newsstands or most churches – which alternates Vatican line-toeing with Vatican-baiting, depending on relations between the Holy See and the idiosyncratic Paoline monks who produce it.

National dailies

Italian newspapers can be a frustrating read. Long, indigestible political stories with very little background

explanation predominate. On the plus side, Italian papers are delightfully unsnobbish and happily blend serious news, leaders by internationally known commentators, and well-written, often surreal, crime and human-interest stories. Sports coverage in the dailies is extensive and thorough, but if you're not sated there are the mass-circulation sports papers *Corriere dello Sport, Gazzetta dello Sport* and *Tuttosport*. Members of Milan's business community are major purchasers of the three big financial dailies, *Il Sole-24 Ore, Italia Oggi* and *MilanoFinanza*.

Corriere della Sera

www.rcs.it To the centre of centre-left, the solid, serious but often dull Milan-based *Corriere della Sera* is good on crime and foreign news. Includes a daily Milan section, which is useful for information on films and cultural events, not to mention strikes, road works etc.

Il Manifesto

www.ilmanifesto.it A reminder that, though the Berlin Wall is a distant memory, there is still some corner of central Rome where hearts beat Red.

La Repubblica

www.repubblica.it The centre-ish, left-ish *La Repubblica* is good on the Mafia and the Vatican, and comes up with the occasional major scoop on its business pages. Has a Milan section.

La Stampa

www.lastampa.it Part of the massive empire of Turin's Agnelli family – for which read the Fiat company – *La Stampa* has good (though inevitably pro-Agnelli) business reporting.

Local dailies

See also *Corriere della Sera* and *Le Repubblica* above. There is currently a rash of free newspapers distributed on the underground. The best is *City*, owned by *Corriere della Sera*, with public transport updates and useful addresses.

Il Giorno

www.ilgiorno.it Owned by the family of Prime Minister Silvio Berlusconi, *Il Giorno* is understandably pro-government... often to a nauseating (when not risible) extent.

Foreign press

The *Financial Times, Wall Street Journal, USA Today, International Herald Tribune* (with *Italy Daily* supplement) and most British and European dailies can be found on the day of issue at most central newsstands; US dailies can take 24 hours to appear.

Listings & small ads

EasyMilano

www.easymilano.it Free bimonthly classified ad mag for the English-speaking community, distributed at consulates.

Hello Milano

www.hellomilano.it A free monthly in English with event and exhibition listings, distributed at the APT office (*see p290*). Includes a Japanese section.

Seconda Mano

The mother of all classifieds (though in Italian), includes ads for car, household and other second-hand sales, plus flat rents and shares. Available daily at newsstands, €1.55.

Radio

The three state-owned stations (RAI 1, 89.7 MHz FM, 1332 KHz AM; RAI 2, 91.7 MHz FM, 846 KHz AM; RAI 3, 93.7 MHz FM, 1107KHz AM) play classical and light music, and also feature endless chat shows and regular, excellent news bulletins.

For UK and US chart hits, mixed with home-grown offerings, try these:
IRRS-Globe Radio Milan 88.85FM
Magic 101 100.950-101.200FM
RADIO 105 105FM
Radio Reporter 103.7FM
RTL 102.5 102.5FM
GammaRadio 95.9FM
Radio DeeJay 106.9FM
Radio Vatican 1260 KHz AM. World events as seen through the eyes of the Catholic Church can be heard in English and Italian in news bulletins at 8.30am, 11am, 4pm and 6.15pm daily.

Directory

Television

Italy has six major networks (three owned by state broadcaster RAI and three belonging to Mediaset, owned by Prime Minister Silvio Berlusconi). When these have bored you, there are any number of local stations to provide hours of compulsively awful channel-zapping fun.

The standard of television news and current affairs programmes varies; most, however, offer a breadth of international coverage that makes British TV news look like a parish magazine.

Money

The Euro replaced the lira as Italy's currency in February 2002. One Euro is worth L1,936.27. There are Euro banknotes of €5, €10, €20, €100, €200 and €500, and coins worth €1 and €2 as well as 1, 2, 5, 10, 20 and 50 cents. Euros from any Euro-zone country are valid in Italy.

ATMs

Most banks have 24-hour cashpoint (Bancomat) machines, and the vast majority accept cards with the Maestro and Cirrus symbols.

Banking hours

Most banks are open 8.30am-1.45pm and 2.45-3.45pm, Mon-Fri. Banks are closed on public holidays, and close early the day before a holiday, usually around 11am.

Bureaux de change

Banks usually offer better exchange rates than private bureaux de change (cambio). It's a good idea to take a passport or other identity document whenever you're dealing with money, particularly to change

travellers' cheques or withdraw money on a credit card. Commission rates vary considerably. Watch out for 'No Commission' signs, as the rate of exchange will almost certainly be bad. Main post offices (see p286) also have exchange bureaux. Travellers' cheques are not accepted.

Many city centre bank branches have automatic cash exchange machines, which accept notes in most currencies (in good condition).

American Express

Via Brera 3, North (02 7200 3694). Metro Cairoli/tram 1, 12, 14, 27. **Open** 9am-5pm Mon-Thur; 9am-5.30pm Fri. **Map** p308 C2.

Thomas Cook

Malpensa Airport Terminal 1 (02 7486 7162). **Open** 6-11pm daily. **Map** p307.
Via Dante 8, Centre (02 8909 6459). Metro Cordusio or Cairoli/tram 1, 24, 27. **Open** 9am-12.30pm, 1-6.30pm Mon-Fri; 10.30am-12.30pm, 1-6.30pm Sat, Sun. **Map** p310 A2.

Credit cards

Italians have a fondness for cash, but persuading them to take plastic has become a lot easier in the last few years. Nearly all hotels of two stars and above now accept at least some of the major credit cards.

If you lose a credit card, phone one of the emergency numbers listed below. All lines have English-speaking staff and are open 24 hours a day.
American Express 800 864 046 (see also above).
Diners' Club 800 864 064.
Visa and Mastercard 800 018 548.
MasterCard Global Service Centre 800 870 866.
Visa International Assistance Centre 800 877 232.
Bank America Eurocard 800 821 001/800 222 464.

Police

Milan's main Polizia di Stato station, the Questura Centrale, is at via Fatebenefratelli 11 (02 62 261). The addresses of others, and of the Carabinieri's

Commissariati (police stations), are listed in phone books under Polizia and Carabinieri respectively. Incidents can be reported to either force.

Postal services

For couriers, see **Business** p280.
Italy's equivalent to first-class post, posta prioritaria, generally works very well: it promises delivery within 24 hours in Italy, three days for EU countries and four or five for the rest of the world. More often than not, it succeeds.

Stamps for all letters are sold at post offices and tabaccai (see p288) only. Most post boxes are red and have two slots, one Per la città (for Milan) and the other Tutte le altre destinazioni (for everywhere else).

The CAI-Posta Celere service (available only at main post offices) costs somewhat more than posta prioritaria and delivers at the same speed, the only advantage being that you can track the progress of your letter on its website (www.poste.it) or by phone (information line 160/service operates 8am-8pm Mon-Sat). Registered mail (raccomandata) costs €2.17 over the normal rate to EU countries.

Local post offices usually open from 8.30am-2pm Mon-Fri, and from 8.30am-1.30pm on Sat and any day preceding a public holiday. They close two hours earlier than normal on the last day of each month. Main post offices have longer opening hours and additional services, including fax.

For postal information of any kind, phone the central information office on 160.

Posta Centrale

Via Cordusio 4, Centre (02 7248 2126). Metro Cordusio/tram 2, 3, 4, 12, 14, 24, 27. **Open** 8am-7pm Mon-Fri; 9.30am-1.30pm Sat. **Map** p310 A2.

Ufficio Posta – Stazione Centrale

*Via Sammartini, North (02 673 95).
Metro Centrale/bus 90, 91, 92/tram
1, 5, 33.* **Open** 8am-7pm Mon-Fri;
8.30am-1pm Sat. **Map** p309 A2.

Queuing

Most Milanese wait their turn
in line courteously, grumbling
their displeasure loudly if the
wait is too long. Queue-
jumpers are given short shrift.

Religion

Anglican

*All Saint's Church, via Solferino 17,
North (02 655 2258). Metro
Moscova/bus 41, 43, 94.* **Services**
Sun 10.30am, usually Wed 7.15pm.
Map p308 B/C2.

Catholic

*San Carlo, piazza Santa Maria del
Carmine 2, North (02 8646 3365).
Metro Lanza/bus 61/tram 3, 4, 12,
20.* **Service in English** 10.30am
Sun. **Map** p308 C2.

Jewish

*Via Guastalla 19, East (02 551
2029). Bus 60, 77.* **Services** vary,
call for info. **Map** p311 A1.

Russian Orthodox

*Via San Gregorio 5, East (02 204
6996). Metro Repubblica or Lima/
tram 1, 5.* **Services** 10am Sun.
Map p309 B2.

Zen Buddhist

*Via Agnesi 18, South (02 5830
6763). Metro Porta Romana/
bus 62/tram 9, 29, 30.* **Services**
10am-noon 2nd Sun of mth.
Map p311 B1.

Relocation

Anyone relocating to Italy is
obliged to procure a series of
forms and permits. EU citizens
should have no problem in
getting documentation once
they are in Italy, but non-EU
citizens are advised to enquire
at their local Italian embassy
or consulate before travelling.
There are agencies that
specialise in obtaining
documents for you – for a
price, of course (see *Pratiche
e certificati-agenzie* in the
Yellow Pages).

Carta d'identità (identity card)

Resident foreigners should have an
ID card. You'll need three passport
photographs, a *permesso di
soggiorno* (original plus a
photocopy), and your passport. The
local branch of the Central Records
Office (see *Anagrafe* in the phone
book) will eventually issue the card.

Codice fiscale (Tax code) & Partita IVA (VAT number)

Anyone living or working in Italy
needs a *codice fiscale*. It is essential for
opening a bank account or setting up
utilities contracts. Take your passport
and *permesso di soggiorno* to the tax
office (see below), fill in a form and
return a few days later to pick up the
card. It can also be posted.
  The self-employed or anyone doing
business in Italy may also need a
Partita IVA. It costs €129.11, and
most people pay an accountant to
handle the formalities. Take your
passport and *codice fiscale* to your
nearest tax office (see below). Make
sure you cancel your VAT number
when you no longer need it: failure to
do so may result in a visit from tax
inspectors years later.
  Addresses of tax offices can be
found under *Agenzie delle entrate* in
the phone book. Further information
can be found by calling the Ministry
of Finance's information line (tollfree
848 800 333) or consulting its website
at www.finanze.it.

Permesso di soggiorno (permit to stay)

EU citizens need one of these if
they're staying in Italy for over three
months; non-EU citizens should (but
usually don't) apply for one within
eight days of their arrival in Italy.
Take three passport photographs,
your passport, and proof that you
have some means of supporting
yourself and reason to be in Italy
(preferably a letter from an employer
or certificate of registration at a
school or university) to the nearest
Questura (for Milan, see *p286*;
otherwise see *Polizia di stato* in
the phone book).

Permesso di lavoro (work permit)

In theory, all non-Italian citizens
employed in Italy need a work permit.
Application forms can be obtained
from the local Ispettorato Provinciale
del Lavoro. The form must be signed
by your employer; you then need to
take it with your *permesso di
soggiorno* and a photocopy back to
the Ispettorato. Don't rush: often the
requirement is waived, or employers
arrange it for you.

Residenza (residency)

This is your registered address in
Italy, and you'll need it to buy a car,
get customs clearance on goods
brought from abroad, and many
other transactions. Take your
permesso di soggiorno (which must
be valid for at least another year) and
your passport to your local *anagrafe*
(see above **Carta d'identità**). Staff
will check that rubbish collection
tax (*nettezza urbana*) for your
address has been paid (ask your
landlord about this) before issuing
the certificate.

Bank accounts

To open an account you'll need
a valid *permesso di soggiorno*
or *certificato di residenza*, your
codice fiscale (see above), proof
of regular income from an
employer (or a fairly
substantial sum to deposit)
and your passport.

Work

Casual employment can be hard
to come by, especially for non-
EU citizens, as document
requirements are more
complicated. English-language
schools often look for mother-
tongue teachers; the best of
these will demand qualifications
and/or experience. Expat
periodicals (see *p285*) have
help-wanted ads. The Friday
edition of *Corriere della Sera*
has a job market supplement,
where many larger companies
and headhunters place ads.
Temporary agencies place call
centre and secretarial help.

Adecco

*Corso di Porta Romana 19, South
(02 7202 2100). Metro Missori/tram
4, 24.* **Open** 9am-7pm Mon-Fri. **Map**
p311 A/B1.

Manpower

*Corso Vittorio Emanuele II 24,
Centre (02 770 741). Metro Duomo
or San Babila/bus 60, 65, 73.* **Open**
8.30am-6.30pm Mon-Thur; 8.30am-
5.30pm Fri. **Map** p311 A1.

Accommodation

House hunting in Milan
is a challenge. Walk the
neighbourhoods that appeal

to you and look out for *affittasi* (for rent) notices on buildings. Check classifieds in *Seconda Mano* (*see p285*) or *Trovo Casa,* the Wednesday supplement to the *Corriere della Sera*. The weekly *Piu' Case* magazine is on newsstands on Friday afternoon. Expat periodicals (*see p285*) also carry rental and for sale notices.

When you move into an apartment, it's normal to pay three months' rent in advance plus another two to three months' deposit, which should be refunded when you move out, although some landlords create problems over this. By law, you have a right to a four-year (plus four more years renewable) contract, registered within 20 days at the Ufficio del Registro in the Agenzia delle Entrate (*see p287*). It's not unusual for owners to demand that your company sign the contract, or to ask you to pay part of your rent under the counter. If you rent through an agency, expect to pay the equivalent of two months' rent in commission.

Safety & security

Milan is, by and large, a fairly safe city. However, like any large city, petty crime is a fact of life: taking the usual precautions with your personal belongings will usually help avert trouble.

Tourists who stand out as such are most susceptible to small-time theft and pickpocketing. Pickpockets often work in pairs or groups and target heavily populated tourist areas and public transport routes, and the international arrival area of Malpensa airport.

Everyone – and lone females especially – should be particularly careful in the Stazione Centrale, Parco Sempione and Arco della Pace areas in the evenings.

A few basic precautions will greatly reduce a street thief's chances:
● Don't carry wallets in back pockets, particularly on buses. If you have a bag or camera with a long strap, wear it across your chest and not dangling from one shoulder.
● Keep bags closed, with your hand on them. If you stop at a pavement café or restaurant, do not leave bags or coats on the ground or the back of a chair where you cannot keep an eye on them.
● When walking down a street, remember to hold cameras and bags on the side of you towards the wall, so you're less likely to become the prey of a drive-by motorcycle thief or *scippatore*.
● If you see groups of ragged children brandishing pieces of cardboard, avoid them or walk by quickly, keeping tight hold on your valuables. They will wave the cardboard to confuse you while accomplices pick pockets or bags.
If you are the victim of a crime, call the police helpline (*see p282*) or go immediately to the nearest police station and say you want to report a *furto* (theft). A *denuncia* (written statement) of the incident will be made for you. You will need the *denuncia* for making an insurance claim.

Smoking

Smoking is not permitted in public offices (including post offices, police stations, etc) or on public transport; though public transport is a smoke-free zone, the rule tends to be applied laxly elsewhere. As this guide went to press a new law banning smoking in restaurants and bars had been introduced and was being fairly strictly enforced. For where to buy cigarettes, *see below* **Tabacchi**.

Study

See also p284 **Libraries**. Milan has two state universities, a highly regarded language institute and two private universities, including the prestigious Bocconi. Most of these offer international

programmes and have agreements with foreign universities. Consult university websites (most of which are in English) to see what's on offer. See also www.graffiti.it/guida aladino/univ_lombardia_sedi for a full listing of university courses available (with helpful links) in Milan and Lombardy.

EU citizens have the same right to study at Italian universities as Italian nationals. However, you will need to have your school diplomas translated and authenticated at the Italian consulate in your own country before presenting them to the *ufficio studenti stranieri* (foreign students' department) of any university.

The Open University also offers degree-level study programmes with tutors throughout Italy. Contact Jane Pollard at (tollfree) 800 790 457/02 813 8048/ j.pollard@open.ac.uk.
Università degli Studi www.unimi.it/engl.
Politecnico di Milano www.polimi.it/english.
Universita' Cattolica del Sacro Cuore www.unicatt.it.
Università Commerciale Luigi Bocconi www.uni-bocconi.it/percorsi_en.htm.
Istituto Universitario di Lingue Moderne www.iulm.it.
There are also universities in Bergamo (www.unibg.it), Brescia (www.unibs.it) and Pavia (www.unipv.it).

Language schools

Consult *Scuole di lingua* in the Yellow Pages.

Tabacchi

Tabacchi or *tabaccai* (identified by signs with a white T on a black or blue background) are the only places to buy tobacco products of any kind legally. They also sell stamps, telephone cards, tickets for public transport, lottery tickets and the stationery required for Italian bureaucracy. Most

Codes

All Italian cellphone numbers begin with 3. (Until 2001 they began with 03 and are still often found written thus). Most fixed-line prefixes in Lombardy begin 03. Scope for confusion is endless. The following is a selection of local fixed-line prefixes, rather than cellphone numbers with a stray zero.

Bergamo 035
Brescia 030
Como 031
Crema 0373
Cremona 0372
Lecco 0341
Lodi 0371
Monza 039
Pavia 0382
Sondrio 0342
Varese 0332

tabacchi keep proper shop hours; many, however, are attached to bars and so can satisfy your nicotine cravings well into the night.

Tax

For VAT rebates on goods purchased in Italy, *see p132*.

Sales tax (IVA) is charged at varying rates on most goods and services, and is almost invariably quoted as an integral part of prices. There are a few top-end hotels that will quote prices without IVA. And some tradespeople will also offer you rates without IVA, the implication here being that if you are willing to hand over cash and not demand a receipt in return, then you'll be paying around 19 per cent (ie the amount you would have spent on IVA) less than the real fee: but note that both you and the vendor risk hefty fines should you fall prey to a policeman demanding to see your receipt.

Telephones

Dialling & codes

All normal Milan numbers begin with the area code 02, and this must be used whether you call from within or outside the city. Phone numbers within Milan generally have seven or eight digits, although some numbers (such as the central operator of a large firm) may have six or less. If you have difficulties, check the directory or ring enquiries (12).

All numbers beginning with 800 are freephone lines (until recently, these began 176 or 167: you will still find old-style numbers listed; replace the prefix with 800). For numbers beginning 840 and 848 (147 and 148 until recently) you will be charged one unit only, regardless of where you're calling from or the length of the call. These numbers can be called from within Italy only; some only function within one phone district.

Rates

The biggest Italian telephone company (Telecom Italia) is one of the most expensive systems in Europe, particularly for international calls.

Keep costs down by phoning off-peak (6.30pm-8am Mon-Sat, all day Sun), by purchasing any of the many cheap-rate international phone cards on sale in most *tabacchi* (see *p288*) and by not using phones in hotels, which charge extortionate surcharges.

Public phones

Milan has no shortage of public phone boxes and many bars have payphones. Most public phones only accept phone cards (*schede telefoniche*); a few also accept major credit cards. Telephone cards are available from

tabacchi (*see p288*), some newsstands and some bars. Beware: phone cards have expiry dates (usually 31 Dec or 30 June).

International calls

To make an international call from Italy, dial 00, then the country code: Australia 61; Canada 1; Irish Republic 353; New Zealand 64; UK 44; US 1. Then dial the area code (for calls to the UK, omit the initial zero of the area code) and then the number.

To phone Milan from abroad, dial the international code (00 in the UK), then 39 for Italy and 02 for Milan, followed by the number.

Operator services

To make a reverse charge (collect) call, dial 170 for the international operator in Italy. Alternatively, to be connected to the operator in the country you want to call, dial 172 followed by a four-digit code for the country and telephone company you want to use (for the UK and Ireland this is the same as the country code above; check the phone book for other countries).

Operator and Italian Directory Enquiries 12.
International Operator 170.
International Directory Enquiries 176.
Communication problems on national calls 182.
Communication problems on international calls 176.
Wake-up calls 114; an automatic message will ask you to dial in the time you want your call, with four figures on a 24-hour clock, followed by your phone number.

Mobile phones

Italian cellphone numbers begin with 3. Note that until mid-2001 they began 03 (*see also above* Codes). GSM phones operate on both 900 and 1800 bands; British, Australian and New

Zealand mobiles work without problems. US mobiles can't be used. Mobile phones can be rented from:

Easy Line
Via Fratelli Bronzetti 1, East (800 010 600). Bus 60, 62/tram 12, 27. **Open** 9am-6pm Mon-Fri. **Credit** AmEx, DC, MC, V. **Map** p311 A2.

Service Group
Corso Lodi 83, South (02 5681 5129). Metro Brenta. **Open** 9am-1pm, 3-7.30pm Mon-Sat. **Credit** AmEx, DC, MC, V. **Map** p311 B1/2.

Fax

Faxes can be sent from most large post offices (*see p286*). Rates are €1.29 per page for Italy or €5.09 for Europe. Faxes can also be sent from some photocopying outlets; the surcharge will be hefty.

Telegrams & telexes

These can be sent from main post offices. The telegraph office at the Posta Centrale (*see p286*) is open 8.30am-8.30pm Mon-Fri and 8.30am-1pm Sat. Or you can dictate telegrams over the phone. Dial 186 from a private phone and a message in Italian will tell you to dial the number of the phone you're phoning from. A telephonist will then take your message.

Time

Italy is one hour ahead of London, six ahead of New York, eight behind Sydney. Clocks are moved forward by one hour in early spring and back in late autumn, in line with other EU countries.

Tipping

Foreigners are expected to tip more than Italians, but the ten per cent customary in many countries is generous even for the richest-looking tourist. Most locals leave 5¢ or 10¢ on the counter when buying drinks at the bar and,

depending on the standard of the restaurant, €1 to €5 for the waiter. In restaurants, check to see if a service charge (*servizio*) is already included, as well as the amount of the cover charge (*coperto*) and calculate the tip based on the quality of service, and the amounts already added to your bill.

Many of the larger restaurants (*see also p112*) now include a 10-15 per cent service charge. Tips are not expected in family-run restaurants, though even here a Euro or two is appreciated. Taxi drivers will be happy if you round the fare up to the nearest whole Euro.

Toilets

By law, Italian bars are obliged to let anyone use their toilets. Buying a coffee or a glass of water will help ensure the loo isn't 'out of order'. Don't expect a bar's restrooms to be clean or have toilet paper. There are modern toilets at or near most major tourist sites, in some metro stations and at the Cadorna railway station; most have attendants and you must pay a small fee. Fast-food joints and department stores also come in handy.

Tourist information

Friendly smiles, patience and printed information are thin on the ground in Milan's main APT office by the Duomo.

Hello Milan, a free English publication available at the APT and consulates, includes a useful map, heaps of information on the city and details of events.

APT
Via Marconi 1, Centre (02 7252 4301/www.turismo.milano.it). Metro Duomo/tram 2, 3, 4, 12, 14, 24, 27. **Open** 8.45am-1pm, 2-6pm Mon-Fri; 9.30am-1pm, 2-5pm Sat, Sun. **Map** p311 A1.

Ufficio Informazioni Turistiche
Stazione Centrale, first floor, North (02 7252 4360). **Open** 9am-6.30pm Mon-Sat; 9am-12.30pm, 1.30-5pm Sun. **Map** p309 B2.

Tours

Autostradale Milan (for info and booking call APT on 02 7252 4301) runs 3hr tours with stops at the Castello Sforzesco and Leonardo Da Vinci's *Last Supper* (€30.99 including entry fees). Tours depart from the APT office. Times vary.
Hello Milano (02 2952 0570/348 600 6298) offers 2hr personalised tours of the city costing €50 per hr.
Tempo Libero (02 607 1009) conducts informative tours on board trams for children aged 5-12 on Saturdays at 2pm and 4pm, Sundays at 10.30am, 2pm and 4pm. Reservations obligatory.
Sophisticated Italy (02 4819 6675/fax 02 481 7877/www. sophisticateditaly.com) organises tours for small groups or individuals to experience Lombard food and wine, gardens, golf courses, and so on. Also organises cooking courses.
Opera d'Arte (02 607 1009/02 6900 0579) organises personalised guided tours of churches and museums.

Visas

EU nationals and citizens of the US, Canada, Australia and New Zealand don't need visas for stays in Italy of up to three months. For EU citizens, a passport or identity card valid for travel abroad is sufficient; all non-EU citizens must have full passports. All visitors should declare their presence to the police within eight days of arrival. If you're staying in a hotel, this will be done for you. If not, contact the Questura Centrale (*see 286*), for advice.

Water & drinking

There are public drinking fountains throughout Italy; in most cases the water is perfectly acceptable to drink. If you have any doubts, opt for bottled water. In bars, specify that you want *acqua minerale* (*naturale* or *gassata*).

When to go

By season

Winter

7 December
Feast of Milan's patron
Sant'Ambrogio (St Ambrose); five-
day 'Oh bej, oh bej' fair in piazza
Sant'Ambrogio culminates; opening
night at the Scala.

Early Dec
Milano Marathon (www.milano
marathon.it). Milan's marathon was
held for the first time in 2001 but
looks like becoming a regular feature.

6 January (Epiphany)
The Wise Men, with thousands of
local followers, process from the
Duomo to Sant'Ambrogio church.

February
Milan's Carnevale celebrations –
exclusively pre-Lenten elsewhere –
stretch to the first Saturday of Lent,
when there's a fancy-dress parade
around the Duomo and city centre.

Sun in early Feb
Vinilmania fair of old and rare LP
records at the Parco di Esposizione
Novero in the suburb of Segrate
(02 7020 0022/www.
parcoesposizioninovegro.it/).

Late Feb
BIT (www.expocts.it/bit/intro.htm)
international tourism trade fair at t
he Fiera (see p100).

Spring

Usually early spring
Settimana dei beni culturali (Cultural
Heritage Week). All Italy's publicly
owned museums and galleries are
free. Check www.beniculturali.it.

Early Mar
Italian designers show their autumn
and winter lines at Modit collections
(02 641 191/www.modaindustria.it).

Third weekend of Mar
Many of Milan's historic *palazzi* are
opened to the public in the Oggi
aperto initiative (information FAI, 02
467 6151/www.fondoambiente.it).

Mid Apr
Stramilano (www.stramilano.it).
Central Milan is closed to traffic as
locals take to the streets for a fun run.

Easter Mon
Flower market in the via Moscova
area near the convent of Sant'Angelo.

Second weekend of May
Pittori sul Naviglio: open-air art
exhibition along the Navigli (see p92).

Late May
Private residences open their
splendid courtyards to the public for
one Sunday in the Cortili Aperti
initiative (02 7631 8634/www.
italiamultimedia.com/cortiliaperti/).

Late May-Sept
The summer season of sporting
events, concerts and nightlife (as well
as family picnics) gets under way at
the Idroscalo park (see map p307).

Last Sun in May
Festa del Caroccio in Legnano (see
p106). Parades in period costume to
commemorate the Lombard League's
1176 defeat of Barbarossa.

Summer

First Sun in June
Giro Italia (www.gazzetta.it). The
final stage of this cycling classic
ends with eight laps between corso
Sempione and the Castello Sforzesco.

July-Aug
Notturni in Villa: a series of concerts
in patrician villas around the city
(02 8912 2383/www.amicidella
musicamilano.it).

First two weeks of June
Festa del Naviglio (see p92): street
artists, concerts, sporting events,
antique markets, regional cooking
and other events along the Navigli.

June-Aug
Milano d'Estate: open-air concerts
and performances in the Parco
Sempione (see p74). Information from
the APT (see p290).

Third Sun of June
Sagra di San Cristoforo: feast of the
patron saint of drivers takes place in
the square in front of the little church
of San Cristoforo (see p92). Decorated
boats float down the Naviglio.

Late June-July
Festival Latino-Americano in the
Forum in Assago (see p168), with
music, crafts and cooking from South
America (www.latinoamericando.it).

Autumn

Second Sun of Sept
Italian Formula One Grand Prix in
Monza (see p103).

Early Oct
Italian fashion designers present
their spring and summer collections
at Modit-Milanovendemoda (02 641
191/www.modaindustria.it).

Late Oct
SMAU: international exhibition of
the latest in multimedia, office and
computer technology at the Fiera.

Public holidays

On public holidays (*giorni festivi*)
virtually all shops, banks and
businesses are closed, although (with
the exception of May Day, 15 August
and Christmas Day) bars and
restaurants tend to stay open. Public
transport is practically non-existent
on 1 May and Christmas afternoon.
Holidays falling on a Saturday or
Sunday are not celebrated the

following Monday; however, if a
holiday falls on a Thursday or a
Tuesday, many people will take the
Friday/Monday off as well, known as
fare il ponte (doing a bridge).

Public holidays are as follows:
New Year's Day (*capo d'anno*),
1 January; **Epiphany** (Epiphania),
6 January; **Easter Monday**
(Pasquetta); **Liberation Day**,
25 April; **May Day**, 1 May; **Feast
of the Assumption** (Ferragosto),
15 August; **All Saints'** (Tutti Santi),
1 November; **Feast of Sant'
Ambrogio**, 7 December;
Immaculate Conception (Festa
dell'Immacolata), 8 December;
Christmas Day (Natale); **Boxing
Day** (Santo Stefano).

Weather

The low-lying Po Valley is
bound on the north by the
Alps, which keep all that
moisture firmly where it is.
Hence the notoriously thick fog
that can bring traffic in and
around Milan to a halt
and close down airports.
Winter in Lombardy can be
bitter, with winds zipping
down from the Alps. Spring
offers warmer temperatures
and blossoming trees while
autumn offers changing
colours and balmy days,
though rain may intrude in late
October and November.
Summer tends to be muggy.

Women

Foreign women will be the
object of attention in Italy, no
matter where they go. Most men
will be attentive, interested and
mostly courteous. You are
unlikely to encounter anything
aggressive. That said, take the
usual precautions in a large
city like Milan. Avoid outlying
areas and don't wander by
yourself at night except in
lively central zones. There are
prostitutes and pushers in the
area around Stazione Centrale
after dark. They are unlikely to
hassle you, but will make your
late-night movements less than
picturesque. A taxi is a good
idea if you're crossing the city
late at night.

Directory

Further Reference

Classics

Catullus *Poems* Uncannily modern musings from Lago di Garda's most famous Roman.

Pliny the Elder *Natural History* Observations of an antique Como native.

Pliny the Younger *Letters* Spirited correspondence of the man who owned several villas around Lago di Como.

Fiction

D'Annunzio, Gabriele *The Child of Pleasure* Autobiographical novel by a bon viveur and *grand poseur* (*see p208*).

Fo, Dario *Accidental Death of an Anarchist* Darkly hilarious take on the fatal 'tumble' of an anarchist from a Milanese police HQ window during an interrogation.

Hemingway, Ernest *A Farewell to Arms* Part of this love 'n' war epic is set in Milan.

Manzoni, Alessandro *I promessi sposi* (*The Betrothed*) The seminal Lombard novel (*see p64*), so ubiquitous you begin to wonder whether it isn't the only Lombard novel.

Shakespeare, William *Romeo and Juliet* Lover-boy is banished to Mantova after unwisely killing his loved-one's cousin.

Non-fiction & travel

Barzini, Luigi *The Italians* Entertaining – if dated – look at how Italians run their lives.

Goethe, Johann Wolfgang von *Italian Journeys* Account of the German poet's adventures in Italy.

Ginsborg, Paul *A History of Contemporary Italy 1943-88* and *Italy and its Discontents*

Excellent insights into what made and makes Italy tick.

Grundy, Isobel *Lady Mary Wortley Montagu* The indomitable 18th-century English traveller spent many years in and around Lovere on Lago di Garda.

Lawrence, DH *Twilight in Italy* Contains wonderful descriptions of Lago di Garda.

Wharton, Edith *Italian Backgrounds* A spirited and intelligent refutation of the 'there's nothing to see in Milan' argument.

See also p160.

Bitter Rice (Riso Amaro; 1948) Tale of exploitation and passion among Lombardy's rice paddy workers.

Goliath and the Barbarians (1959) Mr Universe Steve Reeves beats the barbarian Lombards single-handed in this tacky Stereoscope epic.

A Month by the Lake (1994) The beauty of Lake Como compensates for the turgid four-way tug-of-love (involving Vanessa Redgrave and Uma Thurman) that takes place on its shores.

1900 (1976) Bernardo Bertolucci's two-part opus – shot around Cremona – on the conflict between Communism (good) and Fascism (bad), here both as hammy as each other.

Salò, or the 120 Days of Sodom (1975) Pier Paolo Pasolini's thoroughly nasty S&M allegory of Mussolini's last stand somehow does more to put you off the director than the dictator.

The Tree of the Wooden Clogs (1978) Subsistence farming in turn-of-the-century Lombardy beautifully narrated by Ermanno Olmi.

Verdi Giuseppe (1813-1901), Lombard *per eccellenza*, Verdi gave many of his operas local themes and/or settings: *The Lombards at the First Crusade* (1843), *The Battle of Legnano* (1849) and *Rigoletto* (set in Mantova; 1851) are the most obvious, though many more reflected the tribulations of nations oppressed by foreign rulers, a sore point in Milan in Verdi's time.

Lago di Como Composers' holidays spent on the lake's shores resulted in *Transcendental Studies* (Liszt), *La Sonnambula* (Bellini) and many more works.

www.beniculturali.it The Cultural Heritage ministry's site (Italian only) lists all state-owned museums, galleries, etc, with addresses and opening times, and provides information on temporary exhibitions and initiatives such as the Settimana dei beni culturali (*see p291*).

www.infopoint.it Local transport information site (Italian only): type departure point and destination and it will provide timetables.

www.comune.milano.it and **www.milanocitta.it** Both operated by Milan city council and both in English, these sites provide practical information about the city.

www.provincia.milano.it/ cultura/oltremilano/index. htm and **www.cultura. regione.lombardia.it** Information (Italian only) on every point of cultural interest in the Milan province and Lombardy region respectively.

www.mumi.it All Milan's galleries and museums at a glance (English pending as this guide went to press).

Vocabulary

Italians always appreciate attempts to speak their language, however incompetent those attempts may be.

Note that there are two forms of address in the second person singular (you) in Italian: *lei*, which is formal and should be used with strangers and older people; and *tu*, which is informal. The personal pronoun is usually omitted.

Italian is pronounced as it is spelt.

Pronunciation

a – as in ask.
e – like a in age (closed e) or e in sell.
i – like ea in east.
o – as in hotel (closed o) or in hot.
u – as in boot.
c and g are both soft in front of e and i (becoming like the initial sounds of check and giraffe respectively).
An h after any consonant makes it hard. Before a vowel, it is silent.
c before a, i and u is pronounced as in cat.
g before a, i and u is pronounced as in get.
gl is pronounced like lli in million.
gn is pronounced like ny in canyon.
qu is pronounced as in quick.
r is always rolled.
s has two sounds, as in soap or rose.
sc is pronounced like sh in shame.
sch is pronounced like sc in scout.
z can be sounded ts or dz.

Useful phrases

hello/goodbye (informal) – ciao, salve
good morning – buon giorno
good evening – buona sera
good night – buona notte
please – per favore, per piacere.
thank you – grazie
you're welcome – prego
excuse me, sorry – mi scusi (formal), scusa (informal)
I'm sorry, but… – mi dispiace…
I don't speak Italian (very well) – non parlo (molto bene) l'italiano
I don't/didn't understand (anything) – non capisco/ho capito (niente)
where's the toilet? – dov'è la toilette?
open – aperto
closed – chiuso
entrance – entrata
exit – uscita

Times & timetables

could you tell me the time? – mi sa (formal)/sai (informal) dire l'ora?
it's – o'clock – sono le (...)
it's half past – sono le (...) e mezza
when does it open? – a che ora apre?

Directions

(turn) left – (giri a) sinistra
(it's on the) right – (è a/sulla) destra
straight on – sempre diritto
where is…? – dov'è...?

could you show me the way to the Duomo? – mi potrebbe indicare la strada per il Duomo?
is it near/far? – è vicino/lontano?

Transport

car – macchina
bus – autobus
underground/subway – metro(politana)
coach – pullman
taxi – tassi, taxi
train – treno
tram – tram
plane – aereo
bus stop – fermata (d'autobus)
station – stazione
platform – binario
ticket/s – biglietto/biglietti
one way – solo andata
return – andata e ritorno
(I'd like) a ticket for – (vorrei) un biglietto per…
fine – multa
are you getting off at the next stop? – scende alla prossima?
I'm sorry, I didn't know I had to stamp it – mi dispiace, non sapevo che lo dovevo timbrare

Communications

phone – telefono
fax – fax
stamp – francobollo
how much is a stamp for England/Australia/the United States? – quanto viene un francobollo per l'Inghilterra/ l'Australia/ gli Stati Uniti?
can I send a fax? – posso mandare un fax?
can I make a phone call? – posso telefonare/posso fare un colpo di telefono?
letter – lettera
postcard – cartolina
e-mail – posta elettronica, e-mail
net-surfer – navigatore
courier – corriere, pony

Shopping

I'd like to try the blue sandals/black shoes/brown boots – vorrei provare i sandali blu/le scarpe nere/ gli stivali marroni
do you have it/them in other colours? – ce l'ha in altri colori?
I take (shoe) size … – porto il numero…
I take (dress) size… – porto la taglia…
it's too loose/too tight/just right – mi sta largo/stretto/bene
can you give me a little more/less? – mi dia un po' di più/meno
100 grams of … – un etto di …
300 grams of … – tre etti di …
one kilo of … – un kilo/chilo di …
five kilos of ... – cinque chili di …

a litre/two litres of … – un litro/ due litri di …

Accommodation

a reservation – una prenotazione
I'd like to book a single/twin/double room – vorrei prenotare una camera singola/doppia/matrimoniale
I'd prefer a room with a bath/shower/window over the courtyard – preferirei una camera con vasca da bagno/doccia/finestra sul cortile
can you bring me breakfast in bed? – mi porti la colazione al letto?

Eating & drinking

I'd like to book a table for four at eight – vorrei prenotare una tavola per quattro alle otto
this is lukewarm; can you heat it up? – è tiepido; lo può riscaldare?
this wine is corked; can you bring me another bottle, please? – questo vino sa di tappo; mi può portare un'altra bottiglia per favore?
that was poor/good/ (really) delicious – era mediocre/buono/(davvero) ottimo
the bill – il conto
is service included? – è incluso il servizio?
I think there's a mistake in this bill – credo che il conto sia sbagliato
there's a fly in my soup – c'è una mosca nella mia zuppa
See also p122 **The Menu**.

Days & nights

Monday – lunedì; Tuesday – martedì; Wednesday – mercoledì; Thursday – giovedì; Friday – venerdì; Saturday – sabato; Sunday – domenica; yesterday – ieri; today – oggi; tomorrow – domani; morning – mattina; afternoon – pomeriggio; evening – sera; night – notte; weekend – fine settimana or, more usually, weekend; have a good weekend! – buona domenica!; see you tomorrow/on Monday! – a domani!/ a lunedì!

Numbers & money

0 zero; 1 uno; 2 due; 3 tre; 4 quattro; 5 cinque; 6 sei; 7 sette; 8 otto; 9 nove; 10 dieci; 11 undici; 12 dodici; 13 tredici; 14 quattordici; 15 quindici; 16 sedici; 17 diciasette; 18 diciotto; 19 dicianove; 20 venti; 30 trenta; 40 quaranta; 50 cinquanta; 60 sessanta; 70 settanta; 80 ottanta; 90 novanta; 100 cento; 200 duecento; 1,000 mille.
how much is it/does it cost? – quanto costa/quant'è/quanto viene?
do you take credit cards? – si accettano le carte di credito?
Can I pay in pounds/dollars, with traveller's cheques? – posso pagare in sterline/dollari/con i travellers?

Glossary

Ambulatory a semi-circular aisle generally passing behind a church's main altar

Amphitheatre (ancient) oval open-air theatre

Apse usually semi-circular recess at the high-altar end of a church

Architrave a beam resting across the top of a row of columns

Baldacchino (baldachin/baldaquin) canopy, often over an altar, supported by columns

Baptistery building near a church used for baptisms, often eight-sided

Barrel vault ceiling arch shaped like half-barrel

Baroque artistic and architectural style of the 17th-18th century, in which the decorative element became increasingly florid, culminating in the Rococo (*qv*)

Basilica ancient Roman rectangular public building; rectangular Christian church

Byzantine Christian artistic and architectural style drawing on ancient models developed in the 4th century in the Eastern empire (capital Byzantium/Constantinople/Istanbul) and developed through the Middle Ages

Campanile bell tower

Capitals the decorated head of a column (*cf* Orders)

Cardine (ancient) secondary street, usually running north-south

Carolingian from the period of rule by Charlemagne (emperor 800-814) and his descendents

Caryatid supporting pillar carved in the shape of a woman

Chiaroscuro painting or drawing technique using no colours but shades of black, white and grey

Ciborium dome-shaped canopy over high altar (*cf* baldacchino)

Cloister exterior courtyard surrounded on all sides by a covered walkway

Confessio crypt beneath a raised altar

Cupola dome-shaped roof or ceiling

Decumanus (ancient) main road, usually running east-west

Entablature section above a column or row of columns, including the frieze and cornice

Ex-voto an offering given to fulfill a vow; often a small model in silver of the limb, organ, loved one cured as a result of prayer

Fresco painting technique in which pigment is applied to wet plaster

Gothic style of the late Middle Ages (from the 12th century), of soaring, pointed arches

Greek cross (church) in the shape of a cross with arms of equal length

Latin cross (church) in the shape of a cross with one arm longer than the other

Loggia gallery open on one side, usually with columns and arches on the open side

Lunette semi-circular space above a door or window, often frescoed.

Mannerism High Renaissance style of the late 16th century; characterised in painting by elongated, contorted human figures

Narthex enclosed porch in front of a church

Nave main body of a church; the longest section of a Latin cross church (*qv*)

Orders classical styles of decoration for columns, the most common being the very simple Greek Doric, the curlicued Ionic and the leafy, frondy Corinthian

Palazzo large and/or important building (not necessarily a palace)

Paleo-Christian dating from the earliest days of

Christianity in Italy, ie the early second to the sixth centuries

Panel painting in oils on wood

Piazza (or **largo**) square

Pietà depiction of Christ lying across the Madonna's lap after the crucifixion

Pilaster square column, often with its rear side attached to a wall

Polyptych a painting composed of several panels (cf dyptych with two panels and triptych with three)

Porphyry a deep blood-red coloured marble

Portico a space covered by a roof supported on columns, often in front of a church

Presbytery the part of a church containing the high altar

Pronaos vestibule of a temple, with walls at the sides but open with columns in front

Rococo highly decorative style of the 18th century

Romanesque architectural style of the early Middle Ages (c500 to 1200), drawing on Roman and Byzantine (*qv*) influences

Sacellum (ancient and paleo-Christian *qv*) small chapel for private devotion

Sacristy a room off a church used for storing vestments and vessels

Sarcophagus (ancient) stone or marble coffin

Terracotta unglazed earthenware much used in Lombard architectural decorations

Transept shorter arms of a Latin cross church

Tribune the apse (*qv*) of a basilica (*qv*) or a raised platform at the altar end of a church

Triumphal arch arch in front of an apse (*qv*), usually over the high altar

Trompe l'oeil decorative painting effect to make surface appear three-dimensional

Index

Advertisers' Index

Pleas refer to the relevant pages for addresses
and telephone numbers

	Place of Interest
	Railway Station
	Park
+	Church
	Hospital
	University
—	City Wall
i	Tourist Information
P	Car Park
	Metro Stations :
Ⓜ	Linea 1
Ⓜ	Linea 2
Ⓜ	Linea 3
●	Railway Connection

Maps

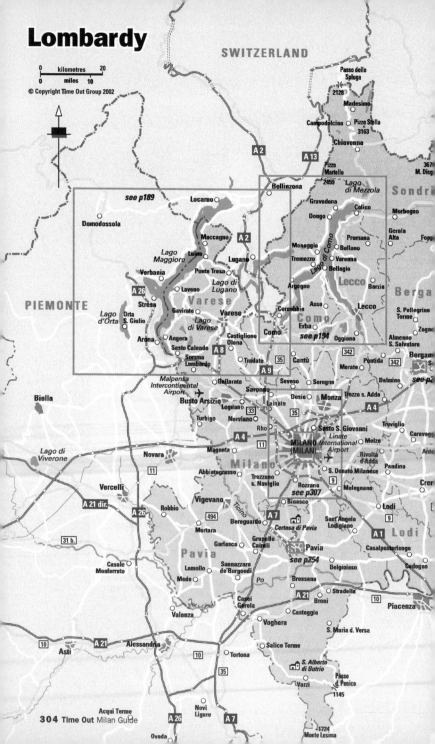

Lombardy

kilometres 20
miles 10

SWITZERLAND

Passo dello
Spluga
2128

Madesimo

Campodolcino   Pizzo Stella
3163

Chiavenna

Pizzo
Martello
2459   Lago
di Mezzola   Sondri

Domodossola

see p189   Locarno

Gravedona
Dongo   Colico   Morbegno

Maccagno   Menaggio   Premana   Gerola
Alta   Fopp

Luino   Tremezzo   Bellano

Lago
Maggiore   Ponte Tresa   Lugano   Varenna
Verbania   Bellagio   Lecco   Berga

Lago di
Lugano   Argegno
A 26   Laveno   Cernobbio   Asso   Barzio
Stresa   Gavirate   Varese   Lecco
Lago
d'Orta   Orta
S. Giulio   Lago
di Varese   Como   Erba   S. Pellegrino
Terme
Como   Oggiono   Zogne
Arona   Angera   Castiglione
Olona   *see p194*   Almenno
S. Salvatore
Sesto Calende   342   Pontida   342   Bergam
Somma
Lombardo   Tradate   Cantù   Merate   Dalmine   *see p*
A 9   35

PIEMONTE   A 8

Biella   Malpensa
Intercontinental
Airport   Gallarate   Seveso   Seregno   Trezza s. Adda
Busto Arsizio   Saronno   Desio   Monza   A 4
Legnano   33   Lainate   35   Truviglio
Turbigo   Nerviano   Sesto S. Giovanni   Melzo   Caravagg
Rho   Linate   Ante
A 4   11   MILANO   International   Rivolta
(MILAN)   Airport   d'Adda
Lago di
Viverone   Novara   Magenta   Milano   Pandino
Vercelli   11   Abbiategrasso   S. Donato Milanese   Crer
A 21 dir.   Trezzano   Melegnano
s. Naviglio   Rozzano   9
A 26   Robbio   Vigevano   *see p307*   Lodi   Lodi
Binasco   A 1   9
494   Bereguardo   A 7   Sant'Angelo
Lodigiano
31 b.   Mortara   Gropello   Certosa di Pavia   Casalpusterlengo
Cairoli   Pavia   Cec
Garlasco   *see p254*   Belgioioso   Codogno
Casale
Monferrato   Sannazzaro   Po
de'Burgondi   Bressana   Stradella   10
Lomello   Casteggio   Piacenza
Mede   Voghera
Valenza   Casei   A 21   Broni
Gerola   S. Maria d. Versa
Pavia
10   A 21   Salice Terme
Asti   Alessandria   S. Alberto
Tortona   di Butrio
10   Passo
Varzi   d. Penice
35   1145

Acqui Terme
Novi
Ligure   A 7
A 26
Ovada   Monte Lesima
1724

Time Out Milan Guide **305**

From 1974, Promoviaggi
has been
the first Agency in Italy
to propose to Company's
marketing strategic taylor
made solutions with prize trip.
Services offered are complete
and abreast with
the time's evolution,
with market and technologies.
Since 1998 Promoviaggi
opened an
Incoming Department
for Incentive Travel,
Business Travels,
Conventions and
Company's Groups.
**Promoviaggi is one of the most
professional Italian DMC
and selects the best venues
and destinations in Italy.**

Smile, is Promoviaggi

Incentive & Motivation
Promoviaggi

Incentive

Convention & Event

Road Show

Congress

Italy DMC

Incentive & Motivation
Promoviaggi

Viale Gian Galeazzo, 3 - 20136 Milano Italy
Tel. +39 02 581891 - Fax +39 02 8373448
www.promoviaggi.it
E-mail: promoviaggi@promoviaggi.it

Greater Milan

Copyright Time Out Group 2002

see p 310

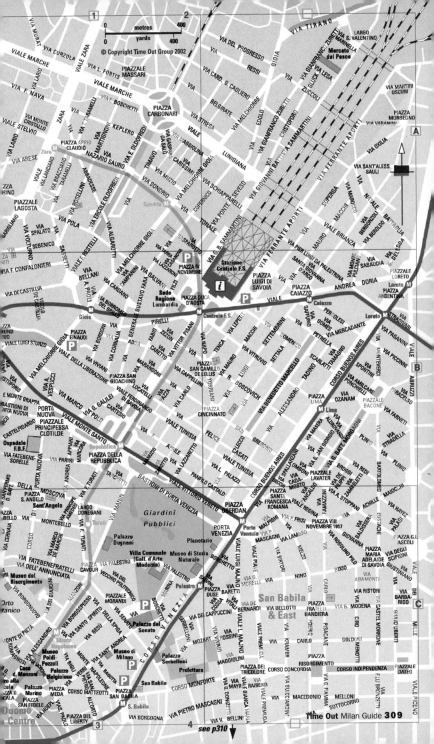

Milan Transport
By kind permission of ATM

Street Index